Hans Henrich Hock

Principles of Historical Linguistics

D1572139

Hans Henrich Hock

Principles of
Historical Linguistics

Second revised and updated edition

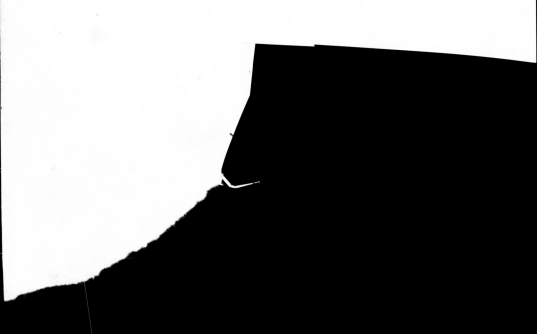

This work appeared originally as volume 34 of the series
Trends in Linguistics — Studies and Monographs.

Mouton de Gruyter (formerly Mouton, The Hague)
is a Division of Walter de Gruyter & Co., Berlin.

♾ Printed on acid-free paper which falls within the guidelines of the
ANSI to ensure permanence and durability.

Library of Congress Cataloging-in-Publication Data

Hock, Hans Henrich, 1938—
    Principles of historical linguistics / Hans Henrich
Hock. — 2nd ed., rev. and updated.
      p.   cm.
    Includes bibliographical references (p.   ) and index.
    ISBN 0-89925-851-4 (pbk. : acid-free paper)
    1. Historical linguistics.
    P140.HG   1991

                                91-10418
                                CIP

n Data

Henrich Hock. —
ork ; Amsterdam :

s. No part
ans

Mouton de Gruyter
Berlin   ·   New York   1991

-012962-0

Typesetting: Arthur Collignon GmbH, Berlin. — Printing: Ratzlow-Druck, Berlin. — Binding: Dieter Mikolai, Berlin. — Printed in Germany.

Preface

The reception of the first edition of *Principles of Historical Linguistics* has been very encouraging, in terms both of published reviews and private comments. Not surprisingly, there also have been many suggestions for revisions and corrections. I am grateful to Mouton de Gruyter for consenting to produce a second, enlarged and slightly revised, edition.

The revision has been kept fairly modest and, with a few exceptions, confined to the Notes and References sections at the end of the book. The bibliographical references in these two sections have been considerably expanded and updated. Other changes, incorporated into the Notes, have been much more limited. Some of these changes concern matters of content and presentation; the rest are confined to correcting misprints that are not self-correcting and major factual errors that managed to survive into the first edition in spite of my attempts to keep such errors to an absolute minimum.

In making the revisions, I have benefited from several reviews of the first edition, extensive personal comments by W. Keith Perceval, and the positive feedback from my colleagues and friends, above all George Cardona, Brian Joseph, Braj B. Kachru, Theo Vennemann, Calvin Watkins, Werner Winter, and Ladislav Zgusta. I owe gratitude also to Lieve van de Walle for helping with the coding of the References. Last, but not least, I am deeply indebted to my wife, Zarina, and my son, Heinrich Sharad, for their support and encouragement. The responsibility of all of these persons is, as usual, limited to what may be good in this book; the responsibility for the rest remains with me.

Champaign, 1991

Preface

Since its pre-nineteenth-century beginnings, historical linguistics has undergone many changes which time and again have led to major revisions and modifications in theory and practice.

Thus, early work was oriented mainly toward comparative morphology. A slow trend toward the 'emancipation' of phonology culminated in the neogrammarians' emphasis on sound change and their claim that sound change is absolutely regular. Combined with the claim that analogical processes may be at work not only in observable history but can be postulated also for prehistoric periods, the neogrammarian approach profoundly changed historical linguistics and greatly increased our understanding of linguistic change. Moreover, under scholars like Delbrück, the neogrammarians produced an impressive amount of research also in historical syntax, especially regarding word order and the use of cases and other morphological categories. This syntactic interest, however, proved to be relatively short-lived.

Though the neogrammarian approach became immensely popular, dissenting voices began to be heard almost immediately. In hindsight, the most formidable among these was Schuchardt who claimed that the neogrammarian distinction between sound change and analogy was spurious and who saw in pidgins, creoles, and other types of 'language mixture' the potential for challenging established views about the development and genetic classification of languages. Until recently, however, Schuchardt's work and claims generally were ignored in 'mainstream' historical linguistics.

Other challenges met a more usual fate: After some initial resistance they were incorporated into 'mainstream' historical linguistics as important modifications or additions to traditional theory and practice. Thus, findings of dialectologists like Gilliéron at first glance suggested that the neogrammarian 'regularity hypothesis' had to be abandoned. Soon, however, dialectological research turned out to provide an important tool for explaining apparent irregularities.

The response was similar as regards the new concepts that were introduced by the structuralists. While following Bloomfield, American structuralism generally remained satisfied with the traditional neogrammarian approach, modified and enriched only by the notions 'phoneme' and 'phonological contrast', the European 'branch' of structuralism provided further and farther-reaching contributions. These included

Trubetzkoy's and Jakobson's concept of 'neutralization of contrast', Martinet's 'functionalism' (with the notion 'chain shift'), as well as Trubetzkoy's and Jakobson's ideas on linguistic 'convergence' phenomena.

The last thirty-odd years have produced the greatest amount of change in the field: Generativism reintroduced the notion 'synchronic rule' into linguistics, a concept which had much earlier been put to excellent use by the Sanskrit grammarians. More importantly, it extended its rule-oriented approach also to historical problems and in so doing provided significant challenges to historical linguistics, but also the potential for considerable enrichment. The most obvious result lies in a strong revival of research on historical syntax; but the areas of phonological and analogical change have also benefited.

At the same time, Schuchardt's, Trubetzkoy's, and Jakobson's earlier work and ideas on language contact have, directly or indirectly, given rise to a very active branch of historical linguistics which is concerned with the general, not just lexical results of language contact, including 'convergence', pidgins and creoles, as well as the relatively new field of research into the nature of 'language death'.

Finally, Schuchardt's early ideas on the relation between sound change and analogy have received partial confirmation in the work of Labov, whose sociolinguistic approach in many important ways has revolutionized our thinking about the nature and motivation of all linguistic change.

These challenges and proposed modifications of the neogrammarian position have clearly changed the field of historical linguistics. At the same time, however, it is remarkable that in the long run they have not so much led to complete 'revolution' in historical linguistic thinking and practice, but rather to modification — by incorporating those concepts that proved useful and important enough to be adopted and rejecting (or ignoring) others.

As a consequence, historical linguistic theory and practice contains a great number of different 'layers' which have been accepted in the course of time and have acquired a permanency of their own. These range from early neogrammarian conceptualizations of sound change and analogy to present-day ideas on rule change and language mixture. To get a full grasp of the principles of historical linguistics it is therefore necessary to understand the nature and justification (or shortcomings) of each of these 'layers', not just to look for a single 'overarching' theory.

The major purpose of the present book is to provide in up-to-date form such an understanding of the **principles of historical linguistics** and the related fields of comparative linguistics and linguistic reconstruction. Chapters 3 to 8 deal with sound change, both in its traditional conceptualization by the neogrammarians and in terms of the more recently developed notions of 'contrast' and 'structure and function'. Analogy is discussed in Chapters 9 to 11, the last of these being devoted to the contributions which generative linguistics can make. Chapters 12 and 13 conclude the coverage of 'internal', non-contact induced developments, by discussing semantic and syntactic change respectively. Language contact is treated in Chapters 14 to 16. Chapter 14 deals with lexical 'borrowing', 15 covers dialectology, and 16 is devoted to such phenomena as convergence, pidgins, creoles, and language death. Internal reconstruction and comparative linguistics are the topics of Chapters 16 to 18. And the last chapter is devoted to a discussion of the general nature and causes of linguistic change.

In addition to this major purpose the book attempts to meet a second goal — to provide a very broad **exemplification** for the principles of historical linguistics. Many aspects of linguistic change have received a broad documentation also in earlier books on general historical linguistics. Compare for instance Paul's extensive coverage of analogical and semantic change, or Bloomfield's rich illustrations of dialectological phenomena. But such coverage usually has not been comprehensive, and especially the area of sound change has generally received only cursory exemplification. The reason, no doubt, was that it could be taken for granted that readers had already studied the linguistic history of at least one language or language family. It could therefore be assumed that they had become familiar with many examples and types of linguistic change, especially with the various types of sound change which was featured most prominently in traditional presentations of language histories. Books dealing with general historical linguistics could therefore be conceived of as providing a broader perspective on linguistic change, not limited to a single language or language family. Moreover, they would naturally emphasize those aspects of linguistic change which received little or no coverage in the histories of individual languages or language families.

For reasons too varied to be discussed here, the field of linguistics has changed such that these earlier assumptions about readers' prior background or familiarity in most cases can no longer be maintained. It is therefore necessary to provide a much broader exemplification than what was customary in earlier works — for all linguistics changes, including sound change.

To accomplish the goals of this book as effectively as possible I have endeavored to adhere to the following guidelines:
(a) Examples should be as accurate as possible. That is, the data should be genuine and they should unambiguously exemplify a given process.

The latter point is not always easy to observe: Many changes, even those which traditionally are often cited as exemplifications of a given process, are in fact analyzable in more than one way. (For instance, examples like Proto-Germanic *uns* going to Old English *ūs* are commonly explained as involving 'loss with compensatory lengthening'. But they may be attributed also to other processes, such as 'weakening' of *n* to some kind of glide and subsequent contraction of that glide with the preceding vowel.) I hope to have succeeded in keeping examples of this type to an absolute minimum.

What is in many cases even more difficult is to find genuine, attested examples in which no changes have taken place other than the one which the example is intended to illustrate. As far as possible, I have tried to highlight the relevant portions of such examples through italicizing or boldface. Elsewhere, readers will have to concentrate on the change under discussion and ignore other developments.
(b) Examples and their interpretation, as well as general theoretical claims, should not be unnecessarily 'controversial' or excessively tied to a particular, possibly short-lived, theory. This concern, of course, is intimately linked with one of the major goals of this book, namely to provide an accurate picture of the various 'permanent' layers of the theory and practice of historical linguistics.

However, this goal is not always easy to implement. For even where there is a 'communis opinio', there will be at least some dissenters. Moreover, there are cases for which no consensus seems to exist (such as the development of 'retroflex' consonants), but where an explanation is possible, along lines which are in essential agreement with general theory and practice. In addition, there are areas where most of the relevant research has been conducted relatively recently, without there having developed a general consensus, but where it is possible to weigh the various arguments and to present what appear to be the most probable findings. (This is especially the case in two areas: The development of pidgins, creoles, and similar forms of language, and the question of the relevance of typology for reconstruction).

In a few cases I have not shied away from providing interpretations of my own, even though they may not (yet) have come to be generally accepted, in order to show how a particular theoretical claim could be made the basis for further fruitful speculation. (This is the case for sections of Chapters 6 and 8 which deal with 'regular dissimilation', 'regular metathesis', and 'initial strengthening'.) Finally, in the chapter on syntactic change I had to relax my rule of avoiding interpretations which might be excessively tied to a particular theory, by employing a rather informal version of Relational Grammar for much of the discussion. The reason for doing so is that this approach makes it possible to provide a fairly consistent exemplification and discussion of a variety of changes as they apply to a "single" grammatical phenomenon (passivization). Moreover, because of its emphasis on grammatical categories, rather than configurations, etc., this approach is quite compatible with traditional treatments of the examined phenomena.

In all of these deviations from my general objective (b), however, I have tried to follow the principle adhered to elsewhere in this book, namely to limit myself to examples and interpretations which I believe I can personally vouch for.

(c) Although this book is intended not as an elementary introduction to the field, but as something like a manual and state-of-the-art report for persons committed to linguistic study and research, I have tried to make it self-explanatory, by defining all concepts and terminology (including methods of transcription and abbreviation). In the absence of any universally accepted terminology and definitions, this practice will, I hope, help to avoid misunderstandings.

Finally, I have the pleasant task of extending thanks to those persons who have helped me in shaping this book.

There are first of all the many former and present students who have taken my courses Linguistics 411 and 412 at the University of Illinois and from whose responses to my teaching and to earlier, prepublication versions of this book I have derived immeasurable benefit. Among these, Lee Becker, Esther Bentur, Rodolfo Cerrón-Palomino, Abby Cohn, Thomas Craven, Karen Dudas, Timothy Habick, Margie O'Bryan, Elizabeth Pearce, Vesna Radanović-Kocić, Jesse Robert Smith, K. V. Subbarao, and William Wallace have been especially helpful and stimulating in the formulation of my ideas. Stephen Schäufele in addition provided the very tangible service of proofing large parts of the manuscript.

I owe gratitude also to many of my colleagues in the field, for general encouragement and for keeping me supplied with their offprints, especially to my departmental colleagues and friends, Eyamba Bokamba, Braj and Yamuna Kachru, Henry and Renée Kahane, C.-W. Kim, Rajeshwari Pandharipande, and Dieter Wanner, and to Robert Austerlitz, Warren Cowgill (whose recent death has been a great loss to Indo-European and general historical linguistics), Wolfgang Dressler, Murray B. Emeneau, Henry Hoenigswald, Brian Joseph, Paul Kiparsky, Bh. Krishnamurti, William Labov, D. Gary Miller, Rocky Miranda, Edgar Polomé, Oswald Szemerényi, Peter Trudgill, and Werner Winter. Special thanks are due to George Cardona and Ladislav Zgusta for their support and friendship. Ladislav Zgusta read and commented on earlier drafts of this book, Werner Winter made helpful suggestions at the galley-proof stage, and Peter Trudgill rendered the same service of support for an early draft of Chapter 16.

I am indebted also to Ram Lakhan Sharma (my guru), S. S. Misra, and Vasudev Dvivedi for their support in my work on modern spoken Sanskrit, and to Michael Clyne, Ingeborg Gutfleisch, Inken Keim, and Bernd-Olaf Rieck for helpful consultations concerning developments in 'Gastarbeiterdeutsch'. Outside the field of linguistics I owe thanks to Michael Sherman (University of Illinois) for support with some of the graphics and to Joseph Benjamin Storch for helping out with Hebrew. The University of Illinois, through its Research Board and its Scholars Travel Fund, has contributed to making my work easier, as have the American Institute of Indian Studies and the American Philosophical Society.

Last, but by no means least, I am deeply indebted to my wife, Zarina, and to my son, Heinrich Sharad, for putting up with me and encouraging me during the all too many years that this book was under preparation. I dedicate this book to them.

Needless to state, the responsibility of all of these persons and institutions is limited to what may be good in this book; the responsibility for the rest lies entirely with me.

Contents

Maps and charts

1. Introduction

ते ऽ सुर आत्तवचसो हे ऽ लवो हे ऽ
लव इति वदन्तः पराबभूवुः। २३ ॥
तत्रैनामपि वाचमूदुः। उपजिज्ञास्यःऽ
स म्लेच्छस्तस्मान्न ब्राह्मणो म्लेच्छेदमूर्या
हैषा वाग्

'The Asuras, deprived of [correct] speech, saying *he lavo, he lavaḥ*, were defeated. This is the unintelligible speech which they uttered at that time. Who speaks thus is a barbarian. Therefore a brahmin should not speak like a barbarian, for that is the speech of the Asuras.'
(Śatapathabrāhmaṇa 3.2.1.23–4)

וַיֹּאמֶר יְהוָה הֵן עַם אֶחָד וְשָׂפָה אַחַת
לְכֻלָּם וְזֶה הַחִלָּם לַעֲשׂוֹת וְעַתָּה לֹא־
יִבָּצֵר מֵהֶם כֹּל אֲשֶׁר יָזְמוּ לַעֲשׂוֹת:
הָבָה נֵרְדָה וְנָבְלָה שָׁם שְׂפָתָם אֲשֶׁר
לֹא יִשְׁמְעוּ אִישׁ שְׂפַת רֵעֵהוּ: וַיָּפֶץ
יְהוָה אֹתָם מִשָּׁם עַל־פְּנֵי כָל־הָאָרֶץ
וַיַּחְדְּלוּ לִבְנֹת הָעִיר:

'And the Lord said, Behold, the people is one, and they have all one language; and this they begin to do: and now nothing will be restrained from them, which they have imagined to do. Go to, let us go down, and there confound their language, that they may not understand one another's speech. So the Lord scattered them abroad from thence upon the face of all the earth: and they left off to build the city.
(Genesis 11.6–8)

1.1. From time immemorial people have been concerned about the fact that language changes and that languages become different as they change. The cause for such change has traditionally been attributed to divine intervention, as in the story of the Tower of Babel. Or it has been ascribed to slovenly, barbarous corruption of speech, as in the case of the Asuras: Instead of uttering the correct Sanskrit *hē rayō hē rayaḥ*, they used the "corrupt" dialectal form *hē lavō hē lavaḥ*. In either case — the ancient Hebrew story of the tower of Babel, or the old Indic tale of the Asuras —, change and diversification is considered highly undesirable, a fall from grace, as it were.

However, in spite of admonitions like 'Therefore a brahmin should not speak like a barbarian', all natural languages change inexorably. Thus, Sanskrit, the language of these brahmins, has over the millennia changed so much that in effect it has been replaced by newer and quite distinct forms of speech: the modern languages of North India, including Hindi, Bengali, and Marathi. And the Hebrew now spoken in Israel is not a straight continuation of the ancient tongue in which the story of Babel has come down to us, but represents a deliberate revival of a language which had long died out in its everyday spoken use. Even the English of Britain and the United States has become changed and differentiated over the past three hundred years.

What is remarkable is that in spite of these changes, in spite of these "corruptions" and the continued "fall from grace", language has not ceased to be intelligible. On the contrary, its current users can, if they choose to or try hard enough, manage to communicate as effectively as those who used language at the time that the stories of the Asuras and the Tower of Babel were composed.

We know now that this is possible because language change is not a completely random, unprincipled deviation from a state of pristine perfection, but proceeds in large measure in a remarkably regular and systematic fashion, without any profound effects on our ability to communicate. We derive this knowledge from the experience of about two hundred years of research into the question of how languages change and how, through divergent changes, they become diversified.

This book is intended to provide an overview of the most important and best-established (or most challenging) findings of that research, ranging from its earliest beginnings to the present time. Although the book is designed for linguists (students and established scholars alike) and therefore does not shy away from discussing fairly technical issues, it does not take for granted a prior familiarity with its topics. For that reason, all necessary concepts and terms will be defined.

1.2. The fact that language changes, and the effect of change can be illustrated by the development of English, as it is reflected in the following versions of the Lord's Prayer. This text has been chosen because of its ready availability in the various stages of English. Moreover, since it encodes the same 'message', it is possible to compare how that 'same message' is expressed differently at different times.

Old English (ca. 950 A.D.)
Fader urer ðu arð [oððe] ðu bist in heofnum [oððe] in heofnas, sie gehalgad noma ðin, to-cymeð ric ðin, sie willo ðin suæ is in heofne ond in eorðo, hlaf userne oferwistlic sel us todæg ond forgef us scylda usra suæ uœ forgefon scyldum usum, ond ne inlæd usih in costunge, ah gefrig usich from yfle.

Middle English (ca. late 14th c.)
Oure fadir þat art in heuenes, halwid be þi name, þi reume or kyngdom come to be. Be þi wille don in herþe as it is doun in heuene. Geue to vs to-day oure eche dayes bred. And forgeue to vs our dettis, þat is oure synnys, as we forgeuen to oure dettoris, þat is to men þat han synned in vs. And lede vs not in-to temptacion, but delyvere vs from euyl. Amen, so be it.

Early New English (A.D. 1534)
O oure father which arte in heven, hallowed be thy name. Let thy kingdome come. Thy wyll be fulfilled, as well in erth, as it ys in heven. Geve vs thisdaye oure dayly breede. And forgeve vs oure treaspases, even as we forgeve our trespacers. And leade vs not into temptacion, but delyver vs from evell. For thyne is the kyngedome and the power and the glorye for ever. Amen.

Modern English (ca. 1985)
Our father who is in heaven, may your name be sacred. Let your kingdom come. May your will be fulfilled just as much on earth as it is in heaven. Give us today our daily bread. And forgive us our transgressions, as we forgive those who transgress against us. And do not lead us into temptation, but free us from sin. For yours is the kingdom and the power and the glory, forever. Amen.

Chart 1.1. Language change

1.3. As we look at these chronologically different versions of the same text we notice quite a number of differences, especially if we compare the earliest with the most recent text. An examination of some of these changes will make it possible to give a brief introduction to the issues which concern historical linguists.

1.3.1. Not all the differences between our sample texts are indicative of language change. In some cases, we are simply dealing with different choices made by different translators in order to convey the same message. Thus, in Modern English, it would have been perfectly possible to write *let your name be sacred*, instead of *may your name be sacred*; and various other words could have been chosen instead of, say, *transgression* and *transgressor*. In fact, the two oldest texts spell out some of the alternatives. Compare Old Engl. *in heofnum* / [= *oððe*] *in heofnas* 'in the heavens' or Middle Engl. *our dettis, þat is oure synnys* 'our debts, i. e. our sins'. The former indicates a choice in grammatical construction (with *in* construed either with the dative or the accusative); the latter recognizes lexical variation (between *dettis* 'debts', a word borrowed from French, and the more native word *synnys* 'sins'). But the listing of alternatives is never complete. Thus, we know from the great majority of other Old English texts that the *Fader urer* of our example exhibits a fairly unusual (but not impossible) construction; ordinarily we would get something like *ure(r) fader* or *ure(r) fæder*, depending on the dialect. In addition to variation of this sort, there may also be differences due to interpolations and other textual corruptions. For instance, the passage *For thyne is the kyngedome ... | For yours is the kingdom ...* of the (Protestant) Early New English and Modern English versions is the result of interpolation in one of the textual traditions of the New Testament. (As the Gothic example further below shows, this interpolation took place at a fairly early period.)

In other cases, the written text may suggest changes which did not actually occur in the spoken language. Or conversely, changes of the spoken language may not be properly reflected in writing. An excellent example in our texts is that of Old Engl. *ure* : Middle Engl. *oure* : Mod. Engl. *our*. The spelling suggests a change in the pronunciation of the initial vowel from Old to Middle English. But we know that this is misleading; for Middle Engl. *ou* is a spelling taken over from the then-dominant French to optionally denote the same long $\bar{u}$ sound as that of Old Engl. *ure*. The real change, from $\bar{u}$ to the modern diphthong, took place after the Middle English period. On the other hand, the final *-e* of Old English was getting lost in Middle English, and the *-e* found at that stage more likely than not is an 'etymological' spelling, a 'silent' letter comparable to the final *-e* which appears in many Modern English words (cf. *give, live, come*, etc.).

Variation of the type Old Engl. *in heofnum | in heofnas* is an ever-present phenomenon in natural language. And inaccurate correspondences between spelling and pronunciation are also quite common, especially in languages with an extended written history. Combined with the absence of native speakers who could inform us about issues of grammar and pronunciation, these factors make the interpretation of the written materials of older languages a difficult task. Fortunately for scholars of historical linguistics, philology, a related branch of inquiry into the history of languages, has provided such interpretations for many of the relevant older languages; and linguists in many cases need no longer concern themselves with this issue. Still, there remain questions of interpretation which have not so far received a satisfactory solution. The Old English 'digraphs' (such as the *eo* of *heofnum*) are a good example: Some scholars consider them diphthongs, others, monophthongs; and both sides support their view with weighty arguments. Within the context of this book we need not worry about such issues of philological interpretation, except that for obvious reasons, forms whose grammatical and phonetic interpretation is still unsettled will not be drawn on as examples for changes in which that interpretation is directly relevant. (Thus, forms like *heofon* will not be used to illustrate changes from diphthong to monophthong, or vice versa. But they may be used as examples of what happens to final consonants, etc.)

However, although philology can be given short shrift in a book like this which is concerned with the linguistics of language change, it should be noted that practicing historical linguists usually cannot divorce themselves from philological work: Quite frequently new insights can be gained only from a better interpretation of textual data.

1.3.2. In the preceding section we referred to the Modern English diphthongization of Old English *ū* in *ūre > our*. This process represents an example of Sound Change, i. e. of change in pronunciation. What is important is that the term 'sound change' has a very specific meaning in historical linguistics, referring only to those changes in pronunciation which are conditioned entirely by phonetic factors.

Sound change thus defined is of considerable importance for historical linguistics. First of all, it is only by knowing how sounds change that we can state with confidence that the similarity between Old Engl. *ūre* and Mod. Engl. *our* is not just fortuitous, but that the two are in fact different historical representations of 'the same word'. This, in turn, permits us to determine what other changes, if any, may have affected our word and its use. (For instance, knowing that *ūre* and *our* are chronologically different forms of the same word, we can state that the syntax of this and similar words has changed from Old to Modern English: While Old English tolerated the order *fader urer* beside the more usual *ure(r) fader*, Modern English usage permits only the order *our father*.)

Secondly, sound change (as defined above) is remarkably regular, so much so that it has been claimed that sound change 'is regular without exceptions'. This claim may have to be modified to some extent, but the fact remains that sound change does operate with a much higher degree of regularity than most other changes. This fact is, of course, a great boon to historical linguists, since it makes the job of tracing linguistic forms through history much easier.

1.3.3. Many changes affecting the pronunciation of words are not conditioned entirely by phonetic factors and therefore do not qualify for being called sound changes. Among these, Analogy plays a very important role.

Analogy can most easily be seen at work in the early stages of children's language acquisition. If for instance a child says *goed* instead of *went*, the form *goed* is made to follow the analogy of the many other past tense forms of English in which -*ed* is added to the verb stem; cf. *walk-ed, smell-ed*, etc. In historical linguistics the term analogy is also used to refer to a number of other, similar developments in which a reinterpretation of the structure of words and their semantic association may play a role. These, too, can be found in early child language, as in the case of the author's child who said *highscraper* for *skyscraper* and, playing with his mother's razor, exclaimed '*Mama, I'm razing myself.*'

In our texts, analogy has played a role in the development of the word for 'heaven'. Ordinarily, Old English final -*n* later was lost after unstressed vowel; cf. OEngl. *ðin* : MEngl. *þi*, archaic Mod. Engl. *thy*, or OEngl. *uœ forgefon* : Mod. Engl. *we forgive*. (The -*n* of MEngl. *we forgeuen* probably is an etymological spelling.) In Old Engl. *heofon*, Mod. Engl. *heaven*, however, final -*n* seems to be retained. The explanation for this 'retention' lies in the fact that the word 'heaven' has, beside the uninflected form OEngl. *heofon*, a number of other, inflected forms, such as OEngl. *heofnum, heofnas*. In these forms the *n* was not final and thus was not subject to loss. It is on the analogy of these forms with retained *n* that Mod. Engl. *heaven* has reacquired its *n*.

1.3.4. Our Middle English text comes from a period after the conquest of England by the French-speaking Normans. The resulting linguistic contact is reflected in the fact that English adopted from French a large amount of vocabulary, such as *reume* (Mod. Engl. *realm*) beside inherited Anglo-Saxon *kyngdom*, or *dettis* (Mod. Engl. *debts*) beside *synnys*. Note also *temptacion* which has replaced old *costung*. This adoption of linguistic items from another language is traditionally referred to as 'borrowing'. Considering that such borrowed items are rarely returned, the terms 'theft' or 'embezzlement' would be more appropriate, but they sound less nice.

The effects of language contact may go far beyond vocabulary borrowing: Through prolonged contact, languages may 'converge',

i. e., become similar in their overall structure. Other results of contact include 'Language Death' (a slow but steady atrophy in the use and structure of a language which is being replaced by another, dominant form of speech) and the development of 'Pidgins' and similar forms of language which are severely reduced in function, structure, and vocabulary.

Social factors play a major role in determining the specific effects of a particular language contact.

1.3.5. Not only the form of words and sentences, but also their meanings may undergo change. In fact, semantics, the meaning of words, is perhaps the most unstable, changeable aspect of language. Even among contemporary speakers, meanings may vary considerably — for individuals and across different speakers. Thus, speakers of Modern English may refer to the sun as a *star* in contexts where they are on their 'astronomically best behavior'; but the same speakers would find it very strange if in bright daylight someone were to say *Look at that beautiful starlight.*

It is therefore not surprising that our texts exhibit a number of Semantic Changes. Where Old English *heofon* could freely refer to both the spiritual 'heaven' and the visible 'sky', Modern English prefers to use different terms for these two concepts. And of these, *sky* cannot ordinarily be used for the usual meaning of *heaven.* The reason for this differentiation probably lies in the fact that English borrowed the word *sky* from Scandinavian, and having done so, 'decided' that if there are two phonetically distinct words, then there must also be some difference in meaning. Other words which underwent semantic change from Old to Modern English are *hlaf* and *sel.* The former survives in the word *loaf*, but the usual word corresponding to OEngl. *hlaf* is *bread* whose Old English ancestor meant 'morsel'. And the word *sell* nowadays can no longer refer to all transfers of property (including giving), but is restricted to commercial transactions.

1.3.6. As noted earlier, Old English permitted both the order *fader ure(r)* and *urer(r) fader*, although the latter was the preferred construction. (The choice of *fader urer* in our text is probably conditioned by the Latin original which had *pater noster.* That is, the motivation lies in something like language contact.) Modern English, on the other hand, ordinarily has only the order *our father.* Syntactic Changes of this sort abound in the languages of the world.

However, linguists in the past have paid much more attention to sound change, analogy, borrowing and other contact-induced changes, and semantic change. As a consequence, we know a good deal more about how these changes operate than about the nature of syntactic change. Recently, interest in syntactic change has increased greatly, mainly because of the prominent role which syntax plays in generative linguistics. While much more work needs to be done, it is possible to outline at least some of the most basic mechanisms of syntactic change.

1.4. The changes briefly outlined in the preceding sections are not unidirectional but can operate in various, sometimes completely opposite directions. Thus in the history of the Scandinavian languages, ancestral **emno-* at an early stage become *javn* with phonetic differentiation ('dissimilation') of the two nasal consonants. In many of the modern dialects, however, the 'dissimilated' *vn* has been re-'assimilated' to a sequence of nasal *m* plus *n*, yielding *jamn*. That is, the development has come full cycle, back to the original *mn*.

Moreover, while all natural languages change, they do not necessarily change the same things at the same time. As a consequence, as communication between different groups of speakers becomes more tenuous or stops altogether, linguistic change may increasingly operate in different directions. Given sufficient time, then, the dialects spoken by these different groups may cease to be mutually intelligible and become completely different languages.

At the same time, this divergent development in many cases does not go so far as to completely obscure the fact that these languages are descended from a common source. In such cases we speak of Related Languages.

As an example compare the Old English translation of the Lord's Prayer (repeated below for convenience) with Old High German and Gothic versions:

Old English (ca. 950 A.D.)
Fader urer ðu arð [oððe] ðu bist in heofnum [oððe] in heofnas, sie gehalgad noma ðin, to-cymeð ric ðin, sie willo ðin suæ is in heofne ond in eorðo, hlaf userne oferwistlic sel us todæg ond forgef us scylda usra suæ uœ forgefon scyldum usum, ond ne inlæd usih in costunge, ah gefrig usich from yfle.

Old High German (A.D. 1022)

Fater unsēr, thu in himilom bist, giuuīhit sī namo thīn. quaeme rīchi thīn. uuerdhe uuilleo thīn, sama sō in himili endi in erthu. broot unseraz emezzīgaz gib uns hiutu. endi farlāz uns sculdhi unsero, sama uuir farlāzzēm scolom unserēm. endi ni gileidi unsih in costunga. auh arlōsi unsih fona ubile.

Gothic (A.D. 311—381)

Atta unsar þu in himinam, weihnai namo þein, qimai þiudinassus þeins, wairþai wilja þeins, swe in himina jah ana airþai; hlaif unsarana þana sinteinan gif uns himma daga, jah aflet uns þatei skulans sijaima, swaswe jah weis afletam þaim skulam unsaraim; jah ni briggais uns in fraistubnjai, ak lausei uns af þamma ubilin; unte þeina ist þiu-dangardi jah mahts jah wulþus in aiwins, amen.

Chart 1.2. Language relationship
(Old English, Old High German, Gothic)

How long such linguistic relationships may remain discernible can be seen by looking at the set of vocabulary correspondences from the major languages of Europe given in Chart 1.3. below. In fact, not only is it possible to recognize the major linguistic groups; within the first and largest one, that of the Indo-European languages of Europe, further subgroups can be established without great difficulties.

One of these is Romance. In the case of these languages we are lucky, in that their (near-)ancestral language, Latin, is attested. We are therefore able to confirm our suspicion that these languages are related, by being descended from a common ancestor through independent, divergent developments.

For the other groups, no such ancestral language is attested. And this is true also for the whole Indo-European language family to which Latin and the Romance languages belong and which outside Europe includes Sanskrit, Persian, Armenian, and others. However, by applying what we know about how languages change we can in many cases 'reverse' the linguistic developments and through 'Comparative Reconstruction' establish what the ancestral language must have looked like.

	'one'	'two'	'three'	'head'	'ear'	'mouth'	'nose'
Breton	ünan	dau	tri	penn	skuarn	genu	fri
Welsh	in	dai	tri	pen	klist	keg	truin
Irish	õn	dɔ	tri	kyan	kluəs	byal	srõn
Icelandic	eidn	tveir	þrīr	hȫfüð	eira	münnür	nēf
Danish	en	tō?	trē?	hōðə	ōrə	mon?	næ̃sə
Norwegian I	ēn	tō	trē	hōvəd	ȫrə	mund	næ̃sə
Norwegian II	ein	tvō	trī	hōvud	öyra	munn	nos
Swedish	ēn	tvō	trē	hṳ̄vud	ȫra	mun	næsa
Dutch	ēn	tvē	drī	hōft	ōr	mont	nȭs
English	wʌn	tuw	θrɪy	hɛd	ɪyr	mawθ	nowz
German	?ains	tsvai	drai	kɔpf	ōr	munt	nāzə
French	æ̃/ün	dö	trwa	tɛ̃t	orēy	buš	ne
Spanish	uno	dos	tres	kaβeθa	orexa	boka	nariθ
Portuguese	ũ	doš	treš	kəbesə	oreλa	bokə	nariz
Italian	un(o)	due	tre	testa	orɛkkyo	bokka	naso
Romanian	un	doy	trey	kap	ureke	gurə	nas
Albanian	nʸe	du	tre	kokə	veš	goya	hundə
Greek	énas	ðyo	tris	kefáli	aftí	stóma	míti
Bulgarian	yedan	dva	tri	glava	uxo	usta	nos
Serbo-Croatian	yedan	dva	tri	glava	uho	usta	nos
Czech	yeden	dva	tři	hlava	uxo	usta	nos
Polish	yeden	dva	tši	gwova	uxo	usta	nos
Russian	adʸin	dva	trʸi	galavá	úxo	rot	nos
Lithuanian	vʸienas	du	trʸis	galvá	ausʸís	burná	nõsʸis
Latvian	viens	divi	trīs	galva	auss	mute	deguns
Finnish	üksi	kaksi	kolme	pā̃	korva	sū	nenä
Estonian	üks	kaks	kolm	pea	wilya-pea	sū	nina
Hungarian	eĵ	kēt	hārom	fő̃/fey	fül	sāy	orr
Turkish	bir	iki	üč	baš	kulak	ayïz	burun
Basque	bat	bi	hirür	bürü	belari	aho	südür

(Notes: (a) Norwegian I and II are the two officially recognized languages of Norway, Bokmål and Nynorsk, respectively. (b) Except for French 'one', the numerals are cited without gender variation.)

Chart 1.3. Language relationship (Major European languages)
(adapted from Greenberg 1957)

2. Phonetics, transcription, terminology, abbreviations

Throughout this book, important new terminology and concepts are introduced in bold face, as for example in the term **'segments'** below.

2.1. Phonetics

In order to understand how sound change operates, it is important to understand something of the nature of speech sounds. For sound change by definition is controlled by the phonetic characteristics of speech. Moreover, in many cases it does not just affect a single sound, but whole classes of phonetically similar sounds at the same time. An elementary familiarity with phonetics is necessary also in order to define such classes of similar sounds.

The following presentation of speech sounds or **segments** does not purport to be exhaustive. It is simply intended to be sufficiently detailed for the purposes of this book. Moreover, some details will be introduced later, in their appropriate specific context.

The easiest way to define and classify segments is in terms of their production or **articulation**; and this is the way which will be adopted here, with only a few exceptions. However, segments can also be classified in terms of their **acoustic** or auditory effects. In fact, it has been argued that sound change is much more sensitive to acoustic than to articulatory properties. But note that while certain changes are explainable only acoustically, for the majority of changes, an articulatory account is at least as feasible as an acoustic one. It seems useful to be able to capture this difference by defining the majority of segments articulatorily, and to reserve acoustic definitions for just those cases in which purely articulatory terminology would be inappropriate or insufficient.

Segments are articulated mainly by modifications of the air passing from the lungs, through the **glottis** (the 'Adam's or Eve's Apple') and the pharyngeal area above it, and then through the oral cavity and through the lips. Depending on where and how they are made, these modifications create different resonances and other modulations in the acoustic transmission of segments.

2.1.1. Stops and place of articulation

The most radical modification consists of a complete blockage of the airflow at one of the points through which it passes. Segments of this sort are called **stops**. Though the direct effect of such an articulatory gesture must be the absence of any audible sound, the blockage leaves an indirect acoustic effect on neighboring segments. And it is this effect which permits the acoustic and auditory identification of different stops, depending on where they are articulated.

Stops can be articulated at various points, or **places (of articulation)**. A closure of the lips produces **labial** stops; in the area of the teeth, **dentals**; further back in the oral cavity, at the 'hard palate', **palatals**; and in the area of the 'soft palate' or 'velum', **velars**. (See chart 2.1. below.)

All of these stops are found in English; cf. the initial segments in *pan, ban* (labial); *tan, Dan* (dental); *church, judge* (palatal); *came/king, game/ ghetto* (velar). But note that the 'palatals' of English are not just simple stops, but palatal or post-dental stops followed by a quite distinct 'sibilant' element. (For 'sibilants' see further below.) Even in languages like Spanish, which have more clearly stop-articulated palatals in words

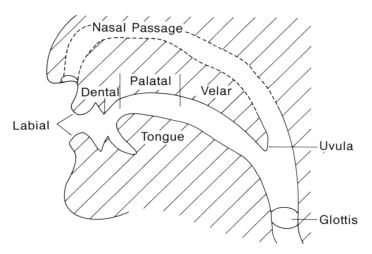

Chart 2.1. Places of articulation and articulators

like *muchacho* 'boy', a certain sibilant-like offglide can be discerned. This **'sibilant offglide'** is a very important, crosslinguistic feature of palatal stops. Note further that the 'dentals' of most English dialects are actually post-dental or **alveolar** and thus different from the 'pure' dentals of languages like Spanish and Italian. Some languages have even more retracted, **retroflex** segments. (Cf. 5.1.6 below for details.) These fine phonetic differences between more or less pure palatals or between dentals and alveolars can for the most part be ignored. They will be noted only where they are crucial for understanding a particular development.

In addition to these segments which occur as regular English speech sounds, other stops can be found in the world's languages. Only one of these will be important for our purposes, and that is the **glottal** stop, produced by closure of the **vocal cords** or **folds** (to membranes in the glottis). Although the glottal stop does not function as a distinctive speech sound in English, or most of the other European languages, it can occasionally be heard in English before initial vowels, especially in emphatic speech. Compare *[?]off with his head*. And German regularly has this stop before (orthographically) initial vowels. Moreover, many dialects of English have the segment for standard *t* in words like *bo[?]le* 'bottle'.

2.1.2. Fricatives and sibilants

A less radical modification than complete blockage of the airflow is that made for **fricatives**: The obstruction is incomplete, but narrows the air passage sufficiently to produce a special friction noise, with specific resonances according to the place of articulation. English has dental and **'labiodental'** fricatives in *think, this* and *fat, vat.* The latter differ from labial stops in that they are not **'bilabial'**, but are produced by an articulation of the upper teeth toward the lower lip. Bilabial fricatives are found in other languages. Thus Spanish has a bilabial fricative for written *v* or *b* (except after nasal or after pause), as in *haber* 'have', *Habana*. (Speakers of English tend to hear this sound variously as *v* or *w*.) Palatal fricatives occur in German *ich* 'I' and North. Germ. *ja* 'yes'; and velars in German *Loch* 'hole' (also Scots Engl. *loch*) and in the Spanish pronunciation of medial *g* as in *ruego* 'I ask'.

Fricatives can be articulated also in the glottal area; cf. the initial segment of Engl. *hound*. But note that *h* can be classified also as a semivowel (see below).

sibilants:

A special subset of the fricatives is constituted by the **sibilants**; cf.
e. g. Engl. *sip, zip* ('dental'), *ship, measure* (palatal or post-dental). These
differ from ordinary fricatives through some ancillary modification of
the air stream which creates a special acoustic effect.

What is interesting is that this effect can be brought about in more
than one way; and different speakers may choose different manners of
production, without being aware of any differences between their own
sibilants and those of other speakers. Thus, in the case of the sibilant
of *ship*, at least two different basic articulatory gestures are found in
English. (Similarly in other languages.) In one of these, the tongue tip
is the major articulator and points up to somewhere behind the dental
area. In the other, the tongue back is the major articulator, arching
against the palatal area; and the tip of the tongue is directed down,
behind the lower teeth. In both types, secondary articulatory gestures
bring about the sibilant effect. These gestures may consist of slightly
curling or folding the tongue lengthwise, or in the tongue's approximating another area of articulation (such as the lower teeth or the velum).
Yet other sibilant-producing gestures are found in other languages. All
of these gestures, however, bring about the 'same' acoustic or auditory
effect, that of sibilant noise which distinguishes sibilants from fricatives.
Sibilants, therefore, are best defined in acoustic, not in purely articulatory terms.

2.1.3. Voicing and aspiration

Except for the glottals, all the segments so far discussed come in
acoustically/auditorily distinguishable pairs, such as *sip:zip*. Articulatorily, they differ in terms of the presence or absence of **voicing** or **voice**,
a feature produced by the 'vocal cords': For **voiced** segments, as in
zip, these membranes come close enough together to be set in vibration
by the airflow. **Voiceless** segments, as in *sip*, lack this vibration, since
the vocal cords are in an 'open' position which produces only the same
kind of glottal friction as in a weakly articulated *h*. (This gesture is
similar to the 'rest position' of the glottis, but the aperture of the latter
is wider.)

The glottal stop comes only in one variety — voiceless. The reason
seems to be that the vocal cords cannot simultaneously produce a stop
and the vibration of voicing. Note however that since the airflow is
interrupted in all stops, voicing should not be articulatable for any

stops. But as *ban* (vs. *pan*) etc. show, 'oral' stops can be voiced. Evidently, some compensatory articulation makes it possible to produce voicing in these segments. Since the glottal friction of voicelessness and the vibration of voicing cannot be produced simultaneously, a voiced counterpart of *h* should likewise not be articulatable. However, some languages, including many of the languages of South Asia, have a 'voiced' *ɦ*. Here again, some compensatory articulation solves the problem. A common device used for this purpose is 'murmur'. Note also that voiceless *h* often is not simply characterized by the absence of voicing, but may involve secondary gestures which produce 'turbulence'.

In English and a number of other languages, voiceless stops generally differ from their voiced counterparts not only by an absence of voicing, but also by being **'aspirated'**, i. e. followed by a brief *h*-like 'offglide'. (In American English, aspiration tends to be limited to the initial voiceless stops of stressed syllables.) Other languages, however, have a contrast between aspirated and unaspirated stops, similar to the English contrast between voiced and voiceless. Frequently such 'distinctive' aspiration is found only with voiceless stops; cf. Class. Gk. *teínō* 'stretch': *theínō* 'kill'. But some languages have a distinction of aspirated vs. unaspirated for both voiceless and voiced stops; cf. Skt. *pala-* (a unit of weight), *phala-* 'fruit', *bala-* 'strength', *bhala* 'indeed'. Note that in languages which distinguish 'plain' and aspirated stops, aspiration tends to be more 'turbulent' than in English; and unaspirated voiceless stops have such a rapid transition from voiceless-stop articulation to the voicing of a following segment that speakers of languages like English tend to hear them as voiced. (Aspiration will generally be marked only for those languages in which it is distinctive.)

2.1.4. Obstruents vs. sonorants; syllabic vs. nonsyllabic

With the exception of the glottal stop, the segments discussed so far in many languages have a contrast between voiced and voiceless. Moreover, languages without such a contrast tend to have only the voiceless segments. Finally, stops and fricatives are articulated with a relatively great obstruction of the airflow. In all of these respects they differ from the class of segments which includes the initial sounds of Engl. *mow, no, lo, row*: Segments of the latter type do not as commonly show a voiced/voiceless contrast. Moreover, if there is no contrast, only the voiced variants are used. And, impressionistically, the airflow seems to be less obstructed; the segments appear to be more 'sonorous'. Given these differences, it is not surprising that the two classes of segments may behave differently in linguistic change. And the similarities within a given class may lead to similar behavior for the members of that class. To capture these similarities and differences, it is useful to distinguish the two classes as **obstruents** vs. **sonorants**.

The two segment classes differ further in their behavior within syllables: Obstruents are much more rarely **'syllabic'**, i. e. the center of a syllable, than are sonorants. In fact, with some marginal exceptions like the [s] of Engl. *psst*, many languages do not permit syllabic obstruents. Sonorants, on the other hand, quite commonly may be nonsyllabic or syllabic, even though standard orthography may not acknowledge this. Thus, the normal pronunciation of English words like *bottle, button, bottom* has syllabic [l, n̩, m̩], without any phonetic counterpart of the orthographically preceding vowel. (It is only in hypercareful speech that a sequence of vowel plus (nonsyllabic) sonorant is heard.)

Some languages, moreover, show systematic alternations between syllabic and nonsyllabic sonorants. Thus in Sanskrit, *r* is nonsyllabic next to vowel, but (generally) syllabic elsewhere; cf. e. g. *kr̥-ta-* 'what has been done' vs. *kr-iyamāṇa-* 'what is being done'.

The subclasses of the sonorants, the nasals, liquids, and semivowels, will be discussed in the following sections.

2.1.5. Liquids

Various *r*- and *l*-sounds are commonly classed together as **liquids**. These include the 'dental' (or more properly, alveolar) [r] of languages like Italian and Spanish, the palatal [λ] of the conservative varieties of the same languages (cf. It. *figlio 'son'*, Span. *ella* 'she'), and the dental [l] of most of the European languages. Moreover, in careful speech, standard French and many varieties of German and other European languages have a **'uvular'** [ʀ]; cf. Chart 2.1 for the location of the 'uvula'. (English, especially in its American varieties, tends to have rather different *r*- and *l*-sounds.) Liquids of the type [l, λ] are distinguished from the [r, ʀ] type as **laterals**.

It is difficult to find any positive articulatory basis for classifying these segments together. However, their behavior in language acquisition and linguistic change suggests that they do form a common class. Thus, a number of languages have lost the distinction between *r* and *l* as the result of sound change; cf. e. g. early Iranian. Others, such as Japanese, simply lack the contrast, with some dialects preferring the pronunciation [l], others (including the standard dialect), [r]. Finally, the difference between 'dental' [l] and [r] generally is one of the last distinctions learned by children acquiring their first language.

2.1.6. Nasals and nasalization, stops vs. continuants

The segments discussed so far are all **'oral'**, in the sense that the airflow (eventually) passes through the oral cavity only. However, lowering the uvula and the adjacent area of the velum permits the air to flow through the nasal passage, creating segments with special nasal resonances.

The most common speech sounds of this type are the so-called **nasals**, segments like the final sounds of Engl. *clam* (labial), *clan* (dental), *clang* (velar; the orthographic *g* is 'silent'); cf. also the palatal [ñ] of Span. *señor* 'sir'. Articulatorily, these segments are simply nasalized stops, differing from oral stops like [b, d, g] only in terms of their **nasalization**. However, as we have seen, in their behavior they differ from oral stops by being sonorants.

Moreover, unlike stops, but like fricatives (including sibilants) and liquids, they are directly identifiable, and their articulation may be audibly extended over a considerable length of time. Accordingly, together with fricatives and liquids they are distinguished from stops by being called **continuants**.

Also other segments may be nasalized, especially the vowels; cf. e. g. Fr. *bon* [bõ] 'good' vs. *beau* [bo] 'beautiful'. Nasalized fricatives and liquids are not as common, but are found in various languages around the world. (Like the nasal stops, they are of course continuants.)

2.1.7. Semivowels/glides; consonantal vs. vocalic

Beside nasals and liquids, the class of sonorants includes also the **semivowels** or **glides**, i. e. segments like the initial sounds of Engl. *wield* and *yield*. As the name semivowel suggests, they are the most vowel-like among the nonsyllabic segments. In fact, evidence from many languages and from linguistic change shows that they are the nonsyllabic counterparts of vowels like the [i] of Engl. *pit* and the [u] of *put*. Thus, just like Sanskrit nonsyllabic [r] alternates with syllabic [ṛ], so nonsyllabic [y] does with syllabic [i]; cf. *ny-avēdayat* 'reported' vs. *ni-vēdayati* 'reports'.

At the same time, because of their close relationship to the vowels, the semivowels may behave in a manner quite different from the liquids and nasals. Thus, for vowel/semivowel alternations like [i/y] the syllabic value seems to be more basic cross-linguistically; but for liquids and nasals, it is the nonsyllabic variant which tends to be more natural. Moreover, liquids and nasals in many changes behave just like the other consonants, while semivowels may act like vowels. To capture this distinction, the terms **vocalic** and **consonantal** have been introduced. The former designates vowels and semivowels. Liquids and nasals, together with fricatives and stops, are covered by the term 'consonantal'.

Beside *y* and *w*, also *h* may behave like a semivowel in certain changes. But note that in others it acts more like a fricative. That is, it appears to have the option of belonging to either of the two segment classes. The reason for its semivowel behavior is that in words like *heat, hit, hate, hat, hot, hoot, hut,* [h] is phonetically identical to the following vowel, except for the fact that it is voiceless and nonsyllabic. And in intervocalic position, [h] similarly is a voiceless and nonsyllabic transition from the preceding to the following vowel. Just like [y] and [w], then, it is vocalic and nonsyllabic.

2.1.8. Vowels — high/low, front/back

Unlike the other classes of segments, the **vowels** (and the related semivowels) are articulatorily confined to just one area, that of the velum. Some scholars, to be sure, use the term 'palatal vowels'; but in articulatory terms, that designation is not accurate.

At the same time, within the very confined velar area, a very large number of vowel distinctions can be made. In the following, only those distinctions will be discussed which will be important for the purpose of this book.

The most basic parameters defining vowel differences are captured by the terms **height** and **frontness/backness**. Of these, 'height' refers to the relative approximation of the tongue-back toward the velum: For the vowels of Engl. *peat, pit; boot, put,* the tongue is relatively close to the velum, and, accordingly, these vowels are referred to as **high**. On the other hand, the **low** vowels of Engl. *pat* and *father*, are articulated with the tongue in its lowest position. Vowels like those of *pet, pate; boat; but*, articulated with the tongue in an intermediate position, have traditionally been referred to as **mid** vowels. In order to make the generalization that for certain processes they behave more like ('non-high') low vowels, for others like ('non-low') high vowels, they are now commonly labeled **non-high/non-low**. ('Mid' will be retained as an alternative designation.)

The terms 'frontness' and 'backness' indicate whether the vowel articulation is made relatively forward or backward in the velar area. **Front** vowels are the vowels in Engl. *peat, pit; pate, pet; pat;* **back** vowels are found in Engl. *boot, boat,* (Brit.) *bought.* In the intermediate position we find the vowels of *just* (adverb; American pronunciation), *but*, and *father*. The traditional term for these is **central**; now they are commonly referred to as **non-front/non-back**. ('Central' will be retained as an alternative.) The [a] of *father*, to be sure, is usually labeled a 'back' vowel in generative linguistics. Phonetically, this is not accurate. True, in linguistic change, [a] often behaves like a back vowel; but this can be accounted for in terms of its being 'non-front'. On the other hand, there are changes in which its behavior is most accurately described as different from both the front and back vowels.

(In some varieties of English, the vowel of *father* is pronounced as a back vowel. Others make no distinction between this vowel and that of *bought*. In fact, the whole area of the low-central and mid- and low-back vowels is characterized by a great amount of fluctuation across different dialects of English. Note, however, that in phonetic transcriptions [a] will always refer to a low-central vowel, as it is found in Germ. *ja*; and [o] to a mid-back vowel as in Germ. *Boot*.)

2.1.9. Vowels — long:short, diphthong:monophthong, etc.

English sets of the type *peat:pit, pate:pet, kook:cook* exhibit yet another difference which is often referred to as **length**, i. e. a difference in vowel duration. The vowels of these sets are then differentiated as [iː]:[i], [eː]:[e], [uː]:[u]. An alternative transcriptional convention, which makes it possible to optionally mark short vowels as not being long, is the following: [ī]:[ĭ] or [i], [ē]:[ĕ] or [e], etc.

For most varieties of English, more than just length is involved, and the vocalic nuclei of *peat, pate, kook* are articulated as **diphthongs**, sequences of a 'steady-state' vowel plus a semivowel or glide. That is, if we transcribe the vowels of *pit, pet, cook* as [ɪ], [ɛ], [ʊ], the transcription of the vowels in *peat, pate, kook* would be [ɪy], [ɛy], [ʊw]. It is also possible to focus on the fact that the steady-state vowel of these diphthongs tends to be higher than the vowels in the corresponding 'short' or **monophthongal** nuclei. Accordingly, we might transcribe [iy], [ey], [uw]. (Some linguists, ignoring the post-vocalic glide, instead use the transcriptions [i], [e], [u].)

Such **qualitative** differences often accompany the **quantitative** distinction of length also in languages like German, where long vowels are steady-state, not diphthongal. And the terms **tense** and **lax** may be used to refer to the combination of qualitative and quantitative differences between long and short vowels. (Some linguists use these terms instead of 'long' and 'short', or for the qualitative differences in such vowels. The relation between vowel height, length, and 'tenseness' will be examined in greater detail in 7.4.5 below.)

Except where relevant, such fine distinctions will be ignored in this book, and transcriptions will focus on the length distinctions. Moreover, following the practice of traditional historical linguistics, long and short vowels will usually be distinguished as [ī]:[i] or [ĭ].

2.1.10. 'Secondary articulations'

Up to this point, vowels have been treated as oral segments. But as noted in 2.1.6, they may also be nasalized; that is, nasal resonances may be superimposed on the vowel resonances produced in the oral cavity.

Superimposed articulations like nasalization typically are produced outside the area of 'primary articulation' and accordingly are called **secondary articulations**. Cross-linguistically, secondary articulations are 'marked': Languages tend to have segments with secondary articulation only if they also have the corresponding 'primary' segments; but many languages only have the 'primary' segments. Thus, English only has oral vowels; French has oral and nasal vowels; but languages with only nasal vowels are exceedingly rare. (Some varieties of English, to be sure, have pervasive nasalization; cf. Midlands British and White Southern American English.)

Another secondary articulation of vowels is **rounding**: In English, back vowels are pronounced with a certain amount of lip rounding, while front vowels lack this rounding. This difference between back, rounded and front, unrounded vowels appears to be crosslinguistically the most unmarked situation. (Rounding, then, differs from other secondary articulations by being crosslinguistically unmarked for a subset of the vowels. But like other secondary articulations, it is produced outside the area of primary articulation.)

Unlike English, many languages (including German and French) have rounded front vowels, beside the unrounded front vowels familiar from English. In this book, the rounded front vowels are designated as [ü], [ö] etc. (Some languages also have a series of unrounded back vowels. These can be ignored in the present book.)

Secondary articulations can be found also in consonants. Beside aspiration, the most important are **'palatalization'** and **'labiovelarization'**. These will be treated in detail in section 5.1.5 below.

2.1.11. Suprasegmentals

Vowels, syllables, and even whole words may be further modified by **suprasegmental** articulations, such as **stress**, **accent**, and **tone**. In transcriptions, stress, accent, and tone are commonly marked over the vowels. But phonetically, they extend over larger stretches. Stress and accent tend to be properties of syllables; tone may range also over smaller and larger domains.

The distinction between stress, accent, and tone is not always easy to make. Stress and accent usually involve relative prominence of a particular syllable compared to other syllables in the same word. Tone, on the other hand, tends to function as a means of differentiating lexical items. But note that different stress or accent placement may also distinguish words, as in Engl. *pervért* vs. *pérvert*. Tone usually involves differences in pitch, but some languages have 'tonal' or 'pitch' accents; and even 'stress' (or 'stress accent') commonly involves pitch beside loudness and other factors. Moreover, historically, it seems to be possible for pitch accent systems to become tonal (or nearly so).

As a consequence, there is a fair amount of terminological uncertainty and fluctuation in the literature. This book does not purport to resolve this uncertainty and fluctuation.

2.1.12. Syllables and boundaries

The notion **'syllable'** has been invoked at various points in this presentation. Phoneticians find it difficult to agree on what it is, articulatorily or acoustically, that constitutes or defines a syllable. However, linguistic change and the synchronic organization of many languages offer abundant justification for the concept.

The basis for syllable structure is the so-called **sonority hierarchy**, cf. Chart 2.2. Syllables are built around a syllabic **nucleus**, the most sonorous element in the syllable. The preceding **onset** tends to be characterized by an increase in sonority toward that nucleus, the following **coda** by a decrease. Complications arise from the fact that various exceptions to these general principles can be found. Some are specific to particular languages. Others tend to be crosslinguistic. (For instance, onsets with stop + fricative are rarer and more 'marked' than fricative + stop onsets, even though the latter violate the principle of increasing sonority.)

Further complications arise in regard to **syllable boundaries**: Given structures of the type *ata, apta*, or *apra*, with two syllabic nuclei, where will one syllable end and the other begin? Here again, only some general tendencies can be stated: If there is only one intervocalic consonant, it will usually be syllabified with the following nucleus (hence the syllabification *a$ta*). In the case of a **cluster** of two consonants, the most general principle is to put the syllable boundary into the middle (hence *apta, apra*). Other tendencies, however, may partially or wholly override this principle. Thus, if the cluster has increasing sonority, it may be syllabified with the following nucleus (hence *a$pra*), especially if the second element of the cluster has a high degree of sonority. Clusters of three or more consonants exhibit even greater cross-linguistic variation. However, within a given language such variation is fairly limited.

Least sonorous:	Stop
	Fricative
	Nasal
	Liquid
	Semivowel
Most sonorous:	Vowel

Chart 2.2. Sonority hierarchy

In many sound changes, **word boundaries** seem to play a
Note however that in most languages there is no constant and cle
identifiable phonetic correlate of the boundaries between words. 'l
creates difficulties for an approach which defines sound change as
conditioned only by phonetic factors. (Chapter 11 shows how word

(a) Consonants (nonsyllabic):

		Labial	Labio-dental	Dental	Palatal	Velar	Glottal
Stops	vl.	p		t	č	k	ʔ
	vd.	b		d	ǰ	g	
Fricatives	vl.	Φ	f	θ, þ	ç	x	h
	vd.	β	v	ð	ɉ	ɣ	ɦ
Sibilants	vl.			s	š		
	vd.			z	ž		
Nasals		m		n	ñ	ŋ	
Liquids				l, r	λ	ʀ	
Semivowels	vd.					y, w	
	vl.					h	

(b) Vowels (syllabic):

	Front Unround	Front Round	Central	Back
High	i (ɪ)	ü (Ü)	ɨ (ɨ)	u (ʊ)
Mid	e (ɛ)	ö (œ)	ə (ʌ)	o (ɔ)
Low	æ		a	ɑ

Notes: (i) [þ] is the symbol for the voiceless dental fricative employed for Germanic; [θ] is used elsewhere. (ii) [ə] = the final vowel of Engl. *sofa*. [ʌ] = the vowel of *but*. (iii) Except for [ʌ], the parenthesized symbols refer to the 'lax' vowels of the type [ɪ] in *bit*. (iv) Parenthesized symbols will be used only for fine phonetic transcriptions.

Chart 2.3. Phonetic symbols and segments classes

boundaries come to play a role in these changes. Prior to that point, the issue will be ignored; and word boundaries will be given as conditions for sound changes.) Pre- and post-pausal **utterance bound-aries**, on the other hand, are phonetic phenomena and may thus be properly invoked as conditions for sound change.

2.2. Transcription

2.2.1. Phonetic transcription

For segmental phonetic transcription see Chart 2.3, which also gives a summary of most of the terminology introduced in 2.1. Phonetic transcriptions are given in square brackets, as in the diacritic examples below.

In addition, note the following diacritics:

- ˜ =   vowel nasalization, as in [ĩ], [ẽ]
- ¯ =   vowel length, as in [ē], [ā]
- : =   vowel length, as in [eː], [aː] (alternative transcription)
- ˇ =   explicit indication that a vowel is short, as in [ĕ], [ă]
- ´ =   accent, as in [mítn̩] 'mitten'
- _ =   syllabicity, as in [mítn̩]
- ‿ =   nonsyllabicity, as in [haį] = [hay] 'high'
- . =   retroflex consonant, as in [ṭ, ḍ, ṛ]
- h   (after a consonant) = aspiration
- y, w   (after a consonant) = palatalization, labiovelarization

Voiceless sonorants will be transcribed as in [m̥].

2.2.2. Transcription of specific languages

Examples from most of the older Indo-European languages will gen-erally be quoted in their standard (or standardized) orthography. In the case of languages not using the Roman alphabet (such as Greek and Sanskrit) the standard Romanization will be employed. Some modifica-tions will be made so as to bring transcription more in line with the phonetic symbols used in this book. (Thus, Sanskrit च, ऩ etc. will be rendered as *č, ǰ*, rather than the *c, j* of internationally established Romanization.)

This approach is made possible by the fact that the 'fit' between spelling and pronunciation is closer in most early languages than in Modern English. Phonetic transcriptions therefore are largely superfluous. Moreover, using standard orthography or Romanization brings this book more in line with the large traditional literature on historical linguistics which generally follows the same procedure. Transcriptions of this type will be cited in italics. But ordinary fonts may be used in numbered examples set off from the text.

The symbols used will have (roughly) the same phonetic values as those in Chart 2.3 above, except for the special conventions noted below:

(a) Proto-Indo-European: *k̑, g̑*, etc. = pre-velar/palatal stops contrasting with 'plain velar' *k, g*, etc. and 'labiovelar' *kʷ, gʷ*, etc.

(b) Latin: *c, q* = [k]; initial *i* before vowel = [y]; *v* = [w]; *ae, au* = [ay, aw].

(c) (Ancient) Greek: ˜ and ´ = different accentuations, as in *oîkoi* 'houses': *oíkoi* 'at home'.

(d) Sanskrit: *ṁ* = a nasalized segment of somewhat controversial interpretation, probably a nasal transition between the neighboring segments. *ṭ, ṭh, ḍ, ḍh, ṣ, ṇ* = 'retroflex' (post-dental) segments contrasting with the pure dentals *t, th, d, dh, s, n*. *ś* = a palatal sibilant. *h* = 'voiced' [ɦ], *ḥ* = voiceless [h] (a segment generally found only at the end of words. *v* = [w] early, later [β] or [v].

(e) Other Indo-Aryan languages: Similar to Sanskrit, except that Middle-Indo-Aryan *ṁ* = nasalization of a preceding vowel. In addition, Modern Indo-Aryan languages have some other retroflex segments, such as the *ṛ* of Hindi.

(f) Slavic and Baltic: *j* = [y]. Early Slav. *ě, a* = (originally) long [ɛ̄, ā]. Slav. *y* = [i]; *ĭ, ŭ* = 'super-short' [ə]-like high vowels ('jers'); *ę, ǫ* = nasal [ẽ, õ].

(g) Germanic: *j* = [y]. *y* = [ü] in Old English and Old Norse. *þ* = [θ] (see Chart 2.3).

2.3. Notation of changes, generalizations

Examples (1)—(8) below illustrate the standard notation of sound change. (Some additional conventions will be introduced later, in the appropriate contexts.)

(1) and (2) are examples of the notation of 'unconditioned change'; (3)—(7) of changes 'conditioned' by a given phonetic environment; (8) of the notation employed to indicate that more than one sound undergoes the same change. Finally, (9) illustrates the convention of **'feature notation'**, employing the articulatory (etc.) phonetic features introduced in 2.1 and summarized in Chart 2.2. (For abbreviations of these features and other conventional symbols employed in change formulations, see 2.7.1 below.)

Specifying the significant presence or absence of particular features (indicated by a + or − before that feature, as in [+ voice]) in many cases enables us to make **generalizations** which a simple enumeration of segments can only adumbrate. Thus, in 'segment notation', (9) would come out as something like (10), with the idea that voiceless labials change into voiced labials, etc., but not into, say, dentals. But in addition to its clumsiness, this formulation does not explicitly state that 'all voiceless stops become voiced between voiced segments'. Moreover, implicit in formulation (9) is the notion that the change from [− voice] to [+ voice] is not just accidental, but is 'conditioned' by the voicing of the **environment**. (But note that in many cases, the same generalization can be made by means of an informal, verbal statement, of the type 'all voiceless stops become voiced between voiced segments'. This alternative procedure is found in most traditional literature on historical linguistics and will frequently be employed also in this book.)

(1)   a > b = 'a changes into b by sound change'

(2)   b < a = 'b develops out of a by sound change'

(3)   a > b / c ___ d = 'a changes into b ... in the environment between c and d' (Variants: a > b / c ___ , a > b / ___ d = 'after c, before d')

(4)   a > b // c = 'a changes into b if preceded and/or followed by c, i. e. if it "neighbors" c'

(5)   a > b / ___ X d = 'a changes into b if d follows, with some unspecified segment or segments X intervening, i. e. not in direct contact'

(6)   a > b / ___ (X) d = 'a changes into b if d follows, with an optional intervening X'

(7)   a > b / ___ C_0 c = 'a changes into b if c follows, with any number of intervening consonants, including none'

(8) $\left\{\begin{matrix} a \\ z \end{matrix}\right\}$ > b / c ___ d = 'Either a or z changes into b between c and d; i. e., both develop the same way'

(9) $\left[\begin{matrix} + \text{ stop} \\ - \text{ voice} \end{matrix}\right]$ > [+ voice] / [+ voice] ___ [+ voice]

(10) $\left\{\begin{matrix} p \\ t \\ č \\ k \end{matrix}\right\}$ > $\left\{\begin{matrix} b \\ d \\ ǰ \\ g \end{matrix}\right\}$ / $\left\{\begin{matrix} \text{vowels} \\ \text{sonorants} \\ \text{voiced fric.} \\ ... \end{matrix}\right\}$ ___ $\left\{\begin{matrix} \text{vowels} \\ \text{sonorants} \\ \text{voiced fric.} \\ ... \end{matrix}\right\}$

Note that in sound change formulations like (1)—(9), the direction of change is indicated by an unshafted arrow (> or <). For analogical change, a shafted arrow (→) is used; and for borrowing, a double-shafted arrow (⇒). (For a different use of →, see Chapter 11.)

2.4. Phonology: contrast, phoneme, allophone/alternant

In addition to the phonetic features of segments, the environments in which they occur, and the classes to which they belong, also their structural relationship to one another may play a role in linguistic change. The branch of linguistics concerned with such structural relationships between segments is referred to as **phonology**.

Perhaps the most important relationship of this sort is the one covered by the term **contrast**. Simplifying matters a little, we can define contrast as the relation between segments which occur phonetically **unpredictably** and which thus can differentiate lexically distinct linguistic items. Thus the occurrence of [p], [t], and [k] in Engl. *pool, tool, cool* is not phonetically predictable, since all three segments are found in the same phonetic environment, before [ūl]. And obviously, it is the

presence of one segment vs. the others which differentiates the three
lexical items. In many cases, contrast can be succinctly demonstrated
by means of **minimal pairs** like [pūl]:[kūl].

What is important is that not all segments have such unpredictable
occurrences. Recall that in section 2.1.7, in arguing for considering *h*
a semivowel, it was observed that its pronunciation varies, depending
on the environment: Before high front vowels it has a high-front
articulation, before low vowels, a low articulation, etc. What remains
constant is the fact that it is voiceless and nonsyllabic. Moreover,
speakers are not normally aware of the fact that its pronunciation varies;
they 'feel' that there is a single, unitary *h*.

The situation is similar for the velars: Close inspection reveals that
the [k] of Engl. *keep* is different from that of *cool*. The former **alternant**
has a front-velar articulation, just like the front vowel [i] which follows
it; the latter has the back-velar and rounded articulation of the following
back-rounded [u]. At this point we can symbolize this difference as [kⁱ]
vs. [kᵘ]. Again, some features of pronunciation are constant, such as
the fact that all the alternants are stops, voiceless, and articulated in
the velar area. And speakers again are not aware of there being any
'different' *k*-sounds.

What makes it possible for speakers to feel this way is first, the
presence of features which remain constant and thus guarantee a certain
degree of similarity between the alternants. Secondly, and equally
importantly, the alternants do not contrast; their selection is predictable:
They are in what is called 'complementary distribution', such that
one occurs where the other(s) cannot occur. (Beside 'complementary
distribution', other criteria may determine absence of contrast. But such
fine details need not concern us.)

Classes of such phonetically similar segments whose selection for a
particular environment is predictable have been called **phonemes**, and
the alternants which constitute such a class are referred to as **allophones**.
Where necessary, phonemic transcriptions can be differentiated
from allophonic and purely phonetic ones by the use of slashes, as in
/k/ (phoneme) vs. [kⁱ] and [kᵘ] (allophones).

Recent developments in linguistics have tended to reject the theory
behind these definitions, but the terminology still is commonly employed.
(The term 'phoneme', to be sure, now is used in a very different
meaning; cf. Chapter 11.) The theoretical foundation for these terms,
the notion 'contrast', has recently been resurrected as an important
determinant of linguistic change.

2.5. Morphology

The notions **morpheme, root, stem, affix, prefix, suffix,** and **ending** are important in the discussion of **morphology**, the analysis of word structure. Morphemes are the smallest meaningful elements of given words, such as the elements *word* and *s* in *word-s*. Boundaries between morphemes will be indicated by a hyphen.

Roots are those morphemes which have the core lexical meaning in a given word, such as *word* in *word-s*, or the *morph-* of *morpheme, morphology*.

Other morphemes are affixes. Depending on their position before or after the root, they are distinguished as prefixes or suffixes, respectively. Thus, the *-eme* of *morph-eme* is a suffix; the *pre-* of *pre-fix*, a prefix. (A third type of affix is the 'infix', as in Lat. *iu-n-g-ō* 'I yoke', made from the root *iug-* of *iugum* 'yoke'.)

If the main carrier of lexical meaning in a given word is morphologically complex, containing a root plus an affix, it is called a stem, such as *word-y* in *word-i-er, word-i-ness*.

Many affixes serve the purpose of lexical or stem **derivation**. Thus the *-eme* of *morpheme* establishes a stem or lexical item which is different from the word *morphology*. In the Indo-European languages, one set of suffixes has a different, non-lexical function. These suffixes serve the purpose of **inflection,** to express such non-lexical notions as the relationship between words to each other within a given sentence. Since these usually are the last suffix in the word, they have been called **endings**.

The non-lexical notions most commonly expressed by Indo-European endings are **number, person,** and **case**. Early Indo-European distinguished three numbers: singular, dual, and plural. Three persons (first, second, third) are differentiated in verbs and pronouns. And the cases relevant for early Indo-European are nominative, accusative, vocative, instrumental, dative, ablative, genitive, and locative.

2.6. Other terminology and concepts

Language can be viewed either as historically developing or as a more or less static, **synchronic** object of investigation. Throughout this book, references will be made to this difference between history (or **diachrony**) and synchrony and to the relationship between these two aspects of language.

The prefixes **'pre'** and **'proto'** refer to earlier stages of linguistic history. 'Proto-' designates a language as being reconstructed, rather than actually attested, as in 'Proto-Indo-European'. 'pre-' indicates an (often inferred) earlier stage of a language, as in 'pre-Modern English', 'pre-Old English', or even 'pre-Proto-Indo-European' (a stage preceding reconstructed Proto-Indo-European).

2.7. Abbreviations and symbols

The following abbreviations and special symbols will be used in addition to the phonetic symbols listed in Chart 2.3. Note however that especially in the chapter on syntax, some other abbreviations may be introduced. They will be defined in context.

Some abbreviatory symbols are used in more than one reference. Thus, N may refer to nasals, to the 'new' or modern stage of a language, to Norse, to nouns, or to nominative. However, the context will make the exact reference clear.

2.7.1. Abbreviations and symbols for sound change and phonological formulations

Note that C and V are commonly used in two overlapping, but distinct meanings. In formulations like (11) they often refer to the features [− syllabic] and [+ syllabic], respectively. On the other hand, in combination with other features, as in (12), they indicate [+ consonantal, (− syllabic)] and [+ vocalic, (+ syllabic)]. (See also section 2.2 on transcription, 2.3 on the notation of changes, and 2.4 for the use of slashes in phonemic transcription.)

(11) C > [+ voice] / V ___ V

(12) $\begin{bmatrix} V \\ -hi \\ -lo \end{bmatrix} > [+hi] / \underline{\quad} \begin{bmatrix} V \\ +hi \end{bmatrix}$

Symbols:

C	[+ cons.] or [− syll.]	C_0	any number of C, incl. none
L	liquid	N	nasal (stop)
R	sonorant	V	vowel
∅	zero	$	syllable boundary
#	word boundary	##	utterance boundary
—	morpheme boundary		

* preceding a linguistic form indicates a reconstructed form
* following a form indicates that the form is not attested or ungrammatical

Feature abbreviations (including nonabbreviated features):

acct.	accent	asp.	aspirated
back		cons.	consonantal
cont.	continuant	dent.	dental
fric.	fricative	front	
glott.	glottal	hi	high
lab.	labial	lat.	lateral
liqu.	liquid	lo	low
long		nas.	nasalized
obstr.	obstruent	pal.	palatal
pltd.	palatalized	round	
sib.	sibilant	son.	sonorant
syll.	syllabic	vel.	velar
voc.	vocalic	voice	

2.7.2. Morphological and syntactic abbreviations

IO	indirect object	N	noun
NP	noun phrase	O	object
PP	prepositional NP	S	subject
V	verb	VP	verb phrase
RC	relative clause		

| 1 | first person | 2 | second person |
| 3 | third person | | |

A(cc.)	accusative	Ab.	ablative
D(at.)	dative	G(en.)	genitive
I(nstr.)	instrumental	L(oc.)	locative
N(om.)	nominative	V(oc.)	vocative

| Aux | auxiliary | | |

| f(em.) | feminine | m(asc.) | masculine |
| n(eut.) | neuter | | |

act.	active	adj.	adjective
adv.	adverb	du.	dual
fut.	future	impve.	imperative
itr.	intransitive	pass.	passive
perf.	perfect	pl.	plural
pple.	participle	prep.	preposition
pres.	present	sg.	singular
tr(ans.)	transitive		

2.7.3. Languages

General prefixes:

Class.	Classical	M	Middle
Mod.	Modern	N	New
O	Old	P	Proto-

(The most usual designations of the old, middle, and modern stages of a given language are O, M, and N, as in OE = Old English, ME = Middle English, NE = New or Modern English.)

Other:

BS	Balto-Slavic	CS	Church Slavic
E	English	G	German
HG	High German	IE	Indo-European
N	Norse	RV	Rig-Vedic (Sanskrit)
W	Welsh		

| IAr. | Indo-Aryan (i. e. Indic) | SCr. | Serbo-Croatian |

Alb.	Albanian	Algonqu.	Algonquian
Am.	American	Arm.	Armenian
Att.	Attic (Greek)	Av(est).	Avestan
Brit.	British	Catal.	Catalan
Celt.	Celtic	Cz.	Czech
Dan.	Danish	dial.	dialect(s), dialectal
Engl.	English	Finn.	Finnish
Fr.	French	Gaul.	Gaulish (Celtic)
Germ.	German	Gk.	Greek (usually ancient Gk.)
Gmc.	Germanic	Go(th).	Gothic
Hom.	Homeric (Gk.)	Hung.	Hungarian
Icel.	Icelandic	Ion.	Ionic (Gk.)
Ir.	Irish	Iran.	Iranian
It(al).	Italian	Jap.	Japanese
Ka.	Kannada (Dravidian)	Kor.	Korean
Lat.	Latin	Latv.	Latvian
Leon.	Leonese (Spanish)	Li(th).	Lithuanian
Ma.	Marathi	Norw.	Norwegian
Pers.	Persian	Pol.	Polish
Port.	Portuguese	Rom.	Romance
Ru(ss).	Russian	Rum.	Rumanian/Romanian
Serb.	Serbian	Sic.	Sicilian
Skt.	Sanskrit	Slav.	Slavic
Sp(an).	Spanish	Swah.	Swahili
Swed.	Swedish	Toch.	Tocharian
Ukrain.	Ukrainian	Ur.	Urdu

(Note that Tocharian comes in two distinct varieties, called A and B.)

3. Sound change:
The regularity hypothesis

3.1. The hypothesis

In the 1870s a group of linguists now generally referred to as the **Neogrammarians** created a lot of attention, controversy, and excitement with the claim that unlike all other linguistic change, **sound change is regular and operates without exceptions**.

Qn of empirical truth ←

This **Neogrammarian** or **regularity hypothesis** led to a great deal of valuable and interesting research. However, as can be expected, such a strong claim did not remain without a good deal of often quite vociferous opposition. And some of that opposition remains valid even today, especially as it extends to some other, related, but ultimately less important claims of the neogrammarians. (Cf. Chapter 20.) However, much of the criticism was misdirected, by attacking the above, bold formulation of the neogrammarian hypothesis, rather than its 'fine-print' version which contains many important modifications.

These modifications concern first of all the definition of **sound change**, not as just any change affecting the pronunciation of words, but as only those changes which take place 'mechanically'. Here, the term 'mechanical' must be understood in opposition to the 'mental' or 'psychological' motivation of other linguistic changes. More prosaically, we can therefore restate the definition of sound change as change of pronunciation which is not conditioned by non-phonetic factors.

Secondly, sound change thus defined is said to take place regularly only at a particular time, in a particular speech community. No claims are made about cross-linguistic regularity. For instance, the change in (1) took place only in English, at some stage prior to the modern period. It did not occur in Old English, which retained initial *k* before *n*; cf. the data in (1). Nor did it affect other (Germanic) languages; cf. NHG *Knabe, Knecht*.

> (1) k > ∅ / # ___ n.
> Cf. OE cnafa [knava], cniht [knixt] : NE knave, knight [nēv, nayt].
> (Elsewhere, [k] is retained, as in OE cyning [küniŋg] : NE king.)

Example (1) illustrates something else which is important about sound change: It may be confined to a particular environment, in which it is perfectly regular. Outside that environment, it just as regularly does not take place. Changes of this type are said to be **conditioned** (by the environment in which they occur). Other changes, which are not confined in this way, are termed **unconditioned**. (For examples of this type, see parts of 'Grimm's Law' below.)

Finally, certain changes are quite commonly, often notoriously, irregular or **sporadic**, even though they are not conditioned by non-phonetic factors. These changes include 'dissimilation' and 'metathesis'; cf. (2) for examples. They will be discussed in greater detail in Chapter 6. (See also Chapter 20 for a possible motivation for the sporadicity of these processes.) What is important is that sporadicity is limited to certain specifiable subtypes of sound change, which therefore can be systematically exempted from the regularity hypothesis.

> (2)   Lat. peregrinus > Fr. pèlerin (dissimilation of r ... r > l ... r)
> Lat. miraculum > Sp. milagro (metathesis of r ... l > l ... r)

With these modifications, it is possible to rephrase the neogrammarian hypothesis as in (3). Clearly, this statement is much more cumbersome and much less exciting than the slogan 'Sound change is regular and operates without exceptions'. But something like it must always be understood as a 'footnote' to the slogan.

> (3)   **Neogrammarian regularity hypothesis restated:** Change in pronunciation which is not conditioned by non-phonetic factors is regular and operates without exceptions at a particular time and in a particular speech community, with possible environmental restrictions. Certain changes (including dissimilation and metathesis) are exempt from this hypothesis.

3.2. Apparent exceptions

Real language is far from regular, and the regularities predicted by the neogrammarian hypothesis more often than not seem to be contradicted by numerous exceptions.

The neogrammarians were keenly aware of this fact. But they claimed that such exceptions are merely apparent contradictions of the regularity hypothesis. In reality, they argued, they are attributable to one of several other factors.

One of these might simply be a wrong formulation of the sound change; a more accurate reformulation would show the change to be regular. A related notion is that the change in question may have been correctly formulated, but that a later sound change in some way undid the effects of the earlier change, thereby creating apparent exceptions.

An even more important source of irregularity is the fact that beside regular sound change, various other changes, such as analogy and borrowing, can apply to any given linguistic form. And these other changes are by definition irregular and will superimpose their own irregularity on the regularity of sound change. In fact, the neogrammarian regularity hypothesis for sound change owes a great deal to the realization that other change is not regular and can therefore be invoked to explain apparent exceptions to sound change.

Examples for these various possibilities of explaining apparent exceptions to sound change will be given in the sections below. At this point, however, it is important to note that the neogrammarian regularity hypothesis has proved to be enormously fruitful, no matter how accurate it may be in fact. For it forces the linguist to look for explanations of apparent irregularity, either by establishing a non-phonetic source or through a better formulation of a given sound change. Either way we learn more about the history of a given language and about the nature of linguistic change than if we subscribe to a view that does not expect regularity in sound change.

3.3. Grimm's Law and Verner's Law: reformulation and additional change

An amazingly regular correspondence between the <u>obstruent systems</u> of Germanic and the other Indo-European languages caught the imagination of linguists in the early part of the nineteenth century. It inspired a great amount of research which slowly removed apparent exceptions to the changes that were responsible for this correspondence. The findings of that research, in turn, eventually provided some of the most important empirical support for the regularity hypothesis.

The correspondences which gave rise to this important development in the history of linguistic science are exemplified by the developments of the initial consonants in (4). (Only one example is given for each segment. The actual number of correspondences runs in the hundreds.) A simplified summary of the correspondences is found in (5).

(4) | PIE | Gothic | Old English | |
|---|---|---|---|
| *pǝtḗr | fadar | fæder/fader | 'father' |
| *tréyes | þreis | þrī | 'three' |
| *ḱm̥tóm | hund | hund(rāþ) | 'hundred' |
| *déḱm̥(t) | taihun | tēon | 'ten' |
| *ǵews- | kiusan | cēosan | 'choose' |
| *bher- | bairan | beoran | 'bear' |
| *dhē | (ga-)dḗþs | dǣd | 'deed' |
| *ǵhew- | giutan | gēotan | 'pour' |

(Examples with initial PIE * *b* are virtually nonexistant.)

(5) | PIE | | | PGmc. | | |
|---|---|---|---|---|---|
| p | t | k | f | þ | x/h |
| (b) | d | g | (p) | t | k |
| bh | dh | gh | b/β | d/ð | g/ɣ |

(PGmc. x/h, b/β etc. indicate allophonic variation.)

The sound changes which account for the above correspondences can be formulated as (6), using modern notation and assuming that <u>what is 'distinctive' about the PIE aspirates *bh, dh, gh* etc. is their</u> <u>aspiration, rather than the presence or absence of the feature [voice].</u> ⎰ next pg
⎱ 6(c)
The changes are known as **Grimm's Law**, after the German scholar

Jacob Grimm who most successfully brought them to the attention of the linguistic community. (They were discovered before him by a Danish scholar, Rasmus Rask.)

(6 a) $\begin{bmatrix} + \text{stop} \\ - \text{voice} \end{bmatrix} > [+ \text{fric.}]$

b) $\begin{bmatrix} + \text{stop} \\ + \text{voice} \end{bmatrix} > [- \text{voice}]$

c) $\begin{bmatrix} + \text{stop} \\ + \text{asp.} \end{bmatrix} > \begin{bmatrix} + \text{voice} \\ - \text{asp.} \\ (\pm \text{fric.}) \end{bmatrix}$

In PIE
[+stop / +asp] sounds
are all [+v]

(The notation ($\pm$ fric.) indicates that the outcome allophonically appears also as a fricative.)

While Grimm and his contemporaries did not fail to be impressed with the great systematicity and regularity of these changes, they did not expect absolute regularity. People, being human beings, were not expected to behave in a completely regular, 'mechanical' manner.

In fact, it was easy to find cases where the above changes did not seem to apply or where other changes appeared to have taken place. Thus, each of the Germanic examples in (7) contains an 'unshifted' voiceless stop, contrary to what change (6 a) would lead one to expect. Worse than that, in addition to the unshifted stops, the first two examples exhibit also instances of PIE voiceless stops which were shifted to fricatives — in accordance with (6 a). These words, then, cannot even be considered systematic exceptions to Grimm's Law. (In (7), attested Latin forms are used instead of the unattested forms of ancestral PIE.)

? vl stop didn't become a fricative

(7) | Latin | Gothic | Old English | |
|---|---|---|---|
| captus | hafts | hæft | 'captured, prisoner' |
| piscis | fisks | fisc[-k] | 'fish' |
| spuō | speiwan | spīwan | 'spit, spew' |
| stō | standan | standan | 'stand' |

Another set of apparent exceptions consists of forms in which the PIE voiceless stops are changed, but where the outcome of the change does not agree with the predictions made by (6 a): Instead of a voiceless fricative we find a voiced segment; cf. (8 a). (In the cited examples, that segment is written as a stop; but just as in the outcomes of the PIE aspirates, there was an alternation between stop and fricative pronunciation.) Again we find that beside this aberrant development, the regular change may be found in the same word, as in the first item of (8 a). Moreover, phonetically and above all semantically closely related words show the regular Grimm's-Law treatment according to (6 a); cf. (8 b). Even within a single paradigm, different forms of the same word may appear with the regular voiceless development according to Grimm's Law, or with the aberrant voicing of (8 a); cf. the examples in (9).

Acced f͞ by Verner's Law

(8)	PIE	Gothic/OHG	Old English	
a)	*pətér	fadar (Go.)	fæder	'father'
	*swekrū́	swigur (OHG)	sweger	'mother-in-law'
b)	*bhrā́tēr	brōþar (Go.)	brōþor	'brother'
	*swékuros	swehar (OHG)	swēor	'father-in-law'

(Note: By a subsequent change, the outcome [h] of PIE [ḱ] was lost in Old English. Even so, the outcome in (b) is different from that in (a).

(9)		Old English	Old High German	Sanskrit
pres. sg. 1		weorþu	wirdu	vártē
past sg. 1/3		wearþ	ward	vavárta
past pl. 3		wurdon	wurtun	vāvṛtúḥ
past pple.		ge-worden	gi-wortan	vavṛtāná-

(PIE root: *wert- 'turn'; OE, OHG meaning: 'become'. Old High German has changed PGmc. *þ to d, and *d to t; but the distinction remains.)

   The evidence thus seems to be overwhelming that in spite of a great amount of systematicity, Grimm's Law was far from completely regular.
   Later researchers showed that this impression is incorrect. First, in (7) and the many other examples which follow this pattern, all instances of unshifted voiceless stop occur in the same environment: after PIE obstruent. And conversely, no shifted voiceless-fricative outcomes are found in this environment. If we *reformulate* the (a) part of Grimm's Law as in (10), then the pattern of (7) ceases to be exceptional and

omes completely regular. Incorporating this reformulation, we ac-dingly rewrite Grimm's Law as in (6').

(10) $\begin{bmatrix} + \text{ stop} \\ - \text{ voice} \end{bmatrix} > [+ \text{ fric.}] \; / \; [- \text{ obstr.}] \underline{\quad}$

(Note: This notation is intended to block the shift just in case the stop is preceded by an obstruent.)

(6') Grimm's Law reformulated:

a) $\begin{bmatrix} + \text{ stop} \\ - \text{ voice} \end{bmatrix} > [+ \text{ fric.}] \qquad / \; [- \text{ obstr.}] \underline{\quad}$

b) $\begin{bmatrix} + \text{ stop} \\ + \text{ voice} \end{bmatrix} > [- \text{ voice}]$

c) $\begin{bmatrix} + \text{ stop} \\ + \text{ asp.} \end{bmatrix} > \begin{bmatrix} + \text{ voice} \\ - \text{ asp.} \\ (\pm \text{ fric.}) \end{bmatrix}$

The second set of counterexamples likewise turns out to be highly patterned and regular, even if more subtle in its special conditioning than the first: In the data of (8 a) and (9), voiced obstruents appear if and only if the PIE voiceless stop occurs in medial voiced environment and if the immediately preceding syllable is unaccented. Elsewhere, the voiceless outcome is found. Compare the difference between the words for 'father' and 'brother' in (8 a/b) and the correlation between Sanskrit accent placement and Germanic voiced vs. voiceless obstruent in (9). (The placement of PIE accent is most faithfully preserved in Sanskrit and Greek. That is the reason for citing Sanskrit data in (9).)

What is interesting is that PIE *s underwent voicing in the same environment as the PIE voiceless stops; cf. (11). This suggests that all Proto-Germanic voiceless fricatives became voiced in this environment, whether they were inherited from PIE (*s) or developed out of earlier voiceless stops by Grimm's Law (PIE *p, t, k > f, þ, x). And data of the type (12) indicate that the same development took place in the context [+ voice] ___ #. In addition, they show that the accentual condition for the change is lack of accent on the immediately preceding syllable. (Without such evidence, the data in (8), (9), and (11) could

just as well have been interpreted as indicating that the accent had to
follow the relevant obstruent.)

(11)

	Old English	Old High German	Sanskrit
pres. sg. 1	cēosu	kiusu	jṓṣē
past sg. 1/3	cēas	kōs	jujṓṣa
past pl. 3	curon	kurun	jujuṣúḥ
past pple.	ge-coren	gi-koran	jujuṣāṇá-

(PIE root: *ǵews- 'taste, enjoy'; OE, OHG meaning: 'choose'. The expected voiced *z* has further changed into OE, OHG *r*. Traces of the earlier
z can be found in Gothic and in the early Runic inscriptions.)

(12) PIE *áyos > PGmc. *áyas > *áyaz > *aiz > OE ār,
NE ore; OHG ēr 'brass, etc.'

Unlike the data in (7), the 'counterexamples' in (8) and (9) and the
data in (11)/(12) cannot be accounted for by a simple reformulation of
Grimm's Law. Rather, an **additional change** must be invoked. This
change, formulated in (13), is named **Verner's Law**, in honor of the
Danish linguist who was the first to propose the correct solution.

[handwritten: OHG kiusu]

(13) $\begin{bmatrix} + \text{fric.} \\ - \text{voice} \end{bmatrix} > \begin{bmatrix} + \text{voice} \\ (\pm \text{stop}) \end{bmatrix} / \begin{bmatrix} + \text{voice} \\ - \text{acct.} \end{bmatrix} \underline{\quad\quad} \left\{ \begin{matrix} [+ \text{voice}] \\ \# \end{matrix} \right\}$

¹ (The notation (± stop) accounts for the fact that in the case of non-
sibilants, the outcome of Verner's Law exhibits the same stop/fricative
alternation as the Grimm's-Law developments of the PIE aspirates.)

[handwritten: ? sie p. 43]

For maximum and most natural generalization, the change is formulated such that it will apply to the outcome of Grimm's Law (as well
as to PIE *s). Moreover, it must precede a change by which Proto-
Germanic replaced the accentual system of PIE (in which the accent
was not restricted to a particular syllable) with a pattern which required
accent on the first syllable of the word. (An informal notation of that
change is given in (14).) Any other ordering of the changes would lead
to incorrect results; cf. the derivations in (15).

(14) $C_0 \, V \, C_0 \; > \; [+ \text{acct.}] \; / \; \# \underline{\quad\quad}$
$\quad\quad\;\; [\pm \text{acct.}]$

(15) PIE   *pətḗr   PIE *pətḗr   PIE *pətḗr
      GL   *faþár   VL   — — —   AS   *pə́tēr
      VL   *fadár   GL   *faþár   GL   *fáþar
      AS   fádar   AS   fáþar   VL   — — —

      Outcome: fádar   fáþar*   fáþar*

(GL = Grimm's Law, VL = Verner's Law, AS = Accent Shift. Relevant vowel changes from PIE to Gothic have been tacitly applied.)

A situation of this sort, where only one ordering of historical changes will yield the correct results, is commonly referred to as **relative chronology**. Note that when linguists establish a relative chronology with the argument that no other ordering will lead to the correct outcome, they are not simply playing around with changes and imposing their own view on history. Rather, it is the history of the language and its development which imposes the solution on the linguist. (But compare Chapter 11 for factors which may interfere with our ability to uncover the relative chronology of linguistic changes.)

3.4. Beyond Grimm's and Verner's Laws: bleeding and feeding changes

At several places in the above discussion, we had to gloss over the fact that changes subsequent to Grimm's and Verner's Laws had obscured the outcomes of these sound changes. In principle, this is no different from what Verner's Law did to Grimm's Law. However, in the case of Grimm's and Verner's Laws the relationship between the changes was fairly simple: The output of one change served as the input of the other. The historical development of the post-Verner's Law obstruent system of Germanic into Old English shows that the relationship between changes may be more complex.

A change shared by all the Old Germanic dialects, except Gothic and the early Runic inscriptions, is the one in (16), which applies to the outcome of Verner's Law. Note that this is an unconditioned change.

(16) z > r (Cf. OE *curun, ge-coren* in (11) and *ār* in (12))

The change in (17) is of more restricted application, being limited
to the group of 'West Germanic' dialects, which includes Old English
and pre-Old High German: As noted earlier, the outcome of PIE *dh- -7 ᵘᵉⱼ (13)
was PGmc. *d/ð, and this was also the Verner's-Law result of PIE
*t > PGmc. *þ. In West Germanic, this alternation between stop and
fricative was eliminated in favor of the stop. Also this change was
unconditional. (Old High German subsequently changed d into t.)

(17)   ð > d (Cf. OE *fæder*)

Subsequent to both of these developments, Old English underwent ᴏᴛ
a set of changes by which fricatives were voiced between vowels and (19)
other sonorants, and devoiced word-finally. Note that PGmc. [h], rather
than being voiced, appears to be lost intervocalically. But this can be
explained from the phonetic nature of [h]: In this position, it is simply
a voiceless, nonsyllabic transition between the preceding and following
vowels. Voicing therefore will make it indistinguishable from its surroundings and effectively bring about its loss.
    These developments are illustrated in (18), and a (consolidated)
formulation is given in (19). (The transcription in (18) is quasi-phonetic.)

(18)   PGmc.   Old English

       *wulf-   wulf   'wolf'
       *wulfōs/z   wulvas   'wolves'
       *hlaiβ-   hlāf   'bread'
       *hlaiβōs/z   hlāvas   'loaves of bread'
       *brōþar-   brōðor   'brother'
       *kaus   cēas   'chose'
       *keusan   cēozan   'to choose'
       *sehan   sēon   'to see'
       *sax   seah [x]   'he, she saw'
       *sēɣun   sæɣon (dial.)   'they saw'
       *burɣ-   burh [x]   'fort'

(19)

$$[+ \text{fric.}] > \begin{cases} [+ \text{voice}] \ / \ \begin{bmatrix} -\text{obstr.} \\ +\text{voice} \end{bmatrix} \underline{\quad} \begin{bmatrix} -\text{obstr.} \\ +\text{voice} \end{bmatrix} \\ [-\text{voice}] \ / \ \underline{\quad} \# \end{cases}$$

There are several considerations which suggest that (19) is chronologically later than either (16) or (17). The facts which are relevant for the present discussion are the following: (i) Changes (16) and (17) do not apply to the outcome of (19); (ii) PGmc. *z and *$\eth$ 'escape' change (19) by going to r and d. That is, only the relative chronology in (20 a) gives correct results for all forms.

(20 a)	PGmc.	keusan	kaus	kuzun	aiz
	(16/17)	– – –	– – –	kurun	air
	(19)	keuzan	– – –	– – –	– – –
	outcome:	cēozan	cēas	curon	ār
b)	PGmc.	keusan	kaus	kuzun	aiz
	(19)	keuzan	– – –	– – –	ais
	(16/17)	keuran	– – –	kurun	– – –
	outcome:	cēoran*	cēas	curon	ās*

The difference in relationship between Grimm's and Verner's Laws on one hand, and our changes (16/17) and (19) on the other is as follows: Grimm's Law **feeds** Verner's Law, by providing inputs for it. Changes (16/17), however, not only fail to feed (19), they actually **bleed** it, by 'removing' possible inputs to (19).

'Additional' sound changes, invoked to account for apparent irregularities in a particular change, therefore are not always to be 'added' after that change. They may precede or follow, and they may bleed or feed it.

3.5. Analogy

With the above modifications, Grimm's and Verner's Laws quite accurately predict the forms found in Old English and Old High German. But in the corresponding modern languages, this is no longer the case, at least in verbal paradigms of the type (9) and (11). Thus, instead of the sibilant/r alternation of (11), Modern German has only r. The English situation is even more noteworthy, for as a result of the medial voicing of (19), Old English had a triple alternation between z, s, and r. Modern English instead has [z] throughout. Compare the paradigms in (21 a). (The first-singular present forms of (11) have here been replaced with infinitives.) In some cases, however, English has retained vestiges of the old alternation; cf. (21 b). And similar relics can be found also in German.

(21 a) OE cēozan, cēas, curon, gecoren : NE choose, chose,   *no more*
                                                chosen [-z-] *z/s/r*
        OHG kiosan, kaus, kurun, gikoran : NHG küren, kor, *alternate.*
                                             gekoren
  b) OE wæs, wæron   : NE was, were *sibilant /r*
      OE lēozan, lēas, luron, geloren : NE lose … beside
                                       forlorn

What has happened is that **analogy** has in virtually all instances eliminated the alternations that were created by Verner's Law. (The specific analogy at work here is called 'leveling'. Note that to be quite accurate, the first applications of this process can be observed as early as Old English and Old High German. But the earliest texts frequently preserve traces of the original form. Compare e. g. early OHG original *sluoh* beside innovated, analogical *sluog*, cf. pl. *sluogun* → later exclusively *sluog : sluogun* '(s)he slew : they slew'.)

That we are dealing with analogy, and not with some (irregular) sound change can be seen from the fact that the German replacement of *s* by *r* and the English generalization of [z] are processes limited to lexical items which earlier had a paradigmatic *s/r* alternation. That is, the notion 'paradigm', a morphological, nonphonetic factor plays a prominent role in these changes. Other words, such as OE *beoran* : NE *bear,* OHG *arlōsen* : NHG *erlösen* 'save, deliver', do not exhibit such changes.

These developments show that analogy can interfere with the outcome of sound change. But because analogy is not a regular process, its interference usually is not regular either. (Contrast the data in (21 a) vs. (21 b).) Moreover, by being sensitive to nonphonetic criteria, it affects only those linguistic forms which are characterized by these criteria. Thus, one of the reasons that E *forlorn* has retained its *r* is that it no longer is 'felt' to be part of the paradigm of *lose*. It therefore is exempt from the analogical processes which affect verbal paradigms.

Here as elsewhere we can extrapolate from such known cases to prehistorical situations: If a language whose earlier history is not known to us shows irregularities similar to those of modern English and

[right margin handwritten notes:]

analogy explained

Interference c̄ sound △

Or . ʔ these sort of comments whose pt of view? c̄ proto-speaker / c̄ investigator?

theoretical assumptn

German, and if these irregularities can be similarly linked to non-phonetic, morphological (etc.) factors, then we may infer that the lack of regularity is attributable to analogy. We have here, then, a very important tool for accounting for apparent irregularities in sound change.

A case in point is Gothic. Like the other Germanic languages, Gothic shows the effect of Verner's Law in words like *fadar*; cf. (8) above. In verbal paradigms, however, Verner's-Law alternations of the type (9) and (11) are virtually non-existent. Instead, Gothic usually shows the voiceless alternant throughout the paradigm; cf. (22a). However, just as Modern English preserves a few traces of the old alternation, so does Gothic; cf. (22b). In English, one of these traces is in the past tense of the verb 'to be', i.e. of a verb which also in other respects is highly 'irregular'. Similarly, Gothic has an (optional) trace of the old x/γ alternation in the otherwise highly irregular verb 'to have, to own'. In addition, English preserves certain relics of the alternation in lexical items which no longer are felt to be in the same paradigm (cf. *lose:forlorn*). And again, Gothic has a similar relic in the words *fra-wairþan* 'become corrupt':*fra-wardjan* 'make corrupt' which likewise belong to different paradigms.

(22 a)   wairþan, warþ, waurþun, waurþans 'become'
         kiusan, kaus, kusun, kusans 'choose'
     b) aih 'he owns' : aigun 'they own'
         wairþan 'become' : frawardjan 'perish'

Given these data and the fact that the absence of Verner's-Law alternations is tied up with the nonphonetic notion 'paradigm', the traditional, 'orthodox' neogrammarian explanation would be as follows: Verner's Law applied with the same regularity in the prehistory of Gothics as it did in the other Germanic languages. The apparent exceptions in (22 a) and similar paradigms are attributable to the workings of analogy.

Note however that beside this 'orthodox' approach, there has continued to be a 'heterodox' countercurrent which would claim that there was no separate analogical development — the Gothic application of Verner's Law was morphologically restricted from the start. In this view, then, there can be such a thing as **morphologically conditioned sound change**. An alternative, but in effect very similar claim would be that a **preventive analogy** interfered directly with Verner's Law (not with its outcome), so as to forestall the development of paradigmatic alternations.

The trouble with arguments of this sort is that they are usually advanced for situations like the Gothic one, where the absence of earlier attested history makes it impossible to show how the irregularities came about. They patently do not work for languages like English and German whose earliest stages show (virtually) complete regularity in the outcomes of Verner's Law, and where it is possible to trace how analogy slowly obscures that regularity. Moreover, in all too many cases it is possible to point to forms like Go. *aih:aigun* which the 'orthodox' approach can elegantly explain as relics of an originally regular sound change. The 'heterodox' view, on the other hand, would have to account for them as 'exceptions' to a sound change which itself is in some sense 'exceptional', in that its application in one morphological category is different from what it is elsewhere. Finally, note that languages like English and German require a distinction between regular sound change and (irregular) analogy. And the interaction between these two types of change not only is perfectly able to account for relics like E *was:were, lose:forlorn*; it is the only acceptable historical explanation of these forms. As we have seen, the same approach is perfectly able to account for the Gothic facts. Proponents of 'morphologically conditioned sound change' or 'preventive analogy' have not explained why languages like Gothic should nevertheless be treated as fundamentally different, as having a third type of morphologically conditioned sound change.

3.6. Borrowing

Doublets like those in (23 a) illustrate another source for apparent irregularity of sound change: The forms in the middle column have undergone Grimm's and Verner's Laws; the ones on the right have not. The latter might therefore be taken as exceptions to these changes. But note the existence of similar doublets (cf. (23 b)) which cannot be explained in this fashion. For here the form on the right side differs from PIE in its initial consonant. One might try to account for forms of this type by some additional (irregular) sound changes.

Linguists realized early that this is not the correct explanation, but that the forms on the right side have been **borrowed** from Latin. And in Latin, PIE initial *bh* regularly changes into *f*; cf. (24). This provides further support for the view that sound change is regular and that apparent irregularity is to be attributed to other processes.

(23) PIE   Modern English   Modern English
 a) *pətér   father   paternal
      *mātér   mother   maternal
 b) *bhrátēr   brother   fraternal

(24) PIE   Latin   Latin derived adjective
      *pətér   pater   paternālis
      *mātér   māter   māternālis
      *bhrátēr   frāter   frāternālis
      cf. *bhéro   ferō
      *bheydh-   fīdō
      ...   ...

In cases like E *father:paternal*, it is relatively easy to determine that the apparent irregularity in Grimm's and Verner's Laws is to be attributed to borrowing. For the differences between Latin and English are great enough to show which word goes back to which source. The situation is a little more complex if a borrowing has been made between more closely related languages, or between dialects of the same language. In many cases, however, even these can be detected.

An example is the following: In Old English, fricatives were voiceless in initial position. And this voiceless articulation is generally retained in Modern English; cf. (25 a). In a small set of words, however, we find an apparently irregular voicing of OE *f* to *v*; cf. (25 b). What is especially striking is that *fox* shows the regular treatment, but *vixen*, its original feminine form, has the voiced outcome.

(25) Old English   Modern English
 a) fætt   fat
      fēoh   fee
      for   for
      fox   fox
      ...   ...
 b) fatu   vat
      fana   vane
      fyxin   vixen

The explanation for the divergent development in (25 a) is that these forms are early borrowings from Southwestern British dialects into the London dialect which was to become the basis for Modern Standard English. In the Southwestern dialects, which include the Somerset [zʌmǝzɛt] dialect, fricatives regularly were voiced by a change which is formulated in (26). In this dialect area, then, we get not only *vixen*, but also *vox*, etc. (Compare the dialect of Squire Jones in Fielding's *Tom Jones*.)

(26) [+ fric.] > [+ voice] / $ ___ V

There are, of course, other instances of initial voiced fricatives in Modern English, such as *vain* and *zeal*. These generally are obvious borrowings. Thus, *vain* is from French, and *zeal* from Greek via Latin. (An exception is the initial voiced fricative of *this, that, the*, etc. The fact that these forms quite commonly are unaccented gave rise to a special sound change which voiced consonants in unstressed environment; cf. 5.3.1 for further discussion. The appearance of voiced fricatives in the stressed variants of these forms, then, is due to analogy.)

3.7. Fast speech, onomatopoeia, taboo

Analogy and borrowing are the most common 'nonphonetic' sources for apparent irregularity. However, some more isolated cases of irregularity are attributable to other factors.

One of these is **'fast speech'**, a term which covers the phenomenon of less clearly articulated, 'slurred' articulation found in accelerated forms of speech. (Note for instance the fast-speech pronunciation of E *can I go?* as something like [ŋaʸgoʷ].) The term may be used also in reference to similar articulary reductions in 'careless', 'tired', etc. speech.

By and large, fast-speech phenomena do not seem to have any lasting effect on linguistic change, which rather seems to take more careful, 'normal' speech as its starting point. However, in certain expressions, especially in 'politeness' terms like those in (27), reductions highly reminiscent of fast speech are encountered quite frequently. One suspects that these forms are 'borrowings' from fast speech into normal speech, and that the motivation for the borrowing is something like the following: Although people want or need to be polite and therefore may use longer, more high-flown forms of address, they do not necessarily want to lose too much time in the process. Reduced, fast-speech versions of these longish polite forms, then, provide the ideal compromise.

(27)   E   madam(e) (from Fr. madame 'my lady') > ma'am
       It. madonna 'my lady' > mon(n)a (cf. Mona Lisa)
       Sp. vuestra merced 'your mercy' > usted 'you (honorific)'

In addition to 'ordinary' vocabulary, most (perhaps all) languages have words which through their segments imitate sounds that we hear around us. Compare Engl. *bow wow, cockadoodledoo* = Germ. *wauwau, kikeriki*, etc. **Onomatopoetic** vocabulary of this sort is often said to be impervious to sound change. Thus, ME *pīpen* (sound made by little bird chicks) should by regular sound change have become NE *pipe* [payp]; instead, it is said, we find *peep* [pīp], with the onomatopoetic high vowel [ī] retained.

An alternative explanation would see in NE *peep* a replacement for expected *pipe*, made in order to reestablish the imitative 'fit' between speech and animal sound. The motivation for the development, then, is imitative, not purely phonetic. The change, therefore, does not qualify for being termed a 'sound change'.

In many cases it is possible to cite evidence which shows this alternative analysis to be superior. For instance, in the case of ME *pīpen*, dictionaries do list its regular outcome *pipe* as a form of Modern English. True, *peep* is the more common variant, but that is to be expected if it is in fact a more clearly onomatopoetic replacement of inherited *pipe*. Note also the even more common forms *cheep* and *chirp*. These suggest that imitation can proceed in more than one way and that consequently, new onomatopoetic forms can be created at any time, independent of what forms may have been in earlier use. Historical developments involving onomatopoeia therefore must be treated with great caution.

Irregularities may arise also as the result of **taboo**: Though languages may differ in what they consider to be too sacred — or too profane — to be uttered in polite company, all languages seem to contain expressions which are considered taboo by their speakers. Nevertheless, speakers often feel an urge or a need to use these words anyway. A common solution to this dilemma lies in **tabooistic distortion**, a deliberate alteration of the segmental structure of a tabooed word. Examples from English are *doggone, (gosh) darn*, or *shoot*, as substitutes for well-known tabooed expressions.

Since this type of distortion is dependent on the nonphonetic, semantic notion of taboo, it cannot possibly apply with the regularity of purely phonetically conditioned sound change.

3.8. Conclusions

This chapter has demonstrated that many apparent counterexamples to the neogrammarian regularity hypothesis can be shown not to be real counterexamples, but to be explainable either through reformulation of sound change and additional sound changes, or through 'nonphonetic', inherently irregular processes like analogy and borrowing.

Here as elsewhere, then, we may extrapolate from the known to the unknown and conclude with the neogrammarians that all apparent irregularities are to be explained in this fashion.

As the discussion in Chapter 20 will show, this latter conclusion needs to be moderated to some degree. Nevertheless, the neogrammarian regularity hypothesis has survived the test of time amazingly well; so well, in fact, that for practical historical work it still provides the heuristically most useful guidelines.

4. Sound change and phonological contrast

4.1. Introductory comment

Sound change, as defined by the neogrammarians, is conditioned entirely by phonetic factors. However, as structural linguists on both sides of the Atlantic realized, its repercussions may go beyond phonetics and affect the phonological structure of language. (And as will be seen in later chapters, phonological structure in turn may influence the direction of sound change.)

4.2. Sub-phonemic change; merger and split

The most straightforward type of change is one which merely changes the features of a given segment, without impinging on its contrastive identity. For instance, parts (b) and (c) of Grimm's Law (repeated as (1) below) have been argued to be 'mere changes in pronunciation' that do not affect phonological structure: Where previously, say, *d* and *dh* contrasted with each other, Proto-Germanic still has a contrast — between *t* and *d/ð*. Compare (2) below for a minimal pair, and (3) for a diagrammatic representation of the developments. (Here as elsewhere in this chapter, ≠ indicates a phonological contrast and ~ allophonic variation; solid lines refer to developments which change contrast; and broken lines represent developments or synchronic variation at the 'sub-phonemic' or 'allophonic' level.)

$$(1\,a) \quad \begin{bmatrix} + \text{ stop} \\ - \text{ voice} \end{bmatrix} > [+ \text{ fric.}] \ / \ [- \text{ obstr.}] \ \underline{\quad}$$

$$b) \quad \begin{bmatrix} + \text{ stop} \\ + \text{ voice} \end{bmatrix} > [- \text{ voice}]$$

$$c) \quad \begin{bmatrix} + \text{ stop} \\ + \text{ asp.} \end{bmatrix} > \begin{bmatrix} + \text{ voice} \\ - \text{ asp.} \\ (\pm \text{ fric.}) \end{bmatrix}$$

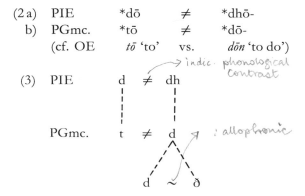

(2 a) PIE   *dō   ≠   *dhō-
   b) PGmc.   *tō   ≠   *dō-
       (cf. OE   *tō* 'to'   vs.   *dōn* 'to do')

→ indic. phonological contrast

(3) PIE   d   ≠   dh

     PGmc.   t   ≠   d   : allophonic

                    d ~ ð

Below the level of contrast, however, things are more complex: Not only has the pronunciation of the segments changed, but the Proto-Germanic outcomes of the PIE aspirates have undergone differentiation into stop and fricative allophones. The term **split** has been introduced to refer to such processes of differentiation.

allophonic split

Just the opposite of this allophonic split is brought about by the West Germanic change of **ð* to *d* (cf. Chapter 3, ex. (17)). That change eliminates the allophonic variation within the phoneme /d/; cf. (4) and (5) below. This converse of split has been called **merger**.

allophonic merger

(4) PGmc.   fadar [-ð-]   dō [d-]   dēdiz = [dēðiz]
     OE   fæder [-d-]   dōn [-d-] dæd   = [dæd]
             'father'   'do'   'deed'

(5)   d   ~   ð

                   \   /
                    V
                    d

4.3. Phonological merger and split

All of the changes so far examined in this chapter are **sub-phonemic** and do not affect phonological structure: No old contrast is lost, and no new contrast is introduced. (Some linguists would accept this interpretation only for the allophonic split and merger, but would consider parts (b) and (c) of Grimm's Law to be phonologically significant since they entail a radical change in the feature system. The problem with this position is that it is not always clear where to draw the line between 'radical' and 'other' change in the feature system.)

Many changes, however, do affect the phonology of a given language by eliminating old contrasts or introducing new ones; that is, we can get **phonologically significant** mergers and splits. And it is these developments which usually are referred to by the unmodified terms 'merger' and 'split'. (Changes of the type (3) and (5), then, are specifically labeled as 'allophonic merger' and 'allophonic split'.)

*z → r

Thus, the change of PGmc. *z to r (Chapter 3, ex. (16)) obliterated the contrast between these two segments, and *z and *r 'merged' into a single phoneme /r/; cf. (6) and (7).

(6)   PGmc.   *aiz-   ≠   *air-
      OE   ār   =   ār
                'metal'   'messenger'

(7)   PGmc.   z   ≠   r

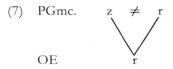

      OE   r

Merger can come about by more complex developments. Consider change (8) below [= (19) of Chapter 3]. As a consequence of its application (and of the change of earlier *β to v), the Proto-Germanic contrast between *f and *β was eliminated. Compare the data in (9) and the left side of diagram (10). The right side of (10) maps out the developments from the purely phonetic point of view and shows that phonological and phonetic developments do not necessarily coincide.

Note that although the two segments merge phonologically, the result is not an invariant segment as in (6)/(7), but a phoneme with two allophonic members. Moreover, disregarding the small phonetic adjustment from *β to v, the change does not eliminate any old phonetic segments or result in any new ones; only the distribution of the segments is altered.

(8)

$$[+ \text{fric.}] > \begin{cases} [+ \text{voice}] \ / \ \begin{bmatrix} - \text{obstr.} \\ + \text{voice} \end{bmatrix} \underline{\quad} \begin{bmatrix} - \text{obstr.} \\ + \text{voice} \end{bmatrix} \\ [- \text{voice}] \ / \ \underline{\quad} \# \end{cases}$$

(9) PGmc.   Old English

    *wulf-   wulf   'wolf'
    *wulfōs/z   wulvas   'wolves'
    *hōf-   hōf   'hoof'
    *hōfōs/z   hōvas   'hooves'
    *grōβō-   grōve   'groove'
    *hlaiβ-   hlāf   'bread'
    *hlaiβōs/z   hlāvas   'loaves of bread'
    *kalβ-   cealf   'calf'
    *kalβizō   cealvru   'calves'

(10)   Phonological development ‖ Phonetic development

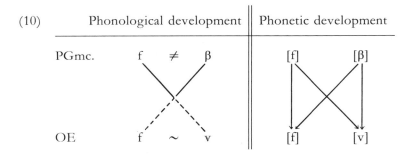

The full phonological implications of change (8) are even more
complex: Recall that in Proto-Germanic, [β] alternated with [b] as
allophones of the same phoneme /b/. And that phoneme clearly was in
contrast with /f/; cf. (11 a). Now, if the allophone [β] merged with /f/,
but [b] did not, then the phoneme /b/ underwent a process of (phonological) split; cf. (12). For /b/ continued to contrast with /f/; cf. (11 b).

(11 a) PGmc.   *banō(n)   ≠   *fanō(n)
    b) OE   bana   ≠   fana
                'murderer'   'flag, vane'

(12) PGmc.

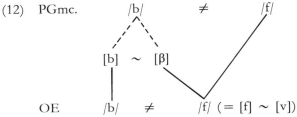

Disregarding the low-level, allophonic variation of OE /f/, diagram (12) represents a classical pattern in which (phonological) split comes about: An originally allophonic split becomes contrastive through merger of one of the allophones with another phoneme. A variant of this development is part (a) of Grimm's Law. As (13) and (14) show, when PIE stops occurred after obstruent and thus did not qualify for (1 a), they merged with the outcome of (1 b). Pattern (14) differs from (12) in that there is no evidence for invoking an intermediate stage with allophonic split. The split and the merger may well have been simultaneous. However, what is shared by both of these scenarios is the fact that split comes to be phonologically significant as the result of a merger, in a pattern of **combined merger and split**.

(13)   PIE   *tr̥no-   *stā-   *dr̥no-
       PGmc.   *þurna-   *stand-   *turna-
       OE   þorn   standan   torn
               'thorn'   'stand'   'anger'

(14)   PIE

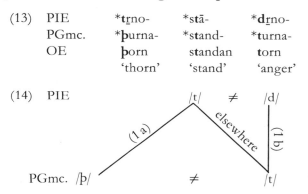

A second way in which split can come about is similar to the scenario in (12), in that it starts out with low-level allophonic alternation. However what triggers the split is not merger, but **loss of** the **conditioning environment** for the allophonic alternation.

This development can be illustrated by the fate of the Old English [f]/[v] alternation along the way toward Modern English. As a result of the changes in (8) and of the merger and split developments in (10) and (12), the allophones of Old English /f/ had (roughly) the distribution in (15); cf. the examples in (16 a). What is important is that at this point, [v] can occur only if a sonorant or vowel follows; its occurrence is 'conditioned' by that sonorant or vowel. Subsequently there was a change in the conditioning environment: Many vowels and sonorants were lost in final syllables. As a consequence, [f] and [v] now can both occur in word-final environment; their relative distribution has ceased to be predictable; they have come to be in contrast. Compare the forms in (16 b) and the diagram in (17).

(15)   OE /f/: [v] / [+ son.] ___ $\left\{\begin{matrix} [+\text{son.}] \\ V \end{matrix}\right\}$

[f] elsewhere, incl. / [+ son.] ___ #

(16 a)   OE   [līf]   [līvlič]   [livyan]
     b)   NE   [layf]   [layvlī]   [liv]
                  'life'   'lively'   'to live'

(17)   OE   /f/

[f]   ~   [v]   / ___ $\left\{\begin{matrix} [+\text{son.}] \\ V \end{matrix}\right\}$

⇓

∅

NE   /f/   ≠   /v/

Note that for split through loss of conditioning environment to occur, it is sufficient that SOME of the conditioning environments be lost. It is not necessary that ALL of them disappear. For instance, in the split of Old English /f/, conditioning environments were lost in forms like *livyan* > *live*, but not in *līvlic* > *lively* and other forms like it. Moreover, [v] becomes a different phoneme not only in forms like *live* (where it has ceased to be predictable), but also in forms like *lively* where the conditioning environment for the voicing has remained. For this and other situations, the slogan 'Once a phoneme, always a phoneme' has been invoked. But see also the next section.

Beside loss, also a simple **change in conditioning environment** can result in split. Examples will be given in 5.1.2 and 5.1.5.

4.4. Neutralization

When Proto-Germanic /z/ and /r/ merged in most of Germanic, the synchronic result was the elimination or **neutralization** of their contrast. For synchronic phonology, however, such cases of complete merger or neutralization are less interesting than partial, environmentally restricted mergers. Compare the German 'final devoicing' in (18) and (19): It leads to the merger of the voiced obstruents with their voiceless counterparts in final position, but leaves the contrast unaffected elsewhere. (Compare the final vs. medial outcomes in (19).)

(18)   [+ obstr.] > [− voice] / ___ #

(19)   OHG   rad   rades   rāt   rātes
       NHG   [rāt]   [rādəs]   [rāt]   [rātəs]
             'wheel'   'of the wheel' 'advice'   'of the advice'

Neutralizations of this type are interesting, in that they cause difficulties for the slogan 'Once a phoneme, always a phoneme': While the distribution of voiced vs. corresponding voiceless stops clearly is unpredictable and contrastive in (initial and) medial position, it is completely predictable word-finally. Only the voiceless 'alternant' of obstruent pairs like /t/:/d/ can occur in this environment. Some linguists therefore invoke a special concept, the **archiphoneme**, to refer to the segments which occur in the position of neutralization. This permits them to capture the native speakers' feeling that, say, the [t] of [rāt] and the [d] of [rādəs] are 'the same sound'. Other linguists insist on identifying the word-final [t] of [rāt] as an allophone of the phoneme /t/ and to account for its relationship to the [d] of [rādəs] as a **morphophonemic alternation**, involving not just phonology but also morphology (in the form of 'word boundary'). Whatever the merits of the arguments on either side, historical linguistics offers many changes which are consonant with the second view, but also some cases where the archiphonemic, environmentally restricted neutralization of a given contrast plays a decisive role. (Cf. e. g. 8.1 below.)

Neutralization can take a variety of synchronic shapes and need not result only from historical merger.

For example, just like German, Sanskrit has word-final neutralization of obstruent voicing. However, instead of a unitary voiceless representation of the archiphoneme, Sanskrit offers a predictable alternation between voiced and voiceless: Word-final obstruents are voiceless before pause or if a voiceless obstruent follows, voiced elsewhere; cf. (20) and (21).

(20)
$$[+ \text{obstr.}] > [- \text{voice}] / \_\_\_ \# \left\{ \begin{array}{c} [- \text{voice}] \\ \#\# \end{array} \right\}$$

$$> [+ \text{voice}] / \_\_\_ \# [+ \text{voice}]$$

(21)	vāk##	:	[vāk]	'speech'
	vāk#tasya	:	[vāktasya]	'that one's speech'
	vāk#asya	:	[vāgasya]	'his speech'
	yug##	:	[yuk]	'yoking'
	yug#tasya	:	[yuktasya]	'that one's yoking'
	yug#asya	:	[yugasya]	'his yoking'

An example of synchronic neutralization not due to historical merger would be the distribution of English liquids after [s]: While /r/ and /l/ clearly are in contrast in most other contexts (cf. *row* and *low*), only [l] can occur after [s]. Hence *slang, slam, slime* are acceptable English words; *srang*, sram*, srime** are not. (Historically, this situation arises from the fact that PIE **sr* changed to **str* in Proto-Germanic, while **sl* was retained.)

4.5. One-to-many, many-to-one replacements

Up to this point we have only looked at 'one-to-one replacements', in which one segment or phoneme changes into another one. However, in diphthongization (as in OE *līf* > NE [layf]), a single segment gets replaced by a sequence; and the converse development is observed in contraction (cf. OHG *bluot* > NHG [blūt] 'blood').

From the phonological point of view, changes of this sort are quite complex. Take for instance the diphthongization of OHG *ī* to NHG [ai]. As (22) shows, this change resulted in merger with old *ei* which likewise became [ai]. However, note that [ai] is bisegmental. The merger therefore was not just with [ai], but at the same time "partly" with [a] and "partly" with [i], either of which can occur by itself, as in [mat] 'worn out' and [mit] 'with'.

(22)	OHG	līb	(h)leib
	NHG	[laip]	[laip]
		'body'	'loaf (of bread)'

Not much seems to be gained by trying to devise diagrams which will take care of the complexities of such changes. Note however that while developments of this sort may involve merger and split, they are substantially different from these processes.

4.6. Extended demonstration

This chapter may be profitably concluded with a summary of the phonological developments affecting the labial stops, from Proto-Indo-European to Modern English. (GL = Grimm's Law, VL = Verner's Law. — (8/10/12) and (16/17) refer to the examples of this chapter in which the respective developments are illustrated and diagrammed.)

(23)   PIE

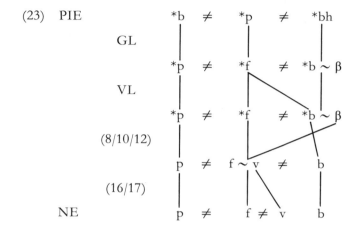

5. Sound change: Assimilation, weakening, loss

Most of the processes covered in this chapter belong to the category of regular sound change. In fact, among conditioned sound changes, these processes make up the bulk of regular change. (Changes which are not normally regular will be specially noted.)

5.1. Assimilatory changes

5.1.1. General; Greek-letter variables (α for variable feature)

The process of assimilation can be illustrated by the history of the word *assimilation*. It is derived from Lat. *assimilāre* 'to assimilate', which in turn is composed of a prefix *ad-*, a root or stem *simil/simul-* 'similar, like', and a verbal suffix *-āre*. In the word *assimilāre*, then, the final *-d* of the prefix has **assimilated**, i. e. become similar in pronunciation, to the initial *s-* of *simil-*; cf. (1).

(1)   d > s / ___ s

In *assimilāre*, the process of assimilation has gone all the way, making the 'assimilated' segment identical in pronunciation to the following *s*. Such a development is referred to as **complete** assimilation. Note that the outcome of this process is a double or **geminate** [ss], with roughly twice the length of a single [s]. (If in languages like English, *assimilation* is pronounced with a single [s], that results from a separate process of degemination, for which cf. 5.2 and 5.3.2.)

Assimilation can also be **partial**, affecting only a subset of a given segment's features. Compare the Sanskrit data in (2) and the Latin examples in (4). The respective sound changes are formulated in (3) and (5). As can be seen, the assimilation of stops to following stops affects only their voicing, and the assimilation of nasals to following stops is limited to their place of articulation. Otherwise, these segments retain their original identity. (The data given here are synchronic, but the changes did take place at some point in history.)

(2) Skt. yu-ŋ-g- + -dhi : yuŋgdhi 'yoke thou'
          yu-ŋ-g- + -tha : yuŋktha 'yoke ye'
          ri-ŋ-k- + -dhi : riŋgdhi 'leave thou'
          ri-ŋ-k- + -tha : riŋktha 'leave ye'

(Note: *yu-ŋ-g-* and *ri-ŋ-k-* have 'nasal infixes' and are derived from the roots *yug-* and *rik-* respectively.)

(3) [+ stop] > [α voice] / ___ [+ stop, α voice]

(4) Lat. in- + primere   : imprimere   'impress'
              + tendere   : intendere   'intend'
              + congruere : [iŋkoŋgruere] 'be incongruous'

(5) N > [α place] / ___ [+ stop, α place]

Examples (3) and (5) introduce a new notational convention, the so-called **Greek-letter variable** notation. This convention is highly useful for many assimilatory processes, and is employed also in the notation of other changes. The more straightforward application of the notation is that in (3). Here the symbol 'α' is understood to indicate that the output of the change has the same feature value ('+' or '−') as the conditioning environment. The notation in (5) extends this notation to place of articulation, which is not statable in terms of a simple '+' or '−'. (5) can be read as indicating that the output of the change has the same feature for place (of articulation) as does the conditioning environment.

The changes examined so far are examples of **anticipatory** assimilation: The segment which is uttered earlier 'anticipates' part or all of the pronunciation of a later segment. The converse development, in which the pronunciation of a segment 'perseveres' into the domain of a following segment, is referred to as **perseverant** assimilation. Examples for this type of assimilation are given in (6) and (7). (6) illustrates complete perseverant assimilation, (7) exemplifies partial perseverant assimilation.

(6) PGmc. *wulnō > *wullō > OE wull 'wool'
              *fulnaz > *fullaz >   full 'full'

(7) Skt. ātman- > MIAr. dial. atpan- 'self'

Note that though anticipatory and perseverant assimilation are both very common processes, anticipation is found more frequently than perseverance.

(Many linguists use the terms 'progressive' and 'regressive' assimilation. But different scholars do not agree on what should be called 'progressive', and what 'regressive'. Some refer to the changes in (6) and (7) as 'regressive', since the assimilating segment 'goes back' to the pronunciation of an earlier segment; others call it 'progressive', since the impetus for the assimilation 'goes forward' from the earlier to the later segment. The terms 'anticipatory' and 'perseverant' have the advantage of being unambiguous.)

In addition to anticipatory and perseverant assimilations, there may also be cases of **mutual** assimilation, in which both involved segments become similar to each other; cf. e. g. (8). But a priori, changes of this type can always be conceived of as proceeding in two steps, one involving anticipatory, the other perseverant assimilation. In fact, (7) shows that some Middle-Indo-Aryan dialects only have perseverant assimilation in the cluster [tm]. It is therefore entirely plausible that (8) came about by the two-step development in (9).

(8) Skt.   ātman- > MIAr. dial. appan- 'self'

(9 a) Perseverant assimilation:

$$\begin{bmatrix} + \text{ stop} \\ + \text{ nas.} \end{bmatrix} > \begin{bmatrix} - \text{ nas.} \\ \alpha \text{ voice} \end{bmatrix} / \begin{bmatrix} + \text{ stop} \\ - \text{ nas.} \\ \alpha \text{ voice} \end{bmatrix} \_\_\_$$

Hence: ātman- > atpan-

b) Anticipatory assimilation:

[+ stop] > [α place] / ___ [+ stop, α place]

Hence: atpan- > appan-

All the examples so far cited have been instances of **contact** assimilation: The two segments involved were in immediate contact with each other. However, developments like the ones in (10) show that **distant** assimilation is also a possibility.

DISTANT usually for vowels

(10) pre-Lat. *penkʷe > *kʷenkʷe > Lat. quīnque 'five'
        *pekʷō > *kʷekʷō >   coquō   'I cook'
        *perkʷus > *kʷerkʷus >   quercus 'oak'

In consonants, such distant assimilation rarely is regular. Example
(10), to be sure, might be considered regular, in that all three words
which qualified for the change did undergo it. But one may well wonder
whether three items are sufficient to establish a pattern of 'regularity'.
At any rate, examples like (11) are much more typical. Here we
find distant consonant assimilation in (a), but no such change in the
phonetically very similar words of (b).

(11 a)	Lat.	*līrium	>	līlium	'lily'
b)		dēlīrium	(unchanged)		'confusion, madness'
		rīdiculāria	(unchanged)		'antics'
		postulāria	(unchanged)		(a ritual term)

The situation is different for vowels, in so far as assimilation between
vowels in neighboring syllables is quite common, and regular. (Cf. the
discussion of umlaut and vowel harmony in 5.1.2—3 below.) That is,
it appears as if for vowel assimilations, intervening consonants 'do not
count', such that vowels in neighboring syllables behave as if they were
in contact.

Note however that examples of such regular vowel assimilation in
neighboring syllables appear to be limited to certain features, especially
usually those of vowel height, frontness, and rounding. Length assimilation
does not seem to be attested as a regular process. Moreover, assimilations between vowels in non-neighboring syllables seem to be just as
irregular as distant consonant assimilation.

Like other sound changes, assimilation often is quite restricted in
scope, as in the case of (6) above, a change limited to _n_ after _l_. But as
(3) and (5) show, the scope of assimilation may be much broader, both
in terms of the class of segments affected by the change and in terms
of the conditioning environment. For instance, (5) applies to all nasals
before all stops. In some languages, assimilation may go even farther
and affect their total structure. Consider the development of consonant
clusters from Old Indo-Aryan (represented by Sanskrit) to Middle Indo-
Aryan (represented by Pali). Whereas Sanskrit permitted a large variety
of **'heterorganic'** clusters like _pt, tp, mn_, almost all Pali clusters had to
be **homorganic**; that is, their members had to have the same place of
articulation. In fact, with the exception of nasal + stop clusters, they
were not just homorganic — they were geminates. This change was
brought about by a number of individual assimilatory processes, only
some of which can be given in (12) below. (Here the feature [manner]

is used to indicate 'manner of articulation', i.e. [stop] vs. [fric.] vs. [nasal] etc. Note that changes (a) and (b) require the use of two pairs of Greek-letter variables. Moreover, (a) must take precedence over (b), such that [r] will undergo (a), not (b). Similar restrictions hold between the other changes.) For examples, cf. (13). *is this Sievers? in effect?* (*is this the mirror effect?*)

(12 a)
$$r > \begin{bmatrix} \alpha\,\text{manner} \\ \beta\,\text{place} \end{bmatrix} \; // \begin{bmatrix} -\,\text{syll.} \\ \alpha\,\text{manner} \\ \beta\,\text{place} \end{bmatrix} \underline{\quad}$$

b)
$$\begin{bmatrix} +\,\text{son.} \\ -\,\text{syll.} \end{bmatrix} > \begin{bmatrix} \alpha\,\text{manner} \\ \beta\,\text{place} \end{bmatrix} \; / \begin{bmatrix} -\,\text{syll.} \\ \alpha\,\text{manner} \\ \beta\,\text{place} \end{bmatrix} \underline{\quad}$$

c)
$$\begin{bmatrix} +\,\text{stop} \\ +\,\text{nas.} \end{bmatrix} > \begin{bmatrix} -\,\text{nas.} \\ \alpha\,\text{place} \end{bmatrix} \; / \begin{bmatrix} +\,\text{stop} \\ -\,\text{nas.} \\ \alpha\,\text{place} \end{bmatrix} \underline{\quad}$$

d)
$$\begin{bmatrix} +\,\text{stop} \\ -\,\text{nas.} \end{bmatrix} > [\alpha\,\text{place}] \; / \underline{\quad} \begin{bmatrix} +\,\text{stop} \\ -\,\text{nas.} \\ \alpha\,\text{place} \end{bmatrix}$$

(13)

	Sanskrit	Pali	
a)	bhartum	bhattuṁ	'to carry'
	patra-	patta-	'wing, leaf'
	sahasra-	sahassa-	'thousand'
	varṣati	vassati	'it rains'
	ārya-	ayya-	'noble'
b)	pakva-	pakka-	'cooked'
	aśvēṣu	assēsu	'among horses'
	namasyati	namassati	'honors'
c)	svapna-	soppa-	'sleep'
	nagna-	nagga-	'naked'
d)	bhaktum	bhattuṁ	'divide'
	prāptum	pattuṁ	'obtain'
	labdha-	laddha-	'taken'

Some assimilations are quite common in the languages of the world. These include voicing assimilations in obstruents; place-assimilations of nasals before stops; height, frontness, and rounding assimilations in vowels. Although there are considerable differences in detail and in the scope of application, most of these differences traditionally have not been considered important enough for being recognized as special subvarieties of assimilation.

A few subtypes of assimilation, however, have received special attention. The most commonly recognized changes of this type are 'umlaut', 'vowel harmony', and 'palatalization'. The reason for according special treatment to umlaut and vowel harmony seems to be that they have a fairly general effect on the vowel system. Umlaut, moreover, frequently leads to new phonological contrasts and thus introduces new phonemes into a given language. And so does palatalization.

These and a number of other special types of assimilation are covered in sections 5.1.2—7.

5.1.2. Umlaut

Umlaut involves the assimilation of a class of vowels to a set of [+ vocalic] segments in an immediately neighboring syllable. It therefore has a fairly general effect on the vowel system. Moreover, umlaut leads to phonological split and frequently introduces new phonemes. (Vowel assimilations not meeting this definition sometimes are also referred to as umlaut. But here as elsewhere, it seems preferable to reserve a special term for the designation of a special phenomenon.)

Perhaps the most 'classical' examples of umlaut come from the early Germanic languages (except for Gothic); cf. (14). Depending on the direction of the assimilation, we can distinguish between **fronting**, **backing**, **raising**, and **lowering** umlaut. (14 a) and (b) offer examples of the fronting of a [− front] vowel to [+ front], by assimilation to a following front vocalic segment. (14 b) also exhibits the raising of [+ lo, − hi] to [− lo, − hi] under the influence of the following [− lo, + hi] vowel. (14 c) exemplifies lowering of high to mid vowels under the influence of a following low vowel. And (14 d) indicates backing (as well as some raising) conditioned by the following back (and high) *u*-vowel. (See chapter 2 for the phonetic values of Gmc. *j* and OE *y*.)

(14)	PGmc.	Old English	
a)	*fulljan-	fyllan	'fill'
	*kūiz	cȳ [kū]	'cows'
	*gastiz	giest [yest]	'guest'
c)	*nistā	nest	'nest'
	*guldā	gold	'gold'

back + raising d)   pre-ON   ON

    *sakū   sǫk [sɔk]   'thing'

    *allum   ǫllum [ɔllum]   'all (pl. D)'

In the majority of cases, the outcome of the change is a new phoneme. And in all cases there has been a phonemic split. Compare e. g. example (15), which also shows that these developments result from a classical scenario of split through loss of conditioning environment. (As usual, split does not require the loss of all conditioning environments. It is sufficient that some of the conditioning environments are lost.)

(15)   PGmc.   kūiz 'cows' :   kūz 'cow'
    Allophonic assimilation   [kũiz]   — — —
    Loss of conditioning
    environment   kũ   (— — —)
    OE   cȳ [kũ]   vs. cū [kū]

The Old Irish developments in (16) and (17) are similar, except that in this case the 'umlauted' vowels merge with other preexisting phonemes. At first sight it might appear that there was no split at all, but just a merger of old /e/ and /i/; cf. the complete agreement in vocalism between (17 a) and (a') on one hand, and between (b) and (b') on the other. But note that the changes in (16) did not affect /e/ and /i/ before the old mid vowel [e]; cf. (17 c) and (c'). In this environment, /e/ and /i/ continued to contrast and remained distinct phonemes. The alternation between [i] and [e] in (a)/(a') and (b)/(b') therefore is morphophonemic, not allophonic. See also the summary in (18).

(16 a) $\begin{bmatrix} V \\ -\text{lo} \\ -\text{hi} \end{bmatrix} > [+\text{hi}] / \underline{\quad} C_0 \begin{bmatrix} V \\ +\text{hi} \end{bmatrix}$

  b) $\begin{bmatrix} V \\ -\text{lo} \\ +\text{hi} \end{bmatrix} > [-\text{hi}] / \underline{\quad} C_0 \begin{bmatrix} V \\ +\text{lo} \end{bmatrix}$

(17)   pre-OIr.   OIr.

  a)   *meli-   mil [mʸilʸ]   'honey'
     *berū   -biur [bʸirʷ]   'I carry'
  b)   *ekwas   ech [ex]   'horse'
  c)   *bereti   berid [bʸerʸəðʸ]   '(s)he carries'

a') *wirī   fir [f^{y}ir^y]   'man (sg. G)'
     *wirū   fiur [f^{y}ir^w]   'to a man (sg. D)'
b') *wiras   fer [f^{y}er]   'man (sg. N)'
c') *ibeti   ibid [iβ^{y}əð^y]   '(s)he drinks'

(18)   */ ___ C$_0$ e   */ ___ C$_0$ i/u   */ ___ C$_0$ a

    *e   >   e   i   e
    *i   >   i   i   e

The whole issue of Old Irish umlaut is complicated by the fact that the conditioning environments for changes (16 a/b) were lost. It is therefore not entirely clear whether it was merger or loss of the conditioning vowels which was responsible for the splits.

Note however that crosslinguistically, umlaut most frequently is conditioned by final syllables. The reason seems to be that word-final position is a highly conducive environment for the loss of segments and syllables, including vowels, the most common conditioning environments for vowel assimilations. Final vowel loss therefore is a natural trigger for making vowel assimilations unpredictable. This certainly is the explanation for Germanic umlaut. That also Old Irish umlaut is accompanied by final vowel loss therefore is probably not just an accident.

The fact that the outcome of umlaut is synchronically unpredictable has important consequences. Like many other morphophonemic alternations, the interchange between umlauted and unchanged vowels easily gives rise to analogical developments which, given enough time, tend to eliminate these alternations. In English, for instance, synchronically 'live' alternations resulting from umlaut are limited to a few irregular noun plurals (cf. *man:men, woman:women, mouse:mice, louse:lice, goose:geese, tooth:teeth.*) (Cf. also Chapters 9 and 10.)

5.1.3. Vowel harmony

Vowel harmony, like umlaut, is an assimilatory process affecting classes of vowels and conditioned by vocalic segments in neighboring syllables. As a consequence, some linguists do not make a distinction between these two processes.

However, if we examine the 'classical' cases of vowel harmony, we find that this phenomenon is sufficiently different from umlaut to merit separate treatment. One of the most striking things about vowel harmony is that in most of the languages that have it, the pattern of vowel alternation goes back to prehistoric times, perhaps even to the proto-language. As a consequence, it is very difficult to find examples in which vowel harmony originates. Linguists therefore are commonly content with giving synchronic data like the Finnish ones in (19), or similar ones from Hungarian or Turkish.

[margin handwritten notes: origin of vowel harmony difficult to find "not q. true" (Paul)]

(19)   Finn.   suoma-lainen 'Finnish'   :   venä-läinen 'Russian'
tuoli-lla 'on the chair'   :   pöydä-llä 'on the table'

A closer examination of the Finnish data will illustrate some of the principles of vowel harmony. As a live process, Finnish vowel harmony operates on the boxed-in vowels in (20). It is triggered by the vocalism of roots and affects the vocalism of suffixes in the following fashion: Vowels of the same height alternate with each other, assimilating to the feature [± front] of the root vocalism. Note that while *i* and *e* do not undergo vowel harmony, they serve as triggers for the process. Cf. the data in (21). (But note that when the root has a combination of *i* and *e* with non-front vowels, the root 'counts' as having [− front] vocalism throughout; cf. *tuoli-lla* in (19).)

(20)

	[+ front]		[− front]	
	[− round]	[+ round]	[− round]	[+ round]
	i	y [ü]		u
	e	ö		o
	ä [æ]		a	

(21)   Root   Adessive   Allative   Partitive
a)   maa-   maa-lla   maa-lle   maa-ta   'land'
b)   pää-   pää-llä   pää-lle   pää-tä   'head'
c)   tie-   tie-llä   tie-lle   tie-tä   'road'

In this (slightly idealized) system, the frontness or backness of the alternating suffix vowels is entirely predictable in terms of the root vocalism. That is, although the vowels participating in the alternation are in contrast elsewhere, that contrast is neutralized in suffixes.

In this respect, then, vowel harmony differs from umlaut, which is
characterized by split, not neutralization. One suspects that it is this
difference which is responsible for the very different behavior of these
two processes of systematic vowel assimilation.

This suspicion is supported by the one reportable case of origination
of a vowel harmony system. As the result of various historical processes,
Old Norse at a certain point had the short-vowel systems in (22).
Whereas stressed initial root syllables had (at least) a five-way contrast,
unstressed syllables offered a reduced, three-point system: The contrast
between high and mid vowels here was neutralized. As often happens
in such neutralized systems, there was a fair amount of dialectal and
chronological variation in the exact realization of the non-low 'archiphonemes' /i:e/ and /u:o/. The *i* and *u* of the transcriptions of (22) and
(23) are found in some of the early Norse dialects; but early Icelandic
has *e* and *o*, only to change them to *i* and *u* in later Old Icelandic.

In a subgroup of the Old Norwegian dialects, high and mid vowels
came to synchronically alternate with each other, with vowel height
determined by the vocalism of the root. We can account for this
development by the sound change in (24). But what is important in
the present context is that this change led to the development of a
system of high/mid vowel harmony out of an earlier system in which
the contrast between high and mid vowels had been neutralized. Moreover, the result of change (24) was a 'locally' predictable alternation
between high and mid vowels. That is, the contrast remained neutralized
in this unstressed position. All that changed is the exact realization of
the non-low archiphonemes.

(22 a)   Stressed: i   u
                          e   o
                               a

     b)   Unstressed: i   u
                               a

(23)   Common   Old Norwegian
       Old Norse   dialects
       ríki   ríki   'country'
       kvæði   kvæðe   'poem'
       urðu   urðu   'they became'
       námu   námo   'they took'

(24) $\begin{bmatrix} V \\ -lo \end{bmatrix}$ > [α hi] / $\begin{bmatrix} V \\ α hi \end{bmatrix}$ C_0 —

While neutralization thus may play an important role in distinguishing vowel harmony from umlaut, it is not the only factor that differentiates the two processes. Recall that umlaut commonly is triggered by the vowels of final syllables, whose subsequent loss makes umlaut unpredictable. In the classical vowel harmony systems, however, the trigger lies in non-final, usually initial and accented roots. In that environment, vowels are quite stable and not liable to be lost. The triggering environment therefore remains stable. As a consequence, vowel harmony can continue to be predictable for centuries. (Norwegian is an exception, in that the dialectal vowel harmony was lost soon after its introduction. However, the reason for that loss does not lie in any significant changes in root vocalism, but in the fact that like most other Germanic dialects, Norwegian began to reduce its final vowels toward [ə] or ∅.)

Note however that beside the clearly distinguished 'classical' cases of umlaut and vowel harmony, less 'classical' systems can be found in many languages. In Finnish, for instance, vowel harmony is synchronically predictable in the majority of cases. However, some exceptions can be found: Recall that the front vowels *i* and *e*, if they do not cooccur with [− front] vowels, trigger the front-vowel realizations in alternating suffixes; cf. (21 c). In examples (25) and (26), however, we find that some forms have this regular vowel harmony, but others do not. The system, therefore, is not completely predictable. ← but Paul has shown how it c'ld be captured. In terms of level-ordering

(25)   Root   Adessive   Allative   Partitive

meri-   mere-llä   mere-lle   mer-ta   'sea'

veri-   vere-llä   vere-lle   ver-ta   'blood'

(26)   teh- 'do' :   teh-dä 'to do' :   teh-das- 'factory'

The terms 'umlaut' and 'vowel harmony' thus refer to two extreme points in the development of systematic vowel assimilations. Intermediate situations can be characterized in terms of how much they deviate from these cardinal points.

5.1.4. Contraction

Taken by itself, the very common process of vowel **contraction**, as in
(27), can be described as assimilatory. This becomes especially clear if
we ignore the issue of syllabicity, as well as differences in transcription
and analysis, and follow the transcriptional convention of (27′): Diphthongs here are written as sequences of non-identical vowels, and long
vowels as the equivalent of two identical short vowels. Example (a),
then, is a case of anticipatory assimilation; (b), one of perseverance;
and (c), one of mutual assimilation.

(27 a)	PIE	*bheyd-	>	PGmc.	*bīt-	'bite'
b)	PGmc.	*bait	>	OE	bāt	'(s)he bit'
c)	PIE	*aydho-	>	Skt.	ēdha-	'fire wood'

(27′ a)		*bheid-	>		*biit-	
b)		*bait	>		baat	
c)		*aidho-	>		eedha-	

Note however that treating contraction as assimilatory might be
taken to require analyzing its logical opposite, diphthongization, as
being a dissimilatory process. As the discussion in 6.1.3 will show,
there are certain difficulties with such an analysis. It is not clear whether
these difficulties are sufficient for rejecting an assimilatory explanation
of contraction.

(Some linguists distinguish between 'monophthongization' and 'contraction'. The latter term tends to be reserved for the conversion
of heterosyllabic vowels into monosyllabic long monophthongs or
diphthongs. — The elimination of 'hiatus' between heterosyllabic vowels is an interesting phenomenon. But as section 7.2 will show, hiatus
is eliminated by a number of different processes. Among these are
contraction (as defined in this book) and 'gliding', an independently
required process which does not necessarily yield diphthongs; cf. 7.2.2,
ex. (30). The distinction between 'monophthongization' and 'contraction' therefore does not seem to be required.)

5.1.5. Palatalization and labiovelarization

The term palatalization crops up in many linguistic discussions, but in an almost bewildering variety of uses. Thus, any of the developments in (28) may be referred to as palatalization:

(28 a)   pre-BS   *minyō   >   Lith.   miniù [mʸinʸú]   'I remember'

Classical Latin [kentʊm]   >   OCS   mĭn'ǫ [mʸĭnʸõ]   'I remember'

   b)   Lat.   centum   >   It.   cento [č-]   'hundred'

   c)   Lat.   centum   >   Fr.   cent [s-]   'hundred'

   d)   PIE   *kʷe   >   Gk.   te   'and'

In some sense, this usage is justified. For all of the above examples have undergone the process of palatalization. In (28 b−d), however, that process has been followed — and obscured — by other changes which quite commonly apply to palatalized segments. This section investigates the nature of these changes, as well as the process of palatalization which gives rise to them, and the related process of labiovelarization.

Palatalization consists in the partial assimilation of a consonant to a neighboring front vocalic segment. Phonetically, this assimilation manifests itself in a non-segmental [y]-like onglide and/or offglide. The usual notation in this book is as in (28 a) above, with superscript *y* following the palatalized consonant. After vowel, however, palatalized consonants tend to also have a [y]-like onglide. A more accurate transcription of Lith. *miniù* therefore would be something like [⁽ʸ⁾mʸiʸnʸú].

Labiovelarization similarly is brought about by the partial assimilation of a consonant to a neighboring back and rounded vocalic segment, is phonetically characterized by a non-segmental [w]-like on- or offglide, and is transcribed by means of a superscript *w* after the labiovelarized consonant.

Like umlaut, palatalization and labiovelarization become phonologically significant through some other process which makes them unpredictable. Most usually, this process consists in the loss of some of the conditioning environments. But other scenarios are possible. The examples in (29)−(31) represent the most common developments leading to distinctive palatalization. In (29), the loss of postconsonantal [y] makes palatalization unpredictable. In (30), final vowel loss leads to 'phonemic' palatalization and labiovelarization. And in (31), a merger of non-high vowels (formulated in (32)) brings about a contrast between palatalized and non-palatalized velars before *a*-vowels.

(29)   pre-Balto-   Allophonic   Contrastive
       Slav.   stage   stage

       *minyō   > *[m^{y}in^{y}yō]   > Lith. miniù [m^{y}in^{y}ú]   'remember'
                                     > OCS mĭn'ǫ [m^{y}ĭn^{y}õ]   'remember'

(30)   pre-   Allophonic   Contrastive
       Old Irish   stage   stage

       *wiras   > *w^{y}eras   > *w^{y}er   > f^{y}er   'man' (sg. N)
       *wirī   > *w^{y}ir^{y}ī   > *w^{y}ir^y > f^{y}ir^y 'man' (sg. G)
       *wirū   > *w^{y}ir^{w}ū   > *w^{y}ir^w > f^{y}ir^w 'man' (sg. D)

(31)   pre-   Allophonic   Contrastive
       Sanskrit   stage   stage

       *penke   > *penk^{y}e   > *pank^{y}a   > pañča   'five'
       *gegome   > *g^{y}egome   > *g^{y}agāma   > ǰagāma   'went'

(32) $$\begin{bmatrix} V \\ -\,hi \\ -\,lo \end{bmatrix} > [+\,lo]$$

Just like other assimilatory processes, palatalization and labiovelarization are more commonly anticipatory than perseverant. In addition, a number of other limitations and tendencies need to be mentioned.

First, of the two processes, labiovelarization seems to be less common. Moreover, once introduced, it seems to be less stable and to be lost more easily than palatalization. Thus, the palatalization of Old Irish has survived to the present day, even if in somewhat changed form. Labiovelarization, however, disappeared so early that some linguists have doubted that it ever existed. (See also 7.3.5 below.)

Secondly, also palatalization tends to have certain restrictions: It is most frequently found with velars and/or dentals, i. e. with 'lingual' or tongue-articulated consonants. (Thus, change (31) is limited to velars.) It is more rarely introduced on labials and, if introduced, is more easily lost. (Thus, Polish has lost palatalization on final labials, but has retained it on dentals; cf. (33). Other 'avoidance maneuvers' will be discussed in 7.3.5 below.) The reason for this difference seems to be that the articulatory gesture for palatalization, as well as for the front vowels

tongue articulated

which give rise to it, is 'lingual' and therefore homorganic with velars and dentals, but not with labials.

(33)   Common Slav.   Polish   cf. Russian

golǫbʸ   gołąb [gowõb]   golubʸ   'pigeon'
dʸĭnʸ   dzień [dzʸenʸ]   dʸenʸ   'day'

Palatalization tends to be 'governed' by a hierarchy of conditioning environments; cf. (34). The most conducive environment is [y], the least conducive one, [æ]. Moreover, palatalization before a segment that is low in this hierarchy generally entails palatalization also before the segments that are higher up. Thus in early Romance, non-velars palatalize only before [y]. The velars palatalize before [y], as well as before front vowel. But in Vegliote, this process seems to have been limited to before [i]-vowel. Most dialects have palatalization before both [i]- and [e]-vowels. And in Gallo-Romance, even [a] > [æ] induced palatalization, but with an outcome different from the one before other front vocalic segments. (Cf. Lat. *circāre* > OFr. *cercher* [serčer], whence NFr. *chercher* with [č] > [š] and distant assimilation of initial [s] to [š]. Engl. *search* is a borrowing from Old French.)

(34)   [y]   Cf. Romance non-velars
       [i]   Cf. Vegliote velars
       [e]   Cf. most Romance languages
       [æ]   Cf. Gallo-Romance

Finally, as already noted, palatalization frequently gives rise to other developments which obscure its effects and which are often terminologically confused with palatalization. Compare (28 b—d).

The most important of these developments is that of (28 b), namely the change of palatalized dentals or velars to palatal articulation. The motivation for this development seems to be phonological, and not just purely phonetic: As palatalization becomes unpredictable and as consequently palatalized and nonpalatalized segments come to be in contrast, there is a tendency to mark this new phonological distinctiveness by an increase in phonetic distinctiveness. This process has been called **polarization**. For velars and dentals, such polarization is accomplished most easily by the shifting of the palatalized segments toward the palatal area of articulation: Articulatorily, they are similar to palatals in that palatalized velars are more 'frontish' and palatalized dentals

more 'backish' than their nonpalatalized counterparts. This is matched
by a similar acoustic affinity between palatals and palatalized velars and
dentals.

If by this process, palatalized velars and/or dentals become palatals,
they become possible candidates for another common change, that of
assibilation. As noted in section 2.1.1 above, palatals are characterized
by an inherent sibilant-offglide. Many languages remain content with
just having this offglide; cf. e. g. the Italian example in (28 b). But by
a process of 'segmentalization' (cf. 7.1.1 below), the offglide frequently
becomes a fully segmental sibilant. The result is a cluster of the type
[čš], with a significant sibilant component. Now, sibilants can be
articulated either with a basic palatal gesture, or with the tongue tip
placed upward, into a post-dental position; cf. 2.1.2. And by assimilation, the preceding stop element may show similar variation, resulting
in an alternative articulation [tš] for the cluster. This essentially is the
state of affairs for the English initial obstruent(s) in *choose*. (Note that
the palatalization which gave rise to this [čš]/[tš] took place before the
Old English period, and that OE *cēosan* was pronounced as something
like [čēozan].)

Clusters of the type [tš], in turn, are liable to undergo a process of
'cluster simplification' (cf. 5.3.2 below), which may lead to the loss
either of the stop element or of the sibilant element. Item (28 c) above
presents an example of stop loss; (28 d) exemplifies the rarer alternative
of sibilant loss.

Many languages thus run the full course, from palatalization to the
eventual sibilant or dental-stop outcomes; cf. (35). But having gone
one step along this line of potential development does not force a
language to undertake the other steps. In the case of velar palatalization,
for instance, Lithuanian has stopped at step (a), Italian and Sanskrit at
(b), and English at (c).

(35 a)   Palatalization
    b)   Polarization, shift to palatal articulation
    c)   Assibilation
    d)   Cluster simplification of assibilated cluster to either sibilant
         or stop.

Note that also non-assimilatory processes can lead to the development
of palatals. Thus, Lat. *ll* has yielded palatal [λ] in much of Western
Romance. The reason for this development seems to be acoustic: Latin

had a 'clear' [l]-articulation in the geminate *ll*, but a retracted and velarized 'dark' [ł] in forms like *alter* 'other'. Perhaps because of the split of the Latin velars into velars and palatals, this difference between clear and dark *l* could be acoustically reinterpreted as one of palatal vs. velar. As a consequence, forms like Lat. *illa* wind up as Span. *ella* [eʎa], while *alter* changes into **autro* > Span. *otro*.

5.1.6. Retroflexion

Retroflex consonants like Skt. *ṭ, ḍ, ṣ* have been treated by many linguists as something unusual and mysterious. In fact, however, they are neither very unusual nor mysterious.

Like many other features, **retroflexion** may exhibit considerable phonetic variation between different languages, dialects, or even speakers. What is shared by retroflex consonants is that they are articulated with the tip of the tongue. (But note that this is a possible articulation also for dentals.) The area in which that articulation is made, however, may range from alveolar to about the boundary between the hard palate and the velum. Similar variation can be observed for another feature that tends to be present in retroflex articulation. This feature consists in a curling back of the tongue at the point of articulation. Examples of such variation can be found in the pronunciation of English [r], which may range from quite alveolar to very retracted with a high degree of tongue tip curling. The first articulation is characteristic of many varieties of British English; the other extreme can be found especially in certain American English dialects. Similarly, certain varieties of South Asian Hindi and Urdu have alveolar articulation for 'retroflex' stops, but a much more retracted articulation for the retroflex flap [ṛ]. Other varieties of Hindi-Urdu, and other South Asian languages, have highly retracted articulation for all retroflex consonants.

Once we realize this phonetic variability of the feature [retroflex], we see that retroflex-like consonants are found in many languages, even if we exclude completely alveolar articulations. As noted in 2.1.2, the sibilant [š] in many individual speech varieties is articulated with the tongue tip against a post-dental area, and thus has something of a retroflex articulation. Similarly, many varieties of English have a post-alveolar, retroflex articulation for orthographic *r*.

However, in many languages such retroflex articulations are limited to just one segment (cf. Engl. [r]) or to the sibilants, in which retroflex may merely be an alternative to palatal articulation. As a consequence, these retroflex consonants tend to be ignored.

What cannot be ignored are situations in which a whole class of retroflex segments contrasts with dentals and other consonant classes. And such 'distinctive' retroflexion appears to be limited to non-European, 'exotic' languages like Sanskrit and many other languages of South Asia. It is this apparent limitation which has given retroflexion the aura of being unusual and mysterious.

The limitation, however, is only a matter of appearance. In reality, retroflexion is found in many European forms of speech. The only difference is that it has not found its way into the standard varieties of the European languages, but is limited to local and regional dialects.

The processes by which distinctive retroflexion has been introduced are not particularly surprising. In many cases they are entirely parallel to the developments which lead to distinctive palatalization, involving low-level assimilation, loss of predictability, and polarization.

The assimilation which gives rise to this development frequently is one of dentals next to [r]. In order to understand the nature of this assimilation it is important to realize that unlike the 'dental' stops, [r] for physiological reasons cannot be articulated as a dental. Its most 'forward' articulation, therefore, is alveolar.

In many languages, then, otherwise dental segments assimilate to neighboring [r] and become alveolar. As long as the [r] stays around, this alveolar pronunciation remains predictable. Loss of the [r], however, will make the distribution of dental and alveolar alternants unpredictable and contrastive. At this point, polarization can set in and increase the phonetic distance by shifting the alveolars to retroflex. Compare for example the dialectal British English development in (36) which can be accounted for by means of the scenario in (37). (Here as elsewhere in this section, [d̪] etc. = dental, [d] etc. = alveolar, [ɖ] etc. = retroflex.)

(36)   cord [kɔ(ː)rɖ] > [kɔːɖ]

(37)   Allophonic   Loss of conditioning
                assimilation   environment and polarization
        [kɔːrd̪] >   [kɔːrd] >   [kɔːd] >   [kɔːɖ] (≠ cod [kɔ(ː)d̪])

The earlier allophonic stage postulated for these English dialects is actually attested in Modern Icelandic, which has not yet reached the stage of contrast. And the relevance of the notion 'polarization' is

demonstrated by the Hindi and Urdu varieties which have alveolar
realization for the retroflex stops, but retracted pronunciation for the
retroflex flap [ɽ]: The latter has to have a retracted articulation in order
to retain its contrast with alveolar [r]. The stops, on the other hand,
are phonetically distinct from the dentals, even if they are articulated
as alveolars. Cf. (38).

(38) Dental   Alveolar   Retroflex

    [t̪, d̪]   ≠   [t, d]

               [r]   ≠   [ɽ]

Even more complex developments are found in Central Norwegian
and Swedish dialects, in which the developments in (39) have led to a
triple contrast between dental, alveolar, and retroflex. ([ł] refers to a
'dark', retracted form of [l], which had developed as a postvocalic
allophone of dental [l].)

(39) Starting point: t̪, d̪   rt̪, rd̪   łt̪, łd̪
    Assimilation: — — —   rt, rd   łt, łd
    Loss of conditioning
    environment: t̪, d̪   ≠   t, d   ≠   ţ, ḍ

Distinctive retroflexion can be introduced also by non-assimilatory
processes. As noted in the preceding section, much of Western Romance
changed Lat. *ll* to palatal [λ]. In Sicilian and Sardinian dialects, as well
as in Asturian Spanish, the outcome is retroflex, as in Lat. *stēlla* > Sic.
[stiḍḍa]. The most likely explanation is that this represents a specialized
development of the normal palatal [λ]: The dialectal Spanish changes
in (40) show that it is possible for [λ] to change into a palatal stop.
Such a stop, in turn, is liable to become assibilated [ǰž]. And since
retroflex is a possible variant of palatal articulation in the sibilants, the
variant [ḍz] may arise. The attested [ḍd] of Sicilian can then be gotten
by simple assimilation. Compare (41) for a summary of these complex
(and somewhat speculative) developments.

(40) Span. [eλa] > dial. [eya] > dial. [eǰa] 'she'

(41 a) [λ]   >   [y]   >   [ǰ] (cf. (40))
  b) [ǰ]   >   [ǰž]   (assibilation)
  c) [ǰž]   /   [ḍz]   (variation in sibilant articulation)
  d) [ḍz]   >   [ḍd]   (assimilation)

5.1.7. Final devoicing

Word-final environment is a position which is especially vulnerable to change. Most of the changes that affect it are of the weakening or loss variety, which will be examined in the following sections. One change, however, is commonly explained as assimilatory, namely **final devoicing**, the unvoicing of obstruents in final syllables.

Final devoicing is perhaps not the most obvious example of an assimilatory process. For 'word boundary' is not a phonetic environment to which segments could assimilate. But if we take prepausal position as the starting point for the development, this difficulty can be removed: At the end of an utterance, the vocal cords commonly return to their rest position. And that setting is similar, though not identical to the phonetic setting for voicelessness. In this environment, then, obstruents can become voiceless by assimilation. (For further discussion, see 11.1.1 below.)

An example of this process has already been cited in Chapter 4, ex. (18/19). It is reproduced as (42) and (43) below. A similar change is the word-final fricative devoicing of Old English, exemplified in Chapters 3 (ex. (18)/(19)) and 4 (ex. (8)/(9)).

(42)   [+ obstr.] > [− voice] / ___ #

(43)   OHG   rad   rades   rāt   rātes
        NHG   [rāt]   [rādəs]   [rāt]   [rātəs]
               'wheel'   'of the wheel' 'advice'   'of the advice'

Examples (42)/(43) show that final devoicing commonly neutralizes the contrast voiced : voiceless.

5.2. Lenition/weakening

Among non-linguists, the perhaps most commonly cited cause for sound change is 'laziness'. While this is a dubious explanation for the great variety of changes that are found in the world's languages, it seems to be singularly appropriate for the class of changes which has been termed **weakening** or **lenition**. What the otherwise quite disparate changes covered by these terms share is a 'relaxation' or 'weakening' of articulatory effort, something that has been called 'the lazy-tongue phenomenon'.

This relaxation of effort may take many different forms. The most radical one consists in **loss**, as in (44). But between the full presence of a segment and its ultimate loss, intermediate stages can often be observed, in which the pronunciation of the segment becomes increasingly relaxed and less distinct from its environment. Compare for instance (45)—(47). In (45) and (46), the first step consists in intervocalic **voicing**, a process which could be taken to be assimilatory, but which also can be viewed as a relaxation of effort: The switching of vocal-cord setting from voiced to voiceless and back to voiced is abandoned in favor of an articulatorily simpler, single gesture of voicing. (The issue of the relationship between assimilation and weakening will be taken up again later.) The second step diminishes oral contact by **fricativization** or **gliding**, changing the voiced stop to fricative or even to glide. And only then comes the final stage, the total disappearance of the 'offending' segment. (This is indicated by a Ø.) Other scenarios are seen in (47)—(49). (47) first has fricativization, then voicing, and finally loss. In (48), the first step is loss of oral contact (**'oral depletion'**), but retention of glottal friction. And this is followed by loss. And in (49), a similar first step gives way to a voicing process by which the voiceless glide [h] changes into voiced [y] (spelled *i*).

(44)   Lat. vidēre > Span. veØer 'see'

(45)   Lat. pacatum > (*)pagado > Span. [paɣaðo]
        > dial. [paɣaØo] 'pacified, pleased'

(46)   Skt. mata- > MIAr. dial. mada-
        > dial. maya- > late MIAr. maØa- 'thought'

(47)   Colloqu. Span. at$las > [aθ$las] > [að$las]
        > [aØ$las] 'atlas'

(48)   Span. las aguas [las aɣwas] > dial. [lah aɣwah]
        > [la(**h**) aɣwaØ] 'the waters'

(49)   (Lat. pōst >) *pos > *poh > Ital. puoi 'thereupon, then'

Other changes which have been referred to as weakening include **degemination**, **rhotacism**, and **flapping**. These are illustrated in (50), (51), and (52), respectively.

degem.   (50) Lat. ci**pp**us > Span. ce**p**o 'pole; branch'
                 ra**tt**us >   ra**t**o 'rat'
                 va**cc**a >   va**c**a 'cow'

rhotacism (51 a) PIE   *eso̅ > *ezo̅   > Lat. ero̅ 'will be'
           b) Span. desde [dez$ðe] > dial. [der$ðe] 'since'

flapping (52) Engl. better [betər]   > dial. Am. Engl. [beɾər]

Chart 5.1 attempts to summarize the total network of possible changes. The changes apply from top to bottom, along a **weakening hierarchy** largely defined by a combination of increased voicing and sonority. (Cf. the sonority hierarchy in Chapter 2, Chart 2.2.) A broken line indicates a possible, but not actually observed change. For notational convenience, dentals have been chosen to represent the different segment classes (as in *t* = voiceless stops), flaps are included among the liquids, and lines leading to Ø have been omitted. (Excepting the geminates, probably all segment classes can go directly to Ø, without having to go through intermediate segmental stages.)

Note that nasals do not figure in this chart. That is because under weakening, their (nasal) stop characteristics take precedence over their sonorant qualities. As a consequence they tend to undergo the same kind of changes as the stops; cf. e. g. (53 a) and (b). The former has fricativization, the latter, flapping. The effect of the stop characteristics of nasals manifests itself also in other respects. For instance, weakening of oral stops in many languages is blocked next to nasal; cf. e. g. (54). (Ex. (a) shows that there was a general process of medial weakening, even next to sonorant; (b) illustrates the lack of weakening after nasal.) Presumably the reason for this blocking is assimilatory: fricativization and many other types of weakening would make the oral stop heterorganic with respect to the neighboring nasal stop. (Cf. (58/59) below for a parallel.)

    (53 a) Skt. kamala- > dial. NIAr. [kaβ̃al] 'lotus'
                            (> [kãβal] by transfer of nasalization)
        b) Skt. manaḥ   > dial. MIAr. maṇo [maɾ̃o]

    (54 a) Lat. vidēre   > Span. veØer 'see'
                 ardo̅rem >   [arðor] 'ardor, heat'
        b)   cantando̅ >   [kantando] 'singing'

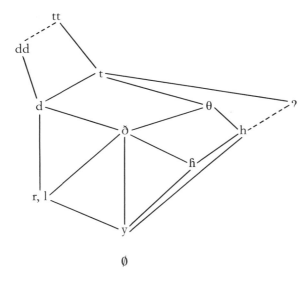

Chart 5.1. The weakening hierarchy

Beyond the perhaps overly impressionistic notion of 'relaxation of effort', there is other, more formal evidence which suggests that all the changes summarized in Chart 5.1 are aspects of one and the same process.

First, these changes have a strong tendency to occur in just two environments: medial intervocalic (or intersonorant) position and word- or syllable-final environment. Changes in medial position are found in (44)–(46), (50), (51 a), (52)–(54); word-final changes in (48) and (49); and syllable-final changes in (47) and (51 b). (Weakening may occur elsewhere, but does so less commonly.)

Secondly, different types of weakening processes often apply in a parallel fashion, within the same language or in closely related ones, for the same segment class or for phonetically closely related ones. Thus, where some American English dialects flap intervocalic *t* (cf. (52) above), others voice it in the same environment; cf. (55). Similarly, in early Welsh and Irish, both belonging to the 'Insular' branch of Celtic, medial stops were weakened. In Irish, the process was one of across-the-board fricativization; but Welsh fricativized only its voiced stops, while its voiceless stops underwent voicing. Cf. the examples in (56). (Old Irish also had medial stop degemination; cf. (89) below for an example.) The Welsh examples further show that phonetically closely related segment classes may undergo different processes of weakening.

(55)   Engl. better [betər] > dial. Am. Engl. [bedər]

(56)   PIE   *tewtā   *bhew**d**i-
a)   pre-OIr.   *tō**θ**ā   *bō**ð**i-
       (OIr.   túath [tuəθ]   búaid [bʷuəðʸ])
b)   pre-MW   *tūdā   *būði-
       (MW   tud [tɪd]   budd [bɪð])
                  'people'   'victory'

Finally, except for final devoicing, no other process typically limited to medial or syllable- and word-final environment goes upward on the weakening hierarchy, contrary to the direction of our weakening processes. (And devoicing is not found medially.) That is, the weakening hierarchy is not just a convenient summary of developments, it predicts the direction of development for a class of sound changes and in so doing, defines these changes as a class. (Changes like [ɦ] > [h], [w] > [v] are apparent counterexamples, but they are not limited to medial and final environment. Cf. 7.3.3 and 7.3.6. For certain conditions under which fricatives may be secondarily realized as stops, cf. 4.2, ex. (4/5), as well as the discussion of (58/59) below.)

As noted earlier, medial voicing can be interpreted not only as a weakening change, but also as a case of assimilation. This raises the question whether the other weakening changes can likewise be considered assimilations. The argument can be made that they are, in that the developments down the weakening hierarchy make segments more similar to the voicing and sonority of the neighboring vowels and sonorants. However, the argument can easily be reversed. For assimilation can be considered a special type of weakening, in which the distinctly different articulatory gestures required to articulate phonetically different segments are made less distinctly. Given that weakening tends to be restricted to medial and final environment, while assimilation is not so restricted, it is perhaps best to treat the two phenomena as related, but different processes.

Note finally that weakening, like any other type of sound change, may at times be subject to arbitrary phonetic restrictions. For instance, the pre-Old English medial voicing of Chapter 4 (examples (18)/(19)) is restricted to the class of fricatives, including the sibilants. Old Norse had a similar medial voicing of fricatives, but excluded the sibilants; cf. (57).

(57) PGmc. *broþar > ON broðir   'brother'
            *slahan >   *slaØa > slā 'slay' (for [h] > Ø,
                                            cf. 3.4) etc.
      vs.   *keusan >   kjōsa   'choose' (with un-
                                            changed [s])

In dialectal Oscan-Umbrian, ancient Italic relatives of Latin, medial voicing affected only sibilant [s]; but in Latin it affected the other fricatives as well, except that [h] seems to have remained unchanged. (But perhaps orthographic Latin h = voiced [ɦ].) Compare the summary in (58). Note that the Latin medial outcomes of the non-glottal fricatives generally change into stops; cf. (58 a). But (58 b) preserves the fricative. Note also (58 d), with stop only next to nasal (cf. the parallel in (54) above). These facts suggest that the stops in (58 a) result from earlier voiced fricatives, probably by means of the developments in (59): Medial voicing leads to the voiced fricatives β, ð, γ which after nasal stop assimilate to oral-stop b, d, g (cf. the parallel in (54) above). In the case of the labials and dentals, the resulting allophonic variation between voiced stop and fricative is eliminated in favor of the stop (cf. 4.2, ex. (4/5) for a parallel). For the labiovelar, we need to assume a process of 'segmentalization' of ^{w} to w (cf. 7.1.1 below), followed by 'cluster simplification' (cf. 5.3.2).

(58) | PIE | Proto-Italic | Osco-Umbrian | Latin |
|-----|--------------|--------------|-------|
| a) *bh | f | f | b |
| *dh | θ | f | b/d |
| b) *gh | x > h | h | h |
| c) *s | s | z | z > r |
| d) *g^wh | x^w | f | gw (after N) |
| | | | w (elsewhere) |

[cf. *sneyg^{w}h-es > Lat. nīvis 'snow (sg. G)'
    *sni-n-g^{w}h- >   ninguit 'it snows' (with nasal infix)]

(59) | PIE | Proto-Italic | pre-Latin | Latin |
|-----|--------------|-----------|-------|
| *bh | f | β/b | b |
| *dh | θ | ð/d | d |
| *g^wh | x^w | γw/gw | w/gw |

(The environmentally conditioned development of Proto-Italic θ > b is ignored.)

An arbitrary environmental restriction is illustrated in (60 a); cf. the formulation in (60 b).

(60 a)   OE gæderian   >   NE gather   [-ð-]
           fæder   >   father   [-ð-]
           weder   >   weather [-ð-]
           etc.
  b)   d > ð / V ___ (V) r

5.3. Loss

5.3.1. Loss and weakening

As we have just seen, **loss** frequently is the ultimate and most extreme outcome of weakening. It is therefore tempting to consider all loss to result from weakening. This view seems to be supported by the fact that loss is especially common in word-final environment, one of the most conducive environments for weakening.

Possible counterarguments are (i) that loss is not restricted to the typical medial and final environments of weakening, but may apply freely in other positions as well; and (ii) that loss affects also vowels, for which no weakening developments have been documented so far. But neither argument is conclusive. While weakening most readily applies medially and finally, it can apply also elsewhere; cf. (61 a). And just as in medial and final position, the ultimate outcome of such weakening may be loss; cf. (61 b). Similarly, vowel loss frequently goes through intermediate stages with 'reduced' or 'weakened' vowels, most notably [ə] or voiceless vowels; cf. (62). (In (62 b), [ⁱ] = voiceless [i].)

(61 a)   PIE *pro   >   Avest. fra   'for(ward)'
          *treyes >   θrayō 'three'
  b)   PIE *so   >   Gk.   ho   >   dial. Øo 'that'
          *sem >   hen   >   Øen 'one'
(62 a)   Lat. causa   >   OFr. chose [-ə] >   NFr. chose [-Ø]
                                  'thing'
  b)   Ital. spaghetti > dial. spaghettⁱ >   spaghettØ
                                    'spaghetti'

An especially close relationship between vowel weakening/loss and consonant weakening/loss is suggested by the fact that both types of processes frequently operate in **clitic reduction**: Many languages have morphological elements called **clitics** which take an intermediary position between full words and affixes. Consider for instance Engl. *n't* (in *this isn't true*): Like ordinary words, it has a definite lexical meaning (negation) and can thus be listed in the dictionary; but unlike ordinary words, it behaves more like an affix in that it cannot occur by itself, as a full utterance, but must 'lean on' an ordinary word which serves as its **host** (such as *is* in *this isn't true*). In many cases, clitics coexist with non-clitic full-word variants, such as Engl. *n't* beside *not*. What is important in the present context is that unlike these fuller forms, clitics typically are unaccented. Moreover, presumably because of their accentual reduction, they also tend to become phonetically reduced, by weakening processes which may affect vowels and/or consonants. Clitic vowel reduction is illustrated in (63 a), loss in (63 b); consonant weakening in (63 c), loss in (63 d); and (64 d) shows clitic reduction both in vocalism and in the consonants.

(63 a)	NE	he wás [wɔz]	:	he wàs [wɔz]	
b)	NE	he ís [iz]	:	he's [-Øz]	
c)	OE	þè [þe] man	>	NE the [ðə] man	
	vs.	þíng	>	thing [θ-] (unchanged)	
d)	PGmc.	*ìst	>	OE isØ (> NE [iz] with [s] weakened to [z])	
	vs.	*wáist	>	wāst (with retained -t)	
e)	NE	he hád, he wóuld	:	he'd [-Ød]	

It is not certain, however, whether all loss proceeds through such intermediate weakening stages. Moreover, certain types of loss have functional characteristics which make them sufficiently distinct from other changes to be treated as a category by themselves. As in the case of weakening and assimilation, the way of caution therefore lies in treating weakening and loss as related, but different processes.

The following sections are devoted to the discussion of subtypes of loss that have been considered worthy of special note in the literature.

5.3.2. Cluster simplification and degemination

The most vulnerable environment for consonant cluster reduction, or **cluster simplification**, is the word-final position, where processes of the type (64)/(65) and (66)/(69) frequently severely reduce the number of permissible consonants (cf. Sanskrit) and the types of permissible clusters (cf. Greek). As (68) beside (66) shows, in such overall processes of final cluster restriction, **degemination** may function the same way as other cluster simplifications.

(64)   Skt. $C_0 > \emptyset$ / VC ___ #

(65)   pre-Skt.   *bharants   >   bharan   'carrying' (sg. N m.)
                    *vākṣ   >   vāk   'speech' (sg. N f.)

(66)   Gk. [+ stop] $> \emptyset$ / ___ #

(67)   pre-Gk.   *tod   >   to   'that'
                   *paid   >   pai   'child' (sg. V)
                   *kērd   >   kēr   'heart'
                   *wanak   >   (w)ana   'king' (sg. V)
          vs.   *wanaks   >   (w)anaks 'king' (sg. N)

(68)   pre-Gk.   (*paids   >)   *paiss   >   pais 'child' (sg. N)

(69)   Greek permissible and non-permissible final obstruents:

Single obstruents	Clusters
s	ss*
t*	ts*
p*	**ps**
k*	**ks**

Also word-initial position is frequently affected by cluster simplification; cf. e. g. the English examples in (70). The most vulnerable clusters in this environment are the geminates. In fact, cases like (71), with actual attestation of an earlier geminate, are so rare that it is commonly believed that developments which would introduce initial geminates 'skip' the geminate stage and directly go to the non-geminate representation. In light of the evidence of (71), that seems to be an unnecessary assumption.

(70)   OE   cnoccian   >   NE   knock [∅n-]
              cnāwan   >   know [∅n-]

(71) pre-Gk.   *kˈwā-mn̥-   ptoli-
      dial. Gk.   ppāma-   ttoli-   (assimilation)
      other dial. pāma-   toli-   (degemination)
                  'possession'   'town, city'

(None of these forms are Attic-Ionic. *ptolis* is attested in Homer; its *t* is of controversial origin.)

Medial cluster simplifications like (72)/(73), though quite common, are considerably less frequent than final and initial simplifications. The reason seems to be that medial clusters tend to be distributed over more than one syllable, as in VCCCV = VC\$CCV. The clustering within each of these syllables therefore tends to be relatively small.

(72) [+ obstr.] > $\emptyset$ / [+ cons.] ___ [+ obstr.]

(73) ON   fylgði > NIcel. [fɪlØðɪ] 'followed'
           æskði   >   [aisØtɪ]   'wished'
      vs. sagði   >   [saɣðɪ]   'said'

The sensitivity of cluster simplification and degemination to syllable structure is further illustrated by (74), which accounts for the fact that Latin had medial degemination after long vowels and diphthongs, but not after short vowels; cf. (75). (In (74), C' is used to identify articulatorily identical consonants; VV is used as a cover term for both long vowels and diphthongs. For the latter convention cf. 5.1.4 above.)

(74) C'C' > C' / VV ___ V

(75) OLat. caussa > Class. Lat. causa 'thing, cause'
           (*)vīssus >   vīsus 'seen'
      vs. sĕssus   (unchanged)   'having sat'

5.3.3. Loss with compensatory lengthening

In the majority of cases, loss affects only the segment that is undergoing the change. Sometimes, however, loss is accompanied by the lengthening of a nearby syllabic segment. This process has been called **loss with compensatory lengthening**: The lengthening is considered to be a **'temporal compensation'** for the duration or **'mora'** of the lost segment. Put differently, the mora of the lost segment reattaches itself to a nearby syllabic segment, thereby lengthening it. (Since most languages do not permit 'overlong' vowels, this process usually does not affect long vowels. Cf. also 5.4.6 below.)

Behind this explanation lies a notion which goes back at least to the fifth century B.C., to the phonetic/phonological literature of the Sanskrit Prātiśākhyas. This is the idea that segments make a phonologically significant and in some ways quantifiable contribution to the length of syllables or words. Recent phonetic work has provided empirical evidence for the notion of temporary compensation. (Efforts to extend the notion beyond the domain of the word have been less successful.)

Changes like those in (76) and (77) are often used to exemplify loss with compensatory lengthening. Compare (78) for an attempt at formulating the developments in (77). (M = 'mora'; a solid line indicates an inherited or current association of the mora; a broken line, an abandoned association.)

(76) PGmc. *gans-   > OE gōs   'goose'
           *anþar-   >   ōðer   'other'

(77) PIE   *sisdō   > Lat. sīdō   'sit down'
            *nisdo- >   nīdus   'nest'

(78) PIE   ni   s   do-
                                 M
      Segmental loss   ni | do-
                                 Ø
                                 M
                                /⋮
      Mora reattachment   n i Ø   do-
      Length   n   ī   do-

Some linguists have argued that these developments can just as well be explained by a scenario of syllable-final weakening, followed by contraction; cf. (79). ([h] here is considered to function as a voiceless semivowel, which then contracts with the preceding vowel in the same way as other semivowels.)

(79) PIE   ni   s   do-
      Weakening   ni   h   do-
      Contraction   n   ī   do-

Evidence that this is a possible interpretation is provided by examples like the dialectally different outcome of older English [ər] as either lengthened [ə̄] or [ə] + glide [y]; cf. (80). The assumption would be that either [hə̄d] results from earlier [həyd] through contraction, or that [hə̄d] and [həyd] have a common source, with weakening of [r] to something like [h].

(80)   [hərd]   'heard'
   a) Most 'r-less' dialects: [hə̄d]
   b) Older New York,
        Atlanta, New Orleans   [həyd]

Other examples, however, are not amenable to an interpretation along the lines of (79), but only in terms of temporary compensation. Compare e. g. (81)—(83). (81) is an example of degemination with compensatory lengthening. Note that there is no evidence that such degemination proceeds through a stage in which the first segment is realized as a glide. (82) involves the loss of a segment in a neighboring syllable. Contraction therefore is out of the question.

(81)   pre-Hindi   *satt   >   Hindi   sāt   'seven'
                      *kamm   >   kām   'work'

(82 a)   PSlav.   *bogŭ   >   (pre-)SCr.   bōg   'God'
                      *bobŭ   >   bōb   'bean'
   b)   Hung.   *kezü   >   kēz   'hand'

The compensatory lengthening in (83) is a little more complicated. It compensates not for the loss of a segment, but for the fact that loss of syllabicity here affects syllable mora count: Within syllables, the domain of mora counting usually begins with the syllabic nucleus and may extend into the coda; segments in the onset, however, do not contribute to the mora count. The gliding of *ē* and *i* to *j* [y] removes these segments from the nucleus into the onset and thus leaves their mora unattached. Reattachment to the following vowel, then, results in the lengthening of that vowel.

(83)   ON   sēa   >   sjā   'see'
          bioða   >   bjōða   'bide'

Since temporary compensation is the only possible explanation for examples like (81)—(83), loss with compensatory lengthening must be recognized as an established historical phenomenon. A priori, 'compensatory' scenarios like (78) therefore cannot be rejected as possible accounts for examples like (76) and (77). But as noted, 'weakening' scenarios like (79) are also possible. Excepting the rare cases where positive evidence is available in favor of a weakening scenario, the analysis of such examples must be considered ambiguous.

word final vowel loss   medial syll vowel loss   initial vowel loss

5.3.4. Apocope, syncope, aphaeresis

Like consonant loss, vowel loss is more common in certain environments than in others.

Word-final position is as vulnerable an environment for vowels as it is for consonants and consonant clusters. Compare for instance (62) above. Vowel loss in this environment is commonly referred to as **apocope**, but note that the term is commonly used to refer not only to loss in 'absolute' final environment (i.e. before #, as in (62)), but also to developments as in (84a), where the environment is 'final syllable' (or ___ C_0 #). There is some justification for using the same term for both types of vowel loss. For in many languages, both processes are found to take place at roughly the same time; cf. (84a/b). However, in many cases there is a distinction, such that final-syllable vowels 'protected' by a following consonant (or by some subclass of the consonants) do not undergo loss; cf. (84c) (= (14d) above). If the term apocope is used for both processes, it is therefore necessary to distinguish them in terms of environmental restrictions.

(84a)	OE	stānas	>	NE	stones	[stōnØz]	
		hlāvas	>		loaves	[lōvØz]	
b)	OE	nama	>	NE	name	[nēmØ]	
		bana	>		bane	[bēnØ]	
c)	pre-ON	*sakū	>	ON	sǫkØ	[sɔk]	'thing'
		*allum			ǫllum	[ɔllum]	'all (pl. D)'

Apocope, however defined, often has various restrictions placed upon it. A common restriction is sensitive to the number of syllables in a word. Cf. e.g. (85), where apocope applies in trisyllabic (or longer) words, but not in disyllabics.

(85) PIE *bheresi > OHG birisØ 'you (sg.) carry'
          *mori   >   meri   'sea'

bur : esti   ìst   ← Hock ignores this —
                                    ie ignores ē

moraic effect / constraint (handwritten)

In all of the examples so far referred to, apocope affects unaccented
vowels. This typically is one of the conditions for apocope (as well as
syncope and aphaeresis). However, it is not a necessary condition. As
(86 b) shows, even accented vowels can be lost. (Their accent then is
reassigned to a preceding accentable segment. In Lithuanian, where
postvocalic [m] is accentable in the context of (86 b), this results in the
accentuation marked by the symbol ˜.)

(86 a) Lith. mőterimi   > mőterim 'by the women'
     b)   dukterimì [í] > dukterim̃ 'by the daughters'

The term **syncope** refers to vowel loss in a medial syllable, such
that the syllable in which loss occurs is flanked on both sides by other
syllables. Compare example (87) and the formulation in (88). Note that
in addition to syncope, example (87) shows the effect of a number of
other changes. These are listed in (89) in (roughly) chronological order.
(See also 11.1.1 below.)

(87) pre-OIr. nắmeddas > [nắβ̃ᵞØdᵞa] 'enemies' (pl. A)

(88) $V > \emptyset$ / [V, + acct.] C_0 ___ $C_0 V C_0$ ___ $C_0 V$ ...

(89) nắmeddas
      nắβedas   Weakening
      nắβᵞedas   Palatalization
      nắβᵞeda   Final $s > \emptyset$
      nắβᵞØda   Syncope
      nắβᵞdᵞa   Assimilation of feature [+ palatalized]

Unlike apocope, syncope is found in a number of apparently irregular,
sporadic changes. Compare for instance (90 a) vs. (b). However, in
many cases it is possible to attribute the irregularity to other factors.
Thus, in the case of Greek *oimai*, one suspects a form with fast-
speech or clitic reduction. Compare the accentual reduction of the
corresponding Engl. *I think* in parenthetical contexts like *He is, I think,
a little bit crazy*. If all examples of apparent irregularity can be explained
away, syncope may turn out to be as regular as apocope, after all. At

any rate, examples like (87) are quite common and show that syncope can be regular.

(90 a) Gk. oiomai   >   oimai   'I think'
   b)   maiomai   (no change)   'I endeavor'

Initial vowel loss or **aphaeresis** usually is irregular. In many cases it appears to be a fast-speech phenomenon; cf. (91). In others, it seems to result from a wrong analysis of 'contracted' forms; cf. (92) and (93). In either case, it is a process outside the usual domain of sound change, a fact which may well explain its irregularity.

(91) Engl.   arithmetic   >   'rithmetic

(92) Class. Gk. ommátion   >   NGk. máti 'eye'

(93) Class. Gk.   to ommátion   'the eye'
      Contraction   tommátion
      Reanalysis   to mmátion
      Other changes   to máti
      Hence: máti   'eye'

5.3.5. Loss of features, loss of contrast, final neutralization

Up to this point, the discussion has focused on segmental loss. Features, however, can be lost, too. Thus in Latin, the Indo-European 'labiovelar' stops lost their feature of labiovelarization before obstruent. Moreover, in the same environment, aspiration was lost. Combined with the medial weakening of (58/59) above, as well as other changes, this led to the forms in (94).

(94) PIE   *sneyg^{w}h-s *sneyg^{w}h-es 'snow'
                                                             (sg. N, G)

      Loss of labiovelar   *sneygh-s   — — — —
      Loss of aspiration   *sneyg-s   — — — —
      Voicing assimilation *sneyk-s   — — — —
      Aspir. > Fric.   — — — —   *sneyx^{w}es
      Weakening   — — — —   *sneywes
      Other changes   nīks   nīvis

Feature loss of this type causes certain difficulties. Although traditional linguists may talk about 'loss of aspiration' etc., the term 'loss'
by itself is usually reserved for segmental loss. More recent approaches
to linguistics in effect do the same thing: The symbol ∅ is used in
formulations of segmental loss. Developments like our 'loss of aspiration' are accounted for by the manipulation of features, in formulations
like (95).

(95)   [+ obstr.] > [− asp.] / ___ [+ obstr.]

One of the reasons for not recognizing a separate category of feature
loss may lie in a preoccupation with processes as they affect 'segments'.
But there are other possible justifications. One of these is the fact that
once we use feature notation, processes like (95) are not substantially
different from changes like voicing assimilation and final devoicing; cf.
(96) and (97). Changes like (96), however, are difficult to conceive of
as involving 'loss' in any phonetically meaningful sense.

(96)   [+ obstr.] > [α voice] / ___ [+ obstr., α voice]

(97)   [+ obstr.] > [− voice] / ___ #

It is only in a phonological sense that loss can be said to play a role
both in changes like (96) and (97) and in developments like (95) and
the (unformulated) 'loss of labiovelarization': All of these changes lead
to **loss of contrast**. Thus, (95) neutralizes the contrast between aspirated
and unaspirated stops; and (96) and (97) eliminate the contrast between
voiced and voiceless.

What is interesting is that there are a number of neutralization
processes which seem to be limited to word- and syllable-final environment, i. e., to the same context which plays a major role in weakening
and segmental loss.

Such **final neutralization** is not limited to final devoicing (for which
see 5.1.7). Also final weakening may lead to neutralization, as in (98).
(The process is illustrated as a change from PIE to Latin. In fact,
however, it may have taken place within the prehistory of PIE.)

(98)   PIE *to-d   > Lat.   (is-)tud   'that'
          *s(i)yēt > OLat. siēd   'would be'

Beyond these fairly well understood processes, a number of other
neutralizations are found in final environment. The two most common

of these are illustrated in (99) and (100). In (99), the place distinctions of nasals are neutralized word-finally, but not in other environments. (100) gives examples of final neutralization between labials and velars. (As the first example in (100 a) shows, 'final' here includes consonants in the coda, even if they are not in absolute final position.)

(99)	Span.	albúm 'album'	corazón 'heart'
	Standard	[alβún]	[koraθ/són]
	Dial.	[alβúŋ]	[koraθ/sóŋ]
	(vs. plural	[alβúmes]	[koraθ/sónes])

(100 a)	Dutch	luft	>	[luxt]	'air'
		nif$te	>	[nix$tə] 'niece' (cf. inherited [axt] '8')
b)	Engl.	[lax]	>	laugh [lā/æf] (cf. inherited *off*)

The processes in (99) and (100) are not very well understood from the (articulatory) phonetic point of view. The velar/labial alternation in (100) has however been connected with a well-known acoustic affinity between velars and labials, for which the acoustically based feature [+ grave] has been invoked. In and by itself, this affinity — or the feature 'grave' — does not provide an explanation for the change. However, this affinity can be made the basis for a speculative explanation, if we consider that the interchange between velar and labial seems to be limited to word-final and syllable-final (or coda) environment:

As noted earlier, final environment is a common position for weakening. Now, phoneticians tell us that the first step in weakening consists in a less forceful and distinct articulation. (This has sometimes been termed 'implosive' articulation.) In velars and labials, such a less forceful articulation might reduce their acoustic identifiability to the point where the listener can only recognize them as [+ grave], without being able to determine to which subclass (velar or labial) they should be assigned. One way out of this dilemma, then, would lie in arbitrarily selecting one or the other alternative as the representation for all instances of final [+ grave] segments.

If this explanation for the velar/labial interchange is correct, then a similar acoustically-based hypothesis can be proposed for the interchange between final nasals. The only difference would be that for nasals, weakening would have to be assumed to affect the recognition of all placement distinctions. Listeners would then be able to recognize that they are nasals, but not whether they are labial, dental, velar, etc.

5.4. Tonogenesis

5.4.1. General

Since many of the processes which lead to the origination of tones are closely related to the other changes discussed in this chapter, it seems appropriate to cover tonogenesis at this point. At the outset, however, a cautionary note must be struck: As observed in 2.1.11, the distinction between tone and (pitch) accent is not very clearly defined. Some of the developments discussed here therefore may be classified by other linguists not as tonogenesis, but as the origination of a new pitch accent system. However, since pitch is involved in both developments, there seems to be no need to be overly concerned about this problem. Note also that this chapter does not attempt to cover the manner in which tonal systems develop further, once they have come about. (In these further developments, assimilation between tones seems to play an important role, as well as many of the processes discussed in the following sections.)

Except where noted otherwise, the acute accent (´) will indicate high tone; the grave (`), low tone; and mid tone will be left unmarked.

5.4.2. Consonantal quality and tonogenesis

Crosslinguistically, vowels tend to have a lower fundamental frequency next to voiced consonants than next to voiceless ones. As long as the conditioning environments remain unchanged, this tonal difference stays at the predictable, allophonic (or 'allotonic') level. But just as in the case of umlaut, palatalization, retroflexion, etc., a change in the conditioning environment can make the tonal difference unpredictable and contrastive.

An example of this development can be found in Tibeto-Burman Jingpho: In the Eastern dialects, high and low tone are fully predictable in terms of the voicing of the following consonant: high before voiceless, low before voiced, mid if no consonant follows. In the Southern dialects, final consonants are lost and tone becomes contrastive; cf. (101).

(101)   Eastern   Southern
        sháh   shá
        shàɦ   shà
        láh   lá
        làɦ   là
        la   la

Some linguists have argued that tonogenesis of this type can be induced only by consonants in the onset of the syllable. But example (101) suggests that segments in the coda can also induce tone. And similar developments have been observed in Polynesian Kate.

Moreover, there is evidence which suggests that a more accurate assessment would be as follows: Both onset and post-nucleus consonants can induce tone, but onset consonants have a greater effect. Tonogenesis, then, is not directly linked to the relative position of the inducing consonants. Rather, the link is an indirect one: Tonal differences become contrastive through changes in the inducing consonants. In some languages, these changes may take place in the onset, in others they may affect post-nucleus position. In fact, there are cases where changes both in onset and in post-nucleus consonants make tonal differences contrastive.

Consider the case of Panjabi: Corresponding to Hindi words with voiced aspirates or [ɦ], Panjabi shows words with unaspirated, voiceless stops or Ø (for medial [ɦ]) plus a tonal distinction between 'high' and 'low'; cf. (102). And that tonal distinction is tied to the location of the Hindi voiced aspirate or [ɦ]. (Let us use the symbol [H] to refer to the class of voiced aspirates and [ɦ].) 'High' tone occurs where Hindi [H] follows (cf. (a)), 'low' tone, where it precedes (cf. (b)).

(102)   Hindi   Panjabi
    a) rāhī   rā́ī   'passenger'
        lābh   lā́p   'profit'
    b) ghoṛā   kòṛā   'horse'
        ghar   kàr   'house'
        dhol   tòl   'drum'

Now, we know that the voiced aspirates and [ɦ] of Hindi are inherited and that the Panjabi tones are an innovation. We can then explain the 'low' tone in (b) as induced by the voicing of the originally preceding

[H]; and its unpredictability results from the deaspiration and devoicing of [H]. But what about the 'high' tone in (a)?

As it turns out, Hindi provides the basis for an explanation. Acoustic phonetic studies of Hindi have shown that this language has very similar tonal contours to what we find in Panjabi, except that they are at the allophonic, not at the phonemic level. What is especially interesting are the pitch differences in disyllabic words; cf. Chart 5.2. We can observe that both initial [H] and medial [H] have a lowering effect on the fundamental frequency. But that effect is greater for initial than for medial [H].

It is this difference in lowering effect which seems to be responsible for the distinction between 'high' and 'low' tone. Moreover, the terms 'high' and 'low' must be read as relative to each other: both are actually lower than the pitch on sequences without [H] ('[-H] patterns'). (This is the reason for consistently putting the terms 'high' and 'low' in quotation marks.) In addition to pitch level, [H] and [-H] patterns also differ in pitch contour: Both [H] patterns have a 'flatter' contour than the [-H] pattern, whose pitch falls down more sharply in both syllables. Presumably the lowering of the fundamental frequency leaves less acoustic 'space' for modulation. Finally, for all three contours, the tonal differences are properties not just of individual syllables, but of whole words.

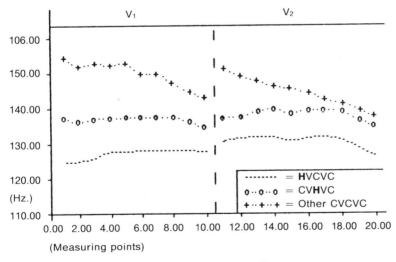

Chart 5.2. Allophonic tones in Hindi
(Adapted from Purcell, Villegas, & Young 1978)

The phonologically distinct Panjabi situation is very similar to the allophonic one of Hindi. 'Low' tone is lower than 'high' tone, and both differ in contour from the [-H] pattern. Unlike Hindi, however, Panjabi 'high' and 'low' tones are no longer significantly lower than the [-H] pattern. It appears that with phonological contrast has come a reinterpretation of what is phonologically significant: 'High' and 'low' differ from each other in pitch; what distinguishes both of them from the [-H] pattern is contour, not pitch.

5.4.3. Contraction and tonogenesis

In languages with pitch accents (perhaps also with stress), contraction of heterosyllabic vowels may lead to contrastive tonal contours, cf. example (103) from Greek. (Note that [A] here refers to an '*a*-coloring laryngeal' which disappears intervocalically and undergoes loss with compensatory lengthening in syllable-final environment. In both cases it imparts *a*-color to a neighboring *e*-vowel. For typographic reasons, length is marked by [:] in the transcription of Greek forms. Low pitch is marked on relevant unaccented vowels.)

	(103)	PIE	*bhug-éA	*bhug-éA-es	'flight'
					(sg. N, G)
			bhug-ā́	*bhug-á-às	
		Contraction	— — — —	bhugâ:s	
		Other Changes	phugé:	phugê:s	

Along with the segmental contraction of [aa] to [ā], the suprasegmental sequence of high pitch on [-á-] and low pitch on [-às] likewise contracts, producing a high-low or falling pitch (marked by ˆ). As a consequence, we now get a phonetically unpredictable contrast in pitch contours over long vowels.

What is interesting is that instead of an expected phonetic distinction between high level pitch in [phugé:] and falling pitch in [phugê:s], we get a distinction between rising and falling pitch. This can be explained as being due to polarization, in response to the fact that the tonal contrast is phonologically distinctive: A phonetic distinction between rising and falling tone encodes the contrast more clearly than one between level and falling tone.

It should be noted, however, that if we choose a **'mora representation'** for the Greek long vowels, it is possible to express the distinction between rising and falling tone in terms of a single pitch accent. In this notation, long vowels are treated as 'bimoric', consisting of a sequence of two identical short vowels. (Cf. the similar convention in 5.1.4.) Rising-tone [é:] could then be represented as [eé] (with accent on the second mora), falling-tone [ê:], as [ée] (with accent on the first mora). Even so, (103) shows that contraction has the potential of introducing unpredictable contour tones.

5.4.4. Pitch assimilation and tonogenesis

Many languages with pitch accent have low-level assimilations whereby unaccented, low-pitch syllables that are neighbors of accented, high-pitch syllables will partially or completely assimilate to the high pitch of these accented syllables. If, then, a subsequent change leads to loss of conditioning environments, contrastive tonal patterns may result.

An example of this development is found in the history of Vedic Sanskrit: At a certain stage, unaccented syllables partially assimilated to the high pitch of the preceding accented syllable. (The resulting falling pitch is traditionally transcribed with the grave accent (`).) By a later change, [i] was lost in the environment C___y V. As (104) shows, this loss made the occurrence of a following falling pitch unpredictable and therefore contrastive.

(104)	pre-Vedic Skt.	vr̥kíyas	:	rāyás
	Partial pitch assim.	vr̥kíyàs		— — —
	i > ∅ / C ___ y V	vr̥kyàs		— — —
	Hence contrast:	vr̥kyàs	vs.	rāyás
		'wolf' (sg. Gf.)		'wealth' (sg. G)

5.4.5. Loss with compensatory tone

Closely related to the preceding phenomenon is the fact that in many languages the loss of (final) syllables may result in tonal contrast on the preceding syllable.

It is possible to conceptualize this development as akin to loss with compensatory lengthening. And in fact, loss with compensatory lengthening may go hand-in-hand with the development of 'compensatory' tonal distinctions. But the process is no doubt aided by earlier low-level assimilations (or similar effects) on the preceding syllable. (For these developments, cf. the preceding section and 5.4.7 below.)

An example involving both compensatory lengthening and compensatory tone is (105) (cf. also (82) above). As the result of these developments, (pre-)Serbo-Croatian acquired contrasting contour tones on long vowels. (As in the case of Greek, it is possible to represent this contrast in terms of different placement of a single high-pitch accent; cf. the mora representations in (105). But that analysis does not seem to be available for the developments in (107).)

(105)   PSlav.   *bógŭ   *bòbŭ
         (pre-)SCr.   bôg   bŏb
              =   [bóòg]   [bòób]
                       'God'   'bean'

A similar development, but without compensatory lengthening, seems to be responsible for the contrasting word tones of Norwegian and Swedish. This contrast has a number of dialectally different realizations. However, the tonal contours found in Stockholm Swedish (cf. (106)) seem to come reasonably close to what the contrast must have looked like soon after it came into being.

(106)   Tone I   Tone II

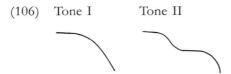

There are a number of conflicting hypotheses about the origin of this tonal contrast. The most plausible one links the contrast with the fate of vowels in the 'post-tonic' syllable (i. e. the syllable immediately following the accented first syllable). Post-tonic vowel loss correlates with Tone I. Tone II results where the post-tonic vowel is not lost (although it may be shortened). Cf. the Swedish data in (107). (Tone I is marked by a preceding [1], Tone II by [2]. Proto-Germanic accented vowels are set off in boldface. Swedish length has been ignored.)

(107)   PGmc.   Swedish

  a) Tone I: *stainaz   ¹sten   'stone'
              *dōmiðē   ¹dömde   'judged'
              *langizō   ¹längre   'longer'
  b) Tone II: *bundanaz   ²bunden   'bound'
              *dagōz   ²dagar   'days'

This correlation can be explained by the scenario in (108): Prior to the change, words of more than one syllable exhibit a step-wise descent in fundamental frequency. (Cf. the similar Hindi [-H] pattern in Chart 5.2.) Loss of post-tonic vowels leaves the lower pitch of these vowels unattached. Reassociation with the preceding syllable then brings about a rapidly falling contour on that syllable. But where post-tonic vowels remained, the old step-wise descent is retained. (The developments in (108) are sensitive to the pitch of the post-tonic syllable, not of syllables that may follow it. Pitch on these later syllables therefore is ignored.)

(108)

Stage I: dō mi ðē   da gōz

Syncope: dō mØ ðē   da gōz

Reattachment: dōmØ ðē   da gōz

Outcome: ¹dömde   ²dagar

Contrast arises from the fact that as the result of these and other changes, Tone I and Tone II can both occur in the same, disyllabic environment; cf. *¹dömde* vs. *²dagar*. (The pitch contour of original monosyllabics like *vet* (< PGmc. *wait*) apparently was sufficiently similar to the contour of (secondarily) monosyllabic words like *¹sten* that they were assigned the same tone.)

Interestingly, the Norwegian/Swedish tonal contrast is mirrored in Danish by the presence or absence of a glottal stop (called 'stød'): Tone I words have glottal stop, Tone II words do not; cf. (109). (The word for 'winter' is a borrowing from Low German which like other borrowings has been assigned Tone I in the Scandinavian languages.)

(109)   Swedish   Danish

            [1]vinter   ven^ʔdər   'winter'
            [1]man   manʔ   'man'
    vs.   [2]sommar   sɔmər   'summer'
            [2]bringa   breŋə   'bring'

This development is found elsewhere (e. g. in Latvian). It seems to be linked with the rapid pitch change in Tone I words. Possibly the required rapid adjustment leads the vocal cords to 'catch', producing a glottal stop. Perhaps the development has a perceptual basis: The rapid pitch change may result in acoustic discontinuities which are perceptually reinterpreted as created by a glottal stop.

5.4.6. Overlength and tone

In most languages, length is a 'binary' phenomenon: Vowels either are 'long', or they are 'short'; no other length distinctions are made. As a consequence, contractions and compensatory lengthenings usually change the quantity only of short vowels, since long vowels cannot be further lengthened.

However, a minority of languages permit a triple distinction, between 'short' (or 'monomoric'), 'long' (or 'bimoric'), and 'overlong' (or 'trimoric'). This is for instance the case in a number of Northern German dialects in which loss with compensatory lengthening has changed originally short vowels into long ones, and originally long vowels into 'overlong' ones.

As it turns out, such **overlength** not only is crosslinguistically rare, it is also fairly unstable, once introduced. In many of the Northern German dialects, overlong vowels therefore were shortened (often to a length intermediate between that of the old long and short vowels).

What is interesting in the present context is that such a shortening frequently is accompanied by the imposition of a rapidly changing tonal contour, a so-called broken tone. Presumably this results from the fact that the intonational contour of the earlier overlong vowel is 'mapped' onto the shortened vowel and in the process gets condensed and distorted. An example is given in (110). (ū3 = trimoric, overlong [u], ˆ = 'broken tone'.)

(110)	Stage I:	hūse	:	hūs 'house'
	Loss with comp. length:	hū3s	≠	hūs (sg. D, N)
	Shortening with comp. tone:	hûs	≠	hūs

see also eg. in notes 10/28 p. 3

5.4.7. Accent retraction and tonogenesis

Many languages seem to have a constraint against high pitch on utterance-final syllables. This has been plausibly explained as due to the fact that the crosslinguistically unmarked, most common pattern of sentence intonation is characterized by falling pitch at the end of the utterance. If, then, a word with final high pitch appears in utterance-final position, a conflict arises between its high pitch and the low pitch of the sentence intonation. A common response to this conflict lies in the **'retraction'** of the high pitch from word-final position to a preceding syllable or mora. This retraction, in turn, may be generalized to other syllables and thus lead to a general accent retraction.

An example of this process is found in Serbo-Croatian: An earlier pitch accent system opposed a rising 'intonation' on long vowels to a high level pitch on short vowels. This system is preserved very nicely in the majority of the Čakavian dialects; cf. (111 a) and (112). In a subgroup of these dialects, however, words with long vowel in their final syllable have undergone accent retraction at the end of the utterance, such that the accent shifted from the second vowel mora to the first; cf. (111 b). Elsewhere, the rising intonation is retained. In the Štokavian dialects, the accent retraction has been generalized to all occurrences of such words; cf. (111 c). (The conventional accent symbols are retained in (111); their phonetic value is indicated by the mora notation.)

(111 a)	Čakavian	krãl^y	=	[kraál^y]	'king'
b)	Čakav. dial.	krâl^y	=	[kráal^y]	/ ___ ##
		krãl^y	=	[kraál^y]	elsewhere
c)	Štokavian	krâl^y	=	[kráal^y]	

Štokavian has generalized this accent retraction beyond the long vowels, so as to apply also to words with accented short vowels. But since short vowels have only one mora, the retraction does not remain confined to the accented vowel, but 'spills over' into the preceding syllable, if any. Of course, if no syllable precedes, the accent retraction is blocked. Compare the developments in (112).

(112) Čakavian   Štokavian

a) otvorít   otvòriti   'to open'
    otvórī   òtvorī   '(s)he will open'
    vodá   vòda   'water' (sg. N)

b) vódu   vódu   'water' (sg. A)

(For typographic reasons, the symbols ´ and ` are used for conventional ῀ and ῾. In Čakavian, ` indicates short accented vowel; in Štokavian, `` = 'rising intonation' on short V, ` = 'falling intonation' on short V.)

What is interesting is that the accent retraction in (112) leads to an intonational contrast in accented short vowels, between rising intonation on syllables which have received the accent and falling intonation where the accent was retained; cf. (112 a) vs. (b). This distinction is difficult to account for simply in terms of accent shift; for short vowels are monomoric. As a consequence, accent shift should not introduce a contour tone, but should replace low with high pitch. We would therefore expect the same accentuation in *voda* and *vodu*.

In order to explain the change, we need to assume that prior to the accent shift there had been a low-level partial assimilation of pre-tonal syllables to the high tone of the accented syllable. (Cf. the similar Vedic assimilation in 5.4.4 which, however, affected post-tonal syllables.) The resulting rising intonation, then, became contrastive as the result of accent retraction. (Cf. *vóda* vs. *vòdu*.) Finally, polarization led to a falling realization for the accent of 'unshifted' syllables.

6. Sound change:
Dissimilation, haplology, metathesis

Except where noted, the changes discussed in this chapter normally are irregular or sporadic. Section 6.3 deals with the conditions which seem to be conducive for the regular application of dissimilation and metathesis.

6.1. Dissimilation

6.1.1. General

The logical opposite of assimilation is **dissimilation**, a differentiation of segments with similar or identical pronunciation. Compare the examples of nasal dissimilation in (1).

(1a) illustrates an early Germanic development of anticipatory dissimilation of the first of two nasals, changing it into a non-nasal continuant (which in Old High German became a stop). Although this process was very wide-spread in early Germanic, examples like (1b—e) show that it did not apply regularly, in all possible cases. (1c) and (1d) further illustrate that in some of the Germanic dialects, and at different periods, an alternative, perseverant process could apply. The whole situation is complicated by the assimilations in (1e). These seem to have applied where *m* and *n* were in contact and had 'escaped' the early dissimilation of (1a). (Similar assimilations took place later in some of the Germanic dialects, some of them undoing the effects of (1a).)

(1)	PGmc.	OE	OHG	Old Saxon	
a)	*emna-	ev(e)n	eban	eβan	'even'
	*heman-	heovon		heβan	'heaven, sky'
	*stemna-	stevn			'prow, stem'
b)	*stemna-	stemn		stemn	'prow, stem'
c)	*heman-		himil		'heaven, sky'

d)	*samanō-		samanōn	'to gather'
			> MHG	
			samelen	
e)	*stemna-	stemm	stamm	'stem, trunk'

(Proto-Germanic vowel alternations are ignored. Old English has variation between [vn] and [mn] in many, but not all words with orignal *mn*.)

As the examples in (1) show, like assimilation, dissimilation can be anticipatory or perseverant, in contact or at a distance. However, cases of mutual dissimilation do not seem to be found.

Moreover, the distinction between complete and partial assimilation has no clear counterpart in dissimilation. True, we can find differences in the degree of dissimilation. For instance. in (2a) the liquid *l* changes to [-liquid] *d* in anticipation of an *l* that follows later in the word; but in (2b) the feature [liquid] remains and (perseverant) dissimilation affects only the feature [lateral]. The only process which could be considered a 'complete' dissimilation is **dissimilatory loss**, as in (3a). (Examples like (3b) show that like other dissimilatory processes, dissimilatory loss is typically irregular. Its behavior therefore is quite different from the loss processes discussed in the preceding chapter.)

(2a)	Greek	*Leukaliōn	>	**D**eukaliōn	(proper name)
b)		*Leukaliōn	>	Leuka**r**iōn	(proper name)

(3a)	Engl.	library	>	[laybØerī]	
b)		contrary		(unchanged)	

Dissimilation is disproportionately common with liquids. Compare examples (2) and (3), as well as (4) below. As noted in section 2.1.5, the difference between [l] and [r] is one of the last distinctions learned by children acquiring their first language. One suspects that this is the reason for this relative 'instability' of the liquids vis-à-vis dissimilation. (Cf. also 6.2, as well as 7.3.1.)

(4)	Latin	Spanish	
	arbore-	arbol	'tree'
	rōbore-	roble	'strength'
	sartore-	sastre	'tailor'
	(priore-	prior (unchanged)	'prior')

6.1.2. Haplology

A special type of dissimilatory loss consists in the loss of a whole syllable before or after a phonetically similar or identical syllable; cf. examples (5) and (6). This process is referred to as **haplology.**

Example (6) shows that the two syllables need not be identical. What seems to be required is that (a) the consonants be identical and (b) the sequencing of consonant and vowel be the same. (Thus, [-phi$pho-] can undergo haplology, and so can [-er$ar-]; but a sequence like [-er$ra-] cannot.)

(5)   Lat. *nutrītrīx > nutrīx   'nurse'

(6a)   Hom. Gk. amphiphoreús
             > amØphoreús   'two-handled pitcher'
  b)   Lat. trierarchus
             > trierØchus / triØarchus   'captain of a tri-
                                          era'

6.1.3. Diphthongization

Section 5.1.4 has presented arguments for considering contraction to be assimilatory. One might therefore be tempted to interpret its logical opposite, **diphthongization**, as being a dissimilatory process.

This interpretation works very nicely for examples like (7a), especially if we use mora notation for transcribing long vowels and diphthongs (cf. (7b)). In the present example, diphthongization then can be analyzed as dissimilation of the first of two neighboring [i]-vowels.

(7a)   OE   bītan   > NE bite [bayt]
             rīdan   >   ride [rayd]
  b)   =   biitan   >   bait
             riidan   >   raid

Diphthongization, however, is not limited to long vowels, but may affect short vowels as well. Compare for instance example (8). In cases like these, a dissimilatory analysis is less attractive: We would have to assume that single segments can undergo something like 'internal differentiation'.

(8) Lat. nostrum   >   Span. nuestro 'our'
           terra   >   tierra   'earth'

Some other considerations argue against considering diphthongization to be dissimilatory. First, several other, non-dissimilatory explanations of diphthongization have been proposed, including developments similar to the ones discussed in 7.1.1; cf. also 7.4.5. (At this point, it does not seem possible to determine which of these is the best or most explanatory account.) Secondly, diphthongization differs in its behavior from ordinary dissimilatory processes by usually being a regular sound change, just like assimilation, weakening, and loss. All other dissimilatory processes, however, ordinarily are irregular.

6.2. Metathesis

Transpositions of segments as in (9), (10), and (11a) are a frequent phenomenon. Developments of this type are referred to as **metathesis**.

(9) PGmc. *aiskō   >   OE ēascian/ēaxian [-sk/**ks**-]
                          NE ask/dial. **aks**
            *fiskas >   OE fisc/fix [-sk/**ks**]

(10) Lat. parabola   >   Span. palabra 'word'
          periculum >   peligro 'danger'

(11) Old English   Modern English
  a) bridd   >   bird
     frist   >   first
     þridde   >   third
  b) þrysce   >   thrush
     bricg   >   bridge
     crisp   >   crisp

(Since metathesis had begun to operate in pre-Old English, Old English often had variants, as in *þridde/þirde*.)

Like dissimilation, metathesis is usually irregular. Compare for instance the coexistence of changed and unchanged forms in the Old English outcomes of (9) or the unchanged residue in (11b). (The change in (10) seems to be limited to two examples.)

And like dissimilation, metathesis is disproportionately common with liquids. (For parallels and a possible motivation, cf. 6.1.1, as well as 7.3.1.) Example (10) illustrates one common process, the interchange of liquids amongst each other. Another common development is found in (11), namely the metathesis of neighboring vowels and liquids. The latter process seems to be limited to sequences of short vowels and liquids. No cogent examples of metathesis between long vowels and liquids appear to be attested.

6.3. Regular dissimilation and metathesis

As the preceding sections have illustrated, dissimilation and metathesis ordinarily are irregular or sporadic processes. However, it has been noted that some of the most 'shining examples of regularity' come from this class of notoriously irregular changes. This raises the question of whether we can establish specific conditions under which these processes can apply in a regular fashion.

Little work has been done in this area. The hypotheses that will be presented below must therefore be considered tentative. However, they do suggest the directions in which future research might look.

One of the most 'shining examples' of regular change is Grassmann's Law, the dissimilation of aspirated stops that are followed by other aspirates within the same word. Cf. the formulation in (12) and the examples in (13). As the examples in (13b) show, Grassmann's Law can apply to more than one segment per word. In effect, it eliminates all but the rightmost aspirate in a given word. Moreover, (13c) suggests that Grassmann's Law is bled by another change that deaspirated and devoiced stops before *s*. This change is formulated in (14). Compare the relative chronology in (15). (But see section 11.8 below for a historically more accurate look at the relative chronology of these changes.)

(12) [+ stop] > [− asp.] / _____ (X) [+ asp.] (= **GL**)

(13) PIE   Sanskrit
  a) *bhudhyetoy   budhyatē   'is awake'
  b) *bhebhowdhe   bubōdha   'was awake'
  c) *bhewdhsyeti   bhōtsyati 'will be awake'
      *bhudhs   bhut   'awakening'

(14)   [+ stop] > [− asp, − voice] / _____ s (=**deasp.**)

(15)   PIE   bhudhs   bhudhs

         deasp.   bhuts   GL   budhs
         GL   − − −   deasp.   buts
         Other changes: bhut   but*

   Greek had a similar, but apparently independent process of regular
aspirate dissimilation. (This process is likewise referred to as
Grassmann's Law.) As the data in (16) show, this change also affected
Gk. *h* (<PIE **s*). Moreover, it was bled by a process of deaspiration
before *s*, and was fed by a process which changed the PIE aspirates
into distinctively voiceless segments. Compare the formulation in (17),
where, [+ asp., ± segment] is an ad-hoc device to cover both segmental
[h] and non-segmental aspiration. (Note that there is no crucial ordering
between (17a) and (b): Depending on whether (17b) is formulated with
or without the feature [-voice] in its output, it can precede or follow
(a), or be simultaneous with it, for that matter.)

(16)   PIE   Greek

         *dhidhēmi   tithēmi   'put'
         *ǵheǵhewa   kekheua   'poured'
         *dhrighs   thriks   'hair' (sg. N)
         *dhrighos   trikhos   'hair' (sg. G)
         *seghō   ekhō   'have'
         *seghsō   heksō   'will have'
         (cf. *so   ho   'that one')

17a)   [+ asp.] > [− voice]
   b)   [+ stop] > [− asp., (− voice)] / _____ s
   c)   [+ asp., ± segment] > ∅ / _____ (X) [+ asp.]

   Like its Sanskrit counterpart, the Grassmann's Law of Greek at one
point could apply to more than one aspirate and in so doing, limited
the feature of aspiration to just one segment per word. Similar effects
have been observed for other dissimilatory processes involving such
glottal features as aspiration, voicing, or 'glottalization'. This is interesting, for such a 'cumulative' application and effect does not seem to be
encountered in the ordinary, irregular dissimilatory processes.

Assuming that this correlation between glottal features on one hand and cumulative application and effect on the other is not just accidental, one can propose the hypothesis in (18).

(18)   **Hypothesis I:** Dissimilation can become a regular process if it affects glottal features and if its application establishes a general limit on the occurrence of such features within the structure of words.

This hypothesis, however, is not sufficient to cover the whole range of regular dissimilatory processes. Also non-glottal dissimilations may be regular. (In the following, diphthongization will be ignored. As noted in 6.1.3, this process may not be dissimilatory in nature.)

Compare for instance (19) from dialectal Old Norwegian. By this regular dissimilatory process, the Common Old Norse back vowel [ɔ] (written *ǫ*) was changed to [-back] *a* before a syllable containing the back vowel *u*, as in *ǫllum* > *allum* 'all (pl. D)'

(19)   ɔ > a / _____ C_0u

Several things are interesting about this change: First, it undoes the effect of an earlier '*u*-umlaut'. Secondly, it does so only where the conditioning environment *u* remained. Where the conditioning environment is lost, the change does not take place. Compare (20) for a summary of relevant data and developments. (*u*-umlaut here is presented as a two-stage process of assimilation and apocope.)

(20)	pre-ON	allaz	allū	allum	'all' (sg. N m., f., pl. D)
	assimilation	— — —	ɔllū	ɔllum	
	apocope (etc.)	all	ɔll	— — —	
	Common ON	all ≠	ɔll	ɔllum	
	dissimilation	— — —	— —	allum	
	dial. ONorw.	all ≠	ɔll	allum	

Now, what is important is that as a result of the apocope which made *u*-umlaut unpredictable, [a] and [ɔ] came to contrast in forms like [all] and [ɔll]. On the other hand, the contrast was neutralized in forms like [ɔllum], where the conditioning environment [u] had remained: Of the two segments [a] and [ɔ], only the latter could occur in this context in Common Old Norse. It is in this position of neutralization, then, that the dissimilation of (19) occurred. Moreover, (19) did not eliminate the neutralization of the contrast between /a/ and /ɔ/ in forms like [allum]. Also after the change, only one of the two segments could appear in this context — namely [a]. That is, the process simply changed the phonetic realization of the 'archiphoneme' /a : ɔ/.

The Nupe developments in (21) are perhaps to be analyzed in the same fashion, since also here, the features [palatalized] and [labiovelarized] are lost only where they are predictable; cf. (21 a). They remain where they are contrastive, as in (21 b). But note that these developments are similar to changes affecting segmental [y] and [w] next to front or back vowels, respectively. And as 7.1.1 will show, in this environment, segmental [y] and [w] may not only be lost, they may also be 'gained'. Processes of this sort therefore may have to be analyzed not as dissimilatory, but in terms of the notion of 'imprecise' or 'wrong timing' developed in 7.1.1.

(21 a)   changed: eg^{y}i   >   egi   'child'
                        eg^{w}u   >   egu   'mud'
     b)   unchanged: eg^{y}a 'blood' ≠ eg^{w}a 'hand' ≠ ega 'stranger'

The case of (22) (example in (23)) is more clearly dissimilatory. But unlike the developments in (19)/(20) — as well as in (21) —, this regular dissimilation does not undo the effects of an earlier sound change by which the contrast between [l] and [d] would have been neutralized. Still, synchronic neutralization of contrast does play a role: Both before and after the change, /l/ — the input to the change — and /d/ — the output — do not contrast in the position before /n/. Just as in the earlier examples, the dissimilation has merely changed the phonetic realization of the archiphoneme /l:d/. (Certain environmental restrictions are ignored in the formulation of (22).)

(22)   l > d / _____ l

(23)   OIcel. all > NIcel. [adl] 'all' (sg. N m.)

Many, perhaps all other examples of non-glottal regular dissimilation follow the same pattern. It is therefore possible to establish the following second hypothesis:

(24)   **Hypothesis II:** Non-glottal dissimilation can be regular if the input and the output of the change do not contrast in the environment of the change.

Regular metathesis likewise seems to apply only under certain specifiable conditions. These are stated in the hypothesis of (25). (The hypothesis requires certain minor modifications. But these need not detain us here.)

(25) **Hypothesis III:** Metathesis can be regular if it serves a specific structural purpose.

That structural purpose may be of a very general, phonological nature, as in (26) and (27). In (26a), length metathesis compensates for mora loss in a pan-Greek process of pre-vocalic shortening, cf. (26b). And the regular vowel + liquid metathesis of South and West Slavic helps implement the pan-Slavic 'open-syllable conspiracy' (for which see 8.5 below).

(26a) Att.(-Ion.) Gk.   basilēŏs   >   basilĕōs   'king' (sg. G)
   b) Other Gk. dial.   basilēos   >   basilĕos   'king' (sg. G)
      All post-Hom.   basilēōn   >   basilĕōn   'king' (pl. G)

(27) PSlav.   *gor$dŭ   >   gro$dŭ/gra$dŭ 'city'
              *mel$ko   >   mle$ko/mlĕ$ko 'milk'

Most commonly, the 'specific structural purpose' of regular metathesis lies in converting phonologically or perceptually 'marked' structures into more acceptable ones.

Thus, clusters of the type dental stop + [l] seem to be in some sense 'marked' or 'unstable', and many languages eliminate them, especially if they are 'tautosyllabic' (i.e. if they occur in the same syllable). Cf. the discussion in 7.3.8 below. (28) illustrates how metathesis eliminated such clusters at a certain stage in the development of Spanish. (Note that by analogical developments, Modern Spanish has restored the order *dl* in a few forms like OSpan. *dalde* → NSpan. *dadle*.)

(28) pre-OSpan.   *tidle   >   OSpan. tilde   'title'
                  *kabidle   >   cabilde 'chapter'
                  *espadla   >   espalda 'back'
                  *dad-le   >   dalde   'give him'

Regular metathesis may also serve to eliminate clusters which do not conform to the preferred ordering of segments within syllables in terms of the sonority hierarchy (cf. 2.1.12 above). For instance, in the prehistory of Modern Persian, apocope introduced word-final clusters of obstruent or nasal + [r]. The increasing sonority of these clusters violated the tendency toward decreasing sonority in the coda. Metathesis eliminated the 'marked' structures and replaced them with 'unmarked' ones. Cf. (29). (An alternative approach to eliminating such clusters is anaptyxis; cf. 7.1.3 below.)

(29) MPers.   čaxra asru namra
      apocope   čaxr   asr   namr
      metathesis   čarx   ars   narm   (= NPers.)

Certain apparent examples of regular metathesis do not seem to be governed by Hypothesis III above. Compare e. g. (30), whose transposition of labial stop and [y] cannot be argued to serve any particular structural purpose. Examples of this type seem to be limited to clusters involving [y] and [w]. Moreover, they appear to be restricted to languages with independent evidence for a general process of palatalization or labiovelarization. One therefore suspects that rather than resulting from metathesis, changes like the one in (30) result from 'segmentalization' of the non-segmental on- or off-glide of palatalized and labiovelarized consonants; cf. (31). For further details cf. 7.1.1 and 7.3.5.

(30) Lat. (sapiat >) *sapya > OSpan. (*)saipa [ay]
                              > NSpan. sepa 'would know'
(31) *sapya > *sap^{y}a [sa^{y}p^{y}a] > (*)saypa (> sepa)

7. Sound change:
Epenthesis, elimination of hiatus,
other changes

The changes discussed in this chapter are less unified in their behavior than the ones of the two preceding chapters. What they share is only negatively definable: With a few exceptions, they have no clear affinities with the processes dealt with in Chapters 5 and 6. Moreover, unlike the changes of chapter 5, the majority of processes discussed here do not have any clear articulatory motivation. — Except where noted, the changes are regular.

7.1. Epenthetic changes

Epenthesis is most easily defined as the opposite of loss: Where loss deletes segments in a given environment, epenthesis inserts segments. Compare the formulations in (1).

(1a) Loss: $Y > \emptyset \ / \ X \ \underline{\quad\quad} \ Z$
  b) Epenthesis: $\emptyset > Y \ / \ X \ \underline{\quad\quad} \ Z$

A certain difficulty lies in the fact that the epenthetic development of consonants is sometimes distinguished from that of vowels as epenthesis vs. **anaptyxis** (or 'svarabhakti'). Moreover, consonantal and vocalic epenthesis tend to be rather different in their behavior and motivation. For that reason it is convenient to use **epenthetic changes** as the cover term, and to reserve the term epenthesis for the epenthetical development of consonants.

7.1.1. (Consonantal) epenthesis

Examples (2) and (3) illustrate what nowadays usually is meant by the term '(consonant) epenthesis', namely the development of an oral stop between a nasal stop and a [-nasal] consonant.

(2a)   pre-Gk. *anros   > an**d**ros   'of a man'
  b)   pre-Gk. *amrotos > am**b**rotos 'immortal'

(3)   pre-Lat. *dēmsei > dēm**ps**ī   'took away'

Developments like these have been plausibly explained as resulting from 'incorrect' or '**wrong timing**' of articulatory gestures. In (2a), for instance, the transition from nasal *n* to the following oral *r* is not accomplished all at once. Instead, the gesture of nasality is discontinued before the stop articulation comes to an end. The result is a stretch of oral dental stop. Compare the diagram in (4). The situation is very similar in (2b). But in this case, the nasal differs from the liquid not only in orality and by being a stop, but also by being [+ labial]. And in situations like these, the epenthetic oral stop seems to always have the placement features of the nasal. That is, what is decisive is the timing of the gesture for nasality. Other features of the nasal stop remain intact.

(4)

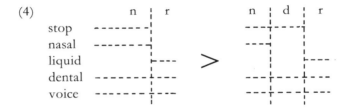

Example (3) takes the differences between nasal and oral segment one step further, by introducing a difference in voicing. The outcome again is typical, but a little more difficult to explain: The epenthetic stop has the placement features of the preceding nasal but the voicing of the following obstruent. We cannot account for this simply as a premature switch to [-nasal]. For in that case we might expect a voiced epenthetic stop. We may try to account for the voicelessness by a separate process of voice assimilation before the voiceless *s*. However, the existence of intermediate stages with voiced stop so far does not seem to have been demonstrated. Perhaps, then, the voicing assimilation is an automatic concomitant of epenthesis.

Even more complicated are epentheses like the one in (5). Nothing in the feature system with which we have been operating so far will be able to explain such changes as instances of wrong timing. The key to an explanation lies in more fine-grained phonetic observation: Trilled or flapped [r] sounds require a certain amount of closure for their production. Wrong timing of this closure, then, produces the epenthetic stop. (In addition, note that here again, the epenthetic stop agrees in voicing with a neighboring obstruent; but in this case the obstruent precedes.)

(5) PIE *swesr- > PGmc. *swestr- (> NE sister)

In much of 19th-century literature on historical linguistics, the term 'epenthesis' was used for what at first looks like a very different process: the introduction of a segmental [y] glide before or after palatalized or palatal segments, and a similar appearance of segmental [w] next to labiovelarized sounds. (These glides often are orthographically represented as *i* and *u*.) Compare (6)−(9) for examples. In (6), the development takes place before a palatal. A similar change is found in (7). Examples (8) and (9) show analogous developments after palatalized or palatal segments. As (6) and (9) show, the conditioning environment can be either a palatal or a palatalized consonant.

(6) Am. Engl. dial. [mæš]   > [mæyš] 'mash'
                    [mežər] > [meyžər] 'measure'

(7) Latin   pre-OF   Old French
a) plangit   > *plañit   > plaint   'complains'
   pugnum   > *poñu-   > poing   'fist'
   vocem   > *vokʸe-   > voiz   'voice'
b) rationem > *ratʸone- > raison   'reason'
   potionem > *potʸone- > poison   'poison'

(8) Latin   pre-OF   Old French
   carum   > *kʸæru-   > chier [čy-] 'dear'
   canem   > *kʸæne-   > chien [čy-] 'dog'
   (vs. mare > *mære-   > mer (not mier) 'sea')

(9) (pre-Balt. *pēuti- >) *pʸautʸi > Lith. pjauti [pyautʸi]
                                                        'cut'

Though these **glide epentheses** look very different from the processes in (2), (3), and (5), they can be explained by the same principle: The non-segmental [y]-like on- or off-glide of palatalized segments and an acoustically similar effect next to palatals becomes segmental through wrong timing. (Mutatis mutandis, the same development accounts for segmental [w] next to labiovelarized segments.) Such a change from non-segmental, 'feature' status to fully segmental articulation can be referred to as **segmentalization**.

Example (9) is especially interesting. First, the glide epenthesis here in effect eliminates palatalization on the initial segment. Secondly, in Lithuanian, the process is limited to initial labials. Now, as noted in 5.1.5, palatalization of labials is both rare and unstable. (Cf. also 7.3.5 below.) The Lithuanian glide epenthesis therefore may well be a device for eliminating the crosslinguistically unstable palatalization of labials.

In this respect it is interesting that developments such as (10a), with apparent glide metathesis next to labial, are a common phenomenon in languages with an (otherwise) very general process of palatalization. And note that in Romance, palatalization affected all dentals and velars (with the apparent exception of [r], which like the labials does not easily 'accept' palatalization; cf. 7.3.5).

> (10a)   Lat. sapiat > *sapya > pre-OSpan. (*) saipa > sepa
> 'would know'
> b)   Lat. rationem > *ratyone- > OFr. raison 'reason' ·

Developments of this type are now commonly interpreted as metatheses. 19th-century linguists, on the other hand, tended to refer to them as (glide) epentheses. Circumstantial evidence is on the side of the latter interpretation: As noted, such changes are common in languages with independent evidence for palatalization. (Elsewhere, examples seem to be nonexistent or rare.) Secondly, changes like these may be found with segments that are unambiguously palatalized or palatal. Compare for instance (10b) = part of (8a), reformulated so as to bring out the parallelism with (10a), omitting the intervening stage with palatalized [t^y]. Thirdly, if they are environmentally restricted, they seem to apply most readily to labials and other segments which crosslinguistically are 'uncomfortable' with palatalization. (This is for instance the case in Spanish; cf. (10a).) Finally, there is the parallelism of developments like (9) which likewise are restricted to labials. And these developments can only be accounted for as epenthetical.

The reformulation of (10a) in (10′a) therefore might be a more accurate scenario; cf. the parallel developments in (10′b). (In these reformulations, both the onglide and the offglide of palatalization are marked.)

(10′a) sapiat   > *sapya   > *saᵞpʸya > *saᵞpʸa > (*)saipa
   b) rationem > *ratyone- > raᵞtʸyone > raᵞtʸone > raison

Also nonsegmental, 'secondary' articulations can apparently be introduced by wrong timing. For instance, in many languages, including
Modern English and German, pre-vocalic (or pre-sonorant) voiceless
stops have acquired the feature of **aspiration**. This has been explained
as **'delayed voicing onset'**; cf. the diagram in (11). (Here and in (12)
and (13), a raised [ʰ] is used to indicate the nonsegmental status of
aspiration.) A similar explanation (in terms of something like 'premature
voicing offset') is possible for the rarer phenomenon of **preaspiration**;
cf. the Icelandic example in (12). (Note that by segmentalization of [ʰ]
and degeminatory cluster simplification, Icelandic [ryeʰtta] tends to
develop into [ryehta].)

(11)

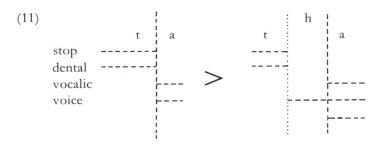

(12) OIcel. rētta > NIcel. [ryeʰtta] 'straighten'

A conceptualization of aspiration as delayed voicing onset will account very nicely for a crosslinguistic tendency for syllable-final, word-
final, and pre-obstruent stops to be unaspirated, or for aspirated stops
to lose their aspiration in these environments. (For the latter development, cf. e. g. 5.3.5, ex. (94).) For in these positions, aspiration cannot
be realized as delayed voicing onset over a following vowel or sonorant.
   What complicates matters is that languages like German and British
English do have word- and syllable-final aspiration. We may try to
account for this as a generalization of the aspirated allophones at the
expense of the unaspirated ones. But the fact remains that contrary to
the 'delayed voicing onset' hypothesis, aspiration can occur word-
and syllable-finally. The explanation seems to lie in the compensatory
development of a nonsegmental stretch of vocalic articulation that
supports the aspiration.

Moreover, it has been noted that aspiration, once introduced, tends to be articulated not just as delayed voicing onset, but also with a certain amount of 'turbulence' (produced by additional articulatory gestures). This turbulence is especially noticeable in languages with distinctive aspiration, such as Hindi and other South Asian languages. The fact that aspiration in these languages is much 'heavier' than in languages like English and German may be attributed to the principle of polarization.

Historically, aspiration may result also from processes other than delayed voicing onset. In Korean, for instance, syllable-final [h] meta-thesized with a following voiceless stop. But the outcome was not a sequence of voiceless stop + [h], but a single aspirated voiceless stop segment; cf. (13). We can look at this as a process of **desegmentalization**: Through wrong timing, segmental [h] becomes nonsegmental aspiration. (Alternatively, the process can be interpreted as one of 'consonantal contraction'.) Desegmentalization of [h] seems to be common in languages like Korean, which have a pre-existing contrast of aspirated and unaspirated segments.

(13)   Kor.   *manh-ta   *mantha > mant^{h}a 'be much'
                 *noh-ta   > *notha   > not^{h}a   'set free'

Wrong timing, then, can result both in segmentalization and desegmentalization. This raises the question whether a similar duality of behavior can be found at the purely segmental level, such that wrong timing not only leads to the introduction of segments, but also to loss or 'eclipsis'.

Some evidence suggests that eclipsis is a possibility. For instance, in many varieties of English, words like *cents* and *sense* have the same pronunciation. In some of these varieties, both are pronounced as [sents], with the development of an epenthetic oral stop in *sense*. Others instead have [sens] for both words. We can look at the latter pronunciation as an instance of cluster simplification in *cents*. However, the fact that a third variety of English seems to have free variation between [sens] and [sents] for both words should give us pause: It seems simpler to relate the two variant pronunciations to each other by a single process of wrong timing (resulting either in epenthesis or in eclipsis) than to attribute them to two very different phonetic processes.

Further evidence for eclipsis as an alternative to epenthesis may perhaps be found in examples like (14) and (15), if we interpret these changes as instances of wrong timing vis-à-vis the feature of syllabicity. (This, of course, requires a certain extension of the notion 'wrong timing'.) (14) shows a 'gain' of non-syllabic [y] and [w] before corresponding syllabic front and back vowels respectively. (The central vowel [a] remains unaffected.) The converse development is found in (15). Both developments are fairly common, although like all other changes they often operate only under specific environmental restrictions. Thus, the development in (14) is limited to initial position and the one in (15a) is restricted to the environment between consonant and front vowel.

(14)	Kannaḍa	ondu	>	wondu	'one'
		eradu	>	yeradu	'two'
(15a)	Lat.	*kapyō	>	capiō [y]	'catch' (sg. 1)
	vs.	*kapyis	>	capØis	'catch' (sg. 2)
b)	PGmc.	*wulfaz	>	ON Øulfr	'wolf'
		*wullō	>	Øull	'wool'

A crosslinguistic tendency to depalatalize palatalized segments before front vowel and to delabiovelarize labiovelarized segments before back vowels may well be the nonsegmental counterpart of the segmental eclipses in (15). (This process is illustrated in section 6.3, ex. (21).)

The epenthetic and ecliptic developments covered in this section share a certain similarity with assimilation. For the basic mechanism responsible for epenthesis and eclipsis, the wrong timing of articulatory gestures, can be conceived of as underlying also assimilation. For instance, the change of *ad-similāre* to *assimilāre* can be accounted for in terms of a wrong timing of the gestures required to differentiate *d* and *s*. Certain loss developments (such as cluster simplification) can be similarly attributed to wrong timing, and so can some weakening processes, especially loss, degemination, and medial voicing. But note that other weakening changes (such as fricativization or oral depletion of the type [t] > [ʔ]) are not so easily conceptualized as resulting from wrong timing. Even certain instances of dissimilation and metathesis are analyzable as resulting from wrong timing. (For instance, the proper sequencing of consonants within a cluster, such as OE [fisk] vs. [fiks], is a question of timing.) But again, other dissimilatory and metathetical processes do not lend themselves readily to such an analysis. (Compare e. g. the dissimilation in PGmc. **heman-* > OHG *himil,* or distant metatheses.) As in the case of assimilation and weakening, or of weakening and loss, epenthesis/eclipsis and the processes treated in the two preceding chapters are perhaps best treated as related, but different developments.

7.1.2. Excrescence

While consonant epenthesis attributable to wrong timing ordinarily is regular, one superficially similar type of consonant insertion is notoriously sporadic. This development, traditionally distinguished from 'epenthesis' by the term **excrescence**, is illustrated in (16), (17), and (18).

(16)	PGmc.	**habuk-*	> NHG	Habicht	'hawk'
		*ak^wuz-	>	Axt	'axe'
(17)	ME	middes	> NE	(a)midst	
	OE	betwihs	>	betwixt	
(18)	NE	no	> informal	[nōʔ] or [nōp]	

As these examples show, excrescence consists in the word-final insertion of a stop. Its explanation seems to be as follows: At the end of an utterance, the organs of speech ordinarily return to their rest position. But occasionally, especially in emphatic speech, speakers may terminate their utterance more abruptly, by a sudden closure somewhere in the vocal tract. Most commonly, this closure is made in the dental area, resulting in a dental stop; cf. (16) and (17). But as (18) illustrates, the closure can be made also elsewhere. The irregularity of the process, then, is attributable to the fact that its articulatory basis is only an occasional, not a normal phenomenon in utterance-final position.

7.1.3. Anaptyxis

With a few exceptions, the motivation of epenthetic vowel insertion or **anaptyxis** appears to be quite different from that of consonant epenthesis: As noted in 7.1.1, the latter can be accounted for in terms of the articulatory concept of 'wrong timing'. This explanation, however, is conceivable only for a very small minority of anaptyctic changes, namely those in which a vowel is inserted between a stop and another consonant, as in (19): In order for stops to be pronounced with an audible release, they must in this environment be followed by a nonsegmental 'pseudo-vowel' that 'carries' the release. Segmentalization of this nonsegmental element could then result in a fully segmental vowel. (Cf. example (20) in which the pseudo-vowel is transcribed as [ᵊ].) Notice however that the same kind of nonsegmental vocalic element appears with released final stops, whether they occur by themselves or as part of a cluster. But single final stops do not ordinarily seem to give rise to anaptyctic vowels.

(19)   PGmc.   *taiknã > *taikn   > OE tācen 'token'
               *akraz   > *akr   >   æcer   'field'

(20)   *akr   [akᵊr]   > [akər]   > [æker]

More than that, an explanation along the lines of (20) will not work for cases like (21), (22), and (23), where the anaptyctic vowel is not preceded by a stop. Rather, in the majority of cases, the motivation of anaptyxis seems to lie in the elimination of consonant clusters, as an alternative to cluster simplification.

(21)   PIE   *r̥kstos   > Lat. ursus, Gk. arktos 'bear'

(22)   Engl. athlete [æθlīt] > substandard [æθəlīt]

(23)   Lat.   spiritus   > Span. espiritu   'spirit'
              schola   >   escuela   'school'

The environments in which anaptyxis is most likely to apply are (i) next to consonantal sonorants that occur in the context of (24), and (ii) in certain clusters which crosslinguistically tend to be avoided, such as dental stop or fricative + [l]. (For clusters of this type, cf. also sections 6.3 and 7.3.8.) For (i), cf. e. g. example (20); for (ii), (22).

(24) $\left\{ \begin{matrix} \# \\ C \end{matrix} \right\}$ ——— $\left\{ \begin{matrix} \# \\ C \end{matrix} \right\}$

Examples (21) and (23) require additional comment. (21) is similar to (20) in having a sonorant in the context of (24). However, the sonorant of (21) is syllabic and thus does not enter into a cluster with the following consonant(s). However, as noted in 2.1.7, liquids and nasals crosslinguistically are more naturally nonsyllabic than syllabic. By inserting a vowel — a segment which is most naturally syllabic —, anaptyxis permits the liquid to 'revert' to its more natural nonsyllabic value. (It is a priori possible to account for the loss of syllabicity in [r̥] by the process of 'desyllabication', for which cf. 7.2.2.) However, intermediate stages of the type [ur̥], [ar̥] seem nowhere to be attested. The loss of syllabicity therefore may be a concomitant of anaptyxis.) Note that instead of having anaptyxis, some languages simply replace (certain) sonorants by vowels, as in (25).

(25a)   PIE   *dek̂m̥   >   Skt. daśa, Gk. deka
   b)   Skt.   *kr̥ta-   >   MIAr. kita- 'done'

Example (23) is of a different nature. In the discussion of syllable structure (section 2.1.12) it was noted that crosslinguistically, initial stop + fricative ('TS') clusters are rarer than fricative + stop ('ST') clusters, even though the latter violate the principle of increasing sonority in syllable onsets. The reason for this preference for ST clusters may well be perceptual: Stops are less clearly perceptible before obstruent (as in TS) than before vowel and sonorant (as in ST + sonorant/vowel). Even so, initial ST clusters do violate the principle of increasing sonority sufficiently enough that many languages eliminate them. Of the different possible approaches to doing so, the most popular seems to be the **prothesis** illustrated in (23), i. e. the insertion of an anaptyctic vowel in front of the ST clusters. As the result of this process, the cluster not only ceases to be initial, but its members usually are distributed over two different syllables; cf. (26). Anaptyxis into the ST cluster, as in (27), is less commonly employed.

(26)   [$sk(h)o$la$]   >   [$eskwela$]

(27)   Panjabi st̪ēšan > sat̪ēšan 'station'

> (This process is limited to borrowings with initial ST.)

7.2. Syllabication, desyllabication, elimination of hiatus

7.2.1. Syllabication

Where consonant clusters contain a nonsyllabic sonorant, an alternative to cluster simplification or anaptyxis consists in **syllabication**, i. e. in making the sonorant syllabic. Thus, the wide-spread Slavic loss of the ultra-short vowels *ĭ* and *ŭ* (the 'jers') resulted in Old Serbo-Croatian and Czech structures of the type (28), with syllabic sonorant. (The mark of syllabicity is lacking in the standard orthography.)

(28)　OCS　　OSCr.　　OCzech

brŭzŭ　brz　　brzý　'rapid'

dlŭgŭ　dlgĭ　dlhý　'debt'

However, as noted in the preceding section, in the environment between consonants, syllabic sonorants frequently are subject to anaptyxis and desyllabication, or to replacement by a vowel. And such was the fate of some of these syllabic Serbo-Croatian and Czech sonorants; cf. the modern outcomes in (29).

(29)　NScr.　NCzech

brz　　brzý

dug　　dlúhý

7.2.2. Desyllabication, etc.

Just as consonant clusters are often eliminated or reduced, so **hiatus**, the clustering of syllabic segments, is generally avoided. (Most commonly, such clusters arise from the loss of intervening nonsyllabic segments. But diphthongization apparently can lead to similar results; cf. (31) and (33) below.) One of the mechanisms for eliminating hiatus is contraction (cf. 5.1.4). Other common processes are the following: (i) **desyllabication**, i. e. the loss of syllabicity of one of the syllabic segments. In the case of [+ vocalic] segments, this process is also referred to as **gliding**. Compare (30) and (31) for exemplifications. (ii)

glide insertion, i. e. the development of a homorganic glide next to a high vowel that occurs in hiatus. Cf. e. g. examples (32) and (33) below. (iii) **vowel truncation,** i. e. the loss of one of the vowels, as in example (31). (Other devices may also be found, such as the insertion of a glottal stop or of some other segment. But it is not clear to what extent all of these alternative processes are regular sound changes.)

(30) Lat. sapiat   > PRom. *sapya- 'would know'

(31) Lat. bonum   > Ital. *buɔno > South.   Ital.   [buǫno] 'good'
                                    > elsewhere [bu̯ɔno] (= [bwɔno])

(32) Skt. kṛta- > kita- > later MIAr. kia- > Hindi kiyā 'done'

(33) SCr. dial. běla   > biela   > bijela [biyela] 'white'

(34) Gk. dial. kaleontes   > kalØontes 'the calling ones'

7.3. Instability of segments

A number of frequently encountered changes can be attributed to an inherent **'instability'** of certain segments and segment classes. For some of these segments, the instability manifests itself in first-language acquisition, in that unstable segments are mastered quite late. (Cf. e. g. the remarks on the liquids in section 2.1.5 above.) Some other segments can be conceived of as articulatorily relatively 'unnatural' or 'marked'. (Cf. 5.1.5 on the lack of 'homorganicity' between palatalization and the labials.) But for a number of other segments or segment classes, no such explanation seems to be possible at this point. All that can be done is to note that they are much more liable to be replaced than other comparable segments and segment classes.

7.3.1. Liquids

The relative instability of the liquids has been noted on several occasions; cf. 2.1.5 on first-language acquisition and related issues, 6.1.1 on dissimilation, and 6.2 on metathesis. Several other developments attest to this instability:

In many languages, children have been observed to occasionally substitute uvular [ʀ] for 'dental' (i. e. alveolar) [r]. Developments of this sort have become standard in many varieties of French, German, and Portuguese. Interestingly, uvulars also tend to be fairly unstable, and 'uvular' [ʀ] is now frequently realized as a velar fricative, as in Fr. *rouge* [ɣuž].

Both 'uvular' and 'dental' *r* (whatever their exact realizations) have a strong tendency to be lost in the coda of syllables. Frequently that loss proceeds through an intermediate 'centering' glide which can be transcribed as [ə]. Cf. e. g. the usual British English pronunciation of word like *there* as [ðɛ(ː)ə] or [ðɛ(ː)Ø], and similar pronunciations in many varieties of German.

Many dialects of Spanish tend to neutralize the contrast between word- or syllable-final [r] and [l]. Cf. e. g. the substandard Puerto Rican pronunciation of *Puerto Rico* as [pweltoxi$ko]. (The voiceless velar fricative [x] in the second word is a replacement via uvular [ʀː] of the 'tense' and often voiceless word-initial [rː] of Standard Spanish.)

Some languages completely neutralize the contrast between [r] and [l]. Thus, ancient Iranian merged PIE [r] and [l] into [r]. Cf. example (35). (A similar merger probably took place in the closely related Indo-Aryan. But secondary developments have obscured the effects of the change.)

(35) PIE *swel- > Avestan hvar- 'sun'
        *ster- >   star- 'star'

Lateral [l] has a strong tendency to develop a retracted, velarized, sometimes retroflex variant [ɫ] in syllable coda; cf. e. g. the difference between (Brit.) Engl. *lick* [lik] and *ilk* [iɫk], as well as the discussion and developments in 5.1.5 and 5.1.6.

Note however that except for this tendency toward retraction, [l] seems to be considerably more stable than [r]. The latter is much more commonly replaced by other segments (such as [ʀ] etc. or [ə]). See also 7.3.5 below for the instability of palatalized [r]. One suspects that this is motivated by a greater articulatory complexity of [r]. While the articulation of [l] may be 'unusual' because of its lateral, rather than central contact, that of [r] seems to require a much greater amount of 'fine tuning': The tongue tip must be raised just the right amount, close enough to a stop position to create a sufficient obstruction, but not so close as to block airflow. Moreover, its tension must be adjusted for just the right degree of rigidity. Too much — or too little — tension will prevent the correct trilling or flapping effect.

7.3.2. Sibilants

As noted in 2.1.2, sibilants are phonetically more complex than simple fricatives, in that they require an additional articulatory gesture. Moreover, their primary articulation is open to considerable variation. Distinctions between sibilants therefore tend to be among the last to be mastered in first-language acquisition. This relative complexity is reflected in a relatively high degree of historical instability.

Thus, sibilants seem to be second only to the liquids in their propensity to undergo the usually sporadic processes of dissimilation, metathesis, and distant assimilation. Cf. e. g. Engl. *ask/aks* etc. (section 6.2, ex. (9)), or examples like (36) below.

(36) OF cercher [serčer] > NFr. chercher 'search'
                                    [šerše]
      pre-Lith. *seši   > Lith. šeši   'six'
                 *sešuras >   šešuras   'father-in-law'
      pre-Skt.   *svaśura > Skt. śvaśura- 'father-in-law'
                 *śasa-   >   śaśa-   'hare, rabbit'

Sibilants also are more vulnerable to weakening than most other segment classes, not only in the usual medial and final positions, but also initially. Among the ancient Indo-European languages, Iranian, Armenian, Greek, and Welsh exhibit initial weakening of *s*; cf. the reflexes in (37) of various formations made from the PIE root *sem-* 'one (and the same)'.

(37) PIE   Avestan   Armenian   Greek   Middle Welsh
      *sem- hama-   homos
             ha(m)-   ham-   hama
                                   homalos   haval (< *haβal)

Sibilants are also characterized by somewhat unusual replacements. For instance, voiced [z], often the result of weakening, tends to undergo 'rhotacism' and change into [r]. (Cf. section 3.4 for the fate of Verner's-Law [z], and 5.2, ex. (51) for Latin and Spanish examples of rhotacism.) And voiceless [š] has changed to the velar fricative [x] in a number of languages; cf. e. g. (38). The latter development is perhaps linked with the fact that the secondary, 'sibilant' articulation for [š] often consists in a velar approximation by the back of the tongue: The change [š] > [x], then, would consist in turning this secondary gesture into the primary articulation of the segment.

(38)   OSpan. baxo [bašo] > NSpan. bajo [baxo] 'low'

7.3.3 Voiceless velar fricatives and glottal fricatives

The voiceless velar fricative [x] has a very strong tendency to turn into glottal [h], no matter what its historical origins. Thus, many of the modern Spanish dialects pronounce the *bajo* of (38) as [baho]. Note also the allophonic differentiation of Proto-Germanic /x/ into [x] and [h] (cf. section 3.3, as well as example (39) below). Perhaps this close affinity between [x] and [h] is due to the fact that both fricatives tend to be homorganic with neighboring vowels. (Cf. 2.1.7 for [h] and 2.4 for velars in general.)

Although some languages do have a 'voiced' [ɦ], there is a crosslinguistic tendency to prefer voiceless [h], presumably because [ɦ] requires some compensatory articulation to make up for the fact that a simultaneous articulation of glottal [h]-friction and voicing is impossible (cf. 2.1.3 above). A historical reflection of this tendency can be seen in the fact that in many varieties of Hindi, the initial [ɦ] of common Indo-Aryan has acquired a pronunciation not appreciably different from Engl. [h]. (Cf. for example Skt. *haṁsa-*, Marathi [ɦams(a)]: Hindi [hans] 'goose, swan'.) Another indication of the 'markedness' of [ɦ] is the fact that under medial-voicing conditions, [h] commonly disappears, rather than changing into [ɦ]; cf. 3.4 and 5.2 for discussion and examples.)

In 7.1.1 we noted a common tendency to avoid aspiration in word-final, syllable-final, and coda positions. A similar tendency holds true for segmental [h]. On one hand, this may be responsible for the fact that PGmc. /x/ was realized as [x], not as [h] in such 'post-nucleus' environments. (Cf. (39) below.) On the other hand, the tendency manifests itself in a propensity of post-nucleus [h] to be lost. Consider for instance the wide-spread dialectal weakening of Spanish final [s] > [h] > ∅. In many dialects, [h] is possible only when it occurs before a word with initial vowel, while elsewhere it is lost. This difference in behavior results from the fact that in the context / _____ # V, [h] can be 'linked' with the next vowel and become the onset of that vowel's syllable. In so doing, it ceases to be post-nucleus and manages to escape the fate of final [h]. Compare (40) for data and formulation.

(39) PGmc. $x > h \ / \ \left\{ \begin{matrix} [-\ \text{cons.}] \\ \# \end{matrix} \right\} \underline{\hspace{2cm}} \left\{ \begin{matrix} [+\ \text{son.}] \\ V \end{matrix} \right\}$

Hence *xund- > *hund- 'hundred'
       *texun > *tehun 'ten'
But: *axt   (unchanged) 'eight'
       *taux   (unchanged) 'pulled'

(40) Span.   las aguas
      Final weakening   [#lah#aɣwah#]
      Linking   [laha$ɣwah$]
      Final [h]-loss   — — —   ∅
      Outcome   [lahaɣwa]

Even in initial position, [h] is very commonly lost. Compare for instance the fate of Latin [h] in the Romance languages (as in *honorem* > Ital. *onore* 'honor'), a similar loss of initial [h] in the history of Greek, or the Cockney English deletion of initial [h] in forms like *has* [æz].

7.3.4. The dental fricatives [θ] and [ð]

As in the case of the liquids and sibilants, the fricatives [θ] and [ð] commonly are mastered quite late in first-language acquisition. It is therefore not surprising that they should prove to be fairly unstable in linguistic change.

For instance, in the modern Germanic languages, only English and Icelandic have preserved Proto-Germanic *þ, elsewhere it has been replaced; cf. e. g. (41). And Proto-Germanic *ð changed to *d* before the earliest Old English and Old High German documents; cf. 3.4 above.

(41)
PGmc.	NHG	NDutch	NDanish	NNorw.	NSwed.
*þrīz	drai	drī	trē⁷	trī/trē	trē

NEngl.	NIcel.
θrī	þrír

(Except for Icelandic, the modern languages are given in phonetic transcription.)

Many varieties of Modern English furnish similar examples for the avoidance of [θ] and [ð]. For instance, in Cockney and American Black Vernacular English, words like *mouth* are pronounced with final [f]. (Black Vernacular English has [t] as an alternative pronunciation.) And many speakers of American English have initial [d] in forms like *them* and *those*.

7.3.5. Palatalized labials and [rʸ], labiovelar segments

As noted at the beginning of section 7.3, palatalized labials can be conceived of as articulatorily relatively 'unnatural' or 'marked' because of the lack of homorganicity between the gestures for the features [labial] and [palatalized]. Some historical consequences of this markedness have been observed in 5.1.5 and 7.1.1. They can be summarized as follows: Palatalization is less easily introduced on labials than on dentals and velars; and if introduced, it is more easily lost. Such loss can be brought about by glide epenthesis, the segmentalization of the previously nonsegmental palatalizing on- or off-glide. Examples (42) and (43) illustrate yet other processes which bring about the depalatalization of labials.

(42a) pre-Slav. *leubyō > *lʸubʸo > OCS lʸublʸǫ 'love'
   b) Lat. sapiat > PRom. *sapʸa > Romantsch sapča 'would know'
   c) pre-Gk. *klepyō > *klepʸo > Gk kleptō 'steal'
   d) Lat. sapiat > PRom. *sapʸa > pre-Fr. sapča
           > Fr. sache [-š-] 'would know'

(43) Cz. [pʸet] > dial. [tet] 'five'
      [pʸīvo] >   [tīvo] 'beer'

In (42), the 'offending' palatalization is removed by insertion of a more easily palatalized dental segment after the labial and by the transfer of palatalization to that segment. Compare especially (42a). (In Slavic, this process is restricted to palatalized labials occurring before non-front vowels.) This palatalized dental may subsequently become palatal [č] (as in (42b)) which through assibilation may yield the cluster [tš]. Cluster simplification, then, will yield the *t* of Gk. *kleptō*. The French outcome in (42d) can be attributed to even more extensive cluster simplification.

The developments in (43) have been accounted for as perceptual reinterpretations based on an acoustic similarity between palatalized labials and dentals. But they can just as well be explained along the lines of (42), as resulting from dental insertion, followed by cluster simplifications which — just as in (42d) — eliminated the labial element. On the other hand, the acoustic account at this point is unable to explain the developments in (42). However, if the acoustic account could be extended to cover also the developments in (42), then it would provide a more interesting, phonetically motivated explanation for these developments than the dental-insertion analysis.

As noted in 7.3.1, the liquids are relatively unstable in historical change, and among the liquids [l] and [r], [r] is the one that is articulatorily more complex and therefore more susceptible to change. Apparently this articulatory complexity also makes [r] a less stable 'host' for palatalization than other dental sonorants. Thus, Serbo-Croatian has eliminated palatalization on [r], while retaining it for [l] and [n], cf. (44). Similarly, palatalization of Romance [l] and [n] has left clear traces in many of the modern Romance languages; but [r] has left no such traces. Instead, most languages show apparent metatheses which in accordance with the discussion in 7.1.1 are probably to be analyzed as resulting from glide epenthesis. And the response of Italian lies in an apparent deletion of the [r], a development which likewise manages to eliminate (or avoid) patalized [r]. Cf. the data in (45).

(44)	OCS	večer^{y}a	SCr.	večera	'dinner'
	vs.	kol^{y}etŭ		kol^{y}e	'chokes'
		n^{y}iva		n^{y}iva	'field'

(45) Lat. area > PRom. *arya : Span. *ayra > era, Port. eira etc. 'area' = It. aia [aya]

	folia	>	*folya	: It. foglia [-λ-], Fr. feuille
vs.				[-y-] (earlier [λ]) 'leaf'
	vinea	>	*vinya	: Span. viña, Fr. vigne
				[-ñ-] etc. 'vineyard'

Note however that tautosyllabic [ry] likewise tends to be avoided. Thus, conservative varieties of English may pronounce *lure, news*, etc. as [lyūr], [nyūz] etc. But in the case of *rule*, their pronunciation is [rūl], not [ryūl]*.

As noted in 5.1.5, labiovelarization is both rarer and less stable than palatalization. This is probably the reason that the labiovelars which must be reconstructed for Proto-Indo-European have in the individual languages undergone a variety of different changes which in effect eliminated them from the obstruent inventory. Cf. the developments in (46). In some languages (such as Sanskrit), the labial element was lost altogether, leading to merger between labiovelars and plain velars. In others (probably including Latin), the nonsegmental [ʷ] offglide has become segmental [w]. Most of the languages have lost the offglide next to [u]; cf. Gk. *lukos*. Some languages (including Greek) have singled out the labiovelars (but not the plain velars) for palatalization before front vowels. (For the Greek outcome *t* of palatalized *kʷ*, cf. section 5.1.5.) And some languages (cf. Greek and Welsh), focusing on the labial element, have turned the labiovelars into labial stops. (In Greek, this development takes place only in those cases where the labiovelars were not palatalized or changed into [k] next to [u].)

(46)	PIE	*wl̥kʷos	>	Skt. vr̥ka-,	Gk. lukos	'wolf'
		*kʷe	>	Lat. que [kw],	Gk. te	'and'
		*kʷrī-	>	Skt. krī-,	Gk. priasthai,	
					OWelsh prinit	'buy'

7.3.6. The semivowel [w]

Perhaps because of its complex, 'labiovelar' articulation (with rounding at the lips and vocalic articulation in the velar area), this segment has a strong tendency to change toward a purely labial articulation. The first step probably is bilabial [β]. But since labiodental articulation is crosslinguistically preferred for labial fricatives, the eventual outcome commonly is [v]. Compare for instance (47). (Among the modern

Germanic languages, English stands alone in preserving the semivocalic pronunciation of PGmc. *w.)

(47)   PGmc. *windaz   : NHG Wind [vint] or [βint], depending
                                      on dialect
                                      OIcel. vindr, Norw. vind, etc.

A different outcome, *gw*, is found in some languages. This development will be discussed in 8.5 below.

7.3.7. Labials

For reasons that are not well understood, also the labials seem to be relatively susceptible to change. Thus, many languages have curious gaps in their system of labial obstruents. Proto-Indo-European, for instance, is generally believed to have at one time lacked the voiced labial stop. (This accounts for the fact that in the discussion of Grimm's Law (section 3.3 above), no correspondences were cited for initial *b*.) And in quite a number of languages, one of the labial obstruents has undergone loss or weakening, while the corresponding dental, velar, etc. segments remained intact. In Castilian Spanish for instance, initial *f* at a certain point was weakened to *h* (except before [u] and [w]); cf. (48). Other fricatives were not weakened. (Subsequently, the [h] was lost in the majority of the dialects, although it is still written.) Similarly, PIE *p was subject in Celtic to a great variety of weakening changes, including loss. Some of these are given in (49). As a consequence of these changes, [p] disappeared from the inventory of Celtic. (In Welsh, however, the changes in (46) subsequently introduced a new segment [p].)

(48)   Lat.   facere   : (Cast.) Span.   hacer [aθer]   'do'
                      farina   :   harina [a-]   'flour'

(49)   PIE   Old Irish

a) #_____ :
        *peyskos   Ø$\bar{\text{\i}}$ask   'fish'
        *pətēr   Øaθər^y 'father'
        *pro   Øro   'before'

b)   V _____ V:

       *tepe-   teØe- > tē-   'hot'

       *uper   *uØar > *war > far 'over'

c)   V _____ [+ stop]:

       *septm̩   se**x**t   'seven'

       *neptis   ne**x**t   'niece'

d)   V _____ [+ liqu.]:

       *kuprā   -koβra   'desire'

       *d(w)eiplo- dīaβul   'doubt'

(The Irish examples are cited in phonetic transcription, with palatalization indicated only where unpredictable.)

7.3.8. Dental nonsibilant obstruent + [l]

Tautosyllabic clusters of nonsibilant dental obstruent + [l] seem to be very generally avoided. Various mechanisms may serve to eliminate such clusters. Among these are metathesis (cf. 6.3, ex. (28)) and anaptyxis (cf. 7.1.3, ex. (22)). Other approaches are exemplified in (50) and (51a). Example (50) illustrates a common solution, which lies in changing the dental to a nondental, velar stop. In (51a), the problem is solved by a process of **resyllabification** which shifts the syllable boundary such that the dental stop and the [l] occur in separate syllables. (51b) shows the normal Spanish syllabification of stop + liquid clusters.

(50)   PIE   *pōtlom > pre-Lat. *pōklom

                 (> Lat.   pōculum) 'cup'

(51a)   Span.   atlas   [at$las]   'atlas'

  b)   coplas   [ko$plas]   'verses'

               teatro   [te$a$tro]   'theater'

               milagro   [milagro]   'miracle'

7.4. Other changes

This section is dedicated to the listing of a few other common historical processes which could not be easily accommodated in the preceding sections of this chapter.

7.4.1. Gemination; geminate strengthening

As noted in 5.1.1, geminates frequently result from complete assimilation. However, they also frequently arise in intervocalic consonant clusters, most commonly before other, cluster-final consonants; cf. e. g. (52)—(54). The most conducive triggers for this process of **gemination** are the semivowels, the least conducive, the stops. That is, the process is controlled by the triggering segment's relative position on the sonority hierarchy (for which cf. 2.2.12 above).

(52) PRom.   *sapya : It. sappia [-ppy-] 'would know'

(53) PGerm. *sitjan > pre-OE *sittjan > OE sittan 'sit'
                *apla-   > OE æppel, MLowGerm. appel
                *akra-   > OSaxon akkar

(54) Skt.   anya-   > 'dial.'   annya-   'other'
              patra- >   pattra-   'leaf'
              pakṣa- >   pakkṣa-   'wing'

Recent work suggests that gemination may be linked with the fact that especially in intervocalic consonant + sonorant clusters there is widespread variation between the syllabifications VC$RV and V$CRV. (Cf. 2.1.12 above.) A geminated VC$CRV might be conceived of as a compromise between these two competing syllabifications.

Something superficially similar to gemination is frequently observed in (single) intervocalic consonants, mainly in languages with no contrast between single and geminate consonants. In English, for instance, the medial stops of words like *sitting* are usually pronounced such that their closure (or 'implosion') is made in the first syllable and their release (or 'explosion') in the second. The syllable boundary, then, goes somewhere into the middle of such stops. However, such **'ambisyllabic'** intervocalic segments differ from geminates in their quantity: Geminates are (roughly) twice the length of corresponding single segments, but ambisyllabic segments have (roughly) the same length in intervocalic position as elsewhere. Moreover, no cases have been reported of ambisyllabicity leading to distinctive gemination.

Whatever their origin, geminates in many languages undergo a process of **strengthening** which operates in reverse direction from the weakening hierarchy in 5.2. Compare the examples in (55). In developments of this sort there seems to be a secondary association of

the relative 'strength' of geminates with other features or manifestions
of 'strength'.

(55) lat.   Iguvium > *Guvvyo   > Ital. Gubbio
                                          (place name)
      Skt.   śrotavya- > (*)sotavva- > Pali sotabba-
                                          'to be heard'
      Goth.   -laigōn   : OE liccian [-kk-] 'lick'
      OHG   ziga   : OHG zikkīn,   'goat : kid'
              OE ticcen

7.4.2. Vowel lengthening and shortening processes

Several environments are conducive to **vowel lengthening**:
Lengthening often takes place before voiced segments, especially
before sonorants. Thus, in many varieties of Modern English, vowels
are allophonically longer before voiced segments than before voiceless
ones. A change of conditioning environment, in the form of final
devoicing, has made the length difference contrastive in some Appala-
chian American English dialects; cf. (56). At an earlier stage in the
history of English, Old English short vowels were lengthened before
sonorant plus one and only one consonant; elsewhere, they remained
short. Compare the examples in (57). The outcomes of this change
became distinctive by merger with the old long vowels. — Since voiced
consonants tend to be shorter than voiceless ones, vowel lengthening
before voiced segments may be viewed as a compensatory development
which maintains syllabic or word quantity.

(56) bed [beːd] > [beːt] vs. bet [bet] (unchanged)

(57) OE cild   > cīld   (> NE child [ay])
      but cildru = cīldru (unchanged; hence NE children [i])

Vowel lengthening is also very common in **open syllables**, i. e. in
structures of the type / _____ $, where the vocalic nucleus is not
followed by a coda consonant. Also this process was very productive
at a certain period in the history of English. Cf. e. g. the examples
in (58). Like pre-voiced or pre-sonorant lengthening, open-syllable
lengthening can be conceived of as compensatory, giving open syllables
the same quantity as **checked** syllables of the type $C_0VC_0$$.

(58)   OE nă$ma > ME nāme (NE name)

mĕ$te >   mēte (NE meat)

Finally, many languages have vowel lengthening in monosyllabic words, at least if they are accented; cf. e. g. (59). Some linguists have speculated that this lengthening serves to make the quantity of monosyllabics comparable to that of longer words.

(59)   PGmc. *nu   > OE nū   'now'

*hwaz >   hwā 'who'

The various factors favorable to vowel lengthening may interact such that they reinforce or cancel one another. For instance, in the history of German, open-syllable lengthening was restricted mainly to the environment before voiced obstruents, as in (60) below.

(60)   MHG wĕ$der > NHG weder [vēdər] 'neither'

vs.   wĕ$ter >   Wetter [vĕtər] 'weather'

Vowel shortening commonly takes place in the following two environments:

Checked syllables not only tend to inhibit vowel lengthening, they promote shortening. Like open-syllable lengthening, this process was quite active at a certain period of English. Cf. e. g. (61). (However, because of various restrictions placed on both processes, English had no complete merger of the old long and short vowels.) — Like open-syllable lengthening, this process can also be conceived of as involving temporary compensation, making the quantity of checked syllables comparable to that of open ones.

(61)   OE fīf$ta > ME fĭfte   (> NE fifth [i])

vs. fī$ve >   fīv(e) (> NE five [ay])

Word-final position very commonly is characterized by the shortening of long vowels, as in (62a). In many languages, final short vowels are lost at the same time; cf. (62b). This suggests that final vowel shortening is a form of final vowel weakening: Final vowels are reduced by one 'mora' each. In the case of bimoric, long vowels, the result is a short, monomoric segment; in monomoric, short vowels, it is ∅. (This latter account is especially apt for Latvian. For as (62c) shows, final

diphthongs are also reduced by one mora; hence bimoric *-ie* > monomoric *-i*.)

   (62)   pre-Latvian   Latvian

     a) *zemē   > zemĕ   'earth'

         *ruokā   > ruokă   'hand'

     b) *meta   > met∅   'throw'

         *turi   > tur∅   'have'

     c) *baltie   > balti   'white' (pl. N m.)

7.4.3. Effects of consonants on vowels

The most common trigger for changes in vowel quality (such as
lowering, raising, fronting, backing) consists in other vocalic segments,
cf. especially the discussion of umlaut and vowel harmony in sections
5.1.2—3. However, consonants can have a similar effect; cf. example
(63) whose vowel changes are conditioned by the preceding consonants.
Changes of this sort seem to be acoustically conditioned, with the
[+ grave] labials and velars favoring rounding and backing, and the
[− grave] dentals and palatals inducing fronting. Both sets of consonants additionally may have a raising effect. Although processes of the
type (63) are very wide-spread in Middle Indo-Aryan, they do not seem
to have applied in a regular fashion. (Cf. e. g. the absence of *ma* > *mu*
in *majjhima-*.) Perhaps, then, this type of change is not quite as regular
as, say, assimilation or weakening.

   (63) Skt. nimajjati   > Pali nimujjati 'dives under'

             madhyama- >   majjhima- 'middle'

Retroflex consonants often have a backing effect on vowels. (But cf.
(66) below.) Presumably this results from the retracted articulation of
retroflex consonants. For instance, in Central Illinois American English,
all back vowels are getting fronted, except before retroflex [r]; cf. (64).
Moreover, the fact that retroflex consonants often are characterized by
a curling back of the tongue tip may have an assimilatory effect on
neighboring vowels which likewise become retroflex. Thus, according
to many phoneticians, the Standard American English pronunciation
of final *-er* is more like a retroflex vowel [ɚ], than a sequence of [ə] +
[r].

(64)   *boot*   [buwt]   >   [bɨwt]
            foot   [fʊt]   >   [fɨt]
            go   [gow]   >   [gəw]
            cut   [kʌt]   >   [kət]
        vs. *gourd*   [gurd]   (unchanged)
            form   [form]   (unchanged)

(Transcriptions are approximate. 'Long' vowels act as diphthongs in this change; accordingly, they are transcribed as such.)

Other types of consonant-induced vowel changes are less easy to explain. For instance, it is a fact that in many languages vowels tend to lower before [r], [h], and [x]; cf. e. g. (65). What is less clear is why this class of phonetically fairly heterogeneous segments should exert such a lowering influence. Moreover, an opposite tendency can be observed in Hindi, where *a* [ə] tends to be raised and fronted before alveolar [r] and (voiced) [ɦ], as well as before the retroflex flap [ɽ]; cf. (66a). And in the complex 'labial' environment of (66b) — after labial stop and followed by a syllable containing rounded [ũ] —, raising before [ɦ] is combined with backing and rounding.

(65)   Gk.   pateras   >   dial. pataras   'fathers'
               pherein   >   pharein   'carry'
       Goth.   *wirz-   >   wairs [wɛrs-]   'worse'
               *suxtiz   >   sauhts [sɔxts]   'sickness'

(66a) Hindi   varmā   [vɛrmā]   (proper name)
               kahnā   [kɛɦnā]   'to say'
               laṛkā   [lɛɽkā]   'boy'
    b)   pahũčnā   [pɔhũčnā]   'to arrive'

Before nasals, vowels have a common tendency toward raising, as in (67). But nasalized non-low vowels tend to lower, cf. (68). (The latter process has been attributed to acoustic/auditory factors.) A combination of both tendencies is found in certain Southern American English dialects. As in many other English dialects, pre-nasal raising has led to the merger of [e] and [i]. However, the usual outcome [i] here has been lowered to [ɪ] under the influence of nasalization. Compare (69).

(67)   PIE   *bhendh-   >   PGmc. *bind- 'bind'
       OE (*anglisk- >) englisc   >   NE English [ɪŋgliš]

(68)	PRom.	*en	>		*ẽ	>	Fr.	en [ã]	'in'
		*fine	>		*fĩ	>		fin [fɛ̃]	'end'

(69)	Engl.	pen	>	dial.	pin	>	[pĩn]
		pin	>		pin	>	[pĩn]

7.4.4. Unrounding of front vowels

In many languages, front round vowels, once they have been introduced by other changes, tend to become unrounded. Compare for instance (70) below. (Interestingly, English unrounding affected the mid vowel [ö] earlier than the high vowel [ü].)

> (70)   pre-OE *doxtriz > Angl. OE dœhter [ö] > Common OE
>   dehter 'daughters'
>   pre-OE *kuning > Common OE cyning [ü] > ME king
>   'king'

7.4.5. Tenseness, length, and vowel quality

As indicated in the discussion of 2.1.9, there is a fair amount of terminological confusion between terms referring to relative vowel height (as in [e] vs. [ɛ]), length, and tenseness. For most of this book's discussion it was sufficient to ignore differences in vowel height and tenseness and to concentrate instead on vowel length. There are several reasons for doing so: First, phoneticians have difficulties finding an articulatory or acoustic correlate of what linguists have called 'tenseness'. The term therefore can be defined only impressionistically, as greater muscular tension (of the tongue or of the whole vocal tract) than in 'lax' segments. Secondly, there is a strong tendency for tenseness to correlate with the features of length and relative vowel height, giving the impression that the term 'tense' is superfluous: Tense vowels usually are longer than lax vowels; and in languages with distinctive vowel length, long vowels usually are tenser than short ones. Moreover, non-low tense vowels commonly are somewhat higher than the corresponding lax vowels; and all tense vowels tend to be more **'peripheral'** than lax vowels (i. e. more front in the case of front vowels, more back for back vowels, etc.). Cf. the diagram in (71). But since 'tense' very frequently corresponds to 'long', these correlations often can instead be expressed as ones between length and relative vowel height or peripherality.

(71)

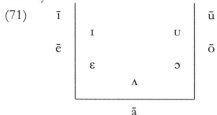

Note however that the correlations between tenseness, length, and relative vowel height are only tendencies. Thus the diagram in (71), where tense/long vowels are on the periphery and, if non-low, relatively higher than their lax counterparts, is a rather idealized representation. Many languages come close to it, but very few conform to it in its entirety.

Consider for instance the vowel systems of Hindi and German in (72) and (73). Hindi makes a nice distinction between peripheral and non-peripheral in the low central vowels. In the mid-vowels, the distinction is virtually non-existent, since [ɛ] and [ɔ] are conditioned allophones of [ə] (cf. example (66) above). (These vowels therefore are put in parentheses.) And in the high vowels, length appears to be the only distinguishing feature. German, here rendered without rounded front vowels, tense and lax *ü* and *ö*, represents the opposite extreme, with non-low vowels having a nice correlation between length distinctions on one hand and tenseness, peripherality, and relative vowel height on the other. In the low central vowels, however, length correlates with tenseness, not with peripherality. But note that long and short [a] tend to be differentiated in terms of relative fronting: in many varieties of German, [ă] is further front than [ā]. This, too, is a common crosslinguistic phenomenon which recurs for instance in conservative French, as well as in Modern Persian (where [ă] has gone to [æ] and [ā] to low back rounded [ā]). (In addition, many dialects of German have an additional long front vowel [ē], given in parentheses, which differs from short [ĕ] mainly in terrms of tenseness and vowel length.)

(72)   ī, ĭ   ū, ŭ
        ē   ō
            (ɛ)   (ɔ)
                    ə
                    ā

(73)   ī   ū
              ɪ   ᴜ
        ē   ō
        (ḗ), ɛ   ɔ
                a, ā

Even more 'atypical' vowel systems can be found. For instance, there is good evidence that at a certain point in the prehistory of Greek, the relative height of long and short mid vowels was as indicated in (74), i. e. entirely contrary to the normal distribution.

(74)   ĕ   ŏ
              ē   ō

The evidence for this distribution comes from linguistic change: In a number of ancient Greek dialects, contraction and compensatory lengthening of short [ĕ] and [ŏ] resulted in long vowels that were higher than the corresponding inherited long vowels; cf. (75). (By a type of change which will be further examined in the next chapter, lengthened [ō] soon after this changed to [ū]; but the inherited long vowel [ɔ̄] was too low to participate in that change.)

(75)   pre-Greek   Attic-Ionic Greek
        tithēmi   [tithɛ̄mi]   'I put'
        tithĕn(t)s   [tithēs]   'putting'
        didōmi   [didɔ̄mi]   'I give'
        didŏn(t)s   [didōs]   'giving'

Developments like those in (75) show that whatever correlations a language might 'choose' to have between tenseness, length, vowel height, and peripherality, these correlations can have important consequences for linguistic change.

Consider for instance the case of Romance. The vowel system which Proto-Romance inherited from Latin was very similar to the German system in (73), except that [ă] and [ā] apparently had no qualitative distinction whatsoever. (In fact, even a long [ɛ̄] seems to have existed, as the result of contraction of Latin *ae* [ay] and other developments.) Subsequently, there was a pan-Romance change which shortened all long vowels. In the majority of dialects, this led to the developments in (76), with the short high vowels and the long mid vowels merging, and with a complete loss of distinction between old long and short [a]-vowels. (To save space, the examples in (76) are limited to the front vowels and [ā/ă] in accented syllable.) If we look at the allophonic differentiation of long and short vowels, these developments make eminent sense; cf. (77).

(76) | Latin | late dialectal PRom. | Spanish | |
|---|---|---|---|
| mīlle | mille | mil | 'thousand' |
| mĭttō | metto | meto | 'put' |
| habēre | aber(e) | haber | 'to have' |
| pĕdem | pɛde | pie | 'foot' |
| cărrum | karru | carro | 'cart' |
| amāre | amar(e) | amar | 'to love' |

(77)

$$
\begin{array}{ccccccc}
\bar{\imath} & & \bar{u} & > & i & & u \\
& \cdots\cdots\cdots & & & & \cdots\cdots & \\
\left.\begin{array}{cc} \ĭ & \ŭ \\ \bar{e} & \bar{o} \end{array}\right\} & & > & e & & o \\
& \cdots\cdots\cdots & & & & \cdots\cdots & \\
\ĕ & \ŏ & > & \varepsilon & & \mathrm{\scriptstyle\jmath} \\
& \cdots\cdots\cdots & & & & \cdots\cdots & \\
\left.\ă/\ā\right\} & & > & a &
\end{array}
$$

Other developments that have been noted are (a) a tendency for tense vowels to rise along the periphery of the vowel system, (b) an often concomitant trend toward diphthongization in tense vowels, and (c) a tendency for lax vowels to fall and to get centralized. Cf. the examples in (78).

(78) | | Old English | Modern English |
|---|---|---|
| a) | cwēn | queen [ī] |
| | dōm | doom [ū] |
| b) | īs | ice [ay] |
| | hūs | house [aw] |
| c) | sŭnu | son [ʌ] |
| | sŭm | some [ʌ] |

The developments in (78a) and (c) can be understood as something like 'exaggerations' of the common tendency toward height and peripherality distinctions between long/tense and short/lax vowels. Diphthongization may likewise be linked to such tendencies, if we assume that the feature [tense] is, by some process of wrong timing, unevenly distributed over a given vowel. In that case, the tense part would rise, and the lax part would lower.

The changes in (78a/b) are part of a major rearrangement in the vowel system of English which has been referred to as the **Great English Vowel Shift**. (Cf. also 8.5 below.) Note that the input to the raising changes in (78a) includes originally short vowels that were lengthened in open syllables (cf. 7.4.2 above). What is interesting is that such lengthened vowels did not necessarily merge with their long counterparts. For just as in many other languages, the short non-low vowels were relatively lower than the corresponding long vowels. Lengthening, then, led to a situation similar to the Romance one in (76/77): Lengthened [ĭ] merged with long [ē] etc.; that is, lengthened non-low short vowels merged with the long vowels that were 'one step lower' in the vowel spectrum. Compare the (original Northern dialectal) developments in (79) with those in (78a/b).

(79)   Old English   dial. ME   Great Vowel Shift/
                                  Modern English

    wicu   wēke   week [ī]
    yvel   ēvel   evil [ī]
    wudu   wōde   wood [u]
                     (with secondary shortening)

8. Sound change:
Structure and function

The concepts of phonological contrast and its neutralization have on several occasions been invoked in the preceding chapters. In many instances, this was done in reference to the results of sound change. But in a fair number of cases, the concepts were invoked in order to account for the direction of change. Compare for instance the relationship between contrast and polarization (sections 5.1.5, 5.1.6, 5.4.4, 5.4.7, 7.1.1), and note the relevance of neutralization for vowel harmony (5.1.3) and one type of regular dissimilation (6.3). Yet other aspects of phonological structure were invoked as conditions for a second type of regular dissimilation, as well as for regular metathesis.

Such **structural** motivations of sound change go beyond (and supplement) the phonetic factors postulated by the neogrammarians. This chapter provides a fuller discussion of the influence of phonological structure and function on sound change.

8.1. Contrast and neutralization

Structuralists have approached contrast and its neutralization in two different ways. As noted in section 4.4, one group invokes a special concept, the archiphoneme, to refer to the segment that predictably appears in the position of neutralization, such as the word-final [t] in (1) below. The other insists on identifying the [t] as an allophone of the phoneme /t/ and accounts for its relationship to medial [d] as a morphophonemic alternation. Let us refer to these two different approaches as the 'archiphonemic' and the 'phonemic' ones.

(1) NHG [rāt] : [rādəs] 'the wheel' : 'of the wheel'
     (cf.   [rāt] : [rātəs] 'advice'   : 'of advice')

Sound change, to a large extent, is on the side of the phonemic approach. Consider for instance the case of Sanskrit palatalization (section 5.1.5, ex. (30/31)). As (2a) shows, palatalization became unpredictable through the merger of non-high vowels into $a/\bar{a}$, for as a result of this merger palatalized and nonpalatalized velars occurred unpredictably in the same context (before low vowel). However, before the high front vocalic segments $i/\bar{\imath}$ and y, the distribution remained predictable: Only palatalized velars could occur; the contrast between palatalized and non-palatalized velars was neutralized. Cf. (2b). Nevertheless, polarization, a process dependent on the notion 'contrast', shifted all palatalized velars to palatals, whether their occurrence was predictable or unpredictable. Cf. the final stages in (2a/b). That is, the palatalized velars of (a) and (b) were treated as members of the same contrastive phoneme; no special allowance was made for the 'archiphonemic status' of [g^y] in (2b).

(2)	Pre-Sanskrit	Allophonic palatalization	Loss of conditioning environment	Polarization/ Change to palatal	
a)	*gegome	*g^{y}egome	*g^{y}agāma	ǰagāma	'went'
b)	*gīwo-	*g^{y}īwo-	(not applicable)	ǰīva-	'alive'

Many other changes attest to the same, 'normal' tendency to disregard the distinction between 'archiphoneme' and 'phoneme' in sound change. However, as already noted, some changes are sensitive to this distinction. Consider for instance the case of Old Norse u-umlaut (sections 5.1.2 and 6.3): Example (3) shows that in Common Old Norse, u-umlaut changed [a] to [ɔ], no matter whether the conditioning environment was lost or not. Here, the 'phonemic' principle prevailed as usual. In a small dialect area of Old Norwegian, however, [ɔ] was changed to [a] in the position of neutralization (before a syllable with retained [u]). That is, the 'archiphonemic' principle was decisive.

(3)	pre-ON	allaz	allū	allum	'all' (sg. N m., f., pl. D)	
	assimilation	— — —	ɔllū	ɔllum		
	apocope (etc.)	all	ɔll	— — —		
	Common ON	all ≠	ɔll	ɔllum		
	dissimilation	— — —	— —	allum		
	dial. ONorw.	all ≠	ɔll	allum		

Changes of this sort may be rarer than those in which the phonemic principle prevails; and perhaps they are limited to certain types of sound change (such as regular dissimilation). Still, they attest to the fact that both the 'phonemic' and the 'archiphonemic' principles can play a motivating role in sound change.

8.2. Functional load

If the notion 'contrast' can influence the direction of sound change, it is tempting to speculate whether there are certain conditions under which contrast is more — or less — likely to exert such an influence. Now, in many languages, there is a considerable difference in the number of words or utterances which any given pair of contrasting segments may distinguish, i. e. in their **'functional load'**. Consider the case of the French nasal vowels [ɛ̃, œ̃, ã, ɔ̃]. Contrasts like the 'minimal triplet' in (4) can be found easily and attest to the fact that the segments [ɛ̃, ã, ɔ̃] have a relatively high functional load. However, contrasts such as (5), involving front-rounded [œ̃], are exceedingly rare. The functional load of this segment thus is very low.

> (4)   sein [sɛ̃]   'bosom' : sans [sã] 'without' : son [sɔ̃]
> 'sound'
> (5)   brun [brœ̃] 'brown' : brin [brɛ̃] 'stalk'

It has been claimed that segments with a low functional load, such as Fr. [œ̃], are more likely to be lost or to lose their identity than segments whose functional load is relatively high. Thus, it is argued, it is not just by chance that in colloquial French, [œ̃] is undergoing a change of unrounding which is leading to its merger with [ɛ̃]. Rather, that merger is the direct consequence of its low functional load.

This claim has been met with a large amount of apparently well founded scepticism. First of all, it is difficult to define what constitutes sufficiently 'low' functional load to threaten the identity of a given segment. Secondly, most of the examples cited in favor of the claim are not particularly persuasive. For instance, the French change of [œ̃] to [ɛ̃] can be attributed to a wide-spread tendency for front rounded vowels to get unrounded; cf. 7.4.4 above. Finally, and perhaps most importantly, many languages have lost contrasts between segments with a very high functional load. One of the most extreme cases is that of Middle-Indo-Aryan: Here, a merger of the Sanskrit sibilants *ś, ṣ, s* into *s*, combined with the pervasive consonant assimilations alluded to in section 5.1.1 (exs. (12/13)), led to a massive loss of 'high-load' contrasts. Thus, MIAr. *satta* can reflect any one of the clearly distinct Sanskrit forms in (6); and similar neutralizations abound throughout the lexicon. Unless and until cases of this sort can be accounted for, the concept 'functional load' must therefore be considered of very limited usefulness in the area of sound change.

(6) MIAr. satta : Skt. sapta 'seven'
                       śapta 'cursed'
                       sakta 'followed, attached'
                       śakta '(having been) able'
                       satta 'having sat' (byform of *sanna-*)

8.3. Phonological symmetry; margin of safety

The vowel systems in section 7.4.5, examples (72) and (73) display a remarkable degree of **symmetry**. This is by no means an isolated incident, for crosslinguistically, phonological systems tend toward symmetry: Systems like (7) and (8) are quite common in the world's languages, but systems like (9) and (10) are quite unusual, especially (9b).

(7) Sanskrit stops:

p	t	ṭ	č	k
ph	th	ṭh	čh	kh
b	d	ḍ	ǰ	g
bh	dh	ḍh	ǰh	gh

(8) Old Norse unstressed vowels:

    i   u
        a

(9 a) p   k
       b   d   g

   b) p   k
                   kh
             d
       bh

(10)   i
                        o
             a

This tendency toward symmetry has been explained as a striving for 'economy': Symmetrical systems make the most economic use of phonetic/phonological features. Thus, in (7), the two features of aspiration and voicing combine to encode four phonological contrasts per place of articulation. In (9b), the same features are present, but the maximum number of distinctions in any one place of articulation is two.

Symmetry, however, is not the only relevant criterion. For systems like (11) may be symmetrical, but they are less common than those of the type (8). The preference for type (8) systems has been plausibly attributed to a tendency to have the largest possible **margin of safety** between contrasting segments so that they can be acoustically/perceptually distinguished with maximum efficiency. (It is this tendency which underlies the process of polarization.)

(11)   e   o
             a

Though symmetry and maintaining a margin of safety between contrasting segments may be a universal tendency, sound change often leads to asymmetrical or underdifferentiated systems. That is, these tendencies do not provide restrictions for sound change. However, they may act in response to sound change, motivating further changes which eliminate underdifferentiation or lack of symmetry.

For instance, certain dialects of Old Norse (especially Early Old Icelandic) had an unstressed vowel system of type (11), rather than (8); cf. section 5.1.3. Perhaps this system resulted from the tendency for lax vowels to lower (cf. 7.4.5). But whatever the reasons for its origination, system (11) was short-lived: Later Old Icelandic replaced (11) by the more differentiated system in (8).

Similarly, the Celtic developments leading to the elimination of PIE
*p (cf. 7.3.7) introduced a **gap** in the system of Proto-Celtic stops. In
the 'British' branch of Celtic (which includes Welsh, Cornish, and
Breton), this gap was 'filled' by the change of **kʷ* to *p* (cf. 7.3.5). Old
Irish, which did not participate in this change, eventually (after some
hesitation) filled the gap with borrowings from Latin (cf. 14.3.1 below).
Note however that PIE **gʷ* changed to *b* in all of Celtic, without any
motivating gap in the system. And in early Old Irish, this change
introduced a second gap in the system — which later was eliminated
by a sound change of *kʷ* to [k]. The effects of these developments are
summarized in (12), with gaps marked as **Ø**.

(12) dialectal PIE   Proto-Celtic   British Celtic

p	t	k	kʷ	**Ø**	t	k	kʷ	p	t	k
b	d	g	gʷ	b	d	g	gʷ	b	d	g

Early OIrish   Later OIrish

Ø	t	k	kʷ	p	t	k
b	d	g	**Ø**	b	d	g

Even more complicated developments have been attributed to the
tendency to make phonological systems symmetrical and to establish a
sufficient margin of safety. One of the most famous cases is the manner
in which the asymmetry in (13) was resolved in various Swiss German
dialects. Compare the systems in (14)—(16). (These represent the North,
East, and West/Center dialects, respectively. Note that in (13), (15), and
(16) [a] is classed together with the back vowels, as being [-front].)

(13) i   ü   u
      e   ö   o
      ɛ
      æ   a

(14) i   ü   u
      e   ö   o
      ɛ   œ   ɔ
              a

(15) i   ü   u
      e   ö   o
      ɛ   œ   ɔ
      æ   a

(16) i   ü   u
      e   ö   o

          æ   a

What is interesting is that, as in the case of Old Irish [p], the developments leading to these more symmetrical systems only in part consisted of sound changes. For instance, the developments leading to the contrast *o* : *ɔ* in (14) and (15) included sound change and interdialectal borrowing processes of the type that will be discussed in Chapter 15. And the front rounded vowel [œ] owes its origin to analogy.

Moreover, the system in (15) comes very close to being 'overcrowded', leaving a very narrow margin of safety between the vowels in both the front and non-front series. And there is a large amount of evidence which suggests that such overcrowded systems, whatever their origin, tend to give way to systems in which the margin of safety is greater.

Consider for instance the Romance system in section 7.4.5, example (77), reproduced below in simplified form as (17). This system was characterized by three degrees of vowel height. Most of the Romance languages, however, reduced this system through various developments, most notably through diphthongization. Thus, Spanish eliminated [ɛ] and [ɔ] by diphthongizing them to *ie* and *ue*; cf. e. g. (18). That is, diphthongization seems to have been motivated as a means of reducing '**overcrowding**' and thus of increasing the margin of safety between contrasting segments.

(17) i   u
      e   o
      ɛ   ɔ
          a

(18) *pɛde > pie   'foot'
      *bɔnu > bueno 'good'

The back-vowel area seems to be especially vulnerable: First, many languages tolerate a 'three-term' system (with three degrees of vowel height) in the front vowels, but not in the back vowels. Cf. e. g. the dialectal German long-vowel system in (19). Secondly, many languages with three-term systems in both the front and the back vowels reduce only the back-vowel system, very commonly through fronting of the high back vowel; cf. e. g. the early Attic-Ionic Greek development in

(20)/(21). (Cf. section 7.4.5, ex (75) for the developments that gave rise to the three-term system which forms the basis for this development.) Similar **u-fronting** to [ü] or [ũ] has taken place in French, Portuguese dialects, Dutch, Swedish, Icelandic, and many other languages. Fronting of [ū] to central [ɨ] is found in Slavic, and a similar change of [uw] to [ɨw] is found in many regional varieties of English. (Such fronting may affect both long and short [u], as it did in Greek. However, it is frequently restricted to long [ū], as for instance in Slavic. Modern Icelandic is unusual in limiting the process to short [ŭ].)

(19) ī   ū
      ē   ō
      ɛ̄
            ā

(20) pre-Attic-Ionic   Early Attic-Ionic
      ī, i   ū, u   ī, i   ū, ü
      ē, e   ō, o   ē, e   ō, o
      ɛ̄   ɔ̄   ɛ̄   ɔ̄
            a, ā   a, ā

(21) pre-Att.-Ion. *mūs > Att.-Ion. [mũs] 'mouse'
                     *lukos >   [lükos] 'wolf'

This common process of *u*-fronting has been plausibly linked to an interaction between two factors: One is the general tendency to maintain a margin of safety between contrasting segments. The other consists in the more specific, physiological fact that the area in which back vowels are articulated is narrower than the corresponding front vowel area; cf. (22). This **asymmetry** of the vocal organs makes differentiation more difficult for the back vowels. *u*-fronting, then, provides an 'escape valve' to relieve overcrowding.

(22)

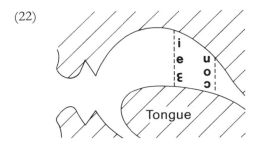

8.4. Chain shifts

The process of *u*-fronting frequently has very interesting consequences. For instance, the early Attic-Ionic system of (20) above very soon gave way to the system in (23). This change was brought about by the raising of early [ō] to [ū]; cf. (23').

(23)   Early Attic-Ionic   Later Attic-Ionic

       ī, i   ū, ü   ī, i   ū, ü   ū

       ē, e   ō, o   ē, e   o

       ɛ̄   ɔ̄   ɛ̄   ɔ̄

                     a, ā   a, ā

(23')   Early-Attic.-Ion. [didōs] > later [didūs] 'giving'

We can account for this development as being motivated by the tendency toward symmetry: *u*-fronting creates a gap in the back-vowel system, and the process of (23') has the function of filling this gap. (Though the resulting system still is not completely symmetrical, it is more 'balanced' than the earlier one.)

Developments like this, in which one change within a given phonological system gives rise to other, related changes, have been referred to as **chain shifts**. And if such shifts are motivated by a gap which 'drags' other segments into itself, they are called **drag chains**. (An alternative term, pull chain, is generally avoided, presumably for tabooistic reasons, in order to avoid the suggestion of a toilet fixture.)

Similar drag-chain developments have occurred in many other languages, including French. Perhaps the most interesting case is that of Swedish. For first of all, more than one segment undergoes raising, and secondly, the change has taken place so recently that we have much more detailed information about its staging than for, say, Attic-Ionic or early French. The first change, after the very early process of *u*-fronting, was a shift of old [o] toward the gap left by the fronted [u]. After taking an intermediate position between [o] and [u] it soon reached 'cardinal' [u] position. As this was being accomplished, old [ɑ] began to rise toward the position of the old [o], first reaching a position close to [ɔ]. The shift to [o] has now been completed for most speakers. (The developments just described affected the old long vowel system. But length marking has been omitted for typographic reasons.) The raising changes, then, clearly are fairly gradual response developments, each one directed at filling the gap left behind by an earlier change.

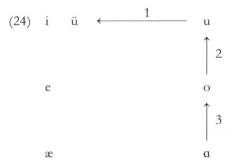

(The numbers next to the arrows indicate the sequencing of changes.)

There is some controversy as to whether beside drag chains, there can also be **push chains**. The concept of push chains can be best illustrated by renumbering the arrows in (24), such that the first change is the one of [ɑ] toward [o] via [ɔ]. This change, then, decreases the margin of safety between old [ɑ] and [o]. As a consequence, [o] shifts toward [u], which in turn is fronted to [ü] in order to retain its own margin of safety vis-à-vis old [o].

The major difficulty with the notion 'push chain', and the reason for its controversial nature, is the following: Drag chains are supported by a good deal of empirical evidence, in terms of observable sequences of events. But no such empirical support seems to exist for push chains. Note however that while push chains may lack empirical support, the overcrowding which gives rise to *u*-fronting and to the ensuing drag-chain developments commonly results from the 'push' of a new segment into the back vowel system. In Swedish, this push consisted in the backing of old low-central [ā] into [ɑ] position. (See 7.4.5 for this backing tendency of long [ā].) In Greek, it consisted in the emergence of the new long vowel [ō] through compensatory lengthening etc.; cf. 7.4.5, ex. (75).

Drag-chain developments are not the only possible consequences of *u*-fronting. In some languages, the gap left by the fronting of [u] may be filled from the 'outside'. For instance in early Slavic, [ou] etc. contracted to [ū], thus making up for the fact that old [ū] had gone to [i].

What is more interesting is the fact that *u*-fronting may lead to yet another type of chain shift which can be referred to as a **solidarity**

chain. Thus the wide-spread fronting of [ʊw] to [ɨw] in Southern and Midland American English has in certain Central Illinois dialects led to a chain shift by which all back vowels are fronted (except before [r]); cf. 7.4.3, example (64), which is reproduced in part as (25) below.

(25) boot [bʊwt] > [bɨwt]
      foot [fʊt]   > [fɨt]
      go   [gow]   > [gəw]
      cut   [kʌt]ʼ > [kət]

(Transcriptions are approximate. 'Long' vowels act as diphthongs in this change; accordingly, they are transcribed as such.)

Similarly, in the white working-class dialects of many large northern cities in the United States the low front vowel [æ] is diphthongized and raised under certain conditions. In Chicago, this change has given rise to a classical drag-chain shift of [ɑ] toward the position vacated by [æ]; cf. (26). In New York, however, a solidarity-chain development has led to the diphthongization and raising of [ɑ]; cf. (27).

(26) Jan   [ĵæn]   > [ĵɛən]
      John [ĵɑn]   > [ĵæˀn]

(27) after   [æftə(r)] > [eəftə(r)]
      coffee [kɑfi]   > [kɔəfi]

In both Chicago and New York, these developments tend to lag behind the change which originated the development. In Chicago, the fronting of [ɑ] generally has not quite reached the position of [æ], hence the transcription [æˀ]. In New York, the raising is less extreme for the back vowel than for the front vowel. In both cases, then, we are clearly dealing with response phenomena. But there is one important difference. The Chicago change can be accounted for as another instance of filling a gap in a preexisting system. The New York change, however, helps bring about a new system, by **generalizing** a sound change from one segment (low-front [æ]) to a phonetically related one (low-back [ɑ]). In the Central Illinois shift, the generalization is even more sweeping: from one back vowel to all back vowels.

8.5. Phonological pattern, conspiracies

In the preceding chapters we have examined numerous changes which
affect word or **syllable structure**: Cluster simplification (5.3.2), anap- *Vowel insertion*
tyxis (7.1.3), syllabication (7.2.1), and resyllabification (7.3.8) may reduce consonant clusters within syllables or words; contraction, desylla-
bication/gliding, glide insertion, and vowel truncation help eliminate
vowel clusters; cf. 7.2.2. Maximal application of these processes would
lead to phonological patterns of the type CVCV(...), with alternating
[− syllabic] and [+ syllabic] segments; but very few languages have
patterns of this 'ultimate' simplicity. More commonly we find that
languages approximate the CVCV type by exhibiting patterns of the
type (C)CVCCVC(C), etc., with consonant clusters limited to two (or
three) members, and frequently with the restriction that initial and final
clusters must be smaller.

While reduction of clusters, thus, may be a common tendency in
linguistic change, most languages go about implementing this goal in
a rather haphazard way, reducing some clusters (such as Engl. initial
kn- > [n-]), but retaining others (such as Engl. initial [kl-, kr-] in
clam, cram). Moreover, processes like epenthesis may increase consonant
clustering (as in Gk. **anros* > *andros*), and medial consonant loss will
introduce new vowel clusters.

In some languages, however, we find much more radical and consistent modifications of the **phonological pattern** of words and/or syllables. What is interesting is that in many cases, these modifications are
implemented not by a single change, but by a number of phonetically
quite different processes. The only thing which such changes share is
that they 'cooperate' or 'conspire' to bring about a general modification
of the phonological pattern. Shifts of this sort accordingly are nowadays
often referred to as **conspiracies**.

Consider for instance the '**Pali two-mora conspiracy**': Old Indo-
Aryan, as represented by Sanskrit, permitted syllables of one, two, or
even three moras, as in (28). (Mora count, as usual, begins with the
syllabic nucleus. Short vowels (= V) have one mora; long vowels (=
VV) two moras; and a consonant in the coda adds another mora. For
greater clarity, numbers below the line keep track of the mora count
in the relevant syllables.)

(28a) One mora: ma$ta-   'thought'
                      1
    b) Two moras: maanasa-   'related to the mind'
                      12
                      man$tum   'to think'
                      12
    c) Three moras: mii$maaṁ$sa$tē 'inquires'
                      123

In early Middle Indo-Aryan Pali, however, three-mora syllables were no longer permitted. They were turned into permissible two-mora structures by means of three phonetically quite distinct processes. One of these shortened long vowels, as in (29). A second change was cluster simplification which removed the syllable-final consonant together with its mora; cf. (30). A third process inserted an anaptyctic vowel. This made it possible to resyllabify consonants from the coda of trimoric syllables to the onset of the next syllable. And once in onset position, the consonants no longer were in the domain of mora counting. Cf. (31).

(29) Vowel shortening:

      Sanskrit   Pali
      mii$maaṁ$sa$tē   vii$mamsati 'inquires'
           123   12
      raaj$ñaḥ   rañ$ñō   'of a king'
           123   12

(30) Cluster simplification:

      diir$gha-   dii$gha-   'long'
           123   12

(31) Anaptyxis and resyllabification:

      raaj$ñaḥ   raa$ji$nō   'of a king'
           123   12

Several considerations support the contention that the elimination of three-mora syllables is not just an accident, but that the developments in (29)—(30) actually 'conspire' to bring it about. First, Sanskrit one- or two-mora syllables remained essentially unaffected, as in Skt. *ma$ta-* : Pali *ma$ta-*, Skt. *man$tum* : Pali *man$tuṁ*. (But see below.) Secondly, there does not seem to exist any principled way of predicting which

Sanskrit three-mora word will undergo which of the changes in (29)—(31). In fact, some words were affected by more than one change; cf. e. g. Skt. *raajñaḥ* : Pali *raññō* beside *raajinō*. Therefore, none of the three changes, taken by itself, is regular — even though all three processes belong to categories of sound change which ordinarily are regular. But what is regular and predictable is the fact that all Sanskrit three-mora syllables are converted into acceptable two-mora configurations. Finally, independent evidence attests to the functional equivalence of the two-mora VC outcomes of (29) and the two-mora VV outcomes of (30): In many cases where Sanskrit has a VV two-mora syllable, Pali (optionally) offers a VC structure, and vice versa; cf. e. g. (32).

(32) Skt. nii$ḍa- Pali nii$ḷa- / **niḍ$ḍa-** 'abode, nest'
        12   12   12

        har$tum   hat$tuṁ / **haa$tuṁ** 'to hold'
        12   12   12

Another famous example of the cooperation of a number of phonetically unrelated changes toward a common goal is the **Slavic open-syllable conspiracy**: While Proto-Indo-European had both open and checked syllables, early Slavic permitted only open syllables. Processes which served to convert checked into open syllables included syllable-final consonant loss, vowel-liquid metathesis, anaptyxis, resyllabification, and word-final consonant loss or anaptyxis. Cf. (33)—(37). Some of these processes were pan-Slavic, others were dialectally restricted, and the changes in (37b) seem to have been limited to just a few words or morphological categories (in only some of the dialects). Here, too, regularity does not necessarily lie in the individual changes, but rather in the effect of these changes on the overall structure of the language.

(33) Loss of syllable-final consonant:

   *sup$no- > pan-Slav. sŭ$nŭ 'sleep'
   *sed$lo- > dial. se$lo/sě$lo 'seat'

(34) Vowel-liquid metathesis:

   *gor$do- > dial. gro$dŭ/gradŭ 'city'

(35) Anaptyxis (in the context V [+ liqu.] _____ CV):

   *gor$do- > dial. go$ro$dŭ 'city'

(36)   Resyllabification:

*mes$ti-	> pan-Slav.	me$sti	'to throw'
*sed$lo-	> dial.	se$dlo	'seat'

(37a)   Word-final consonant loss:

*ḱle$wos‡	> pan-Slav.	slo$voØ	'word'
*tod‡	> pan-Slav.	toØ	'that'
*eǵ‡	> dial.	jaØ	'I'
*bhe$ret‡	> dial.	be$reØ	'will carry'

b)   Word-final anaptyxis:

*eǵ‡	> dial.	(j)a$zŭ	'I'
*bhe$ret‡	> dial.	beretŭ	'will carry'

The effect of phonological pattern on sound change may well extend beyond such conspiracies. For instance, there is reason for speculating that also **'initial strengthening'** changes like those in (38a) and (39a) are motivated by aspects of phonological pattern: They seem to be restricted to initial sonorants. Moreover, they appear to be found only in languages with independent evidence for medial weakening in the obstruents; cf. (38c) and (39b). At the same time, these languages tend to preserve medial sonorants without weakening; cf. e. g. (38d) and (39c). This suggests that initial strengthening results from a generalization of the obstruent pattern 'strong initial segment : weak medial segment' to the sonorants, so as to bring about **pattern symmetry**; cf. (40). (In (38a), initial strengthening results in segments which are identical to the medial reflexes of the corresponding Latin geminates, cf. (38b). In (39), strengthening consists in changing the sonorants into acoustically similar stops.)

(38a)	Lat. rēgem	Span.	[r̄ey]	'king'
	leōnem	Catal., Leon.	[λeon]	'lion'
	nārēs	Leon. dial.	[ñaris]	'nose'
b)	lat. terram	Span.	[tier̄a]	'earth'
	illa		[eλa]	'she'
	annum		[año]	'year'
c)	Lat. vidēre	Span.	veθer	'to see'
	habēre		[aβer]	'to have'
	pacatum		[payaðo]	'pleased'
	cippus		cepo	'pole, branch'
d)	Lat. amarum	Span.	amaro	'bitter'

(39a) Skt. ya-   dial. MIAr. ǰa-   'who (rel.
                                              pron.)'
       vasanta-   basanta-   'spring (sea-
                                              son)'
   b) Skt. mata-   dial. MIAr. mada, maθa 'thought'
       kṛtaka-   kidaya, ki(y)aθa 'done'
   c) Skt. karōti   dial. MIAr. kara(d)i   'does'

(40) Medial   Initial

      Weaker obstruent : Stronger obstruent
      Weaker sonorant   : X = Stronger sonorant

The evidence of Insular Celtic is especially interesting and suggests
that the above explanation is on the right track: Here we find medial
weakening not only of obstruents, but also of one sonorant, namely
[m]; cf. (41). And this is the one sonorant which does not undergo
initial strengthening in any of the Celtic languages; cf. (42). Presumably
the lack of initial strengthening in [m] is due to the fact that through
medial weakening it already participated in the pattern of (40). (Celtic
strengthening to a large extent consists in devoicing. In Irish, the
liquids and [n] are lengthened. And in Welsh, initial [w] is strengthened
by the prefixation of a velar stop. Irish long [l] is represented as [lː];
palatalization and labiovelarization have been left unmarked.)

(41) PIE *tewtā   OIr. [tuəθ]   MW [tid]   'people'
           *bhewdi-   [buəð]   [bið]   'victory'
           *nemos   [ñeβ̃]   [nev]   'sky'

(42) PIE *wiros   [fer]   [gwir]   'man'
                          (via *[βer-]
           *rowdhos   [r̄uəð]   [r̥ið]   'red'
           *ligh-   [lːiɣið]   'licks'
           *lapsa-   [l̥axar] 'gleaming'
           *newyos   [ñaue]   'new'

Note that initial devoicing has been invoked also for obstruents. But
the cases that have been cited seem to be amenable to alternative
explanations. The case of Lac-Simon Ojibwa is typical. Here, a medial
contrast between voiced and voiceless is synchronically neutralized in
initial position. The result is the coexistence of two contrasting patterns:
one with non-alternating voiceless obstruents, the other with medial

voiced vs. initial voiceless obstruent; cf. (43). Historically, however, this situation does not arise from initial devoicing, but from medial weakening (degemination of geminates, voicing of non-geminates) and inintial cluster simplification (in the form of degemination); cf. the summary in (44). (For ease of exposition, dentals have been chosen to represent the contrasting obstruent series.)

(43)   Lac-Simon Ojibwa:

	Medial	Initial
	t	t
vs.	d	t

(44)   Early Ojibwa:

	Medial	Initial
	tt : t	tt : t
Initial simplific.	— — —	t = t
Medial weakening	t : d	— — —

8.6. Teleology

Most of the developments examined in this chapter are directed toward a goal. The goal may be rather modest, such as keeping a margin of safety between contrasting segments. But some goals consist in a major rearrangement of phonological structure.

There has been some controversy whether such goal-oriented or **teleological** developments have any historical reality or whether they are not rather figments of the imagination of historical linguists. For one may well ask how, say, the first generation of speakers, making the first step in a goal-oriented series of shifts, can possibly know — or control — what further changes will be undertaken by future generations of speakers. However, the existence of empirically well attested series of changes like the ones in Swedish, Central Illinois, Chicago, and New York (cf. (24)—(26) above) show both that such changes are possible and how they can take place: A first change gives rise to a later response change which in turn may lead to yet other responses. By and large, then, the teleology does not consist in any preconceived 'grand plan' or 'strategy' but evolves through a series of 'tactical decisions', in response to the situation prevailing at a given time.

In a few cases, however, something more seems to be involved: As noted earlier, the Pali Two-Mora Conspiracy was brought about by the 'cooperation' of three phonetically quite different changes. (Cf. (29)–(31).) Moreover, taken by themselves, none of these changes was regular; only the conspiracy was regular. Similarly, the Slavic Open-Syllable Conspiracy was implemented in part by non-regular changes (cf. especially (37b)). Cases like these seem to require the assumption that at a certain point the results of various 'tactical decisions' along the way may build up enough 'critical mass' to establish a clear goal for further changes, and that from that point onward, all that matters is the accomplishment of that goal, no matter whether this is brought about by an irregular application of otherwise regular sound changes. The very regularity of these conspiracies, however, shows that they are not just the figments of linguists' imaginations and that, whatever their explanation, they must be accepted as genuine historical developments.

Chain shifts and conspiracies are theoretically important in historical linguistics in that they provide an explanation in principle for similar wholesale rearrangements of phonological systems or patterns, even if the evidence now available may not permit an unambiguous identification of the sequencing of events which gave rise to these rearrangements. For instance, Grimm's Law, with its wholesale shift of the PIE stop system, probably came about through some kind of chain shift, although we may never be able to establish with certainty whether this shift was of the drag-chain, push-chain, or solidarity-chain variety, or a combination of these.

In some cases, we can do better, even if some of the details may not be clear. Thus, it is probable that the Great English Vowel Shift was at first motivated by overcrowding, brought about by open-syllable lengthening; cf. 7.4.5, exs. (78a/b) and (79), reproduced as (45) and (46) below. For as (47) illustrates, lengthened vowels and original long vowels did not necessarily merge; open-syllable lengthening therefore added long vowels to the system of English. It is further likely that a diphthongization of old long [ī] and [ū] was a first response to this overcrowding, even though we may not be able to pinpoint the exact phonetic nature of that diphthongization. (Possibly, [ū] was first diphthongized, because of the asymmetry of the vocal area (cf. 8.3). In that case, the diphthongization of [ī] might be a solidarity phenomenon.) Finally, the raising shifts in the remaining long vowels (as in (45a),

(46), and (47) can be accounted for as drag-chain phenomena, even though — again — some details of these changes may not be entirely certain.

(45) Old English   Modern English

a) cwēn   queen [ī]
    dōm   doom   [ū]
b) īs   ice   [ay]
    hūs   house [aw]

(46) Old English   dial. ME   Great Vowel Shift/
                                  Modern English

      wicu   wēke   week [ī]
      yvel   ēvel   evil [ī]
      wudu   wōde   wood [u] (with secondary
                                          shortening)

(47) Old English   stān   nǎma
      Allophonic differentiation   stān   nǎ<mə
      Open-syllable lengthening   — — —   nā<mə
      Raising/Final outcome   stōn   nēm
                                       'stone' 'name'

9. Analogy:
General discussion and typology

Whereas sound change can be accounted for in purely phonetic or phonological terms, other changes that affect the phonetic structure of words are sensitive also to non-phonetic/phonological factors. Among these, **analogy** plays a very important role.

As traditionally defined, analogy is eminently conditioned by non-phonetic factors: Its most common function is to make morphologically, syntactically, and/or semantically related forms more similar to each other in their phonetic (and morphological) structure. It has been claimed that only by recognizing and accepting this distinction between analogy and sound change were the neogrammarians able to establish their claim that sound change is regular.

This chapter is devoted to a discussion of the processes that have been traditionally recognized as analogical. (Chapter 11 will deal with cases of 'non-traditional' analogy, i.e. with developments which traditional historical linguists have found difficult to account for and therefore have tended to ignore. The behavior of these changes differs considerably from most of the ones discussed in this chapter.)

9.1. Systematic processes:
Leveling and four-part analogy

As in the case of sound change, analogical processes differ in terms of the regularity with which they apply. However, there the similarity ends. Even the most systematic analogical changes ordinarily come close to being regular only after centuries or even millennia. The difference between systematic and nonsystematic types of analogy, thus, is merely one of degree.

Still, two processes, **leveling** and **four-part analogy**, tend to be considerably more regular or systematic than most of the other changes. The reason for this systematicity seems to lie in the fact that they often operate within well-defined and fairly broad parameters. In the case of leveling, that parameter is the notion '**paradigm**', i. e. the set of inflected forms of a given word. And since most words belong to inflectional classes, characterized by the same paradigmatic structure, leveling has the potential of affecting whole classes of words. Four-part analogy ordinarily serves to generalize or extend a morphological '**pattern**', such as the pattern of plural derivation in Engl. *arm, book, car* ... :*arm-s, book-s, car-s* ... And again, such patterns commonly are the properties of whole classes of words.

9.1.1. Leveling

Leveling consists in the complete or partial elimination of morphophonemic alternations within paradigms. (For a broader definition see 9.1.4. below.) The motivation for this development has been plausibly captured by the slogan '**one meaning — one form**'. Alternations which do not seem to signal (important) differences in meaning therefore tend to be eliminated.

Thus, the Old English paradigm of the verb 'choose' (and others like it) had a morphophonemic alternation between [s], [z], and [r]. In Modern English, the alternation has been eliminated in favor of the alternant [z]. Cf. (1). A similar change is found in (2), except that unlike English, German has generalized the alternant [r]. As a consequence of these and other levelings, the lexical item 'choose' now has a constant consonantal 'skeleton' (E [č ... z], G [k ... r]).

(1)		Old English	Modern English	
	pres.	cēozan	choose	[z]
	past sg.	cēas	chose	[z]
	past pl.	curon	chose	[z]
	past pple.	(ge-)coren	chosen	[z]

(2)		Old High German	Modern German	
	pres.	kiusan	küren	'choose'
	past sg.	kōs	kor	
	past pl.	kurun	koren	
	past pple.	(gi-)koran	gekoren	

As noted in 3.5, the effects of Verner's Law began to be leveled out as early as Old English and Old High German. But the earliest texts often preserve traces of the original situation. Often these traces consist in the coexistence of the old form with the innovated form, as in (3). **Doublets** of this sort are very common as transitional stages in all analogical change. Occasionally, however, they may persist for a longer period. In such cases, they are often subject to the analogical process of blending (cf. 9.2.1 below), or they become differentiated in function and meaning (cf. 10.1.4 below.).

(3)		Early OHG	Later OHG
	past sg.	sluoh/sluog	sluog 'slew'
cf.	past pl.	sluogun	(unchanged)

It is only over the course of more than a millennium that English and German have 'succeeded' in nearly eliminating all traces of the alternations. Even today, however, some forms have 'escaped' the development; cf. forms like NE *was* [z] : *were* [r]. **Relic** forms of this type, again, are a common phenomenon in analogical change and attest to the inherent irregularity of analogy.

Leveling in (1) and (2) is not limited to the consonants: English and German have also given up the root vowel alternation in the three past-tense forms; cf. (1′) and (2′). Interestingly however, leveling did not extend to the present tense. The reason for this difference is not difficult to see: The vowel alternation between present and past marks a major distinction, between different tenses. The other alternations mark relatively minor distinctions, within the past-tense system.

(1′)		Old English	Modern English
	pres.	cēozan	choose
vs.	past sg.	cēas	chose
	past pl.	curon	chose
	past pple.	(ge-)coren	chosen

(2′)		Old High German	Modern German
	pres.	kiusan	küren
vs.	past sg.	kōs	kor
	past pl.	kurun	koren
	past pple.	(gi-)koran	gekoren

Given only the data of $(1/1')$ and $(2/2')$, there is no strong reason to choose vowel, rather than consonant alternation, to mark the present : past distinction. However, consonant alternation is limited to just those verbs in which Verner's Law or some other change resulted in split. Vowel alternation, on the other hand, is not restricted in this way, but is found in many other verbs which lack consonantal alternations; cf. e. g. (4). Leveling, thus, may be sensitive not only to whether a given morphophonemic alternation is important, but also to whether it is general.

(4)			Old High German	Modern German
	pres.		biutan	bieten 'bid'
vs.	past sg.		bōt	vs. bot
	past pl.		butun	boten
	past pple.		(gi-)botan	geboten

As the root-vowel developments in (1), (2), and (4) show, leveling need not affect an entire paradigm. It may be limited to a particular **sub-paradigm**. English is especially instructive in this regard. For beside the leveling in (1), which affected the entire past-tense (sub-) paradigm, English in many cases had developments as in (5). Here leveling is restricted to the **'finite'** past-tense paradigm, i. e. to those past-tense forms which indicate the person and number of the subject of a given sentence. The non-finite participle, on the other hand, remained unaffected by the process.

(5)		Old English	Modern English
	pres.	rīdan	ride
	past sg.	rād	rode
	past pl.	rīdon	rode
	past pple.	(ge-)riden	ridden

The scope of leveling may be even more circumscribed: In its inflection of the verb 'to be', Sanskrit inherited from PIE a morphophonemic alternation between a 'full-grade' form *as*- and a '∅-grade' form *s*- (i. e. ∅*s*-). Pali continues this alternation in the third-person forms; but in the first and second persons, the full-grade form *as*- has been generalized through leveling. Compare example (6).

(6)		Sanskrit	pre-Pali	Pali
sg.	1	as-mi	*as-mi	amhi
	2	asi	*asi	asi
	3	as-ti	*as-ti	atthi
pl.	1	Øs-maḥ	*as-ma	amha
	2	Øs-tha	*as-tha	attha
	3	Øs-anti	*Øs-anti	santi

(Morpheme boundaries are indicated where possible; the second singular has a synchronically irregular form. The 'pre-Pali' forms may be fictional, but they are useful for illustrating the relevant analogical developments, without interference by the fairly far-reaching sound changes which separate Pali from Sanskrit.)

The relationship between sound change and analogy has often been characterized in terms of the following paradox: 'Regular sound change creates morphological irregularity, because it applies without consideration for morphological factors. Analogy, an inherently irregular process, attempts to reestablish morphological regularity.' Strictly speaking, this paradox applies only to the relationship between sound change and leveling. And even here, the relationship between the sound change which created 'irregularity' and the leveling which removes it may be a very remote one. Thus, the morphophonemic alternations in the Old English and Old High German root vowels and the related root vowel alternations in the Sanskrit verb 'to be' go as far back as Proto-Indo-European, and the changes which gave rise to them must have taken place even earlier. The Germanic and Pali levelings therefore are reactions delayed by millennia.

As the subsequent sections will demonstrate, other analogical changes have very different motivations and may only incidentally be directed at morphophonemic alternations created by (regular) sound change.

9.1.2. Four-part analogy

Four-part analogy is the most systematic sub-type of **proportional analogy**. Like other sub-types it operates on the basis of a 'proportional model' of the type (7), generalizing a **pattern of morphological relationship** between given forms (say, *a* and *a'*) to forms (such as *b* and X) which previously did not exhibit this pattern. For example, it is as the result of this process that the plural of English *cow* today is *cows*, instead of the earlier *kine* (which now survives only marginally, in 'old-fashioned' poetic usage). As example (8) shows, the change generalizes the pattern of plural formation found in other English words, such as *stone : stone-s.*

(7)   a   : a′
       b   : X = b′

(8)   stone : stone-s
       cow   : X = cow-s

Note that for changes of this sort to take place, there must be a morphological relationship between the words which make up the proportion. Proportions based on purely phonetic/phonological similarities such as the one between *ring* (verb) and *king* (noun) in (9) do not normally give rise to analogical developments.

(9)   ring   : king
       rang   : X = kang*

To be referred to as 'four-part analogy', a proportional analogy must operate as in (8): A pre-established relationship of **synchronic derivation** between a **'basic'** and a **'derived'** form (such as singular → plural) is extended to another lexical item, resulting in a new derived form.

To have the potential of applying with a fair amount of systematicity, four-part analogy must satisfy a number of additional requirements. One of these is that the proportional model for the change should be a pattern of derivation, not limited to merely one lexical item. For instance, the analogical change in (8) is not motivated just by the model of *stone : stone-s,* but by the pattern in (8′). Formulations as in (8) usually are only convenient 'abbreviations' for fuller formulations of the type (8′).

(8′)   stone : stone-s
       arm   : arm-s
       dog   : dog-s
       ...   : ...
       cow   : X = cow-s

The condition most conducive to systematic application of four-part analogy is **productivity**: In most languages, certain morphological categories are more productive than other, alternative formations. Usually, these categories are characterized by much larger membership than competing formations. (Cf. e. g. the *s*-plural and *ed*-past tense in English.) But this may be more a symptom than a cause of productivity. For it is not entirely clear how a particular morphological category becomes productive. In English, for instance, it might be argued that the *s*-plural was 'simpler' and more clearly marked than other plural formations: OE -*as*, the ancestor of NE -*s*, unambiguously marked nominative/accusative plural; cf. (10a). In a number of other inflectional classes, the form of the nominative/accusative plural was not distinct from the corresponding singular (cf. (10b)) or was identical to various non-nominative singular forms (cf. (10c)). And some classes formed their plural by the more 'difficult' process of morphophonemic alternation in the root vowel, cf. (10d). But it is doubtful whether simplicity and clearer marking are sufficient to make a formation productive; for in spite of the fact that the -*an* of (10c) is not limited to the nominative plural and thus does not function as a clear marker for that case form, the -*an*-plural enjoyed a great amount of popularity in Middle English, strongly competing with the -*(a)s*-plural of (10a) and even attracting some earlier (10a) formations; cf. e. g. OE *scoh : scōas* vs. ME *schoo : schoon* (beside *schoos*).

(10)		Singular	Plural	
a)	N/A	stān	stānas	'stone'
b)	N/A	word	word (-**Ø**)	'word'
c)	N	guma	guman	'man'
	G/D/A	guman	A guman	
d)	N/A	fōt	fēt	'feet'

Whatever may be the historical reasons for a particular category's becoming productive, once productive, it is more likely to be generalized by four-part analogy than other, less productive categories. The popularity of the English *s*-plural, for instance, is seen in the increasing replacement of Latin/Greek plurals, as in (11). (In some cases, there is still variation between the old and new forms, in others, the replacement is a fait accompli.) On the other hand, Latin/Greek plural forms rarely, if ever, replace older *s*-plurals.

(11)   forum   : fora   → forums
       stadium : stadia   → stadiums
       cactus : cacti   → cactuses
       octopus : octopodes   → octopuses

Perhaps even more importantly, the popularity of the *s*-plural can
also be seen in speaker's reactions to new, analogical formations: If
these forms are modeled on productive patterns (as in (12a)), they may
elicit friendly — or patronizing — correction, but they are found to be
completely intelligible. However, if they reflect unproductive patterns
(as in (12b)), they may either evoke the same reaction as a pun (as in
spice = spouses) or, in the majority of cases, meet with complete
incomprehension. One suspects that it is this difference in speaker's
reaction which is responsible for the difference in historical productivity.

(12a) mouse : mice   → mouses*
       foot   : feet   → foots*
   b) spouse : spouses → spice*
       house : houses   → hice*
       book   : books   → beek*

Note however that productivity is not an absolute, but a gradient
phenomenon: While some patterns, such as English *foot : feet* or *go :
went*, are completely unproductive, many others show at least some
degree of productivity. For instance, beside the *octopodes/octopuses* of
(11), a common alternative plural of Engl. *octopus* is *octopi*. This preserves
some of the 'irregularity' commonly associated with Latin-sounding
words, but uses the plural ending which is more 'regular' in this
irregular category. Similarly, the development in (13) generalizes a more
regular pattern of irregular English past-tense formation. There are
even some (rare) cases of less productive patterns replacing more
productive ones; cf. (14a) and (b). The exact reasons for these 'contrary'
developments are not always clear; but the development in (14b) is
probably motivated by the fact that the word *dwarf* is most commonly
used in fairy tales and that other, similarly irregular plurals abound in
this context.

(13)   bring :   brought   : brought
       → dial. brang/brung : brung

cf.
sing : sang : sung
ring : rang : rung
etc.

or
fling : flung : flung
cling : clung : clung
etc.

(14a)   OE   NE
        dȳvan   dive
        dȳv(e)de   dived   → dove   (cf. drive : drove)
   b)   dwarf   : dwarfs → Am. E   dwarves

cf.
elf   : elves
wolf   : wolves
...   ...

As the examples so far examined show, four-part analogy commonly draws words from one, often less productive paradigm into another, often more productive one. However, four-part analogy can operate also interparadigmatically, generalizing a morphological option from one word class to another. (Even morphophonemic options and patterns may be generalized, cf. 9.1.5, ex. (44) and (48) below.) For instance, as the result of various (partly analogical) developments, early Vedic Sanskrit wound up with two ways of forming the nominative/accusative plural of neuter *n*-stems, one using the ending -*ā/ă*, the other, -*āni*. In the neuter *a*-stems, the inherited suffix of the nominative/accusative plural was -*ā/ă*. The fact that the two classes of neuters thus partially agreed in their mode of forming the nominative/accusative plural then gave rise to the four-part analogy in (15) which made the two classes agree entirely. Outside the nominative/accusative plural forms, however, neuter *n*- and *a*-stems remained completely distinct, cf. e. g. the different endings in the nominative/accusative singular (*nām-a* : *yug-am*) or the genitive singular (*nām-naḥ* : *yug-asya*).

(15)   *n*-stem neuters   *a*-stem neuters

N/A pl.   -ā/ă : -āni   -ā/ă : X = -āni
(cf.   nāmā/ă, -āni 'names'   yugā/ă → yugā/ă, -āni
                                         'yokes')

The effect of four-part analogy does not exclusively lie in the replacement of old forms by newer, more productive ones. The process may also serve to **coin** completely novel forms or **neologisms**. For instance, words like *re-realignment, re-research* can be formed quite freely on the basis of the pattern in (16). Many such words remain 'nonce-formations', never making it into the dictionaries. But others gain limited or even general currency. Many technical terms in linguistics and other fields have came about in this fashion, such as the syntacticians' *sentencehood* (cf. *nation : nationhood*) or this book's *syllabification* (cf. *verify : verification*). Many others have entered general usage, such as *personalize* or *finalize* (cf. *radical : radicalize*).

(16)   affirm   : re(-)affirm
       analysis   : re(-)analysis
       ...   : ...
       realignment : X
       research   : Y

This 'creative' use of four-part analogy is often preceded and triggered by morphological **reinterpretation**. Consider the case of Engl. *hamburger*: The term at first was similar to *wiener* or *frankfurter*, designating the place from which the food originated. Along the way, however, it was (somewhat vaguely) reinterpreted as containing the word *ham* (even though ordinarily it is made of beef) plus an element *-burger* 'meat patty (or the like)'. Relevant models of word formation then could give rise to the generalization of this element to create new words; cf. e. g. (17). (The development may have been aided by a process of ellipsis (cf. 9.2.1 below) which reduced words like *cheese hamburger* to *cheeseburger*. But this development in turn presupposes a semantic reinterpretation of *-burger* as somehow equivalent to the fuller *hamburger*. — The eventual use of *burger* as an independent word in its own right results from backformation, a process which will be discussed in 9.2.5 below.)

(17)   sandwich : cheese sandwich, taco sandwich, ...
       -burger : X, Y, ...

Earlier reinterpretations of this sort have given rise to English suffixes like *-hood, -dom, -ly*: Their Old English antecedents *hād, dōm, līc* could still be used as independent words, with the respective meanings 'character, condition', 'judgment, power, realm', 'body, likeness; like'. However, in compounds their function could be reinterpreted as being that of derivational suffixes; cf. (18). Four-part analogy, then, provided the vehicle for their extension to new contexts, such as *nationhood, sentencehood*, etc.

(18) cīld-hād   'child condition'   → '(condition of) childhood'

      frēo-dōm   'realm of the free'   → '(state of) freedom'
      man-līc   'having the likeness of a man'   → 'manlike, manly'

Reinterpretation and four-part analogy may also be involved in establishing lexical sets like the onomatopoetic expressions in Chart 9.1.

	-ack	-am	-ang	-ap	-ash	-atter
b-			bang (16)		bash (18)	batter (14)
cl-	clack (16)	clam (18*)	clang (16)	clap (14)	clash (16)	clatter (11)
cr-	crack (14)				crash (15)	
d-			dang (19•)		dash (13)	
fl-	flack (14*)	flam (18*)		flap (14)	flash (16)	flatter (14*)
p-			pang (16)		pash (14*)	patter (14)
pl-				plap (19*)	plash (16)	
r-		ram (14)		rap (14)	rash (15*)	rattle (14)
sl-		slam (17)		slap (17)	slash (14)	slatter (17*)
sm-	smack (16)				smash (18)	smatter (14)
sp-			spang (16•)			spatter (16)
spl-					splash (18)	splatter (18)
sw-	swack (14•)				swash (16)	swatter (16•)
wh-	whack (18)	wham (20)	whang (19)			

(This listing is limited to onomatopoetic verbs; some of these may be homophonous with non-onomatopoetic words. Numbers after entries refer to the century of first attestation. An asterisk after a number indicates that the form is obsolete as an onomatopoeia; a raised dot, that the form is limited to certain dialects. *rattle* is included under the assumption that it is dissimilated from * *ratter*; cf. Germ. *rattern* beside *ratteln*.)

Chart 9.1. Systematic onomatopoeia in English

Vocabulary of this sort is notoriously difficult to deal with: First, as noted in 3.7 above, historical developments involving onomatopoeia ordinarily must be treated with caution, because of the possibility of independent, 'spontaneous' creation. Secondly, linguists generally feel uncomfortable about the morphological proportions which would be required in order to derive words like, say, *clack* by four-part analogy, cf. (19). There is a general feeling that words of this type are not morphologically complex, and that therefore there can be no such proportions as (19). For the 'morphemes' which would have to be postulated for such proportions differ considerably from ordinary morphemes: Since we cannot state a clear lexical meaning for, say, *cl-* or *-ack*, they cannot be roots. Nor can they be affixes, since they serve neither to mark syntactic relations nor to derive new stems from preexisting roots or stems. Moreover, it is possible to account for words like *clack* by means of analogical processes which do not require morphological proportions of the type (19): They can be explained as resulting either from 'blending' (cf. (20) and the fuller discussion in section 9.2.1 below) or from 'contamination' (cf. (21) and 9.2.2 below).

(19)   fl-atter   : fl-ack
        cl-atter   : X = cl-ack

(20)   flack **X** clatter → clack

(21)   clatter   : flack
        → clatter : clack

However, in spite of these difficulties, one suspects that four-part analogy is involved to some extent: It is perfectly clear that the pattern in Chart 9.1 is the result of secondary developments. Of the forty-four items, only one (*clatter*) goes back to Old English; and even that word comes from the very last century of the period. The majority (29 items) developed within a timespan of three hundred years, from the 14th to the 16th century. Even more importantly, the pattern which resulted is highly systematic, in that the initial elements (*b-*, *cl-*, etc.) and the final elements (*-ack*, *-am*, etc.) exhibit a remarkable freedom of combinability. In this respect the pattern in Chart 9.1 differs markedly from other sets of onomatopoetic vocabulary.

It is difficult to believe that such a fairly rapid development of a highly systematic pattern of onomatopoeia can result from blending and contamination alone. For these two processes belong to the notoriously sporadic and non-systematic types of analogy. Nor can the pattern result from an independent, spontaneous creation of onomatopoeia. Rather, the systematicity of the pattern requires the operation of four-part analogy, in addition to these other, less systematic processes. This does not necessarily mean that the proportion in (19) is morphological, in the ordinary sense. It may well rest on a (transitory) reinterpretation of words like *flatter, flack, clatter* as being morphologically composite. Note moreover that even if four-part analogy probably is involved in the development of the general pattern, we cannot be certain whether a particular individual word (such as *clack*) results from the operation of four-part analogy (cf. (19)), blending ((20)), or contamination ((21)); a priori, it may have arisen by any of these processes.

9.1.3. The relationship between leveling and four-part analogy

In most cases it is possible to tell whether a given analogical development is to be attributed to leveling or four-part analogy. But there are situations in which the decision is less certain. For instance, the development in (22) can be accounted for either as leveling (elimination of the morphophonemic root vowel alternation) or as resulting from the four-part analogy of patterns like *warm : warmer*; cf. (23). (The comparative form in the latter pattern had a different suffix vowel in Proto-Germanic and thus lacked the umlaut of forms like *elder*.)

(22) Old English   Modern English

 lang : lengra > long : lenger → longer
 eald : ieldra > old : elder   → older
                            (beside relic *elder*)

(23) Proto-Germanic   Old English   Modern English

 *warm- : warmōza- > wearm : wearmra > warm : warmer
 *ald- : aldiza- > eald : ieldra > old : X =
                                             older

Whereas in some cases it may simply be unclear whether leveling or four-part analogy is involved, in others it is quite certain that the two processes are cooperating with each other. The effect of this cooperation can have very drastic effects, such as in Latin, where in one inflectional subclass, analogical change has − like sound change − applied with virtually complete regularity, within a fairly short period. The inflectional class is that of the non-neuter *s*-stems of disyllabic or longer (= 'polysyllabic') words; the alternation which gets leveled out is one between *s* and *r*. The external model consists in a subset of the (likewise) non-neuter *r*-stems, whose inflection is almost identical, except for the fact that their *r* does not alternate. Compare (24).

(24)   *r*-stems   *s*-stems

sg. N   sor-or   : hon-ōs → Class. Lat. hon-o**r**
    G   sor-ōr-is   : hon-ōr-is
    D   sor-ōr-ī   : hon-ōr-ī
    A   sor-ōr-em   : hon-ōr-em
        etc.
        'sister'   'honor'

While leveling was just about completely regular in polysyllabic non-neuter words, no such regularity is found in other *s*-stems: The monosyllabic non-neuters generally resist leveling; cf. (25). And the polysyllabic neuters have leveling in some forms, and retention of the alternation in others; cf. (26). The reason for this different behavior lies in the fact that there are no monosyllabics or neuters in the *r*-stems. Leveling, therefore, here is not supported by four-part analogy and must proceed at the usual, rather slow pace, and with the usual lack of regularity.

(25)   OLat. flōs, flōris : Class. Lat. flōs, flōris (unchanged)
                                                        'flower'

(26a) (*)robus → robur 'power'
       roboris
       roborī
       etc.
   b) corpus (unchanged) 'body'
       corporis
       corporī
       etc.

A more complex cooperation between leveling and four-part analogy is seen in the historical development of the PIE neuter *o*- and *s*-stems into German: Example (27) gives the relevant PIE forms. (The exact PIE root shape for 'calf' is not certain. ∅ indicates absence of case ending. The *-es/os-* of the *s*-stems is a derivational, 'stem-forming' suffix, not a case ending.)

(27)   *o*-stem neuters   *s*-stem neuters

sg. N/A ǵr̥n-om 'corn, grain'   golbh-os-∅   'calf'
     G   -oso   -es-os
     D   -ōy   -es-ey
pl. N/A   -ā   -es-ā
     G   -ōm   -es-ōm
     D   -omis   -es-mis

Regular linguistic change (including loss of some unaccented final syllables in trisyllabic words vs. retention in disyllabics; cf. 5.3.4) transformed these paradigms into the sets of (28), indirect traces of which are found in early Old High German. The normal OHG pattern, however, is that of (29). Here leveling has eliminated the stem alternation between *kalb-* and *kelbir-* in the singular. At the same time, four-part analogy has introduced the clearly characterized and distinct dative and genitive singular endings of the *o*-stems. The result is a new paradigm, with polarization between the singular and plural forms.

(28) sg. N/A korn-∅   kalb-∅
           G   korn-es   kelb-ir-∅
           D   korn-e   kelb-ir-∅
      pl. N/A   korn-∅   kelb-ir-∅
           G   korn-o   kelb-ir-o
           D   korn-um   kelb-ir-um

(29) sg. N/A kalb-∅   (cf. korn-∅)
           G   kalb-es   (cf. korn-es)
           D   kalb-e   (cf. korn-e)
      pl. N/A   kelb-ir-∅   (unchanged)
           G   kelb-ir-o   (unchanged)
           D   kelb-ir-um (unchanged)

A subsequent reinterpretation of the -*ir*-suffix as a plural marker gave rise to a massive four-part analogical extension of the pattern of (29) to most neuters, including original *o*-stem forms like *korn*; cf. (30). (The modern orthography is used here, so as to show that this extension generalized not only the ending, but also the vowel alternation.)

(30) kalb : kälb-er
      korn : X = körn-er

The development of the German *o*- and *s*-stems raises two additional issues concerning the relationship between leveling and four-part analogy. First of all, the leveling from the pre-Old-High German *s*-stem paradigm in (28) to the one in (29) is not limited to the morphophonemic alternation in the root vowel, but affects the total stem alternation *kalb-* : *kelbir-*. Leveling, thus, can extend into the area of morphology, i. e. territory more usually covered by four-part analogy. Conversely, the four-part analogy in (30) extends not only the domain in which a particular affix can be used, it also generalizes a morphophonemic alternation, thus 'trespassing' into the area normally covered by leveling.

Such morphological levelings and morphophonemic four-part analogies are less common than the usual morphophonemic leveling and morphological four-part analogy. But they do occur elsewhere, as will be demonstrated in the next two sections.

9.1.4. Morphological leveling

Leveling of root alternations is found in examples like (31) and (32). In (31), the alternation is the result of 'suppletion', the suppletive use of different roots or stems for different forms of the 'same word' (cf. e. g. E *go* : *went*, where *went* is an old past tense of *wend*, as in *wend one's way*). In (32), alternation results from radically different developments of vowels and consonants in stressed and unstressed syllables. — Example (32) further illustrates that in some cases, both members of an alternation can be generalized through leveling, resulting in two competing words, each with its own paradigm. (As usual, the two words are secondarily differentiated in meaning: *dîn-* 'take the main meal, dine', *déjeun-* 'take breakfast, lunch'. The original meaning seems to have been 'stop one's fast or one's hunger'.)

(31)   OHG   ubil   : wirs-iro   : wirs-isto
→ NHG   übel   : übl-er   : übel-st-
          'bad'   : 'worse'   : 'worst'

(32)   Latin   Old French   Modern French
   pl. 1 *disiēiūnámus   **disn**-ons   dînons AND déjeunons
   sg. 1 *disiēiúnō   **desjun**-e   dîne   AND déjeune

Leveling of stem alternations can be seen in (33): In Sanskrit verbal morphology, certain formations were built on stems which in turn were composed of a root plus a stem-forming affix; cf. the present-tense form in (33). Other formations, such as the (past) participle, were made directly from the root, without any intervening affixes. In Middle-Indo-Aryan Pali, this discrepancy in formation began to be eliminated through leveling of the present stem into 'root formations' like the participle.

(33)   Sanskrit   Pali

    pres.   man-ya-tē   mañ(-)ña-ti

    pple.   ma-ta-   ma-ta- beside mañ̃-ita-

While cases like these differ from ordinary leveling by affecting more than just morphophonemic alternation, they are not incompatible with it. All we need to do is redefine leveling as the elimination of (unimportant) morpheme or stem alternations within paradigms.

However, under certain, much rarer, conditions, leveling seems to be able to eliminate the paradigmatic 'alternation' between different inflectional affixes, such as the different endings for person and number within verbal paradigms. Consider for instance the development of the verbal plural endings in the 'Ingvaeonic' subgroup of early West Germanic, which includes Old English, Old Frisian, and Old Saxon:

In the most productive present-tense verbal paradigm of early Germanic, the suffix vowel alternated between *i* and *a*, cf. the archaic Gothic pattern in (34). (Here and in the following examples, there are certain dialectal differences in the morphology of the first singular, as well as of the endings that follow the suffix vowel, but these need not concern us here.)

As the Old High German data in (35) show, West Germanic eliminated this alternation in the plural, through ordinary, morphophonemic leveling. (This development may have been 'encouraged' by the fact that it made it possible to morphologically distinguish the second plural from the third singular.)

In Ingvaeonic, however, loss of *n* in the context V _____ [+ fric.] led to the morphological merger or **syncretism** of the second and third plural endings; cf. (36). The Ingvaeonic response was a complete elimination of the distinctions between plural endings, by leveling the third/second person ending throughout the plural; cf. e. g. the early Old English paradigm in (37). (Four-part analogy generalized this leveling also to the past tense.)

(34)   Gothic:

	sg.			pl.	
	1	bair-a		1	bair-**a**-m
	2	bair-**i**-s		2	bair-**i**-þ
	3	bair-**i**-þ		3	bair-**a**-nd

(35)   Old High German:

	sg.			pl.	
	1	bir-u		1	ber-**a**-mēs
	2	bir-**i**-s		2	ber-**a**-t
	3	bir-**i**-t		3	ber-**a**-nt

(36)   Ingvaeonic:

	sg.			pl.	
	1	bir-u/beor-u		1	*ber-**a**-m
	2	bir-**i**-s		2	*ber-**a**-þ
	3	bir-**i**-þ		3	*ber-**a**-nþ > -**a**-þ

(37)   Early Old English:

	sg.			pl.	
	1	beor-u		1	ber-**a**-þ
	2	bir-**i**-s		2	ber-**a**-þ
	3	bir-**i**-þ		3	ber-**a**-þ

Developments of this sort are difficult to reconcile even with the revised definition of leveling. For the different inflectional affixes within a paradigm are distinct, different morphemes, not variants of a single morpheme or stem.

To account for the fact that inflectional affix leveling nevertheless is possible, it might first be argued that affixes differ from root or stem morphemes by not having any specific lexical 'meaning'. This argument might be followed up with the following hypothesis: Paradigms are not just combinations of roots or stems with different, individual affixes, but with an 'inflection', and the individual affixes, then, are different (syntactically conditioned) morphological realizations of that 'inflection'. Under this view, the variation between inflectional affixes would become more similar to the morphological alternations in (31)—(33), and leveling would appear less unusual.

Note however, that this explanation is speculative at best. Moreover, there is evidence which suggests that inflectional affixes ordinarily are treated as separate, distinct morphemes. Thus, analogical developments which affect one inflectional ending do not necessarily apply to other endings of the same paradigm. For instance in (38), the Verner's-Law alternation between *s* and *ȝ* is leveled out in favour of *ȝ* in the nominative singular (with subsequent word-final loss of -*ȝ*); but in the nominative plural, it is the voiceless alternant *s* which gets generalized.

(38)   Proto-Germanic   Old English
    sg. N wulf-as/z   *wulfaz > wulfØ 'wolf'
    pl. N wulf-ōs/z   *wulfōs > wulvas

A preferable explanation would be as follows: The Ingvaeonic syncretism of second and third plural endings in (36) brought about a situation
in which the distinction between these two persons could no longer be
unambiguously conveyed by the endings. A further, indirect consequence was the fact that verbal plural endings as a whole no longer
functioned effectively as grammatical markers. At the same time,
Ingvaeonic (like the other Germanic dialects) was changing from a
system in which personal pronouns could be 'omitted' and verbal
endings could be used alone to mark different persons, to a system in
which personal pronouns became obligatory; cf. (39). Under these
circumstances, verbal endings became increasingly **redundant**, duplicat-
ing the information conveyed by personal pronouns. It is apparently
this special conjunction of functional redundancy and morphological
syncretism which made possible the Ingvaeonic affix leveling.

(39a) Early: *(ek) berō, (þū) beris, ...
   b) Later: (OE) ic beoru, þū biris, ...
              'I carry, you carry, ...

This hypothesis is supported by many similar developments in other
languages, although the actual details may differ. Thus, while Gothic
clearly distinguished personal endings in the active verbal paradigm
(cf. (34) = (40a) below), it did not do so in the corresponding passive:
As (40b) shows, the singular does not distinguish between first and
third person; and the plural makes no distinctions at all.

(40a) active:
        sg. 1 bair-a   pl. 1 bair-a-m
            2 bair-i-s   2 bair-i-þ
            3 bair-i-þ   3 bair-a-nd
   b) passive:
        sg. 1 bair-a-da   pl. 1 bair-a-nda
            2 bair-a-za   2 bair-a-nda
            3 bair-a-da   3 bair-a-nda

This is in striking contrast with the ancestral PIE paradigm which clearly distinguished between the different persons; cf. (41a). And with the possible exception of the first and third plural (where sound change may have led to syncretism), the expected Gothic paradigm likewise has clearly distinct affixes (except for the third singular and second plural); cf. (41b). (The paradigm in (41a) actually is post-PIE, but pre-Germanic. For ease of exposition, it is assumed that certain analogical changes have applied which have parallels in other languages and which bring the paradigm as close as possible to the one in (40b). The implicit developments from (41a) to (41b) have similarly been simplified.)

(41a)   "PIE"

        sg. 1 *bher-oy   pl. 1 *bher-o-medhoy
            2 *bher-e-soy   2 *bher-e-dh(w)oy
            3 *bher-e-toy   3 *bher-o-ntoy

    b)   expected Gothic:

        sg. 1 *bair-a   pl. 1 *bair-a-nda
            2 *bair-i-za   2 *bair-i-da
            3 *bair-i-da   3 *bair-a-nda

The massive leveling of personal endings in (40) can be accounted for as follows: The inflected passive of (40)/(41b) was moribund in early Germanic. In fact, Gothic is the only Germanic language which still preserves a full passive paradigm; elsewhere, the only synchronically productive passive formation is 'periphrastic', with an auxiliary (AUX) plus the past participle; cf. (42). Even in Gothic, however, such periphrastic passives are found; cf. (43). It appears that the competition of this more productive formation relegated the old inflected passive to the status of a secondary and somewhat redundant formation which therefore was free to undergo extensive morphological leveling.

(42)   OE   hē   is   (ge)boren
       OHG er   ist   (gi)boran
       ON   hann er   borenn
                   AUX pple.
       'he is (being) carried'

(43)   Go.   bairada / baurans ist
           infl. pass. pple.   AUX (periphr. pass.)
           'he is (being) carried'

(Note that while affix levelings like the Ingvaeonic and Gothic ones above are common in situations where syncretism and functional redundancy come together, they are not a necessary development. Modern German, for instance, has obligatory pronoun use, as well as syncretism between the first and third plural endings, as in pl. 1 *wir gehen,* 2 *ihr geht,* 3 *sie gehen.* But there has been no affix leveling; the second plural has retained its distinct form.)

9.1.5. Morphophonemic proportional analogy

The extension of morphophonemic alternations by four-part analogy is not limited to the example in (30). In the history of German, for instance, root-vowel alternations resulting from umlaut were generalized in many other morphological categories; cf. (44). (This is in striking contrast to English, where such alternations tend to be eliminated; cf. examples (22/23) above).

(44) Old High German   New High German

    gast   : gesti   Gast   : Gäste
    boum : bouma   Baum : X = Bäume
                                (expect: Baume*)

Or consider the case of the fate of word-final *r* in certain varieties of British English: At a certain point, many dialects of English lost *r* in syllable-final (or coda) position; cf. (45). Word-final *r* ordinarily was also syllable-final, and as a consequence generally was lost. But if followed by a vowel-initial word, it could be resyllabified into the onset of the following syllable and thus escape loss; cf. (46). In certain varieties of British English, the resulting word-final alternation between *r* and Ø was extended also to other words which never had word-final *r*, cf. (47). (Presumably, the *r* of expressions like [ðə mætə-r-iz] was reanalyzed as serving to avoid hiatus between word-final and word-initial vowels.)

(45) r > Ø / V _____ (C₀) $

    cf. carting   [kar$tiŋ]   >   [ka(:)$tiŋ]
          cart   [kart$]   >   [ka(:)t$]

(46) the matter was   [ðə$mæ$tər$wɔz] > [ðə$mæ$təØ$wɔz]
      the matter is   [ðə$mæ$tə$riz]   (no change)

(47)   the matter   [əØ] was   :   the matter [ər] is
       the idea   [əØ] was   :   X = the idea [ər] is

A similar development is found in the history of French: A word-final alternation between *t* and *Ø* that originally was limited to certain verbs was extended to others in which the alternation was not originally motivated; cf. (48). (Also this development seems to have been brought on by a reinterpretation, namely that -*t*- was serving to avoid hiatus between verb-final vowel and the initial vowel of the pronoun *il*. However, a later loss of word-final [ə], spelled -*e* (as in *chante*) has obscured the situation.)

(48)   OFr.   est   :   est-il   chante   :   chante-il
       s > Ø   εt   :   εt-il   — — —   — — — —
      Final-*t* loss   ε   — —   — — —   — — — —
      Hence alternation: εØ   :   εti(l)
      Four-part analogy: εØ   :   εti(l)   chanteØ   :   X = chanteti(l)
                      'is'   'is he' 'sings'   'sings he'

Examples like (47) and (48) are interesting on two counts: First of all, within the morphologically defined context in which they took place, they are completely regular. Thus, in the British English varieties which had the change in (47), *r* is inserted between all word-final and word-initial vowels. (There are English dialects, to be sure, in which *r*-insertion is irregular; but the context is different, and the development results from a very different analogical process, namely hypercorrection; cf. 9.3, ex. (97) below.) Similarly, Standard French *t*-insertion is completely regular between originally vowel-final verb and following vowel-initial words like *il*.

Secondly, although the developments in (47) and (48) are instances of (very) systematic proportional analogy, they do not conform to the definition of four-part analogy adopted earlier. For (unlike for instance (44)), they apply not to related morphological forms, but only to morphophonemic alternations within certain morphologically defined, phonological environments. Moreover, in ordinary four-part analogy, the left side of the proportion is morphologically basic, the right side, a derived form (cf. 1.1.2). In proportions like (47) and (48), on the other hand, it is difficult to decide whether *Ø* or the full segment (*r* or *t*) is more basic. One might be tempted to claim that since the proportion is 'solved' on the side of *r* or *t*, the full segment must therefore be derived, and Ø basic. But this is a post-hoc argument and therefore suspect. A more satisfactory approach, which also accounts for the complete regularity of changes of this sort, will be offered in Chapter 11.

9.2. Non-systematic processes

The changes discussed in this section differ from leveling and four-part analogy by being notoriously non-systematic or sporadic. In the majority of processes, this sporadic behavior is a consequence of the fact that by their very nature, these changes apply to just one or two (rarely more) words at a time. The sporadicity of one process, backformation, stems from different, more specific factors which will be dealt with in the discussion of the process.

Although taken by themselves, the processes discussed in this section affect just one or two words at a time, some of them may occasionally give rise to quite systematic morphological changes. This is the case if derivational or inflectional morphemes are affected, for through four-part analogy such morphemes can be freely attached to a large number of different lexical items. Some examples of such developments are given in the discussion of the individual processes.

9.2.1. Blending, portmanteau formation, ellipsis, periphrasis

Blending consists in the development of a morphological 'compromise' between two forms with identical or similar meaning which are perceived as being in competition with each other. Often this competition results from other analogical processes, as in the examples of (49). (49a) is frequently found in children's language, as a compromise between 'correct' *feet* and four-part analogical *foot-s*. (49b) is a similar compromise between an Old English mode of plural formation and the *n*-plural which as noted in 9.1.2 was quite productive in Middle English. (In some varieties of American Black Vernacular English, the pattern of (49a) is found extended to virtually all irregular plurals with stem-vowel alternation; cf. (50). One suspects that somewhere along the way, forms like those in (49a) were reanalyzed as a special mode of plural formation, with vowel alternation plus plural ending -*s*, and that this pattern then was generalized by four-part analogy.)

(49a)   feet **X** foot-s   → feet-s

b)   (OE cildru >) ME child(e)**r X** child**en** → child**ren**

(50)   BVE feet   → feet-s

men   → men-s

women   → women-s

etc.

Competition can also result from (near-)synonymy, as in the common non-standard English expression of (51).

(51)   **regardless X ir**respective → **irregardless**

One of the most interesting uses of blending is found in cases like (52) and (53), for here the process is used in a quite deliberate fashion, in order to coin new vocabulary for semantic areas somewhere in-between the ones covered by the 'competing' terms.

(52)   **breakfast X lunch** → **brunch**

(53)   **chuckle X** snort → **chortle**

(from Lewis Carroll's *Jabberwocky*)

The examples so far presented share the feature that blending consists in the **'amalgamation'** of (parts of) the competing words. A less subtle alternative consists in the simple juxtaposition or **compounding** of the competing words. For instance, in certain areas of the United States, the competition of two regional expressions for 'soft drink' was resolved by the compounding in (54).

(54)   soda **X** pop → soda-pop

Compounding and amalgamation are not the only possible responses to the competition between related forms. There is some evidence which suggests that under certain conditions, such forms may 'cancel each other out', leading to the avoidance of either of the competing forms. In many varieties of American English, for instance, there is a tendency toward replacing the inherited past tense *awoke* by four-part analogical *awaked*; cf. (55). Uncertain as to which of these is the correct form, many speakers avoid the past tense form altogether, as in (56).

(55)   awake: awoke → awaked (cf. bake : baked ...)

(56)   Well, he awaked ... uh ... he awoke ... uh ... **he got up** at seven.

Such avoidance maneuvers are especially common with words which are not part of one's active vocabulary, although one may know them from other, often written, contexts. For instance, many speakers of American English consider the historically correct past tense of *forgo* to be downright ungrammatical (cf. (57a), but are equally or even more uncomfortable with the regularized form in (57b). If asked about the correct past-tense equivalent of *he forgoes* ..., they respond with expressions like (57c).

(57a)   He forwent doing the experiment*
    b)   He forgoed doing the experiment**
    c)   Well, he didn't do/decided not to do the experiment

In affixes, compounding seems to be the preferred manner of resolving competition, presumably because these morphemes generally are too short for amalgamation. Compare for example (49b) above which, concentrating only on the affixes, can be reformulated as in (58). Affix compounding has in many languages led to the introduction of new morphemes which, through four-part analogy, have acquired considerable productivity. Early Germanic, for instance, had several competing modes of forming diminutives, including the suffixes in (59a). Blending of these suffixes led to the introduction of new, productive diminutive suffixes into the derivational morphology of German; cf. e. g. (59b).

(58)   -(e)r **X** -en → -ren

(59a)   OHG   -il-   (cf. nift   'niece' : niftila   'little niece')
             -īn-   (cf. magad 'girl' : magadīn 'little girl')
    b)   -il- **X** -īn- → -ilīn-

Hence NHG *Mägd-elein* 'little girl', *Kind-lein* 'little child', etc., etc.

While affix competition thus does not commonly lead to amalgamation, something very similar to amalgamation is found in the case of neighboring affixes that are phonetically similar or identical, but morphologically distinct. Compare for instance the case of English plural and genitive -*s*. Taken by itself, each of these two affixes can attach to noun stems, as in (60a/b). However, the expected combination of the two suffixes in the genitive plural does not materialize: Only one [s] is found in this context; cf. (60c).

(60a)   chap : pl.   chap-s   [čæps]
   b)   chap : sg. G chap's   [čæps]
   c)   chap : pl. G chaps's   [čæps], not [čæpss]

Situations of this sort are found quite frequently. Historically, they seem to originate from various types of sound changes, including contraction, degemination, dissimilatory loss, and haplology. Somewhere along the way, however, they get reinterpreted as morphological, rather than phonological. In English, for instance, the 'amalgamation' of *ss* into *s* is fully productive only in the genitive plural. The juxtaposition of stem-final *s* with the plural marker -*s*, for instance, results in a very different structure, with [ə] or [ɨ] separating the two *s*-segments; cf. (61).

(61)   loss : pl. losses [lɔsəz] or [lɔsɨz]

Moreover, as a (reinterpreted) morphological process, this type of amalgamation can be generalized to new words, or to new morphological contexts. In English, for instance, the reduction of plural *s* + genitive *s* is not limited to inherited words, but is automatically generalized to new words. If for instance a new word, such as *ayatollah*, is borrowed into English and if that word acquires the productive plural affix -*s*, the formation of the genitive plural is predetermined: it must be *ayatollahs'* with a single final [s].

Amalgamations of this sort evidently do not result from blending, since there is no meaningful 'competition' between, say, 'plural' and 'genitive'. It is therefore useful to distinguish them from blendings by the term **portmanteau**. (This word is often used as synonymous with 'blending'; but it is here used with a distinctly different meaning.)

At the same time, portmanteaus are similar to blendings, in that they simultaneously convey two different 'meanings'. For the 'meaning' of the final *s* in forms like *chaps'* is not just 'plural' or 'genitive', but 'genitive plus plural' (cf. the diagram in (62)), and it is this combined meaning which is extended to new forms like *ayatollahs'*.

(62)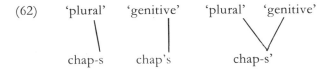

There is yet another process which can introduce forms that simultaneously convey the meanings of two earlier distinct forms, namely **ellipsis**. Ellipsis is often treated as a form of semantic change, because it is normally brought about by semantic reinterpretation or semantic fading. At the same time, however, it has a clear impact also on the formal structure of words.

Consider for instance the change in (63): The starting point is a compound consisting of the elements *male* and *chauvinist* and signifying that the person designated by the compound is an ardent advocate of male supremacy, much as the term *chauvinist* by itself denotes a person who overzealously advocates the supremacy of her/his own country or culture. Through continuous and increasingly unreflecting use of the word in this compound, the original, more general meaning of *chauvinist* begins to fade; it gets to be reinterpreted as having the narrower meaning 'ardent advocate of male supremacy'. This in turn makes the word *male* redundant. It is at this point that ellipsis steps in and eliminates the seemingly redundant part of the compound. The result is that *chauvinist* now conveys the combined meaning which *male* and *chauvinist* contributed to the earlier compound.

(63)   male chauvinist → chauvinist

The effect of ellipsis may occasionally extend beyond word structure. Thus, early French had expressions like (64), in which negation was expressed by the particle *ne*. Beside these, there also occurred sentences of the type (65), whose objects could be used both in their literal meanings and in a more extended, transferred meaning, giving some kind of emphasis to the negation. Over time, the literal meaning of some of these words began to fade, and so did their function as emphasizers. This was the case especially for *pas* which came to be reinterpreted as being simply one part of a 'discontinuous' — and somewhat redundant — marker of negation *ne ... pas*; cf. (66). This has led to a growing tendency, especially in colloquial French, to replace *ne ... pas* by the less redundant, elliptic *pas*; cf. (67). As a consequence of this change, the old negation is in effect being replaced by a word which originally had no negative connotations whatsoever. Moreover, while the old negation preceded the verb, the new one (*pas*) follows. (Similar changes have taken place in the medieval Germanic languages. Cf. also 13.3.2, ex. 112 and 16.3.6 below.)

(64) il   ne   vait/va   'he doesn't go'
      il   ne   sai   'he doesn't know'
           NEG   Verb

(65) il   ne   vait/va **pas**   'he doesn't go a **step** = **at all**'
      il   ne   sai   **rien** 'he doesn't know a **thing**
                                    = **anything** at all'
           NEG   Verb   Obj./emphasizer

(66) il   ne   va   pas   'he doesn't go'
      il   ne   sait   pas   'he doesn't know'
           NEG   Verb   NEG

(67) il   va   pas   'he doesn't go'
      il   sait   pas   'he doesn't know'
                 Verb   NEG

Typically, however, ellipsis affects the structure of (compound) words. Thus, in addition to (63), English has acquired innumerable other expressions through the process of ellipsis; cf. for instance the examples in (68).

(68) motor car   → car
      ambulance (motor) car   → ambulance
      Damask (= Damascus) fabric   → damask
      China porcelain   → china
      United States of America   → United States
      United Kingdom of Great Britain
      and Ireland   → United Kingdom

As examples like these show, ellipsis not only eliminates seeming redundancy, it also serves to shorten otherwise quite lengthy expressions. There is good reason to believe that this is an additional and very important motivation for ellipsis. For we can observe similar shortening processes applying to long words which are not amenable to ellipsis. Compare for instance the examples in (69). Developments of this sort have been referred to as instances of **clipping**. Note that they differ from such processes as ellipsis and blending by lacking any formal and/or semantic basis; their only motivation seems to be the shortening of words. As a consequence it is difficult to conceive of them as 'analogical'. But it is even more difficult to classify them as sound changes or as instances of semantic change.

(69) automobile   → auto
      mathematics   → math
      laboratory   → lab
      telephone   → phone
      omnibus/autobus   → bus
      raccoon   → coon
      influenza   → flu

Even more removed from analogical change, or any other ordinary linguistic change for that matter, is shortening by means of **acronyms** such as those in (70). Developments like these are common in modern, literate societies, where they can easily be based on the first letters or letter combinations of the written form of words. (These letters may than be pronounced as separate 'words', with the standard phonetic value of their names, or they may be combined into new words which are pronounced like ordinary, traditional words with the same or similar spelling.) Note however that early Sanskrit made similar abbreviations within an oral tradition, by combining the initial and final syllables and/or segments of longer expressions; cf. (71). (The input of (71) is a list of the personal endings of verbs. The output is used as the name for the whole set of endings and, secondarily, also for anything characterized by these endings, i. e. as a technical term for 'finite verb'.)

(70) E **U**nited **S**tates   → US [yū es]
         kitchen **p**atrol   → k.p. [kē pī]
         radio **d**etecting **a**nd **r**anging   → radar
      G **Fla**gzeug-abwehr-**k**anone   → Flak 'anti-aircraft gun'
         Geheime **Sta**ats-**po**lizei   → Gestapo 'secret state
                                                          police (of the Nazis)'

(71)   tip-tas-jhi-sip-thas-tha-mib-vas-
       mas-t(a)-ātām-jha-thās-āthāṁ-
       dhvam-iḍ-vahi-mahiṇ   → tiŋ

While shortening and the avoidance of redudancy are common tendencies in linguistic change, the opposite development is perhaps just as frequent, namely the substitution of longer, **periphrastic** expressions for shorter, morphologically or syntactically simpler forms. In some cases, such periphrasis is the result of analogical change; cf. e. g. the dialectal American English *soda-pop* of (54) above. More often, however, it is syntactic and semantic in origin. Most languages offer alternative expressions to convey (roughly) the same information, one morphological and compact, the other syntactic and periphrastic; cf. e. g. (72) and (73).

(72)   to apply   : to make an application
       to bathe   : to take a bath
       to sicken   : to make sick
       to return   : to go/come back
       the application   : the act of application
       cleverer   : more clever

(73)   Lat. Romā (Abl.)   : dē Romā   'from Rome'
             Romam (Acc.)   : ad Romam   'to Rome (goal)'
             Caesare (Abl.)   : per Caesarem   'by Caesar'
             Caesarī (Dat.)   : ad Caesarem   'to Caesar (recipient)'

Most of these periphrastic expressions have no effect on morphology; they simply continue as optional alternatives to the morphologically simpler expressions. However, it is a common phenomenon that some of these expressions do have morphological repercussions, in that they replace the morphologically simpler forms. Thus in the history of Latin, the forms on the right side of (73), with preposition plus case-form of the noun, increasingly were used in preference to the simple case-forms on the left. And in most of the Romance languages, they completely replaced the simple case forms, eventually leading to a system without any nominal case distinctions. (The development of systems without nominal case distinctions was no doubt aided by syncretism and leveling, processes which have been discussed in 9.1.4 above. However, these would not have been sufficient. In the pronouns, for instance, some case distinctions survived, as in the French accented third-singular masculine pronoun *il* (N), *lui* ('oblique') and the corresponding clitic pronoun *il* (N), *lui* (D), *le* (A).)

9.2.2. Contamination

Contamination is similar to blending in that it results from the interaction between semantically closely related forms. But unlike blending, it does not lead to a compromise form. Rather, it consists in one form becoming phonetically more similar to the other, related form, without losing its distinct identity. Cf. for instance the examples in (74) and (75). (The input for (75) consists of the words as they would have been borrowed from French without contamination.)

(74)   PRom.   *gravis 'heavy' : *levis 'light'
        →   *grevis 'heavy' : *levis 'light'

(75)   male : *femelle
        →   male : female

As these examples show, contamination occurs frequently in 'antonyms', pairs of words with related, but opposite meanings. It is also commonly encountered in the numerals; cf. the examples in (76).

(76)   PIE   *septm̩   *oktō   *newn̩   *dek̑m̩
        Lat.   (septem)   *noven   decem
                                    → novem

        Gk. dial. hepta   oktō
                            → hoktō
        Lith. → septyni   *aštuo   *nevyni
                            → aštuoni
                                       *nevyni   dešimt
                            → devyni

What is interesting about antonyms and numerals is that they are not only related semantically, but are often uttered in close juxtaposition, as in expressions like *Is that person male or female?* or as in 'rattling off' numerals in the process of counting. Note moreover that contamination is much more common between closely neighboring numerals than between numbers which are separated from each other by several others or which, say, are related by an operation like multiplication or division. These facts suggest that contaminations may well start out as distant assimilations, comparable to speech errors of the type (77). Unlike ordinary speech errors, however, they become accepted into the lexicon because they encode a semantic relationship.

(77)   **sh**ort-sleeved **sh**irts made of **s**eersucker
                        > **sh**ort-sleeved **sh**irts made of **sheersh**ucker

Although blending and contamination can be clearly distinguished in principle, the distinction is not always clear in practice. For instance, is the common non-standard English expression in (78) the result of contamination (a), or blending (b)? Similar questions might be raised in connection with example (53) and many others. (Cf. also the discussion of the data in Chart 9.1, section 9.1.2 above.)

(78 a)   irrelevant : un**reve**aling (cf. **reve**lation)
          → ir**reve**lant
    b)   **irrelevant X** unrevealing → **irrevelant**

Some linguists therefore do not make the distinction between blending and contamination. However, cases like (74)—(76) are clearly different from the blendings in (49/50) and (52/53), both in terms of their motivations and in their effects. (For instance, *brunch* is a compromise between *breakfast* and *lunch*, not just a phonetically altered form of either of these two words. On the other hand, *female* is not a compromise between *male* and **femelle*, i. e. a term for some kind of hermaphrodite; rather, it is a form of **femelle* altered to bring out its semantic relation with *male*.) Here as elsewhere, we must be prepared for the fact that the evidence often is not clear enough to permit an unambiguous choice between different possible analyses. But such ambiguities should not be taken to imply that the differences between these analyses are meaningless or nonexistent.

As in the case of blending, the short (two- or three-segment) nature of affixes favors a less subtle application of contamination, in which distant assimilation affects the whole affix, not just a part. And like the results of affix blending, the outcomes of such affix contaminations may become quite productive as the result of generalization by four-part analogy. Compare for instance the development in (79), which gave rise to a new nominal nominative plural suffix *-oy* in the masculine *o*-stems of Greek, Latin, pre-Old Irish, and probably also Lithuanian and Latvian. In Latin and Greek, four-part analogy extended this pattern of nominative plural formation also to the morphologically related feminine *ā*-stems; cf. e. g. (80).

(79)   PIE *t-**oy** w̥lk^w-**ōs** → dial. *t-**oy** w̥lk^w-**oy** 'those wolves'
        Cf. e. g. Gk. h**oi** luk**oi**, Lat. istī lupī 'the/these wolves'

(80)   Gk. *tons lukons : *tans korwans   (pl. A)
              *hoi lukoi   : X = h**ai** korw**ai** (pl. N)
                              replacing expected *hās korwās
              'the wolves'   'the maidens'

9.2.3. Recomposition, recutting

The operation of sound change frequently obscures the structure of compounds and other morphologically composite configurations, making it difficult to identify the morphological identity of the elements that make up these constructions. Consider for instance the case of E *daisy*: An earlier compound of *day's* and *eye*, a metaphorical expression for the sun to which the flower was compared, it became NE [dézī], rather than [dézay], because unstressed [ī] did not participate in the Great English Vowel Shift (for which see 7.4.5 and 8.6). Cf. (81). In the process, its compound structure was effectively obliterated.

(81)   OE dæges ēage > ME dais ei(e) > NE daisy [dézī]
        vs.   ēage >   ei(e) >   eye   [áy]

Similar differences in the treatment of stressed and unstressed syllables led to the outcomes *bosun/bo's'n* [bōsn̩] (spelled also *boatswain*) and *hussy* in (82a). However, in the case of the second word, **recomposition** has stepped in and 'restored' the compound by re-combining the normal synchronic forms for 'house' and 'wife'. (Beside reflecting sexist attitudes toward women, the difference in meaning between inherited *hussy* and restored *housewife* results from the usual tendency to differentiate competing doublets of relic and innovated formations; cf. 10.1.4 below.) The situation is similar in (82b), except that no doublets resulted.

(82a) ME bắtswein   hŭswīf   (cf. hŭs, wĭf)
       NE bosun, bo's'n   hussy   (cf. house, wife)
                        → housewife
    b) OE órc-yeard   círic(e)yeard   (cf. círice, yéard)
       NE orchard   *churchard   (cf. church, yard)
                        → churchyard

Recomposition may likewise be involved in the alternative, more 'transparent' Modern English pronunciations of *forehead* and *toward* in (83). However, these pronunciations can also be explained as due to the spelling of these forms.

(83) NE forehead [fɔrɪd] or [fɔ(r)hɛd]   (cf.fore [fɔ(r)],
                                                head [hɛd])
          toward   [tɔ(r)d] or [tʊwɔ́(r)d] (cf. to [tʊ], ward
                                                [wɔ(r)d])

In some cases, the operation of sound change merely obscures the exact location of morphological boundaries. In English and many other languages, for instance, word-final consonants often are 'resyllabified' with a following word-initial vowel, as in (84a). Other configurations may yield the same phonetic structures; cf. (84b). The resulting ambiguity of structures like [ə$nēm] has in the history of English given rise to a number of mis-interpretations, such as the ones in (85).

(84a) an aim [ə$nēm]
    b) a name [ə$nēm]

(85)   ME an ēk(e)nam(e) : NE a nickname
           a nap(e)ron   :   an apron

Recuttings of this sort are very similar to reinterpretation, except that they affect the phonological structure of morphemes or words, not their function. Although typically sporadic, recutting may like blending and contamination lead to more systematic results if it applies to affixes.

One of the most far-reaching effects of recutting is found in (86)—(89): At an early, prehistoric stage of Polynesian, passive verb forms were transparently derived from the corresponding active by the affixation of *-ia*. Loss of final consonants in the active made the derivation opaque, for now the passive differed from the active not

just by the presence of *-ia*, but also of an additional consonant. Cf.
(86). Synchronically, the assignment of this consonant is ambiguous; it
could either be analyzed as part of the root (the historically correct
interpretation), or as part of the suffix (historically incorrect). Cf. (87).
As it turns out, the latter analysis was preferred in the various Polynesian languages. This analysis, however, had important consequences,
for as a result of the recutting, the passive morpheme wound up with
a great amount of morphophonemic alternations; cf. (88). In Maori, we
can observe the first beginnings of a leveling process which is eliminating this alternation; cf. (89). Other languages have completed the
leveling and now have a non-varying passive suffix (such as Hawaiian
-ʔia).

(86)		Active	Passive	
	prehistoric:			
		*awhit	*awhit-ia	'embrace'
		*hopuk	*hopuk-ia	'catch'
		*maur	*maur-ia	'carry'
		*whaka-hopuk	*whaka-hopuk-ia	'cause to catch'
		*whaka-maur	*whaka-maur-ia	'cause to carry'

$$C > \emptyset / \underline{\qquad} \#:$$

awhi	— — —
hopu	— — —
mau	— — —
whaka-hopu	— — —
whaka-mau	— — —

(87)   Synchronic analysis:

a)

awhi	awhit-ia
hopu	hopuk-ia
mau	maur-ia
whaka-hopu	whaka-hopuk-ia
whaka-mau	whaka-maur-ia

b)   or

awhi	awhi-tia
hopu	hopu-kia
mau	mau-ria
whaka-hopu	whaka-hopu-kia
whaka-mau	whaka-mau-ria

(88)   Morphophonemic alternations:

-tia/-kia/-pia/-mia/-ŋia/-ria/...

(89)   Incipient leveling in Maori:

awhi	awhi-tia
hopu	hopu-kia
mau	mau-ria

but

whaka-hopu	whaka-hopu-tia	(for earlier -kia)
whaka-mau	whaka-mau-tia	(for earlier -ria)
etc.		

9.2.4. Folk etymology

In cases like NE *housewife* or *churchyard* (cf. example (82) above), recomposition has restored an etymologically correct compound structure. In many instances, however, historically accurate recomposition may be difficult or impossible. Consider for instance the case of Old English *sām-blind* 'half blind' and *brȳd-guma* 'man of the bride'; cf. (90). In Old English, both were transparent compounds. The former was composed of the adjective *blind* plus a prefix *sām-* 'half' which recurs in other forms (cf. *sām-bærned* 'half-burned'). The latter consisted of *brȳd* 'bride' and *guma* 'man', both of which could also be used as independent words. Along the way toward Modern English, however, *sām-* and *guma* disappeared as independent lexical items, and as a consequence of this lexical loss, the compounds of (90a) became synchronically opaque. They 'looked' like compounds, for the medial clusters [-mbl-] and [-dg-] normally are found only in morphologically complex structures. Moreover, the elements *-blind* and *bride-* were semantically and phonetically recognizable as identical to the independent words *blind* and *bride*. But the elements *sam-* and *-gum* had become unrecognizable and 'meaningless'. At this point, something akin to recomposition stepped in, namely **folk etymology** (also called **popular etymology**). This process reasserted the compound structure of our two words by identifying their opaque elements with synchronically attested independent words which were (i) phonetically similar and (ii) vaguely compatible in meaning; cf. (90b). And in so doing, it gave to these words the (synchronic) 'etymology' which they previously lacked.

(90a) OE forms   sām-blind   brȳd-guma
       Expected NE forms: samblind*   bridgum*
   b) Folk etymology: → sand-blind → bride-groom

Interestingly, folk etymology can apply not only to old compounds that have become opaque through lexical loss, but also to words which simply 'look like' compounds. For instance, English acquired the words in (91a) through borrowing, the first from French, the second from Algonquian. The French word clearly is not a compound, and whatever the native morphological structure of the Algonquian word, it certainly was different from that of its English reflex. In English, however, both words 'look like' compounds: The Algonquian word because of its medial cluster [-tč-], the French one by being trisyllabic and having two full, 'unreduced' vowels. The folk-etymological response is seen in (91b).

(91a) Fr. carriole   Alg. otček
   b) E carry-all   woodchuck
          '(covered) carriage'   'ground hog'

Folk etymology sometimes affects only part of an opaque word. Compare for instance the fate of the borrowing in (92). (In certain varieties of English, however, the folk etymology has been made complete, through the replacement of *andiron* by **handiron**.) Moreover, many forms which are or look like opaque compounds remain unchanged; cf. e.g. Engl. *cranberry* (originally *crane-berry*).

(92) Fr. andier : ME aundyre 'fire dog' (metal support for
          fireplace grill)
       → NE andiron

9.2.5. Backformation

Backformation at first appears to be radically different from the other sporadic changes and more like four-part analogy. For like four-part analogy it is proportional in nature and generalizes a pattern of morphological relationship. Compare for instance the development in (93) which has led to the replacement of older *orient* in many of its former uses.

(93)   operation   : operate
        orientation : X = orientate

There is, however, one important difference between backformation and four-part analogy: Whereas in the latter process, the newly created form is a synchronically 'derived' formation (cf. 9.1.2 above), in backformation, it is the 'base form' of a synchronic derivation. For instance, in (93), the verb *operate* is the base form from which *operation* is synchronically derived as a noun of action (or state). The historical development in (93), thus, goes 'backward', contrary to the normal direction of derivation. This difference apparently is sufficient to bring about very different reactions: Four-part analogical forms involving productive derivational processes, such as *foots*, might elicit an indulgent or condescending smile, but new backformations like the one in (94) are more likely to be met with a groan, or with a remark like *You can't say that; that's awful/that's not English* — even if they involve productive derivational processes. The difference in reaction, in turn, is probably responsible for the difference in historical behavior.

(94)   NE operation   : operate
        backformation : X = backformate (?)

Like other analogical processes, backformation may be brought on by reinterpretation. Thus, Old English had a word *pise* 'pea', pl. *pisan*, which over time came to be used only in the singular, as a mass noun like *rice*. (Cf. the relic in the nursery rhyme, *Pease porridge hot*.) In the meantime, phonetic change had taken its toll, and the word was pronounced as something like [pēz]. At this point, its final [-z] was reinterpreted as a plural marker, and the backformation in (95) yielded the modern singular form *pea*. (Similar changes have taken place in Engl. *cherry* from Fr. *cerise* [-z] and *riddle* from OE *rædels*.)

(95)   bean-s : bean
        pea-s   : X = pea

9.3. Hypercorrection

The analogical changes so far discussed are all motivated intra-dialect-ally, by the morphology (etc.) of the dialect in which they take place. However, some analogical processes are motivated by the structure of another, external dialect, which for some reason is considered to be more prestigious. Changes of this sort are referred to as **hypercorrection**.

In English, for instance, many nonstandard dialects have forms like *thinkin'* [θiŋkn̩] instead of the *thinking* [θiŋkiŋ] etc. of the standard dialects. Because many nonstandard speakers consider the latter pronunciation more prestigious, they tend to substitute standard [-iŋ] for their own [-n̩]. But not knowing the correct contexts for this substitution, they may overapply it, as in (96). (Note however that substitutions of the Y-type are quite rare; this particular hypercorrection tends to be limited to verbal forms.)

(96) thinkin'   : thinking
      readin'   : reading
      takin' [tēkn̩]   : taking
      taken [tēkn̩]   : X = taking
      kitchen   : Y = kitching

Similar developments are found in many varieties of American English: Whereas the *r*-less pronunciation of words like *cart* and *car* is prestigious in British English, in American English the older, 'r-ful' pronunciation has come to be felt to have greater prestige, and speakers from *r*-less dialects tend to affect an *r*-ful pronunciation. However, here again, the correct parameters for this substitution are not known, and hypercorrections such as those in (97) result. (Note that speakers who pronounce *saw* as [sɔr] may well pronounce other words, such as *raw* or *flaw* without [r]. This lack of consistency is quite usual in hypercorrections.)

(97) [gaːd] : [gard]   'guard'
      [gaːd] : X = [gard] 'God'
      [sɔː]   : [sɔr]   'sore'
      [sɔː]   : Y = [sɔr]   'saw'

Hypercorrection can also apply across different languages. For instance, prior to its contact with Greek, Latin had no voiceless aspirated stops. As a consequence, early borrowings from Greek omitted aspiration, as in Gk. *porphura* ⇒ Lat. *purpura* 'purple'. However, as time progressed and as Greek got to be considered a language of education and wisdom, the speakers of Latin tried to affect the more correct Greek pronunciation. Thus, a later borrowing, the adjective *porphyreticus* '(made of) purple' shows up with the Greek voiceless aspirate (as well as with a vowel spelling *y* which is intended to render the Attic-Ionic pronunciation of *u* as [ü]). Hypercorrection, then, began to impose aspiration even on native Latin words, cf. (98).

> (98)   purpura : porphyra   'purple'
>   pulcer   : X = pulcher   'beautiful'

As the formulations in (96)—(98) show, hypercorrection is a proportional process, like four-part analogy and backformation. But by operating across dialect (or language) boundaries, it differs from both.

9.4. Analogy and phonological contrast

With the possible exception of Latin aspiration, all the examples of analogical change cited so far have taken place at the 'phonemic level': They have rearranged the distribution of contrasting segments, but they have not affected the distribution of allophones or created new phonemes. Even the hypercorrect development of Latin aspirates probably did not create new phonemes, since prior to this change, aspirated stops no doubt had already been introduced through borrowings from Greek.

Because analogical change does in fact most commonly operate at the phonemic level, it is tempting to hypothesize — and has occasionally been claimed — that analogy cannot take place at the allophonic level or create new phonemes.

However, that claim is dubious. First of all, consider the West Germanic change of *ð* to *d*. As noted in 4.2 above, this change eliminated the allophonic variation between [ð] and [d] within the phoneme /d/. Although this change is not conditioned by any non-phonetic or non-phonological information, it accomplishes very much the same thing as the morphophonemic process of leveling: It eliminates alternation.

Note also the explanation for initial sonorant strengthening advanced in 8.5, example (40), reproduced below as (99). The development is indistinguishable from proportional analogical changes, except that, again, no nonphonetic information (except word-boundary) is required. In perhaps the majority of cases, the outcome of the change merges with another, distinct phoneme, such as in Catalan and Leonese Spanish *leonem* > *ʎeon* (cf. 8.5, ex. (38)); it might therefore be considered to be a rearrangement at the phonemic level. In some cases, however, such as the dialectal Spanish change in (100), its result is a new segment which, depending on the particular phonological theory one might espouse, is either a new allophone or a new phoneme. Note moreover that some Spanish dialects have extended — or 'leveled' — the change of *y* to *ǰ* to other environments; cf. (101).

(99)　Medial　　　　　　　Initial

　　　Weaker obstruent　:　Stronger obstruent
　　　Weaker sonorant　:　X = Stronger sonorant

(100)　yo　>　ǰo　'I'
　　　 ya　>　ǰa　'already'

(101)　(calle [ʎ] >)　[kaye]　>　[kaǰe]　'street'
　　　 (ella　[ʎ] >)　[eya]　>　[eǰa]　'she'

And as noted in 8.3 (ex. (13/15), in a number of Swiss German dialects, the vowel system was made more symmetrical by the analogical introduction of a new segment [œ].

Since all of these changes are primarily motivated by phonetic and phonological considerations, one might try to argue that they are not truly analogical and that therefore they do not invalidate the claim that analogy can take place only on the phonemic level. It is of course possible to argue instead that changes like these show that the distinction between sound change and analogical change is either spurious, or at least not absolute. But leaving aside this issue, which will be reexamined in Chapter 20, it is possible to cite some evidence which suggests that even morphologically motivated analogy can operate on allophones and/or create new phonemes.

For instance, certain Eastern-Seaboard American English dialects at one point had the allophonic length alternation in (102). Subsequently, the vowel length of verbal forms like *pad* was generalized to other verbal forms in which it was not originally motivated; cf. (103a).

Homophonous nouns, however, remained unaffected; cf. (103b). The length generalization thus clearly is morphologically restricted and therefore cannot be considered as case of purely phonetic or phonological generalization; it must be viewed as an instance of morphological leveling and/or four-part analogy. But as the difference between [pæːdiŋ] (verb) and [pædiŋ] (noun) shows, that morphologically conditioned analogical change has made length unpredictable and thus phonologically contrastive.

(102)   Before final voiced segment Elsewhere

       pad [pæːd]

                                    padding [pædiŋ] (noun/verb)

                                    pat   [pæt]

                                    patting [pætiŋ]

(103a)   Verb:

         Leveling: [pæːd] / [pædiŋ] → [pæːd] / [pæːdiŋ]

         Four-part analogy: [pæt]   : [pætiŋ]

                            [pæːd] : X = [pæːdiŋ]

vs. b)   Noun: [pædiŋ] unchanged

Or consider the case of the Sanskrit *r*-stems: Their expected accusative and genitive plural forms are as given in (104). Early Sanskrit preserves a trace of this pattern in the genitive plural form *svas-r-ām* 'of the sisters'. Elsewhere, however, we find the forms in (105). These differ from the corresponding forms in (104) by having a long syllabic sonorant *r̄*, an inserted nasal in the genitive plural, the accusative plural ending -*s* or -*n* (rather than -*as*), and a previously nonexistent gender distinction in the accusative plural. All of these differences can be explained by a single development: four-part analogy on the model of the *i*- and *u*-stems — which have the long syllabic sonorants *ī* or *ū*, an inserted nasal in the genitive plural, the accusative plural ending -*s* or -*n*, and a gender distinction in the accusative plural; cf. the relevant *i*-stem forms in (106). (The difference in the form of the inserted nasal (*ṇ* vs. *n*) is attributable to the difference in environment: *ṇ* occurs after *r*, *n* after other segments.)

(104)   pl.   A   m.   *pit-r-as   'fathers'

              f.   *māt-r-as   'mothers'

          G   m.   *pit-r-ām

              f.   *māt-r-ām

(105) pl. A m. pit-ŕ̥-n
         f. māt-ŕ̥-s
      G m. pit-ŕ̥-n-ām
         f. māt-ŕ̥-n-ām

(106)

			i-stems	*r*-stems
m.	pl.	I	agn-i-bhis 'fires'	pit-r̥-bhis
		A	agn-ī-n	X = pit-ŕ̥-n
		G	agn-ī-n-ām	Y = pit-ŕ̥-n-ām
f.	pl.	I	mat-i-bhis 'minds'	māt-r̥-bhis
		A	mat-ī-s	X = māt-ŕ̥-s
		G	mat-ī-n-ām	Y = māt-ŕ̥-n-ām

What is important in the present context is the fact that the developments in (106) took place both in dialects which already had a long syllabic r̥̄ from other sources, and in dialects which lacked the segment. In the latter dialects, which form the basis for Classical Sanskrit, the four-part analogical change in (106) thus introduced a previously nonexistent phonological contrast; cf. the near-minimal pair in (107).

(107) pitr̥̄nām 'of the fathers' : r̥̄nam 'debt, guilt'

10. Analogy:
Tendencies of analogical change

While the preceding chapter has examined the types of analogy, this chapter is concerned with the question whether there are any natural tendencies or directionalities in analogical change. Any answers to this question, even if incomplete, will first and foremost increase our understanding of linguistic change. Secondly, they might also be helpful in choosing between alternative possible analyses. Everything else being equal, we would select that analysis which better agrees with what is known to be more natural.

Two Polish scholars, Jerzy Kuryłowicz and Witold Mańczak, have dealt most comprehensively with this issue. This chapter, therefore, is organized mainly around their hypotheses. Though both of the same nationality, the two scholars are far apart in their approach to the problem.

Kuryłowicz's work is essentially introspective, based on the feeling for the direction of analogical changes which he had acquired over many years as a practicing historical and comparative linguist. The major emphasis of his work is on morphology. And his resulting generalizations are stated as 'laws'.

Mańczak, on the other hand, based his observations on a statistical investigation of the analogical changes postulated in standard hand-books on the historical grammar of various European languages. (Some of these observations are based on very large data collections, but the data basis for others is quite limited.) His emphasis tends to be more on the phonological nature of words and morphemes, including their length. And his generalizations are stated as tendencies.

10.1. Kuryłowicz's 'laws' of analogy

Kuryłowicz originally postulated six 'laws' which in his view govern the application and direction of analogical changes. These 'laws' are not intended to predict when analogical change will happen, but rather

what will happen if there is analogical change. (Like most other traditional historical linguists, Kuryłowicz was fully aware of the fact that
this is the best we can do; a prediction of when change will or must
occur is impossible.)

10.1.1. The first 'law'

(I) A bipartite marker tends to replace an isofunctional morpheme
consisting of only one of these elements, i. e. a complex marker
replaces a simple marker.

Example (1) may serve to illustrate what is meant by this 'law': Old
High German had several inflectional classes for masculine nouns; cf.
(1a). Through regular sound change, these would be reflected in
Modern German as (1b). Instead, we find the pattern in (1c), with
generalization of the pattern of *Gast : Gäste* and not of *Baum : Baume*.
The former pattern has the **bipartite** or **complex** plural marker [-ə]
PLUS root-vowel alternation or umlaut. The latter has a **simple** marker
consisting only of the ending [-ə]. And as (1) demonstrates, it is the
bipartite or complex marker which has been generalized, not the simple
one.

(1a) OHG   gast : gest-i   'guest(s)'
                      boum : boum-a   'tree(s)'
   b) NHG (expected) Gast : Gäst-e   [gast] : [gestə]
                      Baum : Baum-e* [baum] : [baumə]
   c) NHG (attested) Gast : Gäst-e
                      Baum : Bäum-e

Similar developments can be found elsewhere. But examples (2) and
(3) illustrate a very different common tendency, namely to generalize
simple markers at the expense of complex ones.

(2a) OE   wearm : wearm-ra
                      lang : leng-ra
   b) NE (expected) warm : warm-er
                      long : leng-er*
   c) NE (attested) warm : warm-er
                      long : long-er

(3a)	OHG	sg.	1	gib-**u**	:	fạr-**u**
			2	gib-**ist**	:	fer-**ist**
			3	gib-**it**	:	fer-**it**
		pl.	1	gẹb-**am**	:	fạr-**am**
			2	gẹb-**at**	:	fạr-**at**
			3	gẹb-**ant**	:	fạr-**ant**
b)	NHG	sg.	1	gẹb-**e**	:	fạhr-**e**
			2	gib-**st**	:	fähr-**st**
			3	gib-**t**	:	fähr-**t**
		pl.	1	gẹb-**en**	:	fạhr-**en**
			2	gẹb-**t**	:	fạhr-**t**
			3	gẹb-**en**	:	fạhr-**en**
				'give'		'go, drive'

Example (2) shows that English generalizes the simple comparative marker *-er*, without preceding root-vowel alternation. (Cf. also 9.1.3, examples (22/23).) And (3) demonstrates a similar development in the German first singular present, where the older bipartite marker of words like 'give' is replaced by a simple marker created on the analogy of the pattern of words like 'go, drive'. (Bipartite markers are retained where the paradigm of 'go, drive' likewise has bipartite markers; cf. the second and third persons singular.) The combination of (1) and (3) further shows that one and the same language may at times obey Kuryłowicz's first 'law', and disobey it at other times. This issue will be considered again in later sections of this chapter.

At this point, it might however be mentioned that Kuryłowicz's first 'law' has greater relevance if we ignore the 'letter of the law' and instead consider its 'spirit', which is that <u>forms which are more 'clearly'</u> <u>or 'overtly' marked tend to be preferred in analogical change</u>. As the further discussion in this chapter will show, this broader concept of **'overt marking'** will turn out to be better justified than Kuryłowicz's overly narrow notion of 'bipartite marking'.

10.1.2. The second 'law'

(II) Analogical developments follow the direction 'basic form' → 'derived form', where the relationship between basic and derived forms is a consequence of their spheres of usage.

10.1.2.1. 'Basic' → 'derived'

The first part of this 'law' is simply a restatement of the conditions which proportional analogy must meet in order to be called four-part analogy and in order to have the potential for systematicity (cf. 9.1.2 with example (8/8')): It must extend a relationship of 'synchronic derivation' between a 'basic' and a 'derived' form to other lexical items, resulting in a new derived form.

Of the above examples, both (1) — which agrees with Kuryłowicz's first 'law' — and (2) — which disagrees with it — conform to this part of the second 'law'. (The case of example (3) is more complicated, since it is by no means clear whether or why one of the two paradigms should be considered more 'basic'.)

In fact, most (intradialectal) proportional analogy conforms to this principle, and so do at least some non-proportional changes. (But see also below.) For instance, recomposition (cf. 9.2.3) affects compounds that are 'derived' by the process of compounding and makes the component parts of these words agree more closely with the corresponding and more 'basic' independent words. Similarly, in folk etymology, opaque compounds or words that look like compounds are remade into transparent compounds of more 'basic' independent words that are synchronically attested.

However, in much or even most of non-proportional analogy, it is difficult to see how Kuryłowicz's second 'law' could apply, and in many cases there is clear evidence that in fact it does not apply. (But see also the next section.)

Thus, in most cases of contamination, it would be difficult to establish which of the two terms involved in the change is more basic. Consider for instance the common phenomenon of contamination in numerals (section 9.2.2, example (76)): There is no principled way in which we can establish that, say, the numeral '7' is more basic than '8'.

The inapplicability of Kuryłowicz's second 'law' is especially evident in the case of leveling. As developments like those in (4) show, closely related languages, starting out from the same Verner's-Law basis, may level in entirely opposite directions. There is thus no predetermined directionality. Moreover, contrary to the provisions of the second 'law', German levels the *r*-alternant of the 'derived' past tense formations into the 'basic' present tense.

(4)   OE cēozan, cēas, curon, (ge)coren : NE choose, chose,
chosen

OHG kiosan, kōs, kurun, (gi)koran : NHG küren, kor,
gekoren

Developments like these suggest that the applicability of Kuryłowicz's second 'law' of analogy is restricted to certain analogical developments. Most prominent among these is proportional analogy. In addition, also recomposition and folk etymology seem to obey the 'law'. But a case could perhaps be made for considering these two processes to be proportional as well. For instance, we can motivate the replacement of opaque *hussy* by transparent *housewife* (9.2.3, ex. (82)) in terms of a proportion of the type (5).

(5)   post + man : postman
house + wife : X = housewife

Within the area of proportional analogy, however, one process does not follow the pattern suggested by Kuryłowicz's second 'law', namely backformation. For as noted in 9.2.5, this process affects the basic, not the derived term of a proportion.

At the same time, it has also been noted that backformation is much less frequent and systematic than four-part analogy. If, then, we take Kuryłowicz's second 'law' of analogy as a statement not of immutable law, but of general tendency or naturalness in proportional change, then the first part of this 'law' can be considered empirically well justified: It essentially restates the traditional wisdom that four-part analogy is more common and in some ways more 'natural' than backformation.

10.1.2.2. The 'sphere-of-usage' provision

The provision that 'the relationship between basic and derived forms is a consequence of their spheres of usage' likewise covers territory familiar to earlier historical linguists. The import of this provision is as follows: Of any given set of forms or morphological classes, the one which has a greater sphere of usage is more 'basic' than the others.

Rephrased in this manner, the sphere-of-usage provision accounts for the fact that productive patterns are more likely to be generalized than unproductive ones. For as observed in 9.1.2, productive morphological categories tend to have a larger membership than less productive ones. However note the existence of isolated developments in the opposite direction, such as Engl. *dive : dived* → *dive : dove*. These provide further evidence that Kuryłowicz's 'laws' are tendencies, rather than exceptionless rules.

The sphere-of-usage provision likewise covers the traditional wisdom that '**basic vocabulary**' tends to be more resistant to analogical change than other vocabulary. Crosslinguistically, certain words are more 'basic' or indispensable for human communication and survival than others, no matter what the accidents of cultural surroundings. This basic vocabulary includes 'function words' like *and, or, but,* pronouns such as *I, you, this,* verbs and nouns referring to basic activities or phenomena such as *eat, sleep, do; sun, moon, rain.* Notice in this regard that, as observed in 9.2.1, pronouns proved more resistant to the Romance loss of case distinctions than did the nouns. The case is similar in English; cf. pronominal *I : me : my* with three case distinctions vs. nominal *man : of man/man's,* with two distinctions at best.

The issue of resistance to analogical development is interesting and important also from another point of view: The Romance (and English) loss of case distinctions involves a great amount of what in section 9.1.3/4 has been called morphological leveling. The fact that the more basic pronouns were not affected by these leveling processes suggests a certain revision of the conclusions reached in the preceding section: While basicness may not make a particular form or formation the basis or **pivot** for leveling, it seems to enable it to **resist** leveling. This conclusion is supported by a large amount of other evidence, some of which will be presented in the further dicussion of this section. This resistance may appear to lend additional justification to Kuryłowicz's second 'law' of analogy. However, as formulated, that law addresses only the question of what can be a pivot for analogical change, not the issue of resistance. Note moreover that the notion 'resistance to paradigmatic leveling' must be qualified. It is applicable and justified only in cases of partial leveling. Complete paradigmatic leveling, such as the one in example (4) above, may affect even basic forms.

Also the notion 'resistance of basic vocabulary to analogical change' needs to be qualified. It does not imply an absolute immunity from analogy. First of all, there are cases where basic vocabulary is affected by analogical processes that originated in less basic vocabulary. For instance, in Latin the distinctly pronominal genitive and dative singular forms in *-īus, -ī* often are replaced by the corresponding nominal forms; cf. (6). Resistance thus is only a tendency. Even more commonly, basic vocabulary may undergo its own peculiar analogical developments, which do not affect other lexical items; cf. for instance the dialectal American English development in (7). Examples like these demonstrate that resistance, where it is found, applies to analogical developments that originate in non-basic vocabulary. It does not preclude changes limited to basic vocabulary.

(6)   Lat. sg. A dominum : illum
             sg. G dominī   : X = illī (beside older *illīus*)
             sg. D dominō   : Y = illō (beside older *illī*)
                    'lord'   'he, that one'

(7)   my   : mine
      your   : X = your'n
      our   : Y = our'n
      ...   ...

While some of the territory covered by the sphere-of-usage provision is quite familiar to traditional historical linguistics, the provision potentially covers a much wider area. Moreover, by including productivity, basic vocabulary, and other factors under one single term, it makes an important generalization.

Consider for instance languages of the Indo-European type, with case distinctions between a 'nominative', 'accusative', and other, 'oblique' cases. In such nominal systems, the nominative tends to be more basic than the other cases — everything else being equal. (For an example where 'everything else' is not 'equal', cf. 10.1.5 below.) This hierarchy of basicness can be derived from the sphere-of-usage provision: In systems of this sort, the nominative is the most 'unmarked' case and will be used exclusively (or at least preferentially) in contexts (i) — (iii) below in which, a priori, other cases could just as well be employed. As a consequence, its sphere of usage is less circumscribed than that of other cases.

(i) In naming or identifying persons or objects, sometimes even if the verb of the question eliciting this act of naming might otherwise govern a different case. Thus, dictionary entries tend to be given in the nominative case.

(ii) In contexts of 'noun-phrase extraction' or 'prolepsis', such as Engl. *the boy, I see his dog,* not *the boy's, I see his dog.*

(iii) As the case of the subject of (non-passive) sentences. Note that while the case of other nominal constituents (such as the accusative of direct objects) can be conceived of as 'governed' by another element in the sentence (such as the verb), the subject is not governed by other overt constituents. A priori, its case marking therefore should be 'free'.

Diachronic consequences of the basicness of nominative case can be seen in the fact that for instance in Latin, the pivot for transfer from one nominal inflectional class to another ordinarily is the nominative singular, not other case forms. Thus the agreement of nominative singular forms in paradigms like the ones in (8) has led to the (optional) inflectional transfers in (9). The fact that the pivot is the nominative singular, rather than plural, is the consequence of another hierarchy of basicness which will play a role also in other, later examples: In languages with number distinctions, the singular is the most basic formation.

(8)

		o-stems	consonant stems
sg.	N	puer	pater
	G	puer-ī	patr-is
	D	puer-ō	patr-ī
	A	puer-um	patr-em
	Ab.	puer-ō	patr-e
pl.	N	puer-ī	patr-ēs
	G	puer-ōrum	patr-um
	D	puer-īs	patr-ibus
	A	puer-ōs	patr-ēs
	Ab.	puer-īs	patr-ibus
		'boy'	'father'

(9a) *o*-stems: socer, socr-ī, ... → socer, socr-is, ...

      pater   : patris   'father'

      socer   : X = socris   'son-in-law'

  b) cons. stems: pauper, pauper-is, ... → pauper, pauper-ī, ...

      puer   : puerī   'boy'

      pauper   : X = pauperī   'poor'

Example (19) illustrates resistance of the nominative singular to analogical processes: An alternation -wō(n)/won/un- has been leveled out in Lithuanian, except in the nominative singular.

(10)   PIE   Lithuanian

sg. N   *ḱwō(n)   šuo
    A   *ḱwon-m̦   šun-ī
    G   *ḱun-es   šun-(e)s
    D   *ḱun-ey   šun-i(e)
        ...   ...

pl. N   *ḱwon-es   šun-(e)s
    A   *ḱwon-n̦s   šun-is
    G   *ḱun-ōm   šun-ū
        ...   ...

In verbal systems based primarily upon tense distinctions, the present tends to be the most basic. This again can be related to the sphere-of-usage provision: Generic statements usually are put in the present, rather than any other tense. Thus, *The horse **is** a four-legged animal* is a more likely generic statement than *The horse **was** a four-legged animal*. (But note that similar generalizations do not seem to be possible for systems primarily based upon aspect, i.e. (roughly) the feature which differentiates Engl. *I go to school* from *I am going to school*.)

Diachronic consequences of the basicness of the present tense can be seen in (11) and (12). While the development in (11a) has not become acceptable in Standard English, it is at least intelligible. Developments in the opposite direction are just about uninterpretable (cf. (11b)), except those involving the most productive derivational processes. (12) illustrates present-tense resistance to the leveling of the Verner's-Law alternation between *h* and *g*. (Note however that this resistance was temporary. In Modern German, the *g* has been leveled throughout the paradigm: *schlagen, schlug, geschlagen*.)

(11a)   dial. Am. E sing   : sang   : sung
                     bring   : X = brang : Y = brung
     b)   brought : bring
                     sought   : X = sing*
                     taught   : Y = ting*

(12)		Early/pre-OHG	Later Old High German
pres.	slāhan	slāhan	'beat, slay'
past sg.	sluoh	sluog	
past pl.	sluogun	sluogun	
pple.	(gi)slagan	(gi)slagan	

However, if tense is only optionally marked, the sphere-of-usage provision may bring about very different results. Thus, at an early stage in the development of Indo-European, present tense was optionally marked, as in the endings in (13a). The unmarked or *i*-less forms in (13b), which could be used for both present and non-present tenses, therefore had a greater sphere of usage and thus were more basic. (In some of the Indo-European dialects, these unmarked forms could be optionally marked by a prefixed 'augment' *e-* if they were used with past-tense reference; cf. e. g. (14a/b).) As a consequence, in early Indo-European, developments like the four-part analogical generalization of the non-past second singular *-s* to the corresponding present tense in (14) were not uncommon. Subsequently, however, present-tense marking became obligatory and by way of polarization, the (indicative) *i*-less forms took on past-tense value. (In dialects with optional augment *e-*, this prefix soon became obligatory in the new past tense formation.) At that point, the present became more basic, and analogical developments tended to proceed in the opposite direction; cf. e. g. the generalization (in (15)) of the Latin present-tense third-singular ending *-t* to the past tense.

(13)   sg. 1   2   3   pl. 3

a)   -m-i   -s-i   -t-i   -nt-i
b)   -m   -s   -t   -nt

(14a)   pre-Greek: non-present   : present
          sg. 3   (e-)pher-e-∅   : pher-e-i   'carry'
          sg. 2   (e-)pher-e-s   : pher-e-hi
                               > pher-e-i

b)   Analogy:
          sg. 3   (e-)pher-e∅   : pher-ei∅
          sg. 2   (e-)pher-es   : X = pher-eis

c)   Common Greek: non-pr. → past : present
          sg. 3   ephere   : pherei
          sg. 2   epheres   : phereis

(15a) pre-Latin   present   past
       sg. 2   am-ā-s   : am-ā-b-ā-s 'love'
       sg. 3   am-ā-t   : am-ā-b-ā-d
    b) Latin   > am-ā-b-ā-∅
       sg. 2   am-ā-s   : am-ā-b-ā-s
       sg. 3   am-a-t   : X = am-ā-b-a-t

In addition, the indicative mood is more basic than the imperative or other modal formations which have a more circumscribed sphere of usage. Active voice similarly is more basic than passive. And third person forms are more basic than the forms of other persons.

The latter fact may appear surprising. For first of all, in Latin and Greek, the first person singular is used as the citation forms of verbs. And secondly, we tend to think of the human race as rather self-centered and as therefore inclined to considering the first person singular as most basic. However, in terms of actual usage, third-person forms are used with considerably greater frequency than any other forms of the paradigm. Thus, even when we express our own cherished opinion in the first person (as in *I think that* ...), the opinion itself is more likely to be expressed in the third person (such as ... *it will rain tomorrow*). Moreover, many verbs can be used only in the third person singular, such as *It is raining, snowing*; but there seems to be no class of verbs which can be used only in the first singular. Finally, crosslinguistically, the third person is most commonly used in generic statements, such as *The horse is a four-legged animal, One might say that* ..., *People/they say that* ..., *It is said that* ... It is interesting in this respect that at least one ancient language, Sanskrit, used the third person singular form as citation form and referred to it as *prathama-*, i. e. 'first (person)'.

This basicness of the third person, especially if it is combined with the basic number category 'singular', likewise has diachronic consequences. One example is found in the development of (14) above, in which the third person serves as the pivot for change. However, unambiguous examples of this type are not easy to come by. Thus, the origin of the (pre-)Greek third person singular ending *-e-i* in (14) is fairly controversial. Some linguists have accounted for it by a four-part analogy in which the second person serves as the pivot. And (15) provides clear evidence for the second person serving as the pivot for a change in the third person. True, the affected form is in the synchronically nonbasic past tense. Moreover, the generalization of overtly marked *-t* at the expense of *-∅* may be interpreted as a consequence of the tendency toward overt marking, the spirit of Kuryłowicz's first 'law'; cf. the preceding section. Still, example (15) does not fit in very well with the notion that the third person is the most basic form in the paradigm.

Perhaps the most striking well-documented example in which a third person singular serves as the pivot for analogical change is the one in (16), where all forms of the verb 'to be' have been remade on the basis of the third-singular form, except the third plural. But note that this development can only very vaguely be motivated by a four-part analogical proportion: If Old Polish *jest* is reinterpreted as having a ∅ ending, the model of (17) might suggest that the other forms of this verb should be composed of *jest* plus the relevant personal endings. However, the endings which this model would produce (cf. (17)) are different from those which are actually found (cf. (16)). The latter are identical to the clitic forms of the verb 'to be' given in (18). The manner in which these clitics got attached to the third singular form can perhaps be accounted for as a combination of compound-blending and four-part analogy; cf. (19). And in this process, the analogy of (17) may have played a certain role. But the required proportion is rather different from the usual formulae of proportional analogical processes. With all of these special assumptions and qualifications, the change in (16) becomes a rather dubious example of a third person singular serving as the pivot for proportional analogical change. And as noted earlier, only in proportional analogy does basicness determine possible pivots for change.

(16)		OCS	OPol.		NPol.
sg.	1	jes-mĭ	jeś-m	→	jest-em
	2	jes-i	jeś	→	jest-eś
	3	jes-tŭ	jes-t	=	jest
pl.	1	jes-mŭ	jes-my	→	jest-e**śmy**
	2	jes-te	jeś-cie	→	jest-e**ście**
	3	s-ǫtŭ	są	=	są

(17)	sg. 3	da-∅		jest-∅
	1	da-m	X =	jest-(e)m(*)
	2	da-sz	Y =	jest-(e)**sz***
pl.	1	da-my	Z =	jest-(e)**my***
	2	da-cie	Σ =	jest-(e)**cie**/jeście*
		'give'		

(18) Clitic forms:

    sg. 1 -em
        2 -eś
        3 $\emptyset$
    pl. 1 -eśmy
        2 -eście
        3 $\emptyset$

(19) sg. 3 jest$\emptyset$ = jest + $\emptyset$ (clitic)
      1 X   = Y = jest + -em (clitic)
      ...   ...

While the evidence for third persons serving as pivots in proportional change thus is rather meager, there is good evidence that third persons tend to resist analogical developments. Thus, in the Polish developments above, both third-person forms, singular and plural, remain unchanged. Similarly, the earlier, pre-Slavic leveling of the singular root alternant *es- > jes- to the plural failed to affect the third plural; cf. (20). (Cf. also the resistance of the third plural in the similar Pali leveling in 9.1.1, ex. (6).)

(20)
		Proto-Indo-European	Proto-Slavic
sg.	1	es-mi	jes-mǐ
	2	esi	jes-i
	3	es-ti	jest-tǔ
pl.	1	**s**-me/os	**jes**-mǔ
	2	**s**-te	**jes**-te
	3	s-e/onti	s-ǫtǔ

10.1.3. The third 'law'

(III) A structure consisting of a basic member and a subordinate member forms the foundation [i. e. serves as a pivot] for a basic member which is isolated, but isofunctional.

One of the examples which Kuryłowicz's uses to illustrate this 'law' is given in (21). Here the root of pl. 1 *lev-ons* seems to be the 'basic member' and the suffix *-ons*, the 'subordinate member'. The expected outcome [lyεv] of Old French sg. 2 *lieves* appears to be the 'basic isolated member' (in that it lacks an overt 'subordinate' ending), but 'isofunctional' (by being marked for person, just like the first plural). And as the example shows, in Modern French the expected [lyɛv] has been remade to *lèves* [lɛv] on the model of the vocalism of pl. 1 *levons*.

(21)   OFr.   sg. 2   lieves   :   pl. 1   levons   'lift'
       NFr.   lèves   :   levons

Examples like these make it appear that this 'law' is intended to account for the fact that leveling may affect more basic forms (such as the second singular in (21)). Note however that such developments are in direct conflict with Kuryłowicz's second 'law'. Kuryłowicz seems to suggest that this conflict is a natural consequence of the fact that morphemes can enter into proportional and non-proportional relationships with each other.

However, if this 'law' is intended to account for the possibility of leveling, its fomulation is inadequate. For as formulated, it is incapable of accounting for the leveling in (4) above, reproduced here as (22). At most, it might be able to account for leveling in the past-tense forms, where *cēas/kōs* can be taken to be 'basic and isolated' and *curon/kurun* is interpretable as 'basic + subordinate member'. But leveling in the present tense or in the past participle cannot be explained. Moreover, neither this 'law' nor any other can account for the fact that English and German leveling proceeded in completely opposite directions in spite of the fact that the two languages started out with the same morphology and morphophonemic alternations.

(22)   OE cēozan, cēas, curon, (ge)coren   :   NE choose, chose,
                                                chosen
       OHG kiosan, kōs, kurun, (gi)koran   :   NHG küren, kor,
                                                gekoren

10.1.4. The fourth 'law'

(IV) When as a consequence of a morphological [= analogical] change, a form undergoes differentiation, the new form takes over its primary ('basic') function, the old form remains only in secondary ('derived') function.

This 'law' addresses the question of what happens if after an analogical change has taken place, the old and the new forms continue to coexist. (Cf. the discussion of doublets in 9.1.1.) It sums up the traditional wisdom that such doublets usually are secondarily differentiated, such that the new form takes over the basic and productive meaning or function, while the old form survives in secondary, nonproductive, or marginal contexts. (It is because of this knowledge that scholars concerned with recovering linguistic prehistory through reconstruction seem to devote an inordinate amount of time hunting for forms which are synchronically marginal, aberrant, or 'unmotivated'. For it is forms like these which are most likely to preserve traces of archaic patterns which elsewhere have been analogically replaced by innovated, more productive patterns.)

Kuryłowicz's fourth 'law' can be seen in action in pairs like the following, where the innovated forms (on the right) invariably have the more basic, productive meaning or function.

(23) hussy   : housewife
      brethren : brothers
      elder   : older

Examples like these can be proliferated ad infinitum. Genuine counterexamples are not easy to find. The only major exception lies in blendings that have been created to designate a meaning intermediate between the meanings of two other, preexisting words, such as *brunch* = 'a meal which has characteristics of both breakfast and lunch'. Presumably, because such words are created to convey a new meaning, differentiation is built into the very change by which they arise. There is thus no need for further, secondary differentiation.

What is easier to find are examples which seem to neither confirm nor disconfirm the 'law'. This is especially common in cases where doublets result from leveling in two different directions, such as (24) and (25). What is interesting is that in cases of this sort, meaning differentiation does not seem to follow any consistent pattern. Thus in (25a), neither of the two forms is significantly more productive or unmarked than the other, in (25b) the form in -*ow* is more productive or 'alive', and in (25c) the form in -*ow* is marginal. Note that this lack of directionality actually supports Kuryłowicz's fourth law of analogy: Since both resulting paradigms contain old and new forms, they should have an equal chance of becoming productive or marginal.

(24)   pre-Lat. sg. N   *deiwos > deus   'divine, divine being, god'

            G   *deiwī   > dīvī

→ Lat. sg. N   deus 'god' beside   dīvus 'divine'
        G   deī   dīvī

(25)

		OE	ME	NE	
a)	sg. N.	sceadu	schade	shade	shadow
	pl. N	sceadwe	shadwe/ow	shades	shadows
b)	sg. N	mǣd(u)	mede	mead	meadow
	pl. N	mǣdwe	medwe/ow	meads	meadows
c)	sg. N m.	hālig	hali	holy	
	pl. N m.	hālge	halwe/ow		hallow

(cf. Halloween = All Hallow E'en 'All Saints Eve')

(Note: Some of the leveling may have begun in Middle English)

A genuine counterexample is perhaps found in the development of (26). The change in (26a) reflects the fact that Latin neuters commonly became masculines in the Romance languages. The development in (26b) involves a less common reinterpretation of the old neuter plural in -*a* as a feminine singular in -*a*. If we consider the latter change to be the major innovation (because it creates a new, parallel paradigm), then we have here a case in which the innovated form, *graine*, has the more restricted meaning 'seed (grain)', while the older form, *grain*, has the less restricted, more basic meaning 'grain, kernel, etc.' However, one may well wonder whether the change from neuter to masculine was not just as much an innovation as the one to feminine. In that case, the situation would be the same as in (24) and (25), with either innovated form having a priori equal chance of becoming productive or marginal. Other potential or published counterexamples run into similar difficulties.

(26)   Latin   Analogical develop-   French outcome
                          ment

a)   grānum (neuter)   → *grānus (masc.)   grain 'grain, etc.'
     pl. grāna   *grānī

b)   grāna (neuter pl.)   → *grāna (fem. sg.)   graine 'seed'
                     pl. *grānae

Recently, however, Kuryłowicz's fourth 'law' of analogy has come under new attack which is buttressed by an impressive and massive array of counterexamples. These include items like those in (27) in which, it is claimed, 'a form is regularized in some special function but remains irregular in its "primary function". These behave exactly the opposite way from what Kuryłowicz's principle predicts.'

(27)   Primary Function   Special Function   *Maple Leafs*

a)   teeth   Sabertooths (tigers)

       leaves   silverleafs 'white poplars'

b)   mice   Mickey Mouses 'police cars'/'trivialities'

c)   wolves   wolfs 'aggressive men'

       worse   badder 'tougher'

At first blush, these examples (which can easily be multiplied) seem to constitute a formidable indictment of Kuryłowicz's fourth 'law'. But closer examination reveals that they have no bearing whatsoever on the 'law'. For the distinction 'primary function' vs. 'special function' is not a consequence of the regularization process; it predates it. Put differently, forms like *silverleafs* are not based on *leaves* or the corresponding singular *leaf*. In fact, the proportion required for such a development is downright preposterous; cf. (28c). Rather, it is based on *silverleaf*; cf. (28b). That form, in turn, is derived from *leaf* by the process of compounding; cf. (28c). And it is this process of derivation which imparts to *silverleaf* its 'special function', just like, say, the addition of plural *-s* imparts to *leaves* its 'special function' of being a plural. Note however that such processes as compounding or pluralization do not create the kind of doublets which Kuryłowicz's fourth 'law' is concerned with. (The examples in (27c) and perhaps also in (b) are slightly different, in that there is no overt morphological derivation in *wolf* 'aggressive man' vs. *wolf* (animal). However, also here the semantic differentiation precedes the regularization of the plural.)

(28a)   silver + leaf   → silverleaf

         cf. red + beard   : redbeard

b)   staff   : staff-s

         ...   ...

         silverleaf   : X = silverleafs

c)   staff   : staff-s

         leaf   : X = silverleafs (??!)

While forms like those in (26) have no relevance for Kuryłowicz's fourth 'law', they do have some bearing on his second 'law' as modified in section 10.1.2.2 above: They are in perfect agreement with the notion that basic formations (such as *leaf*) are more resistant to analogical developments than are derived forms (like *silverleaf*).

10.1.5. The fifth 'law'

(V) In order to reestablish a distinction of central significance, the language gives up a distinction of more marginal significance.

The import of this 'law' is quite transparent and its effect is readily illustrated. Consider for instance the example in (29a): Regular sound change created a situation in the prehistory of Spanish in which nominative singular and nominative/accusative plural had the same endings; only the accusative singular had a different form. As a consequence, the paradigm failed to distinguish number in the nominative forms. This unbalanced relationship was remedied by the replacement of the nominative singular on the analogy of the relationship between the accusative forms; cf. (29b). Note that this analogy affects the nominative singular, the most basic form in the paradigm in terms both of case and of number. It thus goes radically counter to the direction specified by the second 'law' of analogy. However, the present 'law' justifies the development; for the singular/plural distinction is considered to be more basic than overt case distinctions.

(29a)   Latin   Spanish
        sg. N   clāvis   >   *llaves → llave
        A   clāvem   >   llave
        pl. N   clāvēs   >   llaves
        A   clāvēs   >   llaves
    b) Analogical development:
        A   llaves   :   llave
        N   llaves   :   X = llave

This 'law', thus, reminds us that there may be a ranking between different 'basic' formations. Some distinctions are more important than others; and analogical change may serve to reestablish such distinctions.

The only problem with this 'law' is that it does not tell us which distinctions are more basic than others. It is true, in the Indo-European languages, number distinctions seem to be generally more 'vigorous' than case distinctions. Similarly in the verbs, number distinctions seem to be more basic than person distinctions. Consider for instance the 'Ingvaeonic' syncretism in verbal plural endings discussed in 9.1.4, ex. (36/37). These precede by several centuries the syncretism in number which we find in the past tense of Modern English or in the entire verbal inflection of Modern Danish, Swedish, and Norwegian. And tense distinctions tend to be most faithfully preserved. (Thus, even Modern Danish, Swedish, and Norwegian retain tense distinctions, in spite of the fact that they have entirely lost the earlier distinctions both of person and of number.) Even in Indo-European, however, we can only speak of tendencies, not of exceptionless 'laws'. For instance, many of the colloquial varieties of Modern German and French exhibit a syncretism between simple and 'compound' past tenses (cf. (30)), in spite of the fact that both languages preserve verbal number distinctions and a fair amount of person distinctions, as well. And similar developments have been observed in other languages. Perhaps even more importantly, it is not clear to what extent these tendencies hold in non-Indo-European languages.

> (30)   Literary/archaic German   Colloquial German
>
>   ich ging   'I went'   ich bin gegangen 'I went'
>   ≠ ich bin   = ich bin gegan-
>   gegangen   'I have gone'   gen   'I have gone'

10.1.6: The sixth 'law'

(VI) The first and second term of a proportion [can] belong to originally different systems: one belongs to a prestige dialect, the other to a dialect imitating it.

This 'law' provides for the possibility of hypercorrection, for which see the examples given in section 9.3 above. The only contribution which Kuryłowicz makes in this context is the claim that in proportions of this sort, the native dialect is basic, the imitated dialect, derived (in his technical sense). This observation is intuitively appealing, since one's native dialect would naturally appear to be primary. Moreover, a redefinition of this sort makes it easier to account for 'reverse hypercorrections' of native speakers of a prestige dialect when trying to imitate a less prestigious dialect. For instance, speakers of Standard German tend to produce forms as in (31) when attempting to imitate Bavarian dialect. For some of these speakers the imitation may in fact be motivated by prestige considerations; they may consider it desirable to speak Bavarian, so as to be socially accepted in Bavaria. Others, however, may imitate the dialect merely in order to tell somebody else 'how those Bavarians speak' or even for the purpose of derision.

(31)   Standard German   Bavarian

ein(s) [ain(s)]   [oạn(s)]   'one'
zwei   [tsvai]   [tsβoạ]   'two'
drei   [drai]   X = [droạ]   'three'
                   vs. correct [drɛi]

The only difficulty with Kuryłowicz's redefinition is that the Standard German speakers who are guilty of such hypercorrections are not necessarily native speakers of the standard dialect. Their own native dialect may be a different, generally northern non-standard dialect of German, or even a foreign language. The term 'native' therfore needs to be replaced by something like 'primary' dialect.

10.2. Mańczak's 'tendencies' of analogical change

Mańczak proposed nine hypotheses concerning the natural direction or tendency of analogical change. These hypotheses were formulated in response to Kuryłowicz's 'laws' of analogy and thus logically presuppose them. It is therefore possible to discuss them more briefly, by way of reference to the fuller discussion of Kuryłowicz's claims.

10.2.1. The first 'tendency'

(I) Excepting the forms of a paradigm, longer words more frequently are remade on the model of shorter words than vice versa.

Of the numerous examples which Mańczak adduces in favor of this hypothesis, virtually all are such that the 'shorter' form also happens to be the 'basic' form in Kuryłowicz's sense. This includes forms which become basic through reinterpretation, as in the English folk etymology *brŷdguma* > **bridegum* → *bridegroom* on the model of uncompounded, more 'basic', *groom*; cf. 9.2.4, ex. (90). This 'tendency' therefore agrees with the predictions made by Kuryłowicz's second 'law'.

10.2.2. The second 'tendency'

(II) Root alternation is more often abolished than introduced.

This 'tendency', for which Mańczak amasses a very large amount of evidence, covers the phenomenon of leveling. And as Mańczak correctly points out, this widespread tendency toward leveling is in direct conflict with the development in examples like (1), reproduced below as (32), which Kuryłowicz used to exemplify his first 'law' of analogy. For examples of the latter type generalize, rather than level root alternations.

(32a)	OHG	gast	:	gest-i	'guest(s)'			
		boum	:	boum-a	'tree(s)'			
b)	NHG (expected)	Gast	:	Gäst-e	[gast]	:	[gestə]	
		Baum	:	Baum-e*	[baum]	:	[baumə]	
c)	NHG (attested)	Gast	:	Gäst-e				
		Baum	:	Bäum-e				

Mańczak's second 'tendency' provides an important and necessary note of correction to Kuryłowicz's claims. For as the discussion in 10.1 has shown, Kuryłowicz's laws by and large work fairly well for proportional analogical developments, but not for leveling. However, Kuryłowicz must have been aware of such contrary developments, for as noted in 10.1.3, his third 'law' apparently was designed to deal with leveling, albeit unsuccessfully. Moreover, even if root alternations may be more commonly eliminated than generalized, the fact remains that there are quite a number of cases in which alternations are generalized. It thus appears as if the conflict between the two scholars may be irreconcilable. (But note the discussion in 10.3 below.)

10.2.3. The third 'tendency'

(III) Excepting cases where there is one word with ∅-suffix and another with a clearly marked suffix, longer inflectional forms are more often remade on the model of shorter forms than vice versa.

This 'tendency' is similar to the first one, except that it applies to inflectional forms, whereas the first 'tendency' deals with words. In many of Mańczak's examples, the shorter forms are more basic in Kuryłowicz's sense. Cf. e. g. (33), where the longer — and less basic — infinitive and similar forms are remade on the model of the shorter — and more basic — third person singular. In other cases, however, the morphological facts are none too clear; even the force of many examples is uncertain. It is therefore difficult to evaluate the appropriateness of this hypothesis.

(33)

	Latin	pre-French		French	
sg. 3	calefacit	calefat		chauffe	'heat'
inf.	calefacere	calefacere	→ calefare	chauffer	

10.2.4. The fourth 'tendency'

(IV) ∅-endings are more frequently replaced by full ones than vice versa.

This well-supported 'tendency' accounts for instance for the generalization of the -er-plural in German neuters; cf. (34) as well as 9.1.3, ex. (28/30). And compare (35) for a similar development in English. But note that the 'tendency' is in perfect agreement with the spirit behind Kuryłowicz's first law of analogy, namely the preference for more overt marking.

Mańczak's hypothesis nevertheless is valuable. For it demonstrates that the tendency toward more overt marking is not restricted to Kuryłowicz's claimed preference for bipartite over simple markers. (Example (34) happens to involve generalization of a bipartite marker, but as (35) shows, the major motivation is replacement of the ∅-plural ending. Interestingly, English has retained such ∅-plurals in the case of the words for certain animals, such as *sheep, deer*. Moreover, having been reinterpreted as a special property of this class of nouns, ∅-marking

has even had some productivity; cf. e. g. OE *fugol : fuglas* 'bird : birds'
vs. NE *fowl : fowl/Ø*.)

(34)		Old High German	Modern German
	sg. N/A	kalb : wort	Kalb : Wort
	pl. N/A	kelb-ir : wort-Ø	Kälb-er : X = Wört-er

(35)		Old English	Modern English
	sg. N/A	stān : word	stone : word
	pl. N/A	stānas : word-Ø	stone-s : X = word-s

10.2.5. The fifth 'tendency'

(V) Monosyllabic endings are more frequently replaced by polysyllabic ones than vice versa.

Also this hypothesis agrees with the spirit, and in many cases even
with the letter of Kuryłowicz's first law.

10.2.6. The sixth and seventh 'tendencies'

(VI) The forms of the indicative more frequently bring about the
remaking of other moods than vice versa.

(VII) The forms of the present more frequently bring about the
remaking of the other tenses than vice versa.

These 'tendencies' cover some of the corollaries of Kuryłowicz's
sphere-of-usage provision. But the latter covers much larger territory.
Moreover, the early Indo-European remakings of present by non-
present forms (cf. 10.1.2.2, ex. (14)) are difficult to reconcile with
Mańczak's sixth 'tendency', whereas for Kuryłowicz, they are natural
consequences of the sphere-of-usage provision.

10.2.7. The eighth and ninth 'tendencies'

(VIII) If there is a difference between the inflection of a geographic
noun and a common noun, which otherwise are similar, the local

cases generally present an archaic character, while in the non-local cases innovations are more common.

(IX) If a paradigmatic form of a geographic noun undergoes an analogical change under the influence of another form of the same paradigm, the starting point of that change more often lies in the local cases than in the non-local ones.

Also these 'tendencies' agree with the sphere-of-usage provision of Kuryłowicz's second 'law': In geographical nouns, locational cases tend to be used more commonly than others (including the nominative). Thus, though one might say things like *Chicago is a nice city, Chicago is awful*, expressions like *He's going to Chicago, He lives in Chicago, He is from Chicago* are probably more frequent.

An example of this interesting special corollary to Kuryłowicz's second 'law' is the fact that the names of many German, French, Italian, etc. place names have the form of old locational cases; cf. (36)—(38). In these names, the old locational case has become the nominative singular or base form. Note, however, that in a goodly number of other place names, such as G *Mühlheim, Freising*, the old nominative singular form seems to have been generalized. (Note that the *-ing-* of words like *Kissingen* and *Freising* originally had the same function, that of naming the descendants of the town founder or of a clan leader. Similarly, the *-haus-* of *Schaffhausen* and the *-heim* of *Mühlheim* have near-identical meanings: 'house' and 'home', respectively.) What explains forms like *Freising* and *Mühlheim* is probably the fact that beside their more specific membership in the class of place names, they also belong to the more general, overall class of nouns. They may therefore follow the latter, more general pattern (in which the nominative singular is the most basic form), rather than the specific pattern of place names.

(36)		Old High German	Modern German
	pl. D	kissing**um**	Kissing**en** (sg. N)
	pl. D	scafhūs**um**	Schaffhaus**en** (sg. N)
vs.	pl. D	stein**um**	Stein**en** (pl. D of *Stein* 'stone')

(37)		Latin	French
	pl. D	Turrīs	Tours (baseform)
		Aquīs	Aix
vs.	sg. N	aqua	eau 'water'

(38)		Latin	Italian
sg.	D	Florentiae	Firenze (base form)
pl.	D	Aquīs	Acqui (base form)
vs. sg.	N	aqua	acqua 'water'

10.3. Evaluation and reconciliation; the polarity principle

Of Kuryłowicz's six 'laws', the one that seems to hold up best is the fourth, for which genuine counterexamples are hard to find. This 'law' therefore provides a very reliable guide to historical linguistic research.

Also the second, fifth, and sixth 'laws' appear to be pretty sound. But note that for the fifth 'law' to be fully meaningful, more would have to be known about the criteria which determine the relative basicness or centrality of different morphological categories. And as noted in 10.1.6, the sixth 'law' needs to be further modified to account for hypercorrections not based on one's native dialect.

The second 'law' likewise has a number of shortcomings. As formulated, it is applicable only to proportional changes. It acquires more general validity if it is extended to cover also the phenomenon of resistance to analogical change. Even then, it can only be considered a tendency, not a 'law'. For resistance to analogical change is not absolute. Moreover, backformation runs completely counter to the 'law'. At the same time, if the 'law' is taken as a statement of tendency, the relative rarity of backformation would follow naturally.

The second 'law' is especially significant because of its sphere-of-usage provision. As the discussion in 10.1.2.1, as well as in 10.2.6/7 has shown, this provision makes it possible — and mandatory — to define the concept of basicness not merely on the basis of overt morphological marking (as in E *book : book-s*), but also where such marking is absent and even in cases where the overt marking is contrary to the derivational direction (as in E *(s)he sing-s : they sing-Ø*, where the basic, 'unmarked' third singular present is morphologically marked, while the 'derived' plural lacks a morphological marker).

The third 'law', however, is opaque and thus offers no helpful insights. Even if it were certain that it was intended to cover leveling, its formulation is not able to account for many, perhaps most, cases of leveling.

It is precisely because of the issue of leveling that the first 'law' likewise runs into difficulties. At the same time, however, the spirit behind it, namely that there is a tendency toward more overt marking, seems to be well justified. This has been shown especially in the discussion of Mańczak's fourth and fifth hypotheses.

Most of Mańczak's hypotheses are in essential agreement with Kuryłowicz's second 'law' and therefore add little to our understanding of analogical change.

However, his fourth hypothesis is significant because of its implication that the tendency toward overt marking is not limited to Kuryłowicz's 'bipartite' markers.

Mańczak's second 'tendency', the tendency toward eliminating morphophonemic root alternations, constitutes a significant and potent counterclaim to Kuryłowicz's first 'law', at least in so far as the latter affects bipartite markers involving a morphophonemic change in the root. This 'corrective note' to Kuryłowicz's 'laws' of analogy and their heavy emphasis on proportional processes is Mańczak's most important contribution. And the contrasting claims of Kuryłowicz's first 'law' and Mańczak's second 'tendency' constitute the area where the two scholars are farthest apart.

However, Mańczak's claim that his second 'tendency' disproves Kuryłowicz's first 'law' cannot be accepted. For even if root alternations may be more commonly eliminated than generalized, the fact remains that there are quite a number of instances in which such alternations are generalized. Mańczak's second hypothesis cannot do any more than brand examples of this sort as statistical deviations. Kuryłowicz's first 'law', on the other hand, suggests a motivation for these developments, namely the tendency toward more overt marking.

The proper evaluation of Mańczak's and Kuryłowicz's conflicting claims seems to be that both have pointed to important and equally valid, general tendencies in analogical change: On one hand, we have a tendency toward more overt marking, toward the clarification or maximalization of morphological contrast; cf. Kuryłowicz's first 'law' and the spirit behind it, as well as his fifth 'law'. On the other hand, there is a rival tendency toward simplification and regularization of the more phonological aspects of morphology, i. e. of morphophonemic alternations. We can explain these opposing tendencies as stemming from what has been called the **polarity of language**, the fact that language has a dual aspect, with one side concerned with meaning, the other with phonological form. And this, in turn, derives from the fact that the purpose of language is to convey meaning through phonological form. As a consequence, what may be useful or desirable from the point of view of one of these two aspects or 'poles' (such as, say, more overt morphological marking) may be undesirable or may complicate matters on the other side.

There is however a second, possibly complementary, way of looking at this situation: The development of 'bipartite' markers in accordance with Kuryłowicz's first 'law' is 'useful' in so far as it leads to more overt marking in larger, morphologically complex entitities (such as the German plural *Bäum-e*). But at the same time, it obscures the morphological identity of some of the individual morphemes which make up that larger entity (thus, German has two different forms, *Baum-* and *Bäum-*, for one and the same morpheme). Mańczak's second 'tendency', on the other hand, leads to unique, unvarying phonological representations of individual morphemes and thus to a more direct relationship between meaning and form. (Cf. the slogan 'One meaning — one form'.) But in so doing it may require sacrificing important morphological contrasts in the larger, morphologically complex, forms that are composed of these individual morphemes. Under this alternative view, then, both leveling and the tendency toward overt marking are motivated on the meaning side of language, but by different aspects of meaning.

This alternative, entirely meaning-based view is appealing for a number of reasons. First, as noted in 9.1.3/5, the distinction between leveling and proportional analogy is not absolute. Not only can the two processes cooperate, we also find morphological (rather than just morphophonemic) leveling, as well as morphophonemic proportional analogy. Developments like these suggest that leveling and proportional analogy are more closely related than often thought. (In fact, some linguists have tried to use proportions not only for four-part analogy, but also for leveling.) Secondly, beside the opposing tendencies of leveling and proportional analogy, we find another set of opposing tendencies, namely the tendency toward redundancy (or 'periphrasis') on one hand and toward ellipsis on the other; cf. the discussion in 9.2.1. These two tendencies bear a certain resemblance to the motivations behind Kuryłowicz's first 'law' and Mańczak's second 'tendency', namely the tendency toward more overt marking and the tendency to eliminate or reduce (morphologically unimportant) alternations. At the same time, however, it is quite clear that both redundancy and ellipsis are semantic, not phonological, phenomena.

Whichever of these two views may be more correct, we must recognize the existence of two opposed, but equally valid, tendencies in analogical change. While this observation may not be particular helpful as a guideline for historical linguistic analysis, it does contribute to our understanding of the nature of linguistic change.

11. Analogy and generative grammar

As noted in Chapter 9, analogy traditionally has been defined as a process which is eminently conditioned by non-phonetic factors: morphology, syntax, and/or semantics. However, there are other types of change which like traditional analogy consist in secondary responses to the operation of sound change, reanalysis, etc., but which involve morphological information only in a very general, non-specific fashion (such as word boundaries) or even purely phonetic information (such as syllable boundaries).

Traditionally, a number of these changes have been subsumed under sound change, under the assumption that word boundary is a phonetic environment. Certain other changes have been dealt with as analogical, such as the British English generalization of the word-final $r/\emptyset$ alternation (cf. 9.1.5, ex. (45/47)). However, the complete regularity of such developments usually was not accounted for. In the case of other, more complex, developments, traditional historical linguists often found it very hard to explain what was going on.

This chapter will deal with processes of this sort and will show that especially the last-mentioned, 'complex' developments can be more readily accounted for by means of synchronic rules as they are posited in generative phonology. In the process of this discussion, there will also be an evaluation of claims made by generative phonologists concerning the nature of sound change and analogy.

11.1. Background

This section addresses in greater detail the problems which traditional approaches to historical linguistics run into. The subsections will present developments of increasing complexity; and the changes discussed in the final subsection will be of a complexity which virtually defies a traditional account.

11.1.1. Word boundary in sound change

Many sound changes, as traditionally formulated, involve word boundary as a critical conditioning environment. However, since sound change is defined as not being conditioned by nonphonetic (or nonphonological) factors, the inclusion of word boundary in sound change formulations must be considered suspect. For word boundary (#) does not ordinarily have any unique phonetic representation. For instance, in English, it may coincide (a) with silence at the beginning or end of an utterance (marked by ##); (b) with the boundary of a phonological phrase, i. e. a slight break or slow-down, often but not necessarily preceded by a rise in pitch or intonation (marked by /); or (c) with no appreciable phonetic realization at all. Compare for instance the 'word boundary' after *immoral* in the examples under (1). (Note that these examples are assumed to be spoken at a normal rate of speech; in very slow, deliberate speech, each word might be followed by /.)

(1 a)   Let me conclude by saying that racism is immoral ##

   b)   Torture and human rights violations are immoral / no matter who commits, commissions, or condones them

   c)   The most immoral regimes have been founded on religious, racial, or social extremism

A good example of this traditional way of using word boundary as an environment for 'sound change' is final devoicing. As noted in 5.1.7, this very common process cannot be explained as assimilatory if word boundary is taken to be the conditioning environment. However, in utterance-final, prepausal position, the change can be accounted for as an assimilation. In fact, many languages, including many varieties of English, have at least a slight decrease of voicing in utterance-final obstruents, even though elsewhere, word-final obstruents remain unchanged.

The question, then, arises as to how in many languages, this prepausal development can become a general word-final process. The most plausible answer is that this is the result of analogical generalization or **extension**. (In generative linguistics, the term 'generalization' is commonly used for a different, synchronic phenomenon. To avoid confusion, historical generalization processes will be referred to as 'extensions'.)

Since prepausal environment normally coincides with word-final position, prepausal devoicing may lead to the word-final morphophonemic alternation of obstruents between voiceless (before pause) and voiced (elsewhere); cf. (2 a). Such an alternation can be eliminated in two ways. Either the voiced, non-prepausal alternant is extended. (In this case it may appear as if there has been no change at all.) Or the voiceless, prepausal alternant is leveled into all word-final environments. It is by this latter process, then, that languages seem to acquire word-final devoicing; cf. (2 b).

(2) OHG   tag 'day'
a) pre-NHG   tak / ___ ##
            vs.   tag / ___ #   (elsewhere)
b) NHG   tāk / ___ #

A similar explanation can be given for the process of syllable-final devoicing. Although unlike word boundary, syllable-final position is a phonetic environment, its phonetic properties do not seem to be conducive to devoicing. In fact, languages with syllable-final devoicing are quite rare. Rather, also in this case devoicing seems to result from leveling: Since ## usually coincides with syllable boundary ($), devoicing may be extended also to this environment. The result of this process is found in many varieties of Standard German (cf. (3 b)), although others have only word-final devoicing. In many dialects, the developments in (3 b) are limited to slow, hyper-careful speech. But for words like *radle*, certain dialects only have forms with syllable-final devoicing. In these dialects, *tl* and *dl* cannot be tautosyllabic but must always be separated by a syllable boundary. (Cf. 7.3.8 for the tendency to avoid such clusters.)

(3) NHG Redner 'speaker'   radle 'I go by bycicle'
a)   [rē$dnər]   [rā$dlə]
b)   [rēt$nər]   [rāt$lə]

Many other changes can be similarly motivated as extensions of originally prepausal developments. Compare, e. g., the various extensions of originally utterance-final accent retraction in 5.4.7 above.

While developments like these can be accounted for as levelings, they differ from ordinary leveling in one very interesting and important respect: Like sound change, they take place in a completely **regular** fashion, not with the irregularity expected even in the most systematic analogical processes. Moreover, like sound change and unlike ordinary analogical change, developments like the ones in (2) and (3) appear to be quite sweeping, affecting all qualifying words at roughly the same time. It is therefore not surprising that they are commonly treated as regular sound change, not as secondary, analogical extensions of originally more limited sound changes.

It should be noted, however, that many changes for which word boundary has been claimed as a conditioning environment may in fact be sound changes, but attributable to other, purely phonetic factors. For instance, the loss of Engl. [k] in words like *know* (cf. 5.3.2, ex. 70) vs. its retention in *acknowledge* etc. is commonly accounted for as in (4 a) and (5 a). But an alternative analysis in terms of syllable position is readily available; cf. (4 b) and (5 b). In this alternative analysis, the retention of [k] in *acknowledge* results from the fact that in medial position, [k] and [n] would be separated by a syllable boundary. As a consequence, [k] does not occur syllable-initially and thus fails to qualify for the change.

(4 a) $k > \emptyset \ / \ \# \ \underline{\quad} \ n$
   b) $k > \emptyset \ / \ \$ \ \underline{\quad} \ n$

(5)   know   acknowledge
   a)   #kn-   #Vkn-
      Change (4 a) #∅n-   — — — —
   b) $kn- VknV-
      Change (4 b) $∅n-   — — — —

Similarly, Old Irish syncope (cf. 5.3.4) has often been formulated in terms of word position, as in (6 a). However, the formulation in 5.3.4, ex. (88) = (6 b) below is preferable, since it accounts not only for examples like (7 a) (= 5.3.4, ex. (87)), but also for developments as in (7 b) below, where the accented syllable does not happen to be the first syllable in the word. (Palatalization and certain other fine phonetic details have been left unmarked in these examples.)

(6 a) $V > \emptyset \ / \ \# C_0 V C_0 \ \underline{\quad} \ C_0 V C_0 \ \underline{\quad} \ C_0 V \ ...$
   b) $V > \emptyset \ / \ [V, + \text{acct.}] \ C_0 \ \underline{\quad} \ C_0 V C_0 \ \underline{\quad} \ C_0 V \ ...$

(7 a) pre-OIr. námeddas   > [náβ∅da] 'enemies' (pl. A)
   b) pre-OIr. nīs-éssberodd > [ni-éb∅rəd] 'they do not speak'

11.1.2. Regular leveling I

Regularity and 'sweeping' application is not limited to cases like the extension of prepausal devoicing, but may be found also in developments which are much more clearly analogical.

Compare for instance the British English extension of the $r/\emptyset$ alternation in (8) and the discussion in section 9.1.5 above.

(8)   the matter [ə$\emptyset$] was   :   the matter   [ər] is
    the idea   [ə$\emptyset$] was   :   X = the idea [ər] is

A similar, but slightly more complex development is the following from the history of German: Word-final devoicing was introduced as early as Middle High German (through sound change and analogical extension); cf. (9). Between Middle High German and the modern period, another development took place, namely the loss of final [-ə]. It appears that this loss originally had different environmental restrictions in the different dialects. There is reason to believe that in some of the dialects, syllable structure played a role, such that [-ə] was lost after disyllabics, but not after monosyllabics. But leveling and dialect mixture have brought about a situation in which [-ə] is obligatorily lost in certain contexts, optionally lost in others, and ordinarily retained in a third set of contexts; cf. (10). What is interesting in the present context is the fate of obstruents which become word-final through this **'ə-loss'**. Given that final devoicing had taken place much earlier than ə-loss, one would expect the forms in (10 a/b) to appear without final devoicing, cf. (11 a). What we find instead are forms with final devoicing; cf. (11 b). (Here as elsewhere in this chapter, **FD** = final devoicing.)

(9)   OHG   tag   :   pl.   taga   'day'
    MHG   tac [tak]   :   tage

(10)   pre-NHG   NHG
(a)   sg. D   Montage   :   Montag   'Monday'
(b)   sg. D   Tage   :   Tage/Tag   'day'
(c)   pl. N   Montage   :   Montage   'Mondays'
    Tage   :   Tage   'days'

(For ease of exposition, forms are cited orthographically. -e = [-ə].)

(11) OHG   sg. N tag   sg. D tage
              FD   tak   — — —
          pre–NHG   tāk   tāgə
              ə-loss   — — —   tāg
      a) Expected NHG   tāk   tāg
      b) Attested NHG   [tāk]   [tāk]

The final devoicing in forms like sg. D [tāk] can again be accounted for as resulting from analogy: The historical process of ə-loss brought about a word-final morphophonemic alternation between voiced and voiceless obstruents. Leveling then eliminated this alternation by extending the voiceless alternant, just as it did in examples (2) and (3) above.

This interpretation is supported by studies from the turn of the century which show what appears to be an intermediate stage in dialects which in respect to final devoicing are closely affiliated with Modern Standard German. In this intermediate stage, the word-final obstruents of forms which have undergone ə-loss exhibit an alternation between the inherited voicing and an innovated, analogical voiceless pronunciation. On the other hand, words like the nominative singular, which never had the [-ə], have no such alternation. Cf. example (12).

(12) Older   sg. N tak   sg. D tagə
      Dialectal   tāk   tāg/tāk

What is interesting is that this intermediate stage appears to have been very short-lived. The general development consists in a fairly sweeping and completely regular replacement of the expected voiced obstruents by the analogical voiceless ones.

A very different development has taken place in many of the Southern German dialects. Here the general tendency is to have final voicing, not only in forms with earlier final -ə, but also in forms like the nominative singular; cf. (13).

(13) Older   sg. N tak   sg. D tagə
      Southern   tōg   tōg

This situation cannot be accounted for by the assumption that these dialects never had final devoicing. Rather, the final voiced obstruent of the nominative singular must be the result of leveling. For first of all, some words of the type *tag* appear with voiceless, rather than voiced final obstruents; cf. (14 a). These words, then, have leveled the voiceless, rather than the voiced alternant. Secondly, final obstruents are always voiceless in uninflected adverbials of the type (14 b). Words of the latter type are especially instructive, in that they are **'non-alternating'** in origin: Unlike nouns and verbs, these adverbial formations had no inflectional endings and therefore could not acquire a voiced/voiceless alternation through ə-loss. They are therefore not likely to be remade through paradigmatic leveling.

(14 a)		sg. N	sg. D	base form	inflected form
	Earlier	herd	herdə	yuŋg	yuŋgə
	Attested	hɛrt	hɛrt	yuŋkx	yuŋkx
		'stove'		'young'	

b) OHG sīd > MHG sīt > Southern dial. [sɛyt] etc. 'since'

A very similar development is found in Yiddish, an originally Southern German dialect. What is especially interesting is that in this language it is possible to trace the history of the development. And this history is markedly different from what we find in the more northern-based Standard German and related dialects. Far from being sweeping and regular, leveling here proceeds at the slow, word-by-word, and rather irregular pace which one would expect in 'traditional' analogical change.

There is thus a considerable difference between the 'northern' and 'southern' responses to the alternations introduced by ə-loss. Traditional historical linguists could — and contrary to some recent misconceptions, did — recognize both types of developments. However, accounting for both of them as leveling, i. e. in terms of one and the same process, made it difficult, if not impossible to explain why one type of development is just about as regular as sound change, while the other is characterized by the typical irregularity of traditional analogy.

11.1.3. Regular leveling II

Even more complex cases of 'non-traditional' analogical extension can be found. Cases of this sort cause the greatest difficulties for traditional historical linguists. In some cases, scholars can be seen groping for a solution and finally giving up. In other, more successful cases, they may talk about the extension of a particular pattern, but without specifying the analogical model for that extension.

The following examples from Slavic, especially from Polish, may serve as an illustration of complex developments of this type.

After the loss of the so-called jers (for which cf. 2.2 (f)), which in effect undid the Slavic open-syllable conspiracy (cf. 8.5 above), the Slavic dialects re-acquired word-final obstruents. These obstruents in turn underwent final devoicing in the majority of languages. As a consequence, there arose morphophonemic alternations of the type (15).

(15)   moroz   sg. G   moroza   'frost'
    Ru.   moros   moroza

Up to this point, the situation is no different from the word-final devoicing in German (cf. (2) above). However, in some of the Slavic languages (Russian, Polish, Czech), a complication enters into the picture: Word-final obstruents optionally are voiced, rather than voiceless, if the following word begins in a voiced obstruent (other than *v* < semivocalic *w*) and if the two words in question are semantically and/or syntactically closely connected. Cf. (16).

(16)   moroz byl   'there has been a frost'
    Ru.   moros byl
        beside   moroz byl

Moreover, the same option exists for originally voiceless obstruents, such as *mot*, sg. G *mota* 'spendthrift'; cf. (17).

(17)   mot byl   'he has been a spendthrift'
    Ru.   mot byl
        beside   mod byl

In these languages, then, earlier final voiced and voiceless obstruents have the outcomes in (18).

(18)   [+ voice] beside [− voice] / ___ # [+ obstr., + voice]
        [− voice] / ___ # [+ obstr., − voice] and elsewhere

In order to try to account for the innovated voiced alternant, let us introduce the following terminology. Alternations of the type (16/18), which are conditioned by segments that occur across a word boundary, are referred to as **external sandhi**. Alternations as in (19), which do not include word boundary in their conditioning environment, are called **internal sandhi**. (The term sandhi, lit. 'putting together', originated in the essentially generative grammar of the ancient Indian grammarians. But it is now widely used both by generativists and by non-generativists.)

We can try to account for the dialectal Slavic innovation in (16) and (17) as being modeled on the inherited internal sandhi of obstruent voicing in (19). Here, the voicing contrast is neutralized before obstruent, such that obstruents must agree in voicing with the following obstruent.

> (19) Ru. žëg 'he burned'   : žgla 'she burned'
> tak 'so'   : tagže 'also'
> babušek (pl. G)   : babuška (sg. N) 'grandmother'
> verëvok (pl. G)   : verëfka (sg. N) 'string'
> (These forms are cited in a quasi-phonetic transcription.)

The extension of this internal-sandhi pattern to external sandhi can then be motivated by the morphophonemic proportional analogy in (20). However, here as elsewhere, we need to ask ourselves why unlike traditional analogical developments this change should be regular, in the sense that it affects all qualifying segments. What complicates matters even more is the fact that this regular change is optional for all qualifying segments. That is, we have here a case of 'regular optionality'.

> (20)   Internal obstruent sandhi : External obstruent sandhi
> [− voice] / __ [+ obstr., − voice] : [− voice] / __ # [+ obstr., − voice]
> [+ voice] / __ [+ obstr., + voice] :   X   / __ # [+ obstr., + voice]

A further development has taken place in the Polish dialects of Cracow and Poznań. Here word-final obstruents are obligatorily voiced before ALL following word-initial voiced segments. The result is an external-sandhi distribution as in (21). Compare (22) for some examples of word-final voiced obstruents before # plus voiced non-obstruent.

> (21)   [+ voice] / ___ # [+ voice]
> [− voice] elsewhere

(22) pre-Polish   rud lutsk^{y}i   bok levɨ
      General Polish   rut lutsk^{y}i   bok levɨ
      Cracow, Poznań   rud lutsk^{y}i   bog levɨ
                        'human race'   'left side'

This development is even more difficult to account for in traditional terms. We can vaguely talk of an extension of the voiced/voiceless alternation. We can perhaps try to account for it more formally as an instance of leveling of the voiced alternant to all instances of # plus voiced segment; cf. (23). But the parameter for that leveling is entirely phonetic (except for the fact that a word boundary is involved). But if it is leveling, one may ask why the process extended an alternant which even before # plus voiced obstruent had earlier been only optional. Why did it not simply eliminate the word-final alternation between voiced and voiceless obstruents? Note moreover that the outcome of the change is a pattern without any precedent in the language, since in internal sandhi, the alternation between voiced and voiceless obstruents is limited to the environment before obstruent.

(23)   ___ # [+ voice, + obstr.]   ___ # [+ voice, − obstr.]
             [+ voice] beside [− voice]   [− voice]
        →   [+ voice]   [+ voice]

Finally, here again we must wonder why this 'leveling' is regular, unlike traditional, typically irregular leveling.

As will be shown in the rest of this chapter, a generative approach to linguistics makes it not only easier to account for complex developments like the Polish ones, it also makes it possible to explain why certain 'leveling' processes are regular and thus differ from ordinary, traditional analogical changes.

11.2. Purpose and methods of generative phonology

In the preceding, historically oriented, section, German final devoicing has played a significant role. Let us now consider this phenomenon from a synchronic point of view.

The result of the historical process of prepausal devoicing and its extension to word-final (or syllable-final) position is that in Modern German, forms like *Rad* 'wheel' and *Rat* 'council/counsel' no longer are distinct. Both are now pronounced as [rāt]. In spite of this phonetic identity, however, native speakers of German tend to deny that the two forms are pronounced the same and to insist that the first ends in a [-d], while the second has [-t]. The question surely must arise as to what is the basis for this reaction.

It is questions of this sort which **generative phonology** tries to address. More generally, the purpose of generative phonology (and generative grammar as a whole) is to characterize native speakers' (subliminal) knowledge of the grammar of their language. This knowledge, it is assumed, permits speakers not only to assert that what is phonetically identical is grammatically different (and vice versa), but also to make judgments concerning the correctness of given utterances, and perhaps most importantly, to learn to speak (or to acquire) their own native language.

In the view of generative grammar, this grammatical knowledge should be characterized by a system of rules which relate different formations to each other and which ultimately 'map' meaning into phonetic structure. Associated with this rule system is a lexicon containing, at the minimum, the lexical items of the language, together with various features or markings which determine or govern their interaction with the rule system.

These assumptions are shared by all present-day schools of generative grammar. Where these schools differ is in respect to more specific issues such as the questions of what are permissible rules, how morphological vs. phonological generalizations should be accounted for or 'captured', etc. These differences will be of no consequence for the subsequent presentation, which instead will focus on the most basic and probably most generally shared assumptions and practices of generative phonology — to the extent that they are relevant for historical linguistics.

Let us now return to the question of German final devoicing and the native speakers' assertion that [rāt] 'wheel' and [rāt] 'council/counsel' are really different, the first one ending in [d], the second one in [t]. It is not altogether difficult to find out what this assertion is based on: While the nominative forms of the two words are identical, other forms, such as the genitive singular and nominative plural, differ in their root-final consonants. As (24) shows, one root ends in [d], the other in [t]. When native speakers claim that [rāt] 'wheel' has a final

-[d], they merely assert the identity of this form with the [rād-] which appears in forms like [rād-əs]: In spite of their phonetic differences, [rāt] and [rād/rēd-] share the same meaning and thus are the 'same word' (or different realizations of the 'same word'). The situation is similar for [rāt]:[rāt-/rēt-] 'council/counsel'.

(24) sg. N rāt   rāt
      sg. G rād-əs   rāt-əs
      pl. N rēd-ər   rēt-ə

Generative phonology tries to capture this 'sameness' by positing a single **'underlying form'** /rād/ for the word 'wheel' and by stating that this form is realized **'on the surface'** as [rād], [rēd], and [rāt]. To account for the realization of word-final /d/ as [t], and for the fact that all other word-final obstruents are realized voiceless, generative phonology then invokes a (synchronic) **rule** of the type (25). The application of this rule is illustrated in the synchronic **derivation** in (26). Note that as the formulation in (25) and application in (26) show, the rule makes the generalization or 'predicts' that all obstruents, whether underlyingly voiced or voiceless, are realized as voiceless in word-final environment. Further, the rule can be said to relate the different surface forms of the word to each other, as well as to the corresponding underlying forms.

(25) (FD) [+ obstr.] → [− voice] / ___ #

(26)   /rād#/   /rād-əs/   /rāt#/   /rāt-əs/
      FD   rāt   − − −   rāt   − − −
      Surface: rāt   rādəs   rāt   rātəs

To account for the [ē] of forms like pl. N [rēdər], a different rule is needed. No attempt will here be made to formulate this rule. Suffice it to state that the environment for the rule is more complex than the one for final devoicing. It involves a good deal of morphological information (such as 'before the plural suffixes [-ər], [-ə]'), as well as lexical markings (so that [rāt] 'council/counsel' gets the plural form [rēt-ə], while [tāk] 'day' has [tāg-ə] without vowel change).

Some linguists have expressed grave reservations concerning the notion 'synchronic rule'. For that reason it may be useful to point to at least one piece of evidence which strongly argues for the existence of rules, i. e. of generalizations in speakers' grammars, rather than sheer memorization of facts and forms: It is a commonly observed fact that in early stages of first-language acquisition, children have no problem with the morphology of 'irregular' forms like *go:went, sleep:slept*. At a somewhat later stage, children seem all of a sudden to 'perversely unlearn' everything they have learned so far. For now they come up with forms like *goed* and *sleeped*. In fact, however, there is nothing perverse about this. What children have done at this stage is to realize that there is a general rule for past-tense formation, namely to add the dental suffix [-d]/[-t]/[-ɪd] to the verb root. This is shown by the fact that they now can freely produce past tenses from verbs which they might never have heard before, such as *disobey* or *trust*. What they have not yet worked out, however, is the fact that this rule needs to be constrained so as not to apply to certain 'irregular' verbs which either must be memorized (such as *go:went*) or which follow from more restricted, **'minor rules'** (such as *sleep:slept*). Put differently, they have not yet learned that certain forms must be **marked in the lexicon** for not undergoing the rule and/or for undergoing a different, minor rule. This task is accomplished only later, in a much more gradual fashion.

What is important here is that children clearly progress from sheer memorization to rule formulation. There is of course good reason for this. For if children were to continue to laboriously memorize each verb with its corresponding past tense, they would have to spend an inordinate amount of their childhood (and beyond!) on this task alone. But this would still open up to them only one very small, perhaps minor part of their language. There are other tasks to tackle, such as nominal plural formation, derivational morphology (as in *derive:derivation:derivational*), syntax, and a whole universe of meaning/semantics — not to mention the acquisition of innumerable other, non-linguistic skills, or such non-purposive activities as fantasy and play. The formulation of rules helps to reduce this burden of memorization and thus to make manageable the task of learning one's first language.

The importance of rule formation is by no means a recent insight. For instance, one of the leading neogrammarians has stated that 'few of the sentences which we speak have been memorized; most are constructed at the spur of the moment ... [on the basis of] rules [which] are abstracted subconsciously from the patterns [that we hear].' Even as early as the second century BC, one of the Sanskrit grammarians illustrated the usefulness of rules and the need for them by means of the following parable.

Lord Indra, chief of the gods and infinitely more capable than humans, asked Lord Bṛhaspati, preceptor of the gods and infinitely more powerful than mortal instructors, to teach him the Sanskrit language. Lord Bṛhaspati, trying to oblige him, began to enumerate the forms of Sanskrit. But in spite of the superhuman abilities and efforts of these two gods, Bṛhaspati could not accomplish his task even in a thousand divine years (which far exceed a thousand human years). For us poor mortals, with our limitations in capacity and time, this approach will surely fail. It is therefore that we need a grammar that formulates rules or generalizations, which will make it unnecessary to memorize every single form.

11.3. Sound change and phonological rules

The example of German final devoicing shows that generative phonological rules may look very similar to sound changes. To some degree, this should not come as a surprise. For the formulation of sound changes (in terms of features etc.) adopted in this book borrows heavily from generative phonological practice. On the other hand, generative phonology has greatly benefited from the work of traditional historical linguists, who may not have been using the same formalism, but who were as much concerned with phonological generalizations (in terms of segment classes etc.) as are generative phonologists. In fact, many early synchronic analyses of generative phonology were nothing but (properly modified) sound changes, formulated with a shafted arrow ($\rightarrow$), rather than an unshafted one ($>$).

However, it is precisely for that reason that many early analyses failed as proper generative statements. For the relationship between sound change and generative phonological rules is by no means direct. In fact, in many cases it is tenuous at best. This is due to the fact that the goals of historical and generative descriptions are very different: The former 'map' surface structures of one chronological stage into surface structures of a later stage; they try to describe historical events. Generative descriptions, on the other hand, relate synchronically alternating forms to each other; they try to account for speakers' synchronic knowledge of their language.

As a consequence, generative statements will cover only part of the territory taken up by sound change, namely those changes which result in split and thus, potentially, in synchronic alternations. Other sound changes lead to **'restructuring'**, i. e., to a change in underlying forms. Consider for instance Grimm's Law; cf. (27).

(27 a) $\begin{bmatrix} + \text{ stop} \\ - \text{ voice} \end{bmatrix} > [+ \text{ fric.}] \ / \ [- \text{ obstr.}] \ \underline{\hspace{1cm}}$

b) $\begin{bmatrix} + \text{ stop} \\ + \text{ voice} \end{bmatrix} > [- \text{ voice}]$

c) $\begin{bmatrix} + \text{ stop} \\ + \text{ asp.} \end{bmatrix} > \begin{bmatrix} + \text{ voice} \\ - \text{ asp.} \\ (\pm \text{ fric.}) \end{bmatrix}$

Of the three parts of this historical change, only (a) has a chance of resulting in a synchronic rule, since it brings about a split between (unshifted) voiceless stops and (shifted) voiceless fricatives. The other two parts do not introduce any alternations. And since without alternations, there is no motivation for a synchronic rule, the outcomes of these changes are 'restructured' (as in PIE */ǵews-/:PGmc. /keus-/ 'taste, choose').

Even in the case of the first part of Grimm's Law, many of the lexical items undergoing the change will be restructured with underlying voiceless fricatives, since these words do not happen to occur in contexts which would have brought about a morphophonemic alternation. Thus, PIE **trie-* 'three' changes into non-alternating PGmc. **þri-* = /þri-/. Similarly for the systematic exceptions to this part of Grimm's Law, such as PIE *stā 'stand':PGmc. **stand-* = /stand-/ 'stand'.

The forms in which (27 a) did lead to synchronic alternations are quite few. Moreover, in many cases, Verner's Law further complicates the synchronic alternations. For instance, the fact that the PIE participial suffix *-*tó*- was accented leads to the alternations in (28), where the form on the left reflects the conditioned non-application of (27 a), and the one on the right, the application of Grimm's Law **(GL)** plus Verner's Law **(VL)**.

(28) Pre-Gmc.   *tonk-tó-   *nose-tó-
      GL   þanx-tá-   nasi-þá-
      VL   — — — —   nazi-ðá-
      Other changes:
      Goth.   þāh-ta-   nasi-da-
      OE   þōh-ta-   nere-da-
                      'thought'   'saved'

As a result, the synchronic alternation is between voiced stop or fricative and voiceless stop (*d* or *ð* and *t*). The voiceless fricative *þ* no longer plays any role.

Moreover, there are good synchronic reasons for assuming that it is the *d* or *ð*, not *t*, which is synchronically underlying. For the voiced alternant is environmentally less restricted than the voiceless one. As a consequence, the underlying forms for the items in (28) are as in (29), and the applicable synchronic rule must be formulated as in (30).

(29)　Goth.　/þāh-d/ða-/　　/nasi-d/ða-/

$$(30)\quad \begin{bmatrix} +\text{ fric.} \\ +\text{ voice} \end{bmatrix} \rightarrow \begin{bmatrix} +\text{ stop} \\ -\text{ voice} \end{bmatrix} / \begin{bmatrix} +\text{ obstr.} \\ -\text{ voice} \end{bmatrix} ---$$

A comparison between (30) and (27 a) will readily reveal the extent to which synchronic rules and historical sound changes may differ in formulation. In fact, if we disregard some fine details concerning the feature [voice], the synchronic rule in this case is virtually the exact opposite of the historical change. The latter converts (voiceless) stops into fricatives, IF NOT preceded by obstruent; the former realizes (voiced) fricatives as stops, IF preceded by obstruent. This particular relationship between synchronic rule and historical change is often referred to as **rule inversion**. However, given that synchronic rules may be in almost any conceivable relationship to historical sound change, it seems arbitrary to single out this one relationship by giving it a special name.

The synchronic formulation of German final devoicing in (25) illustrates another possible difference between sound change and synchronic rules: As noted in section 11.1.1, there is good reason for assuming two steps in the historical development, namely (i) prepausal devoicing and (ii) extension of devoicing to word- or syllable-final environment. Synchronically, however, there is no motivation for invoking two such steps. All the speaker needs to account for is that word- or syllable-finally, obstruents are realized voiceless. It is immaterial how this situation came about historically. Synchronic rules, thus, may incorporate the results of analogical change.

Even borrowing can introduce synchronic phonological rules. Consider for instance the alternations in (31). These arose through palatalization in the history of French. Through borrowing, English acquired a fairly large number of lexical items exhibiting this alternation, enough to require English to have synchronic rules which relate these alternants to each other — even though the alternations are not attributable to any native sound change or analogy.

(31) allege [-ǰ]   :   allegation [-g-]
      longitude [-ǰ-]   :   elongate [-g-]
      electricity [-s-]   :   electric [-k]
      edifice [-s]   :   edification [-k-]

In spite of these quite formidable differences between historical changes and synchronic rules, generative phonology is by no means irrelevant for historical linguistics.

This is not to say that everything can be accepted that has been claimed by generativists concerning the relevance, or even superiority, of generative linguistics as compared to traditional historical linguistics. In fact, generative phonology itself has changed its position in many ways, to one which now is much closer to traditional historical linguistics than what it started out with. The following discussion will focus on the highlights of this issue of the relevance of generative phonology to historical linguistics.

11.4. 'Grammar change', 'rule addition', 'simplification'

Early generative phonology made a very strong claim, namely that the traditional, surface-oriented approach to historical linguistics is unacceptable and must be replaced by one which considers all linguistic change to be **grammar change**, i. e., change in the rule system of the language (and in the feature markings of its lexicon). Moreover, it was claimed that all such change operates in favor of **simplification**.

In this early view, the traditional notion of sound change was replaced by that of **rule addition** at the 'end of the grammar', i. e., after all other phonological rules.

Traditional analogy was said to be largely a matter of change in lexical markings. Thus, if an earlier English plural form *kine* is replaced by *cows*, this is attributed to the fact that before the change, *cow* had to be lexically marked as not undergoing the productive *s*-plural rule. The change that triggered the appearance of *cows*, then, consisted in the removal of that lexical marking. And this development, it was argued, simplified the grammar in that children learning the language now no longer have to memorize that *cow* is marked as '[- *s*-plural]'.

In addition to such changes in lexical marking and to the notion 'rule addition', several other processes of grammar change were invoked. These will be discussed in sections 11.5—7. At this point, it is useful to take a closer look at the claims that have been mentioned so far and to examine how well they hold up.

11.4.1. 'Rule addition' vs. sound change

As for the notion that sound change is 'rule addition', the principal difficulty lies in unconditioned, non-split changes such as (27 b/c): Since these do not bring about any synchronic alternations, it is difficult to see how there can be a corresponding synchronic rule. (This issue will be considered again in Chapter 20.) Moreover, as we have seen, even in the case of changes which do result in alternations, the resulting synchronic rules may differ considerably from the historical changes which gave rise to them.

Finally, even if this issue were somehow resolved, there seems to be no good empirical reason for considering such 'added rules' to be simplifications in the grammar. On the contrary, to the extent that they result in splits (or mergers, for that matter), they may well complicate the grammar. Thus, Grimm's and Verner's Laws complicated the grammar of the participial ending; cf. (28). Prior to these changes, the shape of the suffix was an invariant *-*tó*-, and no synchronic rule was required. After the changes, it alternated between -*ta*- and -*d/ða*-, thus requiring the rule in (30) above.

It is now generally acknowledged that sound change does not simplify grammar, and generativists tend to distinguish between **primary change** (earlier 'rule addition' = traditional sound change) and other, **secondary changes**. Only the latter are considered to simplify grammar. Note that this change in thinking brings the generative approach much closer to traditional historical linguistics.

11.4.2. 'Grammar change' and surface analogy

Concerning the treatment of what corresponds to traditional analogy, generative phonology likewise turns out not to be superior to traditional historical linguistics. True, analogical replacements such as that of *kine* by *cows* can be explained as a change in lexical marking, and that explanation has a certain intuitive appeal. However, they can also, in an equally intuitively appealing manner, be explained as resulting from four-part analogy extending the productive pattern of English plural formation: It has repeatedly been noted that children, when told that, say, *swang* is not the correct past tense of *swing*, may come up with proportional counterarguments like '*sing, sang* — *swing, swang*'. Here, then, we can at best argue for a 'stand-off' between the two approaches.

However, there are other changes which the traditional approach is able to explain, but which cannot be meaningfully accounted for under the notion 'grammar change'. Consider for instance developments like Engl. *male:*femelle → male:female*. (Section 9.2.2, ex. (77).) The traditional approach can explain this change as a case of contamination of one linguistic form by another, semantically closely related, form. A generative analysis, however, can do no better than note that there has been a 'restructuring' of **femelle* to *female*. No grammatical rule (or lexical feature) is involved in the change.

The problem of analogical changes which do not have a grammatical-rule correlate is not limited to 'minor', non-systematic processes like contamination. It can also be encountered in the case of proportional analogy. Consider for instance the pre-Sanskrit extension of the nominative/accusative plural neuter suffix -*āni* from the *n*-stems to the *a*-stems; cf. (32) as well as section 9.1.2, ex. (15).

(32)   *n*-stem: nām-ā/ă   :   nām-āni 'names'
       a-stem: yug-ā/ă   :   X = yug-āni 'yokes'

While this development can easily be accounted for by means of the four-part analogy in (32), it is not possible to explain it in terms of a 'grammar change': In terms of the rule system of (pre-)Sanskrit, the endings of the *n*-stem *nām-an-* must be accounted for on the basis of an underlying stem-forming suffix -*an*-, whereas the corresponding forms of the *a*-stem *yug-a*- require an underlying suffix -*a*-. Consequently, the attested endings must be accounted for by very different rules. For the *n*-stems these rules can be informally stated as in (33); for the *a*-stems as in (34). The overlap between these two sets of rules is minimal.

Moreover, an extension of the rules for the suffix *-āni* from the *n*-stems to the *a*-stems would yield something like (35), not the actually attested *-āni*.

(33) *n*-stems:
  (a) Suffix -ā/ă: nām-an
        (i) Drop final *n*   nām-a
        (ii) Optionally lengthen suffix vowel   nām-ā/ă
  (b) Suffix -āni: nām-an
        (i) Lengthen suffix vowel   nām-ān
        (ii) Add *-i*   nām-āni

(34) *a*-stems:
     Suffix -ā/ă: yug-a
        (i) Optionally lengthen suffix vowel   yug-ā/ă

(35) *a*-stems with rules of (33 b):   yug-a
        (i) Lengthen suffix vowel   yug-ā
        (ii) Add *-i*   yug-āi
        Other rules   yug-ai*

While the rule system thus cannot be held responsible for introducing the new plural ending in *yug-āni*, it had to account for it, once it had been introduced. There is reason to believe that this was done by means of the rules in (36). These rules differ from the ones in (33 b) and (35) by the addition of a conditioned *n*-insertion process. By being sensitive to the presence or absence of /n/ in the underlying form of the suffix, this rule makes it possible to derive the ending *-āni* for both the *n*-stems and the *a*-stems.

(36)

		nām-an	yug-a
i)	Add *-i*	nām-an-i	yug-a-i
ii)	Lengthen suffix vowel in open syllable	nām-ān-i	yug-ā-i
iii)	Insert *n* after suffix vowel, unless suffix contains underlying /n/	— — — —	yug-ā-n-i
	Surface	nāmāni	yugāni

Evidence for this formulation of the rules comes from their further extension to the nominative/accusative plural neuter of other inflectional classes, such as the *as*-stems or the present-participle *ant*-stems; cf. (37). Note that in a certain, morphologically definable subset of the *ant-*

stems, a 'later' rule of 'n-drop' eliminates the /n/ which blocked (36 ii) and (iii) from applying.

(37)		man-as	bhar-ant	da-dh-ant
	Rule (36 i)	man-as-i	bhar-ant-i	da-dh-ant-i
	Rule (36 ii)	mans-ās-i	— — — —	— — — —
	Rule (36 iii)	man-ā-n-s-i	— — — —	— — — —
	n-drop	— — — —	— — — —	da-dh-at-i
	Surface	manāṁsi	bharanti	dadhati
		'minds'	'carrying'	'putting'

However, while the starting point for this far-reaching development clearly was a surface proportional analogy, the extension of this mode of plural formation to inflectional classes like the *as*-stems and *ant*-stems can hardly be attributed to surface analogy. For it would be difficult to see how a surface pattern could motivate, say, the placement of the nasal before the *s* of *manāṁsi*, or the lack of such a nasal in *dadhati*. True, the absence of surface *n* in the latter form could be motivated by observing that this subclass of the *ant*-stems obligatorily 'drops' underlying /n/. But this generalization itself is more easily stated in terms of a rule (note the terms 'drop' and 'underlying') than in terms of surface patterns. Moreover, even if the underlying /n/ is 'dropped', a surface analogy should be expected to analogically 'reinsert' the nasal, on the model of forms like *bharanti*. Finally, note that the conditions for suffix-vowel lengthening can be stated only in terms of the fairly 'abstract' structures of (36) and (37). On the surface, the lengthening in *manāṁsi* (checked syllable) and its absence in *dadhati* (open syllable) could not be motivated.

This extended example shows that in order to account for analogical change, we need both the traditional, surface-oriented and the generative, rule-oriented approach. (Note also that in this case we have an example of genuine 'rule addition', namely the *n*-insertion rule. However this grammatically motivated rule does not get added at the 'end of the grammar', but quite 'early', near the underlying level, and before a number of other phonological rules, such as the *n*-drop of (37).)

11.4.3. Leveling and the 'paradigm condition'

One type of traditional analogical change causes even more general and consistent difficulties for the early generative view of linguistic change as grammar change and as being oriented toward simplification. This is the process of leveling.

Consider again the Verner's-Law alternations in the Old English verbal system. For roots with the alternation between sibilant and *r*, we find the Old English attestations in (38). Certain verbs have completely retained the expected alternation (cf. (38 a)), others have eliminated it in part of the paradigm but retained it elsewhere (cf. (b)), and a third set has leveled the sibilant throughout the paradigm (cf. (c)). (Examples are cited in normal orthography, without indication of sibilant voicing. — In the case of the word for 'rise', the leveling may have been aided by dissimilatory tendencies; cf. *riron, *(ge)riren. See sections 3.5, 9.1.1, and 10.1.2.2 for discussion of incipient leveling in prehistoric English and German.)

(38)	pres.	past sg.	past pl.	past pple.	
a)	cēosan	cēas	curon	(ge)coren	'choose'
	-lēosan	-lēas	-luron	-loren	'lose'
	frēosan	frēas	fruron	(ge)froren	'freeze'
b)	wesan	wæs	wǣron	*(ge)weren	
				→ (ge)wesen	'be'
c)	lesan	læs	*lǣron	*(ge)leren	
			→ lǣson	→ (ge)lesen	'pick, read'
	rīsan	rās	*riron	*(ge)riren	
			→ rison	→ (ge)risen	'rise'

Now, at a certain prehistoric stage, not far removed from the actually attested Old English, there must have been a rule of the type (39) which accounted for the alternation between sibilant and *r*. And at that time, the rule was a regular process, within its morphologically highly restricted environment.

$$(39) \quad s \rightarrow r \; / \; \begin{bmatrix} V \\ + \text{ root} \end{bmatrix} \underline{\quad\quad} \begin{bmatrix} \underline{\quad\quad\quad\quad\quad} \\ + \text{ 'strong verb'} \\ + \text{ past} \\ \left\{ \begin{matrix} + \text{ plural} \\ + \text{ participle} \end{matrix} \right\} \end{bmatrix}$$

However, as (38) shows, leveling began to take its toll. This development led to a simplification in the surface structure of the language, namely the elimination or reduction of morphophonemic alternations. But in terms of the synchronic rule system, leveling cannot be accounted for as a simplification. (In fact, it cannot be accounted for at all.) Rather, the process leads to a definite complication in the grammar. For as a result of leveling, certain items must now be lexically marked as exceptions to rule (39). Moreover, in words of the type (38 b), the lexical exception marking cannot be 'categorial' but must be restricted to the subcategory of the past participle.

As time progresses and more and more items undergo leveling, matters become even more complicated. For at a certain point, when about half of all eligible words have the alternation, while the other half does not, the question must arise whether the rule should still be considered a **'major'** rule (with exceptions marked in the lexicon) or a more 'complex', **'minor'** rule, limited to an increasingly smaller number of items which must be specially marked in the lexicon for undergoing the rule.

From this point onward, it is of course possible to conceive of leveling as simplification, since it can be said to remove the lexical markings required to 'trigger' a particular word's undergoing the minor-rule version of (39). But this stage results only from an earlier phase of grammar complication. Moreover, ultimate simplification may take centuries to accomplish. In English, to be sure, that stage may now have been reached. For through continued leveling, the alternations which motivate something like rule (39) have in effect been eliminated. Only one synchronic alternation remains, namely *was:were*; and this one may be considered memorized, rather than generated by rule. But note that such memorization in a certain sense is more 'complex' than rule-based generation.

Facts like these have led generative phonologists to introduce the notion **'paradigm condition'** as a motivating factor for linguistic change. But note that the notion 'paradigm' on which this condition is based does not have a meaningful correlate in the rule systems of most approaches to generative phonology. In effect, then, it is a label for leveling, not an explanation. At the same time, however, the acceptance of leveling as a process not conditioned by the grammatical rule system has brought generative phonology closer to the surface-oriented approach of traditional historical linguistics.

11.5 Rule extension

A much more important and lasting contribution to historical linguistics than the claims so far discussed consists in the basic principle of generative phonology that alternations are to be accounted for by rules (unless they are limited to just one or two lexical items, as in the case of Engl. *was:were*). In section 11.4.2, we have seen one example in which this rule-oriented approach of generative phonology has been useful, namely the extension of the Sanskrit nominative/accusative plural formation in the neuters. While this development began as a clearly surface-oriented analogical change, its further extension can be motivated only in terms of a fairly abstract rule approach. In the following, it will be shown that this contribution of generative phonology is useful for historical linguistics also in dealing with the developments discussed in section 11.1.

Let us first look at the case of final devoicing in German, general Slavic, etc.: As noted earlier, the probable starting point for these developments is prepausal position. Now, once prepausal devoicing has applied, it introduces a regular word-final alternation between voiceless obstruents (before pause) and voiced obstruents (elsewhere). This synchronic alternation must be accounted for in terms of a rule; cf. the formulation in (40). And such a rule, once introduced, can be extended to new environments, such as syllable-final or word-final position; cf. (41).

(40)   [+ obstr.] → [− voice] / ___ ##

(41)   [+ obstr.] → [− voice] / ___ # (or / ___ $)

At first sight, this rule-extension analysis may seem to be a mere formalization of the traditional notion of leveling. And as the preceding section has shown, the process of leveling itself is something which is difficult to account for in generative phonology. Closer examination shows that this appraisal is incorrect.

The development which is involved in the extension of final devoicing is quite different from ordinary leveling: It does not require the notion 'paradigm'. Rather, it is governed by the notions 'utterance boundary', 'word boundary', and 'syllable boundary', only one of which is morphological. Moreover, while it does eliminate alternations in word-final or syllable-final positions, it actually increases alternation in many individual words. Thus, prior to the extension of final devoicing, words like G *Tag* 'day' had a voiceless alternant only prepausally, i. e. in a fairly restricted context. But after the extension, the voiceless alternant appears in all occurrences of sg. N [tāk] (vs. pl. N [tāgə]), as well as in forms like the adjective [tēk$liç] 'daily'.

In addition, unlike ordinary, paradigm-based leveling, the extension of final devoicing is eminently explainable in terms of phonological rules. True, the motivation for the rule extension from (40) to (41) does not lie directly in the formulation of (40), but in the fact that utterance boundary usually coincides with word or syllable boundary and that an extension of the rule to the latter context eliminates a certain alternation. But a leveling explanation requires the same motivation.

The most important consideration, however, is the following: If we account for the change from (40) to (41) as a **rule extension**, then we are able to explain the fact that this type of development differs markedly from ordinary leveling by its great regularity and by the sweeping nature of its implementation. That is, we can claim that the regularity of the process results from the fact that it extends a rule, not just a pattern found in one or two particular words or inflectional classes.

Taking a broader view, we might further claim that the regularity of analogical change is tied up with the **regularity of** the **parameters** controlling or motivating the change: most regular when it takes place in terms of rules, intermediate when controlled by well-defined and general surface patterns (leveling and four-part analogy), least regular when motivated by poorly or very narrowly defined surface patterns (as in blending and contamination). (Here as elsewhere, the fact that backformation is typically irregular, even if applying vis-à-vis productive processes, requires a special explanation, along the lines of Kuryłowicz's second law of analogy.)

The concept of rule extension can be invoked for many similar regular and sweeping analogical developments. In some of these developments, the rule extension is preceded and/or accompanied by **reinterpretation**. Compare for instance the British English extension of word-final ∅/r alternation in words with original final *r* (section 11.1.2, ex. (8)): At a certain point, the alternation must have been reinterpreted as a process of insertion, rather than deletion. Compare the sound change in (42) with the rule in (43). For it is only through an insertion rule that we can get the extension of ∅/r alternation to forms like *idea* that did not originally end in *r*. (See section 9.1.5, ex. (45) for discussion of the sound change. Note that alternations could arise only where *r* was word-final and thus could either be syllable-final or linked into the onset of a following vowel-initial word.)

(42) $r > \emptyset / V \underline{\quad} (C_0) \$$

(43) $\emptyset \rightarrow r / V \underline{\quad} \# V$

The situation is similar, but slightly more complicated in the case of the Russian, Polish, and Czech final obstruent developments of section 11.1.3, ex. (16/18). Recall that as a result of this development word-final obstruents had the distribution in (44).

(44)   [+ voice] beside [− voice] / $\underline{\quad}$ # [+ obstr., + voice]
       [− voice] / $\underline{\quad}$ # [+ obstr., − voice] and elsewhere

We can account for this pattern as follows: As noted in section 11.1.3, these Slavic languages not only have an external sandhi resulting from the historical process of final devoicing, they also have an inherited internal sandhi of obstruent voicing; cf. ex. (19) above. The synchronic rules accounting for these alternations would have to be formulated as in (45) and (46 a) respectively. These two rules are motivated by two patterns of alternation which in principle are quite different, one involving any word-final obstruent, the other, any obstruent that occurs before another obstruent. However, if the latter rule is interpreted as applicable not only internally, but also with intervening word boundary (cf. (46 b)), then the two processes come into conflict in the context of (47). This can be illustrated by the derivations in (48): In the majority of contexts, the two rules are mutually exclusive. In the context / $\underline{\quad}$ # [+ obstr., − voice], both rules can apply, and the results of both applications are identical. However, as the rightmost derivation of (48) shows, in the context of (47), both rules can apply, but with different results. (Note that (48 a) and (48 b) merely illustrate the applicability of each of the two rules. No suggestion of 'rule ordering' is intended.)

(45)   **FD**   [+ obstr.] $\rightarrow$ [− voice] / $\underline{\quad}$ #

(46)   **Assim.**
       (a)   [+ obstr.] $\rightarrow$ [α voice] / $\underline{\quad}$ [+ obstr., α voice]
       (b)   [+ obstr.] $\rightarrow$ [α voice] / $\underline{\quad}$ (#) [+ obstr., α voice]

(47) / __ ‡ [+ obstr., + voice]

(48)		/bt/	/pd/	/b‡‡/	/p‡‡/	/b‡t/	/p‡d/
(a)	FD	— —	— —	p‡‡	p‡‡	p‡t	**p‡d**
(b)	Assim.	pt	bd	— — —	— — —	p(‡)t	**b(‡)d**

It appears that this conflict was 'resolved' by the optional application of either of the two rules in the context of (47) and that it is this optional rule application which is responsible for the pattern in (44).

Here again, the observed regularity of the development can be explained as due to the fact that we are dealing with rule-governed changes, not just with the extension of surface patterns. Moreover, unlike the surface account in (20) above, the present rule approach explains the (regular) optionality of voicing assimilation and word-final devoicing in the context of (47).

The further development in dialectal Polish shows even more clearly the usefulness of the generative rule-extension approach. What we need to assume at the outset is that in these dialects, the competition between FD and Assim. was resolved such that Assim. obligatorily took precedence in terms of application. (This seems to entail the assumption that Assim. was 'reordered' after FD. The issue of rule reordering will be discussed separately, in section 11.6.) This change in rule precedence would lead to the derivations in (49).

(49)		/brat‡/	/lud‡/	/brat‡bił/	/lud‡bił/
	FD	brat‡	lut‡	brat‡bił	lut‡bił
	Assim.	— — —	— — —	brad‡bił	lud‡bił
	Surface	brat	lut	brad biw	lud biw
		'brother'	'ice'	'there was	'there was
				a brother'	ice'

The resulting surface patterns, however, could be reanalyzed as being produced not by a combination of FD and Assim., but by a (bipartite) single rule of Final Voice Neutralization (**FVN**); cf. (50). This rule treats the voice assimilation in forms like [brad biw] as a phenomenon separate from the internal-sandhi voice assimilation in (46 a). Instead, it 'captures the generalization' that the contrast between voiced and voiceless is neutralized in final position, with voicing predictable in terms of the phonological context. Notice that this rule will convert the underlying forms of (49) into the same surface forms as does the derivation in (49); cf. example (51).

(50)   [+ obstr.] → [+ voice] / ___ # [+ obstr., + voice]
                   [− voice] elsewhere

(51)
	/brat#/	/lud#/	/brat#bił/	/lud#bił/
FVN	brat#	lut#	brad#bił	lud#bił
Surface	brat	lut	brad biw	lud biw

On this background we can explain the dialectal Polish developments in section 1.1.3, ex. (21/22) as a simple case of rule extension: Instead of being limited to the context / ___ # [+ obstr., + voice], rule (50) was extended so as to voice final obstruents before ALL following word-initial voiced segments; cf. (52) and the derivations in (53). (Contrast these with the derivations in (51′), which would result from applying the old FVN rule to the same underlying forms.)

(52)   **FVN′:**   [+ obstr.] → [+ voice] / ___ # [+ voice]
                               [− voice] elsewhere

(53)
	/brat#/	/lud#/	/brat#bił/	/lud#bił/	/rud#lutski/	/bok#levi/
FVN′	brat#	lut#	brad#bił	lud#bił	rud#lutski	bog#levi
Surface	brat	lut	brad biw	lud biw	rud lutskʸi	bog levi
	'brother'	'ice'	'there was a brother'	'there was ice'	'human race'	'left side'

(51′)
	/brat#/	/lud#/	/brat#bił/	/lud#bił/	/rud#lutski/	/bok#levi/
FVN	brat#	lut#	brad#bił	lud#bił	rut#lutski	bok#levi
Surface	brat	lut	brad biw	lud biw	rut lutskʸi	bok levi

It must be admitted that there are several other conceivable ways of getting from the general Slavic to the dialectal Polish situation. One such scenario would consist of the rule extension of Assim. in external sandhi so as to apply obligatorily and before all voiced segments.

What is shared by all of these possible explanations is that they operate in terms of rule extension, not simply in terms of surface patterns. For complex developments like these, rule-extension scenarios have the advantage that rules provide more explicit 'models' (comparable to the paradigmatic or proportional 'models' of traditional analogy) in terms of which one can try to explain a particular change. Moreover, a rule-based approach makes it easier to account for the various, sometimes conflicting synchronic generalizations which motivate a given analogical change. It is precisely the absence of such models which has in many cases made it impossible for traditional historical linguists to find a satisfactory explanation. In addition, here as elsewhere the rule-based approach enables us to account for the fact that unlike ordinary analogical processes, the Polish developments are completely regular.

11.6. 'Rule reordering', 'rule loss'; opacity/transparency

In addition to rule addition and rule extension, generative phonologists also have argued in favor of the notions 'rule reordering' and 'rule loss'. Many, perhaps most of the early examples in favor of the concept 'rule reordering' are amenable to different explanations and thus are of doubtful cogency. However, a certain residue remains which suggests that this concept may be a lasting contribution to historical linguistics, even if it may require some modification. The concept 'rule loss', on the other hand, must apparently be viewed with some suspicion.

To illustrate the notion **rule reordering**, let us take another look at the case of German final devoicing and ə-loss. As noted in 11.1.2, the historical sequencing of these two processes was as in (54); the expected outcome of earlier *tag* and *tagə* should therefore be as in (54a). But instead, Standard German has the forms in (54b).

(54)	OHG		sg. N tag	sg. D tage
		FD	tak	− − −
	pre-NHG		tāk	tāgə
		ə-loss	− − −	tāg
a)	Expected NHG		tāk	tāg
b)	Attested NHG		[tāk]	[tāk]

Since the pattern of (54b) is completely regular, the development which gave rise to it should be statable in terms of rules, not of surface patterns. It is here that the concept 'rule reordering' comes in:

Both historical developments, FD and ə-loss, are reflected as synchronic rules. For final devoicing, a rule is required because of synchronic alternations like sg. N [tāk] : pl. N [tāgə]. A rule of ə-loss is needed to account for the fact that for many speakers of Standard German, the dative singular ending [-ə] is only optionally lost, resulting in alternations of the type sg. D [tāg-ə]:[tāk-Ø]. Given these rules, the pattern in (54b) can be accounted for as resulting from the reordering of these two rules; cf. (55), where (a) gives the earlier, historically motivated order, while (b) shows the effect of reordering.

(55)			sg. N /tāg/	sg. D /tāg-ə/
a)		FD	tāk	— — —
		ə-loss	— — —	tāg
		Surface	tāk	tāg
b)	vs.	ə-loss	— — —	tāg
		FD	tāk	tāk
		Surface	tāk	tāk

As for the motivation for this reordering, an early view maintained that it lies in the concept of **rule maximalization**: Grammars whose rules are maximally applicable (i. e. which apply to the largest number of potential inputs) were considered to be more 'highly valued' than other grammars. Therefore, if there is to be a change, it will be in the direction of greater rule application.

Allied concepts are the notions of **feeding** and **bleeding** rule relationships and their negative counterparts, non-feeding and non-bleeding: Rules are in a feeding relationship if the output of one rule provides inputs for the other. A rule 'bleeds' another rule if its application deprives the latter of potential inputs. (Cf. 3.4 above for historical counterparts of these synchronic rule relationships.) Rules can apply maximally if they are in a feeding or in a non-bleeding relationship. Thus, in the historically expected scenario of (55 a), ə-loss is in a non-feeding relationship with FD. The change from (55 a) to (55 b) remedies this situation by placing ə-loss in a feeding relationship to FD, thus permitting FD to apply to a larger set of possible inputs.

The very different Southern German and Yiddish developments in (56) (= ex. (13) in section 11.1.2) were attributed to a different historical development, **rule loss**: The rule of FD was said to have been given up, resulting in a clear simplification of the grammar.

(56)	Older	sg. N	tak	sg. D	tagə
	Southern		tōg		tōg

The concept of maximal rule application soon was attacked within the framework of generative phonology, and so was the notion that bleeding rule relationships tend to be replaced by non-bleeding ones. In response to this largely theory-internal criticism, a new criterion was proposed as the motivation for rule reordering, namely the concept of **opacity** and its positive counterpart, **transparency**.

The precise definition of opacity and transparency has undergone several revisions. However, the basic idea behind the terms has remained constant. This is the notion that a rule is 'opaque' if it is 'contradicted' by surface evidence, i. e. if there is surface evidence which does not agree with the 'predictions' made by the rule. Because of this 'surface contradiction', opaque rules are said to be less easily learned by children. A change which brings about a more transparent situation will therefore be preferred.

For instance, in the older scenario of (55 a), FD predicts that all word-final obstruents are voiceless. However, the ordering of ə-loss after FD brings about forms in which final devoicing does not apply. In these forms, then, the prediction of FD does not hold. On the other hand, the reordering in (55 b) permits FD to apply transparently, such that its predictions hold true on the surface.

But not only the reordering in (55), also the rule loss in (56) is considered to be attributable to the 'transparency principle': It is argued that in these dialects, the opacity of FD is resolved by eliminating the rule altogether.

As this brief discussion shows, the 'transparency principle' is more than just a revision of the older 'maximalization principle'. In situations like the German one, where one set of dialects reorders, another loses a rule, the new principle makes it possible to provide a general explanation for developments which otherwise seem to be completely unrelated. In addition, the notion 'transparency' seems to be intuitively more appealing than the rather formalistic concept 'maximalization'. At the same time, it should be noted that here again, a revision in the generative approach brings it much closer to the surface and thus to the area which was of major concern to traditional historical linguistics.

However, as far as the actual analysis is concerned (rather than the principles behind it), the account of German final devoicing and ə-loss cannot be accepted without modification. And these modifications suggest serious flaws in the concept 'rule loss' and a probable revision in the account of 'rule reordering'.

Let us begin with the Southern German and Yiddish 'rule loss'. As the discussion in 11.2.1 has shown, the 'southern' response to the alternations introduced by ə-loss is very different to what we find in the 'north'. Rather than being a regular and sweeping development, it proceeds at the slow, word-by-word, and rather irregular pace which one would expect in 'traditional' leveling. It is thus no different from the slow elimination of the English Verner's-Law alternations (cf. 11.4.3). In either case, a rule eventually is 'lost' from the grammar. (Actually, some Yiddish dialects seem to still have traces of the original voicing alternations.) But that loss is not a primary mechanism of change. Rather, it is merely the eventual outcome of a slow process of leveling which results in what would be more accurately described as **'rule atrophy'** or **'rule fading'**. And since no other, more cogent examples of sweeping and regular rule loss seem to be found, it may very well be that all cases of alleged rule loss must be considered the final result of rule atrophy.

The concept of rule reordering seems to hold up better. For as noted in section 11.1.2, the 'northern' change from (55 a) to (55 b) seems to have been sweeping and certainly is completely regular. It is true, within the framework of generative phonology, an alternative, 'rule insertion' proposal has had some currency. According to this proposal, ə-loss was not added at the 'end of the grammar' and subsequently reordered. Rather, it was 'inserted in the middle of the grammar', before the rule of final devoicing. However, this analysis becomes dubious in view of the dialectal German evidence in 11.1.2, ex. (12) = (57) below. If ə-loss had in fact been 'inserted' prior to FD, the dative singular forms should have the same invariant voiceless final obstruents as the corresponding nominative forms; cf. the derivation in (55 b). The fact that they do not is compatible only with the 'standard view' according to which ə-loss was 'added after' FD.

(57) Older   sg. N   tak   sg. D   tagə
       Dialectal   tāk   tāg/tāk

However, the competition between voiced and voiceless word-final obstruents in these dialectal dative singular forms suggests a different alternative to rule reordering, a process which can be referred to as **rule reapplication** or **rule reaffirmation**. Under this view, reapplication of FD **(FD')** in the dative singular forms reaffirmed the predictions made by that rule and thus eliminated the opacity in (55 b).

At first, this development evidently was only optional; cf. (57) and the derivations in (58). And because of the optionality of reapplying FD, there is a strong motivation for keeping FD and FD' as separate processes. However, once reapplication becomes obligatory, a scenario with both FD and FD' becomes redundant, since its outcome is exactly the same as one in which only FD′ applies; cf. (59 a/b). At this point, there is no motivation for new speakers to invoke both rules. Instead, they can be expected to opt for a grammar of the type (59 b). (The change from (59 a) to (59 b) may possibly be viewed as evidence that there are cases of regular 'rule loss', after all. However, given the close relationship, if not identity, between FD and FD′, it might be more accurately interpreted as something like 'rule consolidation'.)

(58)		/tāg/	/tāgə/
	FD	tāk	— — —
	ə-loss	— — —	tāg
	FD′ (opt.)	— — —	tāk
	Surface	tāk	tāk/tāg

(59 a)		/tāg/	/tāgə/
	FD	tāk	— — —
	ə-loss	— — —	tāg
	FD′ (obl.)	— — —	tāk
	Surface	tāk	tāk

b)		/tāg/	/tāgə/
	ə-loss	— — —	tāg
	FD′ (obl.)	tāk	tāk
	Surface	tāk	tāk

If we extrapolate from the present, empirically well supported analysis, it is possible to argue that all instances of apparent rule reordering may actually be the ultimate outcome of 'rule reapplication' or 'rule reaffirmation'. Further research is needed to determine whether this claim can be maintained or whether there are cases which unambiguously exclude a rule reapplication scenario.

Even so, there can be no doubt that some kind of rule-based development is responsible for the 'northern' response to ə-loss. For only such a process can provide a satisfactory explanation for the regularity and sweeping nature of the change.

11.7. Morphological opacity and the polarity of language

Most definitions of opacity and transparency look at the surface effect of phonological rules. However, just as in the case of traditional analogical change (cf. 10.3), what may be useful or desirable from the point of view of the phonological (or phonetic) side of language may be undesirable or complicate matters on the morphological (or semantic) side. For instance, the 'reordering' of FD after ə-loss eliminates surface exceptions (to FD), but at the same time it eliminates a distinction between different case forms (dative vs. nominative singular). Put differently, the change makes the phonological rule FD transparent, but renders morphological case distinctions more opaque.

On the basis of well-chosen synchronic examples, it has been argued that certain rule orderings are motivated by considerations not of phonological, but of **morphological opacity**. One suspects that also historically, there may be some rule-governed effects of the tendency to avoid morphological opacity. Little actual research has been done in this area. However, some examples suggest that this suspicion may be correct. (It is much easier to find examples which can be explained in terms of traditional analogical processes, but do not require the assumption of rule change or rule extension.)

Some of the best possible examples can be found in the history of the development of Sanskrit external sandhi. But as the following discussion will show, though these examples may be suggestive, they are not always conclusive.

For instance, as the result of various historical developments, Sanskrit at one point wound up with the two rules in (60 a/b) which apply in the order in which they are given. The first of these contracts vowels of like quality (whether short or long) into a corresponding long vowel. The second drops word-final *y*, *w*, and *s* after an *a*-vowel and before the initial syllabic segment of a following word. (A systematic exception to this latter rule is found in those cases where the next word begins in short *ă*. Here, -*ay*#*a*- results in -*ē*-, -*aw*#*a*- and -*as*#*a*- in -*ō*-. These exceptional developments will be ignored in the following discussion.)

$$(60\,\text{a})\quad \textbf{(Contr.)}\quad \breve{\bar{V}}'\ \breve{\bar{V}}'\ \rightarrow\ \bar{V}'$$

$$\text{b)}\quad \textbf{(Loss)}\quad \left\{ \begin{matrix} y \\ w \\ s \end{matrix} \right\}\ \rightarrow\ \emptyset\ /\ \breve{\bar{a}}\ \underline{\quad}\ \#\ [+\,\text{syll.}]$$

The effect of these rules is illustrated in (61). As the derivations show, Contr. is rendered opaque by the application of Loss, for the latter creates uncontracted vowel clusters to which Contr. cannot apply. Moreover, these uncontracted surface forms violate a very general constraint against surface hiatus. (There are, in the long history of the language, altogether some two or three violations of that constraint in internal sandhi. Elsewhere, internal-sandhi hiatus is eliminated by a veritable conspiracy of rules.)

(61)	/dēva#āpnōti/	/dēvas#āpnōti/	/dēvay#āpnōti/
Contr.	dēvāpnōti	— — — — —	— — — — —
Loss	— — — — —	dēva āpnōti	dēva āpnōti
	'O god, he reaches'	'the god reaches'	'he reaches (into) god'

There would thus be ample motivation for a reordering of the two rules. Standard Sanskrit, however, has steadfastly refused to do so. It is tempting to argue that the reason for this refusal is that reordering would eliminate morphological contrasts, such as the distinction in (61) between the vocative singular on one hand and nominative and locative singular on the other. That is, the principle of morphological transparency here brings about a resistance to reordering. (Cf. 10.1.2.2 for the similar resistance of basic morphological categories to traditional analogical change.)

Note however that non-standardized Sanskrit and early Middle Indo-Aryan have (optional) contraction where Sanskrit refuses to contract. It is possible to argue that in these 'vernacular' dialects, the phonological transparency principle has won out over the morphological one.

However, the difference between Standard Sanskrit and the 'vernacular' dialects can also be attributed to a different factor, namely a well-known sociolinguistic polarization between these two different varieties of Indo-Aryan. There are a number of other areas where this polarization between the traditional, orthodox standard language and the more innovative vernaculars has had linguistic repercussions. Thus, the earliest attested Indo-Aryan, Vedic Sanskrit, had two competing instrumental plural endings in the *a*-stems, *-ais* and *-ebhis*. Later Standard Sanskrit generalizes *-ais* (except in one pronoun), while the Middle-Indo-Aryan vernaculars generalize descendants of *-ebhis*. (Cf. also 15.1 below.)

The situation is clearer in another area of Sanskrit external sandhi, although the developments involved are more complex: In the prehistory of Sanskrit, final *-ns* changed to *-n* in most environments. However, in early Vedic Sanskrit, *s* was retained before a word with initial voiceless dental stop. (And before such a retained *s*, *n* changed into *ṁ*.) The result was an alternation between word-final *-n* and *-ṁs*; cf. (62 a). But word-final *-n* which derived from different sources did not participate in this alternation; cf. (62 b) and (62 c). The putative underlying forms of this stage of the language are given on the right side of example (62); and the applicable rules are formulated in (63). (Rule (63 a) accounts for the alternations in (62 a), rule (63 b) for those in (62 c). The word *tadā* 'then' has been chosen to illustrate what happens before a word with initial voiceless dental stop. The environment ## suggests the more common or 'basic' pattern which is found elsewhere.)

(62)   pre-Sanskrit   Vedic Sanskrit

  a) sg. N vidvāns 'knowing' vidvān##   /vidvāns/
                        vidvāṁs#tadā
      pl. A aśvāns 'horses' aśvān##   /aśvāns/
                        aśvāṁs#tadā

  b) sg. V rājan 'king' rājan##   /rājan/
                        rājan#tadā
      pl. 3 abharant 'carried' abharan##   /abharan/
                        abharan#tadā

  c) sg. 1 abharam 'carried' abharam##   /abharam/
                        abharan#tadā
      sg. A aśvam 'horse' aśvam##   /aśvam/
                        aśvan#tadā

(63 a) s → ∅ / ___ # ["— voiceless dental stop"]
    b) m → n / ___ # [+ stop, + dent.]

In later Sanskrit, several things happened. First, words of the type (62 a) were reinterpreted as having underlying final /-n/, presumably because this is the most common form of the word; cf. (65 a). Consequently, the alternation between *-n* and *-ṁs* was reinterpreted as resulting from a process of *s*-insertion, cf. (64). Finally, this rule was extended to other words in underlying /-n/; cf. (65 b).

(64) ∅ → s / n ___ # [+ stop, + dent., − voice]

(65)   Classical Sanskrit:

a)	sg. N	/vidvān/	vidvān##
			vidvāṁs#tadā
	pl. A	/aśvān/	aśvān##
			aśvāṁs#tadā
b)	sg. V	/rājan/	rājan##
			rājaṁs#tadā
	pl. 3	/abharant/	abharan##
			abharaṁs#tadā
c)	sg. 1	/abharam/	abharam##
			abharan#tadā
	sg. A	/aśvam/	aśvam##
			aśvan#tadā

However, as (65 c) shows, *s*-insertion was not extended to words with underlying /-m/, which had surface -*n* only before dental. Note that as a result, rule (64) became phonologically opaque, for forms like *abharan#tadā* do not show the inserted *s* which this rule would predict. At the same time, however, the non-extension of (64) to forms of this type in many cases prevented morphological opacity. For it permitted morphological contrast of the type sg. 1 /abharam/ 'I carried' : pl. 3 abharan/ 'they carried' to remain also before words in initial voiceless dental stop, even if in phonetically different guise (as *n* vs. *ṁs*).

Examples like this suggest that the notion 'morphological opacity' may play a role in linguistic change. But note that if the interpretation is correct, the effect of 'morphological opacity' is one of blocking the extension of a rule. Similarly, in the case of example (61), morphological opacity, if it was involved at all, had a blocking effect. Cases in which morphological opacity triggers rule extension or rule reordering seem to be very difficult to come by. Without such positive evidence, however, there may be some doubt as to how valid the concept of morphological opacity is for historical linguistics. For a priori, the non-extension or non-reordering of a rule may just as well be due to 'inertia'. Clearly, then, further research is needed before it can be considered certain that the concept of morphological opacity is relevant for rule-based linguistic change.

11.8. Rule reordering and relative chronology

We have seen that many synchronic rules are remarkably similar, or even identical to the historical changes that gave rise to them. If, then, synchronic rules can be reordered (whether directly or by rule reapplication), there are obvious and significant repercussions for the historical notion of 'relative chronology'.

Consider for instance the case of German final devoicing and ə-loss. If our historical information were limited to Old High German and Modern Standard German, we might very well conclude that the relative chronology of these two processes was as in (66). As we have seen however, this 'relative chronology' is historically incorrect. The correct development is the one in (67). (Differences in vowel length are left unmarked in (66) and (67).)

(66)   OHG   tag   tage
        e-loss   — — —   tag
        FD   tak   tak

(67)   OHG   tag   tage
        FD   tak   — — —
        MHG   tak   tagə
        ə-loss   — — —   tag
        Reordering   tak   tak

Rule reordering, then, has obscured the effects of linguistic change to the extent that a historical interpretation based solely on the evidence of the Old High German input and the Modern German output leads to the wrong results.

In the German case, we have enough evidence on intermediate stages to come up with the historically correct analysis. However, where such evidence is lacking or difficult to come by, the potential for incorrect analyses becomes greater.

For instance, as noted in 6.3, Grassmann's Law **(GL)** seems to have interacted in Sanskrit with a sound change of deaspiration **(deasp.)**; cf. the examples in (68) and the formulations in (69). And the evidence in (68) suggests that the relative chronology of GL and deasp. was such that deasp. took place before GL; cf. (70). This is in fact the interpretation that is found in many historical analyses.

(68) PIE   Sanskrit
  a) *bhudhyetoy   budhyatē   'is awake'
  b) *bhebhowdhe   bubōdha   'was awake'
  c) *bhibhudhseti   bubhutsati   'wants to be awake'
      *bhudhs   bhut   'awakening'

(69) deasp. [+ stop] > [− asp., − voice] / ___ s
      GL   [+ stop] > [− asp.] / ___ (X) [+ asp.]

(70) PIE   bhudhs   bhudhs
         deasp.   bhuts   GL   budhs
         GL   − − − −   deasp.   buts
      Other changes: bhut   but*

Early Vedic Sanskrit and comparative Indo-Iranian evidence suggests
that this relative chronology is incorrect and that the correct historical
development was as follows:

At some time in the prehistory of Indo-Iranian, medial aspirate +
voiceless obstruent underwent a process known as Bartholomae's Law
(BL); cf. (71) and (73 a). (The formulation in (71) is merely intended
to summarize the 'facts'. There is some controversy about the precise
phonetic developments which converted earlier aspirate + voiceless
obstruent clusters into clusters of unaspirated stop + aspirated obstruent.) Word-finally, on the other hand, all aspiration and voicing
distinctions were neutralized; cf. (72) and (73 b). At a later period,
Grassmann's Law applied, producing the pre-Vedic forms in (73). (The
ẓh of example (73) is a voiced aspirated sibilant. Aspiration is not as
common in sibilants as it is in stops, but it does occur in actually
attested languages; cf. e. g. 5.4.2, ex. (101).)

(71) BL $\begin{bmatrix} + \text{stop} \\ + \text{voice} \\ + \text{asp.} \end{bmatrix} \begin{bmatrix} + \text{obstr.} \\ - \text{voice} \end{bmatrix} > \begin{bmatrix} + \text{stop} \\ - \text{asp.} \end{bmatrix} \begin{bmatrix} + \text{obstr.} \\ + \text{voice} \\ + \text{asp.} \end{bmatrix}$

(72) $[+ \text{obstr.}]_0 > \begin{bmatrix} - \text{voice} \\ - \text{asp.} \end{bmatrix} / \_\_ \#$

(73)   PIE   IIr.   pre-Vedic
  a) pple.   bhudh-to-   bhud-dha-   bud-dha-
      desid. bhi-bhudh-se-ti   bhu-bhudh-zha-ti bu-bud-zha-ti
  b) noun   bhudh-s   bhut-s   bhut-s
  c) pres.   bhudh-ye-toy   bhudh-ya-tai   budh-ya-tai
      perf.   bhe-bhowdh-e   bhu-bhaudh-a   bu-baudh-a

The alternations created by these historical changes had to be accounted for by synchronic rules. And since up to this point nothing has happened to obscure the effect of the changes, we may assume that the synchronic rules were identical in format to the historical changes that gave rise to them. (The exact formulation of the rules is immaterial for the present discussion.)

From pre-Vedic to actually attested Vedic, however, a change took place which did obscure the effect of our historical changes. This was the development formulated in (74). (This change is connected with a 'mini-conspiracy' which eliminated all voiced sibilants in Sanskrit.) The effect of this change was to make the synchronic equivalent of Grassmann's Law opaque. For while the desiderative form in (75 a) has undergone Grassmann's Law in the context / ___ X [− asp.], the structurally similar noun form in (75 b) has not.

(74 a) zh > s
   b) [+ stop] > [− voice] / ___ s

     (Change (b) may actually be a reaffirmation of an inherited rule of voicing assimilation.)

(75)   pre-Vedic   Vedic

a) pple.   bud-dha-   bud-dha-
     desid.   bu-bud-zha-ti   bu-but-sa-ti
b) noun   bhut-s   bhut
c) pres.   budh-ya-tai   budh-ya-tē
     perf.   bu-baudh-a   bu-bōdh-a

As it turns out, forms like *bu-but-sa-ti* survive only in traces, even in the earliest Vedic language. The productive pattern, and the only one acceptable in post-Vedic Sanskrit, is of the type *bu-bhut-sa-ti* with aspirate on the root-initial consonant just as it is found in *bhut*. What has happened is that the synchronic rules corresponding to (72) and (74) have been 'collapsed' into a single rule of deasp. (cf. (76)) and that rule has been ordered before Grassmann's Law. It is this rule collapsing and partial reordering which is responsible for the pattern in (68), i. e. for the pattern on which the incorrect historical analysis and relative chronology in (69/70) are based. (In addition, there is evidence that at this point the synchronic counterpart of Grassmann's Law was reformulated as 'aspirate throwback', rather than aspirate dissimilation. A discussion of this matter is beyond the scope of the present discussion.)

(76)   deasp.   [+ stop] → [− voice, − asp.] / ___ {s, #}

The case of Grassmann's Law is highly instructive. For here the evidence which makes it possible to provide the historically correct account is not readily accessible, as it was in the case of German final devoicing and ə-loss. Rather, it is 'hidden away' in a few obscure early Vedic 'exceptions'. It is therefore not surprising that many analyses of Grassmann's Law have arrived at historically incorrect conclusions.

The implication is obvious: If sound changes result in enough synchronic alternations to motivate 'productive' corresponding synchronic rules, a reordering of these rules may suggest historically incorrect relative chronologies.

But note that where changes result in few alternations or are entirely 'restructured', relative chronologies are not likely to be obscured by rule reordering and thus can be considered trustworthy.

11.9. Summary and conclusions

Many of the early claims of generative phonology concerning the nature of linguistic change are either unacceptable or in need of revision. Thus it is by no means certain that all linguistic change leads to grammar simplification. On the contrary, many changes complicate the grammar. Nor can the claim be accepted that all linguistic change is 'grammar change'. As we have seen, even changes which may have far-reaching grammatical implications may be motivated by surface patterns, rather than the grammatical rule system. Moreover, leveling and the less systematic analogical processes cannot be meaningfully accounted for as grammar change. Finally, the early claim that sound change is 'rule addition' and thus on a par with other rule changes must be − and has been − given up: We need to recognize a fundamental difference between 'primary' sound change and 'secondary' analogical change.

At the same time, for many well-attested analogical developments the generative, rule-oriented approach seems to provide a better explanation than the traditional, surface-oriented approach. For it provides an explanation for the fact that these changes, unlike other analogical developments, are regular and sweeping. In addition, for many developments of this sort the rule approach provides a clear 'model' to motivate the changes and thus makes it easier to account for them than traditional surface-oriented analyses.

Also the notion 'rule reordering', even if it may always be the result of 'rule reapplication', seems to be sound and valuable. Moreover, it has obvious implications for the notion 'relative chronology'. On the other hand, the allied notion of 'rule loss' must be viewed with some suspicion, since it may in all cases be the ultimate outcome of a much slower process of 'rule atrophy' due to leveling. As for the motivation of rule reordering, the notion of phonological transparency and opacity appears to be useful. What still needs to be determined is whether an alternative notion of morphological transparency and opacity can likewise exert a positive influence on rule change.

Beyond its two contributions of rule orientation and the notion of rule reordering, generative phonology has a more general relevance for historical linguistics. Like other approaches which emphasize grammatical systems, it forces the historical linguist to consider the repercussions of linguistic changes on the grammar, rather than merely examining each change by itself, in a quasi-atomistic manner. There is reason to believe that this can be beneficial both to historical and to synchronic linguistics.

12. Semantic change

12.1. Background

It is generally agreed that language conveys meaning. However, a difficulty arises from the fact that the number of meanings which might be conveyed through language — given 'world enough and time' — is without bounds, is in effect infinite. At the same time, human beings are capable of producing only a limited, clearly finite, set of speech sounds. More than that, even if there were no limitations on our production, there certainly are limits on our understanding and processing the infinity of mostly completely novel linguistic symbols which would be required to encode an infinity of possible meanings.

To some degree this difficulty is remedied by the fact that meaning is conveyed not directly, through separate speech sounds for each meaning, but indirectly, through an open-ended, but in effect finite, set of conventional linguistic symbols (lexical items). (The conventionality and 'arbitrariness' of these symbols becomes clear if we consider the word for 'dog' in various languages. As example (1) shows, even closely related languages may 'choose' phonetically very different forms.) These are supplemented by a finite set of rules (syntax) which permit the combination of these symbols into larger structures and ensure that the meanings of these larger structures are not simply a composite of the meanings of the lexical items which they are composed of. Moreover, the lexical items themselves are 'constructed' out of even smaller sets of likewise conventional 'buildings blocks' (phonemes and morphemes) whose combination, again, is governed by a finite set of rules (phonology/morphology). As a consequence, meaning can be conveyed economically, with a very limited set of speech sounds (somewhere between 25 and 125) which, thanks to the lexicon and the rules of syntax, combine into a virtual infinity of possible sentences. It is this economy, then, and the conventional nature of the 'building blocks' and of the rules for their combination which make it possible for us to communicate at all.

> (1)   E dog, G Hund [hunt], Fr. chien [šyɛ̃], Sp. perro, It. cane [kane], Lith. šuo, Hindi kuttā, etc.

However, it seems that there is a certain price to pay for this economy and for the conventional nature of language: Although they permit us to utter a virtual infinity of sentences with at least some hope of being understood, they simultaneously place a clear limit on the meanings which we can convey without ambiguity. Put differently, language provides too broad-meshed a net to capture all the fine distinctions of meaning which we may want or need to express at any given moment.

It is apparently in order to compensate for this restriction that we permit a great degree of 'sloppiness' in meaning: The same phonetic expression is allowed to convey quite different shades of meaning, or even completely unrelated meanings, provided that the linguistic, social, and cultural contexts make it possible to recover something approximating the intended meaning. Consider for instance the sentence in (2). This expression may convey very different shades of meaning depending on whether *Jack* is in kindergarten, first grade, high school, or college, or devoted to calligraphy, or to composing poetry or prose. Moreover, there are in English at least three radically different meanings attached to the phonetic configuration [rayt], the base morpheme of *writer*, namely the meanings which orthographically are differentiated as *write, right*, and *rite*. (For some people there is a fourth meaning, that of *wright*, as in *playwright, wainwright, cartwright*.)

(2)   Jack is a good writer

In this case, there is a clear difference between the lexical item *writer* on one hand and the phonetic configuration [rayt] on the other: In spite of their great diversity, the different meanings of *writer* are clearly relatable and can be accounted for as special 'connotations' or 'uses' of a single lexical item. On the other hand, the different meanings of phonetic [rayt], which can be glossed as 'write', 'right', 'rite' (and 'wright'), are quite distinct from each other; they are the 'basic' or 'core' meanings of different lexical items. It is customary to distinguish these two types of situation as **polysemy** and **homonymy**, respectively.

To complicate matters further, the boundary between these two situations is by no means clear-cut. Thus, British English uses the word *reader* to refer to an academic rank (roughly equivalent to that of an American associate professor). Is this an instance of polysemous use of the same word which occurs in expressions like *He's a slow reader*? Or is it a different, homonymous word? Different individuals might well have different interpretations: To some, a *reader* is properly so named, because he 'reads = lectures'. To others, the similarity between the two 'words' may be intriguing, even tantalizing, but not resolvable into polysemy. While in the case of *reader*, many speakers might opt for polysemy, in cases like *ear* (of grain) beside *ear* (organ of hearing), very few would adopt such an interpretation, although some might at least try. In fact, there seems to be a general tendency to explore the possibility that two phonetically identical expressions might also be lexically identical.

Even if we agree that they are identical, our troubles are not over. For we may then have to worry about which of the two different meanings is the more basic one. In cases like *reader*, this does not appear too difficult: The meaning 'academic rank' clearly seems to be more specialized and therefore derived. However, the case is different in example (3) below: Are planets, comets, meteors, or even the moon properly referred to as stars? (Cf. the expressions in (4).) And what about the sun? If so, what is the basic meaning of *star* and what is derived? Naive speakers may well consider it proper to refer to fixed stars, planets, comets, and meteors as *stars*, but not to the moon or the sun. On the other hand, speakers with some grounding in modern astronomy may exclude not only the moon, but also the planets, comets, and meteors from the range of meanings of *star*; but they might well include the sun, since it is a '(fixed) star'. Still, even such 'astronomically sophisticated' speakers would find it very strange if in bright daylight somebody pointed at the sun and uttered the sentence in (5). And (6) would be considered completely inappropriate when uttered at the sight of the rising sun. Conversely, even more 'naive' uses of the word *star* nowadays tend to exclude meteors. Finally, most speakers are able to live quite comfortably with both the 'naive' and the 'astronomically sophisticated' core meanings, shifting from one to the other as the context requires.

(3)   star : (a) 'luminous natural objects in the night sky, in-
                  cluding the planets, comets, and perhaps the
                  meteors'
             (b) 'fixed stars, i. e. self-luminous bodies, including
                  the sun'

(4)   evening star = 'the planet Venus'
      shooting star = '(comet,) meteor'
      falling star = 'meteor'

(5)   Look at that lovely star in the sky

(6)   Star light, star bright, first star I see tonight ...

Similar **inclusive** and **exclusive** meanings can be found for the word *animal*; cf. (7). And again, speakers may accept any or all of these different meanings (as for instance in the expressions (8)—(10)) without any feeling of contradiction.

(7)   animal = (a) 'any breathing, mobile, food-consuming organism (excepting certain "plants" which come uncomfortably close to this definition)'
       (b) 'mammals, birds, reptiles, amphibians, fish'
       (c) 'mammals and birds'
       (d) 'mammals'

(8)   This powder kills noxious insects, but is harmless to humans and animals.

(9)   It's incorrect to call bacteria 'bugs', because bacteria are plant-like, but bugs or insects are animals.

(10)   Whales aren't really fish, they're animals.

In short, we seem to be prepared to live with a great degree of polysemy. And this polysemy entails a large amount of **semantic overlap**. (Thus, the two meanings of *star* overlap in the area of 'fixed stars which are seen in the night sky'. And in its more inclusive meaning, *animal* overlaps the meaning of, say, *insect*.) Moreover, we accept a great deal of individual variation in the area of semantics.

In fact, we seem to be much more ready to face semantic diversity or even confusion than the logical opposite, the semantic identity of phonetically non-identical expressions, i. e. **synonymy**. True, as a result of semantic overlap, language is full of near-synonyms, such as *unconscious* and *subconscious*. However, total synonymy is rare. There usually is some **semantic differentiation** in terms of the linguistic, social, or cultural contexts in which two words can be used. Thus, in the context of (11), *unconscious* is acceptable, but *subconscious* is not. Cf. section 10.1.4 for the similar phenomenon of differentiation in analogical change. But note that where in analogical change, the direction of differentiation can ordinarily be predicted, no such predictability seems to exist for purely semantic differentiation.

(11)   She knocked him _____

(In certain language uses, especially in poetry, there is a greater tendency than in ordinary language to treat words as synonymous, so as to avoid repetition and 'monotony'. In some poetic traditions, such as the Sanskrit one, this has been carried to an extreme. At the same time, however, poetry tends to exploit differences in connotations which might be ignored in ordinary language. Moreover, poetry may at times simultaneously treat words as synonymous and different in connotation. Some varieties of Sanskrit poetry, for instance, glory in this 'schizophrenic' treatment of meaning.)

Given that meaning is so diversified and 'shifty', it should come as no surprise that many schools of linguistics have tried to exclude it from the scope of linguistic inquiry. And it should likewise not be surprising that it is much more difficult than in other areas of historical linguistics to make statements on natural tendencies of linguistic change. Nevertheless, historical linguistics cannot ignore semantic change. For unless we can relate words such as OE *hlāf* 'bread' and NE *loaf* not only phonetically, but also semantically, it is impossible to trace many historical developments and to do meaningful historical linguistic research.

12.2. The basis for semantic change

As noted, polysemy and semantic overlap are a pervasive feature of language. Associated with these is the fact that there may be variations in the range of meaning of given words, from inclusive to exclusive. At the same time, total synonymy is rarely tolerated, there usually being some degree of semantic differentiation.

12.2.1. Metaphor

What makes it possible for lexical items to be used in this 'fuzzy', overlapping fashion is above all the concept of **metaphor**, in the broadest possible definition of the term: We can use a given item to refer to some new meaning by implicitly or explicitly claiming a semantic relationship or similarity between its established and its intended new meaning. An example at the most elementary level would be the following: We may use sentence (2) above in the meaning that Jack faithfully corresponds with his family and friends, because the act of writing is closely linked with this activity.

The term metaphor is of course more commonly used for less elementary extensions of meaning which require a greater and more daring or conscious semantic 'leap', at least when they first arise. An example is the use of *clear* in sentences like (12), as a metaphoric extension of the meaning which we find in (13). And we can overtly express this metaphoric relation by stating something like (14).

(12)   His statement was clear (to us)

(13)   The water is clear

(14)   His statement was clear as water

Several special subtypes of metaphor are often distinguished. Two closely related subtypes are **metonymy** and **synecdoche**. The former extends the use of a word to refer to things or activities which are considered closely associated with the meaning of that word, such as the examples in (15). The latter refers to a given semantic notion by naming its most prominent or salient part; cf. (16). Sometimes, metaphors of this sort may be humorously or ironically employed where they are totally inappropriate, cf. the synecdoches in (17). Other common metaphors are **hyperbole** or exaggeration (cf. (18)), **litotes** or understatement (cf. (19)), and **euphemism** (cf. (20)). Also ellipsis is often listed in this context, but in this book it has been treated under analogy (cf. 9.2.1).

(15)   The Surf'n'Turf wants   = the person who ordered the
       his bill   'Surf'n'Turf' (= steak and lobs-
                                ter) dinner wants his bill
       The Scalpel   = nickname for a 'scalpel-happy'
                                medical doctor
       Pulpit   = clergy

(16)   The Nose   = the person with the prominent nose

      Hands   = laborers whose hands and arms are considered their only important asset for physical labor

(17)   Curly   = nickname for a person who is bald

      Speedy   = nickname for an exceedingly slow person

(18)   I'm **terribly/awfully/frightfully**   sorry
      He was **sorely** disappointed
      This is the **most unique** (!) experience you'll ever have

(19)   I fell a **bit** under the weather
      The danger is **not inconsiderable**
      A couple of people   = several, but possibly more than two people

(20)   sanitation engineer   = garbage hauler
      pre-owned automobile = used car
      pacified village   = village that has been forced to side with 'us'
      liberation   = killing or putting into 'reeducation camps' people who sided with 'them'
      final solution   = 'elimination' of Jews, Gypsies, and other 'undesirables'

Metaphor thus saliently refers to non-linguistic, 'real-world' similarities (whether real or imagined). However, the relationship between sound and meaning usually remains an arbitrary one. That is, it is merely a matter of convention that in English it is the phonetic sequence [hænd] which refers to a body part and then, by metaphorical extension, also to laborers. Contrast the phonetically very different Spanish *mano* 'hand', as well as the fact that the Spanish metaphorical counterpart to E *hands* 'laborers', namely *bracero*, is based on a slightly different body part, with a pronunciation very different from E *hand*, namely *brazo* 'arm'.

12.2.2. Onomatopoeia, synesthesia

In certain lexical items, the relationship between sound and meaning appears to be more direct and non-arbitrary. The most obvious relationship of this sort is found in **onomatopoeia**, such as the English expression for the rooster's crow, *cockadoodledoo*. True, even here there is a large element of arbitrariness, as can be seen by the fact that in other languages, roosters 'crow differently'; cf. the examples in (20). Still, speakers who have such onomatopoetic expressions in their language generally are satisfied that there is a striking similarity between the linguistic expression and the non-linguistic, real-world sound which it imitates and that therefore the relationship between sound and meaning is direct and 'real'. The linguistic item acts as a metaphor for its real-world reference. A useful term for this kind of relationship is **iconicity**: the linguistic term is an **icon** (a 'likeness') of the thing which it denotes.

(20)   E cockadoodledoo, G kikeriki, Dan. kykeliky [kükelikü], Swed. kukeliku, Fr. cocorico/coquerico/coquelico [kokor/ər/əlikó], Span. quiquiriquí [kikirikí], Lith. kakaríeku/ka-kariekú, Ru. kukarekú, Hindi kuk(a)r̥ūkū, Marathi ku-kručku, Lingala kokolikó; cf. Finn. kukku kiekuu (lit. 'the rooster crows')

There is a strong tendency in onomatopoeia to associate certain phonetic segments or segment sequences with certain types of sound. Some such associations may be rather language-specific. (This is the case, for instance, for many of the examples in section 9.1.2, Chart 9.1.) Others seem to be more common or may even constitute cross-linguistic tendencies. Thus, many languages have pairs or sets of onomatopoetic expressions in which one side has an [i] vowel and refers to relatively high-pitch noises, while the other side has low or back vowels that signal a corresponding lower-pitch noise. Examples may either be of the type (21), with minimal or near-minimal pairs, or of the type (22), where the onomatopoetic expressions differ also in terms of their consonants, etc. (As examples like Germ. *krächzen* with front and non-low [ε] show, some lexical items may not quite fit this pattern. Such examples are put in parentheses. Note that the glosses in (21/24) are only approximate.)

(21a) Engl. drip   drop
              chip   chop
              sniffle   snuffle
              sip   sup (now obsolete)

   b) Germ. girren   gurren   'coo'
              knirren   knarren   'crackle, creak'
              bimmeln   bammeln   'ring (of bells)'
              quieken   quaken   'squeal, quack'

   c) Hindi čīčī   čūčū   'chirp, squeak'
              ṭikṭik   ṭukṭuk   'a ticking noise'
              ṭinṭin   ṭanṭan/ṭunṭun 'a ringing noise'

(22a) bird noises:

   Engl.   cheep, (chirp,) peep,   : caw, coo, hoot, whoop
           twitter
   Germ.   girren, piepsen, zirpen,   : krah (krächzen), gur-
           zwitschern   ren, heulen [hɔ̈ülən]
   Hindi   čīčī (čēčē, ṭē)   : čūčū, kāw
   Kota   čikčik, čivkčivk   : kaka, gugr(gr)

   b) laugh:
   Engl.   giggle, snigger, snicker, : laugh, guffaw, chortle,
           titter   cackle
   Germ.   kichern, wiehern   : lachen (brüllen)
   Hindi   ṭhīṭhī, hīhī, khīkhī,   : hāhā, hāsnā, aṭṭ(a)hās,
           khilkhil   ṭhaṭhānā, ghurghurākar
                                        hāsnā

There is a less forceful tendency toward similar 'sound symbolism' in other areas of the vocabulary. Consider for instance the English and German vocabulary for 'shine, twinkle, etc.'. As the examples in (23) show, a high front vowel generally is associated with a more 'vibrant' or 'pulsating' light effect. (Phonetic exceptions again are put in parentheses. Possible semantic exceptions are indicated by a following question mark.) Hindi exhibits a similar pattern, although the [i] vocalism is more restricted; cf. (24). But note that many of the Hindi lexical items that correspond to English and German [i]-words have palatal stops whose acoustic effect is similar to that of high front vowels.

(23) Engl. flicker, glimmer, glisten, : flame, flare (?), flash (?),
            glitter, shimmer, twin-   glare, (gleam), glow,
            kle   lightning (?), shine,
                                         sparkle (?)

     Germ. blitzen (?), flickern, flit- : flackern, flammen, fun-
            tern, glimmern, glitzen,   keln (?), Glanz (glän-
            schimmern   zen), (glimmen, glü-
                                          hen), leuchten [lɔüçtən],
                                          scheinen

(24) Hindi j̈hilmilānā   'shine with quick vibration (such
                             as hot air over a desert or a light
                             shining through haze)'
            ṭimṭimānā   'flicker'
     vs.   j̈agj̈agānā   'glitter'
            j̈hakj̈hakānā   'sparkle (as of sequins)'
            j̈hamj̈hamānā   'sparkle (also of sounds)'
            j̈hamaknā   'sparkle (also of sounds)'
            j̈amaknā   'be bright'
            čamčamānā   'glare'
            dhakdhakānā   'blaze'
            dhagdhagānā   'flare up'

The similarities between (21/22) and (23/24) are not limited to the
opposition between [i] vs. other vocalism. Both English and German
have a suffix-like element *-er(-)* in onomatopoetic words, as well as in
words referring to 'visual effects'; cf. (25). And Hindi shows a wide-
spread use of reduplication in both sets of vocabulary; cf. (26). (The
suffix *-ānā* serves to turn onomatopoetic expressions into verbs.)

(25) Engl. twitter, snigger, snicker, : flicker, glitter, shimmer
            titter
     Germ. zwitschern, kichern,   : flickern, flittern, glim-
            wiehern   mern, glitzern, schim-
                                          mern, flackern

(26) Hindi ṭin-ṭin(ānā), ṭun-ṭun(ā- : ṭim-ṭimānā, j̈ag-j̈agānā,
            nā), khil-khil(ānā), ...

One suspects that these similarities are the result of the transfer of
acoustically-based onomatopoetic patterns to other areas of perception

and sensation, by a metaphoric process which is frequently referred to as **synesthesia**. Similar developments can be observed in non-onomatopoetic vocabulary, as in Engl. *a shrill red, a quiet blue*. Specifically, the use of high front vowel to designate 'high-frequency' or 'high-vibration' visual effects may be attributed to the relatively 'high pitch' of the vowel [i].

Synesthesia is at work also in other areas of the vocabulary. Consider for instance the metaphorical expressions in (27), where words of sense perception and sensation are extended into the area of 'cognition'. What is common to the examples of this type as well as the ones in (25/26) is a semantic extension from the more **concrete** or tangible **to** the more **abstract** or intangible, a development which recurs in many other areas of the lexicon; cf. e. g. (28).

(27)   Engl.   grasp 'understand'
        Germ.   (er)fassen 'grasp; understand'
        Lat.   comprehendere 'grasp, collect; understand'
        Skt.   avagacchati 'understands (lit. "goes down into")'

(28)   Engl.   **head** of a family
                  foot of a hill/mountain
                  mouth of a river
                  shoulder of a road
                  the **root** of all evil
        Germ.   **Haupt**stadt 'capital (lit. "head city")'
                  Fuss eines Berges 'foot of a hill/mountain'
                  Rücken eines Berges/Berg**rücken** 'ridge (lit. "back") of a mountain'
                  Bauch einer Flasche/Flaschen**bauch** 'body (lit. "belly") of a bottle'
        Lat.   **caput** 'capital (lit. "head")'
                  pēs montis 'foot of a hill/mountain'
                  caput montis 'top (lit. "head") of a hill/mountain'
        Skt.   **mukha**dēva- 'chief/head god'
                  pada- 'foot; quarter (of a verse, etc.; cf. the **four** feet of cattle)'
                  danta**mūla**- 'pre-alveoli (lit. "tooth root")'

A synesthetic explanation has been proposed also for words like the ones in (29), in which the sound [i] appears to be associated with smallness. Various explanations have been offered for this association, ranging from the 'narrow' or 'thin' sound of [i] to the fact that [i] is articulated with a relatively small opening of the lips. Perhaps, however, the association is a secondary one, based on the fact that small or young animals and persons tend to emit higher-pitched sounds than larger or older ones. At any rate, the tendency toward this type of semantic extension is fairly weak, as can be seen by the fact that the vowels of, say, Engl. *big* and *small* are exactly the opposite of what one would expect.

(29)   Engl. itsy-bitsy, teeny, wee, pip-squeak

This explanation has been further extended to account for the [i]-vocalism in diminutive suffixes of the type (30), or even for the feminine suffix *-ī* found in Sanskrit and later Indo-Aryan languages; cf. (31).

(30)	Engl.		baby, Johnny, ...	[-ī/ĭ]
	Swiss Germ.		müəs-li	'cereal (dimin.)'
			Hans-li	'Johnny'
	Goth.		gum-ein [-īn]	'little man'
	Gk.		paid-i-on	'small boy'
	It.		bamb-ino	'little child'
	Span.		perr-ito	'little dog'
(31)	Skt.	vṛka- (m.) : vṛkī (f.)	'wolf'	
	Hindi	čhōṭā (m.) : čhōṭī (f.)	'small'	
		laṛkā (m.) : laṛkī (f.)	'child' (i.e. 'boy' : 'girl')	

Counterexamples to this tendency toward the use of [i]-vowels in diminutive and feminine suffixes are even more wide-spread than the ones for the synesthetic use of [i]-vowels to denote smallness in lexical items.

Thus, Lithuanian has a synchronically very active system of diminutive formation; but only two out of eight diminutive affixes have [i]-vocalism; cf. (32). In fact, the majority of suffixes contain an [u]-vowel. Similarly, the earliest Indo-European diminutive suffixes seem to have been *-lo- and *-ko-, both without [i]. And the synchronically 'live' diminutive suffix of Hindi is *-ū*, not *-ī*; cf. (33).

(32)   -ik^{y}ē-
      -īt^{y}a/īt^{y}ē-
  vs. -el^{y}a/el^{y}ē- or -ēl^{y}a/ēl^{y}ē-
      -ul^{y}a/ul^{y}ē-
      -ut^{y}a/ut^{y}ē-
      -uk^{y}a/uk^{y}ē- (with or without palatalization of preceding
                 C)
      -ūkšt^{y}a/ūkšt^{y}ē-
      -už^{y}a/už^{y}ē-

(33) čhōṭā 'small, little'   : chōṭū 'little one (dimin.)'
      bāp   'father'   : bāpū   'father (dimin.)'
      gītā   (female name)   : gītū   (id., deminutive)

As far as feminine affixes are concerned, -*ī* is productive in Sanskrit and especially in the modern Indo-Aryan languages, but not in the other members of the Indo-European language family, which prefer low-vowel -*ā*. This casts considerable doubt on the 'synesthetic' explanation of -*ī*. There are, to be sure, Hindi doublets like the ones in (34), where the feminine forms in -*ī* denote a smaller variant of the -*ā*-form. However, even in the examples of (34a), it is not always clear whether the form in -*ā* is 'basic' and the form in -*ī* a 'derived' diminutive. And in (34b) it is clearly the form in -*ā* which has a special connotation. One suspects, therefore, that -*ī* does not function as a diminutive suffix. Rather, the contrast between -*ī* and -*ā* in these words appears to be secondarily modeled on the similar morphological contrast between female/feminine and male/masculine forms in human nouns (cf. (31)). And the motivation for this secondary extension seems to lie in stereotypical associations between sex and size. As a consequence, differentiations can be made in both directions, from 'smaller' to 'larger' and vice versa.

(34a) ǰūtā   'big shoe'   : ǰūtī   'small shoe'
       katōrā   'big bowl'   : katōrī   'small bowl'
       ghaṇṭā   'big bell'   : ghaṇṭī   'small bell'
   b) čīṭā   'big black ant'   : čīṭī   'ant'

12.2.3. Taboo

There is one other area in which speakers treat the relationship between words and meanings as iconic, not as arbitrary. This is the area of **taboo**, where the linguistic term behaves as if it were a metaphor of its non-linguistic, real-world point of reference: The 'name' becomes confused, in a very striking and salient manner, with the 'thing' (or person) which it denotes.

What is subject to taboo may differ from culture to culture. But whatever the cultural differences, tabooed expressions tend to be avoided. At the same time, however, complete avoidance commonly is not possible, since on many occasions we will have to refer to the tabooed notion after all. A common avoidance strategy is to replace the tabooed item by a different, frequently euphemistic expression which is semantically appropriate. But the new expression, in turn, tends to become taboo, since it is likewise felt to be too closely linked with the tabooed point of reference. The consequence may be a chain of ever-changing replacements, a constant turnover in vocabulary. Thus, in English and many other languages, there is a strong tendency to place a taboo on terms for excrements, or for the location where they are deposited. Some of the effects of this taboo can be seen in the plethora of current English terms for 'toilet' cited in (35). (The list is by no means exhaustive.)

(35)   bathroom, john, ladies'/men's room, lavatory, loo, powder-room, toilet, W.C., washroom

12.3. Mechanisms and causes for change

Many of the phenomena described in the preceding section as the basis for semantic change are at the same time also mechanisms and causes for change. Especially onomatopoeia, other synesthetic developments, and taboo may act as very powerful agents for linguistic change.

12.3.1. Onomatopoeia, synesthesia, taboo

Onomatopoeia frequently occasions the undoing of sound change, such that the iconic relationship between real-world reference and linguistic symbol is restored. For instance, it has been argued that onomatopoetic considerations are responsible for the fact that the normal Modern English word corresponding to ME *pīpen is peep, not the expected pipe. (Cf. 3.7 above.) Similar effects can be seen in synesthetic vocabulary referring to size (cf. (36)). And it is at least possible that the increasing use of diminutive suffixes with [i]-vocalism in English, early German, and Romance resulted from similar synesthetic considerations. Moreover, there is one reported case in which the stereotypic association of smallness with 'female' ultimately had a profound effect on agreement marking: In archaic varieties of the modern Indo-Aryan language Konkani, words for females ordinarily 'impose' feminine agreement marking on qualifying adjectives. But diminutives, which are charac-terized by a neuter ending -ū, take neuter agreement, whether they refer to males or females. Compare example (37a). In certain dialects, however, the meaning of the diminutive neuter noun čēḍū 'child' was specialized to refer only to female children, i. e. young girls. Subse-quently, the agreement marking associated with čēḍū was reinterpreted as marking 'young female' (rather than 'diminutive') and extended to other, originally feminine-gender nouns when they refer to 'young females'. Compare (37b). What is interesting is that the result of this change is a system in which -i is the unmarked feminine agreement suffix, while youngness is marked by the lower vowel -ɛ̄, contrary to the 'synesthetic' expectation.

(36a) Engl. tiny (16th c.) : teeny (18th c.)
    b) PGmc. *lutila- 'small' > OE lytel, OHG lutzil, etc.
        vs. Goth. leitils [ī], OE (variant) lītel, ON lítell

(37a) bhoyn 'sister' : dhakṭ-i bhoyn 'little sister' (f.)
       čēḍ-ū **'child'** : dhakṭ-ɛ̄ čēḍ-ū 'little child' (n./dimin.)
    b) bhoyn 'sister' : dhakṭ-i bhoyn 'little sister' (unmarked f.)
       čēḍ-ū **'girl'** : dhakṭ-ɛ̄ čēḍ-ū 'little girl' (**young f.**)
       Hence:
       bhoyn 'sister' : dhakṭ-ɛ̄ bhoyn 'little sister' (**young** f.)

Even more pervasive can be the effect of taboo. First, as noted in the preceding section, taboo can lead to a constant turnover in vocabulary, such as in the English expression for 'toilet'; cf. (35) above. In some societies, the effect may be much more far reaching. For instance, it has been argued that the difficulties of tracing Tahitian vocabulary to its Proto-Polynesian sources are in large measure a consequence of massive taboo: Upon the death of a member of the royal family, every word which was a constituent part of that person's name, or even any word sounding like it became taboo and had to be replaced by new words. (It appears that this massive and constant vocabulary renewal was accomplished not only by metaphorical meaning extensions in native vocabulary, but also by large-scale borrowing.)

Interestingly, in the case of some tabooed words, lexical replacement may affect not the tabooed words, but innocent homonyms. This is especially noticeable with many of the 'Anglo-Saxon' or 'four-letter' words of English which, though tabooed in polite company, are used quite frequently — and with gusto — in more 'macho' and almost deliberately impolite contexts. Thus, in American English, the animal names *ass* and *cock* were replaced by *donkey* and *rooster*. Such replacements seem to be motivated by the desire not to be perceived as uttering a tabooed word under the wrong social circumstances. Similarly, earlier English had a fair number of words with short vowel in the context [f _____ k]; cf. (38). Except for the well-known taboo word (not listed in (38)), none of these have survived as independent words, presumably in large measure because they sounded too similar to the tabooed word. (Dates given in parentheses refer to the last attestation of given items. Interestingly, most of the words died out in the Victorian area, when the taboo against words with sexual connotations was at its acme. It is from this period of English that we get expressions like *white meat* and *dark meat* for 'chicken (etc.) breast' and 'legs/thighs'.)

(38)   fuk (a sail) (1529)
       fac 'factotum' (1841)
       feck 'effect, efficiency' (1887) (now only 'Scots Engl.' *feck-
       less*)
       fack/feck (one of the stomachs of a ruminant) (1887)
       feck(s)/fack(s) '(in) faith, (in) fact' (1891)

An alternative to lexical replacements of this sort is **tabooistic distortion**, a deliberate 'mispronunciation' of a tabooed word which enables speakers to utter the word without 'really' saying it. Compare the English examples in (39). The last two sets of examples reflect another common taboo, against 'taking the name of the Lord in vain'.

(39) Oh, shoot! Sheet!
Darn it! Goodness gracious! Doggone it! What in tarnation?!
Good-bye (for older *(may) God be with you*)

12.3.2. Reinterpretation

Outside the area of onomatopoeia, synesthesia, and taboo, **reinterpretation** is probably the most important mechanism of semantic change. We have already seen this process at work in the Konkani development of (37), as well as in the discussion of analogy (cf. e. g. section 9.1.2).

In many cases, reinterpretation is precipitated by other linguistic developments, including sound change and metaphor, and even by extralinguistic, social or cultural changes. These will be examined in closer detail in the following sections. At this point it is useful to note that reinterpretation can operate without such prior, 'precipitating' changes.

A famous and often-quoted example of such 'free', 'unprecipitated' reinterpretation is that of NE *bead*. Its Old English ancestor *(ge)bed* had a markedly different meaning, namely 'prayer', just like its Modern German cognate *Gebet*. The reinterpretation by which this word acquired its modern meaning must have taken place in the context of a practice which was very common in medieval times and which until recently was still wide-spread among Catholics: the practice of counting or keeping track of one's prayers by means of the pellets on a rosary. Within this context it was possible to reinterpret a statement like (40) to refer not to prayers, but to the pellets on the rosary.

(40) I'm counting my beads

12.3.3. Sound change and shift in meaning

One of the developments which may precipitate semantic reinterpretation (as well as other semantically based changes) is sound change. Consider for instance the case of Engl. *daisy*: As noted in 9.2.3, this word originally was a compound of *day's* and *eye*, a metaphorical expression for the sun to which the flower was compared. However, because sound change applied differently in stressed and unstressed syllables, this word developed into NE [dḗzī], not [dēzay]; cf. (41). And in the process, its relationship to *day* and *eye* was obscured to the point that *daisy* was 'bleached' of its metaphorical meaning. It therefore had to be reinterpreted as an underived, non-metaphorical lexical item.

(41)   OE dæges ēage > ME dais ei(e) > NE daisy [dḗzī]
       vs.   ēage >   ei(e) >   eye   [áy]

Semantic change is not limited to cases of phonological 'divergence'. Also 'convergence', resulting in homonymy, may trigger semantic change. As noted in section 12.1, one common reaction lies in exploring the possibility that two phonetically identical expressions might also be lexically identical. In cases like (42), most speakers will probably opt against reinterpreting the two homonymous forms as a single, polysemous lexical item. (But note that for the many Americans whose familiarity with 'ears of grain' is limited to edible corn (or maize) cobs, the identification becomes easier, since such 'ears of corn' are comparable to many animal ears in size and — with some semantic 'good will' — also in shape.) Cases like (43) are more promising, and speakers not familiar with the different spellings of the two terms are often surprised when they find out that they are written differently. A case of successful reanalysis is given in (44).

(42)   PGmc.   *auzō   > NE ear (body part)
               *ahiz/ahuz >   ear (grain-bearing part of a
                                       plant)

(43)   (OFr.   mareschal   ⇒) ME mareschal
                                      > NE [ma(r)šəl] marshal
       (OFr.   marcial   ⇒) ME marcial
                                      > NE [ma(r)šəl] martial
       (cf. NE *field marshal : court martial,* both used in military
       contexts)

(44)   pre-Skt.   *meth-   > Vedic Skt. math-   'rob'
                  *menth/mṇth-   >   manth/math- 'whirl,
                                                          shake'
       → Class. Skt. math- 'whirl, stir, shake, "shake down" =
       rob'

Instead of leading to a reanalysis of originally distinct words as being identical, homonymy sometimes results in a very different development, namely the replacement of one of the two homonymous items. This development is most frequently found in cases of so-called **homonym clash**, where the phonological merger of lexical items results in excessive ambiguities.

One of the most famous cases is the one in (45): Through sound change, Lat. *gallus* 'rooster' and *cattus* 'cat' merged in Gascon French. One can well imagine the ambiguities that this merger must have brought about, especially in a farming context where it makes a considerable difference whether it is the cat or the rooster that has entered the hen house. The response was similar to one of the 'avoidance maneuvers' in taboo: It consisted in a variety of dialectally different replacements of the word for rooster.

(45)   Lat. cattus 'cat'   > Gasc. Fr. gat
          gallus 'rooster' >   gat
                      →   [azã] (orig. 'pheasant')
                           [begey] (orig. 'vicar')
                           [put] (orig. 'chick')

In some cases, the replacement of 'clashing' homonyms may be only partial; cf. (46). What is interesting is that in such cases of semantically-based change, the relic forms survive in marginal function, just as they do in analogical change. (Note that *let ball*, a term in tennis, is often replaced by folk-etymological and more 'transparent' *net ball*.)

(46)   OE lǣtan 'permit'   > NE let
          lettan 'stop, hinder' >   let → stop, hinder, ...
      NE relics: without let or hindrance
                 let ball

12.3.4. Other linguistic change and shift in meaning

As noted in 10.1.4, doublets resulting from analogical change usually are differentiated, such that the new form takes on the synchronically productive meaning or function and the old form survives in marginal function. It may be argued that there is a difference between the differentiation in (47a) and (47b): In (a) we are dealing with simple formal differentiation as the motivation for semantic specialization. In (b), on the other hand, a semantic, metaphorical differentiation had taken place even before the analogical replacement of the comparative *elder* by *older*. The latter change, then, led to the semantic **isolation** of the originally metaphorical expression *elder* and to its reinterpretation as a distinct lexical item in its own right. As a consequence, church officers nowadays do not have to be 'old' (or older than the rest of the congregation) in order to be called *(church) elders*.

(47)   pre-NE   old : elder → older
   a)   Relic I: elder (as in: elder brother, sister)
   b)   Relic II: elder (of the church/community)

Lexical obsolescence likewise can engender the isolation of originally metaphorical expressions and their reinterpretation as basic, underived words. For instance, in medieval soldiers' slang, battle was referred to as the smashing of pots or cups (= heads) into shards. This brought about the metaphorical extensions in (48a). Subsequently, the basic terms for 'cup' and 'shard' became obsolete, so that the Modern German and French words in (48b) have lost their metaphorical flavor. In fact, they have become the normal words for 'head', while the older terms (Fr. *chef*, G *Haupt*) survive in marginal, frequently metaphorical function. (Cf. e. g. the use of G. *Haupt* in *Hauptstadt*, ex. (28) above). Interestingly, in this metaphorical expression, the synchronically normal word for 'head', *Kopf*, would be inappropriate.)

(48a)   OFr.   test   'pot, potsherd' : test   'head (metaph.)'
   MHG   kopf   'cup'   : kopf   'head (metaph.)'
   b)   NFr.   tesson   'shard'   : tête   'head'
   NHG   Tasse   'cup'   : Kopf   'head'

Also borrowing can lead to the isolation and reinterpretation of originally polysemous expressions. For instance, when the German word *Angst* 'fear, anxiety, anguish' was first used in the German-language writings of Freud, it was employed in its fairly broad, ordinary-language range of connotations. However, upon being borrowed into English, the word *angst* came to be used as a technical term of Freudian psychology, with a very specialized range of meanings. (German-born Freudians have deplored this semantic narrowing, considering it a falsification of Freud's view.)

12.3.5. Social and cultural change and semantic shift

Since meaning is established by way of reference between linguistic signs and the 'real world', any change in the 'real world' can affect the meaning of words. In the majority of cases, such semantic shifts are a secondary consequence of social, cultural, etc., changes. But at times the semantic shift may be the very vehicle for such changes.

For instance, negative attitudes of Americans of European descent toward fellow-citizens of African origin for a long time brought about a situation in which any term used for Afro-Americans quickly acquired negative, derogatory, or insulting connotations. Just as with tabooed words, the response until recently consisted in a constant turnover in the words designating Afro-Americans, ranging from *Ethyopian, African, Colored, Negro, Afro-American* to the six-letter obscenity still commonly used as a term of insult. This linguistic turnover was in the nineteen-seventies brought to a halt by a conscious and deliberate redefinition of the word *black*: Where previously this word had negative and derogatory connotations, even among Afro-Americans, it was now redefined by the 'Black-Power Movement' as a word with neutral or even positive connotations, completely on a par with the word *white* which traditionally had been employed in reference to Americans of European origin. And since then it has replaced all of its predecessors, including *Afro-American,* as the most commonly used, neutral term for Americans of African descent.

The more usual, non-deliberate effect of social change is exemplified in cases like the redefinition of, say, Brit. Engl. *king* from 'absolute monarch' to '(figure)head of government' or of Am. Engl. *governor* from 'administrator of a British colony' to 'elected head of a state of the Union'. Redefinitions like these result from a common tendency to retain old terms even if the points of reference for these terms undergo considerable social, cultural, etc. change.

The effects of cultural change can be seen in the semantic developments which words like *car, lorry/truck*, or *tire* have undergone as the result of motorization. Consider also the case of Gmc. **wrītan* 'scratch, carve, make incisions': In early Germanic, this verb was appropriately applied to the art of writing runes, for runes were generally scratched or carved into wood, bark, or rock. With the advent of Christianity came a different mode of writing, namely on parchment and by means of a quill. But in spite of the fact that letters now ordinarily were no longer 'carved', the old term for writing was retained in Old English and Icelandic. This retention, however, in effect severed the semantic link between 'scratch, engrave, etc.' and 'write'. The consequence was a semantic split: OE *wrītan*, OIcel. *ríta* 'write' were now reinterpreted as words in their own right, different from *wrītan, ríta* 'scratch, engrave, etc.' (English subsequently lost the latter word; but Modern Icelandic retains it as a separate word, a 'mere' homonym of *ríta* 'scratch'.)

12.4. Results of semantic change

As the use of the term 'split' in the preceding paragraph shows, it is possible to classify some of the results of semantic change under headings familiar from sound change. Thus, beside the split of **wrītan* 'scratch, engrave, etc.; write runes' into *wrītan/ríta* 'scratch, engrave, etc.' and *wrītan/ríta* 'write', we also get mergers as in the case of Skt. *math-* 'stir' and *manth/math-* 'rob' → *math-* 'stir; rob'; cf. (44) above.

12.4.1. Broadening and narrowing of meanings

But note that such 'clean', clear-cut developments are not very common. Usually, semantic shifts tend to be just as 'fuzzy' as their synchronic basis, leading not to 'mergers' and 'splits', but merely to the **broadening** or **narrowing** of the range of meanings. For instance, the fact that in British English, *king* is now used to refer to a (figure) head of state does not prevent the term from being employed in reference to absolute monarchs. Rather than replacing one meaning with another one, the change broadens the meaning of *king* to cover the range of both '(figure) head of state' and 'absolute monarch'. Similarly, when Germ. *Angst* was borrowed into English as a technical term in Freudian psychology, all that happened was a narrowing of its meaning, not a complete semantic replacement.

12.4.2. Meliorization and pejorization

One effect which is common and interesting enough to have been specially noted in the literature is that the value judgments attached to particular words can change: As the result of semantic change, the connotations of words may become more positive (**meliorization**) or more negative (**pejorization**).

Consider for instance the case of OHG *marheskalk*, borrowed into French as *maresc(h)al(c)*: Its original meaning was 'farm or stable hand in charge of the horses'. Now, horses were very important war equipment in medieval times. As a consequence, the meaning of *maréchal* was reinterpreted as 'person in charge of important war equipment'. A series of semantic extensions, presumably via 'person in charge of horses and other war equipment' and 'person in charge of horses, other war equipment, and troops' eventually led to the fact that Fr. *maréchal* (and also the English and German borrowings *marshal, Marschall*) are used to refer to high military officers, etc. A similar development, perhaps significantly in the same social context, is that of OE *cniht* 'boy; servant' to NE *knight*. (This semantic shift seems to have involved the following steps: 'boy' → 'servant' → 'military servant or follower of a king or nobleman' → 'member of the lower nobility'; cf. the similar development in G *Knappe* 'boy' → 'page of a nobleman, esquire'.) This meliorization has counterparts in similar, chronologically and socially parallel developments in other European languages, such as G *Ritter*/ Fr. *chevalier*/Span. *caballero* 'horse-rider' → 'knight, nobleman'.

On the other hand, the fact that OE *cniht* means not only 'boy, youth', but also 'servant' reflects a different, pejorizing tendency which likewise has parallels elsewhere. Thus, *Knecht*, the German cognate of OE *cniht*, NE *knight*, has the meaning 'servant, stable/farm hand', or even 'serf'. Similarly, in many varieties of English, the word *boy* is used in reference to inferiors or servants. An even farther-reaching development is found in OE *cnafa* 'child, youth' which via 'servant' eventually turned into NE *knave* 'villain'. And note that the word *villain*, used to gloss NE *knave*, likewise is a pejorization of a word whose original meaning was 'belonging to the villa/estate or to the village', i.e. 'servant, serf' or 'peasant = serf'.

The development of such thoroughly negative connotations or meanings may simply reflect a stereotypical distrust of servants' honesty or loyalty. But other pejorizing changes suggest a different explanation, namely that the major motivating force behind such pejorizations is the contempt in which western and many other societies tend to hold those who are weaker or less fortunate.

Consider for instance the fate of ME *sely*: Like its German counterpart *selig*, this word originally meant 'blessed, blissful'. By semantic extension, it came to be used in the meaning 'innocent, helpless, defenseless', as in Matthew Arnold's *silly sheep*. But eventually, its meaning was reanalyzed as 'innocent, helpless', hence 'unwary, incautious' and therefore 'stupid'. This development is by no means isolated. Thus, Fr. *crétin* 'feeble-minded, stupid' is in origin a dialectal development of Lat. *christiānus* 'Christian'. The development from 'Christian' to 'stupid' presumably took place via an intermediate stage 'person who in true Christian fashion turns the other cheek when attacked'.

Note in addition the recurrent and pervasive pejorization of terms referring to women, the so-called 'weaker sex': This change is not limited to *hussy* (for which see 9.2.3 and 10.1.4 above). A similar development is found in OE *cwene* : early NE *quean* 'hussy, whore' or OHG *thiorna/diorna* 'girl, young woman, virgin' : NHG *Dirne* 'prostitute, whore'. Moreover, notice that there is a plethora of other negative terms for women who do not live up to the strictest moral standards (such as E *slut, slattern, whore*), but few if any for men with similarly loose morals. (In fact, the few terms that do exist, such as E *stud*, tend to have 'macho', but positive, rather than negative connotations.)

The interest of such developments of meliorization and pejorization evidently lies in the fact that they tell us a lot about past cultural and social history, and probably also about certain pervasive social attitudes.

12.4.3. Taboo

What must be of perhaps even greater interest to the historical linguist is the pervasive effect which taboo can have on linguistic change. (Similar, but less far-reaching, effects are found also with onomatopoeia and synesthesia, as well as in 'homonym clashes'.)

As noted earlier, one common consequence of taboo lies in lexical replacement. And in some societies, this replacement can take place on a massive scale. A different response lies in tabooistic distortion, which may considerably alter the phonetic shape of tabooed lexical items. Since linguistic reconstruction crucially depends on the establishment of lexical cognates, such tabooistic replacement or distortion may considerably or even severely limit our ability to reconstruct.

A case in point is the Indo-European word for 'tongue': Given that all (or almost all) human beings have tongues, we can be sure that there must have been a word for 'tongue' in Proto-Indo-European. And there is good comparative evidence for the existence of such a word in the proto-language. However, as far as the phonological shape of this word is concerned (especially of its initial consonant), the comparative evidence is quite uncertain. Compare the data in (49), where the forms on the right side indicate the possible PIE sources for the attested forms on the left. (Note that the stem-final alternation between *-*wā* and *-*ū*- can be accounted for in terms of a well-established PIE morphophonemic alternation. In a number of languages, the non-initial stop could be derived from more than one possible source. In such cases, that form has been chosen which best agrees with the majority of the other languages.)

(49)	Oscan	fangvā	*dhn̥ǵwā
	Lat.	lingua	*ln̥ǵhwā (?)
	OLat.	dingua	*dn̥ǵhwā
	OIr.	teng(a)e	*tn̥ǵhwā-
	Gmc.	*tungwō	*dn̥ǵhwā
	OCS	językŭ	*n̥ǵhū- (i. e. Øn̥ǵhū-)
	Lith.	liežuvis	*leyǵhū- (?)
	Skt.	ǰihvā	*ǵ(h)iǵhwā (?)
	Av.	hizū	*siǵhū
	Toch. B	kantwo	*ǵ(h)/kn̥t/d(h)wā

Now, it is perhaps possible to eliminate some of these various reconstructive possibilities. Oscan *fangvā* might for instance be explained as resulting from a metathesis of the feature 'aspiration' (i. e. *dhn̥ǵwā < *dn̥ǵhwā). Similarly, the Tocharian word can be explained as resulting by metathesis from an earlier form *t/d(h)n̥ǵhwā. For the initial *l-* of Class. Lat. *lingua* we might refer to *lacrima* : OLat. *dacrima*. However, the change of initial *d-* to *l-* does not otherwise recur in Latin and is therefore quite anomalous. A different explanation, which would derive the *l-* by contamination from the semantically related verb *lingō* 'lick', is therefore perhaps preferable. And such an explanation is almost certainly to be assumed for Lith. *liežuvis*; cf. *liežu* 'lick'.

Even with these assumptions, however, we are unable to account for the root vocalism *i* of Sanskrit and Avestan. And even more importantly, we cannot establish what was the initial consonant (if there was any): Latin and Germanic suggest *d-*, Old Irish *t-*, Old Church Slavic *Ø*, Avestan *s-*, and Sanskrit perhaps *ǵh-*. Finally, what remains unexplained is why this word should have undergone so many unusual, metathetical or contaminatory changes.

Given our knowledge about early Indo-European society, it is probable that these difficulties result from tabooistic distortion: First, for our linguistic ancestors, the tongue was the organ of speech (= language) par excellence. This is for instance reflected in expressions like *the English tongue* 'the English language', or Lat. *lingua* 'tongue, language' (the indirect source of NE *language*). Being the organ of speech, the tongue was imbued with magical powers, just like speech itself. For speech made it possible to name things or people and by naming them, to have power over them. As a consequence, the word for the organ of speech could be subject to the same kind of taboo as the word(s) for God in the Judeo-Christian tradition. If, then, reference had to be made to the tongue, tabooistic distortion made it possible to do so without actually uttering the awesome word. This explanation gains in plausibility if we consider that the words for a number of other important body parts, such as the heart and the kidneys, likewise have undergone unexpected and deviant phonetic developments in a number of the Indo-European languages.

12.5. Shifts in semantic fields

By and large, semantic change operates in a rather random fashion, affecting one word here (in one way), and another form there (in another way). Given the 'fuzzy' nature of meaning, this is of course not surprising. What is surprising is that there should be any instances at all in which semantic change exhibits a certain degree of systematicity. But some such cases can be found.

First of all, whole semantically related areas of the lexicon may undergo obsolescence or semantic change at about the same time. Most commonly this is the result of some radical change in culture or society. Thus, the effective replacement of the horse and buggie by the automobile brought about a great amount of semantic change (as in *car, truck/lorry, tire*) and/or obsolescence (as in *thill, snaffle*).

Also gradual change can have far-reaching effects, if it permeates the entire society and culture. For instance, the rise of medieval feudalism led to a large amount of semantic change to accommodate old terms to the new social context. Compare again the meliorizing changes in *marheskalk/mareschal, cniht/Ritter/chevalier/caballero*, etc. Or consider the hunt-oriented semantic redefinitions in (50) which seem to have arisen in the more specific context of medieval and early modern British feudalism.

(50)   OE fugol 'bird'   : NE fowl
             deor   'animal' :   deer
             hund   'dog'   :   hound

It is often said that in such cases, whole **semantic fields** are affected by change. However, even here we usually do not encounter a high degree of regularity or systematicity. For lexical items generally belong to several semantic fields at the same time. And membership in one field may in any given case outweigh membership in another field. Thus, where OE *cniht* underwent feudal meliorization to *knight*, OE *cnafa* experienced pejorization to *knave*. In the meantime, the German cognates developed in just about the opposite direction, with *Knecht* being pejorized to 'servant' and *Knappe* acquiring the more favorable meaning 'page of a nobleman, esquire'.

There are, however, semantically highly structured portions of the vocabulary, such as the system of kinship terms (*father, mother, son, daughter*, etc.), the system of numerals, names for days of the week, etc. And these constitute fairly well-defined and coherent semantic fields. It is in these areas that we can — and do — most readily find instances of systematic shifts which affect whole semantic fields.

An excellent example of the results of such a shift (or series of shifts) is the sociolinguistically differentiated recategorization of meal-time names in Jamaica; cf. (51). (The sociolinguistic dialects are: (i) Upper Middle Class; (ii) Lower Middle Class; (iii) Estate Laborer; (iv) Peasant Farmer. The relative size of the meal designated by a given term is indicated as follows: H = heavy, M = medium, L = light.)

	5−7 a.m.	11−Noon	4−6 p.m.	7−8:30 p.m.	10:30−Midnight
(51)					
i)	breakfast (M)	lunch (M)	tea (L)	dinner (H)	supper (L)
ii)	breakfast (M)	dinner (H)	supper (M)	supper (L)	
iii)	tea (L)	breakfast (M)		dinner (H)	
iv)	tea (L)	breakfast (H)	dinner (M)	supper (L)	

Without further interpretation, this distribution of meal-time names may not seem to be any less capricious and non-systematic than any other instance of semantic change. However, if we establish the abbreviatory conventions in (52), we can rewrite (51) as (53).

(52a) Time dimension:

$$T^m = 5-7 \text{ a. m.} \quad (\text{'morning'})$$
$$T^n = 11-\text{Noon} \quad (\text{'noon'})$$
$$T^a = 4-6 \text{ p. m.} \quad (\text{'afternoon'})$$
$$T^e = 7-8:30 \text{ p. m.} \quad (\text{'evening'})$$
$$T^l = 10:30-\text{Midnight} \quad (\text{'late'})$$

b) Size dimension:

$$H^l = \text{light}$$
$$H^m = \text{medium}$$
$$H^h = \text{heaviest meal of the day}$$

(53)

	Breakfast	Lunch	Tea	Dinner	Supper
i)	$H^m\ T^m$	$H^m\ T^n$	$H^l\ T^a$	$H^h\ T^e$	$H^l\ T^l$
ii)	$H^m\ T^m$			$H^h\ T^n$	$H^m\ T^a/H^l\ T^e$
iii)	$H^m\ T^n$		$H^l\ T^m$	$H^h\ T^e$	
iv)	$H^h\ T^n$		$H^l\ T^m$	$H^m\ T^a$	$H^l\ T^e$

This rewritten system makes it possible to see a high degree of systematicity in the various reinterpretations which must have taken place. For instance, *tea* always refers to a light meal, no matter when it is taken. Moreover, it must be a light meal which is taken at some time prior to the evening, i. e. in the morning or afternoon. Put differently, the semantic features in (54) must remain constant.

(54) Tea = $H^l\ T^{-e/l}$

Breakfast is a relatively early and medium-size meal for the first three classes. But its exact timing depends on whether *tea*, as the lighter meal, precedes it or not. For class (iv), this meal has the same time slot as for (iii), but it has increased in size. This time-based reinterpretation of the size of *breakfast* in (iv) has the consequence that for this class another generalization does not hold which is valid for the other three classes, namely that *dinner* refers to the heaviest meal, no matter when it is taken. Finally, for the two classes which use the term, *supper* refers to a meal which is lighter and later than *dinner*.

12.6. Outlook

Examples like the one just cited demonstrate that under certain circumstances semantic change can be quite regular and systematic. However,
this should not detract from the fact that in most cases, semantic change
is 'fuzzy', highly irregular, and extremely difficult to predict.

As a consequence, there seem to be no natural constraints on the
directions and results of semantic change. Given enough imagination
— and daring — it is possible to claim semantic relationship for almost
any two words under the sun. This creates difficulties when we need
to evaluate the relative merits of competing historical analyses. In many
cases, these difficulties can be surmounted by a careful philological
investigation of the historical record, for such an investigation may
uncover the route by which particular words changed their meanings.
Where historical records are unavailable or too scanty, the best we can
do is look for evidence that the postulated developments recur elsewhere. However, arguments based on such parallel developments must
be treated with caution, for we must face the possibility that parallels
can be found also for the competing analyses.

13. Syntactic change

Syntax, as currently defined, covers a broad range of phenomena. A number of these have received relatively thorough treatment in traditional linguistics. These include the syntactic use of morphological forms, the order of syntactic elements in a clause, and the combination of clauses into larger structures (i. e. into sentences). Other, more 'abstract' aspects of syntax, however, have not been dealt with as well, such as the relationship between corresponding active and passive expressions or between fully clausal structures and 'reduced', nominal or participial structures. These receive a more satisfactory account in recent generative approaches to syntax. Unfortunately for the historical linguist, however, generative syntax is characterized by a great variety of often radically different theoretical approaches and practical concerns. Moreover, generative syntax exhibits great variability not only 'synchronically', but also 'diachronically', in that — it seems — every five years or so, at least one radically new theory appears on the scene.

This chapter cannot attempt to cover in detail the full range of syntactic phenomena dealt with in contemporary generative syntax, or to do justice to the great variety of its theoretical claims and concerns. Instead, it will concentrate on outlining what appear to be the major factors that govern syntactic change, notwithstanding what particular theoretical framework one might subscribe to.

However, in order to show that syntactic change affects not only the areas covered by traditional linguistics, it is useful to give illustrations also of change in more 'abstract' syntactic phenomena, such as the relationship between active and passive. And the discussion of these changes will be couched in the terminology and concepts of a specific theoretical framework, namely 'Relational Grammar'. (But note that the version of Relational Grammar which will be employed is a fairly informal one.) The choice of this framework should not be taken to indicate that it is considered to be superior to others, but merely as a matter of convenience: In an informal version, its account of the passive (and its relationship to the active) not only seems more 'congenial' to traditional approaches to historical syntax but also requires less explanation and definition of terminology and concepts.

Note finally that in illustrating many of the changes in this chapter it has been necessary to resort to 'made-up' examples, rather than actually attested citations. For it is often impossible to give attested examples which, except for the change in question, correspond verbatim to attested, quotable sentences in a later stage of the language. Though not directly attested, however, such made-up examples do fully conform to the grammar of the relevant linguistic stages.

13.1. Introductory comment

Syntax is much closer to the 'upper' end of the grammar, i. e., to the semantic pole of language, than morphology and especially phonology. In fact, quite a number of syntactic phenomena, such as the difference in word order between (1) and (2), have a clearly semantic function. In the present case, the order in (2) is highly 'iconic', in that it physically 'foregrounds' the **emphasized**, semantically 'foregrounded' word *him* by **fronting** it into the first position of the clause.

(1)   I see him

(2)   Him I see

Moreover, it can be argued that it is the shared basic meaning (namely that there has been some action of 'biting' done to a 'dog' by a 'man') which makes it possible to consider (3), (4), and (5) to be syntactically related to each other. To account for the relationship between these structures, we can then postulate synchronic syntactic processes, such as **passivization** for (4) or 'nominalization' for (5).

(3)   A man bit a dog

(4)   A dog was bitten by a man

(5)   The biting of a dog by a man (is more newsworthy than the opposite)

What is especially interesting is the following: While we can state that (3), (4), and (5) are semantically related, it is more difficult to pinpoint the nature of this relatedness. And it is even more difficult to describe the nature of the obvious differences between these structures.

What, for instance, is the meaning (or 'function') of 'passive' as compared to 'active'?

Or consider the 'truncated' sentence (6) below. Does it correspond
to the non-truncated version in (7) or to the one in (8)? And is it a
man, a cat, cats, or yet some other being(s) or even thing(s) that is/are
bitten in one reading of (6) or is/are doing the biting in the other
reading? Only the speaker knows for sure. And (s)he may intend to be
ambiguous.

(6)   The biting of the dog was terrifying

(7)   The biting of the dog by the man was terrifying

(8)   The biting of the man by the dog was terrifying

That is, as in semantics, we find a good deal of vagueness, fuzziness,
and ambiguity in the relationship between linguistic structures. And at
least some synchronic phenomena are shared with semantics, such as
the 'iconicity' in (2).

Given these facts, it should come as no surprise that also syntactic
change shows many similarities with semantic change. Especially the
principle of reinterpretation plays a great role in both. Moreover, like
semantic change, syntactic change is characterized by a great degree of
unpredictability: It is difficult to establish the natural directions or
constraints of change.

At the same time, syntax differs from semantics by being more
'abstract'. Thus, as noted earlier, the 'meaning' of structures such as
the passive is difficult to define; it is much more 'abstract' than the
fairly 'tangible' meaning of lexical items such as *dog*. It is therefore
convenient to distinguish the 'meaning' and 'semantics' of syntax from
the more tangible meaning and semantics of the lexicon by referring
to them as **function** and **pragmatics**, respectively.

Moreover, while systematicity is the exception, rather than the rule in
semantics, syntax is eminently systematic. For example, the relationship
between (3) and (4), i.e., 'passive', holds not only for these two
sentences and the particular linguistic forms contained in them, but for
a large, in effect infinite class of sentences made up from a virtual
infinity of different linguistic forms.

As a consequence, syntax is highly rule-governed, and syntactic
change tends to be much more systematic and may have more 'abstract',

non-tangible motivations than what we normally find in semantic change.

It is possible, therefore, to see in syntax and in syntactic change a constant tug-of-war between semantic fuzziness, vagueness, and unpredictability on one hand, and grammatical systematicity and generalization on the other.

What further complicates matters is that syntactic change has not been as well researched as other types of linguistic change. In part this is the result of theoretical or practical preference: Traditional linguistics, and as a consequence traditional historical linguistics, placed greater emphasis on phonology and morphology than on syntax. In fact, it has been claimed that before the advent of contemporary generative linguistics, hardly any work had been done in (historical) syntax. This claim holds to a large extent for the 'school' of linguistics that immediately preceded generativism, namely 'American structuralism'. But a goodly amount of syntactic work had been done by earlier 'schools', especially by the neogrammarians. (As a consequence, students of diachronic syntax would be well advised to become familiar with at least some of that work, lest they spend much of their time on reinventing the wheel.)

At the same time, it is true that the work of earlier linguists tended to be confined to 'surfacy' phenomena such as word order, or the use of cases and other morphological categories (**'morphosyntax'**). But even today this is often the best we can do, since the evidence needed to decide questions about more 'abstract' phenomena frequently is not sufficiently attested in the extant texts of earlier linguistic stages.

Even for quite 'surfacy' phenomena such as word order, it is in some languages extremely difficult for linguists to agree on a synchronic analysis of the attested data. (For instance, the question whether the basic word order of Ancient Greek was 'SVO' or 'SOV' is still a matter of controversy.) Without such a synchronic analysis, however, it is difficult to establish what, if anything, has changed — and how or why it has changed.

Finally, even today the number of linguists doing serious work in diachronic syntax, on the basis of well-attested data and well-documented intermediate stages, is very small, especially when compared to the total number of linguists engaged in some kind of syntactic research.

These difficulties further limit our ability to make statements on the natural direction or constraints of syntactic change. If and when, therefore, in the following sections an attempt is made to state the likelihood of occurrence of a particular change, such a statement must always be read with the qualification 'as far as our present limited knowledge of syntactic change is concerned'.

13.2. The basis for syntactic change

As noted earlier, coverage of the full range of syntactic phenomena is beyond the scope of this chapter. The present section therefore is limited to a discussion of those synchronic phenomena and processes which will be relevant for the subsequent discussion.

13.2.1. Basic sentence structure

Most schools of generative syntax subscribe to the view that the basic organization of sentences is in terms of a **'noun phrase'** (**NP**, the subject of the sentence) plus a **'verb phrase' (VP)**, the **'predicate'**. Verb phrases, in turn, contain a 'Verb' **(V)** plus any number of optional or obligatory NPs, which may include the direct object, the indirect object, and various adverbial or prepositional NPs (**PP**s). NPs may consist of a single element, such as a noun (N), or they may contain additional elements, such as adjectives, prepositions, etc. Verbs likewise may be simple or complex. For our purpose, the most important complex Verb constituent consists of an **auxiliary (AUX)** plus a **main verb (MV)**, as in example (9). In structures like (9), AUX ordinarily is **finite**, i. e., marked for person or gender, number, and tense, while the MV is non-finite (an infinitive, participle, or the like).

(9) She   has   gone   *vs.* She had gone
        AUX   MV   AUX MV
        sg. 3 pres.   past
vs. They   have   gone
        AUX   MV
        pl. 3 pres.

In this approach, the syntactic function of a given NP is defined only in terms of its position within sentence tree diagrams of the type given in Chart 13.1. (Example (10) illustrates an alternative to the tree-diagramm representation, namely **bracketing**. For simplicity's sake, this diagram goes only up to the point where VP is 'rewritten' as V + NP.)

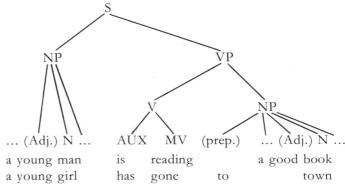

Chart 13.1. Sentence tree diagram

(10)   [[NP] [V + NP]$_{VP}$]$_S$ or more simply: [[NP] [V + NP]]

An alternative, but less common view of basic sentence organization accepts such notions as **subject, direct object, indirect object, verb**, etc., as 'undefined primitives'. For reasons outlined at the beginning of this chapter, the following discussion will generally follow this latter, 'Relational-Grammar' approach. In certain contexts, however, aspects of the alternative, 'tree-diagram' approach will be relevant, especially the basic NP + (predicate) VP analysis and the bracketing approach of (10).

13.2.2. Iconicity, movement processes, and word order

As noted in section 13.1, iconicity is a phenomenon found not only in semantics, but also in syntax, where it may be responsible for the fronting of pragmatically 'foregrounded', emphasized elements. Beside emphasis, fronting may serve other functions. These include establishing the **topic** of a sentence or its **focus**.

The topic typically is a bit of 'old information', something already known to the speaker and presumed to be known also to the hearer.

It is followed by the **'comment'**, the 'new information' which the speaker things worthwhile conveying to the hearer. In some languages, this sequence of topic followed by comment is a very important principle of syntactic organization. In English, on the other hand, other (non-word order) devices are more commonly used, such as in (11).

(11) As far as this film is concerned, I'd rather spend my money on peanuts

The focus of the sentence, often difficult to distinguish from an emphasized constituent or the topic, is that which is most salient to the speaker, that on which the sentence 'focuses'. For example, *A man* ordinarily would be the focus in (3) above, but *A dog* in (4). Here again, alternative devices may be employed, as in (12).

(12) It is him that I see

In many, perhaps most languages, fronting ordinarily affects entire constituents, such as the subject NP in (13). In some languages, however, fronting may be limited to a single word, such that the rest of the NP **'remains stranded'** in its usual position within the clause; cf. e. g. the Vedic Sanskrit example in (14).

(13) **This mangy dog** I don't like at all
  NP

(14) **viśvēbhyaḥ** tām **dēvēbhyaḥ** ālabhantē
  pl. D (adj.) her pl. D (Noun) they seize
  'they seize her for **all** the gods'

If fronting serves to foreground emphasized, topicalized, or focused constituents, one might suppose that **extraposition**, the process of placing a constituent (or part thereof) to the right of an otherwise complete sentence, serves the opposite end. However, this is not necessarily the case. Thus in Hindi the process may signal (a) deemphasis and (b) emphasis; cf. (15/16). That is, in sentences like (16), extraposition in this language is essentially a negative signal, telling the listener to 'expect the unexpected'. (In the case of subjects, extraposition is a fairly common device for signaling emphasis. This probably follows from the fact that, as we will see presently, subjects typically are clause-initial to begin with and thus cannot be further fronted. As a consequence, some other device is needed in order to unambiguously signal emphasis on the subject.)

> (15) mẽ uskō mārũgā
>   I   him will beat
>   'I will beat him' (unmarked)

> (16) uskō mārũgā mẽ
>   him will beat I
>   '**I** (not s. b. else) will beat him'
>   or: 'He'll get a beating (from me)' (or some similar meaning)

Extraposition also makes it possible to add an 'afterthought' to a sentence, as in (17). Moreover, in many languages, extraposition serves merely 'rhythmic' functions, putting 'heavy' or long NPs, which otherwise might excessively interrupt the flow of speech, at the end of the clause. Cf. (18), where (b) is the extraposed version of (a).

> (17) She went to the movie yesterday, with John and Mary

> (18 a) ... putting 'heavy' or long constituents, which otherwise might excessively interrupt the flow of speech, at the end of the clause
>   b) ... putting at the end of the clause 'heavy' or long constituents, which otherwise might excessively interrupt the flow of speech

'Stylistic' **movement processes** like fronting and extraposition thus introduce pragmatically marked syntactic structures. Interestingly, iconic considerations seem to play a certain role even in pragmatically unmarked structures: The three constituents subject **(S)**, verb **(V)**, and (direct) object **(O)** could a priori combine in six different ways; cf. (19). In fact, however, the patterns on the right of (19) are exceedingly rare. Most languages have one of the patterns on the left side as their **basic** (i. e. pragmatically unmarked) **word order**. What these patterns share is the fact that the subject precedes the object. This has been plausibly attributed to the fact that subjects tend to be the pragmatically most salient constituents, either as topic or focus of the clause.

(19) SVO   OVS
      SOV   OSV
      VSO   VOS

This explanation is especially appealing since it explains the preference for S-before-O patterns in terms of a tendency. For though languages tend to have the patterns on the left, some languages have the less common structures on the right.

The tendency for subjects to be clause-initial may perhaps account for another common phenomenon: V-initial languages with basic VSO have a great tendency to employ SVO as a strong alternative order, an order which occurs considerably more frequently than the alternative orders of SVO or SOV languages. This can be attributed to the fact that subjects are the most likely topic or focus of a clause. As a consequence, they are most easily fronted and thus come to occur before the (otherwise) clause-initial verb.

An alternative, or perhaps concomitant, factor accounting for the tendency toward SVO is suggested by another interesting phenomenon about verb-initial languages: O-before-S patterns are considerably more common in V-initial languages than in SVO or SOV languages. This is difficult to explain in terms of fronting or other stylistic movement rules. But it may be linked to the fact that the order VOS has a 'continuous' predicate or VP, while the VP of VSO is discontinuous; cf. (20). It is then perhaps not just due to chance that the alternative SVO of VSO languages likewise offers a continuous VP; cf. Chart 13.1 above.

(20 a)

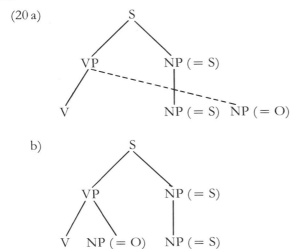

b)

Whatever the explanations, however, one thing appears to be clear: Verb-initial languages exhibit a greater degree of **instability** than SVO or SOV languages.

Basic constituent order tends to be correlated with other orderings. For instance, languages with V before O (i. e. VSO, SVO, etc.) tend to have the order noun + Genitive (N + G), preposition **(prep.)** + N, and AUX + MV; cf. e. g. (21). On the other hand, 'OV' languages (i. e. SOV etc.) tend to have G + N, N + **'postposition' (po.)**, and MV + AUX; cf. (22). However, as (23) shows, these again are merely tendencies: SVO languages like English may have G + N patterns, and in SOV languages like Sanskrit, prep. + N is obligatory for certain **'adpositions'** (i. e. pre- or postpositions) and N + G is a less common alternative to G + N.

(21) English:
  a) SVO: John loves Mary
  b) N + G: The house of Mary
  c) prep. + N: of (prep.) Mary
  d) AUX + MV: John has married Mary

(22) Sanskrit:
  a) SOV: dēvadattaḥ kaṭam karōti
                      'D.' 'mat' 'makes'
                      'Devadatta makes a mat'
  b) G + N: dēvadattasya kaṭaḥ
                      'Devadatta's mat'
  c) N + po.:   dēvadattam prati
                      'D.' 'toward'
                      'toward Devadatta'
  d) MV + AUX: dēvadattēna kaṭaḥ kr̥taḥ asti
                                    MV   AUX
                      'the mat has been made by Devadatta'

(23 a) Engl. G + N: Mary's house
    b) Skt. prep. + N and N + G:
              ā   kumārān yaśaḥ pāṇinēḥ
              prep. N   N   G
        'up to the youth/Cape Comorin [extends] the fame of Pāṇini [India's greatest grammarian]'

It has also been claimed that VO languages normally have relative clauses (RC) which are introduced by relative pronouns (RP) and placed after their 'head noun' while OV languages place relative clauses before their head noun and lack relative pronouns; cf. (24) vs. (25). (In the Tamil sentence of (25), the verb of the relative clause is marked by a special 'relativizing' or 'adjectivizing' affix which turns the clause into an adjectival attribute of the following head noun.)

(24)   [The   house[which Mary bought]$_{RC}$]$_{NP}$ is large
              N   RP

(25)   [[sikāgōvule   tamur   paḍičč-a]$_{RC}$ amerikkaru]$_{NP}$ inge
          'in Ch.'   'Tamil' 'learn'-REL/ADJ.   'Am.'   'here'
       vandāru
       'came'
       'The American who learned Tamil in Chicago came here'

However, this claim was based on an incomplete language sample. More recent investigations have shown that SOV languages may employ several other strategies for relative clause formation. These include the pattern in (26), where the relative clause (marked by a relative pronoun) precedes not its head noun but a correlative main clause (MC, marked by a correlative pronoun = CP). The 'shared' or **'coreferential'** NP of these two structures may be present or 'deleted' in either the relative or the correlative clause. (It is therefore placed in parentheses in example (26).)

(26)   [yah (purusah) katam   karoti]$_{RC}$ [sah (purusah) dēvadattah
        RP 'man' 'mat' 'makes' CP 'man'   'D.'
       nāma]$_{MC}$
       'by name'
       'The man who makes the mat is called Devadatta'

The fact that further research thus disconfirms an earlier claim concerning the correlation between basic constituent order and relative clause formation is significant: It shows that our knowledge about word order patterns (as well as other aspects of syntax) is still quite limited. Moreover, as examples like (23) show, correlations between basic constituent order and other aspects of word order are only tendencies. It is important to remember these facts, since a fair number of dubious historical claims have been made by persons who have taken these correlations to be absolute or near-absolute.

13.2.3. Clitics

As noted in section 5.3.1, many languages have **clitics**, morphological elements which take an intermediate position between full words and affixes. Clitics typically are unaccented and presumably because of their accent reduction, cannot occur by themselves but must 'lean on' a **host**. The word classes which are most likely to have clitic members are the articles, pronouns, (short) adverbs, adpositions, and auxiliaries.

Syntactically, the fact that clitics require hosts can have important repercussions: As long as the clitic is in the scope of a particular constituent, i. e. is syntactically or semantically/pragmatically felt to be closely related to the constituent, that constituent will act as its host; cf. e. g. (27). The only question which might arise is whether the clitic should precede the host (as a **proclitic**) or follow (as an **enclitic**). Thus, the underlined items in (27 a, b) are proclitics, while the one in (27 c) is enclitic.

(27 a)   Engl.   <u>the</u> house
   b)   Gk.   <u>perí</u> dourí 'around the spear'
   c)   Hindi   mēz <u>par</u> 'on (the) table'

However, when clitics are in 'sentence-scope' and thus lack a 'natural' host, there is a problem: Where should the clitic go? Problems of this sort arise especially in the case of short auxiliaries, adverbs, and pronouns which constitute an entire NP.

Recent work shows that there is a crosslinguistic tendency for such **sentence clitics** to be placed after the first element of the clause. (Depending on the language, that element may be the first word, the first NP, or even 'everything that has been fronted'.) In many languages, more than one element per sentence can be clitic, and if these elements are sentence clitics, they may be 'stacked up' into sometimes fairly complex 'strings'. Cf. e. g. the Vedic Sanskrit examples in (28), where (28 d) represents a 'mini-string' of two clitic elements. (Here as elsewhere in this chapter, clitics will be marked by an **E**. Note that (28 a) contains also an NP-scope clitic, *iva* 'like'.)

(28 a)   sá   nah   pitā́   iva   ... sūpāyanáh bhava
   'this =   E   'father'   E   'of easy   'be'
   you'   'us'   'like'   access'
   'Be to us of easy access like a father ... '

b) sácasva   naḥ   svastáyē
   'accompany'   E   'to well-being'
            'us'
   'Be with us for (our) well-being'

c) tébhiḥ   naḥ adyá   pathíbhiḥ ... rákṣa ...
   'by these'   E   'today'   'by paths'   'protect'
            'us'
   'Protect us today by these paths ... '

d) dviṣántam ha asya   tád   bhrátṛvyam abhyàtiriċyatē
   'hating'   E   E   'that'   'enemy'   'is left over for'
     emph. 'his'
   'That remains for his hateful enemy'

13.2.4. Passive

Leaving ordering phenomena behind us, let us take a look at a few other processes and the principles which lie behind them. The first of these is passivization.

13.2.4.1. Formal aspects

Although the process of passivization is found in a vast number of languages, the manner in which it applies and its functions may differ widely. Thus in English, passives ordinarily can be made only from transitives, not from intransitives. That is, there are no grammatical English sentences corresponding to the Sanskrit and German sentences in (30′) and (32′).

Sanskrit, on the other hand, permits passives both from transitives and from intransitives; cf. (29) and (30). The latter lack an overt subject, and the form of the passive verb invariably appears in the morphologically most 'unmarked' form, the third person singular or, in participial forms, in the nominative singular neuter. (Structures like (30′) are difficult to translate into English; hence no translation is given. A rough gloss of (30′) would be 'There is an act of sitting going on, with Devadatta as the agent'.)

(29) dēvadattaḥ kaṭān   karōti
     sg. N   pl. A   sg. 3 **act.**
    'Devadatta makes mats'

(29')   (dēvadattēna)   kaṭāḥ   kriyantē
          sg. I   pl. N pl. 3 **pass.**
          'mats are made by Devadatta'

(30)   dēvadattaḥ   āstē
          sg. N   sg. 3 **act.**
          'Devadatta sits'

(30')   (dēvadattēna)   āsyatē
          sg. I   sg. 3 **pass.**

German similarly permits both transitive and intransitive passives. However, the intransitive passive requires the presence of a 'dummy' pronoun *es* 'it' in clause-initial position if that position is not filled by some other constituent (on this matter, cf. also section 13.3.1.1 below). Moreover, in this type of passive, the agent NP (*von* = 'by' + NP) usually is not specified. Cf. the examples in (31/31') and (32/32').

(31)   Jeder   liest   (die) Bücher
       sg. N sg. 3 act.   pl. A
       'Everybody reads (the) books'

(31')   Die Bücher   werden   (von jedem) gelesen
         pl. N   pl. 3   'by NP'   pple.
                 pass. AUX
       'The books are read (by everybody)'

(32)   Alle   tanzen   hier   / Hier   tanzen   alle
       pl. N pl. 3 act. adv.   adv. pl. 3 act. pl. N
       'All the people dance here'

(32')   Es   wird   hier getanzt   / Hier   wird   getanzt
       'It' **sg.** 3 adv. pple.   adv. **sg.** 3 pple.
       pass. AUX   pass. AUX

In order to differentiate these different passives, it is useful to distinguish two processes: **promotion** and **demotion**.

'Promotion' refers to the process by which a constituent which in the **'underlying'** active is not the subject of the sentence becomes the '**surface**' subject of the passive. Thus in (29'), the object *kaṭān* of (29) has been 'promoted' to subject. And having become the subject, it appears in a different case (nominative, not accusative); and the verb agrees in number (pl.) with that subject, rather than with the singular of the underlying subject. The situation is the same in German (31') vs. underlying (31).

On the other hand, the underlying subject of (29) has undergone 'demotion' in (29'): It no longer 'controls' verb agreement, and it no longer is marked by the nominative case, but by the instrumental. The situation is similar in the German example (31'), except that the demoted subject is morphologically marked by a PP. As examples (29') and (31') show, the demoted underlying subject or '**agent NP**' frequently is 'omitted'. Such passives with omitted or non-specified agent NPs seem to be the norm in many languages, and even in languages like English and German, they seem to be preferred in the more colloquial varieties.

In English, the relationship between promotion and demotion is automatic and can be stated as follows: 'In the passive a constituent is promoted to subject and the underlying subject is automatically demoted.' (Cf. e. g. (3) and (4) above.) The reason for this automatic demotion seems to be that universally, clauses cannot contain more than one subject category. (There may of course be conjoined subjects, as in *Jack and Jill went up the hill*. However, these constitute a single subject category. What cannot occur is something like *The man* (S) *the dog* (S) *were bitten* as the passive of *The dog* (S) *bit the man*.) In English, then, promotion is primary and demotion secondary. Let us refer to this type of passive as the **promotional passive**.

Also for Sanskrit it is possible to state an automatic relationship (but see below). However, because of passive structures like (30'), this relationship is the converse of the English one. In the passive, the underlying subject is demoted and an underlying direct object is promoted into the vacated subject position. In the absence of a direct object, no promotion takes place and the category 'subject' remains empty. Since the passive verb must, for morphological reasons, be marked for number and person, it goes into the 'unmarked' number and person, the third singular. Here, then, demotion is primary and promotion secondary. Let us call this the **demotional passive**.

Languages differ also in terms of what constituents can be promoted to subject. In the examples examined so far, the direct object (DO) has been promoted. And in Sanskrit (but see below), German, and many other languages, this is the only category which can be promoted. But

English can promote also indirect objects **(IO)**, as in (33). Even prepositional, adverbial NPs (PPs) are promotable, but only if the preposition remains 'stranded'; cf. (34') vs. (34").

(33)   She gave John the book
                         IO

(33')   John was given the book

(34)   He tampered with the evidence
                          PP

(34')   The evidence was tampered with by him
                                              prep.

(34")   With the evidence was tampered by him*

This **promotability hierarchy**, with DO on top and PP on the bottom and with IO in an intermediate position, seems to be a crosslinguistic tendency.

However, note that the hierarchy is only a tendency, not an absolute 'law'. Thus in Sanskrit, verbs of motion such as *gam/gacch-* 'go' may take as their goal an NP in the locative or accusative case; cf. (35). If the accusative is selected, this NP is promotable to subjecthood, even if only optionally; cf. (35'). On the other hand, if it is in the locative, it is not promotable; cf. ibid. (Again, English translations are difficult.) Here, then, a PP can be promoted to subject, provided it is in the 'right' case. However, dative-marked IOs cannot be promoted; cf. (36/ 36'). That is, Sanskrit 'skips' one step in the promotability hierarchy.

(35 a)   dēvadattaḥ   grāmam   gacchati
               sg. N   sg. A   sg. 3 act.

      b)   dēvadattaḥ   grāmē   gacchati
               sg. N   sg. L   sg. 3 act.
             'Devadatta goes to the village'

(35' a')   dēvadattēna   grāmaḥ   gamyatē
                sg. I   sg. N   sg. 3 pass.

      a")   dēvadattēna   grāmam   gamyatē
                sg. I   sg. A   sg. 3 pass.

      b')   dēvadattēna   grāmē   gamyatē
                sg. I   sg. L   sg. 3 pass.

(36) tēbhyaḥ dadati
      pl. D pl. 3 act.
      'they/people give to them'

(36') tēbhyaḥ dīyatē
       pl. D sg. 3 pass.

13.2.4.2. Function

As far as the function of the passive is concerned, there is even greater variation, crosslinguistically and even within a single language.

In many languages and uses, the passive may function simply to deemphasize the underlying subject (by demoting it). As a consequence, it may be used to generalize, since non-specification of an agent NP can be interpreted as indicating that any agent can or does perform the action. The passive is therefore very appropriate in various types of scientific discourse in which, say, it is not important by whom a particular experiment was conducted, but only that it was conducted and thus is reproducible by any other researcher.

The demotion and deemphasizing of the agent NP may also be exploited for the purpose of politeness. This may work in two apparently contradictory ways. On one hand, first-person forms are demoted, since 'it isn't polite to place emphasis on oneself'. On the other hand, NPs referring to the person addressed are demoted, since 'it isn't polite or politic to suggest too great a familiarity with the addressee'. Both of these politeness uses of the passive are found in Sanskrit and other 'Eastern' languages. Thus, in Sanskrit (37') is more polite than (37).

(37) bhavān   dadātu
      sg. N   sg.3 impve. act.
      honorific
      'give' (lit.: '(your) lordship should give')

(37') bhavatā   dīyatām
       sg. I   sg. 3 impve. pass.
       honorific

Subject demotion may also be employed to 'de-activate' the verb, as it were; i. e. to make it more like an intransitive. Thus, without an agent NP, (38) can have an intransitive reading 'the crew lost (to their opponents)', rather than a transitive reading 'the opponents/someone defeated the crew'. The result of such an intransitive use of the passive often is a **stative**, i. e. an interpretation of the verbal action as not referring to a process, but to a 'state of being' (which may have resulted from a preceding process). For instance, another possible reading of (38) with deleted agent NP is 'the crew were not victorious, they were losers'. Note however that in English, such intransitive/stative structures cannot occur with specified agent NPs and thus differ syntactically from real passives.

(38)   The crew were defeated (by their opponents)

Also promotion may carry with it certain connotations. As noted earlier, for instance, in sentence (4) above, it is the dog, not the man that is foregrounded. This foregrounding function of the passive appears to be limited to languages like English in which the promoted, surface subject of the passive 'moves' into the preverbal subject position and thus requires movement of the demoted underlying subject into postverbal position. On the other hand, in languages like Sanskrit, where passive is not a 'movement process', promotion does not seem to function as a foregrounding device.

13.2.5. Deletion and ambiguity

Consider again the 'truncated' sentence (6) = (39) below. As noted in 13.1, the interpretation of this sentence is ambiguous: It may correspond to the non-truncated versions in either (40) or (41). And since there is nothing in (39) which tells us what the 'missing NP' might refer to, the sentence is in fact multiply ambiguous.

(39)   The biting of the dog was terrifying

(40)   The biting of the dog by the man, cat(s), ... was terrifying

(41)   The biting of the man, cat(s), ... by the dog was terrifying

Note that the term **ambiguous** or **ambiguity** here is used in a special sense. It does not refer to the vagueness, lack of specificity, or 'fuzziness' inherent in all sentences, such as the fact that sentence (39) leaves unclear which or what kind of dog is involved, or how deep or dangerous the bite was. Rather, it is used to indicate that beyond this inherent vagueness, the derivational 'machinery' of syntax contributes a special, systematic ambiguity by making it possible to associate with a given sentence more than one possible source sentence or more than one possible reading. Let us refer to this phenomenon as **derivational ambiguity**.

Derivational ambiguity can result not only from deletion, but also from other syntactic processes. For instance, in example (42) the ambiguity is attributable to the fact that the scope of *on Monday* may be *The government announced* or *the sale of* ... ; cf. (42'). And it is not really relevant whether according to different syntactic theories, (42) may or may not be considered derived from such sentences as (43) and (44).

(42)   The government announced the sale of surplus butter to New Zealand on Monday

(42' a)   The government announced [the sale of surplus butter to New Zealand] on Monday

   b)   The government announced [the sale of surplus butter to New Zealand on Monday]

(43)   The government announced on Monday that it will sell surplus butter to New Zealand

(44)   The government announced that it will sell surplus butter to New Zealand on Monday

Beside such derivational ambiguity (and in addition to the inherent vagueness of sentences), there is another type of ambiguity which can be referred to as **systemic ambiguity**, i. e. an ambiguity in or about the grammatical rule system.

Recall that in chapter 11 we noted that in order to account for the generalizations needed to learn a language, speakers require a system of rules which relate different formations to each other. Moreover, that rule system must be formulated anew by each speaker on the basis of the utterances that (s)he hears. For only utterances can be observed and thus transmitted from one generation to the other. The rules which account for the utterances, being internalized, cannot be directly observed or transmitted.

Because grammar thus has to be formulated anew by each speaker, it is possible that speakers engage in reanalysis and account for the same surface phenomenon by means of different rules. What is important is that such reanalyses may be extended and thus give rise to novel structures. Compare again the British English reinterpretation of the r/ Ø alternation as resulting from r-insertion and the extension of this process to originally vowel-final words (cf. 11.5).

As it turns out, also syntax offers many examples of such reinterpretations of 'systemically ambiguous' structures.

Consider just one case: Early English, just like German, Latin, and all the other Indo-European languages, permitted only nominative case marking on the 'predicate' NP following the verb 'to be' (and a few other semantically related verbs). Compare for instance (45). On the other hand, after other, transitive verbs, non-prepositional, direct object complements normally are in the accusative, as in (46). Finally, after a few transitive verbs, the complement appears in a case other than nominative or accusative, as in (47) where it is dative. (The discussion here is slightly simplified; for further details and complications see 13.3.1.6 below.)

(45)   þæt is sē   'that is he/him'
            sg. N

(46)   ic sēo hine   'I see him'
            sg. A

(47)   ic help him   'I help him'
            sg. D

Given these facts, two analyses are possible. One focuses on the distinction transitive : intransitive and formulates rules like the ones in (48) for the case marking of post-verbal, non-prepositional complements. Let us refer to this as the 'transitive analysis'.

(48 a)   After intransitive 'be' (and similar verbs), the case of the complement is nominative;
      b)   After transitives, it is accusative;
      c)   Exceptions to (b) are *heolpan* 'help' etc. which take dative (or genitive) instead of the accusative.

A different, 'unitary analysis' accounts for the facts by a single rule. The residue, which is not accounted for by that rule, then is considered exceptional (just as, say, *heolpan* is exceptional in the transitivity analysis). Compare the formulation in (49).

(49 a)   Post-verbal complements are marked accusative;
      b)   Exceptions are *bēon* 'be' (and a few similar verbs), *heolpan* 'help' ... , which take the nominative, dative, or genitive respectively.

While this unitary analysis might be considered inferior to the transitivity analysis by ignoring the otherwise very important distinction between transitive and intransitive, it may be felt to be appealing because of its greater simplicity and generality: Where the transitivity analysis requires two rules plus a statement on exceptions, the unitary analysis gets by with only one rule plus a statement on exceptions. As we shall see, English in the long run preferred the unitary analysis.

13.3. Mechanisms and causes for syntactic change

As observed in the preceding chapter, the synchronic basis for semantic change also functions in large measure as mechanism and cause for semantic change. Given the close affiliation of syntax with semantics, one might expect a similar situation in syntax. However, this is true only to a very limited extent.

The best evidence for the possibility that the synchronic basis of syntax may directly affect syntactic change comes from verb-initial languages. For instance, the documented development of Hebrew from an earlier VSO stage to its present basic SVO order seems to have been initiated by the fronting of topicalized pronoun subjects, one of the most common synchronic processes in syntax. Moreover, the change may have been further motivated by the fact that the order VSO is crosslinguistically unstable, with SVO tending to appear as a strong alternative.

However, even here we must ask whether subject fronting or the common use of SVO as an alternative to VSO is sufficient to bring about a change from SVO to SOV as the pragmatically unmarked structure. The evidence of other syntactic changes suggests that such a change requires an important additional element, namely **reinterpretation**.

13.3.1. Reinterpretation

The following sections will illustrate the interaction of reinterpretation with other factors in bringing about syntactic change. As the discussion will show, the relevant reinterpretations and generalizations tend to be highly language-specific.

13.3.1.1. AUX-cliticization and word order change

The change of earlier SOV to SVO in the Romance and Germanic languages has frequently been attributed to a movement process, namely extraposition. It has been argued that if in an SOV language the object is extraposed, structures with SVO result. However, a closer examination of the historical record shows that the change of SOV to SVO was initiated by a very different process, not only in Romance and Germanic, but also in neighboring Slavic and Baltic, in non-European (but Indo-European) Kashmiri, as well as in certain West African and Sudanic languages. This initiating process consisted in '**AUX-cliticization**' and the shift of clitic AUX into clause-second position. But what is responsible for the ultimate shift toward basic SVO order is reinterpretation.

In early Latin, as well as in early Germanic, the unmarked ordering of AUX in respect to its main verb (MV) was MV + AUX, consonant with the basic SOV order of these languages; cf. e. g. the early Runic Germanic examples in (50).

(50) flagda faikinaz ist
     MV   AUX
'is menaced by evil spirits'

þrawijan haitinaz was
  MV   AUX
'was destined for the throes'

A clear change can be observed in the post-600 AD Runic inscriptions, as well as in Beowulf; cf. (51) and (52a). Here the AUX frequently occurs in clause-second position, with the MV remaining stranded at the end of the clause. (Beside this innovated pattern, older structures of type (50) continue to be found; cf. e. g. (57) below.)

(51) ni s   solu sot, ni s   Akse stAin skorin
    AUX   MV   AUX   MV
'(It) is not hit by the sun, the stone is not cut with a sharp stone'

(52a) Bēowulfe wearð / gūðhrēð gyfeþe
      AUX   MV
'To Beowulf glory in battle was given'

b) Lofdǣdum sceal / in mǣgþa gehwǣre man geþēon
    AUX   MV
    'Through worthy deeds a man shall thrive in every people'

c) þæt wæs wrǣc micel wine Scyldinga
    COP.
    'That was great sorrow for the friend of the Scyldings'

What is interesting about (51) is the phonological form of AUX: While early Runic had the form *ist*, at this point we find clitically shortened *s*. Further evidence for clitic shortening in the verb 'to be' comes from Old English *isØ* and early Old Norse *esØ* vs. PGmc/Runic *ist*; and later Old Norse has *er* with clitic voicing and rhotacism. This phonological evidence suggests that auxiliaries had become clitic and that their shift to clause-second position is attributable to the cross-linguistic tendency for sentence clitics to be placed after the first clausal element.

In the early Old English of Beowulf, clause-second position is by and large restricted to verbs which share with AUX the fact that they tend to be unaccented and semantically/pragmatically of reduced importance. These include the 'modals' (such as *sceal* 'shall, must, ought to') which like AUX play a semantically subordinate role vis-à-vis the MV (cf. (52b)), as well as to the verb 'to be' used as a **copula** (COP), i. e., as a semantically 'empty' linker of the subject and predicate NPs; cf. (52c).

By the time of post-Beowulfian, 'standard' Old English, the pattern of (52) has been extended. At this point, any finite verb may occur in clause-second position; cf. e. g. (53). The fact that the auxiliaries, modals, and copula of (52) are all finite presumably was reinterpreted as being the primary reason for their being placed in second position (rather than the fact that they are clitics). And this synchronic generalization was then extended to all other finite verbs, including MVs. (This process may have been helped by the fact that the copula of structures like (52c) is the only verb of its clause and thus its 'main verb'.)

(53) wē witan ōþer igland hēr be ēaston
     MV
     finite
     'We know another island east from here'

In addition, we can observe the beginnings of the complete shift from SOV to SVO: In structures with AUX and MV, the main verb is beginning to be placed next to its AUX, into the clause-second, usually post-subject position; cf. (54). This process, which took several centuries to run its full course, effectively changed English from an SOV into an SVO language.

The motivation for the change may have consisted in a reinterpretation of patterns like (53) as having the structure SVO. The movement of MV into the position after the AUX then can be viewed as a process which eliminated exceptions to that interpretation. However, an alternative explanation is possible: There seems to be a crosslinguistic preference for continuous, rather than discontinuous constitutents. For instance, it was argued in 3.2.2 that the relative frequency of O before S patterns in verb-initial languages may be linked to the fact that the order VOS has a continuous VP, while the VP of VSO is discontinuous. It is this tendency toward continuous constituents, sometimes referred to as **Behaghel's Law**, which may be responsible for the shift of the non-finite MV to the position after AUX.

(54)   Dryhten wæs   sprecende ðās word tō Moyse
        AUX MV
        'The Lord was speaking these words to Moses'

In the developments outlined above, dependent clauses tended to lag behind, commonly showing verb-final MV + AUX patterns even in 'standard' Old English; cf. e. g. (55). It took several additional centuries before the word order of the main clause was obligatorily extended to dependent clauses. This relative **resistance to change** is consonant with a widely noted tendency for dependent clauses to be more 'conservative' than main clauses in syntactic change. (There is less agreement concerning the reasons for that conservatism.)

(55)   [Ðis synd ðā friðmāl and ðā forword]$_{MC}$ [ðe Æthelred
        COP
        cyng and eall his witan wið ðone here gedōn habbað]$_{RC}$
                                        MV   AUX
        'These are the articles of peace and stipulations which King
        Æ. and all his councilors have undertaken with this army'

Another development, which is more specifically linked to the shift from SOV to SVO via AUX-cliticization, follows from the fact that structures like (52a) = (56a) for several centuries coexisted and competed with structures like (56b). The result of that competition appears to have been the compromise configuration in (56c). (While (56b) and (56c) are not directly attested, the possibility of (56b) is shown by attested Beowulfian structures like (57), and (56c) finds support in the later, 'standard' Old English expression of (58).)

(56a) Bēowulfe wearð / gūðhrēð gyfeþe
       AUX   MV
       'To Beowulf glory in battle was given'
   b) Bēowulfe gūðhrēð gyfeþe wearð
                MV   AUX
   c) Bēowulfe gūðhrēð wearð gyfeþe
                AUX   MV

(57)   ac hē sigewæpnum forsworen hæfde
                MV   AUX
       'but he had put a spell on the (otherwise) victorious weapons'

(58)   þæt hī ðēr mōston wunian
              AUX   MV
       'that they might live there'

The pattern of (51) and (52) is found also in the early stages of other Germanic languages, of Romance, of Slavic, and of Lithuanian, cf., e. g., (59)—(61). And in at least some of these languages we have similar phonological evidence for clitic shortening, such as Lat. *habet* > It., Sp. *ha*, etc., with loss of intervocalic *b* (vs. *dēbet* > *debe*). That is, these patterns seem to have arisen by the same process as the English ones. However, the earliest attested stages of these other languages are comparable to 'standard' Old English, not to the early Old English of Beowulf. As a consequence, in most of these languages the patterns of (59)—(61) are fairly marginal, especially in main clauses. Even in dependent clauses they tend to disappear quite rapidly, being replaced by the more productive, innovated verb-second or SVO patterns of the type (53) and (54). Compare for instance (62). In some of these languages, we also find transitional compromise patterns of the type (56c)/ (58); cf., e. g., (63).

(59) OFr.   vertet est   de terre nee
                 AUX   MV
                 'truth is born from the earth'

(60) Early Slav. starěšinĭstvo esi   s mene snjalŭ
                 AUX   MV
                 'you have taken (my) birthright from me'

(61) OLith.   kaip butu man pats Diewas apreischkies
                 AUX   MV
                 'as if God himself had revealed (it) to me'

(62) Early Slav. čemu este   sŭnjali sŭ mene spačiku
                 AUX MV
                 'why have you taken (my) shirt off me'

(63) OLith.   pats sawe vž yę esti   dawes
                 AUX MV
                 'he has given himself for it'

However, in a small group of languages, comprising German, Dutch, and Frisian, the development toward SVO was not carried through consistently. Rather, the more conservative SOV pattern of dependent clauses was at a certain point reinterpreted and generalized as grammatical marker of dependent clauses, contrasting (by way of polarization) with the verb-second order of main clauses; cf., e. g., the German expressions in (64) and (65). Apparently as a consequence of this retention of SOV characteristics in dependent clauses, these languages to varying degrees have also in main clauses retained an earlier pattern, in which only the finite verb moves into second position, while non-finite main verbs ordinarily remain stranded at the end of the clause; cf. (66).

(64) MC: Er liebt seine Frau
             V
         'He loves his wife'

(65) DC: Alle wissen, dass er seine Frau liebt
                                           V
         'Everybody knows that he loves his wife'

(66) MC: Er hat   seine Frau geliebt
             AUX   MV
         'He has loved his wife'

The result of these development is that Modern German, Dutch, and Frisian have retained a large enough number of SOV features in their basic constituent structure that different linguists (and different schools of linguistics) do not agree on whether the unmarked or basic word order of these languages is SOV or SVO.

At the same time, these languages have in their main clauses a strict synchronic constraint that the finite verb must appear in clause-second position. Moreover, the initial, pre-finite-verb position has been reinterpreted as the position for the sentence topic. (Similar developments took place also in the earlier history of the other Germanic languages, as well as in French.)

This has important consequences: Where for some reason, speakers choose not to specify any constituent as the topic and where as a consequence no constituent is placed in initial position, that position has to be filled with a '**dummy**' element, which in German is the pronoun *es*. We have seen one example in the case of subjectless, purely demotional passives; cf. section 13.2.4.1, ex. (32'). The same phenomenon can be found in active expressions such as (67). In either case, the dummy pronoun *es* provides the 'support' required in order for the finite verb to appear in second position. (Pragmatically, structures of this type by and large function in the same way as verb-initial configurations in the earlier Indo-European languages, for which cf., e. g., (74) in the next section. Most commonly, they serve as a stage-setting device, as in the examples in (67). This suggests that these expressions to a large extent reflect earlier verb-initial constructions which were secondarily made to conform to the predominant verb-second main-clause structure.)

(67 a) Es fliegen die Vögel nach Süden; der Winter steht vor
         V pl. 3 S pl. N
         der Tür
         'The birds are flying south. Winter is waiting at the door'

    b)   Es war einmal ein König, der hatte drei Töchter …
         V
         '(Once upon a time,) there was a king. He had three daughters …'
         (Standard introduction of fairy tales.)

In structures like (67), the *es* clearly is a dummy element, not the subject. For instance, in (67a), the verb agrees in number not with *es*, but with the 'postposed' subject *die Vögel.* Moreover, if in sentences of this type some meaningful, non-dummy element (not necessarily the subject) precedes the verb, *es* obligatorily 'disappears'; cf. e. g. (68).

> (68)   Jetzt   fliegen die Vögel nach Süden
>   'now'   V   S
>   'now the birds are flying south'
>   not: Jetzt fliegen **es** die Vögel nach Süden*

However, in many other structures, an original dummy *es* has been reinterpreted as subject. As a consequence, this *es* does not disappear, but remains in structures analogous to (68); cf. (69a) beside (69b).

> (69a)   Es ist kalt
>   'it is cold'
>
> b)   Heute ist es kalt
>   'today it is cold'
>   not: Heute ist Ø kalt*

What complicates matters is that in structures like (70), in which typically a dative NP indicates the 'experiencer' of a verbal action, the non-initial appearance of *es* is optional. Note that configurations of the type (70b) have an archaic or even obsolescent flavor in Modern German. The innovated structure in (c) thus is in the process of becoming the only permissible configuration.

> (70a)   Es ist mir kalt
>   D
>   'I am cold' (lit. 'it is cold to me')
>
> b)   Mir ist Ø kalt
>
> c)   Mir ist **es** kalt

13.3.1.2. Univerbation and word order change

Also the change from the SOV order of Proto-Indo-European to the VSO of Insular Celtic seems to have resulted from an interaction of reinterpretation with other syntactic phenomena. The background and relevant developments are treated in this section.

Just as in some of the later Indo-European languages auxiliaries became clitics and moved into clause-second position, so in Proto-Indo-European certain pronouns were clitic and occurred in clause-second position. Cf,. e. g., the Sanskrit examples in section 13.2.3, ex. (28).

At the same time, Proto-Indo-European had a class of morphological elements which for want of a better word may be referred to as 'adverbials'. (In the examples below, they will be characterized by the symbol **P**.) Originally independent, adverb-like elements, they gravitate toward new usages in the earliest Indo-European texts. One of these usages is that as adpositions, the other that as 'preverbs' or verbal prefixes. The former results from a reinterpretation of the scope of adverbials as being a particular NP, rather than the whole clause. The latter usage comes about by a reinterpretation of the adverbials as modifying the meaning of the verb.

Compare for instance the different uses of *áti* in the early, Vedic Sanskrit examples of (71). In (a), *áti* functions as an adverb, in (b) it acts more like an adposition modifying *vratám*, and in (c) its function is more that of a modification of the verb's meaning. However, note that in many early cases like these, it is not yet entirely clear whether the adverbial should be interpreted in its original function as adverb, as an adposition, or as a preverb. Thus, (71 b) may alternatively be interpreted with a preverbal reading as 'do-beyond = transgress', and in (71 c) it is possible to get an adpositional reading 'beyond the fires'.

(71 a) áti yáḥ   mandráḥ yajáthāya   dēváḥ
        P 'who' 'pleasant' 'for worship' 'God'
        'which god [is] exceedingly pleasant to worship'

    b) kád   asya áti vratám čakṛma
        'what' 'his' P 'wish' 'we have done'
        'What have we done exceeding = against his wish?'

    c) sá   íd   agníḥ agnín áti astu
        'this' emph. 'fire' 'fires' P 'shall be'
        'This Agni/fire shall be exceeding = shall exceed the fires'

In (71), the ordering of the adverbials is what one would expect, given their (possible) scope: clause-initial for the clausal-adverb reading, next to the NP which it governs in the adpositional reading, and next to verb in the preverb reading. However, early texts show that other orders were possible. For instance, in (72), preverbal *prá* occurs initially but separated from its verb (a), initially and next to its verb (b), non-initially and preceding its verb (c), and non-initially and following its verb (d). (The latter pattern, however, is quite rare.)

(72a) prá prajáyā jā́yēya
       P   V
       'may I "spring off" = be born/be continued through off-
       spring'

   b) prá jā́yasva prajáyā
       P   V
       ' "spring off" through offspring'

   c) yátaḥ prá jajñé índraḥ
            P   V
       'whence was born forth Indra'

   d) árējanta prá mā́nuṣāḥ
       V   P
       'the men trembled (forth)'

Of these different positions, the initial one seems to have been the most original. Other orderings appear to be due either to stylistic movement processes or — more importantly — to the incipient reinterpretation of these adverbials as adpositions or preverbs: As they get reinterpreted as adpositions, they tend to be placed next to their NP in accordance with 'Behaghel's Law'. And in the process of being reinterpreted as verbal prefixes, they tend to be subject to **univerbation**, the morphological counterpart of Behaghel's Law, by which elements forming a single lexical unit become a single word. As a consequence of univerbation, for instance, the post-Vedic, Classical counterparts of (72) are as in (72').

(72'a) prajayā prajāyēya
    b) prajāyasva prajáyā
    c) yataḥ prajajñe indraḥ
    d) prārējanta mānuṣāḥ

One more point is important for understanding the following discussion: Although the basic word order of Proto-Indo-European was SOV, there was also a marked, alternative order, with the verb fronted into clause-initial position. This order was used for emphasis, to focus on the verbal action, or as a stage-setting device. Compare for instance the Vedic Sanskrit example (73), in which the fronting of the verb signals a special emphasis on the verbal action.

(73)   yánti vaí ā́paḥ, éti ā́dityaḥ, éti čandrámāḥ, yánti nákṣatrāṇi
      V   V   V   V
      'the waters move indeed, the sun moves indeed, the moon moves indeed, the stars move indeed'

Note that when more than one element of the clause was fronted in Proto-Indo-European, these elements had to be 'stacked up' at the beginning of the clause; and clitic elements had to follow the first of these fronted elements. Cf. e. g. the Vedic Sanskrit examples in (74). (Verb fronting here serves as a stage-setting device. What follows is quoted direct discourse.)

(74a)   Only verb fronting:

      uvāča ha iyam
      V   E
      'and she said ...'

    b)   Verb and deictic pronoun fronting:

      tad   u   ha uvāča yājñavalkyaḥ
      Pron. E   E   V
      'and concerning that Yājñavalkya said ...'

What is important for the development of Insular Celtic word order is the interaction between the early clause-initial placement of adverbials, the clause-second ordering of clitic pronouns, verb ordering, and univerbation.

Given what has been established so far, Proto-Indo-European can be expected to have had the configurations in (75), where P = adverbial, E = clitic pronoun, V = verb. For (75a), cf. example (72a); for (75b), see (72b) and (74).

(75a)   With P in initial position and verb finally:
          ♯   P (E) ...   V ♯

    b)   With P in initial position and fronted verb:
          ♯   P (E) V ...   ♯

The corresponding patterns without adverbials are those in (75'). (X refers to a word or constituent other than P, E, or V.)

(75'a)   ‡ X (E) ...   V ‡

   b)   ‡ V (E) ...   ‡

As univerbation of P and V set in, the majority of languages opted for putting P next to the verb in its unmarked, i. e. clause-final position. Insular Celtic, however, moved in the opposite direction by ordering V after the initial P (E).

The reasons for this development are complex, but include at least the following elements:

Whereas in most of the other Indo-European languages, relative clauses were marked by full, accented relative pronouns, in Celtic a clitic form of the relative pronoun had come to be used. And this clitic had to be placed in clause-second position. The combination of verb + clitic relative pronoun seems to have been reinterpreted as a special, 'relative' verb form. In effect, then, there was univerbation of verb and relative clitic. (For Old Irish reflexes, cf. 13.3.1.7 below.)

Secondly, clitic pronouns came to play an important role also in the passive: Insular Celtic appears to have started out with a demotional passive; cf. the Old Irish examples in (76) and (77). Reinterpretation of third-singular passive forms with clitic first and second pronouns transformed this passive into a promotional one; cf. example (78). (A further consequence was that the third person passive forms of transitives could be used as promotional passives, as in the second reading of (77). In fact, the first reading is only indirectly attested.)

(76)   tíagar
        sg. 3 pass. itr.
        'let there be going' (lit.: 'let it be gone')

(77)   mórth(a)ir
        sg. 3 pass. tr.
        '(*)there is magnifying'/'he is magnified'

(78)   ní-m-   mórthar
        P E   sg. 3 pass. tr.
           sg. 1
        'I am not magnified' (lit.: 'there is no(t) magnifying me')

Both in relative clauses and in the passive, then, clitics came to be semantically closely linked with the verb and therefore tended toward univerbation with it.

Now, given the pre-existing patterns in (75/75'), the structure which most easily accommodated this univerbation of E and V, as well as the pan-Indo-European univerbation of P and V, is the one in (75b). For here all three elements, P, E, and V, were contiguous with each other and thus could undergo univerbation. For similar reasons, the pattern in (75'a) would be the most successful 'vehicle' for the univerbation of E and V in structures without preverbs.

Once these developments had taken place, however, it was possible to reinterpret the resulting verb-initial order as basic, first for univerbated PEV and VE, then by a fairly simple extension also for PV complexes without E, and eventually — by a bolder, more far-reaching generalization — for all verbs.

13.3.1.3. Other word order changes
Other well-established and well-documented instances of word order change, such as an incipient shift from SVO to SOV in Mandarin Chinese, seem to result from equally specialized — and complex — developments, although the details differ widely.

However, except perhaps for the shift from VSO to SVO, no well-documented major constituent order changes seem to be attributable exclusively to the general movement processes of fronting and extraposition, and to a reinterpretation of the results of these processes as being basic.

13.3.1.4. Relative clauses and rebracketing
There is good evidence that early Germanic relative clauses had the structure in (79): A main clause, optionally marked by a correlative pronoun, was followed by a relative clause with an optional, uninflected relative marker (**RM**). (In the following, only the fate of structures with RM will be discussed. Configurations without RM appear to have had a similar fate; but the relevant developments are hidden in prehistory.)

(79)   [(CP)]$_{MC}$ [(RM)   ]$_{RC}$

Because in this structure the correlative pronoun was semantically linked with the following relative clause, it tended to be placed in clause-final position. (This 'iconic' shift of the relative pronoun next to its referent is of course something very similar to Behaghel's Law.)

Note in addition that the NP of the relative clause which is coreferential with the 'head' NP of the main clause ordinarily is simply deleted; cf. e. g. (80a).

As long as the two coreferential NPs agree in case, this deletion does not create any difficulties; cf. (80a/b). (In (a), both NPs are subjects of their clauses and thus would be in the nominative. In (b), they are direct objects and thus would be in the accusative.) However, where the cases disagree, problems could arise, since the relative marker is uninflected and thus does not indicate the syntactic function of the deleted NP within its clause. In situations of this sort, the general rule is that the deleted NP of the relative clause must be its subject; cf. e. g. (80c/d). Where that is not the case, the relative clause tends to preserve a pronominal 'trace' of the deleted NP, and that pronoun indicates the syntactic status of that NP. Cf. the example in (80e), where the personal pronoun *hine* shows that the 'deleted' NP is the direct object of its clause. (In the examples of (80), the deleted or pronominalized NPs are underlined. Case indications below the text clarify the grammatical status of the correlative pronoun and of relevant NPs, including the deleted or pronominalized coreferential NP of the relative clause. Only Beowulfian Old English examples are given. Similar patterns are found in Old Norse and traces also in Gothic.)

(80a)   ... scōp him Heort naman / sē   þe   Ø his wordes ge-
                                    CP   RM
                                    sg. N   sg. N
        weald wīde hæfde
        'He who widely had power over his word created the name Heort for him'

b) wē þē þās sǣlāc ... / ... brōhton ... / ... : þe   þū Ø
                                                 RM
         pl. A   pl. A
    hēr tō lōcast
    'We brought you this sea booty which you are here looking at'

c) Đā wæs æt ðām geongan grim andswaru / ēðbegēte :
              sg. D
    þām   ðe   Ø   ǣr his elne forlēas
    CP   RM
    sg. D   sg. N
    'Then a grim answer was easy to get for the young one who had earlier lost his courage'

d)   ... līf ēac gesceōp / cynna gehwylcum : þāra   ðe   Ø cwice
                                sg. D   CP   RM
                        pl. G   pl. G   pl. N
      hwyrfaþ
      'he also created life for each of the peoples that move around living'

e)   ... ðǣr gelȳfan sceal / dryhtnes dōme : sē   þe   hine
                                        CP   RM 'him'
                                        sg. N   sg. A
      dēað nimeð
      'there he whom (lit.: "that him") death takes shall believe in the judgment of the Lord'

What is important in the present context is that the correlative pronouns originally were part of the main clause, not of the relative clause. This is seen by the fact that where the cases of the coreferential NPs in the MC and DC disagree, the correlative pronoun has the case marking expected in the MC. Compare e. g. examples (80c) and (d), with sg. D or pl. G 'assigned' by the MC, whereas the relative clause would assign nominative case.

In later Old English, on the other hand, structures are found which are superficially similar to those in (80) but in which the pronoun that appears before the relative marker *þe*/*ðe* gets its case assigned by the relative clause; cf. e. g. (81). In structures of this sort, then, the originally correlative pronoun has become a relative pronoun, and that relative pronoun may be preceded by another, correlative pronoun; cf. (81 b).

(81a)   þā cōm hē on morgenne tō þām   tūngerefan **sē**   þe his
                                        sg. D   sg. N
        ealdormon wæs
        'then he come in the morning to that steward (sg. D) who (sg. N) was his superior'

b)   nēron gelefed him tō gebrūcanne, ne ðǣm   **ðā**   ðe mið
                                          pl. D   pl. N
      him wēron
      'were not permitted to them to eat, nor to those (pl. D) who (pl. N) were with him'

The change from the system in (80) to the one in (81) seems to have come about through reinterpretation of structures like (80a), in which the coreferential NPs of the MC and RC agree with each other in case. (Note that these are the most commonly used types of structures. Configurations with 'case disagreement', such as (80c/e) occur less frequently.) Such structures are 'systemically ambiguous', in that the case of the original correlative pronoun could be assigned by both the main clause and the relative clause. It appears that on the basis of this ambiguity, English opted for the analysis which considers the case of the pronoun to be assigned by the relative clause. This, in turn, required and led to a **rebracketing** of the pronoun from the main clause to the relative clause; cf. (82).

(82)   Old system: [(CP)]MC [(RM)   ]RC
       New system: [   ]MC [(CP)   (RM)   ]RC

Once such a reanalysis and rebracketing had been made, however, structures like (80c/e) became exceptions, since their pronoun case was assigned not by the relative clause but by the main clause. The development of the patterns in (81), then, eliminated these exceptions and thus permitted the new analysis to make correct 'predictions' about Old English relative clause structure.

Interestingly, the evidence of Beowulfian verse structure shows that the rebracketing had already begun. For although syntactically (in terms of case assignment), the correlative pronouns are bracketed with the main clause, phonologically they usually are bracketed with the following relative clause: As for instance the examples in (80) demonstrate, line breaks (marked by /) and caesuras (marked by :) almost invariably separate the pronoun from the main clause and connect it with the relative clause.

The fact that this phonological rebracketing preceded by several centuries the syntactic rebracketing exemplified in (81) suggests that syntactic changes based on systemic reanalysis may go through a considerable period of 'latency' before they finally get implemented.

13.3.1.5. Passive

Also more 'intricate' or 'abstract' syntactic processes such as the passive may be subject to various reinterpretations. We have encountered one such case in the Insular Celtic reinterpretation of clitic pronoun + demotional passive as promotional. (Section 13.3.1.2, ex. (76/78).) A somewhat different development, not from demotional to promotional but vice versa, can be observed in the Sanskrit passive:

Like present-day English, early Sanskrit had a promotional passive. As a consequence, passives could be made from constructions with transitive verbs, but not with intransitives; cf. (83).

(83a)   Transitive:

indraḥ sōmam pibati   sōmaḥ indrēṇa   pīyatē
S   O   act. sg. 3   O → S   S → Instr. NP   pass. sg. 3
'Indra drinks soma'   'The soma is (being) drunk by
                         Indra'

b)   Intransitive:
indraḥ āstē   (no Passive)
S   act. sg. 3
'Indra sits'

Along the way, however, the originally secondary process of subject demotion seems to have been reinterpreted as primary, giving rise to a demotional passive. As a consequence, the later language permits passives both from transitive and intransitive verbs; cf. (83'). (In addition, the later language does not 'reorder' constituents in the passive. Cf. further in 13.3.3.1.)

(83'a)   Transitive:

indraḥ sōmam pibati   indrēṇa   sōmaḥ pīyatē
S   O   act. sg. 3   S → Instr. NP   O → S   pass. sg. 3
'Indra drinks soma'   'The soma is (being) drunk by
                         Indra'

b)   Intransitive:

indraḥ āstē   indrēṇa   āsyatē
S   act. sg. 3   S → Instr. NP   pass. sg. 3
'Indra sits'   ("sitting is done by I.")

The beginnings of this change can be observed in the earliest stage of Sanskrit, where two or three structures like (84) are found. What is interesting about example (84) is that the verb involved is in fact transitive. However, it belongs to a class of verbs whose direct object may be marked either as accusative or as genitive. With accusative objects, these verbs freely passivize; cf. (83a). But with genitive objects, passivization originally does not seem to have been possible. (That is, passivization was sensitive not only to the syntactic status of NPs, but also to their morphological marking.) What seems to have happened in (84) is that passivization has gotten reinterpreted as sensitive not to case marking, but to whether verbs are transitive or intransitive. As a consequence, it is getting extended to all transitives, whether they have accusative or genitive direct objects. However, since promotion remains restricted to accusative-marked objects, the genitive object cannot be promoted. The result is a demotional passive. And this demotional passive, once it has come about in this 'weak spot' of the system, can be extended also to other verbs, including intransitives.

(84)   apāt   asya andhasaḥ   apāyi   asya andhasaḥ
       act. sg. 3 O (sg. G)   pass. sg. 3 sg. G
       'he drank (of) this juice' '(of) this juice was drunk (by
                                    him)' ≈ 'this juice was drunk'

Similarly, the functions of the passive can be reinterpreted. Thus, in the history of Indo-Aryan, many of the Sanskrit passives were reanalyzed as intransitive or stative non-passives; cf. the examples in (85a). (For *dṛśyatē* see also below.) Similarly, in its use as an indication of politeness and deference, the Sanskrit passive imperative was reinterpreted as an honorific active imperative; cf. (85b). (In spite of their formal differences, the Hindi forms in (85) can be derived from the Sanskrit ones by straightforward phonetic and analogical developments.)

(85)   Sanskrit   Hindi
   a) kṛtyatē 'is (being) cut'   kaṭnā   'be in the state of being
                                            cut off, come apart ...'
       dṛśyatē 'is (being) seen'   dikhnā 'be visible'
   b) kriyatām 'let it be done'   kījiyē 'please do (honorific)'
                ≈ 'please do'

However, it is worth noting that as a syntactic category, the passive has survived these and many other changes, in Indo-Aryan and in numerous other languages. In fact, it still remains to be seen whether major syntactic processes like the passive are ever completely lost.

This last statement may at first appear quite dubious to those familiar with traditional historical linguistic studies. For in the history of the

Indo-European languages, as it is often portrayed in the handbooks, the passive is notorious for its instability. Briefly, and by no means exhaustively, the following types of developments can be observed:

(a) Proto-Indo-European did not have a morphologically distinct passive. Rather, there was a so-called **middle voice** whose functions were similar to those of the modern Romance (or Slavic, Scandinavian, etc.) 'reflexive'. The functions included the following:

 (i) **True reflexive**, as in Skt. *bharatē* 'carries for himself' vs. act. *bharati* 'carries (for s. o. else)'. Cf. Fr. *il se lave les mains* 'he washes for himself the hands' = 'he washes his hands' vs. *il lave l'infant* 'he washes the baby'.

 (ii) **Intransitive**, as in Skt. *vardhatē* 'grows (itr.)' vs. act. *vardhati* 'grows (tr.), makes grow'; cf. Fr. *se rouler* 'roll (itr.)' vs. *rouler* 'roll (tr.)'.

 (iii) **Intransitive/stative**, as in Skt. *ramatē* 'is at rest' vs. act. *ramati* 'brings to a rest'; cf. Fr. *se trouver* 'to be found/situated' vs. *trouver* 'find'.

 (iv) **Passive**, as in Skt. *stavatē* 'is praised' vs. act. *stauti* 'praises'; cf. Sp. *se habla Español* 'Spanish is spoken' vs. *(el) habla Español* 'he speaks Spanish'.

 (v) In addition, certain verbs obligatorily appeared in the middle voice, such as Skt. *āstē* 'sits'. These verbs typically were intransitive or intransitive/stative.

Note that depending on the context, one and the same morphological form may have more than one of these different functions. Thus, Skt. *bharatē* may mean not only 'carries for himself', but also 'is carried (off)'.

(b) In Greek and Sanskrit, this use of the middle voice with passive value was soon replaced by a morphologically distinct passive, at least in some of the tenses. Thus, Sanskrit replaced forms like *bharatē* 'is carried (off)', *stavatē* 'is praised' with forms like *bhriyatē, stūyatē*. What is interesting is that at various stages in the history of Sanskrit some of the forms in -*ya*- were not clearly distinct from non-passive, generally intransitive(/stative) forms in -*ya*-. For instance, the form *dṛśyatē* in (85a) above could already in Sanskrit be used in the meaning 'is visible'. Moreover, the intransitive function of these forms was historically primary and the passive value, an innovation. (As a consequence, it is possible that rather than being an innovation, the Hindi *dikhnā* of example (85a) continues an archaic stative form *dṛśyatē* 'is visible'.)

(c)   In Latin and early Germanic, the old middle voice 'became' a passive, i. e., was used only in passive functions, while intransitive (/stative) functions were expressed by other morphological means. (What complicates matters it that Latin retained middle inflection with active, not passive value for some of the verbs which originally had obligatorily been inflected in the middle voice. An example of such a verb is *sequitur* 'follows' = Skt. mid. *sacatē*, Gk. mid. *hepetai*.)

(d)   Already in the earliest Germanic texts, those of Gothic, this passive-value middle voice was in the process of being replaced by other formations; cf. 9.1.4, ex. (41/43). Similar replacements are found in the more or less contemporary Romance, Slavic, and other languages. Various devices may be employed, such as the verb 'to be' plus the past (passive) participle, or the reflexive. (Cf. e. g. Engl. *he was defeated* and the Romance examples given earlier.)

Clearly, then, there has been a great deal of change, including the 'loss' of whole categories. However, the categories lost are not syntactic, but **morphosyntactic**. That is, they do not involve the syntax of the passive, but its morphological encoding. And although the distinction between syntax and morphosyntax is not always clearly made in treatments of diachronic syntax (including the present one), it is important to remember that this difference does exist. While morphosyntactic modes of passive formation may quite frequently be subject to complete loss, there is as yet not convincing evidence that the syntactic category 'passive' (and its contrast with the 'active') has ever been lost.

However, the various morphosyntactic changes outlined above are not without their own interest. For they provide further illustrations of the fact that the functions of the syntactic passive play a very important role in change: As noted in 13.4.2.2, functionally there is a close relationship between intransitive, intransitive/stative, and passive. Clearly, this relationship has again and again made it possible to reinterpret intransitives and intransitive/statives as passives and vice versa. Such reinterpretations are especially easy where underlying subjects are deleted. (Note in this regard that in early Indo-European languages, as well as even in the more colloquial varieties of the modern languages, passives are more commonly used without specified agent NPs.)

The only problem — and it is a problem — is the relationship between reflexive and passive, a relationship which can be observed not just in early Indo-European, but again in Romance, Slavic, Scandinavian, etc.

One speculative, very 'sweeping' explanation might be as follows: Since in reflexive expressions like Sp. *se mata* 'he kills himself', subject and object refer to the same person, they can be reinterpreted as grammatically identical and interchangeable. And if subject and object are interchanged in such structures, the result is a passive reading. This development might be argued to have been aided by the fact that in the early Indo-European languages, as well as in modern languages like Spanish, the subject of an expression like Sp. *se mata* does not have to be specified on the surface. In the process of change, then, this absence could be reinterpreted as an instance of a deleted underlying subject.

The problem with this explanation, however, is that the postulated reinterpretation is not as 'intuitively' appealing as the reinterpretations which obtain between intransitives (etc.) and passives. For instance, there does not seem to be any solid, or even merely suggestive, evidence in favor of such a sweeping reinterpretation.

A more appealing explanation might perhaps be the following. Note that here, too, it is only possible to speculate. At the same time, however, there is at least some circumstantial evidence in favor of that speculation.

Let the starting point consist in verbs like 'roll', 'grow', whose reflexives 'roll oneself', 'grow oneself' can be reinterpreted as intransitives. The immediate result of this reinterpretation would be a contrast between transitive and intransitive, as in early Skt. *vardhati* 'grows (tr.)' vs. *vardhatē* 'grows (itr.)'. Once this point has been reached, the well-known relationship between intransitives and passives can take over and lead to the development of passive functions which can be generalized to other verbs that lack natural pairs of reflexive and non-reflexive forms.

That this development may be on the right track can be seen from the fact that German, a language which normally does not employ reflexive formations to encode syntactic passives, has for a number of verbs an intransitive : transitive contrast which is encoded by a morphosyntactic contrast between reflexive and non-reflexive. Cf. the examples in (86a). In addition, a few reflexives (with stative/intransitive value) come very close to being passives. In fact, in translations with cognate verbs, English uses passive constructions. Cf. (86b).

(86)   refl./itr.   non-refl./tr.

a)   sich drehen   'turn'   drehen   'turn'
     sich ver-   'increase,   vermehren   'increase'
     mehren   have offspring'
     sich setzen   'sit down'   setzen   'set, put, place'
b)   sich (be)fin- 'be found, exist'   (be)finden   'find, deter-
     den   mine'

13.3.1.6. Syntactic ambiguity

Because syntactic ambiguity by definition involves the possibility of more than one interpretation, it might be thought that it is in this area that reinterpretation is most commonly found. It may therefore come as something of a surprise that one type of syntactic ambiguity is not very commonly subject to reinterpretation. This is the type which we have called 'derivational ambiguity'; cf. 13.2.5 with ex. (39/41) and (42/44). The ambiguity of expressions like (42), reproduced below for convenience, appears to be quite stable. The most common change is the development or increased use of syntactic devices which make it possible to avoid the ambiguity, such as rephrasing (42) as either (87a) or (87b).

(42)   The government announced the sale of surplus butter to New Zealand on Monday

(87a) The government announced on Monday the sale of surplus butter to New Zealand
   b) The government announced the sale on Monday of surplus butter to New Zealand

On the other hand, 'systemic ambiguity' is perhaps the major basis for syntactic change. We have seen a few examples in the preceding sections, such as the reinterpretation of clause-second auxiliary position as the proper position for all finite verbs, or the reinterpretation of the early Sanskrit promotional passive as a demotional one. A more complex example is the following.

As noted in 13.2.5, the earlier English expressions on the left side of (88) were amenable to two different synchronic analyses: One, 'transitive' analysis would postulate rules like the ones in (89) (= (48); the other, 'unitary' analysis would operate with rules of the type (90) (= 49).

(88)   Old English   Modern English
a)   þæt is sē   that's him
          sg. N   sg. A
b)   ic sēo hine   I see him
          sg. A   sg. A
c)   ic help him   I help him
          sg. D   sg. A

(89a)   After intransitive 'be' (and similar verbs), the case of the complement is nominative;
   b)   After transitives, it is accusative;
   c)   Exceptions to (b) are *heolpan* 'help' etc. which take dative (or genitive) instead of the accusative.

(90a)   Post-verbal complements are marked accusative;
   b)   Exceptions are *bēon* 'be' (and a few similar verbs), *heolpan* 'help' ..., which take the nominative, dative (or genitive) respectively.

As it turns out, English in the long run opted for the 'unitary' analysis. The basic generalization of this analysis is that post-verbal complements are marked accusative. Older English expressions like (88a) and (88c), therefore, would have to be accounted for as exceptions. And as the Modern English evidence in (88) shows, these exceptions have been eliminated, so that rule (90a) now can apply across the board and mark all pronominal complements accusative. (Note that at this stage the analysis can affect only the personal (and relative) pronouns, since elsewhere, other changes have eliminated case distinctions between subjects and objects. These developments will be further discussed in 13.3.1.8 and 13.3.3.2.)

In structures like (88a), however, another development had to take place first, before (90) — or (89) for that matter — could be applied. For in Old English, just as in the other early Indo-European languages, it was the post-verbal NP which was the subject of structures of this particular type. This can be seen in sentences where the pre- and post-verbal NPs disagree with respect to person or number. As (91a) demonstrates, in such configurations the verb agrees with the post-verbal NP. Assuming that subjects precede their verbs in unmarked structure, sentences of this type therefore must be derived from structures like (91b) by some kind of movement process. (Most probably, the relevant process was an iconic fronting of anaphoric *þæt* to the beginning of the clause which, in combination with a verb-second constraint (cf. 13.3.1.1), requires placement of the subject after the verb.)

(91 a) þæt   eom   ic
        sg. 3   **sg. 1**   **sg. 1**
        'that is I/me'
    b) ic   eom   þæt

Along the way, however, English began to reinterpret preverbal NPs as subjects, according to a rule which can be informally stated as in (92). In structures like (88a), this interpretation was no doubt aided by the fact that the verb can be construed as agreeing with either the preceding or the following NP. (The term 'unmarked' in the formulation of (92) is intended to account for the fact that in structures with 'marked' fronting, such as *Him I like, him* is in the accusative case, even though it precedes the verb.)

(92) The NP preceding the verb in unmarked order is the subject and, if pronominal, is marked nominative. The verb then agrees with this subject.

Once structures like (88a) had been reinterpreted in this fashion and once rule (92) had been formulated, sentences like (91a) had to be treated as exceptions. This exceptionality then was remedied by having the verb agree not with the following, but with the preceding pronoun. The result of this particular change, then, are sentences like (93). And these sentences, in turn, furnished the basis for the application of rule (90a) above.

(93) That   is   I
      sg. 3   **sg. 3**   sg. 1

(In Modern English, structures like (93) continue to coexist with the innovated type (88a). However, in the modern language, these structures seem to owe their existence more to 'puristic' tendencies in nineteenth-century normative school grammar (partly based on Latin models) than to natural internal developments.)

13.3.1.7. Phonology and syntactic reinterpretation
As noted in 5.2, ex. (56), in the prehistory of Old Irish there was a phonetic change of weakening or lenition, converting stops into frica-

tives in medial voiced environments. As many of the conditioning environments for this development disappeared, its outcomes in most cases were phonologically restructured. However, where they alternated with their nonlenited counterparts, that alternation had to be accounted for in terms of phonological rules.

One area in which synchronic phonological rules reflect the historical process of lenition is that of relative clauses. And it is here that the syntactic reinterpretation relevant to the present discussion took place.

In order to understand the change in question, it is necessary to be aware of the fact that the unmarked word order of (pre-)Irish was VSO and that the relative marker *-yo- attached to the clause-initial verb as indicated in (94). (See also 13.3.1.2.)

(94a)   Simple, nonprefixed verbs are followed by *-yo-:
    *V + yo (...)
 b) Prefixed verbs have *-yo- between the prefix and the verb:
    *P + yo + V

In the context P + yo + V, the environment for lenition of root-initial consonants was met. Now, as long as -yo- remained on the surface, that lenition was simply a conditioned morphophonemic phenomenon. However, as a result mostly of syncope, -yo- disappeared in the prehistory of Old Irish, leaving lenition (**L**) of the root-initial consonants as the sole marker of relativization in clauses with prefixed verbs; cf. the historical phonetic development in (95) and the synchronic syntactic evidence in (96).

(95) pre-OIr. *wor-yo-kom-
   Lenition *wor-yo-xom-
   Syncope *wor-y-xom-
   Other changes for-xom- (spelled for-chom-)

(96) din gním for-chomnaccuir
            P L
   'to the' 'deed'   Rel. V
   'to the deed which happened'
   vs. for-comnaccuir (non-relative, non-lenited)

At this point, the phonological process of lenition was reinterpreted as the morphosyntactic marker of relative-clause formation. (That is, a morphophonemic rule was reinterpreted as a 'syntactophonemic' one.) Evidence for this reinterpretation comes from the development of nonprefixed verbs in the observable history of Old Irish: Since in these structures, *-yo-* followed the verb, it could not introduce root-initial lenition. Accordingly, early Old Irish offers examples like (97a), with nonlenited root-initial consonant. Later Old Irish, however, begins to show structures like (97b), with extension of the root-initial lenition of prefixed verbs. (The difference between medial *ln* in (97a) and *ll* in (b) reflects sound change. The endings *-aite* and *-atar* are related to each other as 'active' vs. 'middle voice'. Finally, here as in the prefixed verbs, the original relative marker has in effect been lost, although the endings of relative verbs tend to differ from the corresponding nonrelative endings.)

(97a)   forsnahí   comalnatar [k-]
        'for those' Rel. V
        'for those who fulfill'

   b)   indí   chomallaite [x-]
        'those'   **L**
                      Rel. V
        'those who fulfill'

13.3.1.8. Morphology and syntactic reinterpretation

As noted earlier, beside direct objects marked by the accusative, Old English also had dative-marked direct objects; cf. (98/99). In addition, Old English had expressions like (100), in which *him* is an indirect object.

(98)   Ic   sēo   hīe
       sg. N sg. 1 pl. A
       'I see them'

(99)   Ic   help   him
       sg. N sg. 1 sg./pl. D
       'I help him/them'

(100) Ic   gief   him   (giefe)
       sg. N sg. 1 sg./pl. D (sg. A)
       'I give him/them (a gift)'

All of these expressions could be passivized; cf. (98′)—(100′). But as these examples show, only accusative-marked direct objects could be promoted to subject. (Compare the case marking, as well as the fact that the finite verb now agrees with the promoted plural subject.) Dative-marked direct objects and indirect objects were not promotable. That is, at this stage of English, the passive was demotional. Note, however, that demotional passives from intransitives such as (101′) were very rare. (In all of these passives, the agent NP usually is deleted.)

(98′) hīe   sind(on) (ge)sewen
        pl. N pl. 3
        'they are seen'

(99′) him   is   (ge)holpen
        sg./pl. D sg. 3
        lit.: 'to him/them is helped'

(100′) him   is   giefen
        sg./pl. D sg. 3
        lit. 'to him/them is given'

(101) gif men swā liofaþ
           pl. N   pl. 3
        'if men live thus'

(101′) gif swā biþ   leofod
               sg. 3
        lit. 'if thus is lived'

As early as Old English, however, the morphological distinction between dative and accusative began to disappear. And soon the two categories merged completely. (Cf. section 13.3.3.2 below.) This change, in turn, had important repercussions for the passive:

As the morphological distinction between accusative and dative disappeared, so did the corresponding syntactic distinction(s). Now all objects were reinterpreted as equivalent to each other, whether direct or indirect, whether originally accusative or dative. As a consequence they became promotable and were promoted to subject. Structures like (99′) and (100′) therefore began to be replaced by promotional passives like (99″) and (100″). Moreover, on the basis of such structures, the passive was reinterpreted as promotional, not demotional, a reinterpretation which led to the demise of the rare type (101′).

(99″) He   is   helped (by me)
       sg. N   sg. 3
       They   are   helped (by me)
       pl. N   pl. 3
       but not: Him/them is helped (by me)*

(100″) He   is   given (a gift)
       sg. N   sg. 3
       They   are   given (a gift)
       pl. N   pl.
       but not: Him/them is given (a gift)*

(Interestingly, the same change from demotional to promotional passive has taken place in Northern German dialects and in the Austrian dialect of Carinthia. Here, too, it goes hand in hand with a morphological merger of dative and accusative. One therefore suspects that it is this morphological merger which triggered the syntactic loss of distinction.)

In English, the promotability of objects actually has gone farther. First, indirect objects now are promotable to subject even if marked by the preposition *to*. Secondly, also PPs can undergo promotion to subject. In either case the preposition must remain 'stranded' in its original location. Cf. (102) and (103).

(102) act.:   They sent a letter to him
       pass.: He was sent a letter to

(103) act.:   People stared at him
       pass.: He was stared at

Also these developments had their starting point in early English. A detailed description of the relevant changes is beyond the scope of this chapter. Suffice it to state that the distinction between certain adverbs and prepositions was not as fully made in Old English as it is now. (The situation thus was similar to the early Indo-European one described in 13.3.1.2, ex. (71). But the two phenomena are only indirectly related.) As a consequence, the position of these 'adverb/prepositions' relative to NPs on one hand and to the verb on the other was quite free. All of the orderings in (104) could be found.

(104a)   hēo þā fuhton wiþ Pyhtas
                    V   P   pl. A
         'they then fought against the Picts'
    b)   gefuhton wiþ Walum
         V   P   pl. D
         'they fought against the Welsh'
    c)   ond him   wiþ feaht
             sg. D P   V
         'and fought against him'
    d)   ond wiþ þā   gefuhton
             P   pl. A   V
         'and fought against them'
    e)   ond him   gefeaht wiþ Æþelwulf
             pl. D V   P   sg. N
         'and Æthelwulf fought against them'

It was therefore possible to reinterpret prepositional NPs as direct
objects of verb + adverb combinations. And this, in turn, permitted
promotion of these 'direct objects' to subject of the passive, as in (105),
the Modern English passive counterpart of (104a).

(105)   The Picts were fought against

Note however that although structures like (102), (103), and (105)
began to appear as early as the thirteenth century, the extension of
promotability to prepositional NPs has not yet been completed. For
certain verbs, such as *sleep*, there is still disagreement as to whether
passives of the type (106) are acceptable or not. Moreover, such passives
are unacceptable to most speakers of English if the semantic link
between the verb and the prepositional NP is weak, as e. g. in (107).

(106)   This bed has been slept in by Washington, Jefferson, and
        many other famous people*/?/√

(107)   Chicago has been slept in by him overnight*

13.3.2. Analogy

Analogy and reinterpretation-cum-extension are often difficult to distinguish in syntactic change. It is true, certain developments are quite

clearly analogical in nature. Thus, in section 13.3.1.1, the development of the pattern in (108c) (= (56c) above) was explained as a compromise, i. e., as a **syntactic blending** between the competing arrangements of AUX and MV in the (a) and (b) versions.

> (108a) Bēowulfe wearð / gūðhrēð gyfeþe
>   AUX   MV
>   'To Beowulf glory in battle was given'
>   b) Bēowulfe gūðhrēð gyfeþe wearð
>   MV   AUX
>   c) Bēowulfe gūðhrēð wearð gyfeþe
>   AUX   MV

A similar development has given rise to the Modern German pattern in (109a): Old High German showed a similar incomplete distinction between certain adverbs, preverbs, and prepositions as Old English (for which see (104) above). But unlike in English, the competition between the preverb and preposition functions of these 'adverbials' was optionally resolved in favor of the concomitant use of both the preverb and the preposition. (That is, we are here dealing with an instance of the 'compounding' variety of blending.) Note however that Modern German also permits 'unblended' constructions, such as (109b) (with preposition only), or (109c) (with preverb only). That is, the competition has not been fully resolved. (In colloquial German, however, sentences with specified 'object' NPs definitely prefer pattern (109a) over (109b).)

> (109a) Das Klavier ist nicht **durch** die Tür(e) **durch**gegangen
>   'The piano didn't go (= fit) through the door'
>   b) Das Klavier ist nicht **durch** die Türe gegangen
>   'The piano didn't go (= fit) through the door'
>   c) Das Klavier ist nicht **durch**gegangen
>   'The piano didn't go (= fit) through'

For many other developments, however, it is much less certain whether they should be attributed to reinterpretation (cum extension) or to analogy. These are instances where a syntactic pattern is extended, but in a much slower, less sweeping fashion than in other areas of syntactic change.

An example of this type of change is the following: In Modern English, some verbs are equally 'comfortable' in the blank spaces of all the constructions in (110). Such verbs are *think, declare, believe,* and *know.*

(110a) They/people _____ him to be a crook   (act.)
   b) He is _____ to be a crook   (pass.)
   c) They/people _____ that he is a crook   (act.)
   d) It is _____ that he is a crook   (pass.)

On the other hand, verbs like *regard* are comfortable only in (a/b), and other verbs such as *assert* prefer (c/d). In addition, a number of verbs are more or less well tolerated in (b), (c), and (d), but not − or hardly − in (a).

The table in (111) illustrates the situation more fully. Here 'Infinitive' refers to the constructions in (110a/b), and 'That' to (110c/d). The symbols + and − indicate whether a given verb fits into a particular frame or not. A question mark (?), sometimes in combination with + or −, refers to judgments which are neither clearly + nor −.

(111)		Infinitive		That	
		act.	pass.	act.	pass.
a)	think	+	+	+	+
	declare	+	+	+	+
	believe	+	+	+	+
	know	+	+	+	+
b)	consider	+	+	?	?/+
	regard	+	+	−	−
c)	report	?/+	+	+	+
	feel	?/−	+	+	+
	say	−	+	+	+
	assert	−	?/+	+	+

The explanation for this curious distribution seems to be as follows: Originally some verbs, such as the ones in (111a), could occur in all of the four constructions. Others, such as the ones in (111b), were used only in the 'infinitive' constructions. Finally, there was set (c) which was employed only in 'that' constructions. On the analogy of the semantically related verbs of group (a), then, individual verbs of group (b) could begin to syntactically behave like (a) verbs, adopting − at least tentatively − some of the 'that' constructions. Similarly, the semantic relationship between (c) and (a) verbs could lead to the analogical extension of 'infinitive' constructions to the (c) verbs.

Now, passives tend to be preferred in statements like the ones in (110) where the underlying subject is generic or indefinite. It is this preference which seems to account for the fact that in (111), passives are in the forefront of the analogical extension of the (a) pattern. The result is passives like *He is said to be a crook* which lack corresponding actives. In a language like English, this situation is quite anomalous and might therefore call for remedial action, namely the creation of a corresponding active. In the case of *feel* and *report*, some tentative steps have been made in this direction. But other verbs, such as *say* and *assert*, seem to be in no hurry.

The ultimate outcome is a situation in which every word belonging to categories (c) and (d) has its own, unique pattern of $+$, $-$, ?, or ?/$+$.

Developments like these seem to be much less 'sweeping', much less systematic, and much more 'messy' than the syntactic changes which we have looked at so far.

However, it must be remembered that many, perhaps all of the changes examined in the preceding sections appear to be 'sweeping' only over the course of centuries. In many of them, we can observe (or at least, infer) intermediate stages at which the change in question was less than 'sweeping' or systematic. Consider for instance the slow shift from SOV to SVO (section 13.3.1.1), or the incipient, still incomplete differentiation of 'adverbials' into adverbs, preverbs, and prepositions in early Indo-European (13.3.1.2), or the similar developments and their effects in English and German (13.3.1.8 and this section).

To cite just one more example: While in colloquial Modern French, the change of OFr. *ne* 'not' via *ne ... pas* to *pas* (cf. 9.2.1, ex. (64)−(67)) is virtually completed, Modern Standard French shows a very different, quite 'unresolved', and less than systematic pattern, with uses of *n(e)* by itself coexisting with *n(e) ... pas* or even *pas* alone. Compare the examples in (112). (An asterisk after *ne, pas,* or ∅ indicates that *ne, pas,* or ellipsis is not acceptable.)

(112a)   il n' (∅*) en a (pas*) cure
         'he doesn't care about it'
    b)   il ne (∅*) cesse pas/∅ de parler
         'he doesn't stop speaking'
    c)   il n' (∅*) a (pas*) que deux fils
         'he only has two sons' (lit. 'he has not but two sons')

d) il n' (∅*) a pas (∅*) que deux fils
'he doesn't have only two sons' (note contrast with the preceding)

e) il ne (∅*) vient pas (∅*)
'he doesn't come'

f) ne/∅ vient-il pas (∅*)
'doesn't he come?'

g) (ne*/?) pas (∅*) du bruit
'no noise (please)'

Moreover, recent in-depth studies of completed syntactic changes and of syntactic change in progress show a pattern of minimal change in the beginning stages, with sweeping developments coming about only as a consequence of a long and quite complex series of relatively small-scale generalizations.

Note moreover that even the most sweeping syntactic changes may leave a residue of unchanged archaisms. For instance, although the unmarked major constituent order has changed from SOV to SVO in all of the Romance languages, archaisms with marginal OV order or with clause-final MV + AUX can be found in every language. Cf. e. g. the examples in (113) and (114).

(113)   Fr. sans mot dire
             O   V
        'without saying a word'

(114)   Sic. la pizziliḍḍa vattiata è?
                  MV   AUX
        'Is the girl baptized?'

If, then, syntactic change in general proceeds through quite irregular, nonsystematic stages, the distinction between analogy and reinterpretation-cum-extension becomes highly evanescent, indeed.

13.3.3. Teleology and conspiracy

Like certain types of sound change (polarization, chain shifts, conspiracies), so also certain syntactic changes may be **teleological**, i. e., oriented toward a goal.

For instance, Behaghel's Law and the allied process of univerbation can be considered goal-oriented, in that they bring together elements which syntactically or semantically are closely associated. And as the resulting word-order change from SOV to VSO in Insular Celtic shows, the repercussions of such changes can be considerable.

In the Insular Celtic development, the major change (from SOV to VSO) was an indirect consequence of a fairly minor process (univerbation). At times, however, it seems that teleological considerations can play a more direct role in syntactic change and lead to virtually unprecedented developments. One such case seems to be the following.

13.3.3.1. Subjects and agent NPs in Sanskrit

As noted earlier, the passive of very early Sanskrit was essentially promotional. And so were certain other passive-like structures, including the so-called gerundive or obligational (**Obl.**), the most appropriate device for indicating that somebody 'must' or 'ought to' perform a particular action; cf. (117) for an example. (In the following, the term 'passive structures' will be used as a cover term for both the passive and these other, passive-like structures.)

At this stage, the promoted underlying object, that is the surface subject, acted as the subject of passive structures: First, it normally took clause-initial position; cf. (115). Secondly, it ordinarily 'controlled' reflexivization. That is, it served as the antecedent or point of reference for the reflexive pronoun (**Refl.**), as in (116). Finally, some evidence suggests that it served as the controller of 'absolutive structures'. These structures are reduced clauses that are 'embedded' into 'matrix clauses'. The verb of such structures takes an uninflected, adverbial form, called 'absolutive' (**Abs.**). And the subject of the absolutive ordinarily is deleted. In early Sanskrit, such structures seem to have been grammatically acceptable only if the deleted subject of the absolutive and the surface subject of the matrix clause were coreferential; cf. (117). (In the following examples, **A** = underlying subject/agent, **P** = underlying object/patient.)

> (115) ēṣaḥ dēvaḥ vipanyubhiḥ ... mr̥jyatē
> sg. N   pl. I   sg. 3 pass.
> S = P   A   V
> 'this god is (being) groomed by the praisers ...'

> (116) svēna yuktāsaḥ   kratunā
> Refl. '(having been) yoked'
> 'having been yoked by their own power'

(117)   ... niṣadya ... havyaḥ babhūtha
        Abs.   Obl.   AUX
     '(you) having sat down, you are to be invoked'
     (Not: '(we) having sat down, you are to be invoked (by
     us)'*)

As the Sanskrit passive structures became demotional, however, a
difficulty arose in structures with intransitives. For lacking underlying
objects, they had to become subjectless in the passive; cf. e. g. example
(30′) in 13.2.4.1 above. Moreover, by this point, the obligational had
obligatorily become passive-like. That is, for both transitives and intransitives, it required demotion of the underlying subject. As a consequence, obligationals from intransitives obligatorily lacked a surface
subject. Cf. e. g. (118).

(118)   paśuvratēna bhavitavyam
        sg. I   Obl. sg. N n.
     'one must be cattle-like'
     (lit. '[by one] is to be been cattle-like')

At the same time, absolutive formation became increasingly 'popular'
as a device for clausal subordination. But, as noted, absolutive formation
was controlled by the surface subject of the matrix clause. Therefore,
by all rights, subjectless passive structures from intransitives would have
to be incapable of accommodating the popular absolutive constructions.

It seems that in this situation, the pressure from the increasing appeal
of the absolutive structure was sufficient to lead to a bold syntactic
change: So as to make absolutive formation possible with passive
structures, the underlying subject or agent NP of the matrix clause was
made to serve as the controller of absolutives; cf. (119). As a matter of
fact, agent NPs came to control absolutive formation even when deleted;
cf. (120b). (Note that such deleted agent NPs are either generic, as in
(120b), or 'recoverable' from the context.)

(119)   katam kṛtvā dēvadattēna śayyatē
          Abs. A = sg. I sg. 3 pass.
     '(Devadatta) having made a mat, by Devadatta it is lain (in
     bed)'
     = 'having made a mat, Devadatta lies (in bed)'

364   13. Syntactic change

(120a)   tasmād dīkṣitēna   apigrhya smētavyam
         A = sg. I Abs.   Obl.
'therefore a consecrated person should smile, holding on'
(lit.: 'therefore holding on, by a consecrated person should
be smiled')

   b)   hiraṇyam suvarṇam upāsya agniḥ   ādhēyaḥ
                              Abs.   P = sg. Nm. Obl. sg. Nm.
'having put on a piece of pure gold, the fire should be
replenished'
≈ 'one should put on a piece of pure gold and then
replenish the fire'
Not: '(the fire) having put on a piece of pure gold, the fire
should be replenished'*)

At an intermediate stage in the history of Sanskrit, structures of this
type were especially common with obligationals. This is probably not
by accident: Most passive structures have an alternative active expression, with a surface subject and thus with a ready-made controller for
absolutive formation. Compare for instance (119'), the active counterpart of (119). The availability of such alternative structures, then, made
it possible to 'avoid' the difficulty of absolutive control in intransitive
passives. Obligationals, however, lacked such active counterparts that
could have served as a means of avoiding the difficulty of absolutive
control with intransitive verbs. As a consequence, it was here, in
structures like (120a), that the need for innovation was the greatest.
One therefore suspects that it was this 'weak point' which gave rise to
the innovated system with absolutive control by the underlying, rather
than the surface subject.

(119')   kaṭam kṛtvā dēvadattaḥ   śētē
         Abs. A, S = sg. N sg. 3 act.
'having made a mat, Devadatta lies (in bed)'

This new pattern with 'underlying subject or agent control' seems
to have been first extended to the obligationals of transitive verbs such
as (120b). Subsequent extensions, then, account for the fact that also
other passive structures begin to be attested with agent control of the
absolutive.

These extensions were accompanied by another, more general development: The agent NP of passive structures was reinterpreted as being

the clausal subject also in respect to word order and reflexivization. As a consequence, the unmarked order in later Sanskrit passive structures is as in (121), with the agent NP in clause-initial position. And reflexives now are controlled by agent NPs, not by the underlying object; cf. (122). (Note that here again the agent NP is a controller even if deleted.)

> (121)   dēvadattēna katāh   kriyantē
>   A = sg. I   P = pl. N V = pl. 3 pass.
>   'mats are made by Devadatta'

> (122)   ātmanah pūrvā tanūh ādeyā
>   Refl.   P = sg. N sg. N
>   'one should recover one's previous body'
>   (lit.: '(one's) own previous body is to be recovered (by one)')

At the same time, however, the underlying object continues to act as clausal subject for the purposes of other syntactic processes. For instances, the verb agrees with the patient NP in (120b), (121), (122), and in all other clauses which have a (promoted) patient NP. The outcome, thus, is a system in which 'subject properties' may be divided over different NPs.

What may have helped in the development of this new system is the fact that throughout its history, Sanskrit like many other languages tolerated occasional 'sloppy' absolute constructions, such as the early example in (123). (Structures of this sort seem to involve control not by the subject NP, but by the most 'salient' NP of the clause. That is, they are pragmatically motivated, not syntactically. What is important in the present context is that such structures are used quite rarely. Moreover, in modern languages, where it is possible to get speakers' reactions, their grammaticality usually is considered questionable, and speakers tend to replace them with more 'correct' structures if they have a chance to do so.)

> (123)   striyam drstvāya kitavam   tatāpa
>   Abs.   O/P = sg. A V act.
>   'seeing (his) wife, it burns the gambler'
>   ≈ 'the gambler is in pain, seeing his wife'

It is possible that the earliest layer of the language had occasional 'sloppy' absolute expressions in which the subject of the absolute corresponded to the agent NP of a passive structure, such as (124). (No examples are found in the extant texts of that period.) Constructions of this sort may then have been reinterpreted as having syntactic control by the agent NP, rather than 'sloppy' pragmatic control by a 'salient' NP. However, the fact that it was this pattern, rather than, say, the pattern of (123) that was generalized and extended in Sanskrit requires the special syntactic motivation outlined above.

> (124)   striyam dṛṣṭvāya kitavena tapaḥ anubhavitavyam (*)
> Abs.   A = sg. I   Obl.
> 'having seen his wife, the gambler must feel pain'
> (lit. '…, pain must be felt by the gambler')

13.3.3.2. Conspiracy — English case marking, word order, and passive

At various points in the preceding sections of this chapter, we have noted changes affecting English word order, case marking, and passive formation. Moreover, rules such as (89/90) and (92) relate case marking to word order, and the discussion in 13.3.1.8 suggests a relationship between changes in case marking and passive formation.

There is good reason to believe that these developments are related to each other as part of a quite complex '**conspiracy**' whose ultimate effect was a radical change in case marking, word order, and syntactic behavior, as well as in morphological structure. The individual changes of this conspiracy feed, motivate, and reinforce each other in many intricate ways, only a few of which can be noted below.

Part of this conspiracy was the completion of the change from SOV to SVO. This development made possible, and was in turn reinforced by, the polarizing trends toward reinterpreting unmarked pre-verbal or initial position as subject or subject-like and unmarked post-verbal position as object or object-like. (Cf. the agreement and case marking in Mod. Engl. *That's me.*)

The latter development, in turn, motivated and was reinforced by the merger of dative and accusative markings on objects. As may be recalled, this merger was beginning to take place as early as Old English, where it manifests itself in several ways: First, dative and accusative alternated next to certain prepositions/adverbs; cf. 13.3.1.8, ex. (104). Secondly, a similar alternation can be observed next to certain verbs; cf., e.g., (126) and (127). Thirdly, dative and accusative were morphologically undifferentiated or only optionally differentiated in a number of morphological categories, including nouns such as (125 a) and the first and second person pronouns (cf. (125 b)). (The reasons for these alternations and underdifferentiations are manifold and include the accidental working of sound change and the less accidental effects of analogy.)

(125)   sg. D   sg. A
  a) Nouns: tale = tale   'tale'
               stice = stice 'stitch'
                 ...
  b) Pronouns: mē   mē/mec '(to) me'
               þē   þē/þec '(to) you'

(126) God forgifþ mē/mec
                  D : A (or just A?)
       'God forgives me'

(127a) Cyning hine bæd
           A
        'The king asked him'
   b)   Cyning him bæd
           D
        'The king asked him'

Structures like (126) are especially interesting, since here we have a clear instance of ambiguity: Is the *mē* of this structure a morphological variant of accusative, direct-object *mec*, or is it an example of a dative-marked direct object? (For such dative-marked direct objects, see 13.2.5, ex. (47) with (48).)

It appears that poorly differentiated datives of this sort furnished a 'weak spot', permitting the reinterpretation of certain dative objects as accusatives. Thus, comparative evidence suggests that *forgiefan* origi-nally took dative complements and that the accusative in (126) therefore is an innovation, based on reinterpretation of the ambiguous *mē*.

Beside verbs in which case variation resulted from morphological reinterpretation, there was a limited set of other verbs in which case variation was syntactic and appears to have been inherited. A probable example is found in (127). Verbs of this type must have provided further support for the reinterpretation in (126). Moreover, they made it possible to interpret the pattern in (126) not just as morphological variation in a syntactically accusative-marked complement, but as syntactic variation between dative and accusative complements. At the same time, this interpretation led to a considerable increase in the number of verbs which admitted syntactic variation between dative and accusative complements.

The result of these developments is that structures of the type (126) and (127) both permitted their objects to be promoted to subject in the passive, yielding structures like the (a) variants under (126′) and (127′) beside, or instead of, the non-promoted (b) variants.

> (126′a) ic   eom forgifen
>   sg. N sg. 1
>   'I am forgiven'
>   b) mē   biþ   forgifen
>   sg. N sg. 3
>   'to me is forgiven'
>
> (127′a) hē   gebeden wæs
>   sg. N   sg. 3
>   'he was asked'
>   b) him   gebeden wæs
>   sg. D
>   'to/from him was asked'

It is interesting that the vast majority of Old English passives with apparent promotion of dative objects correspond to active sentences of the type (126) and (127), i. e., with variation between accusative and dative. As a consequence, it is possible that the subjects of such passives are actually promoted accusative, not dative objects. However, the coexistence of, say, (127b) with (127′a) could give rise to the reinterpretation that these subjects result from the promotion of dative objects. And this promotability could then be extended to other dative objects which did not alternate with accusatives. Combined with further phonetic and analogical changes (such as the loss of the case marker *-e* in OE sg. D *stān-e* > NE *stone*), this reinterpretation further weakened the significance of morphological case distinctions and thus reinforced the tendencies toward defining case marking and syntactic status in terms of position in the sentence.

It appears that at a certain point these tendencies to define morphological case and syntactic status by sentence position became powerful enough to trigger the elimination of patterns which did not conform.

This is especially true for the notion (or constraint) that what directly precedes the verb ordinarily must be its subject. In addition to the change in verb agreement and case marking in structures like *That's me*, consider the following additional examples:

(a) In earlier English, the position before the verb was that of the topic of the sentence, and if that topic was different from the subject, the latter had to be placed after the verb; cf., e. g., the 'standard' Old English example in (128), as well as the Modern German parallel in 13.3.1.1, ex. (67/68). In Modern English, however, such structures by and large no longer are permissible. Instead, we usually find sentences like (129) which manage to retain the positioning of the subject before the verb. The older pattern survives only in marginal, syntactically and pragmatically quite limited relics, such as the ones in (130).

(128a) Hēr   wæs   Crist āhangen
        Adv. AUX S   MV
        'Here/at this time Christ was crucified'

  b)   On ðām beoð oft   gemētte þā betstan meregrotan
        PP   AUX Adv. MV   S
        'on it the best pearls are often found'

(129a) At this time, Christ was crucified
        vs. At this time was crucified Christ*

  b)   On it the best pearls are found
        vs. On it are found the best pearls*/?/|/

(130a) Up jumped the monkey ...

  b)   And out of the cake flew Superman

(b) In Old English, the verb *līcian* > NE *like* was construed as in (131): The NP referring to the 'enjoyer' was marked dative and, being more salient than the thing enjoyed, was placed clause-initially. The NP of the thing enjoyed, although the subject of the clause, then was placed after the verb. This is radically different from the modern English situation, where the enjoyer NP is the subject and the other NP is the object of the clause; cf. (132). This change can be explained as follows: As nominal case distinctions and most verbal endings were lost, structures like (131) became ambiguous; cf. (131'a). It was therefore possible to reinterpret the initial NP of (131'a) as its subject, and the post-verbal NP as its object. And given the general tendency toward identifying pre-verbal NPs as subjects, this reinterpretation was a 'useful' one, since it eliminated exceptions to that tendency. However, as a result of this reinterpretation, the retained pronominal case marking of structures like (131′b) became exceptional. The Modern English pattern, then, results from an elimination of these exceptions through generalization of the reanalyzed structure of (131′a).

(131 a)   þām wīfmannum līcoden þā menn
          pl. D   pl. 3   pl. N
          'To the women the men were pleasing'
     b)   hiere   līcoden þā menn
          sg. D pl. 3   pl. N
          'To her the men were pleasing'

(131′a)   The women liked the men
          (I)O   V   S
          → S   V   O
     b)   her liked the men

(132 a)   The women liked the men
          S   V   O
     b)   She liked the men
          S   V   O

13.4. Results of syntactic change

As already noted, major syntactic processes (such as passivization, nominalization, or reflexivization) do not normally seem to be subject to loss, although their scope of application, specific aspects of their formal behavior (such as promotion vs. demotion), or their morphosyntactic encoding may undergo frequent and manifold changes. Compare for instance the Indo-European passive: At some times and in some languages it prefers deleted agent NPs, but at other times and/or in other languages it may freely be construed with specified agents. It may change from demotional to promotional, and vice versa. Still, it has never been lost as a syntactic category.

Similarly it appears that major syntactic processes rarely, if ever, are added to the grammar of particular languages. More often than not, careful examination shows that what appears to be the addition of a new major syntactic process or category is merely a change in scope of rule application, in specific aspects of its formal behavior, or in its morphosyntax. (This, too, holds true for the Indo-European passive. For instance, it has been claimed that the 'Sanskrit passive' is an innovation, not inherited from Proto-Indo-European. However, the statement applies only to the morphosyntax of the passive, namely the appearance of a new present formation in -*ya*-; cf. 13.3.1.5 (d). As a category, the passive was inherited from Proto-Indo-European, morphosyntactically encoded as a 'middle' voice.)

That is, major syntactic processes seem to be quite stable. (There is, however, one probable exception, namely the loss of the passive in pidginization and its reintroduction in the depidginization/creolization process, cf. section 16.4 below.)

On the other hand, it is quite possible to add (or lose) relatively minor processes. A case in point seems to be the following development in American Black Vernacular English.

The starting point for the development seems to have lain in 'truncated' expressions like (133), corresponding to the fuller version in (134). By reanalysis, structures like (133) were interpreted as corresponding to something like (135). This reinterpretation, in turn, furnished the motivation for a new rule (not found in Standard or in White Vernacular English). This rule, which we may call 'negative auxiliary fronting' (**NAF**), then could be extended to other expressions, such as (136) corresponding to (137).

(133)   Ain't nobody gonna touch me

(134)   There ain't nobody who('s) gonna touch me

(135)   Nobody, but nobody ain't gonna touch me

(136)   Cain't nobody do what he can

(137)   Nobody, but nobody cain't do what he can

That (136) is generated by this new rule can be seen from the fact that there is no expression (138) which might correspond to (136) in the same manner as (134) once did to (133).

(138)   There cain't nobody who('s) gonna touch me*

Note that this development may have been facilitated by the fronting of auxiliaries in 'yes/no' questions like (139). However, this interrogative auxiliary fronting is not limited to negatives but applies also to positives, as in (140). NAF, on the other hand, is limited to negatives. Despite their formal similarities, the two processes thus are quite different.

(139)   Cain't he come too?

(140)   Can he come too?

There are examples also of loss of (relatively) minor syntactic categories. For instance, Greek and a number of other Balkan languages are said to have lost the construction of verb + infinitive: While Ancient Greek had structures of type (141), Modern Greek has the constructions in (142). (Cf. also 16.3.3 below.)

(141 a)   thelō   graphein
          sg. 1   inf.
          'I want to write'
     b)   thelō   graphein   ton andra
          sg. 1   inf.   sg. A
          'I want the man to write'

(142 a)   θelo   na   γrafo
          sg. 1 'that' sg. 1
     b)   θelo   na   γrafi   o anθropos
          sg. 1 'that' sg. 3   sg. N

Note, however, that there is reason to believe that this 'loss of the infinitive' was mainly a matter of morphosyntax. True, structures of the type (142) historically are dependent clauses, with conjunction (or 'complementizer') *na* 'that' plus finite verb. But synchronically their behavior differs little from the older infinitive. For instance, like the Ancient Greek infinitive (cf. (143)) they can function as NPs of their clause, usually preceded by the definite article; cf. (144).

(143)   zētēma   tou   einai
                 sg. G def. art.   'to be/being'
        'A question of being'

(144)   zitima   tu   na   ine   enoxi
                 sg. G def. art.   'that' 'are'
        'a question of their being guilty'

Beside such additions and losses of syntactic processes (limited as they may be), we can also find merger, especially partial merger. For instance, in English direct objects, the distinction between accusative-marked and dative-marked complements has been lost completely, and as a consequence, there is no longer any difference between constructions like (145) and (146). Dative-marked indirect objects, however, to some extent remain distinct, in that unlike direct objects, they may be marked by the preposition *to*. But at the same time, they now are as promotable to subject as are direct objects; cf. (147).

(145)		act.	pass.
a)	OE	ic sēo hine	hē is sewen
		sg. A	sg. N
b)	NE	I see him	He is seen
		sg. A	sg. N
(146a)	OE	ic help him	him is holpen
		sg. D	sg. D
b)	NE	I help him	He is helped
		sg. A	sg. N
(147a)	OE	ic gief him giefe	him is giefen giefe
		sg. D sg. A	sg. D sg. N
b)	NE	I give him a gift	He is given a gift
		sg. A	sg. N
		I give a gift to him	A gift is given to him
		PP	PP
			He is given a gift to
			sg. N prep.

Also the interactions of processes may be affected by syntactic change. For instance, in early Sanskrit, surface subjects controlled absolutive formation and reflexivization and took unmarked clause-initial position. That is, at that stage of the language, absolutive formation, reflexivization, and word order rules had to 'follow' the rule of passivization which 'created' these surface subjects in the first place. In later Sanskrit, on the other hand, this rule ordering was not required, since at this stage it was the underlying subjects which controlled absolutive formation and reflexivization and occurred clause-initially.

Finally, it has been claimed that change in major constituent order entails or triggers changes in the ordering of other syntactic elements. For as noted in 13.2.2, SOV tends to correlate with G + N, N +

po(stposition), MV + AUX, etc., while SVO or VSO tend to be 'harmonious' with N + G, prep(osition) + N, AUX + MV, etc.

The evidence of the Indo-European languages suggests that such a diachronic effect of these tendencies is quite tenuous, except for the correlation between major constituent order and the relative order of AUX and MV.

Thus in Kashmiri, the change from SOV to SVO is nearly completed. (It is more advanced than in Standard German.) And the change from MV + AUX to AUX + MV is only slightly less complete. However, G + N and N + po. remain unchanged.

In Modern Lithuanian, the change from SOV/MV + AUX to SVO/ AUX + MV has been completed. Lithuanian also has the 'harmonious' ordering prep. + N. But the latter order prevailed already at a time when SOV was still the basic major constituent order and when AUX had just begun to move into clause-second position. Moreover, the order G + N, which supposedly correlates with SOV, still is the unmarked order, in spite of the fact that SOV has changed to SVO.

Similar developments are found in a number of the Germanic Scandinavian languages. Other Germanic languages, on the other hand, have changed an earlier G + N into N + G. Interestingly, this change has been carried through more consistently in German than in English (cf. (148) vs. (149)), even though German has retained considerably more SOV characteristics than English.

(148a) 'Prepositional genitive':   Das Haus von dem Mann(e)
                                    NP   PP

   b)   'Inflected genitive':   Das Haus des Mannes
                                    NP   sg. G

        (beside marginal, archaic   Des Mannes Haus
                                    sg. G   N
                                    'the house of the man')

(149a) 'Prepositional genitive':   The house of the man
                                    NP   PP

   b)   'Inflected genitive':   The man's house
                                    sg. G N

        (ungrammatical: The house the man's*
                                    NP   sg. G)

Finally, Latin had N + G and prep. + N long before SOV changed to SVO.

The summary in (150) illustrates the large variety of different correlations between major constituent order and the (unmarked) ordering of other syntactic elements. Note that these observations are limited to Indo-European and do not even exhaustively cover all of the Indo-European languages. (The symbol '−' under SOV indicates that the language in question has SVO. Elsewhere it is to be read as in '− G + N' = 'N + G'. An asterisk under MV + AUX indicates the pattern 'AUX in second position, MV at end of clause'.)

(150)	SOV	MV + AUX	G + N	N + postposition
pre-Kashmiri	+	+	+	+
Kashmiri	−	−/*	+	+
O Lith.	+	*	+	−
N Lith.	−	−	+	−
Scand. lgs.	−	−	+	−
OE	+ → ?	*	+	−
NE	−	−	+/−	−
OHG	?	*	+	−
NHG	?	*	−	−
Latin	+	+	−	−
Mod. Romance	−	−	−	−

Now, it is probably not necessary to worry about archaic retentions such as the G + N of Kashmiri, Lithuanian, and Scandinavian languages, or the N + po. of Modern Kashmiri. For in syntactic change as elsewhere, the fact that one step in a given change has been undertaken does not necessarily require that other, possibly related changes be initiated.

What is troublesome, however, are the 'premature' N + G and prep. + N of Latin and the 'premature' prep. + N of Lithuanian and (early) Germanic. For these appeared prior to the change from SOV to SVO.

Of these, the appearance of N + G is the easier to account for. This ordering can be attributed to extension from the order N + A (adjective) and/or N + R(elative) C(lause). These orders, although likewise not 'harmonious' with SOV (which prefers A + N and RC + N or RC + MC), are found in a significantly large minority of SOV languages. (For instance, in one sample, five out of eleven SOV languages had N + A.) In fact, crosslinguistically adjectives and relative clauses tend to follow their head noun, no matter what the basic major constituent order. This has been explained as attributable to the tendency for topics to precede their comments: The head nouns of these constructions are considered the topic, the following elements, the comment. Now, genitives share with adjectives and relative clauses the fact that they are modifiers of nouns or NPs. It is therefore not surprising that the prevailing order N + A and N + RC, i. e. N + Modifier, was occasionally extended also to genitives. (This explanations works well for Romance. It is less motivated for Germanic, which has N + RC, but retains A + N.)

On the other hand, the relation between head noun and genitive can also be conceived of as comparable to that between verb and (direct) object: Just like verbs 'assign' case to their objects, so head nouns assign the case with which their genitive modifiers are marked. As a consequence, changes in the ordering of V and O might conceivably be mirrored by changes in the ordering of head noun and genitive.

The genitive, then, appears to have a dual affiliation: On one hand with other nominal modifiers, on the other with the verb. Perhaps it is this fact which accounts for the differences between the SOV/N + G of Latin and the SOV/G + N of pre-Kashmiri or early Lithuanian.

What is most problematic is the 'premature' appearance of prep. + N in the majority of the Indo-European languages. For crosslinguistically, the relative placement of adpositions shows the most consistent correlation with the relative positioning of verbs. Presumably this is the case because adpositions are very similar to verbs in that they assign case to a 'complement' NP.

A closer look at early Indo-European provides some possible explanation for the relative ordering of adpositions. But that explanation does not succeed in correlating major constituent order with the ordering of adpositions and nouns:

As noted in section 13.3.1.2, in early Indo-European the distinction between prepositions, adverbs, and preverbs was not yet complete. Moreover, these as yet undifferentiated or underdifferentiated 'adverbials' could occur in various positions in the clause, including prenominal and postnominal position. Cf. e. g. (151a) vs. (b) (= 71b/c) above).

(151a)   kád   asya **áti** vratám čak_rma
          'what' 'his' P 'wish' 'we have done'
          'What have we done exceeding = against his wish?'
    b)   sá   íd   agníḥ agnín **áti** astu
          'this' emph. fire 'fires' P 'shall be'
          'This Agni/fire shall be exceeding = shall exceed the fires'

It is therefore not surprising that their 'reincarnations' as adpositions likewise could precede or follow their noun. While the early texts of some of the Indo-European languages (notably Sanskrit and Greek, but also very early Latin) show numerous traces of this early state of affairs, the later tendency is to generalize one order or the other. Sanskrit and a few other languages opted for postpositions. Greek, Latin, and most other languages generalized the preposed variants. However, some traces of the original freedom remained in a number of languages. Compare for instance the preposed *ā* of Sanskrit (section 13.2.2, ex. (23b)) and Latin postposed *cum* in *mē-cum* 'with me'.

Note however that this 'scenario' does not explain why the majority of Indo-European languages opted for prepositions rather than postpositions. Such an explanation must remain somewhat speculative; and several possible scenarios suggest themselves. But interestingly, none of these involves correlation between major constituent order and the relative ordering of adpositions.

Possibly, there was in these languages a polarization, such that postnominal position was assigned to preverbs, while prenominal position was relegated to adpositions; cf. the schematic illustration in (152). But one suspects that a more important element was the fact that the adpositions tended to become (NP-bound) clitics. As such they could become either enclitic or proclitic on their respective NPs. Archaistic patterns of the type (153) suggest that in complex NPs they originally were enclitic on the first word of the NP. (This is an early pattern also for other NP clitics. Compare e. g. the early Sanskrit example in (154) where the first *ča* is enclitic on its noun, while the second *ča* is enclitic on the first word of a complex NP.) However, the fact that in structures of this sort adpositions preceded their head nouns could lead to the reinterpretation that their unmarked order was prenominal.

(152a) Preverb: O [P V]
    b) Adposition: [P O] V

(153) Lat. magnā cum   gloriā
          A   prep. N
          'with much glory'
          quā dē   rē
          RP prep. N
          'concerning which matter'

(154)   tád **agnáyē ča**
         N   'and'
         etád havíḥ parídadāti gúptyai **asyaí ča pṛthivyaí**
                                        'this' 'and' N
         'Thereby he hands over this oblation for protection, both
         to Agni and to this earth'

The evidence of Indo-European word order and word order change,
then, suggests that the correlation between major constituent order and
the ordering of other elements is weak at best. In fact, in the development of Proto-Indo-European 'adverbials' into pre- or postpositions,
it seems to have been entirely irrelevant. This should actually not come
as any surprise. For as noted in 13.2.2, even crosslinguistically, we can
at best talk about such correlations as 'tendencies'.

13.5. Outlook

As noted earlier, syntactic change is the area of historical linguistics
which has been least thoroughly researched. As a consequence, many
statements concerning the general nature of syntactic change must be
considered highly tentative.

Some generalizations, however, are unlikely to be seriously chal-
lenged by future research. One of these is that reinterpretation-cum-
extension is the most important cause for syntactic change. Other
processes, such as analogy or polarization, seem to play a much less
important role or are merely ancillary phenomena.

Another generalization, somewhat more tentative but still quite well
supported, is that syntactic change typically seems to start in a relatively
limited domain. The sweeping generalizations which we can so often
notice by comparing different chronological stages of a given language
seem to result from a sometimes very long and complex series of
extensions, none of which, taken by itself, is really 'sweeping'.

Beyond these two statements, very little of a general nature can be
said about syntactic change. Clearly, what is required is a great deal of
further in-depth studies in languages or language families with a long
and rich tradition of written attestations. The most promising areas for
such research are:

(i) most of the Indo-European languages, especially the Romance and Indo-Aryan languages with their considerable present-day diversification, their attested (near-)ancestors, and their long textual traditions;
(ii) some of the Semitic languages, especially Hebrew and Arabic;
(iii) some of the Uralic languages, above all Finnish and Hungarian;
(iv) Chinese, Japanese, and Korean.

It appears that research in some of these areas is now being conducted with greater vigor than it has been in the past, especially within the various theoretical frameworks of generative linguistics. It is to be hoped that this research will remain vigorous for a long time to come and that it will become as vigorous in, say, Japanese as it has been and still is in many of the Indo-European languages. For certainly, such additional research is urgently needed.

14. Linguistic contact: Lexical borrowing

With the exception of hypercorrection and a few other developments, all the changes examined so far have been intradialectally motivated. Languages and dialects, however, do not exist in a vacuum. There always is at least some contact with other languages or dialects. It is only the degree of that contact which may differ from language to language or dialect to dialect.

A very common result of linguistic contact is vocabulary or lexical **borrowing**, the adoption of individual words or even of large sets of vocabulary items from another language or dialect. Examples of such borrowings or **loans** abound: If a woman is said to put on *rouge*, if a man is called *macho*, if a country is said to engage in *realpolitik*, all of these statements contain borrowings. In these cases it is rather easy to know that the words are borrowings, since even with very little knowledge of French, Spanish, or German, we can tell that the words are of foreign manufacture. However, borrowings can also come from other dialects of the same language. If for instance speakers of Standard (American) English call somebody a *cool cat* or go off to *boogy*, they are using words borrowed from Black Vernacular English, a different dialect of the English language. In the case of such dialect borrowings, it is often difficult to recognize their status as borrowed words, since different dialects of the same language have much fewer and less striking differences than completely different languages. (In addition to lexical borrowing, linguistic contact can have a variety of other effects. These will be discussed in Chapters 15 and 16.)

The terms **dialect** and **language** in this context are used in a sense that is different from their ordinary-language meaning. For instance, in ordinary usage, Standard English is a 'language', while Black Vernacular English is a 'dialect'. In the technical use of the terms, however, Black Vernacular English and Standard English are both dialects of English and thus, from a purely linguistic point of view, on an equal footing. Put very simply, varieties of speech which are relatively similar to each other, whose divergences are relatively minor, are called different 'dialects' of the same 'language'. A language, then, is the ensemble of such dialects — whether they are standard or vernacular, urban or rural, regional or supra-regional. Varieties which differ from each other more noticeably, whose divergences are major, are called different 'languages'.

Ideally, this distinction between language and dialect is based on the notion 'mutual intelligibility': Dialects of the same language should be mutually intelligible, while different languages are not. This mutual intelligibility, in turn, would then be a reflection of the linguistic similarities between different varieties of speech.

Unfortunately, the mutual-intelligibility test does not always lead to clear-cut results. Thus Scots English may at first be quite unintelligible to speakers of the various varieties of Standard American English, and vice versa. True, given enough time (and good will), mutual intelligibility can be achieved without too much effort. But given an even greater amount of time (and good will), and a greater effort, also French might become (mutually) intelligibile for the same speakers of English.

In addition, there are cases like Norwegian and Swedish which, because they have different standard varieties and literary traditions, would be called different languages by most people, including linguists, even though the two standard languages are mutually quite intelligible. Here, cultural and sociolinguistic considerations tend to overrule the mutual intelligibility test. Finally, consider the case of Norwegian/ Swedish vs. Danish. The former two standard languages are said to be quite readily intelligible to speakers of Danish. But the intelligibility is not mutual, since speakers of Swedish and Norwegian find Danish quite unintelligible. Moreover, some speakers of Norwegian and Swedish admit that this lack of intelligibility may be a consequence more of sociolinguistic attitude than of actual linguistic differences.

What these varying results and failures of the mutual-intelligibility test show is that there is no clear line of demarcation between 'different dialect' and 'different language': Linguistic similarity or difference is a matter not of 'yes' or 'no', but of 'more' or 'less'; it is gradient, not discrete. Moreover, mutual intelligibility depends not only on linguistic factors, but also on sociolinguistic ones.

Even so, the terms 'dialect' and 'language' are useful in that they define the extreme or cardinal points of a continuum. If then, in the following discussion certain developments are portrayed as characteristic of 'dialect' contact on one hand, or 'language' contact on the other, it is to be understood that contact between speech varieties with an intermediate kind of relationship will show some of the characteristics of either of the two more extreme types of relationship.

14.1. The substance of borrowing

The first thing which comes to mind when we think of borrowing is the adoption of individual lexical items, such as *rouge, macho, realpolitik*, or *umlaut*.

However, through vocabulary borrowing other linguistic elements may be acquired. Thus, heavy borrowing from French, as well as Latin and Greek (often through the medium of French), has introduced into English words like the ones in (1). Many of these words coexist with other borrowed words from which they are synchronically clearly derived, cf. e. g. (2). They can therefore be analyzed as containing these basic words plus the suffixes *-able/ible, -ation/tion, -ance/ence*. In addition, since these patterns are not limited to just a few words, they must be accounted for by synchronic rules of derivation and morpheme combination. As a result, English has through borrowing acquired a considerable amount of sometimes quite complex morphology. Some of the morphemes thus acquired may remain limited to combining only with other borrowed morphemes, such as the *-duct, -ceive* of (3), words coined in English from borrowed elements, rather than being borrowed in their entirety. But other morphemes can combine with non-borrowed, native morphemes. Thus, *-able* quite freely combines with native roots (cf. (4a)), while *-ation* and *-ance* are less flexible (cf. (4b)). Note that one of the most commonly used derivational suffixes of English, the agential *-er* of words like *singer, baker,* or *transceiver*, ultimately is a loan from (late) Latin *-ārius* ⇒ OE *-ere* (as in OE *leornere* 'learner; disciple').

(1)   equatable, legible, potable
      derivation, deliberation, equation
      deliverance, occurrence

(2)   equate
      derive
      deliver

(3)   trans-duct, trans-ceiv-er

(4 a)   readable, laughable, drinkable
   b)   furtherance, botherance
        botheration

Vocabulary borrowing can also introduce new segments, or new environments for established segments. The latter, perhaps more common development is observed in words like *rouge, prestige* with [ž] in word-final position. (In more established English words, [ž] is limited to medial environment, as in *measure, leisure*.) The introduction of a new segment is found in the pronunciation of *Bach* as [bax] by English-speaking aficionados of Baroque music. Or consider the New York English expression *yecch* [yex] which seems to be of Yiddish origin. Moreover, as noted in chapter 11, borrowing can lead to the introduction of new phonological rules, such as the [k/s] and [g/ǰ] alternations in *electric: electricity, allegation: allege* which entered English through loans from French.

In addition to individual lexical items, collocations of such items, as well as idioms may be borrowed. Thus, French again is the source of such collocations as *court martial* and *marriage of convenience* (The latter loan involves a reinterpretation of Fr. *marriage de convenance* 'marriage by arrangement or agreement' as 'marriage of convenience'.) Similarly, the idiomatic expression *it goes without saying* is a borrowing from French *il va sans dire*.

Such borrowed collocations, in turn, may influence the grammar of the borrowing language. For instance, expressions like *court martial* have introduced into English a new manner of plural formation, with *-s* attaching not to the last word of a noun phrase, but to the non-final 'head noun'; cf. (5). In this particular case the influence is relatively limited and the resulting pattern of plural formation tends to be regularized in more colloquial or vernacular varieties of English; cf. (5′). However, in other cases the influence may be considerably greater. Thus, the French mode of forming comparatives by means of *plus* 'more' plus the simple adjective (cf. (6 a)) has given rise in English to the pattern in (6 b) which came to coexist with the native pattern in (6 c). The competition between these two different modes of comparative formation eventually was resolved such that monosyllabic adjectives take the inherited comparative in *-er*, as do disyllabic ones in *-y*. Many speakers have this pattern also in disyllabic adjectives in *-er*; but for some this is only optional. Adjectives which do not qualify for taking *-er* make their comparatives by means of *more*. Compare example (7). The reason for this specialization seems to be that inherited adjectives tend to be monosyllabic, while adjectives of more than two syllables tend to be of foreign origin. This sets up the pattern '(native) *-er* goes with monosyllabics, (borrowed) *more*, with polysyllabics'. In the case of disyllabic adjectives, no clear tendency is observable, except perhaps that adjectives in *-y* tend to be native and therefore take *-er*. As a consequence, disyllabic adjectives do not exhibit a unified behavior and some, such as *clever*, may fluctuate between the two different modes of comparative formation.

(5)   court-s martial (vs. parade marshall-s)

(5′)   court martial-s

(6 a)   beau   :   plus beau
   b)   beautiful   :   more beautiful
   c)   long   :   long-er

(7)   Monosyllabic: long   :   long-er
        Disyllabic: pretty   :   pretti-er
                clever   :   clever-er/more clever
                handsome   :   more handsome
        Polysyllabic: beautiful   :   more beautiful

From the preceding discussion it may appear as if anything can be borrowed: lexical items, morphemes, morphological rules, phonemes, phonological rules, collocations and idioms, and morphosyntactic processes. To some extent this impression is well justified. Otherwise the examples cited so far would not exist. Still, some distinctions can be made, although these distinctions concern not so much what can be borrowed, as how easily or commonly it can be borrowed.

It is widely known that the most easily borrowed words belong to more specialized forms of discourse, often referring to technology or other phenomena that require a good deal of mental and linguistic abstraction. Compare for instance *nation, inflation, machine, engine, atom, finance*, all of which are borrowings. In fact, this entire book is filled with such borrowings, since linguistics happens to be one of the fields which require a good deal of mental and linguistic abstraction.

Other words, too, may be commonly borrowed, especially the names for new artifacts and other cultural items which are subject to frequent change. Here belong words like *telephone* (made up of the borrowed components *tele-* 'far' and *phone* 'speech') and *lac/laquer* (ultimately from Hindi *lākh* or from its cognate in some other Modern Indo-Aryan language).

On the other hand, other spheres of the vocabulary are less commonly borrowed and seem to require more special motivations in order to be adopted from another language. The most important special motivation

for this kind of borrowing is the notion **prestige**. The special effects
of prestige can be illustrated by the English lexical division of terms
for hooved animals in (8): The forms on the right side are borrowed
from French, in the sphere where French culture and prestige dominated
after the conquest of 1066, namely that of (elegant) dining. And it was
that prestige which motivated the borrowing of special terms for the
animals as they are served 'at table'. On the other hand, the terms on
the left side refer to the area which after 1066 was relegated to the non-
French-speaking community, that of raising and herding the respective
animals. (It is for this reason, for instance, that we get *piggard/pig herd*
and not *porcard/pork herd** etc.)

(8)   cow, bull, ox   :   beef
       calf   :   veal
       pig/hog/swine   :   pork

The same cultural, prestigious influence of the French-speaking court
and its dominance in warfare and the administration of justice is
responsible for the borrowings in (9), many of which replaced native
terms. But note that as in many other similar situations, a fair number
of native terms survived the onslaught of the more prestigious language,
often coexisting with borrowed items; cf. *king, weapons, law* in example
(9).

(9)   Borrowed term   Native term
       royal   king (kingly), queen
       arms   weapons
       justice, legal   law
       court   (yard)
       curfew
       (petit/grand) jury

As in analogical change, **basic vocabulary** tends to resist change
most successfully, even in the face of heavy prestige. This may perhaps
be the reason that the more basic words *king, queen, law* of (9) are native
English words, while the derived terms *royal* and *legal* are borrowed.
It certainly accounts for the fact that in spite of its pervasive and
domineering influence, French contributed virtually nothing in the area
of the most basic vocabulary, such as *eat, sleep; moon, rain; do, have, be;*

this, that, the; and, or, if, when. In addition, it has been noted that verbs are crosslinguistically less easily borrowed than nouns and that if the need for borrowing does arise, many languages instead borrow a nominal form of the verb and employ a native 'all-purpose' verb such as *do, make* as a means of turning that form into the equivalent of a verb. Cf. for instance the Hindi examples in (10), where *karnā* = 'do, make'.

(10)	Sanskrit Verb	Sanskrit Verbal Noun	Hindi borrowing	
	pratiṣṭhati	prasthāna-	prasthān karnā	'depart'
	ārabhatē	ārambha-	ārambh karnā	'begin'
	rakṣati	rakṣaṇa-	rakṣaṇ karnā	'protect'

However, as in analogical change, the resistance of basic vocabulary (and of verbs) is not absolute. Thus, the English pronouns *they, their, them* are borrowings from the Scandinavian spoken by the so-called Danes who had harried England before the Normans and had eventually settled down in the Danelaw. The Old English *hie, hiera, him* now survives only in the colloquial *'em* (as in *Give 'em hell, Harry*) which synchronically has been reinterpreted as a shortened form of *them*. It is from the same Scandinavian source that English also got the fairly basic terms *give, skin, sky*. Similarly, the English conjunction *because* contains the borrowed element *cause* (ultimately from Latin). Moreover, English borrowed a fair number of verbs from French, such as *perceive, receive, derive* etc. However, it is also true that many apparent verbal borrowings from French, especially those in *-ate*, are of a different origin. Some of them, such as *orate*, are the result of backformation. Others are recent adaptations from Latin (etc.), made on the model of the relationship between existing English verbs in *-ate* and Latin verbs in *-āre*, such as *animate : animāre*. However, the starting point for the pattern seems to have consisted in a pattern of borrowing highly reminiscent of the Sanskrit ⇒ Hindi borrowings in (10): Instead of borrowing Latin verbs, English adopted verbal adjectives (or participles) derived from these verbs and turned them into the equivalent of verbs by means of the all-purpose verb *do*; cf. (11). Reinterpretation of the *do* of these structures as equivalent to the *do* of constructions like (12) then made it possible to use forms of this type as verbs in their own right, without the need for a supporting *do*.

(11)

Latin Verb	Latin Verbal Adj.	Early Modern English borrowing
imitāre	imitātum	do imitate
speculāre	speculātum	do speculate
corrigere	correctum	do correct
etc.		

(12) he goes: he does go

Finally, it may be noted that in the area of morphology, derivational morphemes (such as *-able, -ate,* or earlier *-er(e)* from Lat. *-ārius*) are borrowed much more readily than inflectional affixes. Examples of the latter type of borrowing are exceedingly rare, excepting instances where the affix remains limited to (a few) borrowed words, as in the Latin endings of (13). Even so, there are at least some instances where inflectional endings are borrowed, as in the German plural marker *-s* which enjoys a certain productivity in pluralizing borrowed words (cf. (14a)), as well as native names (cf. (14b)). This ending is a borrowing from northern German dialects which are quite distinct from Standard German and its essentially southern dialectal basis.

(13)

Engl.	criterion, pl. criteria
	alumnus, pl. alumni
	alumna, pl. alumnae
Germ.	Christus 'Christ': in Christi Namen
	'in Christ's name'

(14 a)

Auto	:	Autos 'car(s)'
Piano	:	Pianos 'piano(s)'
Jeep	:	Jeeps 'jeep(s)'

b)

Brandt	:	Brandts
Brugmann	:	Brugmanns
Delbrück	:	Delbrücks

14.2. Dialect borrowing

The majority of basic-vocabulary borrowings in English (*they, their, them; give, skin, sky*, etc.) were adopted from the closely related Scandinavian of the 'Danes'; and the plural ending *-s* of Standard German is a loan from northern dialects of German. This may suggest that borrowing from dialects or closely related languages can have more profound effects than foreign-language borrowing. Perhaps there is some truth to this impression. However, as we shall see in section 14.5, the prestige relation between borrowing and '**donor**' language is probably more important.

The major differences between foreign and dialect borrowings, rather, seem to be the consequence of the differences in relationship between dialects of the same language on one hand and different languages on the other. Because of the greater linguistic differences between different languages, the integration of borrowings represents greater difficulties. At least some modification is required to make the borrowed words fit in with the structure of the borrowing language. At the same time, because of the greater linguistic differences between distinct languages, the detection of foreign borrowings generally presents no great difficulties to the linguist. In the case of dialects of the same language, on the other hand, linguistic differences are minor and little structural adjustment is needed. However, the very fact that linguistic differences are minor makes the detection of dialect borrowings considerably more difficult. It is this question of the detectability of dialect borrowings which will occupy us in this section.

The most reliable criterion for establishing that a particular word is a dialect borrowing has already been adumbrated in 3.6 above, in the discussion of the relationship between NE *vat, vixen* and OE *fatu, fyxin*: Find a dialect (such as the Southwestern, 'Somerset' dialects of English) in which the phonological (or morphological, etc.) peculiarities of a suspected borrowing can be considered native. In the case of sound change, this translates into finding a dialect in which a particular change (or lack of change) is regular. Thus, the fact that 'prevocalic fricative voicing' is regular in the Somerset dialects suggests that the Standard English words with fricative voicing are borrowings from these dialects. They are internally '**motivated**' in these dialects, but not in Standard English.

What complicates matters is that dialect borrowing often works both ways, such that features of dialect A may be borrowed into dialect B in some words, while those of B may be borrowed into A in others. It is therefore not always realistic to expect complete regularity of a given sound change in a putative donor dialect. All that is required is that the change in question be significantly more regular.

To strengthen an argument for dialect borrowing, it is useful to give additional, independent evidence for the assumption that there was in fact contact between the putative donor and borrowing dialects and that therefore a borrowing relation was possible. Ideally, there should be some concrete evidence that the dialects were geographically or socially in contact with each other. For instance, in the case of the 'Somerset' dialects and the speech of London, where the English standard language originally developed, we know that the geographic distance is small and that moreover, at certain points in the history of London there was a relatively large population influx from the Southwestern area of England.

Even without such concrete evidence, it is often possible to make a circumstantial argument for contact by demonstrating that there is independent evidence for borrowing in other linguistic forms, with very different phonetic, morphological, etc. characteristics. For instance, in the case of Standard English and the Somerset dialects, one may refer to the fact that the development of Middle English final [x] after non-front vowel to [f] is more regular or wide-spread in the Somerset dialects than in Standard English, where [f] is limited to certain words (such as *laugh, tough, rough*) but absent in many others (such as *dough, though, plough, through*). This additional suggestive evidence for borrowing contact strengthens the argument that words like *vat, vixen* are loans from the Southwestern dialects of English. Obviously, the more evidence of this sort can be amassed, the more plausible will be the case for dialect borrowing.

As a final note it may be added that the principles here outlined for detecting and verifying dialect borrowings may be relevant also in certain foreign-language borrowing situations, especially where the donor and borrowing languages are relatively closely related to each other.

14.3. Foreign borrowing

As already mentioned, the major difficulty with foreign-language borrowings is that the linguistic structures of different languages may
diverge considerably, necessitating in most cases at least some adjustment of loan words to the native structure of the borrowing language.
It is this question of **nativization** which forms the topic of this section.

14.3.1. Phonological nativization

One of the most obvious areas in which nativization is called for is
phonological structure. For in order to be usable in the borrowing
language, loans must first and foremost be 'pronounceable'. At the
same time, phonological nativization is perhaps the area where the most
divergent strategies may be employed to integrate a foreign word into
one's native structure.

The process most commonly mentioned in the literature is the
substitution of the '**most similar native sound**' for a foreign segment
which does not occur in one's native language. In some cases, this
principle is quite straightforward in its application. For instance, a
voiced French fricative (as in *zéro*) is most plausibly nativized as a
voiced English fricative (as in *zero*), even though the French segment
may be more fully voiced than its English counterpart. A slightly more
complicated example is the usual English substitution of [k] for foreign
[x], as in the usual English pronunciation of *Bach* as [bak]: Both sounds
are voiceless velar obstruents; and since English (outside of Scots
English) has no fricative in this area, the stop is the most similar native
substitute.

In many other cases, however, the situation is by no means as simple.
Thus, if English [θ] as in *Thackeray* comes out as [s] in French and
German, but as [t] in many other European languages, the different
choices cannot be fully accounted for by the notion 'most similar
segment'. For all of these languages have both [t] and [s]. True, there
may be differences between some of the [t] sounds. Some are more,
others less dental; some are more, others less aspirated. But these
differences do not seem to correlate with the choice of substitution.
Rather, it appears that [θ] may be felt to be equally similar — and
dissimilar — to both [t] and [s], although in terms of different phonetic

parameters: [s] differs from [θ] by being a sibilant, [t] differs by being a stop. The choice between [t] and [s], then, is arbitrary; and the fact that different languages opt for one or the other substitution seems to result from something like conventionalization. (In fact, the substitution [s] is normal for Germans who have received formal training in English, while speakers without such training frequently substitute [t]. Moreover, some speakers use [f] to nativize [θ], presumably because it is acoustically closer than either [s] or [t].)

What further complicates matters is that at times it is not just one segment which is substituted, but a combination of segments which together can be said to be 'most similar'. Thus, if Fr. *enveloppe* or *salon* are borrowed as Engl. (dial.) [anvəlowp] and [sələn], the nasal vowels [ã] and [õ], single segments in French, are nativized as sequences of the corresponding oral vowels plus nasal segment [n]. Note that here again the selection of [n] as the nasal to be used in nativization is arbitrary. German uses the velar nasal [ŋ] for the same purposes, as in [zaləŋ], even though (in the present case) the resulting segment sequence has no precedent in native structure. Other examples of such a process of 'factoring out' the features of a non-native single segment are the substitution of ME [iu] for Fr. [ü] and of Lith. [ui] for Slav. [i]; cf. examples (15) and (16). In the case of (15), the frontness of Fr. [ü] ist rendered by Engl. [i], and its rounding by [u]. Similarly in (16), the fact that [i] is situated between front [i] and back [u] is the motivating factor for the substitution [ui]. Note however that the actual sequence of the two segments chosen to represent the single foreign sound is arbitrary. There is no inherent reason that English could not have substituted [ui], or Lithuanian [iu].

> (15)   Fr. pur [pür] ⇒ ME [piur] (> NE [pyūr] or [piwr], depending on the dialect)

> (16)   Ru. mylo [milo] 'soap' ⇒ Lith. muilas

In the modern literate languages, nativization quite frequently takes place through **spelling**. For instance, the common English pronunciation [rɔθ(s)čayld] for *Rothschild* [rōtšild/t] is based on the fact that *th* and *ch* usually are pronounced as Engl. [θ] and [č]. Similarly the common English pronunciation of Skt. *sandhi* as [sændī], with [æ] rather than [ə], results from the fact that the word is written with the letter *a* which in this environment usually is pronounced [æ] in English. To forestall such pronunciations, some Indian words with [ə] are alternatively spelled with *u*, as in *Panjāb* : *Punjab*. But interestingly, spellings of this type may give rise to the pronunciation [punȷ̃ab], an apparent hypercorrection based on the fact that the letter *u* is commonly pronounced as [u] in foreign words.

Spelling pronunciation may also be involved in the English substitution [r] for the [ɣ] of French words like *rouge* [ɣuž]: It is only the spelling which seems to account for the English pronunciation with [r]; the French pronunciation would rather call for voiced velar [g]. However, here an alternative explanation ist available; cf. below.

A somewhat less common process might be referred to as **etymological nativization**. For instance, literate speakers of Russian normally nativize foreign [h] as [g], as in *gospital'* 'hospital'. (Unsophisticated speakers may substitute the much more natural [x].) None of the nativization processes so far discussed would account for this substitution. However, if we note that Slavic languages quite closely related to Russian and in intensive contact with it have changed PSlav. *g* to *ɦ* or *h*, an explanation is possible: The relationship between native Russian words and their, say, Ukrainian cognates provides a pattern which suggests that 'foreign *h* corresponds to native *g*'; cf. (17).

(17)   Ukrainian **h**ospod' :   Ru. **g**ospod' 'God, Lord'
etc.

Germ.   **H**ospital :   X = Ru. **g**ospital' 'hospital'
etc.

A similar case is observed in the very early Old Irish substitution of *q* [kʷ] for early Welsh words with *p* which, in turn, in many cases were borrowed from Latin. Compare Lat. *Patricius* ⇒ pre-OW *patrikios* ⇒ pre-OIr. *qatrikias* (> OIr. *cothrige*) 'Patrick'. What motivated the nativization was the fact that in inherited words, Welsh had changed older **kʷ* to *p*, leading to correspondences of the type (18).

(18)   pre-OW   **pē*   :   pre-OIr. **qē* 'who'
etc.

*patrikios :   X = **qatrikias*

It is possible that the case of Fr. [ɣuž] : Engl. [rūž] is to be exlained in a similar fashion: Through earlier borrowings, made at a time when French *r* still had an alveolar pronunciation [r], a correspondence pattern of the type (19) has been established which might motivate the etymological nativization of Fr. [ɣ] as [r].

(19)   Earlier Fr.   [real]   :   real [r]
                         etc.

       Modern Fr.   [ɣeal]   :   real [r]
                         etc.

                        [ɣuž]   :   X = [rūž]

One of the perhaps most sophisticated approaches to nativization is the **system-based** substitution process of Hindi and other modern Indo-Aryan languages by which foreign voiceless fricatives are nativized as aspirated stops, while foreign voiceless stops, even if aspirated, are rendered as unaspirated stops; cf. the summary in (20). (Here as in 5.1.6 above, [t̪] = dental stop, [ṭ] = retroflex.) The beginnings of this process seem to go back to the pre-modern period, to the contact with the Persian and Arabic used by the Muslim conquerors; cf. (21). It can be seen in action even today, in the nativization of English borrowings; cf. e. g. (22).

(20)   f, θ, x   ⇒   ph, th, kh
       pʰ, tʰ, kʰ   ⇒   p, t̪/ṭ, k

(21)   farš(a)   ⇒   pharš(a)   'floor'
       xatm   ⇒   khatam   'finished'

(22)   thermos [θ]   ⇒   t̪harmas
       tin [tʰ]   ⇒   ṭīn
       phone [f]   ⇒   phōn
       proof [pʰrūf]   ⇒   prūph
       concrete [kʰ]   ⇒   kaŋkrīṭ

The basis for this substitution process lies in the very different structures of the Indo-Aryan and foreign obstruent systems: The stop system of, say, Hindi is much richer than that of, say, English, containing both a plain voiceless and an aspirated voiceless series, in addition to a distinction between dental and retroflex stops. On the other hand, English has a richer fricative system, containing [f] and [θ] in addition to the sibilants [s] and [š]; and Persian has the velar fricative [x]. Compare e. g. (23).

(23)   Hindi   English

    p ṭ ṭ č k   p t č k

    ph ṭh ṭh čh kh

        s   š   f θ, s š

In spite of these differences or perhaps because of them, the substitutions in (20/22) manage to retain the distinction made in the foreign donor languages, albeit in a radically altered and completely native guise: Foreign non-sibilant fricatives are nativized as the corresponding voiceless aspirated stops, because the friction noise of these aspirates approximates the acoustic impression of the foreign fricatives. The substitution of unaspirated voiceless stops for foreign voiceless stops, even if the latter are aspirated, then may perhaps constitute an assignment 'by default'. However, as noted in 7.1.1, the distinctive aspiration of languages like Hindi has a much more noticeable turbulence than the non-distinctive, allophonic aspiration of English. (This accounts for transcriptions like [tʰ] for the English words in example (22). English aspiration therefore may perhaps be perceived as not turbulent enough to be considered 'true' aspiration. Finally, the fact that English 'dental' stops are rendered retroflex, while [θ] is nativized as dental [th] finds its explanation in the phonetic nature of the English segments: While [θ] is a genuine dental, Engl. [t] is alveolar, post-dental; and it is this 'post-dentality' which is captured by the post-dental retroflexes of Hindi.

While system-based nativizations like these may be quite rare, substitutions that are sensitive to **phonological structure** or to **phonological rules** are quite common. For instance, many languages nativize foreign borrowings such that they conform to native restrictions on word or syllable structure. Thus, English and other western borrowings in Japanese are quite consistently reshaped in order to conform to the open-syllable structure of careful (or even moderately fast) Japanese speech. This is commonly achieved through anaptyxis, as in the examples of (24a). But it may be accomplished also by other means, such as cluster simplification (as in (24b)) or syllabication of glides (as in (24c)).

(24 a)   Engl. baseball   ⇒ Jap. bēsubōru
            crawl   ⇒   kurōru
    b)   sweater   ⇒   sētā
    c)   quiz   ⇒   kuizu

Similarly, Hindi and Panjabi nativize the 'alien' initial *st* of English words like *station* through prothesis or anaptyxis, as in Hindi *isṭēšan*, Panj. *saṭēšan*.

In cases like Japanese and Hindi/Panjabi, opinions may be divided as to whether the noted constraints are synchronically to be accounted for by rules. However, in other cases there is no doubt that non-permissible structures are eliminated by the application of synchronically productive rules of the borrowing language. For instance, forms like Engl. *trend* violate the German constraint that final obstruents must be voiceless. They are nativized by the application of the rule of final devoicing; cf. (25). On the other hand, inflected forms such as sg. G *Trend-es* [trend-əs] do not undergo the process, since their [d] is not word- or syllable-final.

(25)   Engl. tren**d**   :   Germ.   /trend/
                       FD   [trent]

In this case, then, the foreign form has been adopted (more or less) unchanged in the underlying representation, but the surface form has been nativized by the productive application of final devoicing. However, other possibilities exist, sometimes alongside the one just noted. Thus Welsh has a morphophonemic process of 'lenition' which affects word-initial consonants after certain preceding morphological forms; cf. (26 a). And this process is extended to borrowings such as the ones in (26 b). Now, in the process of borrowing words with initial [v-], Welsh is faced by the difficulty that this segment does not occur underlyingly in native words. The early Modern Welsh response to this difficulty lay in a 'backward' application of the rule of lenition (cf. (26 c)), assigning to such words an underlying initial [b] or [m] on the analogy of the native derivational patterns in (26a).

(26a)   Native Welsh lenition alternations:

Nonlenited	Lenited
p	b
b	v
m	v

b)   Borrowings I:

Paris	Baris	'Paris'
bwth [buθ]	fwth [vuθ]	'booth'
map	fap [vap]	'map'

c) Borrowings II:

vicar ⇒

bicar	ficar [v-]
micar	ficar [v-]

Finally, nativization can also be accomplished by downright **adoption** of the foreign segment or by adoption of the segment in a context in which it does not occur natively. The latter development, for instance, accounts for the final [ž] of Engl. *prestige, rouge,* etc. The former development is found in Hindi, and especially in highly Persianized Urdu, a literary sister-dialect of Hindi. Compare forms such as [fōn], [farš], [xatm] instead of the nativized [phōn], [pharš], [khatam] of (21) and (22).

The case of Old Irish *p* is especially interesting and instructive. As we have seen above, at an early stage (Latin and) Welsh *p* was nativized as *q*, as in *patrikios* ⇒ *qatrikias* (> *cothrige*) 'Patrick'. But at a later point, after *patrikios* had become *pādrigios* in Welsh, Old Irish (re-) borrowed this and other words with *p* by adopting the foreign sound without further modification, as in Olr. *pādr(a)ic*. There is evidence, however, that these new words with unmodified foreign *p* were for some time still felt to be 'foreign', i.e. not completely nativized: The morphophonemic process of lenition (similar to the Welsh one above) for a considerable time failed to apply to this new *p*. At this stage in the development, then, we get sets like the ones in (27a). Only after some time do such words begin to participate in the alternations produced by this rule, such that sets of the type (27b) start to appear. (Note incidentally that *cland* is in fact also a borrowing with original *p*. Ultimately it goes back to Lat. *planta* 'plant', with the semantic development 'plant' → 'fruit, seed' → 'offspring'. But unlike *popul* from Lat. *populus*, this word shows the earlier, full nativization **qlantā*.)

(27 a)	tūath 'people'	:	a thuāth [θ-]	'his people'
	cland 'offspring'	:	a chland [x-]	'his offspring'
	vs. popul 'people'	:	a popul [p-]	'his people'
b)	popul 'people'	:	a phopul [f-]	'his people'

The importance of this Old Irish example is twofold. First, it suggests that 'nativization by adoption' is qualitatively different from the other nativization processes: It does not really nativize at all, but merely 'admits' foreign words into the language without losing track of the fact that they are and remain foreign. It is only after these words have been around for quite some time, have been used often enough, and in enough different and novel contexts, that speakers may slowly begin to lose the feeling that they are not native. Nativization by adoption, then, is not an immediate process, but one of slow, gradual, even grudging, acceptance.

The second important fact about the Old Irish example, however, is that once a word has become nativized (or at least not long thereafter), it is native in every respect and therefore behaves like a native word, by for instance undergoing synchronically productive phonological rules. It will therefore, from that point onward, behave like any other native words also for the purposes of linguistic change. For instance, Old English and Old High German borrowed and nativized the words in (28 a) from Latin. And these loans then underwent the same phonetic developments as native words with the same or similar phonetic structure. Thus the vowel of OE *strǣt* developed just like the one of native *dǣd*; cf. (28 b). The medial *t* of pre-OHG **strātō* had the same fate as the *t* of **lātan*, etc.; cf. (28 c). That is, through whatever routine nativization comes about, it does in fact make foreign words native.

(28 a)	Lat. (via)	strāta	'paved road'	
	⇒ OE	strǣt		
	pre-OHG	*strātō		
b)	OE	strǣt	dǣd	
	NE	street	deed	
c)	pre-OHG	*strātō	*lātan	
	OHG	strāzza	lāzzan	
		'street'	'let'	

14.3.2. Lexical nativization

Nativization is an issue also in the areas of the lexicon and of derivational morphology.

Here again we encounter the possibility of adoption, without morphological modification (although there may be phonetic or phonological nativization). Examples are Engl. *rouge, conceive, compassion, sympathy* which, respectively, are from Modern French, Old French, Latin (via French), and Greek (via Latin and French). Also here, probably, nativization does not take place instantly, but there may be a considerable period during which the word in question is still considered 'foreign'. This is no doubt true for the latest of these borrowing, *rouge*; cf. its 'foreign' final [ž]. Note that in some cases of complete adoption, folk etymology may secondarily lead to greater nativization, as in the case of Algonqu. *otček* ⇒ NE *woodchuck*. Cf. also Fr. *chaiselongue* 'long chair' ⇒ Engl. *chaiselongue* → *chaise lounge/lounge chair*.

The polar opposite of lexical adoption consists in what has been called **loan shifts**. These arise from a shift in meaning of an established native word, so as to accommodate the meaning of a foreign word. That is, a foreign concept is borrowed without its corresponding linguistic form and without the introduction of a new word into the borrowing language.

Examples of this much more subtle and often no doubt undetectable process are the semantic shifts which many older Germanic religious terms underwent in response to the introduction of Christianity through the vehicle of Latin. For instance, the Old English words *heofon, hel,* and *god* acquired new Christian meanings beside, or instead of, their earlier native connotations. These semantic shifts were motivated by the fact that the corresponding Latin terms had a range of meanings which included both Christian and pre-Christian connotations. The partial semantic agreement (or near-agreement) between Latin and Old English then made it possible to extend the Old English meanings into areas which were covered only by the Latin terms. As the formulation in (29) shows, developments of this sort usually operate on something like a proportional model. However, the semantic proportions do not need to be perfect; cf. especially the differences between Lat. *infernum* and OE *hel*.

(29)
Latin			Old English	
caelum	'sky'	:	heofon	'sky'
	'abode of the gods':			'abode of the gods and of warriors fallen in battle'
	'Christian heaven'	:		**X**
infernum	'abode of the dead (below the earth)'	: hel		'abode of the dead who have not fallen in battle (below the earth)'
	'Christian hell'	:		**Y**
deus	'deity'	:	god	'deity'
	'God'	:		**Z**

Occasionally, however, loan shifts may come about in a less straight-forward (and more deliberate) manner: In languages which have a strong tendency to resort to loan shifts, etc., rather than the outright adoption of foreign words (cf. 14.5 below), it is not uncommon that an archaic word which occurs only a few times in old venerated texts — so rarely that its precise meaning is difficult to ascertain — gets revived so as to 'house' a foreign meaning. Compare for example NIcel. *sími* 'telegraph, telegram, telephone', as well as its compounds *rit-sími* 'telegraph' and *tal-sími* 'telephone'. Before its modern revival, the word occurs only four times, in very early, archaic Old Icelandic texts, with perhaps the meaning 'rope', 'thread', 'string', or the like. With a somewhat arbitrary redefinition as 'wire' or 'cable', the word then could be resurrected to translate Engl. *wire, cable* = 'telegram' (etc.).

A process in some ways intermediate between adoption and loan shift is that of **calquing**, i.e. of producing **calques** or **loan translations**: This process consists in translating morphologically complex foreign expressions by means of novel combinations of native elements which match the meanings and structure of the foreign expressions and their component parts. Compare for instance the examples in (30). Like loan shifts, these formations do not introduce foreign elements into the language; but they do introduce new forms. For instance in (30 c), the English term *world view* owes its existence to Germ. *Weltanschauung* 'view, outlook on the world', of which it is a loan translation. But unlike its occasional rival *weltanschauung* it is composed entirely of native elements.

(30a)	Fr.	il va sans dire	:	Engl.	it goes without saying
b)	Engl.	chain smoker	:	Germ.	Kettenraucher
		sky scraper	:		Wolkenkratzer
				Fr.	gratte-ciel
c)	Germ.	Weltanschauung	:	Engl.	world view

The examples in (30b) additionally illustrate that the elements used to translate the component parts of a foreign word usually are put together according to native morphological patterns and processes. For instance, Engl. *chain* corresponds to Germ. *Kette* and *smoker* to *Raucher*. But the German compound is *Kette-n-raucher*, not *Ketteraucher**, in accordance with a productive native process of compound formation. Similarly, French translates Engl. *sky scraper* as *gratte-ciel*, lit. 'scrape-sky', because that is the synchronically productive mode of making compounds corresponding to the English pattern *sky scraper*. Germ. *Wolkenkratzer*, lit. 'cloud scraper', further shows that calques may occasionally be less than exact translations. And the example in (30a) illustrates that even idiomatic, multi-word expressions can be calqued.

Calques are not necessarily limited to structures like (30), in which the component parts of morphologically complex expressions are independent lexical items in their own right. They can also involve affixes. Compare for instance the calques in (31). Here the Latin and German prefixes *com-* and *mit-* translate the Greek prefix *sun/sum-,* and the following noun stems render the Greek *patheia* 'suffering'. Or consider (32), where Old Welsh and Old Irish substitute their native suffixes for the Latin *-ius* of *Patricius*. Such suffix calquing seems to be especially common in borrowings from closely related and therefore structurally very similar languages. (Cf. the close similarity between Lat. *-ius,* pre-OW *-ios,* and pre-OIr. *-ias*.)

> (31) Gk. sum-patheia ⇒ Lat. com-miserātiō, com-passiō ⇒
>   Germ. Mit-leid
>
> (32) Lat. Patric-**ius** ⇒ pre-OW Patrik-**ios** ⇒ pre-OIr.
>   Qatrik-**ias**

It might be added that calquing presupposes a certain familiarity with the donor language and its grammatical structure. Otherwise, it would not be possible to recognize that a given item in that language is morphologically complex.

14.3.3. Nativization of inflectional morphology

The equivalent-suffix substitution in (32) is interesting, since through it, foreign words are integrated into the inflectional system of the borrowing language: The suffix *-ius* is well established in the inflectional system of Latin, where it goes along with a dative singular form *-iō* and other case forms. In the older Insular Celtic languages, however, the suffix does not fit in comfortably with the native systems of inflectional morphology. At the same time, like Latin, the morphosyntax of these languages requires nouns to be inflected for number and case. The substitution of native *-ios, -ias,* then, introduces suffixes which are suitable for inflection (cf. e.g. pre-OIr. sg.D *$Qatriki\bar{u}$) and thus makes it possible to use the borrowed word(s) in a morphosyntactically grammatical manner.

However, this type of nativization is possible only if the donor and borrowing languages have similar grammatical systems. Where the systems diverge, different strategies need to be resorted to, at least in the case of languages which have fairly complex morphological and morphosyntactic systems. In the following, a few of these strategies will be exemplified, as they apply to the question of gender assignment in languages which obligatorily have to mark every noun for gender.

Gender assignment seems to operate in terms of the following parameters: (i) Formal criteria; (ii) general semantic criteria; (iii) considerations of the gender of semantically related native words; (iv) a 'default' class to which words are assigned if none of the other criteria provides a solution.

Consider for instance the case of German borrowings. German has three 'grammatical', semantically largely arbitrary, genders: Masculine, as in *der Mann* 'the man', *der Tisch* 'the table'; feminine, as in *die Frau* 'the woman', *die Tür* 'the door'; and neuter, as in *das Kind* 'the child', *das Mädchen* 'the girl', *das Buch* 'the book'. What complicates matters is that there is no consistent formal distinction between the three genders of German. The best that can be said is that masculines and neuters tend to inflect alike and tend to end in a consonant, while feminines tend to end in a vowel, most commonly in *-e* [ə]. At the same time, however, gender assignment is obligatory and has important repercussions for pronominalization and adjective agreement; cf., e.g., (33). And it is in these 'derived-gender' forms, especially in the pronouns that we find the most clearly marked morphological differences between the three genders.

(33)   Masculine: Das ist ein nett**er** Mann; **er** ist Mediziner.
                      'That is a nice man. He is in medicine.'
                      Das ist ein alt**er** Tisch; **er** kostet viel Geld.
                      'That is an old table. It costs a lot of money.'

        Feminine: Das ist ein**e** klug**e** Frau; **sie** ist Mediziner**in**.
                      'That is a smart woman. She is in medicine.'
                      Das ist ein**e** stark**e** Tür; **sie** hält viel aus.
                      'That is a strong door. It can take a lot (of abuse).'

Neuter: Das ist ein nett**es** Mädchen; **es** gefällt allen.
               'That is a nice girl. All people like her.'
               Das ist ein gut**es** Buch; **es** kostet aber sehr
               viel.
               'That is a good book. But it costs a lot.'

Let us now take a look at how German assigns gender to words
borrowed from other languages. Examples will be drawn from English,
French, and Sanskrit. English has 'natural' or 'sex' gender but no
'grammatical' gender distinctions. French has two 'grammatical' genders, masculine and feminine. Sanskrit appears to be the most similar
to German, by having a three-way 'grammatical' gender distinction
between masculine, feminine, and neuter. However, in terms of its
morphology, the gender system of Sanskrit is no more similar to that
of German than the two-way system of French or the 'natural' gender
system of English. The ordinary tendency, therefore, is not to look to
the donor language for guidance in assigning gender but to rely on the
criteria outlined above. Consider for instance the examples in (34).

(34 a)   Skt. vēda (m.) 'veda; traditional/sacred knowledge'
     b)   Early NFr. garage [garažə] (m.) 'garage'
     c)   Engl. computer
                 babysitter
                 beatnik
                 trend
                 meeting

The Sanskrit and French words in (a) and (b) are masculines and
should not cause any difficulties if German gender assignment were
based on the system of the donor language; they should come out as
masculines. However, formal criteria here are potent enough to cause
serious interference with gender assignment:
     French *garage* and all other French words in *-age* come out as feminine
in German, as in *die Garage,* because of the tendency for nouns in *-e* to
be feminine. (And note that this is only a tendency. For quite a number
of native non-feminine German words end in *-e,* such as masc. *der Recke*
'the hero', *der Rüde* 'the male dog' or neut. *das Auge.* But the existence
of such nouns does not seem to have been sufficient to salvage the
masculine gender of words like *garage,* which rather adopt the more
productive feminine gender of words in *-e.*)

In the case of (34a), the interference comes from the fact that, through earlier borrowings from Latin and Greek, German has acquired many feminines ending in *-a,* such as *die Prima* 'top or senior class in a Gymnasium', *die Aula* 'the great hall'. And these words establish the expectation that words in *-a* should be feminine. As a consequence, the naive gender assignment for *vēda* tends to be feminine. The fact that for educated speakers the gender is masculine reflects the influence of those who know something of the *vēda* and the Sanskrit language in which it is composed. (There is also a minor pattern of Greek borrowings in *-a* that have neuter gender, such as *das Komma* 'the comma'. But as in the case of final *-e,* only the major pattern tends to be generalized.)

The problem of gender assignment is of course greatest in borrowings from languages like English which lack grammatical gender. Here, too, German may draw on formal criteria. For instance, the word *computer* fits in with the native German class of agent or instrument nouns in *-er,* such as *Bäck-er* 'baker' or *Schab-er* 'scraper'. And since nouns of this type are masculine in German, *computer* is assigned masculine gender.

The same expectation would seem to hold for *babysitter.* However, while masculine gender causes no difficulties if the word is used in a generic sense, it becomes rather inappropriate if used in reference to an individual babysitter if, as commonly is the case, that person is female. For in that case, German morphology requires that the form be marked by the suffix *-in,* as in the *Medizinerin* of example in (33). But many Germans would balk at using a form like *Babysitter-in,* presumably because the word *Babysitter* has not been sufficiently nativized to accept native derivational suffixes.

The word *Beatnik* likewise is assigned masculine gender, but for semantic, not formal reasons: For human beings, the masculine gender is normally used (i) to refer to males and (ii) as the unmarked term for persons whose sex is not specified.

The masculine gender assignment for *Trend* is more complex, since general semantic criteria work only in certain areas of the lexicon, especially with words for humans or animates. Moreover, formal considerations provide only negative guidance: Since the word ends in a consonant, it is more likely to be assigned masculine or neuter gender than feminine. However, there are no formal criteria which permit a choice between masculine and neuter. It is here that principle (iii) takes over, namely considerations of the gender of semantically related native words. Native near-synonyms which like *Trend* are monosyllabic and end in consonant are *Zug* and *Hang;* and these are masculine. (There are to be sure also some feminine near-synonyms, such as *Anlage* or *Tendenz;* but these are clearly characterized by feminine suffixes (*-e* and *-enz*), while the formal structure of *Trend* suggests non-feminine gender.)

In cases like *Meeting,* finally, none of the criteria examined so far will unambiguously assign a specific gender. Here the 'default class' provision takes over and turns the word into a neuter, as in *das Meeting.*

There is evidence that similar considerations play a role also in other languages, with very different gender systems. Thus in Swahili, the Arabic word *kitāb* 'book' is assigned to the *ki*-class, as in *ki-tābu,* and makes its plural accordingly as *vi-tābu.* As in the case of German feminine assignment to *Garage,* the assignment of *kitāb* takes place on the basis of the purely formal criteria of the borrowing, not the donor language. (In Arabic, *kitāb* is composed of a root *k-t-b* 'write' and a vocalic morpheme *i-ā* which turns the root meaning 'write' into the noun meaning 'book'.) General semantic considerations decide the assignment of Engl. *settler* to the *m-* (pl. *wa-*) class of human beings: *m-setla,* pl. *wa-setla.* And here, too, we have a 'default class' to which are assigned words that are not classifiable by other criteria. This is the $\emptyset$-prefix class (with $\emptyset$-prefix also in the plural). It is this class which accommodates borrowings like Port. *mesa* [-z-] 'table' $\Rightarrow$ Swah. *mēza,* pl. *mēza.* Although the details differ, the other Bantu languages follow essentially the same routine in assigning gender (or 'concord markers') to foreign borrowings.

14.4. Borrowing from linguistic ancestor

A borrowing relationship which is often overlooked is the one between a language and its linguistic (near-)ancestor. This type of relationship is found between the Romance languages and Latin; between the modern Slavic of peoples belonging to the Eastern Orthodox faith and Old Church Slavic; between modern colloquial Greek (*Dēmotikē* [ðimotiki]) and the more traditional literary language (*Kathareusa* [kaθarevusa]); between modern colloquial Arabic and Classical Arabic; between the modern Indo-Aryan languages (except Urdu) and Sanskrit; etc.

What makes for additional complications is the fact that in many of these languages the ancient, ancestral prestige language for centuries did not become a dead or 'book' language, but continued to be in active use among the educated. This special coexistence between ancient prestige language and modern 'vernacular' is now commonly referred to as **diglossia**. In some cases, such as especially in modern Greece and the Arabic world, the ancient prestige language tends to be employed mainly in written form or in highly formal recitation, while elsewhere the 'vernacular' is used. At the same time, the vernacular normally is not employed in writing. In other traditions, the prestige language can — or could — be employed also in freely spoken form, such as Latin in medieval Europe or Sanskrit in India down to the present time. In principle, such prestige languages are very conservative, resisting the 'normal' linguistic changes which affect the vernacular. However, if they are freely used in spoken form, they often undergo what may be called **vernacularization,** i.e., a certain intrusion of vernacular linguistic features. Thus, spoken Sanskrit has in many areas of India acquired the vernacular pronunciation [ǰ] and [b] for initial *y-* and *v-*. And the vernacularization of medieval Latin led to the compilation of dictionaries which prescribe the 'correct', more classical pronunciation and proscribe the 'incorrect', popular pronunciation.

This coexistence of the ancestral language as a prestigious, educated medium of communication beside the vernacular has a number of very special effects. First, borrowings from the ancestral language may be made repeatedly, at various stages in the development of the vernacular. Secondly, because of the close interaction between prestige language and vernacular, borrowing may be quite intensive. Moreover, even when the ancestral language ceases to be a commonly spoken language, its written influence and prestige may lead to continued borrowing. Finally, the nature of the borrowing relationship undergoes interesting changes: In the early stages, the relationship is more like that between dialects of the same language. But as the descendant languages undergo normal linguistic change and thus become increasingly differentiated from the classical language, the relationship may turn into one between different languages. In addition, along the way, borrowings may be made not from the prestige language in its classical form, but from a vernacularized variant.

The frequent outcome of this situation is the appearance of doublets as in (35), where the forms on the left side are inherited from the ancestral language, while the ones on the right are nativized borrowings.

(35a) Hindi
    dāhin(ā) 'right (hand)'   dakšin 'right hand, south'
    kām 'work'   karm(a) 'deed, action'
  b) Spanish
    leche 'milk'   láctico 'lactic, milk-'
    reja 'grate, grid, grill'   regla 'rule'

The consequences of this continued stream of borrowings from the prestigious ancestral language to its vernacular descendants may, however, be much more far-reaching. Thus as the result of extended and continued borrowing, Latin words containing the sequence *-omVn-* may have at least four different outcomes in Spanish; cf. (36). One of these shows the same development as Lat. *-omn-*, suggesting that *-mVn-* underwent syncope early enough to produce a sequence that could be treated like original *-mn-;* cf. (36a). In a second development, the *-mn-* resulting from syncope has undergone cluster simplification to *-m-;* cf. (36b). This type shares with (36a) the fact that *o* is diphthongized to *ue*. A third type, which apparently entered Spanish after the period of diphthongization, is represented in (36c). Here, *-mVn-* likewise has undergone syncope, but the resulting *-mn-* changes into *-mbr-*. Finally, examples like (36d) represent the sequence *omVn-* in unchanged form.

(36) Latin   Spanish
  a) dominum   dueño   'lord'
    cf. somnum sueño   'sleep'
  b) hominem   ueme   'man' (OSpan.)
  c) hominem   hombre   'man' (NSpan.)
  d) nomināre   nominar 'name, nominate'

The following scenario provides a probable account for this situation: Of the four types, that of *dueño* is most likely to be inherited, since it behaves exactly like inherited *somnum* > *sueño*. The type (36b), on the other hand, probably is the result of borrowing from a spoken Latin which under the influence of the coexisting vernacular had syncope, but which unlike the vernacular left the resulting cluster unchanged. Since the vernacular no longer had the sequence *-mn-* in native words, it nativized *-mn-* to *-m-*. While this borrowing took place early enough to undergo diphthongization, a later reborrowing from (syncopated) spoken Latin arrived too late for that process; cf. (36c). Moreover, in this case a different routine was chosen to nativize *-mn-*. It was changed to *-mr-,* a sequence permitted in the vernacular. And through epenthesis this *-mr-* eventually changed into *-mbr-.* Finally, at a much later stage when Latin had ceased to be commonly spoken, unsyncopated, full forms like (36d) were borrowed with a minimum of nativization.

While in the present case we have enough attested evidence for establishing the above scenario as a probable hypothesis, the question arises as to what we would or could do if for instance there were no attestations of the type *somnum* > *sueño* which provide independent evidence for the treatment of inherited *-mn-*-clusters. In that case it might be a little more difficult to determine which — if any — of the outcomes of *-omVn-* is inherited. True, as a general rule of thumb one might say that the more similar a given form is to what is found in the ancestral language, the more recent a borrowing it is. For inherited words or early loans exist in the borrowing language for a longer period and thus have more chances for undergoing linguistic changes which differentiate them from their sources. Unfortunately, however, in some cases, this rule of thumb may be difficult to apply. For instance, how does one decide whether, say, *(h)ombre* is more — or less — similar to *hominem* than, say, *dueño* is to *dominum?*

As a consequence of the difficulties just outlined, it may in some cases be next to impossible to state with certainty the regular sound changes by which particular segments or segment sequences of the ancestral language developed in the descendant languages. For instance, in the case of the Latin-Spanish correspondences in (37), there can be some difference of opinion as to which Spanish forms owe their existence to direct inheritance from the parent language and which — if any — are the result of borrowing. On the basis of semantics, one might expect the outcomes with *y* to be inherited, since words like *yunto* show greater divergence from Latin. In phonetic terms, however, it is the [y] of these forms which is much closer, in fact indentical, to the *i*-[y] of Latin; and forms like *junto* [xunto] show a more divergent development. We thus do not get consistent results by applying the rule of thumb that what is more similar to the ancestral language must be a borrowing.

(37)   Latin   Spanish

       iam 'still'   ya 'still'   beside jamás 'any more'
       iunctum 'joined'   yunto 'close'   beside junto 'joint, united'

14.5. Motivations for borrowing

In the preceding sections of this chapter we have taken a closer look at borrowing from several different angles: We have examined the subject matter of borrowing and have noted that basic vocabulary and inflectional endings are the least easily borrowed. At the same time, we have observed that even these very basic linguistic elements can be borrowed. What we have not explored is the question of which circumstances are conducive for borrowings of this type.

We have also looked at the different effects and implications of dialect vs. foreign vs. linguistic ancestor borrowing. It is especially in the area of foreign language borrowing that we have noted a very important ramification of borrowing, namely the fact that foreign words need to be nativized. In the various nativization processes one can recognize two recurrent routines. One of these consists in the unmodified **adoption** of foreign words and their morphology and/or phonology. In such cases, nativization results only slowly and almost grudgingly. The other approach, with different sub-routines, can be more properly called nativization, in that it attempts to integrate borrowed words, their morphology, and their phonology into the structure of the borrowing language. We can refer to this approach as **adaptation.** Here again we have not examined the question of which circumstances favor adaptation over adoption or vice versa.

It is by looking at the motivations for borrowing that we can begin to answer these questions.

14.5.1. Need

The motivation for borrowing which perhaps most readily comes to mind is **need**: If the speakers of a given language take over new technical, religious, etc., concepts, or references to foreign locations, fauna, flora, etc., there obviously is a need for vocabulary to 'house' these concepts or references. Compare for instance the English terms in (38).

(38) umlaut   (from German)
      karma   (from Sanskrit)
      gnu   (from Bushman)
      potato   (from Taino)

However, this motivation will hardly be sufficient to account for the difference between adoption and adaptation. And it certainly cannot explain the borrowing of basic vocabulary. (For every natural language is fully equipped with basic vocabulary.) Nor would the notion 'need' account for borrowings like Germ. *Trend* (from Engl. *trend*) or the loan shift of Germ. *realisieren* (itself an ealier borrowing from French) so as to include the meaning 'to recognize, understand, etc.' beside its more original German meaning 'to make real, transform into reality'; cf. (39). For German has perfectly adequate native words with these meanings: *Zug, Hand, Anlage, Tendenz,* etc. for the first word, *einsehen, erkennen, verstehen,* etc. for the second.

(39) English   German

       realize 'make real, etc.'   :   realisieren 'make real, etc.'
              'recognize, etc.'   :   **X**

14.5.2. Prestige

If we look at the context in which these words entered the German language, we can see that the motivation for their getting borrowed was not need, but **prestige**: These new terms or meanings were first used in post-1945 Western German sociology and related social sciences, where they were used in quite conscious imitation of the corresponding English terms. The initial purpose transparently was to indicate to the world — or at least to one's colleagues — one's familiarity with the most up-to-date and prestigious literature in the field; and that literature happened to be written in English. (Even now, the term *Trend* and especially the use of *realisieren* in the meaning 'recognize, etc.' tend to be limited to the somewhat trendy professional jargon of sociologists, pollsters, and journalists.)

As it turns out, prestige seems to be the most important factor deciding what type of vocabulary will be borrowed. This can be illustrated by looking at the prestige relationships of English with three different (groups of) languages with which it has come in contact during the course of its history, and by examining the different borrowing patterns associated with these contacts.

The first such contact to be examined is the one with the Old Norse of the so-called Danes who harried the English before the arrival of the French-speaking Normans and, still in pre-Norman times, eventually

410 *14. Lexical borrowing*

settled in the so-called Danelaw, intermarrying and otherwise acting as equals with the indigenous English population. From this relationship between equals resulted borrowings like *egg, get, give, guest, hit, husband, like, raise, skill, skin, skirt, sky, take,* as well as the pronouns *they, their, them.* Clearly these borrowings affected everyday, even basic vocabulary. Moreover, there are no special connotations (either positive or negative) attached to these loans. One might be tempted to attribute this situation to the fact that at the time of borrowing, Norse and English were mutually quite intelligible and in effect nearly dialects of the same language. However, examples like Standard German *Karre* 'run-down car (as lower-class people might use it)', borrowed from non-standard, uneducated German *Karre* 'car', show that inequality in prestige leads to very different results, in dialect borrowing just as much as in foreign borrowing (for which see below).

The next important contact of English was with the French of the Norman conquerors who arrived as superiors or overlords over the native English (and Anglo-Scandinavian) population. This contact resulted in a much larger amount of borrowings. Moreover, to the extent that special connotations are attached to the loans, they almost invariably reflect the higher prestige enjoyed by the speakers of French: As observed in 14.1, ex. (8/9) above, the borrowings from French tend to cluster in the prestigious areas of the king's court, warfare, administration, etc.

The last contact to be examined is between English and the native American Indian languages of North America, a contact in which — at least from the perspective of the conquering Europeans — there was an unequal relationship, such that English enjoyed a very high, the American Indian languages a very low prestige. This difference, again, is reflected in the types of borrowings that were made from the American Indian languages. The most general sphere of borrowings is that of place names. Thus of the forty-eight contiguous states of the United States, more than half bear names derived from American Indian languages. Compare, for instance, *Illinois, Michigan, Wisconsin.* Even here, however, there is a strong tendency to use European-derived names, such as *New York, Washington, Virginia.* Outside of place names, borrowings most commonly are names for fauna and flora, such as *woodchuck* from Algonqu. *otček.* However, the tendency to adapt European words to the new surroundings is even greater. Compare for instance the word *robin* which in America refers to a bird quite different in size and genetic affiliation from the European bird of the same name.

Finally, other borrowings are even more limited and tend to refer exclusively to American Indian life (cf. *mocassin, teepee, wampum*), very often with derogatory connotations, as in *pow-wow* or *squaw*.

The three contact situations just outlined and the nature of the borrowings associated with them are fairly typical of linguistic contact in general. The different types of relative social status of the 'participants' in such contact situations can be characterized by the terms **adstratum, superstratum**, and **substratum**. Languages of roughly equal prestige, such as English and Norse in early England, are referred to as adstrata. On the other hand, where prestige is unequal, as between the Normans and Anglo-Saxons or between the English-speaking Europeans and the American Indians, the terms superstratum and substratum are used, the former referring to the language with higher prestige, the latter to the one with lower prestige. (In certain approaches to historical linguistics, the term substratum is employed with a rather different meaning. This will be dealt with in 16.1 below.)

Adstratal relationships, then, are most conducive for borrowings of everyday-life vocabulary, even of basic vocabulary. In contacts between languages with unequal prestige, on the other hand, there are greater limitations. Moreover, in such contacts, the borrowings that are made tend to reflect the sociolinguistic status of the donor language: If that language is a superstratum, loans tend to come from the more prestigious sections of the lexicon and their connotations likewise tend to be prestigious. If the donor language is a substratum, loans tend to be more limited to 'need' borrowings (such as new place names) and/or to have derogatory connotations. Note however that the relative prestige of a given language does not affect the question of whether it will replace the other language or be replaced by it: In the above case histories, English successfully ousted an adstratal language, a superstratum, and a substratum. Rather, the question of which of two languages will eventually become victorious seems to be a matter of such factors as numbers, cunning, and ruthlessness. In terms of the eventual outcome, we can therefore dinstinguish between **'weak'**, **'strong'**, and (roughly) **'equal'** ad-, super-, and substrata. This distinction will be of some interest in Chapter 16.

14.5.3. Adoption vs. adaptation — prestige vs. linguistic nationalism

As we have just seen, it is the sociolinguistic notion 'prestige' which determines the sphere of vocabulary most likely to be affected by borrowing. Also the question of what determines the choice between adoption and adaptation seems to find a satisfactory answer only when sociolinguistic factors are considered.

True, one might at first suspect that it is entirely linguistic factors which determine the choice between adoption and adaptation: Adoption would be preferred where the structures of donor and borrowing language are sufficiently similar to permit this process to apply. Elsewhere, adaptation would be preferred. In this regard one might point to the difference between Chinese and English: Chinese heavily favors adaptation, preferring for instance [tyɛn xwa], lit. 'lightning speech', to [tə lü fəŋ] as the rendition of Engl. *telephone*. Similarly, *microscope* is nativized as [šyɛn wey čiŋ], lit. 'display-minute lens'. English on the other hand quite readily adopts foreign words, except for the fact that it usually nativizes their pronunciation; cf. e.g. *macho, rouge, umlaut*. This difference might be attributed to the fact that the structure of Chinese is radically different from that of the European languages, with essentially monosyllabic words (although compounding is possible), with severe restrictions on clusters and on final consonants, and in addition with a rich system of tonal contrast (not marked in the above examples). And as a consequence of its strucutre, the phonetic complexes which would serve to render longer European words such as *telephone* are not just arbitary, purely phonetic syllables, but meaningful lexical items whose native meaning is often difficult to reconcile with the meaning of the foreign word. (For instance, [tə lü fəŋ] literally means 'power-law-wind', which only very vaguely fits the meaning of *telephone*.)

However, it is difficult to determine what makes for 'radical' linguistic differences. For instance, is Japanese with its open-syllable structure and consequently severe restrictions on consonant clustering, as well as with an accentual system quite different from those of the major European languages, significantly less different from English than Chinese? Note that Japanese nowadays quite freely engages in adoption. Or is Modern Icelandic, with a still relatively fully developed system of inflectional morphology, radically different from English which preserves only remnants of such a system, and more different from English than is Japanese? Note that like Chinese, Modern Icelandic resorts to adoption mainly in the case of foreign place names and in terms referring to foreign fauna and flora, such as *Arabi* 'Arab', *Evrópa* 'Europe', *melóna* 'melon'. Elsewhere, adoptions such as *jeppi* 'jeep' are exceedingly rare, the preferred method of borrowing being adaptation, as in the examples in (40).

(40) ljóshvolf   'photosphere'   lit.: 'light concavity'
      samríkismaður '(US) Republican' 'together-state-man'
      síma   'telegram, tele-
                       phone, etc.'   'wire'
      talsíma   'telephone'   'speech wire'
      ritsíma   'telegram'   'write wire'

What is especially interesting is that both in Chinese and in Icelandic, there is evidence that this avoidance of adoption has not always been dominant. At the time when the Chinese adopted Buddhism, mainly through the vehicle of Sanskrit, the considerable structural differences between Sanskrit and Chinese (which if anything, far exceeded those between English and Chinese) presented no obstacle to the adoption of innumerable Sanskrit words. Modern descendants of these loan words include the ones listed in (41). (Note that the nuts of the pipal tree seem to have been used as rosary beads. [phin pho] 'apple' was later replaced by [phin kwo], with [kwo] 'fruit' apparently introduced by folk etymology.)

(41) Chinese   Sanskrit

      [po li] 'glass'   sphaṭika 'crystal, glass'
      [phu thi tsi] 'grape,
      rosary bead'   bodhi 'pipal tree (ficus religiosa)'
      [phin pho] 'apple'   bimba 'disk, orb; a particular fruit'

Similarly, in the pre-Modern Icelandic of the sixteenth through early nineteenth centuries, we find innumerable adoptions of foreign words. These come largely from Danish, but also from Swedish and Norwegian, and — through these Scandinavian languages — from (Low) German. What gave special impetus to these borrowings was that in 1550 Iceland carried through the Reformation and that subsequently the influence of German and Danish religious treatises became very strong. Borrowings include the examples in (42).

(42) borger 'citizen, burgher'   (ultimately from Low German)
      borgmeistari 'mayor'   (ultimately from Low German)
      dedicera 'to dedicate'   (ultimately from Latin)
      disputatia 'dispute'   (ultimately from Latin)

However, with only a few exceptions, these words are no longer found in Modern Icelandic. More than that, at the time that these borrowings were used, they occurred more frequently in personal, informal writings than in more formal texts. (In the former, the ratio between foreign and native words can be as high as $1:10$; in the latter it ranges from $1:30$ to $1:90$.) Still more interesting, even in informal writings, laden with foreign words, the very writers of these texts inveighed against the use of foreign words, since their excessive use was feared to alienate Icelanders from their own traditional and highly revered literature. It is no doubt because of this attitude that the Icelanders of that time used adopted foreign words much more sparingly in their formal writings, where they were 'on their best linguistic behavior'. And the same attitude seems to be responsible for the eventual elimination of most of these words and for their replacement by adaptations, as well as for the modern preference for adaptations, rather than adoptions. Notice that this attitude seems to be very much alive even today, manifesting itself in a rather negative attitude toward the speech of the capital Reykjavik, which is generally considered to be excessively laden with foreignisms.

Very similar attitudes of **linguistic nationalism** can be found in many other languages, although the majority show its effects only in a very inconsistent, intermittent, even erratic fashion.

Consider for instance the case of German. During the Thirty Years' War, most of Germany's cities, towns, and villages had been destroyed, half of its population had been killed, and the sword and the gun, increasingly wielded by foreign troops, ruled supreme. In this context, an enormous amount of vocabulary reflecting the prestige of the foreign powers, especially of the French, had entered the German language. Compare the examples in (43), which were culled from a seventeenth-century German novel.

(43) par dieu 'by god'   (from French)
      Schergeant 'sergeant'   (from French)
      fouragiren 'plunder and rape'   (from French)
      Alamode-Cavalir 'fashionable gentleman'   (from French)
      Salvaguardi 'safeguard'   (from Italian)
      Grandezza 'high style'   (from Italian)

After the war, which ended in 1648, a great number of locally organized clubs emerged which were dedicated to restoring the 'purity' of the German language and in so doing, the self-esteem of the German people, by eliminating all foreign words which had come into the language, no matter what their origin or social connotations. It is as a consequence of their activities that the foreign words on the left side of (44) came to coexist with the German adaptations on the right. However, in spite of the extraordinary circumstances that motivated their organization and activities, these clubs were far from successful in purging the German language of foreign elements. In some cases the proposed nativizations caught on, such as in the case of *liberté de conscience* which was replaced by *Gewissensfreiheit*. Other terms, especially many of the type (43), simply died out as the prestige of foreign nations and their troops came to an end. But in many other cases, the German adaptations merely came to coexist with the adopted foreign words. Thus *Briefwechsel* still coexists with *Korrespondenz* and *Mundart* with *Dialekt*.

(44)   Correspondance   Briefwechsel
       Dialect   Mundart
       Liberté de conscience   Gewissensfreiheit

Nor did the continued efforts of similar clubs and occasional official encouragement or sanction (especially under the Nazis) prevent the influx of new adoptions of foreign words, such as *Salon* 'living room', *Ballon* 'balloon', *Auto* '(motor) car', *Radio* 'radio', *Telephon* 'telephone', *Television* 'television', or even expressions like *petit gens* (lit. 'little people') used to express disapproval of petit bourgeois behavior. (In fact, despite their linguistic-nationalistic tendencies, the Nazis referred to themselves by the adopted foreignism *Nationalsozialist*.) True, some of these adopted expressions, such as *petit gens,* either never caught on widely or were subsequently eliminated. In many other cases, however, also these later foreign expressions continued to be used, often coexisting with their nativized counterparts.

The erratic effect of linguistic nationalism manifests itself also in the manner in which the resulting doublets have been semantically differentiated. As the examples in (45) show, in some cases it may be the adopted borrowing, in others, the adapted word that is the more 'natural' or popular. The other word, then, often is used mainly in 'officialese'. (Thus, people might enter a phone booth which is marked *Öffentlicher Fernsprecher,* but in that booth they use the *Telephon*.) And there is at least one example *(Auto : Wagen)* in which both words are commonly used, with different speakers preferring one or the other term.

(45)	Adoption	Adaptation
	Dialekt (general and technical use)	Mundart (technical use and officialese)
	Salon 'living room' (lower-class)	Wohnzimmer (educated and officialese)
	Auto (general use)	Wagen (general use)
		Kraftwagen (officialese)
	Radio (general use)	Rundfunk (officialese)
	Telephon (general use)	Fernsprecher (officialese)
	Television (TV industry jargon)	Fernsehen 'TV institution' (general and officialese)
		Fernseher 'TV set' (general)
		Fernsehgerät 'TV set' (officialese)
	Kopie 'xerographic copy' (large-city, university)	Ablichtung (small-town, officialese)

(Note: Beside lower-class *Salon* [zalɔŋ] 'living room', there is also an educated *Salon* '(French) salon' with non-nativized or partly nativized pronunciation: [salɔ̃] or [zalɔ̃].)

Examples like these show a common tendency for adaptations to be favored in 'officialese'. In some cases, such as *Wohnzimmer,* also the educated prefer adaptations, presumably because they are more in contact with the formal language of the schools and the style used in official promulgations. This situation suggests a reason for the mixed success of linguistic nationalism in Germany: Linguistic nationalism has been embraced mainly by (a subset of) the elite, traditionally defined as the educated and those in political power. On the other hand, the general populace, as well as many sections of the elite, are less concerned with linguistic nationalism and more with the prestige of foreign, often international, culture and vocabulary. Note in this regard that the adopted foreignisms which have been eliminated most successfully are those which temporarily appealed to certain sections of the elite, but which did not catch on among the general populace, such as *liberté de conscience* or *petit gens.* Essentially the same explanation seems to hold true for the fact that adaptations have caught on with enormous success in technical vocabulary, the domain of the elite; cf. the examples in

(46). Note, however, that these attitudinal and linguistic differences between the elite and the general populace are merely tendencies. Even the educated generally use the adoptions *Radio* and *Telephon,* and adaptations like *Kettenraucher* 'chain smoker' and *Wolkenkratzer* 'sky scraper' are not limited to the elite.

(46)   Sauerstoff (lit. 'sour matter')   'oxygen'
Schwerkraft (lit. 'heavy power/force')   'gravity'
Bauchspeicheldrüse (lit. 'belly-spit gland')   'pancreas'

The situation is quite similar in the other languages of Europe (outside of Iceland). Thus the continued efforts of the prestigious and centralized Académie Française, aided by the political and educational establishment, have met with only limited success in eliminating foreignisms like *redingote* 'riding coat' or *club* (borrowed from 19th-century British English), or the more recent 'Franglais' of mainly American English manufacture exhibited in expressions like *le hot dog, le hamburger.* On the other hand, even English, which seems to almost glory in the adoption of foreign words (except for their pronunciation) and which often prides itself in the resulting large size of its lexicon, clearly has had its 'bouts' of linguistic nationalism, accounting for expressions like *chamber maid* (Fr. *femme de chambre*), *world view* beside rarer *weltanschauung* (cf. above), or *almighty* beside *omnipotent* (Lat. *omnipotens*).

Also outside Europe, the effects of linguistic nationalism commonly are mixed. Thus in Hindi, the attempts to impose 'nativized' terms such as the ones in (47a) have generally been successful only in officialese or in Hindi-nationalist circles. Other adaptations may have wider currency, but tend to have traditionalist connotations; cf. e.g. (47b). On the other hand, the item in (47c) seems to enjoy quite general acceptance, even in the villages, while the corresponding adopted form is limited mainly to the urbanized, westernized elite. What complicates matters is that Hindi 'nativizations' in general are based on Sanskrit, not Hindi material. As a consequence, they may exhibit phonolocial properties quite alien to colloquial Hindi, such as the cluster *-ṁsk-* in *saṁskaraṇ* or the sandhi of *grāmōdyōg = grāma* 'village' + *udyōg* 'industry'. In addition, in many cases there exist alternative 'native' terms of Perso-Arabic origin but now felt to be native, especially by Muslims, such as *daftar* 'office'. And these likewise compete for recognition. Finally, there is an internal sociolinguistic conflict between three groups: (i) Western-oriented speakers. These tend to prefer adoptions from English. (ii) Traditionalists and Hindu-/Hindi-nationalists who advocate the elimination of all foreign traditions and languages and the use of Hindi as India's national language. These insist on 'indigenous', Sanskrit-derived adaptations. (iii) Muslims, but also non-Muslims with a strong attachment to Urdu language and literature. These prefer Perso-Arabic words but show at least some tolerance also toward adoptions from English. (Note that India is not the only area in which borrowings are 'nativized' by means of adaptations based on a language that is not in widely spoken use within the country. For instance, during its highly nationalist phase, Japanese frequently 'nativized' foreign terms by means of vocabulary that had earlier been borrowed from Chinese, as in *den wā* 'telephone'. Presumably, Chinese was felt to be more 'oriental' and thus more 'indigenous' than western languages like English.)

(47)	Adaptation		Adoption	
a)	dūrbhāš	('far speech')	phōn/fōn	'(tele)phone'
	kāryālay	('work abode')	āfis	'office'
b)	sammēlan	('gathering')	mīṭiŋ	'meeting'
	saṁskaraṇ	('putting together')	ēḍišan	'edition'
c)	dūrdaršan	('far view')	ṭēlīvizan	'television'

Even in Israeli Hebrew we find a similar mixed success of linguistic nationalism. This is so in spite of the fact that from the very beginnings of the Hebrew revival in the early part of this century, there was a very conscious, linguistic-nationalist attempt to revive the language in a truly Semitic guise, with total elimination of the various European influences which had over the centuries crept into the oral recitation of Hebrew. It was expected that this total elimination of European influence would free Hebrew and it speakers from the yoke of 1700 years of diaspora and its attendant pattern of second-class citizenship and recurrent persecution. Not even the killing of six million Jews in the Nazi holocaust preceding and precipitating the foundation of the state of Israel, or the continuous state of siege since then, have been able to block the entrance of adopted words like *visa, student,* or *gymnasia* (a type of secondary school). In fact, although the basic idea of reviving the ancient Hebrew language, long extinct in its spoken use, as an every-day, full-fledged spoken language was implemented with remarkable and unparalleled success, the companion idea of reviving a truly Semitic Hebrew, without any traces of western influence has been remarkably unsuccessful even in the area of phonology: Owing to the influence of the European languages spoken by the immigrants, ancient Hebrew segments such as the uvular stop [q] were replaced by sounds such as velar [k] that were native to Europe. Even the arrival of the Sephardic or 'oriental' Jews who had preserved these segments in their traditions of biblical recitation did not prevent this development. Rather, in order to be socially accepted, Sephardic Jews have to adopt the European, non-Semitic pronunciation of the Ashkenazim.

The unqualified success of linguistic nationalism in Modern Icelandic and in post-Buddhist-Sanskrit China, then, is perhaps quite unusual and must be attributed to very special circumstances. In both cases, the immediate reason for this success seems to have been that linguistic nationalism is shared by (virtually) all layers of society.

In the case of Chinese, the underlying cause would seem to be the highly traditional, ethnocentric attitude of the Chinese who consider all outsiders, western or non-western, technologically superior or inferior, as barbarians — in the ancient sense of the word: The Greek word *barbaroi*, the Latin *barbarī*, or the Sanskrit *barbarāḥ* or *mlečchāḥ* refer to people who don't really speak a human language (which a civilized person might understand). All that these foreigners are able to utter is an unintelligible *barbarbar* or worse.

In Icelandic, the underlying reason seems to have been a universal literacy coupled with a genuine fondness and reverence among all the layers of society for their ancient literature which had remained remarkably intelligible to the speakers of Modern Icelandic. (Although a vowel change entirely comparable in the breadth of its application to the Great English Vowel Shift had radically changed the phonology of the language, its nature was such that it did not require a radical change in spelling.) And the elimination of foreign words only increased the archaic nature of the modern language and its closeness to the original texts.

In other societies, the general populace seems to have a more ambivalent attitude toward linguistic nationalism. However, even if its effects may be mixed, there can be no doubt that in most societies, linguistic nationalism provides an important counterbalance to the prestige of foreign culture and vocabulary.

The distinction between linguistic nationalism and foreign prestige is most relevant in the area of the lexicon, accounting for the difference between adaptation and adoption. And it is from this area that the examples in this section were drawn. On the other hand, in the area of phonetics/phonology, adaptation is the rule. Adoptions (such as later

OIr. *p,* Hindi *f,* or educated German [ʒ] as in *Salon* [s/zalɔ̃]) seem to require quite unusual circumstances, where the impact of a foreign language and its prestige is of extraordinary magnitude and thus manages to override the normal tendency toward nativization.

Whatever the details, however, it is clear that the two sociolinguistic notions 'prestige' and 'linguistic nationalism' are the most important factors which determine the manner in which foreign linguistic elements are borrowed.

14.5.4. Argots, taboo

Sociolinguistic considerations are responsible also for more unusual borrowing processes which can be encountered in the case of **argots** on one hand and languages with extensive **taboo** on the other.

In the case of argots or 'secret languages' it is the need for retaining secrecy, i. e. unintelligibility to outsiders, which requires constant renewal of key vocabulary, lest outsiders begin to understand what is being said. And borrowing is one of several possible means toward accomplishing that goal. (Another approach lies in the quite deliberate use of metaphorical extension of the meanings of ordinary-language words, as in Engl. *the heat* 'the police', *grass* 'marijuana', *snow* 'cocaine'. As these examples show, such argot words often are quickly understood by the population at large, necessitating the invention or importation of new key words.) In the underworld languages of Europe, Romani (or Gipsy) was a common source for borrowing; cf. e. g. the German examples in (48). Also Yiddish played an important role in the underworld argots of Central and Eastern Europe; cf. the German words in (49). (The word *Schickse* is especially interesting: In Hebrew and Yiddish, *šiksa* is the feminine counterpart of *šegets* 'gentile, goy'. But through the argot, the word has entered German with a meaning that permits it to be used as an insult also toward Jewish women.)

(48)	Kaschemme	'bar frequented by gangsters'
	Zaster	'money'

(49)	kapores	'broken, apart'
	besäbeln	'cheat'
	Zores	'rabble, riff-raff'
	Schickse	'loose woman'

Argots are not necessarily limited to criminal activities. For instance, it has been argued that the Black Vernacular English words on the left side of (50) are relics of an argot of early slavery, used to keep 'the man' from understanding important communications between the slaves. It has further been argued that these words can be traced to West African Wolof sources; cf. the forms on the right side of (50). (For the semantic development of *honkey* compare the fact that *redneck* is a common derogatory term for (lower-class) whites in the South of the United States, presumably because they turn red in the sun.)

(50) dig 'understand'   dega 'understand'
      (hep/hip) cat '(smart) man'   hep kat 'man in the know'
      honkey 'white (derogatory)'   hong/honk 'red'

Linguistic taboo, if it is massive enough, likewise requires constant lexical renewal. And here again, renewal can easily be accomplished through lexical borrowing, compare section 12.3 above.

14.6. The effects of borrowing

Since the arrival of the French-speaking Normans in 1066, English has had a strong tendency to adopt foreign vocabulary, with adaptation generally restricted to phonology. In fact, as noted earlier, English seems to almost pride itself in the resulting 'enrichment' of its vocabulary. The extent to which borrowing has 'enriched' English can be gauged by the fact that between sixty-five and seventy-five percent of its present-day vocabulary is of foreign origin. Much of that vocabulary comes from Romance, especially French; cf. (51 a). Or it comes from Graeco-Latin sources, but in a shape which clearly is Romance, usually French in character; cf. (51 b). Moreover, there are borrowings like those in (51 c) which come from other Romance sources.

(51 a) place, receive, rouge, veal
    b) hydrogen (Fr. hydrogène; cf. Gk. hudro- 'water' + genēs 'engendering')
        carbon (Lat. carbō, -ōnis, Fr. carbone)
    c) plaza (from Spanish)
        piazza (from Italian)

The effect of these borrowings is especially striking in technical prose, where English and French (and other Romance languages) show a great degree of terminological similarity, whereas German with its adapted *Wasserstoff* 'hydrogen', *Kohlenstoff* 'carbon' etc. appears to be quite different and "Teutonic". As a consequence, one can frequently hear the claim that English now really is a Romance, not a Germanic, language. Further arguments for this claim might be based on the fact that English much more freely than German uses recognizable Romance morphology, even in combination with native vocabulary; cf. e. g. example (4) above. (In German, the suffix *-ieren* is the only recently borrowed morpheme showing any comparable combinability. But even this is limited to just a few lexical items, such as *buchstabieren* 'to spell' from native *Buchstabe* 'letter'. Some borrowed suffixes, to be sure, such as the *-er* of words like *Bäcker* 'baker' or the *-ei* of *Bäckerei*, combine quite freely with native elements. But these are no longer easily recognized as being of foreign origin.)

The claim that English is a Romance language, however, must be considered quite dubious for several reasons: First, the English borrowings from "Romance" are not all from the same language. For instance, the *place* of (51a) and the *plaza* and *piazza* of (51c) all go back to Latin *platēa* 'street' (ultimately a borrowing from Greek); but *place* shows developments peculiar to French, *plaza* to Spanish, and *piazza* to Italian. That is, the "Romance" of English is an amalgam from different Romance languages, not an identifiable sub-group of Romance. Moreover, while the majority of "Romance" borrowings are French in character, they have entered English at various different times, with consequently quite different phonological (etc.) developments in English. Compare for instance Engl. *petty* vs. *petite*, both borrowings from Fr. *petit* (m.), *petite* (f.) 'small', but adopted at different times and consequently with different accentual patterns etc. Consider also correspondences like Engl. *chant* with [č-] vs. Fr. *chant* with [š-]. Here English preserves an Old French pronunciation which in Modern French has fallen victim to cluster simplification. That is, English cannot be identified with any single chronological layer of Romance. Finally and perhaps most importantly, the basic vocabulary and the basic inflectional morphology of English have remained Germanic. Contrast the English words on the left side of (52) with their French equivalents (center column) on one hand and their German cognates (right column) on the other. Note also the differences in verb morphology, as in the formation of irregular verbs of the type (53). Clearly, then, in this most basic, most indispensible, and most frequently used, part of the language, English very much looks like a "Teutonic", not like a "Romance" language.

(52)
I	je	ich
you	tu/vous	du/ihr/Sie
he	il	er
she	elle	sie
it	il	es
do	faire	tun
be	être	sein
eat	manger	essen
drink	boire	trinken
earth	terre	Erde
sky	ciel	Himmel
and	et	und
to	à	zu
of	de	von

(53) English drink (pres.), drank (past), drunk (past pple.)
      German   trinken (pres.), trank (past), getrunken (past pple.)
      vs. French boire (pres.), buvais (imperf.), bus (passé défini), boirai (fut.), bu (past pple.)

The case is quite similar for Swedish (with some sixty-five to seventy-five percent of its vocabulary of foreign, mainly Low German origin) and even for Albanian, with about ninety percent of its lexicon of foreign provenience, coming from Greek, Latin, Slavic, and many other sources. In both cases the basic structure and vocabulary are distinctly native. And as in English, the overall structure of the language, including its lexicon, cannot be identified with any of the source languages for the borrowings, or with any particular chronological stage of these languages.

It appears, then, that lexical borrowing, even on a massive scale, is highly unlikely to lead to a change in the genetic affiliation of a given language. (Cf. also 16.1.3 below.)

On the other hand, as already noted, the adoption of borrowings may be conceived of as 'enriching' the lexicon of a given language, as for instance in the case of English. However, even here it is necessary to proceed with caution. For to the extent that languages make adaptations through calquing (as in Germ. *Wasserstoff* lit. 'water matter' ≈ Fr. *hydrogène* 'water engendering/matter') they expand their vocabulary no less than languages which adopt (such as Engl. *hydrogen*). It is only in the case of loan shifts, such as early English *hell* ≈ Lat. *infernum*, that there is an inherent difference between adoption and adaptation. For the latter does not add any new vocabulary to the language. Moreover, in many cases it leads to a considerable increase in polysemy, to a proliferation of meanings for a given word. Under these circumstances, adoption can be justifiably argued to 'enrich' the language, by making it possible to clearly convey a greater range of meanings. Cf., e. g., example (54) for the considerable polysemy of native German *Zug* vs. the unambiguous meaning of *Trend*.

> (54)   Zug 'trend, tendency'   Trend 'trend, tendency'
>   beside 'pull; draft (of air);
>   train; etc.'

Even in other respects, adoption may 'enrich' a language (in the sense in which the term 'enrich' has just been used). For one thing, not all borrowings are need borrowings which introduce completely new concepts into the language. Many are prestige borrowings that introduce novel linguistic forms for already existing linguistic concepts and their corresponding native forms. Thus when English borrowed from French the adjective *royal*, it already had its own indigenous adjectival formation corresponding to *king*; cf. NE *kingly*. The introduction of the new term *royal* then led to a situation similar to what we find in analogical change, namely the competition between an inherited and an innovated form. And just as in the case of analogy, one possible resolution of the conflict between the two forms lies in linguistic specialization. Thus in the case of *royal/kingly*, the former word became the common, 'productive' adjective corresponding to *king*, while *kingly* survived in more marginal function. Note, however, that unlike what we find in analogical change, the 'innovated', borrowed form may just as easily take on marginal functions, as in *donate* vs. *give*, *observe* vs. *see*. Still, in both cases, the retention-cum-specialization of borrowed and native vocabulary 'enriches' the language in our more technical sense.

A less obvious 'enriching' effect of adopted borrowings is that in many cases they bring with themselves their own, novel morphological inventory and rules for morpheme combination. This is of obvious benefit in the area of word **coinage**, the creation of new linguistic terms to express novel concepts developed within one's own linguistic community. Not only does the borrowed morphology provide an enlargement of the morphological elements and rules which can form the basis for such word coinage; it also often provides a clear signal that the resulting 'neologism' is a technical term, not an everyday word. Consider for instance the case of *automobile*. The word was created from the elements *auto-* 'self' and *mobile* 'moving' which had been extracted from borrowings from Greek and Latin, respectively. The novel combination of these elements into *automobile*, then, signaled the technical nature of the resulting word much more clearly than would have Engl. *self-moving* or Fr. *mouvant par soi* etc.

In fact, perhaps the most important and overriding effect which large-scale adoptive borrowing has had on English is that it has created a quite clearly marked formal distinction between an educated/technological variety or 'register' and other, more everyday registers of the language. And this distinction is quite patent to native speakers, as can be seen from epithets like 'high-falutin' which tend to be given to the former register by speakers who are comfortable only with the everyday registers. Even here, however, it is necessary to add some qualifications: It is only the more clearly Graeco-Latin vocabulary that tends to furnish the basis for the educated/technological register of English, not other borrowings. Contrast the difference in connotations between expressions like *automotive, capability, antidisestablishmentarianism* on one hand and *target practice, royal pain, enterprise* on the other. Moreover, note that the special connotations of the Graeco-Latin loans can be explained in terms of the context in which they were borrowed: Whether they were adopted directly from Greek and Latin, or via French, these words were borrowed from languages which were scholarly prestige languages and in which many of these words had already been used with special scholarly or technical connotations. The connotations of Graeco-Latin borrowings therefore are exactly what one would expect. In addition, recall that in languages like German it is adaptations like *Fernsprecher, Rundfunk* which often have special register connotations. Facts like these suggest that in many cases it is more the 'sphere of usage' (in Kuryłowicz's sense) than the origin of a particular lexical item which determines its special register connotations.

15. Linguistic contact: Dialectology

In the preceding chapter we have examined the question of lexical borrowing in language and dialect contact situations. Linguistic contact, however, is not necessarily restricted to the borrowing of lexical items and the relatively minor structural implications of such lexical borrowings. It may have sometimes far-reaching effects also on general linguistic structure.

This is especially true for the contact between dialects of the same language, at least to the extent that they are in close geographical and/ or social proximity. For under these conditions, contact between the speakers of the dialects is likely to be pervasive and to permeate, on a day-to-day basis, all aspects of their lives. Moreover, the mutual intelligibility of dialects makes structural borrowing quite easy. For there is a great deal of structural agreement to begin with and it is therefore much more difficult than in the contact of distinct languages to maintain separate grammatical identities, as it were. As a consequence there is in most cases a constant exchange not only of lexical items, but also of general structure, i. e., of grammar, as well as of linguistic changes (including sound change) which affect the grammar.

15.1. Prestige and sociolinguistic polarization

Just as in the case of lexical borrowing, prestige differences can accelerate or retard structural borrowing. What complicates matters is that a particular dialect may at the same time be prestigious in relation to some of its neighboring dialects and non-prestigious in relation to others.

15.1.1. Prestige

An example which demonstrates this variable aspect of prestige — in addition to illustrating structural borrowing — is the following. The

most widely-spoken white working-class dialect of Chicago is characterized by the diphthongization of [æ] to [æə] or [ɛə] and the fronting
of old [a] toward [æ]; cf. example (1) as well as the discussion in 8.4,
ex. (26).

(1a)   have [hæv]   >   [hæəv], [hɛəv]
       Jan [ǰæn]   >   [ǰæən], [ǰɛən]
       taxi [tæksi]   >   [tæəksi], [tɛəksi]
       etc.
  b)   Chicago [šikago] >   [šikæ'gō]
       John [ǰan]   >   [ǰæ'n]
       etc.

Within the city of Chicago, this dialect is considered relatively low
in prestige and its changes therefore by and large are not accepted into
other dialects. Outside the city, in 'downstate' Illinois, however, the
change in (1a) has been reinterpreted as a relatively prestigious sign of
'urban-ness' or urbanization. Consequently it is now spreading within
this area, expecially among the younger, more urban-oriented people,
and in more urbanized localities. (For the reaction within Chicago, see
below.)

A more drastic development has been observed in French. Toward
the end of the eighteenth century, Parisian speech had acquired two
sub-dialects, one in which written *oi* was pronounced [wɛ], and one in
which it was rendered [wa]. The latter pronunciation had been common
in lower-class speech as early as the sixteenth century. By the end of
the seventeenth century it had been accepted also into the speech of
the bourgeoisie. However, the prestige dialect of the royal court continued to hold on to the older pronunciation [wɛ]. The revolution of 1789
and subsequent events led to a radical change in prestige relationships.
And when Louis XVIII returned to become king in 1815, he had to
be advised not to pronounce *C'est moi le roi* 'It is I, the king' with
the traditional prestigious [wɛ], but to use instead the new prestige
pronunciation [wa].

A further complication lies in the fact that prestige may lead not
only to the borrowing of features native to the more prestigious model
dialect, but also to hypercorrections which go beyond the patterns of
the model. It is this type of development which is responsible for the
regional U.S. pronunciation of *Missouri* as [mizūrə]: Missouri, as well
as most of the southern half of Illinois, Indiana, and Ohio, had been

settled by speakers coming mostly from the border dialect between Northern and Southern U.S. speech in which final [-ə] regularly had become [-i]. The proportion between dialectal [-i] and more 'standard', Northern [-ə] then led to the hypercorrection in (2).

(2) sody   :   soda
     opry   :   opera
     Missouri :   X

15.1.2. Sociolinguistic polarization

Just as in the case of lexical borrowing prestige finds a counterforce in linguistic nationalism, so in dialect contact, prestige may be countered by **sociolinguistic polarization**. And this force can act not only defensively, by retarding structural borrowing, but also offensively, by engendering developments diametrically opposed to what is found in other dialects or by bringing about something like hypercorrection in reverse.

For instance, the fact that the changes in (1) are highly stigmatized as working-class in Chicago has engendered the following response in much of Chicago speech: Not only does [æ] escape diphthongization and raising, general Midwestern [a] undergoes a backing and rounding development which is diametrically opposed to the working-class fronting. Thus, *Chicago* in these varieties of Chicago English winds up pronounced as something like [šikɔgō]; and as a consequence, the general Midwestern pronunciation [šikagō] is conspicuous by its absence in the very city which carries the name.

Consider also the case of Martha's Vineyard, off the Massachusetts coast: Here the [a] of the diphthongs [ay] and [aw] was centralized toward the position of [ə], apparently in order to reassert linguistically the separate identity of the islanders over against the mainlanders. (This polarization has had political counterparts, sometimes extending to the point where the islanders have threatened secession from the mainland, the Commonwealth of Massachusetts. For further details on the linguistic developments, see sections 15.2.1 and especially 20.10 below.)

Another case has been alluded to earlier, namely the sociolinguistic polarization between Sanskrit and the coexisting Middle Indo-Aryan vernaculars; cf. section 11.7. A closer examination of this relationship may illustrate the rather mixed results which this sociolinguistic attitude may have in perhaps the majority of cases.

There is evidence that Sanskrit and an early form of Middle Indo-Aryan coexisted even in the oldest attested stage of Indo-Aryan. This early evidence comes mainly in the shape of lexical borrowings of the type (3) below. Some of these loans even affected the basic vocabulary and grammatical structure of Sanskrit, such as the neuter interrogative pronoun *kim* whose ending -*m* reflects a general Middle Indo-Aryan replacement of the pronominal nominative/accusative singular neuter ending -*d* by the nominal ending -*m*; cf. e. g. (4). (Note that both Vedic Skt. *kad* and MIAr. *kim* are analogical replacements of an original form *čid* which survives only in marginal function, as a particle of emphasis. Moreover, the Middle Indo-Aryan loan *kim* begins to replace native *kad* even in the earliest Sanskrit texts.) What is interesting about these early borrowings is that they do not suggest any attempt on the side of Sanskrit to differentiate itself from the Middle Indo-Aryan vernaculars. On the contrary, borrowings like *kim* belong to the basic vocabulary of the language and affect its grammatical structure. The fact that such borrowings could be made suggests that the relationship between Sanskrit and Middle Indo-Aryan at this point was an adstratal one.

(3)	Proto- IAr.	Expected Skt.	Expected MIAr.	Attested Ved. Skt.	
	*mṛhus	mṛhuḥ*	muhu(r)	muhur	'suddenly'
	*čid	čid/kad	čim/kim	kim (kad)	'what'

(4 a)	Proto-IAr.		Skt.		MIAr.	
	*tad		tad		taṁ	'that'
	*yad		yad		yaṁ	'which (rel.)'
b)	sg. N m.		sg. A m.		sg. N/A n.	
	śobhanaḥ	:	śobhanam	:	śobhanam	'beautiful'
	yaḥ	:	yam	:	X = yam	
	etc.					

In the later language, however, a very different development is found. We now find instances of 'hyper-Sanskritizations' in which Middle Indo-Aryan forms are given a more 'Sanskritic' form than would be expected on purely phonetic grounds. Some examples may illustrate this phenomenon:

MIAr. *mārisa-* 'friend, worthy man', etymologically corresponding to Skt. *mādṛśa-* 'looking like me', was borrowed into Sanskrit in the form *māriṣa-*. Now, it is perhaps understandable that the etymologically correct form was not substituted, since it is phonetically rather different from the Middle Indo-Aryan word and since, moreover, the two forms differ considerably in their meaning. However, what is interesting is that Sanskrit did not accept the Middle Indo-Aryan word unchanged; for phonetically or phonologically, a form *mārisa-* would have been acceptable. Instead, Sanskrit chose to change *s* into a phonetically more clearly differentiated, hyper-Sanskritizing retroflex *ṣ*, a segment not found in most of the Middle Indo-Aryan dialects. True, there is precedent for aligning MIAr. *s* with Skt. *ṣ*; cf. e. g. Skt. *aśvēṣu* 'among horses': MIAr. *assēsu*. However, as *asi* 'thou art': *asi* shows, also *s* corresponds to MIAr. *s*.

A similar case is that of Skt. (*) *icchuka-* 'desiring' > MIAr. *ucchuka-* which was borrowed in the hyper-Sanskritized form *utsuka-*. Here again, a substitution different from the phonetically most similar one is made, even though *ucchuka-* is phonetically a perfectly acceptable Sanskrit form. Moreover, in this case there is no significant differentiation of meaning which would preclude the substitution of the etymologically correct form. The only explanation is that the substitution *ts* reflects an attempt at 'Sanskritization' by producing a form which could not possibly be Middle Indo-Aryan. (Skt. *ts* regularly changed into MIAr. *cch*, as in *vatsa-* 'calf' > *vaccha-*. And it is of course this correspondence which furnished the model for the hyper-Sanskritizing substitution of *ts* for *cch* in *utsuka-*.)

These lexical/phonological developments are mirrored by morphological polarizations. For instance, in the earliest Indo-Aryan texts, the instrumental plural of the *a*-stems had two competing endings, *-ais* and *-ēbhis*. While Middle Indo-Aryan generalized endings descended from *-ēbhis*, Sanskrit opted for *-ais* (except in the pronominal form *ēbhis* 'by these'). Similarly, it has been observed that out of the three past-tense formations of the early language, the 'aorist', 'imperfect', and 'perfect', Sanskrit tended to continue only the imperfect and the perfect as productive formations, while the Middle Indo-Aryan vernaculars maintained the aorist and imperfect, but lost the perfect except for a few early traces. Compare the summary in (5) below. Another instance of sociolinguistic polarization may perhaps consist in the fact that Sanskrit steadfastly maintains to the present day the number category of the dual (as in *karṇau* '(a set of two) ears' vs. pl. *karṇāḥ* '(several, many) ears'), whereas even the earliest attested Middle Indo-Aryan has lost the dual as a separate category, using the plural instead.

(5)   aorist   imperfect   perfect
        Vedic Sanskrit   √   √   √
        Classical Sanskrit   (moribund)   √   √
        Middle Indo-Aryan   √   √   – – –

At the same time, there is evidence also for continued convergent developments between Sanskrit and Middle Indo-Aryan. First of all, many borrowings from Middle Indo-Aryan into Sanskrit do not exhibit hyper-Sanskritization but are adopted with minimal alteration. Compare for instance MIAr. *mairēya-* with heterosyllabic [a$i] : Skt. *mairēya-* 'intoxicating liquor' with tautosyllabic [ai̯], since hiatus ordinarily is not tolerated word-internally. (MIAr. *mairēya-* is derived from *maira-* which resulted from Skt. *madira-* by regular sound change.) There are also a number of convergent developments in the areas of morphology and syntax. Perhaps the most noteworthy is the tendency of later Middle Indo-Aryan and Sanskrit to replace their remaining, sociolinguistically polarized past-tense formations by a non-finite construction based on the participle in *-ta-*; cf. the examples in (6) and (7). This development is especially interesting because of its far-reaching syntactic repercussions: As the examples in (6) and (7) illustrate, for transitive verbs, the new participial formation requires a passive-like syntactic construction. The underlying subject is demoted and appears in the instrumental case. And the underlying object is promoted to subject; witness its nominative case marking, as well as the fact that the verb agrees with it in case, number, and gender. At the same time, the 'meaning' or function of this new construction is not specifically passive. Rather, the contrast between active and passive here is neutralized. (It is this construction which is the major source for the so-called ergative of Modern Indo-Aryan.)

(6)   Sanskrit

a)   Imperfect   strī   kaṭān   akarōt
                     sg. N f.   pl. A m.   sg. 3
       'the woman made the mats'

(b)   *ta*-pple.   striyā   kaṭāḥ   kṛtāḥ
                     sg. I f.   pl. N m.   pl. N m.
       'the woman made the mats/the mats were made by the woman'

(7)   Pali:

a)   Aorist   itthī   kaṭē   akāsi
                   sg. N f.   pl. A m.   sg. 3
     'the woman made the mats'

b)   *ta*-pple.   itthiyā   kaṭā   kitā
                   sg. I f.   pl. N m.   pl. N m.
     'the woman made the mats/the mats were made by the woman'

Clearly, then, like linguistic nationalism, sociolinguistic polarization is an important force. But just like linguistic nationalism, it leads to mixed results in the majority of cases.

15.2. Patterns of dialect interaction

15.2.1. The Chicago vowel shift

In the preceding section, brief mention was made of the spread of the change [æ] › [æə] etc. from working-class Chicago English to downstate Illinois. This spread first of all is correlated with relative distance from Chicago: The change is taking hold more pervasively in the counties immediately surrounding Chicago than in those which are farther removed. At the same time, because it is associated with urbanization, it is implemented more thoroughly in urbanized than in rural areas. As a consequence, its effect may be stronger in urban locations that are quite far from Chicago than in intervening rural areas. In certain areas, then, the change is spreading in a **discontinuous** pattern.

The extent to which the shift is spreading is reflected not only in the number of speakers or in the frequency with which individual speakers affect the innovated pronunciation beside the older, indigenous one. It is reflected also in the degree to which the individual changes that make up the shift are accepted in a given community and by given speakers. There is reason to believe that in Chicago the shift was implemented through a sequence of the three changes listed in (8), with (a) being the earliest, (c) the latest development. Now, of these changes, the first one has spread to the largest area outside Chicago. The second tends to be restricted to the counties close to Chicago. And the third appears to have the smallest number of adherents outside of Chicago.

(8 a)   æ   >   æə
    b) æə   >   ɛə
    c) a   >   æ'

It appears, then, that in the spread of linguistic innovations, it is the early changes which tend to extend the farthest and most completely, while later changes cover more restricted territory.

Note however that this generalization needs to be qualified to some extend. For there seem to be cases like that of Martha's Vineyard where sociolinguistic polarization obscures the picture: Although the centralization of [a] originated in the diphthong [ay] and was secondarily extended to [aw], it is now most completely implemented in the latter environment. The reason seems to be that the centralization in [aw] has fewer precedents or parallels on the mainland and thus lends itself more readily to becoming an overt marker of sociolinguistic polarization. Fortunately, however, cases like this seem to be relatively rare, so that the above generalization will hold in the majority of cases.

15.2.2. Shift of *ū* in the Low Countries

A classic example of dialect interaction is found in the Low Countries (the Netherlands and Flemish-speaking Belgium). The example is interesting and valuable for several reasons: First, the patterns resulting from the spread of linguistic innovations are fairly complex. Secondly, the changes that gave rise to these patterns took place in observable history. It is therefore possible to correlate geographic patterns with historical processes. Thirdly, the correlations which can be observed in this and other similar situations can be used as a diagnostic tool in the interpretation of similar geographic patterns where the processes that gave rise to them are not known.

Map 1 below shows in somewhat simplified form the distribution of the reflexes of PGmc. *ū* in the early-twentieth century dialects of Dutch and Flemish. This distribution arose from the following historical developments:

At a relatively early, medieval period, old [ū] shifted to [ǖ], probably in Flemish which at that time enjoyed considerable prestige in the area.

From there it spread west, north, and east. On the eastern boundary, its spread was inhibited by the influence of another prestige area, that of the Low German Hanseatic cities which retained unshifted [ū].

Along the border between these two territories, however, there arose 'speech islands' in which the shift of [ū] to [ǖ] took place only incompletely, affecting some words and leaving others unchanged. What is especially interesting is the lexical distribution of shifted vs. unshifted vowels. The former are found in more prestigious vocabulary, such as the word for 'house', [hǖs]; the latter occur in more 'homey' vocabulary, such as [mūs] 'mouse'. Here the prestige of the innovating dialects appears to be reflected in the choice of words permitted to adopt the innovating pronunciation.

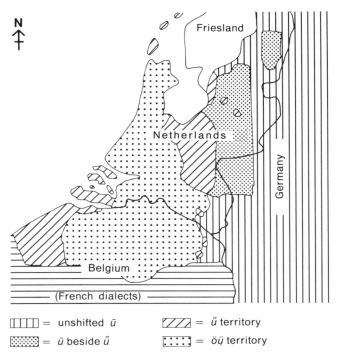

Map 1. Outcomes of long **ū* in the Low Countries (cf. Kloeke 1927)

Similar evidence for the greater prestige of innovated [ǖ] vis-à-vis older [ū] is found also in Friesland, on the northern periphery of the territory. What complicates matters is that the change of [ū] to [ǖ] has arrived here after another change had shifted old [ō] to [ū], as in [vōt] > [vūt] 'foot'. As a consequence, some speakers change not only old [ū] into [ṻ] (as in [hūs] > [hṻs]), but also the secondary [ū] of words like [vūt]. The result is hypercorrect forms with [ṻ], such as [vṻt].

In the sixteenth and seventeenth centuries, a new development affected the area: [ṻ] was diphthongized to [öÿ] in the coastal cities of the Netherlands; and the prestige of these cities led to the spread of this innovation to most of the territory which had participated in the earlier change. Again, however, we find that the change 'peters out', losing momentum on the periphery. As a consequence, parts of the area — in some cases only very small speech islands — retain the older monophthongal pronunciation.

Note that here, as in the case of the Chicago working-class vowel shift, there may be instances of discontinuous spread, skipping over territory that is only incompletely affected by the change. Compare the pockets of solid [ū] territory within the larger [ū/ṻ] area, as well as the [ū/ṻ] enclave in the northwest, in otherwise solidly [ū] territory. The explanation no doubt is similar to the one for the case of Chicago/ downstate Illinois: The [ṻ] pronunciation has become associated with a prestige feature like urbanization which makes for geographically discontinuous spread.

In addition it should be noted that in the early part of this century, as the diphthongal pronunciation had been encroaching on the [ṻ] dialects for several centuries, the pronunciation [ṻ] was still spreading at the expense of old [ū] on the periphery of the dialect area. Such is the case for instance for the Frisian development mentioned above.

This suggests that in many cases the spread of linguistic change takes place at the local level and is independent from innovations that are taking place farther away. It is therefore unaffected by more recent developments in the area where the change originated, even if these supersede the original change.

15.2.3. The Old High German consonant shift

A similar, but in many respects even more complex pattern is found in the case of the 'High German' (i.e., southern, mountain area) shift of the Germanic voiceless stops. In the territory where the shift seems to have originated, in Alemannic, the changes which together implement the shift can be formulated as in (9), disregarding a few minor complications.

(9 a) $\begin{bmatrix} + \text{ stop} \\ - \text{ voice} \end{bmatrix} > [+ \text{affric.}] \quad / \quad \left\{ \begin{matrix} [- \text{ fric.}] \\ \# \end{matrix} \right\} \underline{\quad}$

b) $[+ \text{affric.}] \quad > \begin{bmatrix} + \text{ fric.} \\ + \text{ "fortis"} \end{bmatrix} / \quad V \underline{\quad} \left\{ \begin{matrix} V \\ \# \end{matrix} \right\}$

By the first of these changes, voiceless stops not preceded by fricatives become 'affricates', i. e., stops followed by a homorganic fricatival release, such as [pf], [ts], [kx]. It is probable that an intermediate stage consisted of heavily aspirated stops. The 'affrication' or fricative release, then, results from something like wrong timing, an overlap of the oral articulation (labial, dental, velar) with the glottal friction of the aspiration. (Similar phenomena can be observed in a number of Modern Indo-Aryan languages, as well as in the case of Modern Danish [th] > [ts].)

The second change converts these affricates into the corresponding fricatives. In the formulation of (9b), the feature 'fortis' has been introduced to characterize the fact that the resulting fricatives are consistently distinguished from the older, inherited fricatives by being written as geminates. Moreover, in the case of the 'dentals', a distinction is made between older *s* or geminate *ss* and the *zz* which results from change (9b).

Example (10) illustrates the manner in which the outcomes of (9) are usually transcribed, together with an approximate phonetic interpretation. Note that in the examples below, the traditional orthography will be employed. It is important to recall that *z* by itself (initially and after consonant) refers to an affricate, while doubled *zz* designates the 'fortis' fricative which occurs elsewhere.

(10)	Symbol	Phonetic value	Environment
	pf	[pf]	#, C ___
	ff	[ff]	elsewhere
	z	[ts] (dental)	#, C ___
	zz	[ss] (dental, vs. alveolar *s(s)*)	elsewhere
	ch	[kx] or cluster-simplified [x]	#, C ___
	hh	[xx]	elsewhere

The changes in (9) may be illustrated by the examples in (11).

(11)	Proto-Germanic	Old High German	
	*paid-	pfeit	'tunic'
	*helpan-	helpfan	'help'
	*stump-	stumpf	'stump'
vs.	*hlaupan-	hlouffan	'leap, run'
	*tō	zuo	'to'
	*hert-	herz	'heart'
	*unt-	unz(i)	'unto'
vs.	*lētan-	lāzzan	'let'
	*fat-	fazz	'vat, barrel'
	*þat	thazz	'that'
	*kald-	chalt	'cold'
	*melk-	milch	'milk'
	*ank-	ancho	'butter'
vs.	*makō(ja)n-	mahhōn	'make'
	*ik/ek	ihh	'I'

Outside of Alemannic, the results of the High German consonant shift decrease in generality and regularity as the distance from Alemannic increases. However, with the progress of time, there is an increase of generality and regularity radiating out from Alemannic to the surrounding dialects. That is, there is clear evidence for a continued spread of the shift. A (simplified) representation of the resulting patterns is given in Map 2. For data, developments, and relic forms, cf. Chart 15.1.

As in the case of the Chicago vowel shift and the developments of *ū in the Low Countries, so also here the change radiates out from its original home, losing generality and regularity in the process. The only difference is that the area in which the change 'peters out' is larger and more complex and that the degeneralization of the change largely operates in terms of the phonological classes or elements undergoing the change and of the phonological environments conditioning the shift.

Lexical or overt prestige considerations seem to play only a minor role. But compare the different treatment of the pronominal form *that* vs. nominal *fazz* in areas Va, Vb, and VI. Note that the -*t* of *that* is

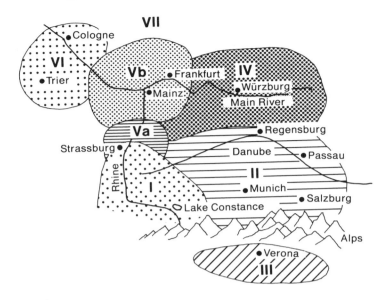

I = Alemannic, II = Bavarian, III = Langobardian,
IV = East Frankish, Va = South Rhine Frankish, Vb = North
Rhine Frankish, VI = Middle Frankish, VII = Low Frankish/Low
German

Map 2. Old High German sound shift

morphologically significant, marking nominative/accusative singular
neuter pronominal forms. In this dialect area, then, the spread of the
Old High German sound shift affected 'content' words but failed to
affect elements that are more deeply embedded in the grammar. Similarly
in Düsseldorf, at the very periphery of the territory, a distinction is
made between the first person singular pronoun and other forms: In
the modern dialect, the pronoun has the form [iç] with shifted velar,
while form like *maken* 'make, do' have unshifted [k]. There is reason
to believe that at an earlier time the dialect belonged to area VI, with
shifted *hh* in all qualifying forms, but that political realignments later
brought it under the sway of the northern dialects with unshifted velars.
As a consequence, [k] was reintroduced in most words, and only a few
basic-vocabulary exceptions managed to retain their earlier fricative
pronunciation.

	#___	r___	l___	N___	V___V	V___#
I	z, pf, ch	z, pf, ch	z, pf, ch	z, pf, ch	zz, ff, hh	zz, ff, hh
II	z, pf, ch	z, pf, ch	z, pf, ch p̣ in relics	z, pf, ch	zz, ff, hh	zz, ff, hh
III	z, p, k > pf, ch	z, p, k > (p)f, ch	z, p, k > (p)f, ch	z, p, k > pf	zz, ff, hh	zz, p, hh > pf
IV	z, pf, k	z, pf, k	z, pf, k p̣ in relics	z, pf, k	zz, ff, hh	zz, ff, hh
Va	z, p, k > pf	z, (p)f, k p̣ in relics	z, pf, k p̣ in relics	z, pf, k p̣ in relics	zz, ff, hh	zz, ff, hh early: that vs. fazz
Vb	z, p, k	z, p, k > pf	z, p, k > pf	z, p, k	zz, ff, hh	zz, ff, hh early: that vs. fazz
VI	z, p, k	z, p, k > pf	z, p, k > pf	z, p, k	zz, ff, hh	zz, ff, hh but: that vs. fazz
VII	t, p, k	t, p, k	t, p, k	t, p, k	t, p, k	t, p, k

Chart 15.1. Outcomes of PGmc. *t, p, k* in the older continental Germanic dialects, grouped in terms of phonetic environments.

The degeneralization of the Old High German sound shift moreover probably does not reflect the sequentiality of changes in the original 'home' dialect (as it did for instance in the case of the Chicago vowel shift). For the patterns of relics or delayed changes are not consistent. Thus in the environment V ___ #, Langobardian (= area III) shows a delayed change in the labial, while Rhine and Middle Frankish (= areas Va, Vb, and VI) have relics in the dental. Rather, it appears that at least in part the degeneralization is governed by considerations of precedent and of relative naturalness: Since all the Germanic dialects had geminate fricatival *ss*, the 'fortis' = geminate fricative outcome in the environments V ___ V and V ___ # had some native precedent in all the dialects and therefore spread most successfully. It is perhaps also for reasons of precedence that ȥ [ts] was accepted with relative ease. For although rare and resulting from secondary developments, a [ts] of independent origin occurred in forms like *Balȥo*, hypocoristic form of *Baldwin* via *Bald-so*. On the other hand, [pf] and [kx] had no direct precedents in native structure. Moreover, it appears that affricates of this sort, especially [kx], are crosslinguistically much less common or 'natural' than [ts]. It is noteworthy in this respect that many of the dialects which accepted [pf] have tended to simplify it to [f]. (In Chart

15.1, this has been indicated for Langobardian, where the development took place very early. But also Rhine and Middle Frankish show early beginnings of this change. At a later stage the change appears also in East Frankish dialects. Note finally that Modern Standard German regularly has [f], not [pf] after [l], as in *helfen* 'help'.) The cluster [kx] seems to be even more marked than [pf]: It did not spread to the Frankish dialects which instead retained [k] in the relevant environments. Also in Bavarian, a strong tendency toward velar-stop pronunciation (with or without aspiration) can be observed. And even in Alemannic, the 'home' dialect for the change, [kx] tends to be unstable, undergoing early simplification to [x] in many of the dialects.

15.2.4. Focal, transition, and relic areas

If we disregard differences in detail, all the cases of dialectal spread that we have examined so far share a general pattern: There is a **focal area** within which the change originates and where, in the case of sound change, the process is (most) regular. This area will include the 'home' dialect of the change. However, it may also include neighboring territory into which the change spread early and thoroughly. On the other end of the spectrum is a **relic area**, or several such areas, which has (or have) not been affected by the spread. In between these, there often is a **transition area** in which the spread 'peters out' or is 'degeneralized'. The extent of this degeneralization may be determined by lexical considerations; cf. Dutch [hūs] vs. [mūs], Rhine Frankish *that* vs. *faʒʒ*. Or it may be conditioned by structural or phonological considerations, such as the general spread pattern of the Old High German consonant shift. The prestige factors which are responsible for the incomplete spread may in some cases remain quite transparent; cf. especially Dutch [hūs] vs. [mūs]. But in many other cases, such as in the majority of dialects accepting the Old High German shift, they may no longer be discernible. What is discernible, however, is the decreased generality and regularity of the change.

Focal areas tend to be geographically or sociolinguistically **central** areas, whereas relic areas tend to be geographically or sociolinguistically **outlying** or otherwise **remote** areas. Thus in the case of the Low Countries, the focal area consisted of the sociolinguistically central, coastal regions. Relic areas are typically found on the periphery, relatively far removed from the focal areas. However, it has been observed that other factors may play a role. For instance, location in a relatively inaccessible mountain area (which may be geographically quite close to the focal area) may turn a dialect into a relic area.

Note moreover that the terms 'focal' and 'relic', 'central' and 'outlying/remote' are relative and have meanings only in respect to a given change. Therefore, a region which may be a relic area for a given change may at the same time be a focal area for another, possibly (but not necessarily) geographically more limited change. For instance, in the early German/Danish dialect continuum, the High German sound shift originated in the south and spread toward the north. At the same time, however, a development which originated in the north was arriving in the south, namely the voicing of fricatives in syllable-initial prevocalic environment. This change is ultimately responsible for the voiced outcome of PGmc. *þ in all the German dialects; cf. *þu > du 'you (sg.)'.

It is important to note this 'relativity' of the terms 'focal' and 'relic', 'central' and 'outlying/remote'. It is true, in some areas there may be just one important center of prestige which for centuries or even millennia may serve as the focal area for a variety of changes which then spread into most of the neighboring dialects. And in cases of that type, certain dialects may for all practical purposes be permanently on the periphery and thus resist the spreading innovations. Situations of this type may give the impression that central areas always show more — and more sweeping — innovations, and outlying areas are always more archaic. However, as the example of the German/Danish dialect continuum shows, this conclusion is not supported by the facts. Moreover, even in areas with a single, stable center of prestige, one may well wonder whether outlying areas are archaic in all respects. Rather, one suspects that they are archaic vis-à-vis the changes which are sweeping the center, while at the same time undergoing unrelated, but sometimes quite sweeping changes of their own. For as stated at the beginning of this book, all languages and all dialects change.

For this reason it seems preferable to determine the focal, relic, and transition areas for a given change on the basis of the specifically relevant evidence, rather than on the basis of preconceived notions as to what should be central or outlying/remote areas.

15.2.5. Dialectology as a diagnostic tool

If determined in the manner advocated in the preceding paragraph, the concepts 'focal', 'relic', and 'transition' area can be valuable tools in accounting for prehistoric situations where we lack attested documentary evidence on the timing and direction of the spread of linguistic innovations. This is especially important in the area of sound change. For establishing a scenario of 'focal', 'relic', and 'transition' areas permits us to explain apparently irregular change as the result of incomplete spread in a transition area. (Here as elsewhere in linguistic contact, our case will be strengthened if we can show that several, not intrinsically related phenomena can be explained as stemming from the same contact relationship.)

For instance, in the prehistory of Indo-Iranian, Slavic, and Baltic, two separate developments took place. In their most regular and general form, they can be formulated as in (12) and (13).

(12)   [+ stop, + 'pal.'] > [+ assibil.]   (Palatal assibilation)

(13)   s > š / RUKI ___   (RUKI)

Change (12) converts Proto-Indo European prevelar stops, commonly referred to as 'palatals', into assibilated clusters of stop + sibilant. These clusters in turn were commonly subject to cluster simplification, usually resulting in some kind of sibilant. (These developments, of course, are identical to the well-known changes that affect palatal or palatalized segments elsewhere; cf. 5.1.5.)

Change (13) turns *s* into *š* after *r*, high vowel *u* or *i* (whether syllabic or nonsyllabic), and velar stop — hence the abbreviation RUKI. This process is especially interesting since it is neither very common nor easily explainable in (articulatory) phonetic terms. (Evidently it is not just a case of palatalization.) Changes of this sort are valuable because they cannot be attributed to common tendencies which could very well have **independent** manifestations in different dialects. Rather, they can only be attributed to **common innovation**. That is, we must assume that a single change is responsible for the fact that *s* turns into *š* in this environment in Indo-Iranian and Balto-Slavic.

A number of other Indo-European dialects, surrounding these 'Indo-Baltic' dialects, do not exhibit either of the two changes. (In the case of the prevelar stops they instead show unassibilated stops which merge with the plain velars of Proto-Indo-European.) These dialects, then, can be considered relic areas.

Within the Indo-Baltic group, however, the generality and regularity of changes (12) and (13) is not evenly distributed. Whereas Indo-Iranian shows the changes in their most complete and regular form, even to the extent that *i* from PIE *$*ə*$ triggers RUKI, Slavic and Baltic exhibit the changes in some forms, while others show unshifted segments. Even doublets can be found, in which the same original root shows reflexes with and without shifted segments. Compare the data in Chart 15.2. (Latin here represents all of the relic dialects. Blanks indicate that a particular languages happens to have no attested cognate of a given word. Note that RUKI-*š* changes into *ş* in Sanskrit and *x* in Slavic. Moreover, in Slavic, RUKI is regularly blocked from applying in the environment before obstruent; cf. *prŭstŭ* 'finger'. Otherwise the change is regular in Slavic, with divergent developments explainable in terms of the environment or by analogy. In Lithuanian, RUKI seems to have been regular after *r*, with divergent developments explainable by analogy or other sound changes. It is not clear what happened after *k̑*. After *i* and *u*, the outcome of *š* is quite unpredictable.)

PIE	Sanskrit	Avestan	Lithuanian	Old Ch. Slavic	Latin
*k̑lew/k̑lu- 'hear, listen'	śru-	sru-	klau-s-ī-ti vs. šlōvē 'fame'	slyšati slava 'fame'	in-clutus 'famous'
*swek̑uros 'father-in-law'	śvaśura-	xvasura-	šešuras	svekŭrŭ	(Gk. hekuros)
*k̑m̥tom '100'	śatam	satəm	šimtas	(sŭto)	centum
*wr̥s- 'top, protrusion'	varṣman-		viršus	vrŭxŭ	verrūca < *rs 'wart'
*pr̥sto- 'sticking out'	pṛṣtha- 'back'	paršta- 'backbone'	pirštas 'finger'	prŭstŭ 'finger'	postis < *rs 'post'
(a)us- 'ear'		uši	ausis	uxo	auris < *-s-
*(a)us- 'dawn'	uṣas-	ušå	aušra/austra		aurōra < *-s-

Chart 15.2. 'Indo-Baltic' and Latin correspondences for PIE *$*k̑*$ and *$*š*$

Keeping in mind the geographical distribution of the dialects, for which see Map 3, we are justified in explaining the Balto-Slavic irregularities as a transition-area phenomenon, resulting from the incomplete spread

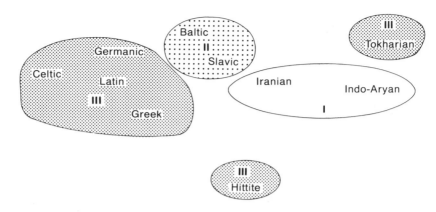

I = Focal area   II = Transition area   III = Relic areas

Map 3. RUKI and palatal assibilation in Indo-European dialects

of changes which originated in Indo-Iranian. Our case is strengthened
by the fact that we have two quite different changes whose spread
follows essentially the same pattern. Moreover, as noted earlier, the
nature of one of the changes (RUKI) is such that independent innovation can be safely excluded as a possible explanation. Only common
innovation will account for the presence of this quite unusual change
in neighboring dialects. Finally, it may be noted that for the same
reason we must rule out an explanation which views the *s* of the non-
Indo-Baltic dialects as resulting from an 'anti-RUKI' change. For it is
very unlikely that such a highly unusual change would have independently operated in the geographically discontinuous peripheral dialects.

15.3. The effect of dialect contact: Isoglosses, 'wave theory', and 'tree theory'

In the preceding section we have observed the patterns that result from
the spread of linguistic innovations. And we have seen that these
patterns can in many cases be quite complex. The complexities would
become even more evident if, in the case of the Old High German
sound shift, we had marked the boundaries or **isoglosses** of the

territory in which any given word or class of words was or was not affected by the spread of the change. Compare for instance Map 4 which does not even account for the Langobardian dialect area, or for minor early relics or readjustments. Thus, areas Va and Vb, South and North Rhine Frankish, are included in the territory with shifted *t* in the pronoun *thazz*, even though at an early stage they show unshifted *that*.

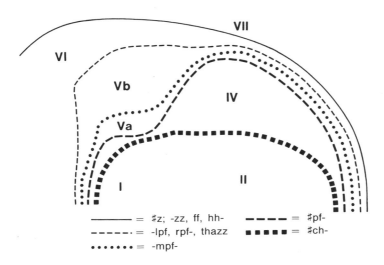

——— = ‡z; -zz, ff, hh-	– – – – = ‡pf-
– – – · – = -lpf, rpf-, thazz	■ ■ ■ ■ ■ = ‡ch-
• • • • • • = -mpf-	

Map 4: Old High German isoglosses

Map 4, however, is still quite incomplete. For at the same time (roughly) at which the Old High German sound shift spread from Alemannic to the neighboring dialects, other changes were spreading in the same territory, but in different directions. And these changes likewise have their own, often quite complex isoglosses.

A more complete representation would look something like Map 5. The added isoglosses reflect the developments and phenomena summarized in Chart 15.3. But also this map is simplified and offers only a glimpse of the real complexity. In part the simplification is deliberate, to ensure at least some degree of perspicuity. To some extent, however, it results from the fact that due to chronologically and geographically uneven attestations, our knowledge of the (late) Old High German dialects is quite spotty. This is especially true for North Rhine Frankish and Middle Frankish. But even elsewhere, chronological difficulties abound. For instance, at the time when the northern change of *ft* to

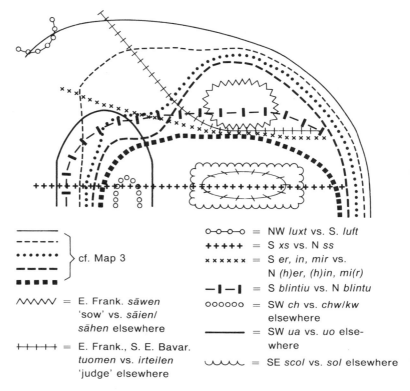

<table>
<tbody>
<tr><td>o—o—o—o</td><td>= NW luxt vs. S. luft</td></tr>
<tr><td>+++++</td><td>= S xs vs. N ss</td></tr>
<tr><td>x x x x x x</td><td>= S er, in, mir vs.
N (h)er, (h)in, mi(r)</td></tr>
<tr><td>—I—I</td><td>= S blintiu vs. N blintu</td></tr>
<tr><td>oooooo</td><td>= SW ch vs. chw/kw
elsewhere</td></tr>
<tr><td>————</td><td>= SW ua vs. uo else-
where</td></tr>
<tr><td>ᴜᴜᴜᴜ</td><td>= SE scol vs. sol elsewhere</td></tr>
</tbody>
</table>

cf. Map 3

〰〰〰 = E. Frank. *sāwen*
'sow' vs. *sāien/
sāhen* elsewhere

+++++ = E. Frank., S. E. Bavar.
tuomen vs. *irteilen*
'judge' elsewhere

Map 5: Old High German isoglosses (more complete coverage)

xt reached Middle Frankish, the earlier change of *xs* to *ss* was already being reversed in the southern part of the High German territory. (This was the result of the northward spread of 'southern' *xs*.) In short, Map 5 should be looked at as an illustration, not as a complete or fully accurate dialect description of (late) Old High German.

The complex, often quite irregular isogloss patterns of Map 5 are by no means unusual. In fact, as time progresses, the dialect map of the High German dialects will become only more complex. If we include all the various lexical borrowings in such a map and allow for enough time of continuous, uninterrupted contact, then the result may well be that **every word has its own history** — the battle cry of the dialectologists, especially around the turn from the nineteenth to the twentieth century.

While it probably is true that in the long run every word has its own history, it is not justified to conclude as some linguists have, that

(a) EFrank. $\emptyset \rightarrow w/[V, -\text{front}]$ ___ V in verbs of the type *sāen > sāwen* 'sow'. Elsewhere other glides (*h* or *y*, spelled *i*) may be inserted, but without any discernible dialectal differentiation.

(b) As a consequence of West (= Middle and Low) Frankish overlordship, a good deal of legal terminology makes its way into the majority of the dialects, such as *irteilen* 'to judge'. East Frankish and Southeast Bavarian preserve the relic *tuomen* 'to judge'.

(c) Low Frankish $f > x$ / ___ C_0 $ spreads to part of neighboring Middle Frankish.

(d) *$*xs > ss$, as in *oxso > osso*. The change at one point reached into Alemannic and Bavarian, but later retreated toward the north.

(e) Where the more southern dialects have pronominal *er* 'he', *in* 'him', *mir* 'to me', *dir* 'to you (sg.)', the northern dialects offer *her*, *hin*, *mī*, *dī*, beside the southern forms, as a transition to the Low German forms, *he*, *hin*, *mī*, *dī*.

(f) Pl. N/A n. *-iu*, as in *blintiu* 'blind things', is replaced by *-u* in most of Frankish, except the Southern portion of East Frankish. (Hence *blintu* 'blind things'.)

(g) Alem. *chw > ch* by cluster simplification, as in *chwedan > chedan* 'speak'.

(h) Until a later 'weakening' process produces *ue* in all the dialects, old *$*\bar{o}$ winds up as *ua* in Alemannic and parts of neighboring South Rhine Frankish, while elsewhere it appears as *uo*. (Hence *ruam* vs. *ruom* 'glory'.)

(i) Apparently through the generalization of unstressed alternants, the majority of the dialects have *sol* 'shall' in late Old High German times, while Bavarian *scol* retains the original cluster.

Chart 15.3. Additional Old High German isoglosses (in the order in which they are listed in the key to Map 5)

therefore the neogrammarian position on the nature of linguistic change is falsified. For in spite of the rather amorphous nature of much of linguistic change, there is also a great systematicity and regularity to language, without which it would be difficult, if not impossible, to acquire — and understand — language effectively. And that systematicity manifests itself most clearly in the regularity of sound change (within its home territory). To ignore this regularity and systematicity would severely limit our understanding of linguistic change.

At the same time, however, it is quite clear that extensive and prolonged contact, as it is frequently found in areas long settled by speakers of the same language, may cause considerable difficulties for the historical linguist. For it can make it next to impossible to **classify dialects** in terms of their genetic relationship.

Our knowledge about the early, largely prehistoric, ethnic relationship between the Germanic tribes that settled Germany would suggest a corresponding system of linguistic relationship which can be represented by the **tree diagram** in Map 6. This diagram would state that, say, the Frankish dialects are more closely related to each other than to any other dialects, because they are descended from a single ancestor, Proto-Frankish, which differs from Proto-Alemannic and Proto-Bavarian by exhibiting certain linguistic developments which are exclusively Frankish, over against other developments which are limited to Bavarian or Alemannic, respectively. Put differently, in this conceptualization of linguistic relationship, the Frankish dialects have a clear and separate identity as the consequence of exclusively shared common innovations. (Cf. 15.2.5 for the term 'common innovation'.) And these innovations in turn reflect a period of exclusively shared common prehistory during which the dialects were in contact only with each other, so that innovations spread only through these dialects.

While there may have been a period during which there was an especially close relationship between the various Frankish dialects, the situation has changed considerably in the attested Old High German period. As Maps 2, 4, and 5 show, at this point, Low Frankish is much more closely allied with Low German than, say, with East Frankish. And the latter dialect shows much closer affinities to the 'Upper German' dialects of Alemannic and Bavarian. Moreover, the Rhine Frankish dialects, especially (southern parts of) South Rhine Frankish, are quite closely aligned with the Upper German Alemannic. Finally, Middle Frankish forms a bridge, as it were, between the High German (i. e. Upper German + East and Rhine Frankish) dialects and Low German. These relationships suggest a tree diagram very different from the one of Map 6.

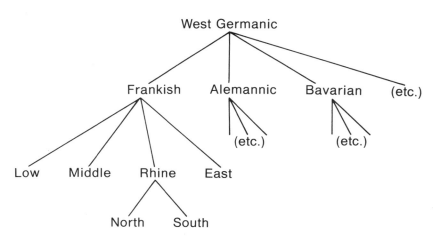

Map 6. Old High German dialects: prehistoric tree diagram

A more adequate representation would be the one in Map 7. This would capture some of the similarities and differences: Middle Frankish is closer to Low Frankish than are the other, Southern dialects, because it 'branches off' nearest to Low Frankish. The situation is similar for Rhine Frankish and Middle Frankish, etc.

Relatively **'flat tree diagrams'** of this type, with mainly binary branchings (vs. the multiple branchings of diagrams like the one in Map 6) and with the dialects arranged in more or less geographical order, account quite nicely for the major patterns that result from the spread of linguistic change, such as the Old High German sound shift. In fact, they typically are indicative of the spread of linguistic innovations in a dialect continuum. But note that they cover only some of the dialectal affiliations. For instance, the diagram in Map 7 does not account for the special relationship between (parts of) Southern Rhine Frankish and Alemannic, or for the special affinities between East Frankish and Bavarian on one hand and Bavarian and Alemannic on the other. More than that, many other isoglosses of Map 5 cannot be captured at all. And diagrams which would account for these relationships would by necessity fail to express some of the relationships that are captured by the diagram in Map 7.

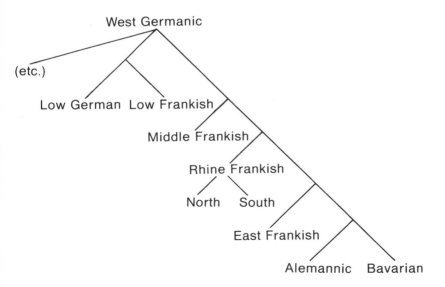

Map 7. Old High German dialects: synchronic tree diagram

In short, the linguistic relationship between neighboring dialects of the same language very commonly cannot be stated in terms of tree diagrams. This is a consequence of the fact that these speech varieties remain mutually intelligible, stay in close contact, and therefore continue to interact with each other on a day-to-day basis, with shifting realignments as political and social circumstances change. It is therefore unrealistic to expect clear, 'tree-diagram' splits in such dialect continua.

Clear splits seem to result only when originally closely affiliated dialects become separated, through migration or radical political and social realignment, such that they cease to be mutually intelligible and become different languages. In such cases, innovations no longer will be shared through dialectal spread. Rather, they will be confined to the (sub-)dialects of the newly differentiated languages. It is in such situations, then, that it is meaningful to talk about exclusively shared innovation and the allied concept of exclusively shared common (pre-) history.

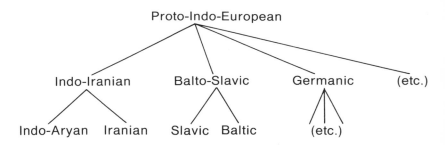

Map 8. (Proto-)Indo-European dialects: tree diagram

It is this type of relationship which is encoded by tree diagrams like the one in Map 8, which presents one view of the genetic classification of the Indo-European languages. Note that this diagram differs considerably from the one in Map 7: First of all, it is not 'flat', but exhibits multiple branchings. Moreover, the branches of the diagram reflect not just one out of many possible innovations. Rather, each branching is supported by a large number of different common linguistic innovations. For instance, the innovations defining the Indo-Iranian branch include the developments in (14), while those defining Germanic include Grimms's Law, Verner's Law, and the development of a new past-tense formation with dental suffix (cf. Engl. *dive : dive-d*).

(14 a)   [+ vel.]   >   [+ pal.] / ___ [V, + front]   (cf. 5.1.5, ex. (31))
   b)   [V, − hi]   >   [+ lo]   (cf. 5.1.5, ex. (32))
   c)   ə > i   (cf. *pətēr > Skt. pitā, Av. pitā)

Even so, also in the case of the relationship between distinct languages, tree diagrams like the one in Map 8 are not fully realistic. For they do not account for the fact that prior to becoming clearly differentiated, these languages must have been mutually intelligible dialects of a larger **dialect continuum**. Differentiation therefore must have set in already before they ceased to be in contact and became mutually unintelligible. Moreover, one suspects that within the earlier dialect continuum, innovations spread in the same fashion as in observable dialect continua, i. e., in a complex, criss-crossing fashion, not in the 'neat' manner suggested by the tree diagram. In short, diagrams of this type fail to capture the truism that languages have dialects.

In fact, as the discussion in 15.2.5 shows, there is clear evidence for innovations spreading across the language boundaries suggested by the diagram in Map 8: RUKI and palatal assibilation were not confined to, say, the Indo-Iranian branch of Indo-European but affected also the Balto-Slavic branch, albeit in an incomplete manner.

Similarly, Balto-Slavic and Germanic share the fact that the contrast between PIE *a, o,* and *ə* is neutralized — in favor of *a* in the case of Baltic and Germanic, in favor of *o* in Slavic. Cf., e. g., the examples in (15). The same set of dialects also has replaced the labial aspirate of certain nominal endings with the corresponding nasal, such as pl. I *bhis* → *mis;* cf. (16). (Sanskrit here presents the usual Indo-European form of the ending.)

(15)	PIE	Lithuanian	Old Ch. Slavic	OHG	
	*aḱs-	ašis	osĭ	ahsa	'axle'
	*okʷ-	akis	oko		'eye'
	ok tō	aštuoni	(osmĭ)	aht	'eight'

(16)	Sanskrit	Lithuanian	Old Ch. Slavic	Proto-Gmc.	OHG
	tē-bhis		tĕ-mĭ	þai-m(i)z	dēm
	'by those'				
	mātr̥-bhis	mōteri-mis	materi-mi	mōdru-m(i)z	muoter-um
	'by the mothers'				

To account for such relationships, diagrams like the one in Map 9 are probably more realistic. Here, languages are presented two-dimensionally as dialect continua. As a consequence it is possible to make at least some provision for the criss-crossing of isoglosses or the spread of linguistic innovations across the boundaries of dialects which eventually wind up as distinct languages. Compare for instance the isoglosses for the changes in (15) and (16), as well as for RUKI and palatal assibilation.

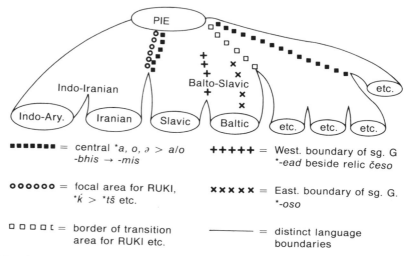

■■■■■■■ = central *a, o, ə > a/o -bhis → -mis	+++++ = West. boundary of sg. G *-ead beside relic *česo*
○○○○○○ = focal area for RUKI, *k̑ > *tš etc.	×××× = East. boundary of sg. G. *-oso
□ □ □ □ ⊏ = border of transition area for RUKI etc.	——— = distinct language boundaries

Map 9. (Proto-)Indo-European dialects: modified tree diagram

In addition, this type of diagram permits a resolution in principle of the long-standing controversy as to whether Baltic and Slavic form a single, Balto-Slavic branch or two separate branches of Indo-European: Some of the exclusively shared innovations of Baltic and Slavic can go back to an early period at which the two dialect groups were still mutually intelligible and in closer contact with each other than with other Indo-European languages and dialects. An example of this type of change is the development of a new past-tense formation in *-ā́-, as in the examples in (17). (Other, later common innovations will have to be explained in terms of the concept of convergence, for which see 16.3 below.)

(17)   present   past
    OCS   beretŭ   bĭr-a [ā]   'gather, collect'
    Lith.   auga   aug-ō < *-ā   'grow'

But also some of the features which differentiate the two groups may well have originated during that early, dialect-continuum, stage and thus may be as ancient as the features which unite the two groups. A probable example of this type of development is the following: In Proto-Indo-European there was originally no distinction between ablative and genitive singular in nominal paradigms; a single ending was used for both. In most inflectional classes, this ending was *-os* or *-s*. In the most productive inflectional class, the so-called thematic nouns (characterized by the suffix *-e/o-*), the suffix was *-so* or *syo* in the majority of the dialects, as in (18a). On the other hand, the pronouns made a distinction between genitive and ablative singular. In the demonstrative *te/o-*, the pronominal stem which was formally most similar to the thematic nouns and which had the greatest tendency to influence its inflection, the endings were distinguished as in (18b) vs. (18c). (The variant *te-sme-ad* will be ignored in the subsequent discussion.)

(18 a)   *deywo-s(y)o   'of/from the god'
  b)   sg. G *te-s(y)o   'of that one'
  c)   sg. A *te-ad (or *te-sme-ad) 'from that one'

The formal similarities between the demonstrative pronoun and the thematic nouns, as well as the fact that the two frequently were collocated, led to a variety of contaminatory developments in a number of different inflectional forms; cf. e. g. section 9.2.2, ex. (79/80) above. What is relevant for the present discussion is that in the genitive/ablative singular, a very wide-spread development was the one in (19).

(19)   *te-ad deywo-s(y)o → *te-ad deywe-ad
      beside   *te-s(y)o deywo-s(y)o   (unchanged)

A number of languages exploited the coexisting patterns in (19) to distinguish ablative from genitive singular in the thematic nouns, with *-ad* serving as ablative ending, *-s(y)o* as genitive. (Cf. e. g. Indo-Iranian, pre-Greek, Latin, possibly pre-Germanic.) And a few languages (most notably Avestan and Latin) extended the distinction to other noun classes. In Balto-Slavic, on the other hand, the situation was resolved differently. Here the inherited lack of distinction between genitive and ablative singular was extended to the pronouns. This syncretism, rather than differentiation (or lack of change), clearly is an innovation common to all of Baltic and Slavic. In terms of the choice as to which of the competing endings should be generalized, however, there are clear differences. Lithuanian, Latvian, and Slavic agree on generalizing the forms in *-ad* for the nouns. This is the choice also for the Lithuanian pronouns. On the other hand, Slavic has the pronominal relic form *česo* 'of what'; and in the other pronouns it offers an innovated ending *-ego/ogo* which perhaps is a replacement of earlier *-eso*. Finally, Old Prussian generalized the suffix *-s(y)o* for both nouns and pronouns. Compare the examples in (20).

(20) OCS   te-go bog-a   (relic: česo 'of what')
      Lith.   tō diev-ō
      OPrus. ste-sse deiva-s (with apocope of *-o after
                               non-initial syllable)

What is most interesting in these divergent developments is that in the nouns at least, Lithu-Latvian goes along with Slavic and not with Old Prussian with which it otherwise agrees closely enough to be classed together as Baltic. In prehistoric times, then, at least some of the isoglosses must have cut across the boundaries which later separate Baltic from Slavic.

The discovery in the late nineteenth century that isoglosses can cut across well-established linguistic boundaries at first created considerable attention and controversy. And it became fashionable to oppose a **wave theory** to a **tree theory**. (Here the term 'wave' refers to the fact that linguistic innovations spread, like waves created by a stone thrown into a pond, from their point of origination to the periphery, slowly losing their momentum and intersecting with the waves created by other innovations.) Today, however, it is quite evident that the phenomena referred to by these two terms are complementary aspects of linguistic change. And the modified, hose-like (or 'truncated octopus'-like) tree model of Map 9 can be considered a means of providing a unified picture of change.

However, in practice, it is generally preferable to use the traditional, simple tree model — if necessary supplemented by synchronic isogloss maps for relevant historical stages. For the actual picture of intersecting isoglosses may in many cases be far too complex to be incorporated into the modified tree model. Compare for instance the display of Proto-Indo-European isoglosses in Map 10. (The last isogloss listed in the key to that map refers to the fate of the Proto-Indo-European cluster *-tt-*. Examples are: PIE *wit-to-* 'known': Av. *vista-*, Gk. *-istos*,

OHG *wiss*, Skt. *vitta-;* Proto-Indo-European **set-to-* 'sat' (pple.): Lat.
sessus, Skt. *satta-;* Proto-Indo-European **et-te* 'you (pl.) eat': OCS *jaste*,
Hitt. *ets-teni*.)

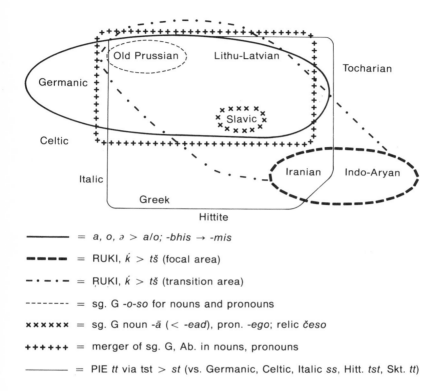

```
          = a, o, ə > a/o; -bhis → -mis

━━━━      = RUKI, ḱ > tš (focal area)

━·━·━    = RUKI, ḱ > tš (transition area)

--------  = sg. G -o-so for nouns and pronouns

xxxxxx   = sg. G noun -ā (< -ead), pron. -ego; relic česo

++++++   = merger of sg. G, Ab. in nouns, pronouns

          = PIE tt via tst > st (vs. Germanic, Celtic, Italic ss, Hitt. tst, Skt. tt)
```

Map 10. (Proto-)Indo-European dialects: isoglosses

15.4. Discontinuous, supra-regional dialects; standard dialects

In the preceding two sections of this chapter we have seen numerous
instances of dialect spread. These included at least two examples —
from Chicago/downstate Illinois and from Dutch/Flemish — in which
the spread was geographically discontinuous. But since the pattern of

spread was not significantly different from what is found between contiguous dialects, no further discussion was required. The reason for this lack of difference may well have been the fact that the source for the spread, its focal area, was in essence a continuous dialect.

In addition to continuous (social or regional) dialects, probably all languages also have at least some **discontinuous, supra-regional** dialects, defined only in terms of social factors which extend across the boundaries of continuous dialects.

15.4.1. Professional jargons

The dialect employed in this text is an example of one variety of discontinuous, supra-regional dialect, namely that of linguists, with its own very specific vocabulary and with at least some conventions of grammatical usage which differentiate it from the other dialects of English. While here the differences may by and large be limited to vocabulary, and grammatical differences may be subtle, there are other dialects which more obviously (and more notoriously) differ from 'normal' English. Consider for instance the dialect of lawyers, with its heavy use of borrowings from French and Latin, as in (21), as well as with certain pecularities in grammar, such as the past tense *ple(a)d* [pled] of *plead* [plīd] and especially the extremely long and complex syntactic strings conjoined by *whereas ... whereas ..., therefore*.

(21)   feme couverte, feme sole
        grand jury, petit jury
        oyez, oyez, oyez (at the beginning of a court session)
        habeas corpus
        nolo contendere, nolle prosequi
        venire (facias)

In addition to such **professional jargons**, there are of course the **argots** or secret languages discussed in 14.5.4 above, which likewise tend to be discontinuous and supra-regional. (To outsiders, in fact, the terminology and grammatical conventions of professional jargons are often as impenetrable as argots. And the impression that they are secret languages, intended to keep outsiders 'out', is in some cases quite correct. At the same time, however, there is in principle good justification for the development of special vocabulary, etc., in specialized fields of inquiry. For the concepts with which such fields are concerned are themselves quite specialized. Similarly, the use of certain grammatical constructions, such as the passive, is highly appropriate in many areas of the sciences. For as noted in 13.2.4.2, the demotion of passive agents makes it possible to state facts that are believed to hold true no matter who observes them.)

Supra-regional professional jargons are not necessarily limited to lawyers, scientists, and other 'professionals'. They are found also in the 'trades' or 'crafts'.

One of the most common trade jargons is the one of sailors and seafarers. But in some ways, this jargon is perhaps unusual: At least in the North Atlantic, the vocabulary of the jargon is highly international, with liberal borrowings back and forth between the languages of all the seafaring nations. And there is reason to believe that Mediterranean nautical jargons had similar characteristics. Moreover, the vocabulary frequently comes not from the standard languages but from coastal dialects. This is especially true for the German element, which comes from the Low German (LG) dialects that differ considerably from southern-based Standard German and are much closer to Dutch and Flemish. A consequence of these special circumstances is that words may be borrowed back and forth several times over; and in many cases it is impossible to determine with certainty which language was the ultimate source for a given term. Compare for instance the English, German, and French examples and their putative sources in (22). (Note that some of the terms in (22) may be used also in non-nautical meanings. In some cases, this is the result of secondary extension, as in Engl. *caboose, freight*. In others, such as perhaps Engl. *average*, we may be dealing with simple homonymy. [In nautical jargon, *average* refers to damage at sea.]).

(22)	English	German	French	
	average	Havarie	avarie	Fr., fr. It., fr. Arabic
	brig	Brigg	brig/brick	Engl., clipped from brigantine (< ?)
	boat	Boot		ME fr. ON
	buoy	Boje	bouée	OFr., via Dutch(?)
	cabin	Kabine	cabine	(OFr. cabane ⇒ Engl. cabin)
	caboose	Kombüse	cambuse	Dutch (< ?)
	fleet	Flotte	flotte	early Gmc. ⇒ Fr. flotte ⇒ Germ.

flotilla	Flotille	flotille	Fr. ⇒ Span. ⇒ Fr. etc.
freight	Fracht	fret	Frisian, via Du./LG
gaff	Gaffel		OFr., fr. Span. or Port.
(larbord)	Backbord	bâbord	LG/Du.?
	Matrose	matelot	fr. Du./LG and/or
	'sailor'		Scand. ⇒ Fr. ⇒
			Du./LG
lee	Lee		Engl.(?), or ON(?)
luff	Luv	lof	fr. ON(?)
packboat	Packboot	paquebot	Engl.
pilot	Pilot	pilote	fr. It., fr. Gk.
road	Reede	rade	fr. ON
schooner	Schoner	schooner	Scots Engl. (?)
starbord	Steuerbord	tribord	early Gmc. ⇒ Fr. (via?)

Although international in character and provenience, nautical jargon can have repercussions on the languages and regional dialects of individual countries. In Germany, for instance, it is responsible for the introduction of a large amount of foreign elements, as well as borrowings from northern Low German which, as noted, differs considerably from the southern-based standard language. And these borrowings have introduced some 'alien' phonological features into Standard German. The most striking of these is the initial cluster *wr-* [vr-] in the examples of (23). The earlier form of this cluster, [wr-], had been lost in the dialects forming the basis of Modern Standard German, just as they were in most of the other Germanic dialects; cf. e. g. (24).

(23)   Wrack [vrak] 'wreck'
        wricken/wriggen [vrikən/vrigən] 'scull (a boat)'

(24)   *wrītan- 'write': NE write [rayt], NIcel. ríta, NHG Reissfeder 'drafting pen'

Other professional jargons can have similar effects. Consider for instance the jargon of German miners, whose roots can be traced back to the early Middle Ages. It appears that in the latter part of the tenth century A.D., Rhine Frankish miners migrated to the linguistically Low German Harz region, bringing with them not only their technique but also the technical vocabulary that went with it. By imparting their skills and their vocabulary to the local 'Low Saxon' population, they laid the foundation for a professional jargon that was not specifically linked to a particular dialect area. Moreover, since new technical terms now tended to come from the local Low Saxon, that jargon soon acquired northern beside southern features. A further shift of the center of mining in the twelfth century, from the Low German Harz region to the linguistically mixed 'Eastern Middle German' area of Meissen and the Erzgebirge added yet another linguistic element. The resulting variety then became the foundation for a national miners language, a supra-regional dialect which eventually coexisted with Standard German and which even had international ramifications.

The vocabulary of the jargon reflects its dialectally composite origin. And as words from the jargon entered the standard language they brought with them pronunciations or meanings which in a number of cases differed from their cognates in Standard German. Compare the data in (24). (The listing under 'Standard German' excludes borrowings from miners jargon.) Especially interesting are *Teufe, (ab)teufen* and *Grus* vs. standard *Tiefe, (ab)tiefen,* and *Graus* (the latter attested in Goethe's works), where miners jargon and standard language exhibit quite different phonological developments. Note also the word *Schlacke,* whose *ck* [k] is rather difficult to explain vis-à-vis the earlier northern attestation *slagge* [g].

(24)	Miners jargon	Standard German	Origin
	Schweif 'entrance of a gallery'	Schweif 'tail'	southern
	Zechstein 'zechstein'	zäh 'tough'	southern
	• Schacht 'mine shaft'	Schaft 'shaft (of spear, etc.)'	northern
	• Schicht 'layer; shift'		northern for 'southern' *Schift* 'shift, change'(?) or southern *Schicht* 'layer'(?)
	Hund/Hunt 'trolley'	Hund 'dog'	southern/northern
	Kaue 'pit head'	(Käfig 'cage', a later borrowing from Lat.)	MHG *kouwe* fr. Lat. *cavea*

Kumpel 'miner'	Kumpan 'friend, buddy'	East. Middle German variant of *Kumpan*
Grus 'coal fragments, slag, grit'	Graus 'gravel'	Middle Frankish (?) or southern, MHG *grūz* with northern lack of *ū > au*?
• Schlacke 'slag(s), refuse'	schlagen 'beat, hammer' or schlack 'slack'?	northern *slagge*; cf. *slagen* 'beat, hammer' or *slak* 'slack' (?)

The items marked by • are especially interesting. For they have remarkably similar correspondences in English miners language; cf. (24). (The English listing is limited to the words as they are used in mining.) Moreover, as (24) shows, English likewise has a variation between voiced [g] and voiceless [k] in the words corresponding to Germ. *Schlacke,* northern *slagge.* Semantically, the relation between Germ. *Schlacke,* Engl. *slack* 'slags, refuse; inferior coal' and *schlack, slack* is supported by the precedent of German miners jargon *Fäule/Feule* 'inferior mineral' (Standard *Fäule* 'rot') and *faul* 'rotten, lazy'. But this will not account for the [g] of *slagge, slag,* which finds a better explanation in Low German *slagen,* NHG *schlagen* 'beat, hammer': *slagge, slag* then is the refuse which results from hammering, either in the pit or in the originally closely associated foundry.

(24)	German	English
	Schacht	shaft (1433: '... factura unius shaft ... pro carbonibus ... lucrandis' = 'for the making of a shaft to exploit coal')
	Schicht	shift (1708: 'The Pit will require ... 4 shifts or horses ...')
	slagge	slag (1552: 'At the furst melting ... was mad ... 288 lbs. of lead besids the slaggs and stones')
	Schlacke	slack 'small or refuse coal' (1440; cf. 1795: 'for all slack or small or inferior coal')

The English evidence, then, does not help to resolve the phonological and etymological problems with *Schlacke.* However, it opens up another dimension: Are the correspondences in (24) due to chance or independent development, or was there contact between German and English miners jargon? Some points might argue for independent innovation. For instance, the *ft* of Engl. *shaft, shift* does not agree with the *cht* of Germ. *Schacht, Schicht*. (But note that the southern form *Schaft* is indirectly attested in early German treatises on mining. The English words, then, might be borrowings from an early, more southern, form of German miners jargon.) On the other hand, there are several arguments which might favor the latter view: First, as English mineral terms like *zechstein* (cf. (23) above) and *blende, feldspar* (Germ. *Blende, Feldspat*) show, there was a certain influence of German mining language on English. Moreover, examples like (25) illustrate the fact that German miners jargon exerted an influence also on other European languages. Finally, if Engl. *slag* is to be derived from a word meaning 'hammer, beat', then its source would have to be (Low) German: The native English cognate, with regular indigenous phonetic and semantic developments, is *slay*.

(25 a)	German	Swedish
	Schicht	skikt
	Schacht	skakt
b)	German	French
	Rückstein	rustine
	Bleimacher	blaymard

Given the fact that in observable history, professional jargons can be seen to introduce phonologically, semantically, etc., deviant elements into particular languages, it must be accepted as a possibility that similar developments may have happened in prehistorical times. The assumption of borrowing from a professional jargon therefore must be considered another possible approach to accounting for apparently irregular sound change, beside analogy, incomplete spread of innovations in transition areas, and 'ordinary' borrowing. Here as elsewhere, of course, it is necessary to give persuasive arguments for such an account.

A possible example of phonetic irregularity attributable to borrowing from a professional jargon may be the fate of Proto-Indo-European initial **y* in Greek: The normal Greek development is the one exemplified in (26), with weakening of **y-* to *h-*. However, in a limited set of items, the development is to ʒ- (= [dz-], [zd-], or [z], depending on the dialect), presumably via [ǰ] with initial strengthening. Compare (27).

(26)   PIE   Greek

       yo- 'who (rel.)'   ho-
       yudh- 'fight'   husminē
       yēkʷr̥t- 'liver'   hēpar

(27)   PIE   Greek

       yes- 'boil, ferment'   zeō
       yewos 'barley (etc.)'   zeiai
       yūs- '(fermented) broth'   zūmēn
       yōs- 'belt, girdle (etc.)'   zōnē
       yugom 'yoke, harness'   zugon
   cf. yewg- 'to yoke (etc.)'   zeugnūmi

The correspondences in (27) have given rise to a great variety of mutually contradictory attempts to account for them in terms of regular sound change. However, these attempts have been flawed either by invoking ad-hoc, special reconstructions for Proto-Indo-European, designed exclusively to account for the difficulties of Greek, or by failing to account for the whole ensemble of ʒ- and h- forms. Moreover, it is not possible to show that, say, the forms in (27) are borrowed from a particular attested dialect of Greek.

However, it is possible to argue that all of the words in (27) involve or affect a certain degree of 'technology', where 'technology' has to be understood within the context of the relevant, quite early prehistoric period. Specifically, the words either refer to processes of fermenting, or common ingredients for certain fermentation processes (such as *yewos 'barley'), or the products of tanning (such as (leather) belts or girdles, or the leather straps of yokes and harnesses). Given these observations, we can then argue that the words must come from a prehistoric supra-regional dialect of brewers and tanners in which the change of *y- to ʒ- may have been a regular feature. While this explanation evidently has to rely on a good deal of speculation, it does show the often overlooked explanatory potential of the concept of discontinuous, supra-regional professional jargon.

15.4.2. Standard languages

The most important discontinuous, supra-regional dialects are **standard dialects** or **standard languages**. Historically, these can be of very different origins:

They can be regional or local dialects which for some reason acquired sufficient prestige to be accepted as standard on a supra-regional basis. Compare for instance Standard French and English which developed out of the educated speech of Paris and London, respectively.

They may develop out of koinés (cf. section 16.2 below), such as the Greek Koiné of Alexandrian times or the Swahili of present-day Tanzania.

They may result from quite deliberate 'language planning' or 'language engineering', as in the case of Nynorsk, one of the standard languages of Norway. This language was deliberately constructed out of elements from conservative rural dialects as an overt sign of linguistic nationalism, a counterforce against the earlier prevailing standard language, Riksmaal or Bokmaal, which in essence was a Norwegianized Danish and reflected the fact that Norway previously had been under the domination of Denmark.

They may also result from a combination of any or all of these different sources. Compare the case of Modern Standard German: The ultimate source of the language was a regional written koiné of the chanceries of various East Central German principalities. It acquired greater currency as the vehicle for Luther's bible translation and of (mainly northern) German protestantism. Subsequently it underwent a certain degree of deliberate archaization at the hands of some of the people who were involved with the attempts to 'purify' the German language of foreign influence. Especially through the literary works of the Romantics and of the 'Classical' writings of Goethe and Schiller, the language acquired wider recognition as a vehicle of German culture, even in Catholic and Calvinist areas which up to that point had been reluctant to embrace it. And its written use by these writers and by contemporary scientists and philosophers increasingly became the model for correct usage, just as the written (and oral) use of educated Paris and London speech had become the model for correct French and English. At roughly the same time, it also became the vehicle for nationalist, largely anti-Napoleonic and anti-French, sentiments, serving as the symbol of an as yet evanescent national unity. And slowly it came to be used also as a spoken language, especially in the northern areas of Germany and in the cities. With increasing spoken use, it finally could become also a native language, for at least some speakers. (Although the details differ, the development of Modern Standard Italian followed a very similar pattern.)

Whatever its origins, however, a standard language soon becomes an entity in its own right, with a supra-regional sociolinguistic basis. As a consequence, for instance, Modern Standard English no longer is tied to (educated) London speech, not even to Standard British usage. Rather, it is the language of those, mostly educated speakers who use it, no matter where they may be located. And some of its linguistic innovations, such as the "haw-haw" variety of the "King's (or Queen's) English" with [ew] etc. for the [ow] or [əw], etc., of other dialects, seem to have no regional basis whatsoever but are limited to sub-varieties of Standard British English.

As is shown by the case of English, which is used in Great Britain, Ireland, the U.S., Canada, Australia, New Zealand, etc., standard languages are not necessarily restricted to a single country. Similarly, German is the standard language of East and West Germany, as well as Austria, and part of Switzerland; and French is standard not only in France but also in parts of Belgium and Switzerland.

At the same time, countries like Norway, Belgium, and Switzerland have more than one standard language: Nynorsk and Riksmaal/Bokmaal, Flemish and French, and French, German, Italian, and Romantsch, respectively.

Moreover, within France, Provençal is clamoring for recognition as a literary standard language, in addition to Breton and Basque; and similarly in Spain, Catalan and Basque claim special recognition. Examples like these show that standard language and 'national' or officially recognized language are not necessarily identical: Those who advocate special 'language' rather than vernacular status for, say, Provençal and Catalan will point to the fact that these languages have a rich literature of their own and thus are distinct from, say, French and (Castilian) Spanish. On the other hand, those opposed to special recognition will argue that these 'dialects' are not officially recognized as national languages, may not be taught in the schools (because they are not officially recognized), etc.

Finally, beside languages like German, French, English, or even Provençal and Catalan, all of which are current in fairly large areas, there may be more regionally restricted standard languages. And these may coexist with the supra-regional standard languages, as well as the local dialects, with different roles assigned to each of these varieties of speech. For instance, in much of German-speaking Switzerland, Standard German is used only for written communication. A regional standard is said to be used for oral communication between speakers from different areas, while elsewhere the local dialect is employed. A similar multi-layered relationship can be found at a certain period of Indo-Aryan. At this point, Sanskrit was the perhaps most prestigious standard dialect. However, some of the Middle Indo-Aryan dialects had likewise acquired supra-regional, prestige-language currency. This was true especially of Pali and Ardhamagadhi, the sacred languages of much of Buddhism and of Jainism, respectively. In addition, there was a later Middle-Indo-Aryan form of speech, called Apabhraṁśa, which likewise had become a literary prestige language. Finally, the Modern Indo-Aryan languages began to develop their own, more regionally defined, standard varieties which, of course, coexisted with the local varieties.

Standard languages often are written languages. In fact, they often may exist only in written form (which of course may be 'read out' or recited). This was the case for instance for early Standard German, and still is the case for Standard German in much of Switzerland. In such cases, standard language and local dialect or 'vernacular' coexist in a diglossic situation. (Cf. also below, as well as section 14.4 above.) However, in preliterate societies and occasionally also elsewhere, standard languages exist only in spoken form. Compare for instance the regional Standard German of Switzerland. An extreme case is that of Vedic Sanskrit, the language of the oldest sacred texts of Hinduism, which until very recently was not put into written form but handed down only through oral tradition — in spite of the fact that the art of writing has been available in India since at least the third century B.C.

At the same time, the fact that many standard languages exist first and foremost in written form may have important repercussions for linguistic change. One of the most common effects is that of **spelling pronunciation**, that is the replacement of the historically justified pronunciation of a given word by one which is suggested by the spelling.

It is this phenomenon which accounts for fact that Engl. *often* frequently is pronounced as [ɔftən], rather than as inherited [ɔf(ə)n]. Similarly, the initial [h] of Engl. *humble* results from spelling pronunciation, the older pronunciation surviving only in rural dialects, such as South. Amer. Engl. *Be 'umble to the Lord*. The same explanation holds true for Brit. Engl. [hɔb] *herb* vs. North. Amer. Engl. [ərb].

The effect of spelling pronunciation may be even more far-reaching. For instance, the somewhat arbitrary spelling distinction between *ä* and *e* in German has in the long vowels led to a historically unmotivated phonetic distinction between [ɛ̄] and [ē] in certain varieties of Standard German. Note that this distinction is entirely motivated by spelling and has no basis in the historical origin of the words in question. Thus we get [ē] both for words with original *e*-vowel and for words with *e*-vowel resulting from fronting umlaut of earlier *a*; and the same holds true for the pronunciation [ɛ̄]. Compare the examples in (28). (However, the distinction does seem to have a linguistic basis in the fact that some of the local dialects make a distinction between [ɛ̄] and [ē]. Confronted with a spelling distinction *ä* vs. *e,* speakers from these dialects probably identified the *ä*-spelling with their [ɛ̄] and the *e*-spelling with [ē].)

(28)	Proto-Germanic	Modern Standard German		Pronunciation
	*erþō	Erde	'earth'	[ē]
	*basi-	Beere	'berry'	[ē]
	*beran-	ge-bären	'give birth'	[ɛ̄]
	*ahiz-	Ähre	'ear of grain'	[ɛ̄]

Here, then, a previously nonexistent contrast was introduced into the language on the basis of orthography. Even more far-reaching effects of orthography on phonology can be observed in Modern Hebrew.

It has also been observed that standard languages, whether written or not, can have a general retarding effect on linguistic change. For what characterizes standard languages is at least a certain degree of standardization. And such standardization then becomes a measurement of correct speech, to which people purporting to speak the standard language must adhere. Standard languages therefore tend to become 'fettered languages' which tend to retain older patterns more tenaciously than vernaculars, especially when such patterns become 'shibboleths'. For instance, Standard German still retains the option of the inflected genitive, as in (29a) or of the dative singular ending *-e* [-ə], while most of the vernaculars have lost the [-ə] of the dative and have replaced the inflected-genitive construction with 'periphrastic' structures of the type (29b) and (c). Compare the similar retention of the dual number in Sanskrit (section 15.1.2 above). It is this conservative character of standard languages which, if left unchecked, will over the centuries bring about the kind of diglossia that we find in the modern Arabic world or in modern Greece; cf. section 14.4 above.

(29 a)   Das Haus des Vaters   'the father's house'
   b)   Das Haus vom Vater   'the house of the father'
   c)   Dem Vater sein Haus   (lit.: 'to the father his house')

In addition to being conservative or 'defensive', standard languages may also go on the offensive, as it were: It is commonly observed that in many contemporary societies the standard languages are in the process of severely threatening the existence of the local, vernacular dialects, or even of replacing them. This is often attributed to the influence of general education and/or of the increased effectiveness of the mass media in penetrating all layers of society. While these may be contributing factors, there are enough examples of similar developments in earlier times (when these factors played a minor role at best) to suggest that we are dealing with a general tendency, which holds true for all languages, at all stages of their development.

The most celebrated and well-known instance of this development is the spread of the Greek Koiné during the Hellenistic period, leading to the replacement of virtually all of the older local dialects. As a consequence, only one present-day dialect can be traced back to an ancient Greek local dialect, namely Tsaconian, a modern descendant of ancient Laconian. And even Tsaconian has a very heavy admixture of Koiné elements. All the other Modern Greek dialects are descended from the Koiné, although they may preserve a few traces of older local, or at least, regional dialects.

Standard languages, thus, can in effect completely eliminate the effects of centuries of continuous dialect interaction. In a manner of speaking, they wipe clean the 'slate' that has been covered by the isogloss residue of centuries of contact.

15.5 Migration and dialect leveling

The dialect interactions which we have examined so far basically involve 'stationary' dialects, whose speakers are fairly well settled. However, throughout the course of history we find entire linguistic groups

468   15. *Dialectology*

migrating to new territories. In the process they may encounter speakers of very different languages, as for instance in the case of the European settlements in the New World. However, they may also enter territories held by speakers of other dialects of the same language. And as in the case of contact with distinct, foreign languages, there may result a complete (or near-complete) replacement of the native dialects by those of the conquering invaders.

The patterns resulting from such a dialect expansion by conquest in many cases look very similar to what we find in the case of the 'peaceful' spread of dialectal innovations. Here, too, we can often distinguish between something like a focal area and relic areas. (There may even be transitional areas, if the influence of the invaders begins to 'peter out' on the periphery.)

A good illustration of this situation can be seen in Map 11, a simplified account of the ancient Greek dialects: Disregarding the

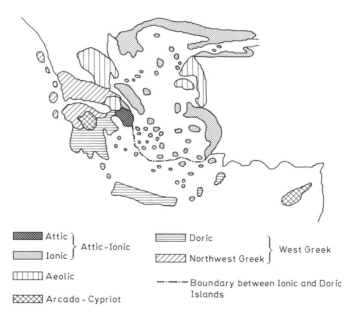

Attic ⎫
Ionic ⎬ Attic-Ionic
⎭

Aeolic

Arcado-Cypriot

Doric ⎫
Northwest Greek ⎬ West Greek
⎭

—·—·— Boundary between Ionic and Doric Islands

Map 11. Ancient Greek dialects

mainland of Asia Minor and its off-shore islands, whose earlier settlement history is less certain, we can observe that a strong wedge of West Greek (i. e. Northwest Greek and Doric) dialects cuts through the territories of Arcado-Cypriot and Aeolic. The still extant members of these two dialect groups are located in typically relic areas: Of the Aeolic dialects, one (Thessalian) is located in the north, at the very periphery of ancient Greek; the other (Boeotian) is wedged into the mountainous and fairly inaccessible area between Northwest Greek, Doric, and Attic-Ionic. In the other dialect group, Arcadian is tucked away into the mountainous, forbidding interior of the Peloponnesus, and Cypriot survives on Cyprus, on the southern periphery of Greece.

From the historical traditions of the Greeks we can discern the reason for this patterning: The West Greek tribes entered Greece as conquerors considerably later than the other Greek tribes. And with their conquest, the West Greek invaders imposed their dialects in the areas which they settled, ousting the older, indigenous Greek dialects in the process. In some cases there is evidence that the ouster was not complete, and that features of the local dialects were incorporated into Doric and Northwest Greek. Evidence for such a development appears to be especially strong in Elean, in the northwest of the Peloponnesus. However, by and large the division between West Greek and the other dialects is quite bold and clear cut, with only a few isoglosses crossing the dialect boundaries between these two groups.

This clear division between neighboring dialects, with a minimum of isoglosses running across the major dialect boundaries, is perhaps the most common outcome of dialect spread by migration. Where we lack sufficient evidence about dialectal prehistory, we can therefore take the existence of such patterns as suggestive of migration, rather than the more 'usual' interaction between stationary dialects. However, since later dialectal interaction can easily give rise to the spread of innovations across these bold, clear-cut isoglosses, such patterns will tend to be short-lived. After a few centuries, then, it may become difficult to decide whether well-defined isoglosses or isogloss bundles that are crossed by a considerable number of less clear-cut isoglosses reflect migration plus subsequent stationary interaction, or the domineering influence of a prestige center in a completely stationary dialect continuum.

In addition to its effects on surrounding dialects and their synchronic relationship, migration can have considerable influence on the speech of the people who are engaged in the migration. It has often been observed that 'colonial' speech, i. e., the speech of groups that have left their homeland and settled in a new territory, has a much smaller degree of linguistic diversity than what is found in dialects which have remained stationary. Thus the differences between the various American English dialects are much smaller than those between the dialects of Great Britain. Moreover, relatively homogeneous dialects occupy relatively large areas in the United States, whereas in Britain, every village may have a dialect markedly different from the neighboring villages. Finally, dialect differences in the Western States, the last-settled area of the United States, are even smaller than on the East Coast or in the Middle West.

To some degree this pattern may reflect the fact that in colonial territory, speakers tend to 'spread out' over a larger territory. But by itself, this factor does not seem to be sufficient to explain the observed differences. Rather, it appears that **dialect leveling**, a process similar to koiné formation (cf. 16.2 below), plays a major role: It is a common occurrence in migration that speakers who in the homeland lived far apart suddenly come into intensive, daily contact. Prior to the migration, local loyalties and patterns of communication prevailed and communication may have been minimal at best. As the result of migration, however, the original local loyalties become reduced in importance, and the job of communicating with the other settlers becomes paramount. Under these circumstances, changes which eliminate excessive differences between different speakers are highly favored, since they make communication and interaction easier. The result is a dialectally much more homogeneous language. The effects of migration, thus, may in some ways be similar to the elimination of dialect differences brought about by the expansion of a supra-regional, standard language at the expense of the local dialects.

Migration, in addition, can lead to a decrease in contact between the speech of the colonizers and that of the homeland. This may often result in a 'relic area' status for colonial speech as compared to the homeland: Innovations which sweep the homeland after the migration may reach colonial territory only incompletely, or not at all. Thus the British English loss of *r* in syllable-final or coda position affected only the New England and Southern states of the U.S., which had remained in closer contact with the homeland. Other areas of the United States remained unaffected. (And as it turns out, it was the speech of these other, *r*-ful areas that eventually became more prestigious and now threatens the originally *r*-less dialects.) Similarly the continued *h*-less pronunciation of *herb* in the United States is an archaism compared to the British spelling pronunciation with *h*. However, here as elsewhere, being a relic area does not offer immunity from all linguistic change. Thus the strongly retroflex pronunciation of American *r,* and changes like the Chicago shift of [æ] to [æə] etc. are testimony to the fact that American English has undergone its own innovatory changes.

Finally, where migration leads to a complete severance of communication between colonial and homeland speech, it can result in the development of quite distinct, different languages: Without continued communication, the separated speech communities are free to change in completely different directions, making independent, unrelated choices out of the plethora of crosslinguistically possible changes. Developments of this sort, then, provide the possible starting point for the interactions between distinct languages which will be discussed in the next chapter.

16. Linguistic contact: Koinés, convergence, pidgins, creoles, language death

Except for koinés, link languages, and the 'substratum' influence of languages on each other, the phenomena covered in this chapter have been subject to systematic investigation only since very recently. As a consequence there is still a great deal of terminological (and no doubt also conceptual) variation and even confusion. Especially the terms pidgin and pidginization have been used almost promiscue in much of the literature, to the point that the heavy admixture of foreign lexical items in English has been referred to as an instance of pidginization.

This chapter intends to show that there are a number of quite distinct patterns of non-lexical interaction between different languages and that there is good reason for believing that the differences between these patterns are correlated with quite distinct sociolinguistic settings.

This is not to say that the distinctions are absolute. Given the great variability of human interaction, it is to be expected that a large number of contact situations will be intermediate in character between (some of) the 'cardinal points' recognized in this chapter. What increases the diversity of the results of contact is the fact that any variety of speech, once established, can be put to different and novel uses. Thus in the preceding chapter we noted the secondary use of some koinés as standard languages. Similarly, there is evidence that pidgins can secondarily be used in koiné or link language function.

It is with these qualifications that the present chapter is offered as a modest attempt at imposing some order on what in the existing literature — and probably also in linguistic actuality — is a very complex subject.

16.1. Link languages, interlanguage, substratum-induced changes, etc.

Just as in dialect continua there are supra-regional forms of speech which facilitate communication across regional differences, so also in the case of distinct languages there often arise supra-regional means of communication. In many cases it is the (more or less) standard varieties of already established languages which serve in this function.

16.1.1. 'Link languages' and their sources

The reasons for the supra-regional use of languages may be quite varied. They may range from dominance by sheer power of conquest, over a combination of political and cultural or technological/commercial predominance, to purely cultural preeminence. Examples of 'conquering languages' are Latin in the Roman Empire and English, French, Spanish in more recent colonial empires. The combination of political and cultural, technological, or commercial predominance is seen in the case of French in eighteenth-century continental Europe, or English in the present, largely post-colonial world. Cultural preeminence was responsible for the great prestige accorded to Greek as a language of wider communication in the Roman Empire — in spite of the fact that the Romans had conquered Greece.

A very different, almost diametrically opposed factor can likewise lead to the selection of a particular language as a supra-regional language, namely its lack of association with any particular linguistic group whose dominance might be perceived as a threat to the identity of other groups. In fact, one might entertain the thought that such 'regionally or communally unmarked' languages are perhaps the optimal solution in situations where political and cultural factors permit a choice. A good case in point is the so-called Sanskrit Renaissance in India:

It has been widely observed that in the early centuries A.D., Sanskrit began to flourish as the unchallenged literary language, common to all the various linguistic and religious groups of India, while earlier its use had been much more restricted. The most plausible explanation for this phenomenon seems to be that this period was marked by an excessive diversification of India in terms of communal, regional, and

religious factors and by a corresponding linguistic diversification. As
a consequence, the following varieties of language coexisted with each
other:

(i) Vedic Sanskrit, the language of traditional religion, used mainly
in recitation and ritual;

(ii) Secular Sanskrit, a spoken and written standard language, used as
a vehicle for scholarship, literature, and administration;

(iii) Various Prakrits which like Sanskrit had become standard languages and which were employed either for very specific types of
secular literature (such as Mahārāṣṭrī for lyrical poetry) or in the
sacred texts of several 'non-traditional' religions;

(iv) A great variety of aborning literary languages which were used only
regionally, including the early forms of the Dravidian languages in
the south of India;

(v) An even greater variety of regional or local vernaculars.

In this highly diversified panorama, secular Sanskrit was the only
language which had no strong regional, communal, or religious affiliations that might have been perceived as a threat to other groups.

Just as elsewhere, linguistic nationalism can act as a counterforce to
the factors just outlined. The relationship and interchange between
these opposing forces can be seen in many of the former European
colonies: On one hand are those who argue for the retention of the
former colonial language as a supra-regional means of communication,
whether as the national language or as an officially recognized co-
national or auxiliary language. Proponents of this view may at least in
part be motivated by a desire to maintain the status which they derived
from the knowledge of the colonialist language, a language not accessible to the uneducated and less privileged. However, another important
factor is that adoption of the foreign language makes it possible to
avoid the often violent consequences of choosing one native linguistic
variety over the others. On the other hand are those who oppose the
former colonial language as an obstacle and insult to their national
identity. Moreover, they can argue that only through the use of indigenous languages will it be possible to make up for the appalling lack of
general education that has been the usual legacy of colonial rule. For
it is unrealistic to expect people to acquire literacy in a language which
is unfamiliar to them. (In actual fact, the arguments for both views are
far from cogent: On one hand, it is in many cases possible to adopt an
indigenous language which is just as 'neutral' as the former colonialists'

language and thus would make it possible to avoid the violent reactions which meet the selection of a regionally, communally, etc., 'marked' language. On the other hand, even if an indigenous language is chosen, that language quite frequently will be unfamiliar to the speakers of other indigenous languages. These speakers, then, will still have to acquire literacy through a non-native language.)

The case of modern India is especially interesting in respect to the interaction between linguistic nationalism and other factors. During the time of British rule, Hindi (in its religiously neutral, 'Hindustani' variety) increasingly came to be the symbol of national unity over against the English of the foreign oppressor. And Hindustani was learned widely throughout India, even in Bengal and the Dravidian south. After independence, however, a great deal of opposition arose to the attempt to replace English by Hindi as the national language. There are several reasons for this reaction.

One of these may be been the following: Independence had been accompanied by the division of former British India into two countries, Pakistan and India. The former had been established as a Muslim state and had made Urdu, the Muslim variety of Hindi-Urdu or Hindustani, its national language. By way of polarization and because Hindi enjoyed greater literary prestige than Hindustani, India opted for Hindi as its designated national language. But unlike Hindustani, Hindi was sociolinguistically marked as a Hindu language. In a secular state with a sizable Muslim minority, the selection of Hindi would consequently have to meet with a certain resistance.

But perhaps the most important factor was the fact that the use of Hindi as national language was felt to constitute a threat by the largest linguistic community to impose its political dominance over the rest of India. This fear was especially great in Bengal and the Dravidian south, areas where it was felt that the regional languages had a far greater literary tradition and prestige than Hindi.

Whatever their motivations, however, for the opponents of Hindi, English became an ideal alternative. For after the departure of the British, it ceased to be a potent threat within India, being natively spoken by only a very small and politically insignificant community.

At the same time, there continue to be strong and outspoken advocates of Hindi, not merely within the territory in which Hindi is spoken natively. As a consequence, the issue of whether Hindi or English should serve as the national language of India remains unresolved to the present day. (Notice that at this point, Sanskrit no longer offers a realistic alternative as national language, since it has become too closely identified as the language of conservative Hinduism.)

Whatever their origin, supra-regional languages may serve many different functions, ranging from national language to merely auxiliary status. A useful term that covers all of this range is **link language**. What distinguishes link languages from other varieties of speech is that they are unmodified, preexisting, and (generally) standard languages, at least in origin.

16.1.2. Interference and interlanguage

As time progresses, link languages may well be modified, often to a considerable degree. This development can be illustrated by the example of Indian English, a language which for most speakers differs considerably from the British model.

What is perhaps most easily affected is the vocabulary, including fixed collocations which would have to be specially listed in the dictionary. The reasons for this often are quite straightforward, such as the need to refer to objects, concepts, etc., for which there are no ready-made terms in the language chosen as a link language. Lexical borrowing, with its various routines of nativization, may serve to bridge this gap as in the Indian English examples of (1a). Some of these borrowings even spread to the English used outside of India; cf. (1b). However, not all lexical innovations are motivated by need. For instance, the Indian English forms on the left of (1c) replace 'native' English expressions like the ones on the right.

(1a) saree
       tahsil   (an administrative unit)
       lathi   'a long bamboo stick used by Indian police for crowd control'
       twice-born   (calque of Skt. *dvi-ja-* 'twice-born; member of the three upper varnas or "castes"')
   b) khaki
       yoga
   c) key bunch   bunch of keys
       God-love   love of God/God's love

However, also grammar may be affected. This is perhaps most strikingly the case in the phonology of Indian English, which is characterized by large-scale substitutions. Among these are the processes which in section 14.3.1 above (ex. (20/22)) were observed as serving to nativize lexical borrowings from English and other foreign languages. As a consequence, expressions like *I am going to the station* may be pronounced as in (2). (In the following examples, only retroflex segments are specially characterized, as in *ṭ, ḍ*. Dentals are left unmarked.)

(2) [aī ēm gōiŋ ṭū da (i)sṭēṣan]

But also the areas of morphology and morphosyntax may be affected. Thus the expression in (2) is more likely to come out without the article, as in (2'). Yet a further deviation from the native varieties of English can be observed in (2").

(2') [aī ēm gōiŋ ṭū (i)sṭēṣan]

(2") [aī ēm ǰasṭ naū gōiŋ ṭū (i)sṭēṣan]

The variant in (2") follows from a tendency toward the morphosyntactic correspondences in (3). (Differences in pronunciation are here ignored.) Though the use of *just now* in examples like (2") and (3c) at this point apparently is not (yet) obligatory, we can observe here the makings of a complete and systematic shift in the formation of the present-tense system.

(3)	British English	Indian English
a)	I know this	I am knowing this
b)	I go to school	I am going to school
c)	I am going home	I am just now going home

What seems to be operative in such 'non-need' modifications of link languages is the same principle which can be observed in second-language acquisition in general. This principle has often been called **interference**, i. e., the influence of one's native language on the structure of the acquired, second language. Thus Ind. Engl. *God-love* may be formed on the native model of Skt. *dēva-bhakti-*, a compound of *dēva-* 'God' and *bhakti-* 'devotion'. And the phonological substitutions in (2) impose on English the phonological structure of Hindi and other South Asian languages.

However, the concept of interference will not be sufficient to account for the correspondences in (3). True, the substitution in (3b) can be explained as a morphological calque of the Hindi expression in (4) or similar structures in other South Asian languages. Here the Hindi participial ending *-tā* is translated by the English participial ending *-ing,* and the auxiliary *hū̃* is matched by its English counterpart *am.* The explanation is similar for (3a).

(4) mɛ̃ (i)skūl ǰā — tā   hū̃
    'I' 'school' 'go'   pple. AUX
    'I go to school'

However, there is no pattern which would directly motivate the type (3c), whose Hindi counterpart is given in (5). For a literary translation of the auxiliary *rahā* of this construction would be 'remained/remaining'.

(5) mɛ̃ ghar ǰā   rahā hū̃
    'I' 'home' 'go' AUX AUX
    'I am going home'

Rather, the type (3c) seems to be motivated as an attempt to retain the English distinction between (3b) and (3c) and — perhaps even more importantly — the corresponding South Asian distinction between (4) and (5), within a grammar which encodes (4) as *I am going to school.* The *just now* which may optionally be used also in the British English version of (3c), then, seems to have been 'recruited' in order to achieve that goal.

Examples like *key bunch* are even more complex: It is not clear that there are any native, Indian precedents for this construction. Rather, it seems that an English pattern of compounding has been extended to new formations.

Modifications of the 'target language' in second-language acquisition thus are not always explainable as resulting exclusively from interference. They can more satisfactorily be accounted for as arising from the fact that language learners must formulate for themselves a grammatical rule system which will account for the target language. The formulation of that rule system, then, will be influenced not only by the speakers' native language but also by their — correct or incorrect — assumptions about the nature of the target language. And in the process, novel structures may arise which are unprecedented in both the native and the target language. To account for this different conceptualization of the second-language learning process and to differentiate it from the older conceptualization as 'interference', the term **interlanguage** has been introduced. It is this term which will be used in the remainder of this chapter.

While interlanguage plays a role in all second-language acquisition, its effects ordinarily are relatively short-lived and limited to individual learners. Moreover, different learners may have rather different interlanguages, even if their native language is the same. However, in cases where the second language serves as a link language and is used in that capacity by generations of speakers, there is a greater chance that interlanguage phenomena may become a permanent feature. This is especially true if the target language is used as in South Asia — as a means of communication primarily between speakers of mutually unintelligible indigenous languages, and not with native speakers of the target language. In situations of this sort, interlanguage phenomena are less likely to be eliminated under the corrective influence of the target language. As a consequence they can become cumulative and the results can become '**institutionalized**' as the linguistic norm of an entire speech community.

16.1.3. Code switching and code mixing

Language contact may lead to several other responses. But these seem to have a lesser effect on linguistic change than interlanguage.

One common response, found especially in persons who are fluently bilingual, consists in switching back and forth between the coexisting languages, such that portions of a given sentence or utterance are in one language, other parts in another language. This process is commonly referred to as **code switching**. The examples in (6) illustrate how code switching works. Example (6a) gives the (pure) Hindi version, while (6b-f) present code switched variants, with the English portions italicized for easier recognition.

> (6a) kahtē hẽ ki ājkal   bahut lōgõ   kō yah
>   'saying' 'are' 'that' 'nowadays' 'many' 'people' 'to' 'that'
>   nahĩ pasand   hẽ ki   rāj̆ nārāin   pāgal kē samān
>   'not' 'pleasing' 'is' 'that' 'Raj Narain' 'fool' 'like'
>   ẽkṭ kar rahā hẽ
>   'act'   AUX 'is'
>   'They say that many people don't like it that Raj Narain is acting like a fool'

b) kahtē hɛ̃ ki ājkal bahut lōgõ kō yah nahī pasand hɛ̃ ki *rāǰ nārāin ɛ̄kṭs lāik a fūl*

c) kahtē hɛ̃ ki *nāvadēz̧ mɛnī pīpal ḍōnṭ lāik iṭ* ki rāǰ nārāin pāgal kē samān ɛ̄kṭ kar rahā hɛ̃

d) kahtē hɛ̃ ki ājkal *mɛnī pīpal ḍōnṭ lāik iṭ dɛṭ*/ki *raǰ nārāin ɛ̄kṭs lāik a fūl*

e) kahtē hɛ̃ ki ājkal bahut lōgõ kō yah nahī pasand hɛ̃ ki *rāǰ nārāin ɛ̄kṭs* pāgal kē samān

f) kahtē hɛ̃ ki ājkal bahut *pīpal ḍōnṭ lāik iṭ* ...

There seem to be definite, probably cross-linguistic parameters determining the syntactic points at which code switching can take place: Switching occurs most easily at major syntactic boundaries (between clauses), as in (b) and (c). (Interestingly, the break may appear both before and after the 'complementizer' *ki* 'that'. That is, *ki* seems to act as a 'linker' which belongs neither to the matrix clause nor to the dependent clause.) Example (d) illustrates the next common pattern, where the break occurs between an adverbial or similarly 'non-essential' element and the rest of the clause. The type (e), with a break between more 'essential' or 'indispensible' constituents of the clause, is much rarer. Finally, examples like (f), in which the break occurs in the middle of a constituent, border on the ungrammatical. (The examples in (6) illustrate another common phenomenon in code switching: Switching tends to be limited to syntax and morphology, without a comparable switch in phonology. And the phonology which is employed throughout such code-switched utterances usually is the property of the speaker's native or otherwise more dominant language.)

Many linguists recognize a parallel phenomenon of **code mixing**. While code switching takes place on the syntactic level, code mixing appears to be a lexical phenomenon. The phenomenon can be illustrated by the *ɛ̄kṭ kar rahā hɛ̃* of (6a), where *ɛ̄kṭ* is Engl. *act*, while *kar rahā hɛ̃* 'is doing' is Hindi and serves to make *ɛ̄kṭ* usable in a Hindi sentence. Examples like this show that code mixing consists of the insertion of 'content words' from one language into the grammatical structure of another.

It is difficult to distinguish this process from lexical borrowing. However, the term code mixing may perhaps be useful to refer to certain varieties of language use in which the admixture of foreign elements is much heavier than in 'normal' borrowing situations, so heavy in fact that virtually all content words are of foreign manufacture, while the native language furnishes only the phonology, morphology, and basic vocabulary. Such varieties of language use are currently quite common in South Asia. In most cases, they are limited to individuals and do not appear to have lasting consequences.

However, it appears that in certain areas of South America, a heavily code-mixed language use has become institutionalized as the norm of a particular linguistic community: At the border between certain Spanish and Quechua speaking territories, a new, **mixed language** is said to have arisen whose vocabulary by and large is Spanish, while grammar and basic vocabulary are Quechua. Although cases of this type appear to be quite rare, they seem to cast doubt on the claim of 14.6 above that lexical borrowing, even on a massive scale, is highly unlikely to lead to a change in the genetic affiliation of a given language. But interestingly, even in this extreme case, genetic relationship as it is understood in historical linguistics is not affected. For such a relationship is determined by the evidence of basic vocabulary and structure; cf. chapter 18 below. The fact that these elements are of Quechua origin would therefore be interpreted as indicating that the language is genetically Quechua and that the heavy Spanish component results from borrowing. And this interpretation seems to be in complete agreement with the historical evidence.

Nevertheless, it is also true that the heavy borrowing involved in code mixing can occasionally have considerable and lasting linguistic consequences. Code switching, on the other hand, does not seem to have been institutionalized anywhere, leading to new varieties of language. Perhaps it plays a certain role in the transfer of syntactic patterns from one language to another. But at this point, even this hypothesis cannot be substantiated by any persuasive evidence.

16.1.4. 'Substratum'

In contradistinction to code mixing and especially to code switching, the effects of interlanguage quite commonly are institutionalized, leading to distinctively new varieties of language. Examples in recent, observable history include Indian English (cf. 16.1.2) and West African English, both used as link languages in their respective areas and both showing phonological, syntactic, and lexical peculiarities which markedly differentiate them from native varieties of English. A less radical effect of interlanguage (between Yiddish and English) can be seen in the special variety of English used in New York by the descendants of

Jewish immigrants. (Institutionalization here seems to be attributable to the fact that until relatively recently, communication with speakers outside the Jewish ghetto was fairly limited. As a consequence, many interlanguage phenomena remained unchecked by the corrective model of the target language.)

Extrapolating from such known cases, many linguists have postulated similar developments in earlier, sometimes prehistoric contacts. The scenario most commonly envisaged is one where contact results from invasion and where one language (usually that of the invaders) eventually replaces one or more indigenous languages. In such situations, it has been claimed, the '**substratum**' of the indigenous languages can have as systematic and far-reaching an effect on the language of the conquerors as, say, the South Asian languages had on Indian English. (Note that the term 'substratum' here is used in a somewhat different meaning from the one introduced in section 14.5.2 above. This different use of the term will be limited to the present discussion.)

Thus it has been claimed that the far-reaching Western Romance weakening, as in (7) below, is to be attributed to a Celtic substratum. For, it is said, the area in which lenition is found is coterminous with the territory settled by the Celts before the Roman expansion. Moreover, similar weakenings are found in attested Celtic languages, such as Old Irish and Middle Welsh; cf. (8). (Compare also section 5.2 above.)

(7)	Latin	Spanish	French	
	amicus	amigo[-ɣ-]	amiØ	'friend'
	vidēre	veØer	voiØr	'see'
(8)	PIE	Old Irish	Middle Welsh	
	tewtā	tūath [θ]	tu**d**	'people'

Similarly the change of Lat. *ū* to Fr. [ü] has been attributed to a Celtic substratum. For again, the Celts held Gaul before the Roman invasion, and a fronting change of **u* is found in Welsh; cf. (9).

(9)	PIE	Middle Welsh	
	*uksen-	ych [ɨx]	'ox'
	*tū	ti [ti]	'you (sg.)'

And the fact that Castilian Spanish and certain Southern French dialects have a change of *f* to *h* (> Ø) in examples like (10) has been explained in terms of a Basque substratum. For, it is said, Basque had no *f* at the point that this change occurred.

(10)   Latin   Spanish
     filius   hijo   'son'
     farina   harina   'flour'

These examples are fairly typical of traditional 'substratist' explanations. However, they also suffer from the typical weaknesses of many, perhaps most, of these explanations.

For instance, it is by no means clear that the lenition found in the relatively late-attested Insular Celtic of Old Irish and Middle Welsh was a feature also of all the Continental Celtic dialects of Gaul and Iberia (which died out very early). Moreover, weakening is found also in many Italian dialects that are spoken in areas not originally settled by the Celts.

As for the French change of *ū* to *ü,* the Celtic fronting of *u*-vowels was restricted to Welsh. And there is in this language no evidence for a front-rounded outcome (although it is possible to invoke such an outcome as an intermediate stage). And here again the change in question has parallels in other Romance dialects where Celtic influence is unlikely to have played a role, such as the Portuguese dialect of Saõ Miguel in the Azores.

The 'substratist' case is perhaps best for the change of *f* to *h*. For the dialects of Spanish and French in which it occurs are both close neighbors of Basque. However, the same change is found also in Italian dialects which are far removed from Basque. Moreover, the change of *f* to *h* is limited to the environment before (non- *u*) vowels. It is difficult to see how this restriction could be accounted for in terms of a Basque substratum, for the Basque absence of *f* appears not to have been environmentally restricted.

At the same time, note that the above changes are by no means unusual and thus do not require an 'unusual' or 'special' substratum explanation. They might therefore just as well be the result of independent innovation: Intervocalic weakening is so wide-spread that it would be more noteworthy to find a language which did not undergo it at some point of its historical development than to find a language which did. The fronting of *u*-vowels likewise is quite common; cf. section 8.3 above. Finally, special weakening developments in labials, though not as common as medial weakening, nevertheless are found in a number of other languages; cf. section 7.3.7. Within these general conceptual categories of sound change, the phenomena in question receive a more satisfactory explanation than in terms of alleged substratal influence.

Perhaps the most striking example of the way in which substratist 'explanations' fail to explain anything is that of retroflexion, a phenomenon most consistently attributed to substratal influence, wherever it is found. This approach has been carried to an extreme in the case of the Sicilian dialectal development of *tr* to *ʈ(r)*: After finding that no known language could be held responsible for this change, one linguist claimed that it must be attributed to an unknown 'substratum X'. Substratist 'explanations' of this sort have to a large extent been responsible for the fact that the phonetic processes leading to retroflexion (cf. 5.1.6) have been largely ignored in traditional handbooks on historical linguistics.

The case for substratist explanations might appear stronger in the case of systematic, overall structural changes such as those brought about by Grimm's Law. For the systematic rearrangement of the English obstruent system in Indian English seems to provide a thought-provoking parallel. However, in the case of Grimm's Law it is difficult to work out what kind of (unknown, unattested!) substratum might be held responsible for the changes in question. One might toy with the idea that the change of voiceless stops to fricatives was brought about by an absence of the corresponding segments in the substrate language. However, the fact that the voiced stops change exactly into such voiceless-stop segments casts considerable doubt on this assumption. Put differently, it would be difficult to explain in terms of a substratum why substitutions were made as in (11a) and not in the more natural and plausible manner of (11b). (For the substitution *dh* ⇒ *þ*, cf. the opposite change in Engl. *þ* ⇒ Hindi *th*, etc. in which the feature 'fricative' is equated with the friction noise of aspirates. Note that the Proto-Indo-European aspirates, although written as voiced *dh* etc., may well not have been distinctively voiced.) A preferable explanation of Grimm's Law therefore would seem to be in terms of a chain shift, as suggested in Chapter 8 above.

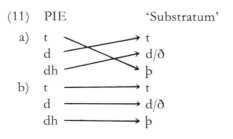

(11)   PIE   'Substratum'

    a)   t   t
          d   d/ð
          dh   þ
    b)   t   ⟶   t
          d   ⟶   d/ð
          dh ⟶   þ

The conclusion therefore must be that although examples like Indian English demonstrate that interlanguage may result in far-reaching structural changes, many (perhaps most) of the commonly alleged prehistoric instances of 'substratal' changes are quite dubious. It is in the more specific areas of koiné formation, convergence, and — to some degree — in the development of pidgins and similar varieties of language that interlanguage plays a more clearly relevant role.

16.2. Koinés

A special type of contact situation, found in many areas of the world, is characterized by the following features: (i) The varieties of speech which are in contact with each other are closely related languages or even mutually intelligible dialects. (ii) For cultural or political reasons, these linguistic varieties are considered by their speakers to be of about equal prestige, each being the proper linguistic vehicle for a group with its own cherished identity. (iii) No outside language suggests itself as a link language. These conditions seem to be the most ideal for the development of **koinés**. (Alternative designations include the term 'trade language'. However, this term is used also in reference to link languages in general, or even to pidgins, etc.)

Put simply, koinés may be defined as deregionalized regional languages or dialects which because of their **deregionalization** become potential vehicles for supra-regional communication in areas meeting the above description. The mechanism for this deregionalization, in turn, seems to lie in interlanguage.

The classical example of koiné is the Hellenistic Koiné (writ large), the *koinē glōssa* 'common language' of the Greece of Alexander the Great and subsequent times. This language transcended the local languages (or rather, dialects) of the various Greek city states and confederations of such states, with their previously jealously guarded separate political, cultural, and linguistic identities.

In nature, this Koiné was essentially a (partially) de-Atticized Attic: It was based on the dialect of Athens, a city which had become one of the most important, perhaps the most important state in Greece, both culturally (in terms of its arts, literature, and philosophy) and politically (in terms of heading the Attic League, the main line of defense against the Persians). Even so, without de-Atticization, its dialect might well not have been acceptable as a link language to the other Greek city states, since accepting it would have smacked too much of accepting also the political predominance or hegemony of Athens. Fortunately however, a de-Atticized version arose. The origin of this form of speech may well have lain in the important harbor of Athens. Here Attic came into daily contact with virtually all the other Greek dialects, especially with Ionic; and therefore an interlanguage variety of Attic could readily develop. The language received further impetus from the contact between different sea-faring Greek city states in the Attic League, where beside Attic, Ionic dialects again played a major role. Whatever its early origins however, this non-standard de-Atticized Attic was ideally suited as a link language, since it could be looked at as unaffiliated with any of the competing standard local dialects.

Some examples may illustrate the way in which the de-Atticization of Attic was accomplished.

While the majority of Greek dialects have -*ss*- as the outcome of earlier -*ky*-, -*khy*-, and other clusters, Attic has -*tt*-, a development shared only by a few dialects of relatively minor importance. (These include neighboring Boeotian and parts of neighboring Euboean, as well as Thessalian and Cretan.) The Koiné instead generally offers the -*ss*- of the majority of dialects, as in the examples of (12a). Similarly, older -*rs*- was assimilated to -*rr*- in Attic and a few other dialects which again were of relatively minor significance (West Ionic, Arcadian, Northwest Greek). Elsewhere, the unchanged -*rs*- prevailed. And here again the Koiné went with the majority pattern, against the idiosyncratically Attic usage; cf. (12b). Attic, together with parts of Ionic, had changed earlier *-*ayw*- into -*ā*- before vowel, whereas the majority of dialects had -*ai*-. And again, the Koiné sided with the majority; cf. (12c). Most of the Greek languages had lost the dual number as an inflectional category, whereas Attic had retained it. The Koiné went with the non-Attic majority by replacing the dual with the plural.

	Attic	Koiné	
(12a)	glōtta	glōssa	'tongue'
	phulattō	phulassō	'guard, watch'
	tettares	tessares	'four'
b)	arrēn	arsēn	'male'
c)	elāā	elaiā	'olive'

In all of the cases cited so far, it might be argued that the forms adopted in the Koiné are simply Ionic in origin. For they are found in all (or most) of the Ionic dialects. Moreover, in spite of their differences, Ionic and Attic are closely related linguistically, as well as close geographic neighbors. And there is a good deal of evidence for close literary, economic, etc., contact between the speakers of Attic and Ionic. Finally, there is one peculiarly Attic-Ionic change, namely that of *$\bar{a}$ to *$\bar{e}$ (with certain environmental restrictions). And here the Koiné is in general agreement with both Attic and Ionic, and not with the pattern of all the other dialects (which had retained unshifted *$\bar{a}$). It might therefore be claimed that the Koiné is simply an Ionicized Attic, that the non-Attic features of the Koiné are Ionic and that their agreement with what is offered by the majority of other dialects is simply fortuitous.

However, some evidence suggests that the situation was more complex. Most telling is the correspondece of Attic *-eōs* : Koiné *-āos*. For *-āos* not only is non-Attic, it also is non-Ionic. Compare (13). (Some Ionic dialects may agree with Attic in having *-eōs*. For the change of earlier *-ēos* to *-eōs* see section 6.3, ex. (26).)

(13) | Attic | Ionic | Koiné | |
|------|------|------|------|
| leōs | lc ᵔs | lāos | 'people' |
| neōs | nē᷍ | nāos | 'temple' |

The model for the *a*-vocalism of the Koiné, then, clearly lies in the *$\bar{a}$* of the other dialects. The exact motivation for this particular choice is less clear.

Perhaps the *$\bar{a}$* received special support from Homeric *lāos* and from the famous *nāos* or 'temple' of near-by Delphi. For in the Homeric epics and in connection with Delphi these words were used with special frequency and/or significance.

However, there may have been another motivation for giving up the Attic type *leōs*: As noted above, elsewhere the Attic *e*-vocalism for old *$\bar{a}$* was left untouched in the Koiné. In the forms of (13), however, the vocalism was accompanied by a peculiar inflection which differed from the normal inflection of the '*o*-stems' to which these words belonged; cf. (14). Moreover, the aberrant inflection was limited to just a handful of nouns. Finally, it was idiosyncratically Attic and lacked any precedent in the other dialects. The Koiné type in *-āos*, on the other hand, was in complete agreement with the ordinary inflection of *o*-stems; cf. (14').

(14) Attic

sg.	N	hippos	leōs
	G	hippou	leō
	D	hippō(i)	leō(i)
	A	hippon	leōn
pl.	N	hippoi	leōi
	G	hippōn	leōn
	D	hippois	leō(i)s
	A	hippous	leōs
		'horse'	'people'

(14′) Koiné

sg.	N	hippos	lāos
	G	hippou	lāou
	D	hippō(i)	lāō(i)
	A	hippon	lāon
pl.	N	hippoi	lāoi
	G	hippōn	lāōn
	D	hippois	lāois
	A	hippous	lāous

Note however that also the Ionic type *lēos, nēos* would fit in perfectly with the usual *o*-stem inflection. The choice of non-Ionic *lāos, nāos* therefore cannot have been governed entirely by morphological considerations. Still, whatever the explanation of this particular choice, we must conclude that the development of the Koiné was a process of de-Atticization, not just of Ionicization.

This development should of course not be conceived of as a conscious one, set in motion in order to de-Atticize, but rather as a slow process of (semi-conscious) selection from the non-Attic features which had fortuitously arisen through the Attic interlanguage used by native speakers of other Greek dialects.

We can see similar processes at work in the development of various African koinés, especially in the Bantu languages. What is interesting is that in many cases the deregionalization is brought about by **selective simplification**, the reduction or elimination of just those grammatical features in terms of which the various languages and dialects involved exhibit the largest disagreement. (It is possible to see selective simplification also in the Koiné replacement of Attic *leōs* by *lāos*.)

For instance, there is good reason to believe that the Bantu languages originally had either a pitch accent which was not bound to any particular syllable, or something like the tonal system of languages like Chinese. However, as the result of linguistic change, the synchronic accent or tone systems differ considerably from one Bantu language to the other. Languages like Swahili and Lingala, which appear to have originated as koinés, instead show a stress accent which is fixed to the next-to-last (penult) syllable of all words. The reason for this simplificatory development may very well have been the fact that by dropping a feature which is idiosyncratically different from language to language, and by substituting in its stead a completely predictable feature, these languages achieved a degree of deregionalization which made them more suitable as koinés. (In addition, there is evidence that these languages underwent some of the simplificatory developments in the 'concord' system which will be discussed presently.)

While in the case of Swahili and Lingala we must depend on speculation, since the developments in question took place prehistorically, similar examples of selective simplification are found in observable history. These include varieties of Swahili and Lingala which have become koinés more recently, after the standard varieties of these languages had acquired the status of 'established' languages in their own right.

These koinés exhibit a considerable simplification in the system of 'concord' prefixes, the area of their morphology which exhibits the greatest degree of idiosyncratic differentiation, both within given languages and across linguistic boundaries: The Bantu languages are characterized by a complex system of nominal classes which are morphologically marked by prefixes. (For some examples cf. section 14.3.3.) Adnominal modifiers (pronouns, possessives, adjectives), as well as verbs must show 'agreement' with these noun class prefixes. Agreement markers, however, in many cases are not identical but may differ considerably, as in the Lingala examples of (15) and (16). (Singular formations are given under (a), plurals under (b). CL = 'class prefix', AG = agreement marker, TA = tense/aspect marker.)

(15a) **mw**-ana **o**-   yo **mo**-lamu **a**-   ko- kweya
      CL   AG   AG   AG TA
      'child' 'this' 'beautiful' 'fall'
      'this beautiful child will fall'

  b) **ba**-na **ba**-ye **ba**-lamu **ba**- ko- kweya
      CL   AG   AG   AG TA

(16a) Ø-ndako e-ye e- lamu e- ko-kweya
    CL   AG AG   AG TA
    'house'
    'this beautiful house will fall'

b) Ø-ndako i- ye n- damu e- ko-kweya
    CL   AG   AG AG TA

(The alternation between *l* and *d* in (16a/b) is regular.)

Moreover, agreement markers differ considerably across linguistic boundaries. Contrast the Lingala examples in (15) and (16) with their Swahili counterparts in (15′) and (16′).

(15′a) m-toto hu-yu m-zuri a- ta- nguka
    CL   AG   AG   AG TA
    'this beautiful child will fall'

b) wa-toto ha-wa wa-zuri wa- ta- nguka
    CL   AG   AG   AG TA

(16′a) Ø-nyumba hi- i n- zuri i- ta- nguka
    CL   AG AG   AG TA
    'this beautiful house will fall'

b) Ø-nyumba hi-zi n- zuri zi- ta- nguka
    CL   AG AG   AG TA

Given these disagreements, it should not come as a surprise that in the course of deregionalization, koinés based on these languages often radically simplify the system. Compare the Kinshasa Lingala examples in (15″) and (16″) with the Standard Lingala and Swahili versions of (15/16) and (15′/16′).

(15″a) mw-ana o-yo ma-lamu a- ko-kweya
    CL   AGTA

b) ba-na o-yo ma-lamu ba-ko-kweya
    CL   AGTA

(16″a) Ø-ndako o-yo ma-lamu e- ko-kweya
    CL   AGTA

b) Ø-ndako o-yo ma-lamu e- ko-kweya
    CL   AGTA

As these examples show, agreement now is marked only on the verb. The demonstrative pronoun and the adjective, on the other hand, no longer show agreement but offer an invariable 'prefix'. And in many cases, the lack of variability in that prefix leads to its being reanalyzed as part of the following root. In some of the Bantu koinés, such as Kituba, the process has gone even farther and has led to the virtual elimination of the whole noun class system. (Here, the one remaining productive use of nominal prefixation has the function of marking plurals, as in *masua*, pl. *ba-masua* 'boat : boats'.)

What is interesting and shows that simplification here is a selective process is the fact that there has been no similar reduction in other areas of the morphology. Thus the Bantu tense/aspect system remains considerably more intact than the class prefixes; cf. the Kinshasa Lingala examples in (15″/16″). And derivational suffixes seem to be the most resistant to change, perhaps because here the intra- and interdialectal differences are smaller and less striking, and thus less in need of deregionalization.

16.3. Convergence

At least until recently, the ideal of modern western societies has been that of the nation-state with a single national language. True, there are a few countries like Switzerland and Belgium with a clear policy of bi- or multilingualism. However, the linguistically inspired strife or even violence which keeps flaring up in Belgium demonstrates how precarious the notion of bilingualism tends to be in modern western society.

In many ways, however, it is this aversion to bilingualism which is anomalous in the world's languages. Large areas of the world are habitually bilingual. (Henceforth the term **'bilingualism'** will be used to cover both bi- and multilingualism.) These include not only the Balkans, South Asia, much of Africa and the New World, but even premodern, especially medieval Europe (cf. 16.3.6 below).

For such a long-standing tradition of bilingualism to arise and to continue, however, one condition must be fulfilled: The languages in contact must not be in such a relation to each other that one is a strong superstratum or substratum which would quickly oust the other(s). (Cf. 14.5.2 for the terms 'strong' and 'weak' superstratum and substratum.) For such a relationship would bring about a quick end to bilingualism. Put differently, a long-standing tradition of bilingualism is most likely to come about and to persist where the languages in contact are more or less equal in strength, especially if they are also more or less equal in prestige. In societies of this sort, the use of different languages in many ways is comparable to the use of different social or regional dialects in monolingual societies: Different varieties of speech are appropriate under different social conditions. One might be used at home, another on the job, a third in religious contexts, etc. But to a large extent their spheres of usage are mutually exclusive; each has its own appropriate 'niche' in society.

16.3.1. Convergence defined

It is in bilingual societies of this sort that a phenomenon can be observed which commonly is referred to as **convergence**, the increasing agreement of languages not only in terms of vocabulary (which may in fact remain quite distinct; cf. 16.3.5 below), but especially in regard to features of their overall structure.

Depending on the nature of their prestige relationship, the convergence between different languages may be **mutual** (between adstratal languages) or **unidirectional** (in an unequal prestige relationship). Situations of the latter kind share certain similarities with the so-called substratum changes discussed in section 16.1.4. However, in the case of convergence, the bilingual contact is much more prolonged. (Still, since length of time is a relative concept, the difference between these two types of contact is probably a gradient one.)

The fact that bilingual contact is prolonged, often extending over more than a millennium, has important consequences. For interlanguage in such situations can have a much more profound effect than in the fairly short-lived 'substratum' situations. This is not simply because interlanguage has a longer time span within which it can operate. Rather, with the passage of time, a syndrome of the following sort will arise: Let the interaction begin with two languages, A and B, producing the interlanguages A^B, based on native knowledge of language A and acquired knowledge of B, and its counterpart B^A. These interlanguages, in turn, will come to interact with each other, as well as with relatively unchanged A and B. The result will be a build-up of increasingly complex and 'mixed' interlanguages. Cf. the illustration in (17) which ignores the continued coexistence of earlier, less 'mixed' varieties. Where the convergence is mutual, it may therefore in the long run be impossible to determine which of the features shared by given languages originated where.

(17) A   B

A^B B^A

A^{BA} A^{BB} B^{AA} B^{AB}

A^{BAA} A^{BAB} A^{BBA} A^{BBB} B^{AAA} B^{AAB} B^{ABA} B^{ABB}

etc.

Note that for convergence of this sort to take place it is not necessary for all speakers of the languages involved to be bilingual, or for all dialectal areas of these languages to be bilingual. For the results of convergence can spread to new speakers and to new dialect areas by the same process which permits other linguistic innovations to spread. (Compare the preceding chapter.)

16.3.2. Unidirectional convergence — Czech and German

Unidirectional convergence evidently is not as complex as mutual convergence, for the direction of change is clearly discernible. It is therefore convenient to start the illustrations with this development.

Among the Slavic languages, Czech stands out by having word-initial accent; cf., e. g., (18). (On this point, Czech is joined by Sorbian which significantly enough is located right within (East) German territory.) It shows unusual developments also in its vowel system; cf. the changes in (19). (Note that the diphthongization of older [ɨ] is limited to the colloquial language.) Moreover, it has completely eliminated the contrast between palatalized *l'* and plain (or velarized) *ł*; cf. (20).

(18) Cz. stárica   : Ru. stárica   'old woman'
           stárina   :   stariná   'ancient times'

(19) Cz. moucha   : OCS mūxa   'fly (insect)'
           mejt [ey]   :   myti [ɨ]   'wash'
           Búh [ū]   : OCz. Buoh   'God'
           bílý [ī]   :   bielý   'white'

(20) Cz. lid   : Pol. l'ud   'people'
           locika   :   łocyka   'lettuce (*lactuca*)'

Now, beginning with the thirteenth century, the Czechs increasingly came under the sway of German-speaking powers. The result was an extended period of bilingualism, mainly on the Czech side, which lasted until the 1930s. It is therefore possible to argue that the developments in (18/20) resulted from contact with German. For German usually has word-initial accent. The German dialects which could exert the greatest influence on Czech had diphthongization of the old high vowels and subsequent contraction of the diphthongs *uo* and *ie;* cf. (21). And these German dialects do not have a contrast between palatalized and velar *l*.

(21)   MHG   hūs   > NHG   Haus   'house'
              līb   >   Leib   'body'
              guet [uǝ] >   gut [ū]   'good'
              lieb [iǝ] >   lieb [ī]   'dear'

More than that, it has been observed that the German changes in (21) took place earlier than the corresponding Czech developments. And perhaps most important, we have the evidence of Jan Hus, the fifteenth-century reformer and apostle of Czech nationalism, who complained that his compatriots were pronouncing the velarized, 'dark' *ł* as a 'clear' *l*, indistinguishable from the old palatalized *l'* [l], 'more Teutonicorum', i. e., in the manner of the Germans.

16.3.3.   Sprachbund — the Balkans

Convergence has even more far-reaching and interesting effects in areas where adstratal languages are in long-standing bilingual contact. Under these circumstances, languages which may be quite distantly related or which exhibit no discernable genetic relationship may come to converge to the extent that they form a group that is structurally quite distinct from the surrounding and/or genetically related languages. Such a group of languages is commonly referred to as a **sprachbund**, i. e. 'language league'. (Another widely used, but not very 'descriptive' term is **linguistic area**. A rarer, but more 'descriptive' alternative is **convergence area**.)

One of the most famous examples of a sprachbund is the area of the Balkans. The members of this sprachbund belong to four genetically quite distinct subgroups of Indo-European: Bulgarian, Macedonian, part of Serbo-Croatian (all Slavic); Rumanian (Romance); Albanian; and Modern Greek.

Some of the features shared by most or all members of the sprachbund are the following:

(a) A post-posed definited article, as in (22). (Greek here shows a different, preposed pattern, as in *o fílos* 'the dear one'.) The articles of the Slavic and Romance Balkan languages have outside relations, such as the demonstrative pronoun *(*)tŭ* 'that' in Slavic or the article of It. *il duomo* 'the house', Fr. *le chat* 'the cat', Sp. *el lobo* 'the wolf'. However, outside the Balkan area, these articles and demonstratives are preposed; cf. Sp. *el lobo* vs. Rum. *lupu-l*. Note further that though the Balkan languages (other than Greek) agree on the placement of the article, they do not agree on the form. Each language employs an indigenous morpheme.

	plain noun	noun + article	
(22)			
Bulg.	voda	voda-ta	'water'
Rum.	lup	lupu-l	'wolf'
Alb.	shok	shok-u	'comrade'

(b) The numerals from 'eleven' through 'nineteen' are formed by means of structures whose literal meaning is 'one upon ten, etc.; cf. (23). At least in Rumanian, this formation is markedly different from what we find outside the Balkans; cf. e. g. Fr. *onze* < Lat. *un-decim* lit. 'one-ten'. On the other hand, also the non-Balkan Slavic languages as well as Hungarian have the construction of (23). Finally Greek again differs by preserving an inherited formation, of the type *en-deka* lit. 'one-ten'.

(23)	Bulg.	edi(n)-na-deset	'eleven'
	Rum.	un-spre-zece	'eleven'
	Alb.	njëm-bë-dhjetë	'eleven' [nyəmbəðyetə]

(c) Infinitival structures tend to be replaced by dependent (or coordinate) clauses; cf., e. g., (24a), as well as section 13.4, ex. (141/142). This development has been carried through most consistently in Greek, Macedonian, and Bulgarian. In Serbo-Croatian, however, it 'peters out', with Serbian generally using the dependent-clause structure and Croatian preferring the old infinitive construction; cf. (24b). The related non-Balkan languages all have structures with infinitives, as in Fr. *je veux écrire*.

(24 a) Mod. Greek θelo   na   γrafo
                     'I want' 'that' 'I write'
                     'I want to write'
   b)   Serbian   hoću   da   pisam
                     'I want' 'that' 'I write'
        Croatian   hoću   pisati
                     'I want' 'to write'

(d) The verb 'want, wish' is used as an auxiliary in the formation of the future tense, except in certain Albanian dialects which use the verb 'have'. Compare the examples in (25). Note that outside Serbo-Croatian, the auxiliary is uninflected and usually followed by the subordinating construction of example (24). (Gk. *θa* is a clitic reduction of the *θelo na* of (24a).) Again the outside languages have very different constructions; cf. (26).

(25) Gk.   θa γrafo
      Rum.   o să scriu
      Alb.   do të shkruaj
      SCr.   pisa-ću
      'I will write' (*'I want to write')

(26) Span. *escribir-é* < *escribir hé* *'I have to write'

While it is quite easy to state that the languages of the Balkans have come to converge in terms of the above features, as well as others not listed, there has been considerable disagreement concerning the exact sources for these features.

True, feature (b) is found also in the non-Balkan Slavic languages and thus may constitute a Slavic contribution to the area.

And there is some reason to believe that Greek may have been the focus for the innovation in (c). For it is here that the development has been carried through most consistently. Moreover, with increasing distance from Greek, the extent to which this feature is found tends to decrease. Finally, in Greek it is possible to trace the beginnings of this process as far back as the Hellenistic Koiné. But note that where the subject of 'want' and the (logical) subject of what is wanted are not coreferential, also non-Balkan languages use 'clausal' rather than infinitival structures. The use of the infinitive in such structures seems to be a feature of the western 'periphery'. Compare (27). Moreover, even with coreferential subjects, colloquial German prefers the clausal type (28a) to infinitival (28b) if the 'subordinate' action contains a modal. It is not clear how these non-Balkan patterns relate to the situation on the Balkans. Perhaps the area in which the feature 'peters out' extends beyond Croatian. However, the infinitival type Engl. *I want him to go* appears to be just as much an innovation as the Greek type *θelo na γrafo*. (It does not seem to be attested before the sixteenth century.)

(27) Germ.   ich will,   dass   er   geht   (vs. ich will ihn   (zu) gehen*)
              'I' 'want' 'that' 'he' 'goes'   'him' 'to' 'go'
              'I want him to go'
      vs. Engl. I want him to go   (vs. I want that he go(es)*)

(28a)   ich will, dass ich gehen darf
        *'I want that I may go'
    b) ich will gehen dürfen
        'I want to be permitted to go'

There are problems also concerning the use of 'wish, want' as a future-tense auxiliary: As noted earlier, some of the Albanian dialects use the verb 'have', instead of 'want, wish'. Now, as examples like (26) show, this is the auxiliary which is employed in non-Balkan Romance. This might suggest closer affiliation of these Albanian dialects with non-Balkan Romance than with the other Balkan languages.

What complicates matters is that a construction morphologically very similar to the auxiliary 'have' is found in the other Albanian dialects, but in a different function. Moreover, historical evidence suggests that at an earlier time the verbs 'want' and 'have' competed with each other as future-tense auxiliaries both in the Balkan languages Greek, Balkan Romance, and Old Church Slavic, and in the non-Balkan Romance languages. The secondary use of 'desiderative' structures like 'want' + infinitive and 'obligationals' like 'have to' + infinitive has precedents elsewhere.

Combined with other evidence (cf. e. g. section 16.2.6 below), this can be taken to indicate that earlier the convergence area was larger. An even larger area is suggested by the fact that early Germanic had a similar variation between 'desiderative' and 'obligational' structures as expressions of futurity. Compare (29) for examples of the auxiliaries which were used.

(29)   OHG   s(k)olan   'be obliged'   wellen   'want, wish'
        OE   sculan   'be obliged'   willan   'want, wish'
   cf. NE   shall   will
        ON   skolu   'be obliged'   monu   'intend'
        Go.   skulan   'be obliged'   haban   'have to'
                (beside *duginnan* 'begin')

It is difficult, if not impossible to determine the source for this earlier use of 'desideratives' and 'obligationals' as expressions of futurity. (There are some indications that it may have developed in a Graeco-Roman sprachbund of late Imperial Roman times.)

The source for the postposed article is likewise uncertain. True, the evidence in (a) above suggests that Greek can be ruled out as a possible source. However, the syntactic behavior of articles in complex noun phrases (consisting of noun plus adjective) has by some scholars been taken to cast doubt even on that conclusion.

In spite of these difficulties, however, and in spite of the fact that many of the features extend beyond the Balkans (or did so in the past), there cannot be any doubt that members of four distinctly different languages groups have converged into a sprachbund.

16.3.4. South Asia

Another famous sprachbund is that of South Asia: Beside Burushaski in the Northwest, for which we have no known outside relations, there are at least three major linguistic families which over the course of millennia have come to show an increasing agreement in a large number of overall structural features. These families are (i) Indo-Aryan and some of the neighboring Dardic and Eastern Iranian languages (such as Pashto), belonging to the Indo-European language family: (ii) the Dravidian languages, which may be related to the Uralic or Finno-Ugric family; and (iii) the Munda languages which seem to be related to Southeast Asian ('Austro-Asiatic') languages like Mon and Khmer. (In fact, one non-Munda branch of Austro-Asiatic is found on the eastern periphery of the South Asian convergence area.) In addition, many features of the sprachbund are found also in the neighboring Tibeto-Burman languages. For the present-day locations of these languages and language families, see Map 12.

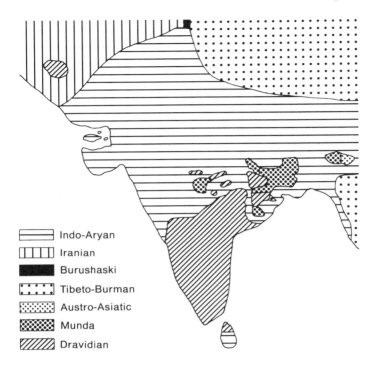

- ▭ Indo-Aryan
- ▭ Iranian
- ▪ Burushaski
- ▭ Tibeto-Burman
- ▭ Austro-Asiatic
- ▓ Munda
- ▨ Dravidian

Map 12: South Asian language families

All of these languages tend to share the following features. Exceptions do occur, such as some Munda languages which lack absolutives, or Kashmiri which has the innovated order SVO (through AUX cliticization, cf. 13.3.1.1.1). But such exceptions are rare.

a) A contrast between dental and retroflex consonants, as in (30);
b) An unmarked SOV order, as in (31);
c) The tendency to use 'absolutives' where European languages would employ dependent or coordinate clauses; cf. (32).

(30) Skt. pāta- 'flight' : pāṭa- 'portion'

(31) Hindi mɛ̃ kitāb paṛh rahā hũ
     'I' 'book' 'read' AUX AUX
     'I am reading a book'

(32) Hindi
  a) kitāb paṛh kē   bɛ̄ṭh lō
     'book' 'read' Abs. 'sit' 'take'
     'having read the book/after you have read the book, sit down'
  b) bɛ̄ṭh kē   kitāb paṛh lō
     'sit' Abs. 'book' 'read' 'take'
     'having sat down, read the book / sit down and read the book'

In addition, many languages have a so-called quotative construction, in which reported speech is marked off by a special word, as in (33). Constructions of this type are now lacking in many of the Indo-Aryan languages, including Hindi and Panjabi, as well as in Brahui, a Dravidian speech island in the northwest, surrounded by Iranian territory. But the presence of a quotative construction in earlier Middle Indo-Aryan and Sanskrit, as well as in the Dravidian languages other than Brahui, shows that this absence is an areal innovation. (The source for that innovation appears to have been Persian which began to play an important role in northwest and north-central India after the Muslim conquest.)

(33) Skt. nakiḥ   vaktā   na   dāt   **iti**
     'no one' 'about to say' 'not' 'shall give' "unquote"
     'No one is about to say "He shall not give".'

There is a continuing controversy as to when the convergence of South Asian languages began and which language group is responsible for the features listed above. Some scholars have argued that Dravidian must be the source, since all four features can be reconstructed for Proto-Dravidian. And, it is claimed, the ancestors of the other languages lacked some, or even all of them. Moreover, since all of the features are found in the earliest attested stage of Indo-Aryan, convergence between Indo-Aryan and Dravidian must have begun in the second millennium B. C.

Other linguists have pointed to evidence which suggests that all four features are indigenous also in Indo-Aryan, even if the retroflex/dental contrast may be an innovation. (Indo-Aryan retroflexion can be accounted for entirely in terms of 'internal' developments along the lines of section 5.1.6. An explanation in terms of convergence with Dravidian is dubious, since we find a good amount of divergence between the systems of Dravidian and Indo-Aryan. For instance, Indo-Aryan has a contrast only between dental and retroflex, while Proto-Dravidian has a triple distinction between dental, alveolar, and retroflex.)

SOV plus absolutive and quotative structures seem to be inherited also in Tibeto-Burman, in Altaic and Uralic, as well as in a number of ancient Near Eastern languages, including Elamite, Accadian, and Sumerian. (Nothing is known about the earlier nature — or affiliations — of Burushaski.) These features, therefore, may have been characteristic of an earlier, much larger sprachbund which has by some scholars been referred to as the Indo-Altaic area.

Only for the Munda languages is there good evidence to believe that some of these features are the result of contact. For the Austro-Asiatic languages of Indo-China have SVO and lack the dental/retroflex contrast. (In addition, some of the Tibeto-Burman languages have secondarily acquired the dental/retroflex contrast; and some of Indo-Aryan has secondarily lost it).

While the evidence for early convergence thus is rather limited, it is much clearer for later periods. For instance, early Indo-Aryan had a voiceless retroflex sibilant *ṣ* which was lacking in Dravidian, while early Dravidian had a retroflex continuant variously transcribed as *ẓ* or *ṛ* which did not have a Sanskrit counterpart. Except for the extremely northwestern dialects, Indo-Aryan lost its idiosyncratic retroflex segment by the Middle Indo-Aryan period through merger with *s* and *ś;* and in most of Dravidian, *ṛ* merged with other *r*-sounds, except in the extreme south.

What is interesting is that the later developments are indicative of a mutual convergence, not of the unidirectional convergence envisaged by linguists arguing for early Dravidian influence on Indo-Aryan. Given the later adstratal relationship between Dravidian and Indo-Aryan and given the parallels on the Balkans (cf. 16.3.3) and in modern South Asia (16.3.5), this is exactly what one would expect. And the fact that the Munda languages appear to have undergone more extensive 'areal' changes can likewise be attributed to sociolinguistic conditions, except that they involve a considerable degree of inequality in prestige: Most of the Indo-Aryan and many of the Dravidian languages have literary, standard varieties and enjoy the status of 'civilized', officially recognized languages. Munda on the other hand is limited to so-called 'tribal' or 'backward' groups and has for centuries been losing ground to both Indo-Aryan and Dravidian. Under these conditions, convergence is more likely to be unidirectional.

16.3.5. Kupwar

The developments discussed in the two preceding sections have come about largely in the unobservable past. The explanations which have been given for them therefore must remain speculative without the support of parallels in observable history.

Fortunately, such parallels can be found. Perhaps the most celebrated of these is the case of Kupwar, a small locality of about 3,000 at the border of the modern Indian states of Maharashtra and Karnataka. Its population consists of four groups whose languages outside Kupwar are clearly distinct:

(a) *Urdu* (Indo-Aryan): spoken by Muslim landholders, a socially prestigious or powerful group.

(b) *Kannada* (Dravidian): spoken by Jain landholders and Hindu craftsmen who likewise hold a fairly high prestige.

(c) *Marathi* (Indo-Aryan): used by Hindu untouchables and landless laborers, i. e., by persons on the lower end of the prestige spectrum. But in addition it is the state language and the primary means of education.

(d) *Telugu* (Dravidian): spoken by Hindu rope makers, a low-prestige group. (This group will be ignored in the following discussion.)

In spite of the obvious prestige differences, these languages coexist without any appreciable threat of one language replacing another. For within its own communal setting, each of these groups or 'communities' sticks to its own language as a mark of its separate identity. (The sociolinguistic relationship thus can be referred to as 'non-integrative adstratal'.) In intergroup relations, however, there is a great amount of bilingualism and multilingualism, expecially among the men and largely, though not exclusively, in favor of Marathi. Moreover, most speakers are at least passively competent in all of the languages of the locality.

This complex and intensive bilingualism is known to have extended over more than 300 years. And during that period it has brought about such a remarkable degree of convergence that the surface structures of the individual languages have become virtually identical. Only the vocabularies and the grammatical morphemes have remained clearly distinct, with borrowing limited to a few lexical items. (Presumably it is this lexical distinction which makes it possible for people to have nearly identical surface structures and still feel that they are speaking different, communally appropriate, languages. This is perhaps not surprising, given that non-linguists, when trying to characterize differences between dialects or languages, find it much easier to talk about different lexical choices than about structural divergences.)

The structural parallelism of the examples in (34) provides just a glimpse of the extent of this convergence. (The underlined words represent one of the rare examples of recent lexical borrowing. The source language is Urdu. Abs. = absolutive marker; TA = tense/agreement marker.)

(34) Ur. pālā   jarā   kāṭ   kē   lē   kē   ā − yā
     Ma. pālā   jarā   kāp   un   ghē   un   ā − lō
     Ka. tāplā jarā   khōd − i tagōnd − i ba − yn
          'greens' 'some' 'cut' Abs. 'take' Abs. 'come' TA
          'I cut some greens and brought them'

Such a high degree of convergence could of course be achieved only by a great deal of structural adjustments in the areas where the languages differ from each other. Thus, Urdu and Marathi both have 'arbitrary' gender, at least for non-human nouns: These nouns may arbitrarily be assigned masculine gender (cf. Urdu *pālā* in (34)), or feminine gender (cf. Urdu *kitāb* 'book'). And Marathi has yet a third, neuter gender. Like Marathi, Kannada has a three-gender system, but with a clear semantic basis for gender assignment: Male humans are masculine; female humans, feminine; and all others, neuter. The similarities and differences of these three systems are summarized in (35).

(35) | | masculine | feminine | neuter |
|---|---|---|---|
| Ur. | ± human | ± human | − − − − |
| Ma. | ± human | ± human | ± human |
| Ka. | + human | + human | − human |

Nominal gender assignment has important grammatical repercussions, for it controls agreement on adjectives and verbs as in example (36). As a consequence, the differences between the Urdu, Marathi, and Kannada systems were not resolved simply by giving up gender marking altogether. Rather, the semantically more transparent system of Kannada was generalized to Kupwar Marathi and Kupwar Urdu. As a consequence, Kupwar Marathi has neuter agreement for non-human nouns that are masculine or feminine in Standard Marathi. And Kupwar Urdu, lacking a separate neuter gender, employs the 'unmarked' mascu-

line gender for the same purpose. Compare the examples in (37). (Here
and elsewhere below, St. = Standard, Ku. = Kupwar variety.)

(36) Ur. ačchī   kitāb   paṛhī
      Adj. f. N f.   V f.
      'good' 'book' 'read'
      '(I) read a good book'

(37) St. Ur.   vahã   nadī   ā-ī
                  f.   f.
      St. Ma.   tith   nadī   ā-lī
                  f.   f.
      Ku. Ur.   hvā   nadī   ā-yā
                                  m.
      Ku. Ma.   tith   nadī   ā-lō
                                  n.
      Ku. Ka.   yalli   hwaḷi   ba-ttu
                                  n.
                 'there' 'flood' 'came'
                 'A flood came there'

In other areas of disagreement, it may be the pattern of Urdu and/
or Marathi which wins out. Thus, Standard Kannada does not have a
verb 'to be' after predicate adjectives. On the model of Urdu and
Marathi, Kupwar Kannada has come to employ a form of 'be' in this
context. Cf. example (38).

(38) St. Ka. ii   mane   nim-da Ø | i-du nim   mana   Ø
      Ku. Ka. id   mani   nimd   eti | id   nimd   mani   eti
      Ku. Ma. hē   ghar   tumčā   hāi | hē   tumčā   ghar   hāi
      Ku. Ur. yē   ghar   tumhārā hai | yē   tumhārā   ghar   hai
               'this' 'house' 'your' 'is' | 'this' 'your'   'house' 'is'
               'this house is yours' | 'this is your house'

Example (38) further illustrates that as in the development of koinés,
convergence may bring about selective simplification: In Standard
Kannada, adjectives and demonstratives appear in two morphologically
distinct forms. One occurs when the form is used as a predicate or as
a noun (cf. *nim-da, i-du*), the other is used elsewhere (cf. *ii, nim*). Kupwar
Kannada has given up this distinction in favor of the predicate/nominal
forms (cf. *id* and *nimd*).

16.3.6. Europe — sprachbund as dialect continuum

Convergence has not always been limited to 'exotic' areas. There is good reason for believing that prior to the development of the notion of the monolingual nation-state, much of medieval and early modern Europe was a convergence area.

One development which swept virtually the whole area is the cliticization of AUX and its movement into clause-second position; cf. section 13.3.1.1 above. The only exceptions are: (i) the Insular Celtic languages, including Breton (originally spoken on the British Isles), which have VSO; (ii) Basque, with SOV; and at an early period, (iii) the Uralic languages (Finnish, Estonian, Hungarian, etc.) which likewise have SOV. (Turkish has retained SOV to the present day.)

A further extension of this development, the shift of all finite verbs to second position, covered the same area, except that German, Dutch, and Frisian generalized verb-final AUX in dependent clauses. The same languages resisted also the last phase of the word order change, the movement of originally stranded non-finite 'main verbs' into the position after clause-second AUX. Cf. again section 13.3.1.1.

Through this change the unmarked word order of most of the Indo-European languages of Europe became SVO. And this order spread also to the Uralic languages which had settled in Europe (Finnish, Estonian, Hungarian, etc.). In Hungarian, however, the spread was incomplete, and older SOV patterns continue to exist beside the innovated SVO.

Other innovations extended over a more limited territory. For instance, Greek, Romance, and Germanic developed a system with contrasting definite and indefinite articles, as in Fr. *l'homme* 'the man': *un homme* 'a man'. But Icelandic and early Insular Celtic, on the (north)western periphery, acquired only a definite article.

Greek, Romance (including Rumanian), and the Balkan Slavic languages Macedonian and Bulgarian share the development of a 'verb-based' system of pronominal clitics, i. e., a system in which the position of clitic pronouns depends on the location or function of the verb: Enclisis is the norm after imperatives, cf., e. g., (39a). Relics of the type (39b) show that at an earlier stage enclisis was normal after any clause-initial verb. Proclisis is found elsewhere; cf., e. g., (39c). (Next to non-finite verbs, the pattern of pronoun placement is slightly more complicated.)

(39a)   Span.   mostrad me   'show me'
        Fr.   dis-le   'tell it'
        It.   mostrate mi 'show me'
   b)   Span.   verémos lo   'we will *see* that'
        It.   disse gli la dama ...   'said the lady to him ...'
   c)   vs. Sp. (yo) te amo 'I love you'
        Fr.   je t'aime   'I love you'
        It.   (io) ti amo   'I love you'

The geographical source of this innovation is not clear.

Yet another innovation is the development of a redundant marker of negation and the subsequent ellipsis of the original negative morpheme, as in (40). This change is found also in German and English (cf., e. g., (41)), as well as in French. (The representation in (41) glosses over the fact that older and newer patterns coexisted and alternated with each other for a considerable time. For the French developments see sections 9.2.1 and 13.3.2 above which also offer a fuller discussion of the individual changes involved in this development.)

(40)   pre-ON I: ne   āt   : ne   āt   eitt-gi
                    neg. V   neg. V   emph.
                    'did not eat'   'did not eat anything'
       pre-ON II: ne   āt   eitt-gi
                    neg. V   neg.
                    'did not eat'
       ON   Ø   āt   ekki
                         V   neg.
                    'did not eat'

(41)   OHG   ne   āzz   : ne   āzz (n)iowiht
                    neg. V   neg. V   emph.
                    'did not eat'   'did not eat anything'
       11th/12th c.: ne āzz ni(wi)ht
                    neg. V   neg.
                    'did not eat'
       14th c.:   Ø   āzz niht
                    'did not eat'

This development appears to have started in the north: In Old Norse, it was virtually complete by about 1000 A. D. German carried it through by the fourteenth century. The English implementation of the process appears to have been a little slower; for Chaucer still has a fair amount of variation. In French, on the other hand, redundant negation becomes obligatory only in the fifteenth century; and ellipsis still has not been carried through consistently.

Finally, a more recent and geographically more limited development appears to be the replacement of the simple past by the present perfect in colloquial French, Romantsch, and southern German. (Cf. 10.1.5 for an example.)

What is interesting about these developments is that in the 'European sprachbund', innovations have spread across language boundaries in just about the same way as they cross dialect boundaries in a dialect continuum. And just as in the case of dialect continua, it is possible to capture the effects of spread by means of isogloss maps. Compare for instance Map 13, which accounts for the effects of some of the above developments by about the sixteenth century. Similar patterns have been observed for other convergence areas. (In Map 13, S Fin. OV/ SOV refers to the peculiar word order type of German, Dutch, and Frisian. — The map has been simplified to some extent. For instance, Finnish, Estonian, and other neighboring Uralic languages are listed as still having SOV, and Hungarian has been ignored altogether. Moreover, Lithuanian is listed as SVO, even though at this point it has only begun to move finite verbs into second position. Similarly, the North African Arabic and Berber dialects are listed as having VSO, rather than the prevailing present-day SVO. In the Arabic dialects, the change from VSO to SVO may have been close to completion by this time.)

Map 14 offers a more detailed account of word order isoglosses in modern Europe and adjacent areas. (For the prevailing SVO, as well as VSO relics, in present-day North-African languages see the discussion of Map 15 below. The German/Dutch/Frisian word order type here is indicated as S (Fin.) OV. And the Hungarian vacillation between SOV and SVO is symbolized as SOV/SVO. Moreover, 'prep.' = preposition + noun and 'po.' = noun + postposition; N + G = noun + genitive, G + N = genitive + noun.)

The interest of this map lies in the fact that it shows even more clearly the similarities between dialect maps and 'sprachbund maps': It is clearly possible to distinguish a large central area with SVO, prep. + N, and N + G which includes the original focal area for the change from SOV to SVO.

In addition there are relic areas which have not been touched by the change, such as the VSO etc. of Insular Celtic or the SOV, N + po.,

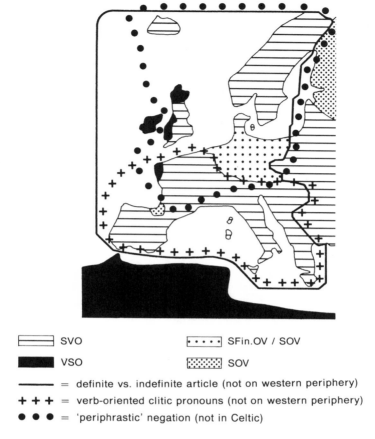

SVO

VSO

SFin.OV / SOV

SOV

——— = definite vs. indefinite article (not on western periphery)

+ + + = verb-oriented clitic pronouns (not on western periphery)

● ● ● = 'periphrastic' negation (not in Celtic)

Map 13:   Some European isoglosses

G + N of Basque, Turkish and other Altaic languages, and the Eastern
Uralic languages. Except for Turkish, a late arrival which juts into SVO
or transitional territory, these relic areas are neatly on the periphery.

The location of the German/Dutch/Frisian and Hungarian semi-relic
areas is a little less typical. Moreover, the geographic proximity of these
two areas is not well accounted for: Is the fact that both are 'semi-
archaic' due to chance, or are the similarities due to common development?

If we disregard this semi-relic area, the remainder of the languages
fit in very well as transition areas: The greater their distance from the

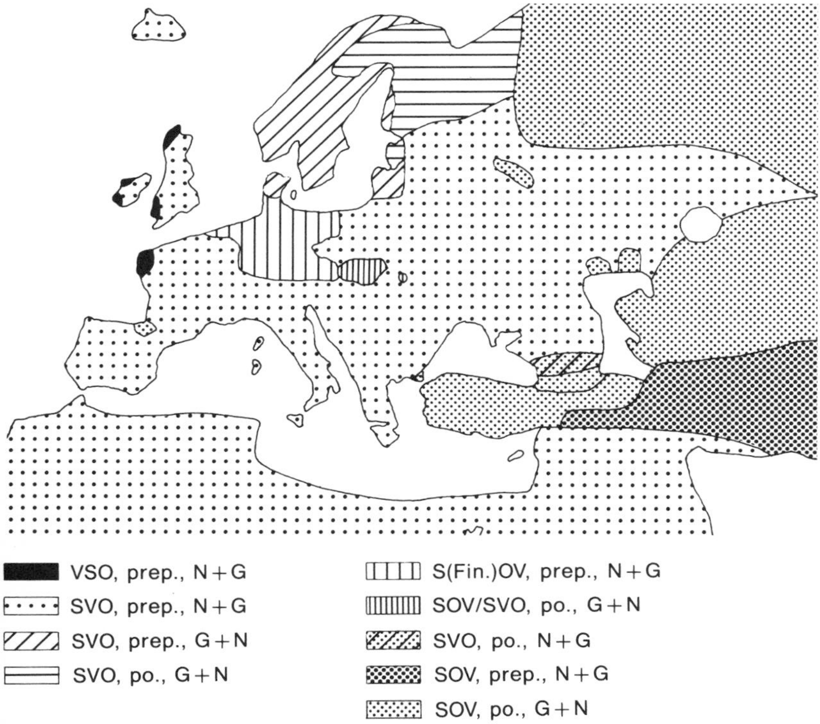
VSO, prep., N+G
SVO, prep., N+G
SVO, prep., G+N
SVO, po., G+N
S(Fin.)OV, prep., N+G
SOV/SVO, po., G+N
SVO, po., N+G
SOV, prep., N+G
SOV, po., G+N

Map 14: Word order isoglosses in Europe and neighboring areas

focal area (and their proximity to the 'eastern' relic area with SOV etc.), the less they are similar to the focal area: Norwegian, Danish, Swedish, and the Baltic languages (Lithuanian and Latvian) have SVO and prep. + N, but G + N. Finnish, Estonian, and other partly 'Europeanized' Uralic languages have SVO, but both G + N and N + po. Similarly, some of the Caucasus languages have SVO and N + G, but postpositions. Finally, Iranian has the patterns prep. + N and N + G of the focal area, but the SOV of its Eastern neighbors. (Recall that the geographically more western Turkish is a relatively recent arrival from the east.)

The similarity between sprachbund and dialect continuum should perhaps not be surprising, for as noted earlier, the use of different languages in bilingual societies is in many ways comparable to the use of different dialects in monolingual societies.

Here as in dialectology, it is possible to extend the notions 'focal area', 'transition area', and 'relic area' from relatively well documented cases like the Continental European shift of SOV to SVO to other similar situations where we lack documentary evidence on the timing and direction of the spread of linguistic innovations.

One area in which such an approach yields interesting results is Africa. As Map 15 illustrates, a large central area of Africa has SVO as its unmarked constituent order, while other word orders are limited to the periphery. This distribution by itself might suggest that the SVO of the central area is an innovation. But note in addition that a number of peripheral languages have the pattern S AUX O MV which, as noted in 13.3.1.1, is a typical chronological transition pattern in the change from SOV to SVO. (In fact, this observation was based in part on the evidence of certain West African languages.) Now, what is interesting is that the type S AUX O MV in a number of East and South African areas is also geographically a transition between SOV and SVO. This agreement between diachronic and geographic evidence provides additional support for the argument that the central SVO is an innovation.

To the extent that earlier historical stages are known, they support this interpretation: The North African SVO clearly is an innovation, replacing the earlier VSO of Berber and other indigenous Afro-Asiatic languages, as well as the language of the Arabic invaders, belonging to the Semitic branch of Afro-Asiatic. In fact, traces of VSO remain in some of the Berber dialects. Semitic Amharic, to be sure, has adopted the order SOV. But this development is attributable to the fact that Amharic migrated into the SOV territory of East Africa. It does not require us to assume a geographical expansion of SOV order.

Even so, some caution might be in order: If we did not have the evidence of VSO relics in Berber, it would be difficult to infer from the present-day geographical distribution that the North African SVO replaces an earlier VSO, not the SOV suggested by the more southern evidence. Clearly, isogloss maps covering vast geographic territory may mask more localized developments. At the same time, however, their evidence cannot be ignored.

Isogloss patterns like those in Maps 14 and 15 are important for several reasons. First of all, they suggest that major changes in grammatical structure can diffuse over large geographic areas through a dialect-like chain of bilingualism. And this diffusion can be completely oblivious of the genetic relationship between languages. For instance, the European spread of SVO, originating in Indo-European languages, has

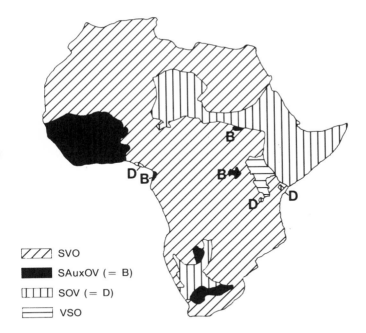

Map 15:   Word order isoglosses in Africa (Based on Heine 1976)

affected some of the Uralic languages but has left the Indo-European Insular Celtic languages untouched. And Proto-Indo-European SOV has been retained in the modern Indo-Aryan languages, no doubt in part because they are located in solidly SOV territory.

The fact that major grammatical changes can diffuse across language boundaries and can ignore genetic affiliations has repercussions also for typology and general theories about the relative 'naturalness' of different patterns. For instance, cursory examination suggests that SVO, SOV, and VSO are not randomly distributed in the world's languages but tend to 'cluster' in particular areas: Beside the focal areas of Europe and Africa, SVO is limited to one other area in the 'Old World', namely part of Austronesia, Indo-China, and China. Similarly, in the same large area, VSO is limited to Insular Celtic, early Semitic and related languages, an apparent relic area in East Africa, and the Austronesian/ Polynesian area. Finally, in addition to Basque and various African relic areas, SOV occurs in a large Central Asian and South Asian territory, as well as in Siberia, Korea, and Japan.

Typological studies must take these geographic facts into consideration. For instance, in trying to establish a representative sample, it is not sufficient to make sure that different language families are equally presented. For as Swedish and Finnish show, geographically neighboring members of different language families may converge in their structure.

Moreover, the dynamics of word order in the Old World must be considered: SVO has replaced earlier SOV in Continental Europe, as well as in large parts of Africa. And the SVO of Modern Chinese likewise seems to be an innovation for earlier SOV. This suggests (i) that the SOV territory at an earlier time was considerably larger than today and (ii) that the wide distribution of SVO in the modern world is a fairly recent phenomenon.

16.4. Foreigner talk, pidgins, trade jargons, and creoles

In the wake of the European colonialization of much of today's Third World, there arose all over the globe a series of speech varieties that are commonly referred to as **pidgins**. These languages in many ways differ radically from any of the other types of language which we have looked at so far. True, also here we find evidence of interlanguage influence from the various indigenous languages. Moreover, one of the major characteristics of pidgins, structural simplification, may be found also in other types of language contact, such as koiné formation or convergence. But in other contact situations, structural simplification is selective and merely serves to eliminate (excessive) linguistic differences. In pidgins, on the other hand, there is a **radical simplification of linguistic structure** and a **radical reduction of vocabulary**. Thus, all inflection, all morphophonemic alternation, major syntactic processes such as passive, and all syntactic embedding tend to be eliminated. And the lexicon of pidgins tends to be limited to 1000 or 2000 words. Moreover, from all appearances, simplification and reduction take place very rapidly, within one or two generations.

Clearly, such developments — and their results — are quite unusual. True, one may claim that Chinese, with its virtual absence of morphophonemic alternations and without any appreciable inflection, shows a similar degree of simplification. But this simplification took millennia to be accomplished. Moreover, Chinese has not lost any major syntactic processes or the ability to embed clauses into other clauses. Most importantly, neither here nor in any of the contact situations which we have looked at so far do we find the radical reduction in vocabulary which is so characteristic of pidgins. (For that reason, it is quite misleading if some scholars claim that English, or languages like Marathi, went through a pidgin phase: There is no evidence whatsoever for the radical vocabulary reduction associated with pidgins.)

Before attempting to establish the processes and special sociolinguistic conditions that give rise to pidgins, it is useful to take a look at a sample of a pidgin text.

The text in Chart 16.1 illustrates many of the features which are characteristic of pidgins:

(a) The vocabulary, limited as it is, is almost exclusively derived from the European (i. e., colonialist) language, in this case from English. Except for the names of places, flora, and fauna, native words like *kanæka* are quite rare.

(b) The reduction of vocabulary requires a much greater degree of polysemy that in 'ordinary' languages. This polysemy to some degree shows up in the glosses and the translation. Compare for instance *kič* from Engl. *catch*, whose meanings range from 'catch' to 'receive', 'get', and many other similar activities.

(c) Vocabulary reduction has considerable grammatical consequences in the case of prepositions and similar function words: Pidgins tend to have just one universal preposition, such as the *(bi)lɔŋ* of our text which variously indicates possession or other genitival relationship, destination, location, etc. In the verbal system, reduction generally manifests itself in the absence of the copula 'be'; cf., e. g., sentence (1).

(d) The elimination of inflection is illustrated by the use of *mī, ɛm*, etc., not only as object pronouns, but also in subject function; cf., e. g., sentences (1) and (10). But note also (f) below. Similarly, there is no inflection for past or present tense, nor is there any third-singular present ending -*s*. (Pidgins derived from languages with richer inflectional systems than English tend to use the infinitive as all-purpose uninflected form of the verb. But other choices may also be encountered. Cf. also 16.4.3 below.) Plural, where it is expressed,

(1) naw bifɔr   lɔŋtaym   mī   plīsbɔy
     'now' 'before, previously' 'long (time)' 'I/me' 'police-boy'

(2) mī stap   æmbunti
     'be continually' 'Ambunti'

(3) ɔrayt, mī stap gud-fɛlə
     'OK'   'good' *

(4) mī no gat   trəbəl
     'not' 'have' 'trouble'

(5) ɔlə kanæka bilɔŋ buš   ī-no stap ɔlsem
     'all' 'native' PREP. 'backwoods' *   'so, same way'

(6) ɔltaym ɔltaym ɔl ī-fayt
     'always'   'all' *'fight'

(7) ɔrayt, baymbay nəmbərwən kīap   ī-hīr- im
     'soon'   'nr. 1; top' 'government official' *'hear' *

(8) nəmbərwən kīap ī-hīr-im finiš, ī-sɛl-   im pæs   lɔŋ   stešən
                              *   *'sell, send, ...' * 'pass, letter' PREP. 'station,
                                                                               post'

(9) nəmbərtū kīap kīč-   im pæs finiš
     'nr. 2; sub-' 'catch, get' *   *

(10) bihayn   ɛm   ī- tɔk   - im mī-fɛlə
     'behind, after, etc.' 'he/him'* 'talk, speak, say' * 'I' *

(11) ɛm ī-tɔk mī-fɛlə ɔltəgɛdər   go   lɔŋ   buš bilɔŋ layn-   im
                 'all (together)' 'go, ...' PREP. PREP. learn, teach, ...' *
     ɔltəgɛdər kanæka

(12) ɔrayt, tū-fɛlə de mī-fɛlə go naw
     '2' *   'day'

(13) mīfɛlə go go go lɔŋ   kanu tūdark
                  PREP. 'canoe' 'dark, night'

(14) tūdark, ɔrayt, mīfɛlə slīp   naw
                            'sleep'

(15) slīp finiš lɔŋ   mɔrniŋtaym mīfɛlə kirəp
         *   PREP. 'morning'   'get up, rise'

Translation: (1) Now, long ago I was a "police boy", i. e., a native policeman. (2) I was/ stayed at Ambunti. (3) OK, I always was good. (4) I did not have/make/get into trouble. (5) [But] all the natives of the backwoods were not always that way. (6) They were always fighting. (7) OK, soon the top government official heard [about this]. (8) When the top government official had heard about it, he sent a letter to the post. (9) The subordinate official received the letter. (10) Then he spoke to us. (11) He said "We will all go to the backwoods in order to teach (a lesson to) all the natives." (12) OK, then we went for two days now. (13) We kept going in the canoe until nighttime. (14) At nighttime, OK, we slept now. (15) Having slept, in the morning, we got up.

(Note: An asterisk (*) indicates elements that are calqued on native structures not found in English. PREP. indicates the all-purpose preposition.)

Chart 16.1: Pidgin sample text (based on Hall 1943)

is characterized not by inflection, but by the addition of separate words; cf. *ɔlɔ kanæka* in (5). (For *mīfɛlɔ* see (f) below.)

(e) Derivational morphology is reduced to compounding, as in *nɔm-bɔrwɔn kīap,* and reiteration or 'duplication' of words, as in *go go go* (cf. sentence (13)). The latter device serves various functions, such as indicating repetition, continuous activity, and emphasis. (Note that forms like *nɔmbɔrwɔn* and *lɔŋtaym* are not compounds in the pidgin but single, unanalyzable lexical items. In some cases, the choice of such longer forms makes it possible to differentiate lexical items; cf. *lɔŋtaym* 'long (duration)' vs. *lɔŋ* (prep.). In other cases, the long forms seem to be attributable to verbal exaggeration by the colonialists. For instance, in many English-based pidgins, *tūmɔč* "too much" is used for 'much, many, etc.')

(f) There is evidence also for indigenous, non-English 'interference' or interlanguage. Thus the use of *finiš* (sentence (9)) to indicate that an action has been completed serves to render a native aspectual distinction which is absent in English. Also the use of *ī-* (cf. sentence (5)) and *-im* (sentence (7)) is calqued on marking conventions of the indigenous languages. The source for these markers appears to be Engl. *he, him;* but note that the same source has also furnished the pronoun *ɛm.* Moreover, *ī-* is not pronominal, but serves as something like an agreement marker on the verb; and *-im* functions as a marker of transitivity. Similarly, the element *-fɛlɔ,* found in various combinations, serves to encode grammatical distinctions not made or differently marked in English. In the case of *mī-fɛlɔ,* for instance, it helps render an indigenous contrast between 'inclusive' (or 'unlimited') *mī-fɛlɔ* 'we = you, I, and others' and 'exclusive' (or 'limited') *yūmī* 'we = you and I (only)'

16.4.1. "Incorrect learning"

Various theories have been proposed concerning the manner in which pidgins originate. One of these, coming in different variants, boils down to the assertion that they resulted from the inability of the "natives" to learn European languages correctly.

However, one must ask why only these "natives" showed this peculiar inabilty, while elsewhere language contact has very different results. In fact, even among these "natives", language contact ordinarily does not result in pidgins. Compare the earlier discussion of African koinés and the convergence in Kupwar.

An additional assumption, often implicit but sometimes explicit, is that "these natives" are genetically inferior to the European colonizers and therefore unable to learn their languages. This claim is without any intellectual merit whatsoever. First of all, now that the attitudes of the former colonizers have undergone at least some change and that the descendants of the "natives" are given a greater chance to learn the complete breadth of the European languages, large numbers of Third-World people are acquiring a complete and excellent mastery of the European languages. Secondly and more importantly, no convincing evidence has been offered in favor of the view that Third-World people are mentally inferior to Europeans. (Recent attempts to furnish such evidence in terms of IQ tests are unacceptable: The "scientific" basis for these attempts is the claim that twins separated at birth and brought up in radically different environments nevertheless have the same IQ, "proving" that intelligence is inherited and not conditioned by social environment. However, the "data" upon which this hypothesis was built turn out to be manufactured and fraudulent.)

Other, non-racist theories claim that pidgins can result through imperfect learning form any contact between speakers of different languages. Here again, however, we must ask ourselves why pidgins then do not arise more commonly and why language contact in so many others cases leads to very different results.

16.4.2. Portuguese 'Proto-Pidgin' and 'relexification'

It has also been alleged that all — or at least most — pidgins are descended from a single source, a Portuguese 'Proto-Pidgin' established at the time of the Portuguese expansion. The other pidgins are then considered to be 'relexifications' of that proto-pidgin: As other nations, with different languages, entered the colonialist scene, they took over the ready-made pidgin of the Portuguese, but adjusted it to their languages by substituting for the Portuguese vocabulary words from their own lexica. (A common variant of this theory has it that the Portuguese Proto-Pidgin is itself a relexification of Sabir, also known as the (original) Lingua Franca, a trade language employed in the Mediterranean of the Middle Ages. The few early attestations which we can find are literary caricatures; however, they do suggest that this language was pidgin-like in its structure.)

The evidence adduced for a Portuguese origin of all pidgins consists mainly in the fact that many, if not most of the non-Portuguese European-based pidgins have certain lexical items which are likely to be of Portuguese origin. Most notable among these are the words in (42). What is important is that *sabby,* clearly Romance in origin, agrees best with Port. *saber* [-b-] 'know', whereas Fr. *savoir* and Sp. *saber* have [v] and [β] respectively. Similarly, *pickaninny* etc. seems to be best derived from Port. *pequeno,* diminutive *pequenino* 'small', while Spanish has *pequeño* with palatal nasal.

(42)	Engl. pidgin	savvy
	Earlier	sabby
	Fr. pidgin	sabé
	Engl. pidgin	pickaninny
	Du. pidgin	pikien
	Span. pidgin	piquinini

Moreover, there are a few pidgins, such as Saramaccan, which seem to have stopped relexifying in 'mid-stream': About 27% of Saramaccan vocabulary is traceable to Portuguese, the rest is mainly of English origin.

Also this theory, however, is open to several doubts and reservations. First of all, even if it were established beyond a reasonable doubt that all pidgins are descended from a single Proto-Pidgin, we must still explain how that Proto-Pidgin came about. The explanations offered on this count have generally not been different from the ones which were rejected in the preceding section.

Secondly, there is at least some evidence which suggests that pidgins in many cases arose independently, rather than through relexification of an established, ready-made pidgin. Thus early documents from the French West Indies show that in the French-based pidgins of that area there was as yet no complete agreement on which form to use as the uninflected, general verb form: Both infinitive (as in *savoir* 'know') and the (morphologically regularized) participle (as in *savé* 'known') still were in competition with each other. It is only later, as the pidgin comes to be more institutionalized and established, that the infinitive form is used across the board, just as it is in the established Portuguese-based pidgins. Had there been simple relexification of an already established pidgin, we would not expect such fluctuations. In addition, pidgin-like languages have been found in areas where Portuguese influence is impossible (such as a highly simplified Russian used by Chinese traders in Russian border towns).

Moreover, the linguistically heterogeneous vocabulary of Saramaccan and a few other similar cases can be accounted for differently: Let us assume that Saramaccan started as a Portuguese-based pidgin. In that case, the English element can be accounted for as the result of vocabulary expansion in the process of 'creolization' or 'depidginization' (cf. 16.4.5). True, in the majority of pidgins, the same language has furnished the basis for both pidginization and creolization. But this merely reflects the fact that in most cases the nationality — and language — of the colonialist/slave-master power remained unchanged. Saramaccan can be explained as an example of what happens when there is a change in power, such that the language which can serve as the source for vocabulary expansion (English) is different from the base language for the pidgin (Portuguese).

Finally, the presence of a few — actually quite limited — Portuguese vocabulary items in the majority of the pidgins that developed in the wake of European colonialism can be explained differently, namely as the result of vocabulary borrowing among the European colonizers and slave traders. The words may have been acquired from Portuguese together with other aspects of the "art" of colonialism and slave trade. Moreover, at an early period slavers' ships from other nations frequently employed Portuguese pilots, and their crews commonly were international in character. That is, we can look at these vocabulary items as part of a conquistador/slavetrader-jargon. (Compare section 15.4.1 above for the North Atlantic nautical jargon.)

That words of this sort, together with their social connotations, can be picked up by people who do not speak a pidgin (or are in the process of relexifying a pidgin) is shown by the fact that *savvy* and *pickaninny* have entered the general vocabulary of English. Similarly, American World War II veterans who fought in Italy and learned a smattering of Italian picked up the word *kapeesh* = It. *capisci* 'do you understand?' and having done so, used that word in other situations in which they were faced with speakers of foreign languages that they did not understand. In fact, many American who have never been to Italy have adopted the word from the veterans and put it to similar uses.

16.4.3. Foreigner talk

The latter type of language use points the way to a more fruitful theory
on the origination of pidgins. For the use of words like *kapeesh* usually
goes hand in hand with several other features which are highly reminiscent of what is found in pidgins: The use of very 'simple' words and
of a rather restricted vocabulary; the tendency to omit inflection or
inflectional elements, as well as function words and the copula 'to be';
repetition and to some extent compounding as a means of amplifying
an otherwise quite impoverished structure and vocabulary. Other features, not necessarily found in established pidgins, are speaking more
loudly and forcefully, the use of a 'heavy' and 'choppy' intonation
(where each word is treated as a sentence in itself), and more than usual
gesticulation. Through this approach, it seems, people feel they can
establish communication with a person whose language they do not
understand and who similarly does not understand their language.

Though there are considerable differences in the degree to which
these features are present in the speech of individuals, the general
pattern is very clear and appears to be universal. This mode of speaking
now is commonly referred to as **foreigner talk**, on the analogy of
'baby talk' in the sense of the 'simplified/reduced language which
grown-ups tend to use when speaking to babies'.

The similarities between foreigner talk and the pidgins which arose
in the wake of European colonialism are too great to be attributed to
chance. One is tempted to believe that there is a direct, causal relationship — that pidgins simply are institutionalized varieties of foreigner
talk.

However, the link cannot be quite so direct. For if foreigner talk is
a very common tendency in linguistic contact, we again must ask why
it is not institutionalized more commonly.

The answer to this question appears to require reference to sociolinguistic factors: Under normal circumstances, the expectation is that a
foreign language (or even several languages in contact) will be learned
to the point of complete mastery. Foreigner talk therefore is only a
transitory, first-generation or first-contact phase. The expansion of
European colonialism brought with it a very different expectation on
the part of (most of) the Europeans: The "natives" were held to be
inferior and thus worthy of colonialist and racist exploitation, even of
slavery. They were therefore also believed to be incapable of correctly
learning the European languages. Under these cicumstances, the use of

foreigner talk was considered not just a transitory phenomenon, but the only proper vehicle for communicating with these "natives".

Another important factor may have been that by providing foreigner talk as the only model which the "natives" could imitate, the Europeans were able to keep them 'in their place'. The use of foreigner talk, then, became a marker of political and social domination.

Recent research has provided evidence suggesting that at least in the case of the Portuguese pidgin there was at a certain time a deliberate decision to use foreigner talk, rather than 'normal' Portuguese: In the early phase of Portuguese expansion down the western coast of Africa, attempts were made to communicate with the local population through interpreters who were familiar with Portuguese and Arabic (which at that time served as the major link language in the northern part of the area). As the Portuguese moved farther south, this approach no longer was feasible. At first, the Portuguese tried to teach their language to members of the local community who would then serve as interpreters. However, after a while, realizing that this was a very time-consuming process, they switched to teaching a simplified, foreigner-talk variety of Portuguese. It is this variety which seems to have been the basis for the Portuguese pidgins.

The importance of sociolinguistic factors can be seen also in a more recent and therefore more observable development: In Germany (and similarly in a number of other European countries), the industrial boom of the sixties led to a heavy influx of foreign laborers or 'guest workers' who were brought in from economically less advantaged countries to do the work which Germans considered undesirable. Most of these 'guest workers' had no prior knowledge of German, and their languages were equally unfamiliar to most of their German supervisors. Out of the foreigner talk employed by the socially more powerful Germans developed a special variety of language called **Gastarbeiterdeutsch** ('guest worker German', abbreviated GAD in the discussion below). This variety of language has undergone a certain degree of institutionalization and may for instance be used by 'guest workers' of different linguistic backgrounds when talking to each other. Moreover, although in the early stages of GAD, native Germans apparently used foreigner talk quite freely with 'guest workers', more recent studies suggest that GAD now is used rather sparingly. That is, foreign laborers no longer seem to need the input of native speakers' foreigner talk for acquiring GAD.

At the same time, however, the sociolinguistic conditions do not seem to be conducive for the development of a fully institutionalized pidgin: In spite of considerable legal difficulties, most foreign laborers try to become integrated into German society and therefore make considerable efforts to learn German more fully. Moreover, most native speakers of German tend to switch to normal, non-simplified German as soon as they feel that a particular foreign laborer has begun to acquire a more than cursory control of the language. It is only among those 'guest workers' who develop a very negative attitude to Germany and to German society (either because of cultural disillusionment or because of the rude, racist behavior of some Germans) that GAD becomes relatively 'fixed'. But then, workers with such a negative attitude usually return to their home countries at the earliest opportunity. As a consequence, their version of GAD has no chance of becoming institutionalized.

The relatively unsettled sociolinguistic nature of GAD is mirrored by relatively unsettled linguistic characteristics. For instance, instead of generalizing a single morphological form as the all-purpose, uninflected form of the verb, it has at least three different formations; cf. (43). Interestingly, each of these can in ordinary German be used to give orders; cf. (43'). It has been observed that the generalization of formations which can be used as imperatives is a common feature of pidgins. Note for instance that the infinitive, commonly used in Romance-based pidgins, can be used as an imperative in the Romance languages. Presumably, this choice reflects the social context in which the more privileged or powerful give orders to the less privileged.

(43)	Gastarbeiterdeutsch	Ordinary German	
a)	mach Arbeit	ich mache/tue die Arbeit	'I do the work'
		wir machen/... die Arbeit	'we do the work'
		ich habe die Arbeit getan	'I did the work'
		etc.	
b)	nix nach Haus gehn	ich gehe nicht nach Hause	'I don't go home'
		etc.	
c)	Tag geschlafen	ich schlafe am Tag/...	'I sleep during the day'
		etc.	
(43'a)	iss deine Suppe!	sg. 2 impve.	'eat your soup'
b)	Essen fassen!	infinitive (distancing)	'get (your) chow'
c)	stillgestanden!	past pple. (military)	'stand still; (stand at) attention'

Moreover, as the examples in (43) show, the relative ordering of object and verb is not fixed. Both VO orders (as in (43a)) and OV orders (as in (43b)) can be encountered. The most probable explanation is the following: Ordinary German has the order VO in main-clause structures with finite verbs, as in the imperative structure of (43′a); but with non-finite verbs, such as the infinitive of (43′b), the order is OV. As a consequence, the specific input provided in German foreigner talk, the imperatival structures of the type (43′), will provide a mixture of VO and OV patterns. (Note that the different orders in (43) cannot be attributed to the interlanguage influence of the foreign laborers' native languages. For whether 'guest workers' are Greek (with SVO) or Turkish (with SOV), both will show just about the same mixture of VO and OV structures.)

16.4.4. Trade jargons

While pidgins and pidgin-like languages such as Gastarbeiterdeutsch arise in an environment of rather extreme inequality, there is evidence that similar types of language can come about under conditions of equality. Interestingly, these different sociolinguistic conditions are reflected in the fact that such **trade jargons** differ from pidgins also in their linguistic characteristics.

One such language may be the so-called Chinook Jargon which used to be employed by trappers and traders in the northwest of the United States and in adjacent areas of Canada. Extant descriptions show that when the Europeans arrived, the jargon was used for relatively short-term trading relations in a sociolinguistic setting of equality. Here, too, we find a great degree of structural and vocabulary simplification, exceeding what one encounters in 'normal' language contact. However, there is an important difference: The vocabulary and the linguistic structures employed, as well as their simplification, were much more variable than those of the 'classical' pidgins. Thus, the vocabulary did not predominantly come from a single source; but a variety of languages contributed to it. Moreover, the extent to which different groups contributed to the vocabulary was subject to considerable fluctuations. Finally, some studies have suggested that the core 'grammar' of Chinook Jargon is best explained as a compromise between the grammars of the various languages of the area, with a large amount of selective simplification. (A recent study, however, proposes that the Jargon started out as a more or less classical pidgin.)

A similar language arose in the north of Norway, as an auxiliary means of communication between Russian traders and Norwegian fishermen during the relatively short fishing season. Just as Chinook Jargon, the language was employed for relatively short-term trading relations between social equals. Here, too, we find considerable reduction in structure and vocabulary. And again, the vocabulary is heterogeneous, with Russian and Norwegian elements roughly mixed, in addition to a few lexical items which seem to have come in from nautical jargon. Moreover, some areas of grammatical structure exhibit the effect of something like selective simplification. For instance, the all-purpose preposition *po* is phonetically more or less identical to the Norwegian preposition *på* and the Russian *po* (although the meanings of these two prepositions are not identical). (Unlike Chinook Jargon, Russenorsk does not offer any evidence for having developed out of an earlier pidgin.)

It is interesting that Sabir, the 'original' Lingua Franca of the Mediterranean, appears to have been more similar to trade jargons like Russenorsk than to the 'classical' pidgins which arose during the period of European colonization. And like Chinook Jargon, it seems to have undergone considerable fluctuations in the predominant sources of its vocabulary.

Trade jargons like Russenorsk and Chinook Jargon give the impression of being semi-institutionalized forms of foreigner talk, without the homogeneity which is found in the fully institutionalized 'classical' pidgins. However, although they differ considerably from pidgins, not only linguistically but also in terms of sociolinguistic attitude, they share one feature: In both types of contact language, there is no expectation of full acquisition of the other's foreign language. What differs is the specific reason for not expecting full acquisition. In the case of pidgins, that reason is the colonialists' notion of extreme social inequality. In the case of trade jargons, on the other hand, the reason is that two or more groups (by design or necessity) engage in a very limited contact which is restricted to just a few activities. What is interesting in this regard is that when the Russian merchants decided to engage in a less limited trading relation with Norway, they sent their sons to Oslo to learn 'proper' Norwegian.

16.4.5. Depidginization, creoles, creole continua

Many pidgin-like forms of language may have developed in the extended history of human language, only to disappear later — usually without any distinct trace. But under certain conditions they have come to be employed in a manner which ensured them a more lasting place in history, as languages of wider communication or even as native languages.

Given their severe limitations in grammar and especially in vocabulary, pidgins and similar varieties of language may be very useful, even appropriate, for the very restricted social conditions in which they arose. However, the limitations are considerable obstacles when languages of this type are to be used in a broader range of social and linguistic contexts. At a minimum, an expansion of context requires a vastly expanded vocabulary which more unambiguously accommodates the large range of meanings ordinarily expressed through language. A certain expansion of grammar seems to be required as well. For instance, some degree of syntactic embedding seems to be necessary to convey more complex ideas or actions without excessive circumlocution. Moreover, major processes like passive tend to (re-)appear.

This process of **creolization** (or perhaps more accurately, **depidginization**) is commonly believed to take place only when a pidgin 'acquires native speakers': That is, in a linguistically highly diversified community, parents begin using pidgin with each other as their only common means of communication, and as a consequence, pidgin becomes the only basis for a new generation of speakers to acquire as a native language. And, it is argued, while the pidgin may have been sufficient as an auxiliary language for the parents, it is clearly inadequate as a native language and therefore must perforce undergo expansion and elaboration. Linguists subscribing to this view will reserve the term **creole** for languages which arose in this manner.

Perhaps developments of this sort took place in the slave-holding societies of the New World, where slave owners, fearful of Africans conspiring against them, apparently attempted to prohibit the use of African languages and force slaves to resort to pidgin. It is perhaps this set of circumstances which led to the development of the slavery argot discussed in 14.5.4. However, there is a fair amount of evidence that such attempts were not always successful. For instance, it is reported that early American fugitive slave patrols frequently had Wolof interpreters, a fact which suggests that instead of pidgin, Wolof and perhaps other African languages were used as link languages among the slaves.

More importantly, it must be seriously doubted whether in non-coercive situations a language as restricted as a pidgin would have been picked up as a native language by large groups of children, or whether it would have been used as the only means of communication in the parental generation. In order for anything of that sort to happen, the pidgin must have undergone considerable prior expansion and elaboration. (According to certain scholars, current developments in Hawaiian Creole are an example of sudden expansion without prior elaboration. The basis for these developments appears to be not a fully institutionalized pidgin, but a relatively unsettled pre-pidgin comparable to Gastarbeiterdeutsch. It is not clear whether or how this language is related to the Hawaiian English-based pidgin which was attested in the last century. Perhaps the present-day 'jargon' represents a secondary use of original pidgin as a means of communication with new immigrants. The historical background for the Hawaiian situation thus does not seem to be fully understood. There are good reasons, then, for being cautious about accepting the Hawaiian developments as typical.)

In fact, there is evidence that creolization or depidginization can take place without a pidgin's 'acquiring native speakers'. Especially illustrative is the case of the varieties of Pidgin English used in Papua New Guinea, Melanesia, and the Solomon Islands. (These are now commonly referred to as Tok Pisin, Neo-Melanesian, and Neo-Solomonic, respectively. But in some writings, the term Neo-Melanesian is used to include Tok Pisin and Neo-Solomonic.)

Like many other pidgins, these languages came to be employed as administrative auxiliary languages used by the European colonial administrations in communicating with a linguistically highly diversified indigenous population, as increasingly popular link languages between the various local communities, and as vehicles for missionary activities. Each of these expanded uses brought with it an elaboration in vocabulary and structure. And it is the intensive use of these pidgins as link languages which seems responsible for the fact that their structure exhibits a great amount of interlanguage influence from the indigenous languages; cf. point (f) at the beginning of 16.4. above. Neo-Melanesian has now become a language of parliamentary debates and of the news media, requiring yet further expansion and elaboration. A similar development has recently begun in Tok Pisin.

526   16. Koinés, convergence, pidgins, etc.

'Acquisition of native speakers', on the other hand, has proceeded at a much slower pace. Even now, for instance, only about five percent of all Tok Pisin users are native speakers. Moreover, the linguistic behavior of native speakers does not seem to differ radically from that of other fluent users. True, native-speaker children seem to speak a faster and more innovative variety of the language; but as they grow up, they adapt to the more conservative norms of the older generation.

Cases like these suggest that creolization ordinarily is a slow, continuous process of depidginization, rather than an almost overnight, 'catastrophic' phenomenon. As a consequence, it would seem arbitrary to reserve the term 'creole' only for those varieties of language which have acquired native speakers.

In many, perhaps most of the attested cases, the vocabulary expansion connected with depidginization has taken place through borrowing from the European language which had earlier formed the basis for the pidgin. Thus, an English-based pidgin tends to be creolized by borrowing from English, a French-based one by borrowing from French, etc. However, as noted in 16.4.2, a shift in political environment may introduce a different source for vocabulary expansion. Moreover, vocabulary closely connected with the native culture of the non-European population frequently is of indigenous, non-European provenience.

Grammatical expansion may result from several factors. One of these is that lexical borrowing may indirectly introduce foreign morphological, sometimes also syntactic structure; cf. 14.1. In this fashion, French-based Haitian Creole has (re-)acquired a distinction between masculine and feminine gender which had been lost in the pidgin stage; cf. (44).

(44)   le lundi (m.)   'Monday'
       la semaine (f.)   'the week'

A perhaps more common source for syntactic elaboration seems to lie in the interlanguage-influence of the native, non-European languages. In addition to the Neo-Melanesian phenomena referred to in point (f) at the beginning of 16.4, note the Haitian Creole situation: A variety of syntactic phenomena, including the placement of definitizers and genitives, and the structure of comparative constructions have been attributed to West African influence. Thus, just like various West African languages (cf. (45)), Haitian Creole places definitizers after their noun phrase, while French — and borrowings from French into the

Creole — place them before (cf. (44)). Moreover, as the examples in (46) show, these definitizers may follow extended noun phrases which contain a postnominal modifying adjective or even a relative clause. (There is some question as to whether the Creole morpheme *-a/la/na/ã* should be traced to a West African source (cf. Ewe *-(l)a*) or to the (preposed) French article *la*.) Interestingly, by having both pre-NP and post-NP definitizers (cf. (44) beside (46)), Haitian Creole has a more complex system than either French or the West African languages.

(45) Ewe   afe -   a
      Yoruba   ile   yen
      'house' DEF.
      'that house'

(46) Hait. Cr. plaf-plaf -   la
      'plop-plop' DEF.
      'the plop-plopping'
      mãgo   mi -   ã
      'mango'   'ripe' DEF.
      'the ripe mango'
      oto   li   vã -   mwẽ -   ã
      'car' 'he' 'sell' 'me'   DEF.
      'the car which he sold me'

Having in this manner acquired the expanded vocabulary and grammar of 'normal' languages, creoles will be synchronically indistinguishable from such other varieties of speech. It is only their historical origination which differentiates them.

In the majority of cases, the result is a 'vernacular' which is used only for ordinary everyday communication, while another language (usually a European standard language) serves as a means of more intellectual and written communication. However, the case of Neo-Melanesian shows that this is not a necessary development. Creoles are just as much usable as intellectual and written languages as any other form of speech, if there is the need.

Where creoles are used as a vernacular, their relationship to the coexisting European prestige language may be of two types: On one side is the relationship between Haitian Creole and French, which can only be described as diglossic. On the other hand, where society is less rigidly stratified, as in the post-slavery English-speaking Caribbean, the result may be quite different. In this environment, an ever-increasing section of the population has found it possible, convenient, or even necessary to become actively bilingual between the creole and the European standard language. Through interlanguage, then, varieties of language have arisen which are intermediate between the European standard and the creole. The ultimate result is what has been called a **creole continuum**, i. e., a range of speech varieties which extend from the more or less pure European language to the more or less pure creole, with all kinds of intermediate varieties which, depending on education, motivation, etc., have a varying admixture of standard and creole elements. The different 'layers' within this creole continuum may then function much like the social dialects of monolingual societies, such that different speakers will show proficiency in a number of different varieties (but not necessarily in all). That is, for all practical purposes, the two languages have merged into a single entity.

16.4.6. Decreolization, Black Vernacular English

The ultimate outcome may be what seems to be found in the case of **Black Vernacular English** (BVE), namely complete **decreolization**, i. e., the more or less full integration of the creole grammar into the grammar of the European language, and the disappearance of the pure creole.

The resulting social dialect may well show relics of the original creole stage; cf. the aspectual marker *done* in (47a) or the lack of gender distinction in (47b). But these are definitely on the wane.

(47a)   he done tole me
  b)   he a nice girl

Other creole features have proved more vigorous, such as the absence of the marker *-(e)d* in the form *tole* of (47a) or the absence of the copula 'to be' in (47b). However, they have done so in a very curious fashion:

In the case of *told*, there is evidence that BVE now tends to have the ending $/-d/$ in its phonological underlying structure. For forms like *lied, teed (off)* have practically invariant final [-d] on the surface. However, where the addition of $/-d/$ results in a final consonant cluster, surface [-d] (or [-t]) is only variably present, as in *clean(ed), walk(ed)*.

Its absence is especially common in forms like *tole* where the vowel change is sufficient to mark the form as the past tense of *tell,* even without the affix.

What seems to have happened here is that the original absence of the past-tense marker has been 'salvaged' to a certain degree by synchronically overextending a rule which is found also in the fast speech of many white speakers of English, namely word-final cluster simplification.

Similarly, the absence of the copula in structures like (47b) has been integrated into the system of European-based English grammar: BVE does in fact have an underlying copula. But that copula is deleted under the same conditions under which standard English 'contracts'; cf. (48). In all those examples in which *is* is italiciaed, standard English cannot contract and BVE cannot omit the copula.

(48)   Standard English   Black Vernacular English

        She's a nice girl   She a nice girl
vs.   She *is*[1]   She *is*[1]
        She isnt' nice, *is* she?   She ain't nice, *is* she?
        The girl I saw yesterday   The girl I saw yesterday
        is nice   *is* nice

([1] response to claim that she is not)

It is through 'integration' of its creole features into an essentially 'standard' English grammar that BVE has become a decreolized dialect of English. Note however that much of the decreolization took place in the American South, based on 'Vernacular (Southern) White English', and not on the standard language. It is this factor which probably accounts for the fact that BVE has been much slower to adopt the third-person singular present ending *-s*. For the absence of this ending (or its generalization throughout the present, as in *we goes*) appears to be an old feature of non-standard white Southern speech, carried over, it seems, from regional dialects of the British Isles. In this case, then, the structure of the European-based speech which was available as a model for decreolization reinforced the pidgin/creole feature of not having inflectional endings.

16.5. Language death

As a consequence of linguistic contact, speakers often give up their native language in favor of another, more prestigious form of speech, whether the latter be the language of a foreign conqueror, a link language, a koiné, a creole, or perhaps even a pidgin. While this much has been known for a long time, the manner in which linguistic communities switch language 'loyalties' and the effects of this switch on linguistic structure were only poorly understood. Traditional linguistic literature may mention the date at which 'the last speaker' of a given language died. But it does not examine questions like 'Who did that last speaker speak to?' or 'What was his/her language like?'

It is only fairly recently that research has begun into this aspect of language contact, which now is referred to as **language death**. As a consequence, findings are limited in number and spotty in terms of the languages and the aspects of grammar that have been studied. Nevertheless, certain very general patterns are beginning to emerge:

Language death commonly does not take place suddenly, within just one generation. Rather, it is a slow process which may extend over more than three generations. Its basis is bilingualism of a sort where a non-native language is considered more prestigious or useful, or may be required in certain contexts (such as school or dealing with governmental authorities). As a consequence, the non-native language begins to be used with increasing frequency and in increasingly larger social contexts, while the native language is employed less frequently and in fewer contexts.

Reduction in use in turn reduces the 'input' on which new speakers of the language can draw in order to formulate their own internalized grammar. While this may not affect the most common constructions in the language, its effects can be greater on structures which are less frequently used. These may now be heard so rarely that learners find it difficult, if not impossible, to internalize rules which correctly account for them.

As a consequence, the new generation of speakers may avoid using such constructions, thus further reducing the input for the next generation of speakers, and so on. In this manner, then, the rule system of the language undergoes a slow process of atrophy. (Studies on language death in very different locations, focussing on very different grammatical phenomena, agree on the fact that grammatical attrition is not across the board or random, but that it takes place in terms of the 'fading out' of rules and that in this process, certain, apparently more 'marked' or 'difficult' rules are lost first.)

What is interesting is that grammatical atrophy is not matched by a similar decrease in vocabulary or in the younger generations' ability to understand older speakers. Passive and active command of the language thus may differ considerably.

At a certain point, the atrophy in the grammatical system 'progresses' to the point that a new generation of speakers no longer is able to formulate an internalized grammar, even to their own satisfaction. The members of this generation, often referred to as 'semi-speakers', fluently understand even their grandparents' speech, but will generally admit that they are unable to speak the language themselves. At this point, then, the transmission of the language has come to an end, the language has effectively died. (One suspects that many of the 'last speakers' mentioned in traditional accounts were in fact the last remaining members of such a generation of 'semi-speakers'.)

17. Internal reconstruction

Up to this point we have considered diachronic linguistics from the 'historical' point of view: We have examined how language changes over time, and we have looked at the factors — both linguistic and extralinguistic — which affect the way language changes. In so doing, we have often drawn on developments originating with Proto-Indo-European, Proto-Germanic, Proto-Slavic, etc., i. e., with languages for which there are no historical attestations. Now that we have gained some understanding of how language changes, we can direct out attention to the question as to how we can have any knowledge about such unattested, ancestral languages.

The means through which we acquire such knowledge is **reconstruction**, a process in which we apply our knowledge of linguistic change so as to in effect **reverse linguistic history**. We can do so by looking for synchronic evidence which points to earlier linguistic change. Such evidence will consist of phonetic (or other) **variation** between forms which can be plausibly assumed to originally have had **invariant** structure. Put differently, reconstruction attempts to reduce synchronic variation to earlier invariance.

Variations of this kind may be of the type (1) below, where within a given language there is a synchronic morphophonemic alternation (in this case, between voiced and voiceless obstruent). Or it may consist of variation across linguistic boundaries (whether dialect or language boundaries), as in (2). In the latter case, the evidence is said to be **comparative**, requiring **comparative reconstruction** to reduce variation to invariance. In cases like (1), the variation is **internal** (to German) and can be reduced to invariance through **internal reconstruction**. (Variation of this sort usually consists of morphophonemic alternations between related forms. However, as will be seen later, other types of variation may motivate internal reconstruction.)

(1) Germ.   [tāk]   : [tāg-ə]   'day : days'

(2) Amer. Engl. [kǽnt] : Brit. Engl. [kānt] 'can't'
     Engl.   father : Fr.   père

It is convenient to begin the discussion of this approach to historical linguistics with internal reconstruction. For unlike comparative reconstruction, it requires less extensive data and thus is accomplished — and demonstrated — more easily. Moreover, comparative reconstruction frequently needs to draw on the insights provided by the method of internal reconstruction.

17.1. Basic assumptions, exemplification

Internal reconstruction attempts to reduce synchronic, language-internal variation to an earlier, prehistoric stage of invariance.

To illustrate internal reconstruction, let us consider the alternations between voiced and voiceless stops in the Latin data of (3).

(3) sg. N   sg. G
     urp-s   urb-is   'city'
     rēk-s   rēg-is   'king'
     etc.

Without any further information, there would be two different ways in which this variation can be reduced to earlier invariance. On one hand, we can reconstruct voiced stops as in (4) and account for the voicelessness in [urps, rēks] as resulting from the common process of voicing assimilation. On the other, we may posit the forms in (5) and explain [urbis, rēgis] etc. as due to the equally common change of medial voicing (or weakening).

(4) *urb-s   *urb-is
     *rēg-s   *rēg-is
     etc.

(5) *urp-s   *urp-is
     *rēk-s   *rēk-is
     etc.

The additional attested Latin evidence in (6), with invariable voiceless stops, makes it possible to choose between these two analyses and to prefer the voiced-stop reconstruction in (4). (The examples in (6), then, are the unchanged reflexes of an earlier contrasting set (6′) with root-final voiceless stops.) For if (5) had been selected, we would be confronted with the difficulty of having to assume that medial voicing applied in (5) = (3), but not in (6). Given that medial voicing is a regular type of sound change, we should expect it to apply in a regular fashion.

(6)   wōk-s   wōk-is   'voice'
       stirp-s   stirp-is   'root'
       etc.

(6')   *wōk-s   *wōk-is   'voice'
       *stirp-s   *stirp-is 'root'
       etc.

It might be argued that the reconstruction in (5) can be salvaged by assuming that words of the type (6) have undergone a leveling process which eliminated the alternations that resulted from medial voicing. However, there are a number of reasons against this argument: First, the general tenet of historical linguistics is to prefer a sound-change analysis over an analogical one. Put differently, analogy is to be invoked only where strictly necessary. In the present case, however, there is no need to invoke analogy, since a perfectly straightforward alternative is available, namely to reconstruct two contrasting sets, (4) and (6') and to account for forms like *urp-s* as resulting from voice assimilation. Secondly, invoking analogy to 'rescue' reconstruction (5) violates 'Occam's Razor' for which see below. A third argument against the 'rescue' version of reconstruction (5) is motivated specifically by the structure of Latin: Closer examination shows that Latin has a contrast between voiced and voiceless stops in all environments, save before (or next to) obstruents; cf. (7) beside (3) and (6). It is only next to obstruents that the contrast is neutralized. Reconstruction (4) explains this situation by postulating an original contrast between voiced and voiceless stops in all environments, and its later neutralization next to (voiceless) obstruents. Reconstruction (5), on the other hand, fails to provide any explanation. In fact, it requires the assumption that the contrast between voiced and voiceless had been neutralized root-finally in the ancestral language, and that the attested contrast in medial environment results from the accidents of irregular leveling.

(7)   ad   'at'   : at   'but'
       grūs 'crane' : crūs   'calf, shin'

From this brief exemplification we can abstract several general principles for internal (as well as comparative) reconstruction. These are detailed in the following sections.

17.1.1. Naturalness

Given two otherwise equally acceptable competing analyses, we prefer the one which postulates more natural or more common processes. For instance, given an alternation of the type (8), we could a priori reconstruct either [k] or [č] as the root-final consonant and derive the other by means of an appropriate sound change. However, since palatalization is a very common and natural process, while the alternative shift of [+ pal.] to [+ vel.] is not, we will prefer the reconstruction with invariant [k], together with the change in (9). (Note that the principle of naturalness is applicable only where there is a choice between a more natural and a less natural analysis. Where there is no choice, as for instance in unconditioned changes, the principle cannot apply. Moreover, in many cases, both competing analyses are equally natural. Compare, e. g., the case of Latin voicing assimilation next to obstruent vs. medial voicing.)

(8)   It. amik-o : pl. amič-i 'friend : friends'

(9)   [+ vel.] > [+ pal.] / _____ [V, + front]

17.1.2. Priority of sound change and regular change

Given a choice, analyses postulating sound changes are more highly valued than analyses which require analogical or other non-phonetic changes. Similarly, everything else being equal, analyses operating with regular changes (sound change and/or rule-governed analogy) are preferred over those which require sporadic or less regular changes. This is true not only in the Latin case of (3) above, but also in examples like (1) = (10) below.

(10)   Germ. [tāk] : [tāg-ə] 'day : days'

Here again, it is a priori possible to postulate two competing reconstructions; cf. (11) and (12).

(11)   *tāk : *tāk-ə

(12)   *tāg : *tāg-ə

In addition to (10), there is a pattern with invariant voiceless root-final obstruent; cf. (13). And this pattern would call for the reconstruction in (13').

(13)   [zak] : [zɛk-ə]   'sack : sacks'

(13')   *zak : *zɛk-ə

The German situation at first sight appears to be entirely analogous to the Latin one and to require the reconstruction in (12) for the pattern in (10), with invariant voiced obstruent in the ancestral language. For again, if we were to reconstruct as in (11), then we would have to postulate developments involving both sound change (medial voicing) and analogy (leveling of the word-final voiceless alternant in cases like (13)).

However, in this case it might be argued that also reconstruction (12) necessitates postulating both a sound change (prepausal devoicing) and analogy (the extension of devoicing to word-final environment); cf. 11.5 above. That is, there seems to be no difference between the two analyses, and therefore no way of choosing between them.

What makes it nevertheless possible to prefer reconstruction (12) is the fact that the extension of prepausal devoicing to word-final environment is a regular, rule-governed analogical development, while reconstruction (11) would require postulating an inherently non-regular process of leveling.

17.1.3. Explanation and structure

Given two alternative analyses, we will prefer the one which provides greater explanation or motivation for the postulated changes, as well as for the attested synchronic facts. Such explanations often refer to issues of over-all linguistic structure.

This principle was invoked earlier, when we decided in favor of reconstruction (4) for Latin *urp-s, urb-is* because the required voicing assimilation explains a general feature of Latin structure, namely the fact that the contrast voiced : voiceless is neutralized next to obstruents.

A similar argument can be made also for the German situation: Reconstruction (12), together with its postulated extension of prepausal devoicing to word-final environment, explains the general fact that in word-final position, obstruents can occur only in voiceless form.

In both of these cases, the notion that reconstructions should be explanatory is only one of several factors which make it possible to choose one reconstruction over the other. The following case from the West African language Nupe makes much more crucial reference to our principle. Moreover, this case shows that the variation which motivates internal reconstruction need not always consist of morphophonemic alternations.

Nupe consonants occur in three varieties, palatalized, labiovelarized, and neutral; cf. (14).

(14) Palatalized   Neutral   Labiovelarized
    C^y i C^w u
    C^y e C^w o
    C^y a   C a C^w a

As example (14) shows, there is a considerable variation or divergence between the contexts in which the three types of consonants can occur. The reconstruction in (15), combined with the changes in (16) and (17), establishes a more balanced system for the ancestral language and provides a historical explanation and motivation for the divergent distributions in the attested system of (14). (The relative chronology of changes (16) and (17) is as indicated; i.e., (16) precedes (17).)

(15)   C i   C u
         C e   C o
         C ɛ   C ɔ
              C a

(16) C > [+ palatalized]   / _____ [V, + front]
      > [+ labiovelarized] / _____ [V, + back]

(17) $\begin{bmatrix} V \\ + lo \end{bmatrix} > \begin{bmatrix} - \text{front} \\ - \text{back} \end{bmatrix}$
(i.e. ɛ, ɔ > a)

(An alternative reconstruction would posit earlier *ya* and *wa* instead of ɛ and ɔ. In this case, change (16) would be followed by the loss of *y* or *w* in the context C _____ V. The objection to this alternative approach would be that it creates a new imbalance in the reconstructed system, by permitting *y* and *w* to occur in the context C_____*a*, but not between consonants and other vowels.)

17.1.4. 'Occam's Razor'

Reconstructions should not violate the maxim attributed to the medieval philosopher Occam that **entia non sunt multiplicanda praeter necessitatem** 'entities (in an argument) are not to be multiplied beyond necessity'. Put differently, the simplest possible analysis is to be preferred, everything else being equal.

The most obvious example of a violation of Occam's Razor would be to propose the reconstructions in (19) for the Latin data in (18). True, we can postulate regular and not necessarily unnatural changes to derive the attested Latin forms from the reconstructed ones; cf. (20). (Thus the changes in (20a) and (b) follow the precedent of Grimm's Law.) However, the analysis clearly violates Occam's Razor by postulating more changes (namely (20a/b)) than is necessary.

(18) urp-s   : urb-is
      stirp-s : stirp-is
      etc

(19) *urbh-s : *urbh-is
      *stirb-s : *stirb-is
      etc.

(20a) [+ stop, +voice]   > [− voice]
   b) [+ stop, + asp.]   > [− asp.]
   c) [+ stop] > [− voice] / _____ [+ obstr., − voice]

The situation would be similar if we were to propose the reconstruction in (21) for the Nupe data in (14), together with the change in (22) which in effect neutralizes the contrast between palatalized and neutral consonants, except before *a*.

(21) C^y i   C i   C^w u
      C^y e   C e   C^w o
      C^y a   C a   C^w a

(22) C > [+ palatalized] / _____ [V, + front]

Again there is nothing unnatural, irregular, or even 'unexplanatory' about the postulated change. But the reconstruction posits more prehistoric segments, segment types, and segment combinations than necessary, given the availability of an alternative analysis.

There are cases, however, where it is not so self-evident as to whether or not a given analysis postulates entities beyond necessity. This is especially true where Occam's Razor comes into conflict with the other principles that have been noted above. Consider for instance the Latin data in (23).

(23)   lau-s   : laud-is   'praise'
      ar-s   : art-is   'art'
      mile-s : milit-is 'soldier'
      etc.

Clearly, the occurrence of either *d* or *t* on the right side of (23) is not predictable. Moreover, we have seen earlier that the other Latin stops exhibit a contrast voiced : voiceless in the same environment and that they can occur before *-s*. For these reasons, there can be no doubt that (23) must be reconstructed as in (24). (The alternation *e : i* in *mile-s : milit-is* is left unresolved.)

(24)   *laud-s   : *laud-is
      *art-s   : *art-is
      *milet-s : *milit-is
      etc.

And from *laud-s* our well-known voicing assimilation would regularly produce *laut-s*. The question arises, however, as to how the expected earlier *-t-s* of all of these forms has changed into the actually attested *-s*. Two solutions suggest themselves. According to one, *t* is simply lost in this environment; cf. (25). The other lets *t* assimilate to the following *s* and then postulates a process of degemination (possibly restricted to word-final position); cf. (26).

(25)   t > Ø / _____ s

(26a)   t > s / _____ s
  b)   ss > s

Both of these solutions operate with regular sound changes; and there is nothing particularly unnatural about the changes of either (25) or (26). In terms of simplicity, solution (25) clearly has the edge; for it postulates a single change, rather than a sequence of two. However, to many linguists' minds, there is a subtle, but clear difference between the genuine explanation of (26) and the "brute-force" manner in which (25) "merely accounts for the facts":

The processes by which (26) accounts for the absence of *t* are very natural and have no 'arbitrary' limitations placed upon them. Moreover, this solution explains why it is the dental stop which is singled out for loss before *s*, while other stops remain (cf. the earlier Latin examples). Solution (25), on the other hand, manages to 'account' for the absence of *t*, but it does so in terms of an 'arbitrarily' restricted process. Moreover, there is nothing in the postulated process or in its formulation that would explain why it is *t* and not some other stop which is lost before *s*. The first of these two points against solution (25) can perhaps be dismissed. For as noted in the discussion of sound change, general phonetically motivated processes, such as for instance weakening, may in individual languages be arbitrarily restricted to just a subset of the environments which 'normally' trigger the change. One might argue that the loss of *t* before *s* is an example of such an arbitrarily restricted change (of cluster simplification). However, the fact still remains that although simpler than (26), solution (25) provides less of an explanation.

There is no absolute agreement among linguists as to whether in cases like this the principle of explanation (or of naturalness or regularity, for that matter) should take precedence over Occam's Razor or vice versa.

As it turns out, in our present case we have Old Latin attestations of the postulated intermediate stage *ss* of solution (26). The historical evidence in this case therefore is on the side of 'explanation', rather than of Occam's Razor. However, there is no guarantee that the principle of 'explanation' (or 'naturalness', or 'regularity') will always lead to a more correct analysis than Occam's Razor.

17.1.5. Justification of reconstruction — statement of changes

As a final note it should be observed that in order to be considered successful, reconstructions (both internal and comparative) must be 'justified' by means of a detailed statement on the changes required to convert the reconstructed forms into their actually attested counterparts.

These changes should, of course, not be in conflict with what we know about the general, natural directions of linguistic change. Thus, outside of certain well-known subtypes, sound change should be regular. And if sound change is to be regular, then split must result from conditioned change. (The notion of random, unconditioned split is logically incompatible with the regularity principle.) In cases of split it is therefore necessary to indicate the phonetic conditions for the split.

In the case of analogical change (or borrowing, where that is a possibility), it is necessary to provide evidence for a plausible motivation (or source) for the development in question. For instance, when dealing with analogy we should be able to identify the parameter and motivation for the change: Is it a specifiable morphological proportion, a particular morphophonemic alternation in an identifiable paradigm, or the model of a specific semantically related form?

17.2. Limitations, comparison with generative phonology

The requirement that changes postulated for a given reconstruction must not conflict with the general, natural directions of linguistic change imposes significant limitations on our ability to reconstruct. For there are many alternations (and other types of variation) that do not lend themselves to a successful internal reconstruction which abides by this requirement.

Consider for instance the English alternations in (27). We may suspect that they go back to an earlier stage at which there was an invariant form for the root 'sing'. However, the fact that the attested root vowels occur in the same phonetic environment makes it impossible to establish by what phonetically motivated processes they developed out of a single, invariant ancestral root vowel. In fact, it is not even possible to decide in a principled fashion which invariant vowel we should reconstruct. Finally, the alternations in question are synchronically quite irregular and restricted, suggesting that what regularity there may once have been has long since been obscured by later developments. (In the present case, the uncertainty to a large extent goes back as far as Proto-

Indo-European: Even at that early stage, when there are clear differences in phonetic environment, the phonetic motivations for most of the morphological alternations are by no means clear or uncontroversial.)

(27)   sing : sang : sung : song

The case is better with examples like (28). True, also here there are some problems about regularity. For beside (28) we find non-alternating sets like (29) and (30). However, further investigation will show that some speakers have the pattern (31) beside, or instead of, (30), etc. Moreover, there are correspondences like the ones in (32), where the alternation does not show up in nominal paradigms but in related verbs.

(28)	noun singular	noun plural	derived verb
	wife	wives	
	half	halves	to halve
	life	lives	to live
(29)	wave	waves	to wave
(30)	staff	staffs	to staff
	roof	roofs	to roof
(31)	roof	rooves	to roof
(32)	belief	beliefs	to believe

As a consequence we can attribute the present-day invariant voiced or voiceless fricatives of sets like (29) and (30) to the operation of leveling, a process which has only partially applied in sets like (31) and (32). Our internal reconstruction therefore needs to explain only the pattern in example (30).

Unfortunately, however, even after thus eliminating the irregularities created by analogical processes, we are still not able to state with confidence (i) whether the alternation $f : v$ should be reconstructed as invariant f or as v, and (ii) more importantly, under which phonetic conditions the reconstructed segment was differentiated into the attested f and v. (Recall that forms like *half* and *halve* offer the voiceless and voiced alternants in the same word-final environment.)

Although cases like these do not lend themselves to successful internal reconstruction, they may be of considerable interest and usefulness in comparative reconstruction. Consider for instance the German/English correspondence sets in (33). Knowing that English has a morphophonemic alternation between *f* and *v* in words like *wife : wives* and that non-alternating *f* or *v* can be attributed to leveling, we can reduce the two sets in (33) to the single set in (34). As a consequence we can now consider the alternation *f : v* a problem of English historical grammar, not of comparative Germanic linguistics. Moreover, where in the absence of the internal evidence of English we might have toyed with reconstructing two proto-segments (one for (33a), the other for (33b)), we are now able to posit a single proto-segment, thus satisfying the principle of Occam's Razor.

(33)		German	English
a)		b	f
	cf.	Stab	staff
		ab	off
		etc.	
b)		b	v
	cf.	Grab	grave
		geben	give
		etc.	
(34)		b	f/v

By not being able to successfully tackle alternations like *sing : sang* etc., or even *wife : wives*, internal reconstruction differs considerably from the generative-phonological procedure of setting up invariant underlying forms. For with the exception of non-recurring, isolated patterns like Engl. *go : went,* generative phonology must account for all synchronic alternations, since presumably they are not just memorized but governed by grammatical rules. Thus in the case of *sing : sang* etc., generative phonology would set up an underlying form /sing/ and derive the other forms by morphologically or syntactically conditioned minor rules, such as (35).

$$(35) \quad i \rightarrow æ \ / \ \underline{\hspace{2cm}} \begin{bmatrix} + \text{ verb} \\ + \text{ root} \\ + \text{ past} \\ - \text{ participle} \end{bmatrix}$$

This difference between internal reconstruction and synchronic generative phonology is a natural consequence of their differences in goals: As noted in Chapter 11, generative phonology attempts to relate synchronically alternating forms to each other and to account for speakers' synchronic knowledge of their language. Therefore it must account for all such alternations, "warts and all". Internal reconstruction, on the other hand, has to abide by the "rules of the game" of historical linguistics, such as the regularity principle and the distinction between sound change and analogy. Moreover, historical linguistics primarily traces the diachronic development of surface forms. For it is surface forms which are handed down from one generation of speakers to another. Underlying forms and rules of grammar, on the other hand, are not directly observable, therefore cannot be handed down directly, and have to be formulated anew by each generation.

At the same time, however, note that because of its limitations, historical linguistics often has to posit reconstructions with 'unresolved' morphophonemic alternations, such as the vowel alternation [ē : ā] in the German example (36). Alternations of this sort then must be accounted for in terms of the synchronic grammar of pre-German, just as much as they are in the grammar of contemporary German, namely by means of synchronic rules similar to the English rule in (35). That is, through the reconstruction of surface forms it is possible to indirectly reconstruct earlier synchronic rule systems.

(36a) Attested German   [gēb-n̩] : [gāp]
   b) pre-German   [gēb-n̩] : [gāb]
                      'give'   'gave'

17.3. Accuracy of the method

In many cases we are able to check the accuracy of internal reconstructions by comparing them with the corresponding forms as they are attested in documented earlier stages of the language. For instance, in the case of Germ. [tāk] : [tāg-ə], reconstructed as *[tāg] : *[tāg-ə], we can point to the invariant voiced root-final consonant in OHG *tag : tag-a*. Cases like these lend a great degree credibility to the method of internal reconstruction.

The perhaps most celebrated confirmation of the method involves an internal reconstruction undertaken in 1879 by de Saussure on the basis not of a modern attested language, but of Proto-Indo-European as it was reconstructed at that time. Moreover, when this reconstruction was made, there was no hope of ever empirically confirming it. Confirmation eventually became possible (some 50 years later), after Hittite was shown to belong to the Indo-European family. For it turned out that Hittite preserved distinct traces of the segments postulated in de Saussure's reconstructive hypothesis.

The framework within which the reconstruction was made was the Indo-European system of **ablaut**, i. e., of the vowel alternations which are the ancestor of the Modern English pattern *sing : sang*, etc. (Note however that de Saussure's reconstruction merely 'streamlined' the ablaut system; it did not propose an earlier invariant stage without ablaut alternations.)

For the majority of forms, ablaut had the following alternants or '**grades**', each of which would occur under particular morphological conditions (although some morphological categories showed variation between different ablaut grades). For instance, verbal nouns in *-ti-* had ∅-grade of the root, 'iteratives' of the type Gk. *phoreō* 'carry repeatedly' had the *o*-grade, etc. (The root used to illustrate the different ablaut grades is PIE **bher-* 'carry'.)

(a) **Basic, '*e*-grade' or 'normal grade'** with *e*-vocalism, as in **bher-ō*: Skt. *bhar-ā-mi*, Gk. *pher-ō*, Lat. *fer-ō* 'I carry'.

(b) ***o*-grade**, with substitution of *o* for the *e* of the normal grade, as in **bhor-eyō* : Gk. *phor-eō* 'I carry repeatedly'.

The common term for the ablaut grades of (a) and (b) is '**full grade**'.

(c) **Extended grade**, with replacement of full-grade *e* or *o* by the corresponding long vowel, as in **e-bhēr-s-t* : Skt. *a-bhār* 'has carried' or **bhōr-s* : Gk. *phōr* 'thief'.

(d) **∅-grade**, with deletion of the basic vowel, as in **bhr̥-ti-* : Skt. *bhr̥-ti-* 'a carrying'.

These alternations are summarized in (37). (Citations are in the form that occurs before non-syllabic segments.) As this summary shows, the ablaut alternations of the vowels can have secondary effects on neighboring sonorants: A sonorant which through the ∅-grade loss of the root vowel comes to occur between consonants is syllabified.

(37) *e*-grade   *o*-grade   extended grade   ∅-grade
      bher-   bhor-   bhēr- / bhōr-   bhr̥-

Let us refer to roots which follow this ablaut pattern as '**aniṭ-roots**', a term used by some of the ancient Indian grammarians for the synchronic reflexes of these roots.

Beside the aniṭ-roots, a different type, the so-called '**seṭ-roots**' had been reconstructed. As the examples in (38) and (39) illustrate, these came in two superficially very different subvarieties. However, both subtypes shared the feature of having the vowel ǝ in some of their ablaut grades. Moreover, both types of roots differ from the aniṭ-roots by showing an unexpected long root vowel or syllabic sonorant in some of their forms. As a consequence, type (38) makes no formal distinction between full-grade and extended-grade forms. Compare the summary in (40). (As in (37), the citations of (40) are in the form that occurs before non-syllabic segments. For typographic reasons, lower-case *r* is used to indicate any sonorant. Short vowels are specially marked, as in *ĕ*.)

(38) *e*-grade = Extended   **dhē,*   as in Gk. *ti-thē-mi* 'put'
      e-grade:
      o-grade = Extended   **dhō,*   as in Gk. *thō-mos* 'heap'
      o-grade:
      ∅-grade: **dhǝ-,* as in Skt. *(d)hi-ta-* (pple.)
                                                           'put, placed'

(39) Normal grade: **terǝ-,* as in Skt. *tari-tum* 'to cross'
      o-grade: **torǝ-,* as in Skt. *ta-tar-a* 'I crossed over'
                                   (with loss of ǝ before vowel)
      Extended
      e-grade: **tērǝ-,* as in Skt. *a-tārī-t* 'has crossed'
      ∅-grade: **tr̥̄-,*   as in Skt. *tīr-ṇa-* (pple.) 'crossed',
                                   Lat. *trā-ns* 'across'

(40)   Aniṭ-roots   Seṭ-roots I   Seṭ-roots II

	Aniṭ-roots	Seṭ-roots I	Seṭ-roots II
e-grade	ĕr	ē	ĕrǝ
o-grade	ŏr	ō	ŏrǝ
Ext. *e*-grade	ēr	ē	ērǝ
Ext. *o*-grade	ōr	ō	ōrǝ
∅-grade	∅r̥	ǝ	∅r̥̄

De Saussure's reconstruction was based on the observation that length and ǝ are in complementary distribution in the seṭ-roots; cf. (41). Phonologically, therefore, the two subtypes of the seṭ-roots were entirely parallel. (Morphologically, to be sure, they differed, in so far as in type I, length appeared in the full grade and ə in the ∅-grade, while type II had the 'mirror-image' distribution. But this was simply due to the fact that the two types of seṭ-roots differed in their phonological structure.)

(41) [+ syll.] _____ C   [− syll.] _____ C
      dhē (length)   dhə
      tr̄ (length)   terə

Given the distribution in (41), it was possible to reconstruct an earlier stage at which ə and length were a single, invariant segment, which de Saussure symbolized as *A*; cf. (42). The later outcomes, then, could be accounted for as resulting from the processes in (43).

(42) [+ syll.] _____ C   [− syll.] _____ C
      dhe**A**   dh**A**
      tr**A**   ter**A**

(43a) A > ∅ (with comp. length) / [+ syll.] _____ C
   b) A > ə / [− syll.] _____ C

This reconstruction accounted not only for the similarities between the two types of seṭ-roots, or for the fact that the full-grade forms of type I roots always have a long vowel (as the result of loss with compensatory lengthening). It also made it possible to operate with an earlier single system of ablaut which applied both to aniṭ- and to seṭ-rules. Compare the summary and derivations in (44). (Here, (a) refers to change (43a), (b) to (43b). The ∅ of the ∅-grade is specially indicated to show the parallelism in formation.)

(44)

		e-grade			∅-grade		
		aniṭ	seṭ I	seṭ II	aniṭ	seṭ I	seṭ II
		bher-	dhĕA-	tĕrA-	bh∅r-	dh∅A-	t∅rA-
a)		— —	dhē-	— —	— —	— —	tr̄-
b)		— —	— —	tĕrə-	— —	dhə-	— —
	Outcome:	bher-	dhē-	tĕrə-	bhr̆-	dhə-	tr̄-

For various reasons, which are interesting mainly to Indo-European specialists, de Saussure went on to distinguish between two reconstructed segments (or **coefficients sonantiques** 'sonorant coefficients'), namely *A* and *O*. Later scholars added a third segment, *E*, or even a larger number. To some extent, the question of the exact number of such segments is still a matter of dispute. However, most Indo-Europeanists would now agree that at least three such segments are required.

At the time that de Saussure postulated his reconstruction, it received a generally quite negative response. Even scholars who initially were in favor soon began to have doubts. The reason to some degree was purely a matter of 'guilt by association': De Saussure's reconstruction was eagerly embraced by linguists trying to establish a genetic relationship between Indo-European and Semitic. These scholars equated the expanded set of de Saussure's 'coefficients sonantiques' with the Semitic 'laryngeals' ʔ, ʕ, *ħ* etc. And though the term **'laryngeal'** eventually came to be accepted as the name for de Saussure's 'coefficients sonantiques', the claim that Semitic and Indo-European are genetically related has to the present day been considered premature, if not dubious, by most Indo-Europeanists and Semiticists.

Another reason for the negative attitude toward de Saussure's analysis, however, was the fact that to the minds of most linguists it was too speculative, abstract, and 'algebraic' or 'mathematical' to be credible within the context of such an eminently 'non-mathematical', human activity as language. The fact that de Saussure did not provide any exact phonetic specifications for his reconstructed segments added to the reservations. For such 'phonetically empty' reconstructions violate the principle that reconstructions should be natural. (To some degree, the question of the phonetic identity of the 'laryngeals' is still unsettled. For the evidence of the attested languages is not clear enough to suggest a phonetic reconstruction which would satisfy all linguists.) Note however that this counterargument is rather weak: The naturalness principle is applicable only if there is a choice between competing analyses. Where no reasonable choice is possible, the principle is moot. But this does not mean that reconstruction, if otherwise well founded, must come to a halt.

As it turns out, after about half a century, enough new evidence had been discovered to make it possible to confirm the essential correctness of de Saussure's reconstruction. By now, the language of the documents of the ancient Hittites (ca. 2000 to 1200 B. C.) had been shown to be Indo-European. And as Kuryłowicz showed in 1927, Hittite offers distinct reflexes for two of the segments postulated by de Saussure and his later followers. Thus, de Saussure's **terA-* 'cross over' corresponds to Hittite **tarh-*.

This unexpected confirmation of de Saussure's hypothesis was perhaps the single most important event that aroused a sense of confidence in the accuracy and value of the method of internal reconstruction. And as Kuryłowicz's identification of Hitt. *h* with some of the 'coefficients sonantiques' or 'laryngeals' became more and more widely accepted, textbooks on historical linguistics began to pay special attention to internal reconstruction.

However, in spite of the fact that the accuracy of internal reconstruction has been confirmed in many cases, there is evidence which shows that occasionally the method will yield inaccurate results.

Consider for instance the German evidence in (45). Sound methodology requires us to reconstruct the corresponding pre-German forms in (46), especially if we consider the parallel evidence of [tāk] : [tāg-ə] etc. in (10) and (13) above. However, earlier German had the pattern (47) for (45a), and words following pattern (45b) appear to be borrowings made after the change by which forms like *bunte* changed into [bundə]. What is important is that the available synchronic evidence gives no clue for this special behavior of earlier *nt* clusters. At the same time, the problem is fairly 'localized' (to earlier *nt*-clusters). The general reconstruction of root-final voiced obstruents (as in **[tāg]* : **[tāgə]*) remains accurate.

(45)		base form	inflected form	
a)		[bunt]	[bund-ə]	'league'
b)		[bunt]	[bunt-ə]	'colorful, variegated'
(46a)		*bund	*bund-ə	'league'
b)		*bunt	*bunt-ə	'colorful, variegated'
(47)	OHG	bunt	bunte	'league'

'Localized' problems of this type seem to be rather common. But as noted, they do not affect the validity of the general reconstruction.

What is more problematic is the effect which rule reordering may have on our ability to engage in internal reconstruction. Consider for instance the case of Grassmann's Law in Sanskrit. The alternations between *budh* and *bhut* in (48) can be accounted for by the internal reconstruction in (49), together with the changes in (50).

(48) budhyatē   'is awake'
      bubōdha   'was awake'
      bubhutsati   'wants to be awake'
      bhut   'awakening'

(49) *bhudhyatē
      *bhubhōdha
      *bhubhudhsati
      *bhudh

(50) deasp. [+ stop] > [− asp., − voice] / _____ s
      GL   [+ stop] > [− asp.] / _____ (X) [+ asp.]

As we have seen in 11.8 above, though the reconstruction in (49) appears to be quite accurate, the changes postulated in (50) are not. The actual developments were considerably more complex and involved also rule reordering. The result of that reordering, however, was to eliminate the evidence which would have made it possible to posit the historically accurate scenario. As a consequence, the structure of Sanskrit has changed to the extent that invoking the correct historical developments would constitute a serious violation of Occam's Razor.

As this example suggests, rule reordering and other rule changes can limit the accuracy of internal reconstruction. In the case of Grassmann's Law, this limitation was of relatively minor consequence, affecting 'only' the postulated changes, not the reconstruction. However, it is quite conceivable that in other cases, rule change may affect the accuracy also of the reconstruction.

In spite of these limitations, however, internal reconstruction is an extremely useful and generally quite accurate tool for the reconstruction of linguistic prehistory. And where outside, 'comparative' evidence is not available, it is the only tool available for this purpose.

17.4. Extended exemplification

To illustrate more fully the manner in which internal reconstruction is undertaken and the kinds of considerations which determine reconstruction, it is useful to look in detail at a larger set of data.

In Lithuanian, *j* = [y] occurs only in the environments listed in (51). It does not occur in the context C _____ V.

(51)   ♯ _____ V
       V _____ V
       V _____ ♯

Consonants other than *j* are palatalized before front vowels. (Palatalization will be marked by an apostrophe, as in g' = [gʸ].) Before non-front vowels, both palatalized and non-palatalized consonants can occur, with one exception: Palatalized dental stops are not permitted before non-front vowels. Note in addition that the feature of palatalization must occur either with all members of a consonant cluster, or with none. That is, there are no clusters of the type *kr'* or *k'r*.

Given this background information, it is possible to tackle the alternations in the partial paradigms of (52).

(52)   sg. N   vargas   kraujes   k'el'es   s'v'eč'es
        V   var'g'e   krauje   k'el'e   s'v'et'e
        G   vargō   kraujō   k'el'ō   s'v'eč'ō
      pl. N   vargai   kraujei   k'el'ei   s'v'eč'ei
        A   vargus   kraujus   k'el'us.   s'v'eč'us
            'misery'   'blood'   'way'   'guest'

The following alternations can be noted:

(I)   rg : r'g' (/ _____ [V, + front]); cf. vargas : var'g'e
(II) a : e   (after C' or j); cf. vargas : kraujes
(III) t' : č' in s'v'et'e : s'v'eč'es

Alternation (I) can be accounted for by reconstructing an invariant *rg*, together with a process of palatalization which affects single consonants or consonant clusters; cf. (53).

(53) C_0 > [+ palatalized] / _____ $\begin{bmatrix} V \\ + \text{ front} \end{bmatrix}$

This analysis can be extended to the synchronically invariant palatalized initial segments of *k'el'es, s'v'eč'es*. In fact, Occam's Razor requires this extension. For otherwise we would have to unnecessarily postulate an earlier contrast between palatalized and non-palatalized consonants before front vowels.

Alternation (II) can be reduced to an earlier invariant *$*a$. For the change tentatively formulated in (54) can be considered a natural process of assimilation (of a to the front quality of the preceding non-syllabic segment).

$$(54) \quad a > e \ / \ \begin{Bmatrix} [+ \text{ palatalized}] \\ j \end{Bmatrix} \ \_\_\_\_\_$$

This analysis permits us to reconstruct a single set of endings for all of the words in (52) and for all the other words which follow the same patterns. Compare (55).

(55) *-as
      *-e
      *-ō
      *-ai
      *-us

At the point we are able to account for all the variations in the paradigms of *vargas* and *kraujas*.

The paradigms of *k'el'es* and *s'v'eč'es* with their root-final palatalization even before non-front vowel endings are somewhat more difficult to account for. But given that synchronically j does not occur in the environment C _____ V, it is possible to postulate earlier forms of the type (56), whose front-vocalic j would naturally motivate the palatalization before the (original or retained) non-front vowels. All that would be required is the very common and natural cluster simplification in (57), a change which has to be ordered after the palatalization process of (53).

(56) *keljas, *keljō, etc.

(57) $j > \emptyset \ / \ C \ \_\_\_\_\_ \ V$

Though this reconstruction does increase the clustering of reconstructed pre-Lithuanian, the resulting cluster is completely natural. Moreover, this analysis appears preferable to the conceivable alternatives. One of these alternatives would consist of reconstructing for pre-Lithuanian a contrast between palatalized and non-palatalized consonants before all vowels, i. e., in a larger set of environments than in Modern Lithuanian. The other would entail giving up the idea of reconstructing a single set of endings for the paradigms in (52). In either case, we would wind up proliferating entities much more than under the proposed analysis.

The analysis still leaves alternation (III) unaccounted for. In this case we may note that the change in (58) is a very common and natural development, while the opposite change is rare at best. Given the precedent of *k'el'es, k'el'ō < *keljas, keljō* etc. we can then posit the reconstructions in (59).

(58) t' > č'

(59) *svetjas, *svetjō, etc.

To correctly derive the attested forms in the paradigm of *s'v'eč'es* we will have to restrict (58) as in (60). Moreover, noting the difference between *s'v'eč'es < *svetjas* and *s'v'et'e < svetje*, we will have to order (60) before (54), i. e. before the process which changes *a* to *e* in the suffix.

$$(60) \quad \text{t'} > \check{\text{c}}' \ / \ \underline{\hspace{2cm}} \begin{bmatrix} V \\ - \text{front} \end{bmatrix}$$

At this point we may want to take stock of what we have reconstructed so far and of the changes that are required to convert the reconstructions into the actually attested forms. The reconstructed roots and endings are given in (61) and (62) and the required changes are listed in (63). (The relative chronology is as indicated, with (a) preceding (b), etc.)

(61) *varg-, *krauj-, *kelj-, *svetj-

(62) *-as
      *-e
      *-ō
      *-ai
      *-us

(63a) $C_0 > [+ \text{palatalized}] \, / \underline{\hspace{1.5cm}} \begin{bmatrix} V \\ + \text{front} \end{bmatrix}$

   b) $j > \emptyset \, / \, C \underline{\hspace{1cm}} V$

   c) $t' > \check{c}' \, / \underline{\hspace{1.5cm}} \begin{bmatrix} V \\ - \text{front} \end{bmatrix}$

   d) $a > e \, / \begin{Bmatrix} [+ \text{palatalized}] \\ j \end{Bmatrix} \underline{\hspace{1.5cm}}$

These reconstructions and changes will account well for the attested Lithuanian facts; cf. the sample derivations in (64). (Here, (a)−(d) refer to the changes under (63).)

(64)   *varge   *svetje   *svetjas   *svetjō
a)   var'g'e   s'v'et'je   s'v'et'jas   s'v'et'jō
b)   − − −   s'v'et'e   s'v'et'as   s'v'et'ō
c)   − − −   − − −   s'v'eč'as   s'v'eč'ō
d)   − − −   − − −   s'v'eč'es   − − −

Moreover, change (63c) can be argued to explain why Lithuanian does not have any palatalized dentals before non-front vowels. However, we might take offense at the formulation of (63c) by noting that non-front vowels do not seem to be a very natural environment for the change *t'* > *č'*.

One alternative would be to consider this to be one of those unexplainable, but regular changes which may occasionally be encountered in working with 'non-sanitized' historical data and developments. Here as elsewhere, however, a more fruitful approach would be to look for a more explanatory analysis.

Accordingly, one might speculate that at a certain stage, *j* was lost only in the environment before front vowel; cf. (63b'). (For precedents and discussion of this type of change, see section 7.1.1 above.) This permits us to reformulate (63c) as (63c'), a change which appears to provide a more natural condition for the change of *t'* into *č'*. Finally we would have to apply (63b) in its original formulation, so as to delete *j* also before non-front vowels. Compare the derivation in (65).

(63b') $j > \emptyset \, / \, C \underline{\hspace{1.5cm}} \begin{bmatrix} V \\ + \text{front} \end{bmatrix}$

(63c') $t' > \check{c}' \, / \underline{\hspace{1.5cm}} j$

(65) svetje   svetjas
  a)   s'v'et'je   s'v'et'jas
  b') s'v'et'e   — — —
  c') — — —   s'v'eč'jas
  b)   — — —   s'v'eč'as
  d)   — — —   s'v'eč'es

There is however another alternative. And this approach makes it possible to retain the original analysis and to reject the derivation in (65) for being unnessarily complex and thus a violation of Occam's Razor: As noted in section 5.1.5 above, palatalization is characterized by a non-segmental *y*-like on- or off-glide. Since such a frontish glide will be more noticeable before non-front vowels, it can be expected to have more noticeable and far-reaching effects in that environment, such as changing a preceding dental stop into a palatal. (This analysis may receive support from the fact that as noted in section 7.1.1 above, there is a crosslinguistic tendency to depalatalize palatals before front vowels, suggesting that the palatalizing offglide may be weaker in this environment than before non-front vowels.)

But whatever the decision concerning the exact route by which *ť* changed into *č'*, the reconstruction and most of the postulated changes seem to be reasonable and justifiable. Moreover, comparative evidence confirms the essential correctness of our reconstruction, for forms like *s'v'eč'es* do in fact reflect earlier forms of the type *svetjas*.

18. Comparative method: Establishing linguistic relationship

'The Sanscrit language, whatever be its antiquity, is of a wonderful structure; more perfect than the Greek, more copious than the Latin, and more exquisitely refined than either, yet bearing to both of them a stronger affinity, both in the roots of verbs and in the forms of grammar, than could possibly have been produced by accident; so strong indeed, that no philologer could examine them all three, without believing them to have sprung from some common source, which, perhaps, no longer exists: there is a similar reason, though not quite so forcible, for supposing that both the Gothick and the Celtick, though blended with a very different idiom, had the same origin with the Sanscrit; and the old Persian might be added to the same family, if this were the place for discussing any question concerning the antiquities of Persia.'

This quotation from Sir William Jones's 'Third Anniversary Discourse, on the Hindus' of 1786 has a double significance for the history of linguistics. On one hand, it provided one of the most important stimuli for research in comparative Indo-European linguistics, a field which soon became the most thoroughly investigated area of historical and comparative linguistics and which to the present day has remained the most important source for our understanding of linguistic change. At the same time, however, Jones's statement is important also for the fact that perhaps for the first time, it offered a very succinct and quite explicit summary of what have turned out to be the basic assumptions and motivations of comparative linguistics: accounting for similarities which cannot be attributed to chance, by the assumption that they are the result of descendancy from a common ancestor, i. e., of genetic relationship.

The historical significance of Jones's statement is not diminished by the fact that even before Jones, there had been some serious and well-taken speculations on genetic relationship between various languages, or even by the fact that some scholars had gone beyond mere speculation, as for instance J. Sajnovics (1770) in his *Demonstratio idioma ungarorum et lapponum idem esse* 'A demonstration that the Hungarian and Lapp languages are the same (in origin)'. And it is only slightly diminished by the fact that there are, from our present vantage point, some naive elements in Jones's claims. Thus we now would not normally expect the ancestral language to continue to be spoken alongside its 'daughter' languages. (But note the diglossia between Latin and Romance, or Sanskrit and Middle or Modern Indo-Aryan; cf. 14.4 above.) More importantly, we now know that even if we exclude chance as a possible factor, not all similarities must by necessity reflect genetic relationship or descendancy from a common ancestor. As the discussion in Chapters 13—16 has shown, they may reflect linguistic contact.

Given these additional insights, which result from nearly two centuries of intensive work in comparative linguistics since Jones made his famous statement, we would now define the goal of comparative linguistics as establishing genetic relationship by showing that the putatively related languages share similarities which cannot be attributed to chance or to linguistic contact and which find their explanation only through the assumption that the languages are descended from a common ancestor.

18.1. Chance similarities, onomatopoeia, etc.

Probably any given pair of languages will offer at least some formally and semantically similar linguistic items whose similarities are simply due to chance. For instance, English and Modern Persian both have a word [bæd] 'bad', with almost exactly the same pronunciation and meaning. Similarly, Modern Greek has a word *mati* 'eye' whose phonetic and semantic resemblance to Malay *mata* is remarkable. Or compare the case of Korean *man* = Engl. *man* or of Mod. Pers. *hūrī* 'beautiful young woman; companion of deceased men in the Quranic paradise' ≈ NHG *Hure* 'whore'. (Note that the semantic difference between the last two words is not in any way unprecedented or unusual. Thus, Germ. *Hure*, Engl. *whore* are quite probably related to Lat. *cārus* 'dear, beloved'.)

In all of these cases, and in many others like them, our knowledge of the earlier history of the languages makes it certain that the similarities do not reflect genetic relationship or borrowing, but are attributable only to chance.

Similarities of this sort are relatively easily eliminated by requiring that similarities or '**correspondences**' not be limited to a few lexical items, but **recur** in a fairly **large set** of other linguistic items.

Moreover, correspondences need not be similar to the point of identity. What is of perhaps even higher diagnostic value are recurrent correspondences of partial similarities (or differences). For the normal result of linguistic change operating independently and in different directions is to differentiate related languages.

Finally, in our search for correspondences, we will put greater faith in the diagnostic value of relatively long forms than short, one- or two-segment forms. For given, say, two languages with twenty consonants and five vowels, the chance of two-segment sequences such as *ba* having a similar meaning is something like one in two hundred. On the other hand, the chance of sequences like *basta* being similar is something like one in 400,000. (These calculations are illustrative only. They are clearly flawed, both mathematically and factually. For instance, they assume that the two languages have identical sets of segments, identical restrictions on the combinability of segments, and identical sets of possible words which can be formed by these segments. In actuality, of course, languages are not limited in this way.)

The chance of unrelated vocabulary items being similar is especially great in the area of onomatopoeia. For though details may differ, onomatopoetic expressions come out remarkably similar in different languages; cf., e. g., the rooster's crow in section 12.2.2, ex. (20), as well as the crosslinguistic tendencies noted in the same section. As a consequence, it is entirely possible that languages independently create (or re-create) phonetically similar expressions for similar noises in the 'real world'. (Cf. also 3.7 above.)

The situation is similar as regards vocabulary items like Engl. *dad(dy)*, *mom(my)*, *baby*, It. *papa*, *mama*, *bambino*, Hindi *bāp*, *mā*, *baččā*. The structure, segmental inventory, and often also the connotations of these words suggest that they come from one variety of 'baby talk', namely the 'words' and meanings which grown-ups assign to the early babbling of infants: Like other items that occur in this kind of language, the words exhibit a strong tendency to have syllabic reduplication (as in *pa-pa*). And the predominance of the vowel *a* and of the consonants *p/b*, *t/d*, *m*, and *n* in these words is a common feature of early babbling. (The difference between the voiced consonants of Engl. *daddy*, *baby* and the voiceless ones of It. *papa* seems to be linked to the fact that the stops of the babbling phase tend to be voiceless, unaspirated, and fairly 'lax'. English speakers apparently interpret the lack of aspiration as indicating voiced stops. [Note that Engl. *papa/pop*, *mama/mom* seem to be borrowings from Romance.] Speakers of languages like Italian or

Hindi, who have unaspirated voiceless stops, can interpret the babbling stops as voiceless. However, their relatively 'lax' articulation makes it possible to alternatively identify them as voiced; cf., e. g., *bambino.*)

Because of the much greater possibility of chance similarities, onomatopoeia and words which can be derived from the babbling-based variety of 'baby talk' are generally considered unreliable evidence in attempts to establish genetic relationship.

18.2. Similarities due to linguistic contact

Having in this manner eliminated the possibility of chance similarities, we may soon be confronted with situations of the type (1). Here it appears as if English is simultaneously and equidistantly related to two quite distinct languages, with — at this point — no evidence for genetic relationship between these two languages. Within certain limits, such a relationship is not at all remarkable in the area of biological genetics. But in genetic/comparative linguistics it is always considered suspect and indicative of probable secondary contact. And in fact, in the present case we know that the correspondences between English and French result from the secondary contact between the two languages after the Norman conquest of England.

(1)
English	French	German
calf		Kalb
veal	veau	
cow		Kuh
beef	bœuf	
swine		Schwein
pork	porc	

Even if we did not have this direct historical knowledge, however, we would be able to make a good case for a borrowing relation between English and French by looking at other vocabulary items, such as the ones in (2).

(2)
English	French	German
to	à	zu
too	trop	zu
two	deux	zwei

twenty	vingt	zwanzig
eat	manger	essen
bite	mordre	beissen
father	père	Vater [f-]
mother	mère	Mutter
three	trois	drei
thou	tu	du

In correspondences of this sort we can quickly observe that there is a very close relationship between English and German, while French generally offers very different forms. True, closer examination now reveals some recurrent similarities which also involve French; cf. the last four words in (2). But it is also quite clear that French here does not show any closer affinities with English than it does with German (or vice versa). Moreover, in the words for 'father' and 'mother', and in many others like them, the similarities between English and German are much more striking than those of either of the two languages with French. The special affiliation of English with French that was suggested by the correspondences in (1) thus turns out to be contradicted by the evidence of additional data.

Moreover, we are now able to adduce further arguments against considering the English/French correspondences in (1) to result from genetic relationship: These correspondences are restricted to certain limited spheres of the vocabulary. The German/English similarities, on the other hand, **pervade the whole vocabulary**, including **basic vocabulary**. And as noted in Chapter 14, borrowing tends to be limited to certain spheres of the vocabulary. In addition, it is often restricted to technical vocabulary. And it has the least effect in the area of basic vocabulary. (But note that kinship terms like Engl. *daddy, papa, mommy* cannot be considered immune to change. For as seen in the preceding section, they may arise independently. Moreover, in the case of the words *papa, mama* = Fr., It., etc. *papa, mama(n)*, Germ. *Papa, Mama*, there is good reason for believing that the words diffused through borrowing.)

Cases like the English/French/German relationship are important because they furnish us with insights that make it possible to detect borrowing in other cases, where we do not have earlier, direct historical evidence indicating a borrowing relationship.

On the basis of such insights, Greenberg (1957) examined a similar 'triangular' relationship between Thai, Sino-Tibetan, and Kadai/Malayo-Polynesian and concluded that the relationship between Thai and Sino-Tibetan must be one of borrowing. His arguments are interesting and add to the criteria which we can use to eliminate borrowing.

'The specific resemblances found with Sino-Tibetan languages always occur in forms found in Chinese, usually to the exclusion of other Sino-Tibetan languages. The specific form, even when found elsewhere, is always very close to Chinese. Moreover, the resemblances cluster in a few semantic spheres, the numerals from 2 to 10 and a few names of metals and domestic animals. In contrast, the resemblances to the Kadai languages and to Malayo-Polynesian tend to recur throughout the family, not just in some single language; are basic; do not concentrate in any particular semantic area; and exhibit an independence of form which excludes any particular Kadai or Malayo-Polynesian language as a source.'

Evidence for possible genetic relationship thus should consist of correspondences which pervade the vocabulary and which include most of the basic vocabulary.

One may ask, however, why linguists concentrate on vocabulary, and not on general linguistic structure. There are two good reasons for not considering linguistic structure as major evidence.

First, as noted in Chapter 16, distantly related languages may as the result of extended bilingual contact come to converge in their general linguistic structure, even to the point of having virtually the same grammar. At the same time, vocabulary remains relatively little affected by such contact. What is especially interesting is that convergence not only has the effect of making distantly related or unrelatable languages structurally more similar. It may also bring about the differentiation of related languages, if they are located in different areas. Thus, as the result of regionally different developments, all three major word order patterns are found in the modern Indo-European languages: SOV in the east, SVO in most of Europe, and VSO among the Insular Celtic languages. (In addition, German, Dutch, and Frisian constitute a sub-area with SOV beside SVO characteristics.)

Secondly, derivational and inflectional morphemes tend to be much shorter than 'independent' lexical items, so that there will be a greater possibility of encountering chance similarities. (In combination with 'lexical' morphemes, however, such inflectional and derivational morphemes may be of considerable interest.)

18.3. Systematic, recurrent correspondences

Having thus reduced the likelihood of chance similarities and of similarities due to linguistic contact, we can strengthen our case for genetic relationship by showing that the correspondences encountered in our putative cognates recur in a **systematic** fashion. That is, there should be a systematic pattern to the correspondences, both in terms of their similarities and in terms of their differences.

Thus, the English/German correspondences in (2), together with those in (3), are characterized by the recurrent phonetic similarities and differences summarized in (4). (Note that similar correspondences are found in a large number of other lexical items.)

(3) English   German
     frost   Frost
     chest   Kiste

(4) English   German

     t   z [ts] (/ $\left\{ \begin{array}{c} C \\ \# \end{array} \right\}$ _____)

     t   ss [s] (V _____ V)

     t   t (/s _____)

If we look at other voiceless stops of English and their German counterparts, we notice similar, even if not entirely analogous, correspondences; cf. (5).

(5) English   German

     pound   Pfund   }
     penny   Pfennig   }   p-   :   pf-

     ape   Affe   }
     hope   hoffen   }   -p- :   -f-

     aspen   Espe   }
     wasp   Wespe   }   -sp- :   -sp-

     cool   kühl   }
     card   Karte   }   k-   :   k-

     make   machen   }
     cook   Koch   }   -k- :   -x-

Systematic and recurrent correspondences of this sort that pervade the whole lexicon, including basic vocabulary, provide fairly conclusive evidence for genetic relationship, since they suggest divergence from a common source by systematic regular sound change (as well as other changes, of course).

18.4. Shared aberrancies

Our case becomes especially persuasive, and to many linguists' minds, proven beyond a reasonable doubt, if we can detect a common '**aberrancy**' shared between the putatively related languages, and characterized by systematic recurrent correspondences. For it is extremely unlikely that such shared aberrancies result from borrowing — not to mention chance.

Shared aberrancies may be morphological/lexical, as in the English/German correspondences of (6). Here we notice a 'suppletion' between the roots used for the simple adjective and its comparative and superlative counterparts. Normally, of course, such suppletion is not found; cf. Engl. *blue, bluer, bluest*, Germ. *blau, blauer, blauest*. Note, however, that suppletion by itself is not sufficient. For as (6) shows, French has a similar suppletion. What is important is that the morphemes involved in the suppletion must be characterized by systematic recurrent correspondences. Correspondences of this type are found between the English and German sets; but the French set does not exhibit any recurrent correspondences with either of the other two sets.

(6) English German French

    good gut bon
    better besser meilleur
    best best- le meilleur

(For the correspondences *-t-* : *-s-*, *-st-* : *-st-*, cf. (4) above. The other correspondences are similarly supported by 'outside' evidence; cf., e. g., the *g-* : *g-* in Engl. *great, give*: Germ. *gross, geben*.)

Aberrancies of this type need not be confined to morphology. For instance, if in the majority of Indo-European languages we find correspondences of the type (7) for the third singular and plural present indicative of the verb 'to be', the shared morphophonemic root alternation between vowel and ∅ must be considered highly suggestive of genetic relationship.

(7)

	Sanskrit	Avestan	Greek(dial.)	Latin	OCSlavic	Gothic
sg. 3	as-ti	as-ti	es-ti	es-t	jes-tǔ	is-t
pl. 3	s-anti	h-anti	(h)-enti	s-unt	s-ǫtǔ	s-ind

18.5. Phyla and isolates: degrees of relatability

For many language groups, the comparative method cannot go beyond establishing a shared aberrancy. A useful term for a group of this sort is **phylum**.

As an example, consider the case of Uralic (a language family which includes Finno-Ugric) and Dravidian: On the basis of reconstructed Proto-Uralic and Proto-Dravidian, it is possible to establish a considerable amount of systematically recurring correspondences in non-technical, basic, etc., vocabulary, with no apparent lexical restrictions. Compare, e. g., the data in (8).

(8)

Proto-Uralic	Proto-Dravidian	
*tay-	*ta(-r)-	'give'
*täm-	*tev-	'fill'
*tuy-	*tur̠-	'river'
*käte-	*kay-	'hand'
*kele-	*kēl-	'speech'
*sükese-	*čuk(k)-	'autumn'
*pekse-	*pak-	'arrow'

In addition we find systematically recurrent phonetic correspondences in the shared morphosyntactic aberrancy of expressing negation by a finite verb; cf. (9). For the original use of this verb, compare the Finnish example in (10), which shows that it is the negation which is inflected for person and number, while the accompanying main verb appears in an uninflected form. (But note that the Finnish root morpheme seems to be an innovation.)

(9)   Proto-Uralic *äl- : Proto-Dravidian *al(l)-
(10) sg. 1 juo-n   : e-n juo (neg.) 'drink'
          2 juo-t   : e-t juo
          3 juo   : ei juo
      pl. 1 juo-mme   : e-mme juo
          2 juo-tte   : e-tte juo
          3 juo-vat   : ei-vät juo

It is true, we find 'negative verbs' also elsewhere, such as in a number of Australian languages. In fact, also Marathi, an Indo-Aryan neighbor of Dravidian, has developed something like a negative verb, presumably by convergence with Dravidian. However, as usual in convergence situations, the form of this negative verb consists of inherited, Indo-Aryan elements (cf. the present stem *nāhī* ≈ Hindi *nahī* 'not'). It is thus quite different and exhibits no systematic recurrent correspondences with either Dravidian or Uralic.

The only reservation which one must have concerning the value of the shared aberrancy in (9) is that the morphemes involved are very short. This raises the specter that we might be dealing with a case of chance similarity.

In the case of other groups of languages, the evidence may be even more limited, such that the similarities which one encounters could very well be the result of borrowing or convergence, or might even be attributable to chance.

Thus there are a number of intriguing correspondences between Uralic and Indo-European, including pronominal forms, as well as verb and noun endings. These similarities include also the word for 'name'; cf. (11). However, outside the very short inflectional affixes (such as sg. A -*m*), the number of such correspondences is very limited. Moreover, there are no shared aberrancies involving systematically recurring correspondences.

(11)   Uralic   Indo-European
      Finn.   nimi   Skt. nāma
      Hung.   nyev   Lat. nōmen
              etc.   etc.

The case apparently is somewhat better for the relation between Uralic and Altaic (a group which includes Turkish and Mongolian). However, here too the vocabulary evidence is relatively limited. And the fact that the two neighboring groups share overall structural features, such as SOV syntax, suffixing of inflectional and derivational affixes (without an alternative prefixing pattern), and vowel harmony, may very well be the result of convergence.

There are many other languages for which there is no probative evidence whatsoever for outside genetic relationships. Languages of this sort are Basque along the western part of the French/Spanish border and Burushaski in Northwest India. Languages of this sort are often called **isolates**. Even more commonly they are referred to as 'unrelated' to any other languages.

Strictly speaking, the term 'unrelated' is not very felicitous; the word 'unrelatable' would give a much more accurate description. For we can never prove that two given languages are not related. It is always conceivable that they are in fact related, but that the relationship is of such an ancient date that millennia of divergent linguistic changes have completely obscured the original relationship.

Ultimately, this issue it tied up with the question of whether there was a single or a multiple origin of Language (writ large). And this question can be answered only in terms of unverifiable speculations, given the fact that even with the added time depth provided by reconstruction, our knowledge of the history of human languages does not extend much beyond ca. 5000 B.C., a small 'slice' indeed out of the long prehistory of language.

The extent to which prolonged divergent developments can obscure genetic relationship can be illustrated by comparing the relative transparency of the relationship between Sanskrit and Old English on one hand, and their modern descendants, Hindi and English, on the other. Compare (12). (The Hindi forms are given in a quasi-phonetic transcription.)

(12)	Sanskrit	Old English	Hindi	Modern English
	ēka-	ān	ēk	one
	dvā(u)	twā	dō	two
	trayas	þrī	tīn	three
	ṣaṭ	seox	čhě	six
	asti	is	hē	is
	sa	sē	vō	he
	vayam	wē	ham	we
	svasar	sweostor	běhěn	sister
	śvaśrū	sweogor	sās	mother-in-law (on wife's side)
	vēda	wāt	jǎntā hē	(he) knows
	pād-	fōt	pãv-	foot

18.6. Comparative reconstruction: language families

The ultimate proof of genetic relationship, and to many linguists' minds the only real proof, lies in a successful reconstruction of the ancestral forms from which the systematically corresponding cognates can be derived. (Note that just as in courts of law, the terms 'proof', 'prove' here are used in the sense of 'establish beyond a reasonable doubt'. In fact, the general tenet of historical linguistics is that all hypotheses, whether they concern genetic relationship, 'language-internal' developments like sound change or analogy, or contact-induced changes, should be established beyond a reasonable doubt. It must be admitted, however, that this tenet is often ignored in practice.)

The success of a reconstruction depends in large measure on how well it conforms to the principles outlined in 17.1.1-5. But it also depends on the extent to which the vocabulary and linguistic structure of the proto-language have been recovered. Reconstructions which recover something like a thousand words plus, say, a fairly complex system of both inflectional and derivational morphology clearly are more impressive and make a better case for linguistic relationship than do reconstructions which manage to recover only a hundred lexical items plus a few morphological patterns. (For instance, recent attempts to prove genetic relationship between Dravidian and Elamite, a long extinct language documented in texts from the ancient Persian empire, have been met with a great degree of scepticism. For although these attempts were accompanied by comparative reconstruction, the attested vocabulary of Elamite is too small to permit reconstructing a sufficiently large number of lexical items, etc., to establish the case beyond a reasonable doubt.)

It is through the procedure of comparative reconstruction, then, that we can establish **language families**, such as those of Indo-European, Uralic, Dravidian, Altaic, Sino-Tibetan, Malayo-Polynesian, Bantu, Semitic, or Uto-Aztecan.

18.7. Realism in reconstruction

Besides thus providing the ultimate proof of genetic relationship, comparative reconstruction also permits us to recover linguistic prehistory, in so far as it **approximates earlier linguistic reality.**

True, it has been argued that reconstructions are nothing but convenient cover formulae, summarizing our understanding of the linguistic relationship between given languages. Two major arguments have been advanced in favor of this claim and against the view that reconstruction recovers (some aspects of) prehistoric reality.

One of these arguments is that we cannot hope to fully reconstruct the ancestral language. For obsolescence of lexical items and grammatical forms is pervasive in language change and may therefore attack related items independently, eliminating them from so many of the related languages that no evidence remains for reconstruction.

Thus the rich Latin inflectional system, with six different cases each in the nouns, pronouns, and adjectives, has in most of the Romance languages been reduced to a distinction between three cases at best (cf. Fr. *je* 'I', *me* 'me', *moi* '(to) me'). And that distinction is virtually limited to the pronouns. To reconstruct any richer inflectional system would therefore be out of the question. Moreover, Latin distinguished between five different classes of nominal inflection, of which only three have survived into the modern Romance languages. Again, reconstructing anything more than three such classes seems to be out of the question.

Lexical items constantly undergo obsolescence or other changes which make successful reconstruction impossible. Compare for instance English *let* 'hinder, obstruct' (section 12.3.3), *thill, snaffle* (12.5), or the Indo-European word for 'tongue' (12.4.3).

The second argument is that comparative reconstruction, by reducing variation to invariance, has to postulate dialect-free proto-languages. Natural languages, however, have dialects. Reconstruction therefore by necessity leads to unnatural proto-languages.

Moreover, it is argued, dialect-free reconstructions not only are unnatural, they are factually incorrect, as is shown by the insights of the 'wave theory':

If we follow the precept of 'reductionist' comparative reconstruction that dialectal or cross-linguistic variation between related languages is to be reduced to earlier invariance, then our Proto-Indo-European reconstructions should include the following:

(13a)   A contrast *a : o : ə*

b)   A set of inflectional endings beginning with *bh-*, such as pl. I *-bhis*

c)   A segment *s* and a pre-velar/palatal series *k̂, ĝ, ĝh*

d)   A genitive singular ending *-os(y)o* in the pronouns

e)   An ablative singular ending *-ad* in the pronouns

f)   A neutralization of the contrast genitive : ablative in the nouns

g)   A cluster *tt*

However, if we look at the early changes which these segments and forms underwent, we see that the isoglosses for these different changes intersect in such a criss-crossing fashion as to suggest a single, dialectally highly diversified proto-language. Compare the discussion in 15.3, together with Map 10, which is reproduced below for convenience.

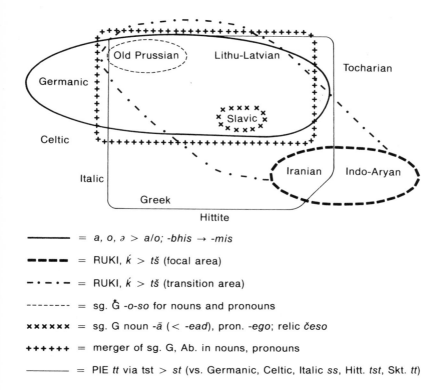

———— = a, o, ə > a/o; -bhis → -mis

▬ ▬ ▬ = RUKI, k̂ > tš (focal area)

— · — · — = RUKI, k̂ > tš (transition area)

- - - - - - - = sg. Ĝ -o-so for nouns and pronouns

× × × × × × = sg. G noun -ā (< -ead), pron. -ego; relic česo

+ + + + + + = merger of sg. G, Ab. in nouns, pronouns

———— = PIE tt via tst > st (vs. Germanic, Celtic, Italic ss, Hitt. tst, Skt. tt)

Map 10. (Proto-)Indo-European dialects: isoglosses

This evidence for a dialectally diversified proto-language, however, is in conflict with the non-diversified language postulated by the 'reductionist' approach of comparative reconstruction.

As it turns out, neither of these two arguments against considering reconstructions to have any realistic value is conclusive.

This is most easily seen in the case of the second argument. True, comparative reconstruction does postulate the invariant segments and forms of (13), and it thus eliminates dialectal diversity. However, this is in respect only to these segments and forms, and only in respect to a particular period. For given the evidence summarized in Map 10, it is also quite clear that at a later period, Proto-Indo-European was dialectally diversified − in respect to these very elements. That is, the comparative method, if properly understood and applied, does make it possible for us to recover some degree of dialectal diversity, for certain prehistoric periods (even if these periods may not be the earliest ones covered by comparative reconstruction). And in so doing, comparative linguistics can be argued to approximate a linguistically realistic situation.

In fact, it is only through comparative reconstruction that we get the evidence which makes it possible to postulate dialectal diversification within the proto-language. For late Proto-Indo-European is no less reconstructed than early Proto-Indo-European.

More than that, it can be argued that only if comparative linguistics treats reconstructed entities and systems as approximating linguistic reality is it possible to establish dialectal diversity for (late) Proto-Indo-European: Real dialects can be meaningfully characterized only in terms of real linguistic differences, not in terms of differences in 'convenient cover formulae'. Put differently, if we want to argue − as we should − that late Proto-Indo-European was dialectally diversified, then we must accept a certain realistic value for the reconstructed entities on whose basis we establish the diversification.

It is true, from cases like the Latin and Romance systems of nominal inflection we know that there are limitations to how much 'reality' we can reconstruct. But comparative Romance linguistics likewise furnishes evidence that the 'slice' of reality which we can reconstruct does closely approximate what is actually found in the near-ancestor of the Romance languages, in Latin (especially in its more vernacular varieties). This is especially true in the area of phonology, where reconstruction has been most successful.

Moreover, as observed in section 17.2 above, through reconstruction we can recover morphophonemic alternations which require synchronic rules within the ancestral language. Similarly the Indo-European ablaut system outlined in 17.3 is the product of reconstruction. Alternations of this sort likewise demonstrate that comparative reconstruction is not so 'reductionist' as to unnaturally (or unrealistically) eliminate all variation from the proto-language.

That is, while we may not be able to reconstruct all of prehistoric reality, we can at least approximate such reality through our reconstruction.

A word of caution is required, however: Close approximations of this sort are possible only where there is sufficient evidence, and even then they will frequently come about only as the result of the cumulative work of many scholars, devoting themselves to a detailed examination and reexamination of the evidence, to searching for additional, previously unnoticed evidence, and to subjecting reconstructions and related hypotheses to constant critical reexamination.

As a consequence, there may be considerable differences between the reconstructions postulated by different generations of researchers. In the history of Indo-European linguistics, for instance, early reconstructions postulated the three-vowel system in (14). The major motivation for this reconstruction seems to have been (i) the fact that Sanskrit presupposes such a prehistoric system and (ii) the mistaken assumption that Sanskrit was the earliest attested and therefore most conservative Indo-European language.

(14) $\breve{\bar{\imath}}$ $\breve{\bar{u}}$

        $\breve{\bar{a}}$

As the discipline 'matured', it became obvious that even Sanskrit required a more complex earlier system, containing not only high and low, but also mid vowels. (For instance, palatalization presupposes a pre-Sanskrit distinction between front-vocalic *e*-vowels and non-front *a*- (and *o*-) vowels; cf. 5.1.5 above.) Accordingly, the system in (15) was postulated.

(15) $\breve{\bar{\imath}}$ $\breve{\bar{u}}$

    $\breve{\bar{e}}$ ə $\breve{\bar{o}}$

        $\breve{\bar{a}}$

The work of de Saussure, Kuryłowicz, and others (cf. 17.3 above) has required further modifications of the reconstructed vowel system. Most instances of long *ī* and *ū* are now considered derived from earlier sequences of short *i* or *u* plus laryngeal. The situation is similar for many instances of *ē* and *ō*. The vowel *ə* is now reconstructed as a syllabic form of one or another laryngeal. And on the basis of equations like Lat. *avus* : Hitt. *ḫuḫḫas* 'grandfather', it has been argued that apparent instances of basic-vowel *a* reflect earlier sequences of '*a*-coloring' laryngeal *A* plus the basic vowel *e* (hence Lat. *avus* < *Aewos). Finally, if we ignore the not yet fully resolved problem of how the PIE ablaut alternation between *e, o, ē, ō*, and *∅* came about, it is possible to reduce the entire system of non-high vowels to just one single vowel, namely *e. In this extreme view, then, the vowel system of early Proto-Indo-European was as in (16).

(16)   i   u

        e

That is, it appears as if our research may have come full circle, back to something very similar to the three-vowel system postulated in the early days of Indo-European linguistics. (Cf. also below.) But note that the most current approach actually must postulate two chronologically differentiated systems: System (15), or something very close to it, in all likelihood belonged to late Proto-Indo-European, after Hittite and several other languages had 'broken off'. System (16), on the other hand, reflects a much earlier stage of (pre-)Proto-Indo-European. The early researchers who postulated system (14) were not aware of this chronological distinction and conceived of their reconstructions as the vowel system of Proto-Indo-European, especially for the late Proto-Indo-European period. Our research, thus, has in fact progressed and not just come full circle. And in this progress, we can expect that our reconstruction has achieved a greater degree of realism.

In addition, the goal of approximating reality as closely as possible provides an important criterion for evaluating competing reconstructions. It forces us to reconstruct systems which are maximally 'realistic', i. e., 'possible' in natural language. And it likewise requires us to postulate linguistic changes that are possible in real languages. For instance, realism might suggest that instead of reconstructing the early (pre-)Proto-Indo-European system in (16), we should postulate the system in (17). For three-vowel systems containing the high vowels *i* and *u* usually include low-central *a* as the third vowel. (Cf. also 19.1 below, as well as the cautionary note in 19.5.)

(17)   i   u

            a

Like the regularity principle in sound change, the principle of realism in reconstruction is highly fruitful, no matter how accurate it may be in fact. For it compels us to look more carefully at the evidence and at alternative interpretations. As a consequence we can expect to learn more about linguistic relationships and the nature of proto-languages than if we subscribe to an approach which rejects the principle.

18.8. Linguistic paleontology, confidence in reconstructions

Through the reconstruction of lexical items we may be able to recover information pertaining to prehistoric culture, society, perhaps even to geographical facts. This use of linguistic reconstructions has been referred to as **linguistic paleontology**.

For instance, the fact that we can reconstruct Proto-Indo-European words for 'horse' (*$ekwos$), 'bovine animal' (*$g^w\bar{o}ws$), 'dog' (*$kuw\bar{o}n$), etc., tells us a great deal about the degree to which the speakers of Proto-Indo-European had succeeded in the domestication of animals. The words for 'cat', on the other hand, look like recent borrowings. This suggests that the speakers of Proto-Indo-European had not yet domesticated cats. (In Latin, for instance, *cattus* is a late replacement for earlier *fēlis*, a word which did not have the specific meaning 'domesticated cat'. Similarly, the corresponding Germanic words, such as Engl. *cat*, have not undergone the Grimm's-Law shift of *k* and *t* to *h* and *þ* and thus seem to have entered the Germanic languages relatively late, after the application of Grimm's Law.)

From similar evidence it can be gathered that the structure of Indo-European society was strongly patriarchal, was organized around the system of clans with (probably elected) chieftains, and worshiped deities associated with the sky (and perhaps with other natural phenomena).

There have also been attempts to establish the 'race' of the speakers of Indo-European. The Nazi-inspired efforts to identify this 'Aryan race' as blond, blue-eyed, and 'Nordic' are especially notorious. However, these and other less racist attempts vastly overestimate the probative value of the available evidence. True, a good deal of evidence suggests that there were among the Indo-Europeans light-haired people with blue or grey eyes. Moreover, in many areas (including not only

India, but apparently also Greece and Italy), the Indo-European invaders were lighter-skinned than the indigenous population, or at least, considered themselves to be lighter-skinned. However, this evidence does not prove that the Indo-Europeans as a whole were 'white', blond (or light-haired), blue-eyed, etc., or that all Indo-European invaders were lighter-skinned than the non-Indo-Europeans. The situation may well have been the same as in present-day Europe, where different areas may present different ratios of blond/blue-eyed (etc.) vs. dark-haired/brown-eyed (etc.), but where no area has an exclusively blond/blue-eyed or dark-haired/brown-eyed population. Nevertheless, because of the greater preponderance of the latter type in Italy, brown-haired/grey-eyed Germans may refer to themselves as lighter (or 'whiter') than 'the Italians' (ignoring the existence of 'perfectly' blond/blue-eyed Italians). The extreme case is perhaps seen in the United States, where members of every 'race' under the sun have come to speak the same language. And skeletal evidence from the Indus Valley Civilization (ca. 2400–1700 B.C.) shows that a fair amount of such 'racial mixture' has always existed and cannot be simply attributed to relatively recent developments.

Attempts have also been made to identify the original home of the Indo-Europeans by means of reconstructed names for fauna and flora. The basic assumption is highly plausible: If we can reconstruct a word which refers to a particular plant or animal, then the speakers of Indo-European must have found that plant or animal in their environment (or close by). Through pollen samples in the appropriate layers of moors and through skeletal remains, it should then be possible to establish the area in which that plant or animal flourished some 5000 to 6000 years ago, at the time when it is commonly assumed Proto-Indo-European must have been spoken. And if we limit our investigation to those plants and animals whose habitat was geographically highly limited or unique, we should be able to pinpoint the exact area in which the speakers of Proto-Indo-European lived.

On the basis of this approach some scholars have claimed that the original home of the Indo-Europeans must have been in an area of central and western Europe, to the west of a line which runs roughly from today's Polish/Russian border to the Crimea. That area is defined by the coexistence of beech trees and birch trees. And it has been claimed that words for both of these trees can be reconstructed.

Of the two terms, the word for 'beech tree' is the more significant one, since it is believed to crucially define the relevant sub-area out of a much larger birch-tree region (which extends considerably farther to the east). The following discussion therefore will concentrate on the word for 'beech'.

The evidence for reconstructing this word is limited to three language groups: Greek, Latin (Italic), and Germanic; cf. (18). These languages offer words which can be derived by straightforward changes from a common Proto-Indo-European source, *bhāgos. To the extent that other European languages have a term for 'beech', it is borrowed from one or the other of these three language groups. (This is the case for instance for MIr. *fagh-vile* or Russ.-Ch. Slav. *buky*. According to one view, a number of Slavic words meaning 'elder' should also be included. But their phonetic shape does not permit considering them descended from the same ancestral form as the words in (18).)

(18) Gk. phēgos   (a kind of oak tree with edible acorns)
      Lat. fāgus   'beech tree'
      Gmc. *bōk-   'beech tree' (cf. OHG buohha, OE bēc)

The claim that the words in (18) are descended from a common Proto-Indo-European source requires the subsidiary assumption that only Latin and Germanic preserved the original form and meaning, and that other languages either retained the word and changed its meaning (cf. Greek) or lost it altogether. Presumably, the semantic change or loss was brought about by migration into areas which lacked beech trees. The fact that the Greek term refers to an oak with edible acorns may be considered significant, since the nuts (or acorns) of beech trees likewise are edible. That is, it can be argued that the Greeks transferred the term *bhāgos* to a tree which shared certain salient characteristics with the tree that was originally designated by the word.

While this 'beech-tree' scenario is possible, it is not probable beyond a reasonable doubt. Several equally possible alternative explanations can be advanced. And the availability of such alternative explanations raises serious doubts about the cogency of the beech-tree scenario.

First of all, Latin (or Italic) and Germanic were neighbors, located in areas with beech trees. It is therefore entirely possible that the meaning 'beech tree' is a common innovation on their part, reflecting the fact that they moved into beech-tree territory. The Greek meaning, then, may represent an archaism. Or alternatively, both the Latin/Germanic and Greek meanings may be innovations, replacing an original reference to some other large deciduous tree with edible acorns or nuts. Consider the different uses of the term *Korn* 'corn, grain' in different areas of Germany: It may refer to wheat, rye, barley, or oats, depending on which was the traditional crop grain of the area. Similarly, different British English varieties use *corn* to refer to wheat or oats, and in American English the term refers to maize.

Secondly and more importantly, the fact that our word is limited to just a few geographically neighboring languages makes it possible that it is a regional innovation, perhaps a borrowing from another, non-Indo-European language originally spoken in the region. The fact that the word looks as if it is inherited from a common Proto-Indo-European source is no obstacle to this assumption. All that needs to be assumed is that the word was borrowed early enough, before the sound changes took place which differentiated Greek, Latin, and Germanic from each other. It is precisely through developments of this sort that Greek and Germanic are generally considered to have come to share the word for 'hemp': Gk. *kannabis*, PGmc. **hanipiʒ*, OE *hænep*, OHG *hanaf*. Note that this borrowing took place early enough for the word to undergo Grimm's Law, the development which most strikingly differentiated Germanic from the other Indo-European languages.

In fact, it may be argued that the 'beech-tree' scenario involves circular reasoning: It assumes that the meaning found in Latin and Germanic is the original one and that the word is inherited. Having done so, it reconstructs an ancestral form **bhāgos* with the meaning 'beech'. The reconstruction then is 'confirmed' by the Latin and Germanic forms and their meanings, while different meanings (cf. Greek) and the absence of the word are attributed to special developments.

There is good evidence which suggests that the way of caution lies in avoiding reconstructions which are merely possible, but not probable beyond reasonable doubt, or — at a minimum — in not putting excessive faith in such merely possible reconstructions.

Consider first of all the case of the Algonquian words for 'alcohol'. These words are synchronically transparent compounds of 'fire' and 'water'. And given what is known about Algonquian comparative phonology, it would be possible to reconstruct an ancestral form from which the individual words are derived. A priori, however, such a reconstruction is merely possible, not necessarily probable. For given the fact that the Algonquian languages inherited from the proto-language a productive process of compounding, as well as the words for 'fire' and 'water', the two words could be freely compounded with each other long after the period of Proto-Algonquian. Historical evidence confirms the latter scenario: The word 'fire-water' diffused through the Algonquian languages at the fairly recent point in history when the Europeans arrived and brought with them the object designated by the term 'fire-water', namely alcohol.

A less 'exotic' example of the same phenomenon is the case of the English/German correlation between words of the type *thereby : dabei, whereby : wobei* which might suggest reconstructions as in (19). However, the fact that both German and English have words which are not matched (20a), or are only semantically (but not formally) matched (20b) by the other language should suggest that it is the morphological pattern which is inherited and not any particular words. This suspicion is confirmed when we look at the history of these structures. Words of the type *thereby* are found in English and German as early as the 9th century; the *whereby* type, on the other hand, appears considerable later. The first, quite tentative attestations are found in late 10th/early 11th-century German and 12th-century English. In both languages, the bulk of the forms is of later manufacture.

(19)	English	German	Reconstruction
	thereby	dabei	*þar-bī (?)
	whereby	wobei	*hwar-bī (?)
	therein	darin	*þar-in (?)
	wherein	worin	*hwar-in (?)

(20)	English	German
a)	whereas	— — — —
	— — — —	wogegen
b)	where-after	wo-nach
	where-with	wo-mit

There are thus considerable **differences** in the degree of **confidence** with which we can reconstruct.

What is reconstructed with the greatest degree of confidence is linguistic structure — above all, phonological structure.

Next come morphemes, especially inflectional and basic-vocabulary morphemes. For as noted earlier, these are least easily borrowed.

Together with these individual morphemes we can reconstruct the patterns which govern their combination. (And similarly we can reconstruct certain syntactic patterns; cf. 19.4 below.) However, specific combinations of morphemes into larger configurations, such as Algonquian 'fire-water' or Engl./Germ. *whereby : wobei,* may very well owe their existence to parallel innovations or to calquing.

Other vocabulary is reconstructed with greatest confidence under two conditions: (i) It is found in (virtually) all the related languages; (ii) its formal characteristics and geographic distribution make borrowing or independent innovation unlikely. Thus, early Skt. *rāṭ,* Lat. *rēx,* OIr. *rí* 'king' are probably inherited from a PIE *$*rēk$-s,* since (i) reflexes of the word are found in geographically very separate areas, on or near the periphery of the attested Indo-European languages, and (ii) the inflection of the word is highly archaic. In Sanskrit, for instance, it is increasingly replaced by the more productive inflectional type *rāj-an-* 'king'.

On the other hand, regionally limited vocabulary (such as the words for 'beech tree') must be considered suspect. Here as elsewhere, Occam's Razor should make us hesitate to 'over-reconstruct'.

18.9. Subgrouping, intermediate proto-languages

As noted earlier, comparative reconstruction and the process of tracing changes from the proto-language to the attested languages make it possible to establish dialects for late Proto-Indo-European. The same process of tracing changes from the proto-language — or **reconstructing backward** (cf. also 19.3) — enables us to establish that some of the descendant languages are more closely related to each other and thus form a special **subgroup**.

Languages of this sort show remarkable agreement in various common developments or innovations which cannot be attributed to chance or to cross-linguistic borrowing. Cf. sections 15.2.5 and 15.3 above.

Thus, all the Germanic languages share the phenomena referred to as Grimm's Law and Verner's Law, the development of a new preterital formation with dental suffix (cf. Engl. *thank : thank-ed),* and a large number of common vocabulary innovations (cf. example (21)). Most of these innovations are not very commonly found in the world's languages and therefore are unlikely to result from independent, parallel developments. And many of the lexical innovations affect basic vocabulary, where parallel, independent borrowing would be quite unlikely. They therefore require the assumption of a period of exclusively shared prehistory, during which the Germanic dialects were in close contact with each other, but not with the rest of the Indo-European languages. In short, they argue for positing a common ancestral language, Proto-Germanic, an **intermediate proto-language** which existed at some time between the period of Proto-Indo-European and the earliest attestations of differentiated Germanic dialects.

(21)   Proto-Indo-European   Proto-Germanic

          *pō/pī-   *drink-   'drink'
          *dō/də- = *deO/dO-   *geb-   'give'
          *rēk-s   *kuningaz   'king'

Notice that only common innovations are indicative of such a special relationship. Common archaisms (or inheritances) can be found between any two members of a larger language family. In fact, sometimes they survive best in quite distantly related members of the family, located on or near the periphery; cf. the case of early Skt. *rāṭ*, Lat. *rēx*, OIr. *rí* 'king' in the preceding section.

At the same time, it is not always easy to establish whether given common innovations are to be attributed to a period of exclusively shared prehistory or to diffusion between different members of a dialect continuum within the proto-language. (Compare the discussion in 15.3 above.) As a consequence, some subgroups are posited with greater certainty and unanimity than others. In Indo-European, for instance, the Indo-Iranian, Slavic, Germanic, etc., subgroups are established with great confidence. On the other hand, disagreement continues about whether special Balto-Slavic or Italo-Celtic subgroups should be postulated.

Because of the existence of such subgroups and of intermediate proto-languages (IPLs), some linguists have insisted that reconstructions should first be done for each of the subgroups, and that the 'superordinate' proto-language (SPL) should then be reconstructed on the basis of the reconstructed IPLs. In this way, the latter languages would be established in their own right, rather than as a kind of afterthought to the reconstruction of the SPL.

In many cases, such an approach is no doubt appropriate — as an initial step. This is especially obvious in cases like the possible relationship between Dravidian and Uralic: Had we concentrated merely on the attested languages (which in Uralic go back five hundred years at most), then linguistic change would have brought about such a great differentiation that the evidence for Dravido-Uralic relationship would be extremely tenuous. The reconstructed languages (Proto-Uralic and Proto-Dravidian), on the other hand, get us back to a time depth at which differentiation had a lesser effect and where the possible relationship therefore becomes more transparent. That is, the reconstruction of IPLs may be useful in so far as it provides greater time depth and thus brings us closer to the SPL.

However, once genetic relationship is established, it is preferable to proceed with reconstructing the SPL on the basis of the actually attested languages.

For first of all, by considering all the available evidence, we may be able to reconstruct for the SPL items which by Occam's Razor we might have had to exclude from the IPLs. For instance, within Germanic there is just one language, Old Norse, which has the word *svilar* referring to brothers-in-law whose wives are sisters of each other. Occam's Razor would prevent us from reconstructing this form for Proto-Germanic. If further reconstruction had to proceed from Proto-Germanic, without consideration of its individual daughter languages, we would miss the connection with the dialectal Greek *aelioi*, a word with the same meaning as *svilar*. We would therefore fail to reconstruct the PIE word **swelio-* from which both the Norse and the dialectal Greek words can be derived. Such an approach, however, would be patently wrong. For the kinship term in question is of such highly specialized reference that the correspondence is not likely to result from borrowing (or chance). And since otherwise Greek and Germanic are not closely related members of the Indo-European family, common innovation is not likely. Under these circumstances, reconstruction seems to be the only acceptable solution.

A second argument against basing reconstruction on IPLs would be that subgroups are logically establishable only after we have reconstructed the SPL. For it is exclusively shared deviations from the SPL which define subgroups and their intermediate proto-languages: Subgroups require the prior establishment of the larger group. (This argument, however, is perhaps less cogent than the first. For in many cases we are able to set up subgroups quite readily, by simple inspection. Consider the ease with which it is possible to discern the Celtic, Germanic, Romance, Albanian, Greek, Slavic, and Baltic subgroups of Indo-European on the basis of the seven vocabulary items in Chapter 1, Chart 1.3. Still, in cases like Baltic and Slavic, the question of whether there was a special relationship can be settled only in terms of common deviations from the proto-language — if it can be settled at all.)

19. Comparative reconstruction

The last chapter has demonstrated the importance of comparative reconstruction for establishing genetic relationship, for subgrouping related languages, and also for approximating prehistoric reality. This chapter is devoted to the actual methodology of comparative reconstruction.

In many ways, comparative reconstruction is not different from internal reconstruction, which has been discussed in Chapter 17. Both methods have the same goal, namely to reduce synchronic variation to earlier invariance and in so doing, to recover prehistoric linguistic stages. Both methods also share principles which in many cases make it possible to choose between alternative analyses: We prefer analyses which (i) are more natural or realistic (cf. 17.1.1, as well as 18.7); (ii) operate with regular changes (17.1.2); (iii) are more explanatory (17.1.3); and (iv) do not violate Occam's Razor (17.1.4). In both approaches we are required to justify our reconstruction in terms of a detailed account of the linguistic changes which relate the reconstructed forms to their attested counterparts. And these changes must conform to the general 'rules of the game' of historical linguistics: Except for certain subtypes (e. g., dissimilation), sound change should be regular, and analogies and borrowing should be motivated by plausible models or sources. (Cf. 17.1.5.) Finally, in both methods we primarily reconstruct surface forms, although through the reconstruction of alternating surface forms we may recover evidence for synchronic rules in the pre- or protolanguage; cf. 17.2 above.

19.1. Special characteristics and problems of comparative reconstruction

In spite of their similarities, comparative and internal reconstruction differ in several important ways. These differences and their consequences will be discussed in the present section.

The goal of comparative reconstruction is not only to recover (or approximate) prehistoric linguistic reality, but also to establish genetic relationship. And when reconstruction is used for this purpose, it is not sufficient to demonstrate a general relationship between given languages or dialects. Rather, it is necessary to establish specific relationships between their forms and structures — through reconstruction of the corresponding ancestral forms and structures. The more we can reconstruct, i. e., the more we can account for similarities which cannot be due to chance, the more successful will be our demonstration of genetic relationship. At the same time, however, the need to establish relationship through reconstruction must be counterbalanced by considerations of Occam's Razor and the principle of realism. As the last chapter has shown, these two principles put certain limits on our reconstructions: We must not over-reconstruct.

There is another important difference between internal and comparative reconstruction: The data base for the latter approach is considerably larger. Not only because we are considering data from more than one language or dialect, but also because we are not restricted to just those linguistic items which happen to have morphophonemic alternations. Our task is much more like working on an entire language — multiplied by the number of languages which we are considering.

This greater complexity of goals and data basis is responsible for the fact that in comparative linguistics we may occasionally have to accept analyses which are not entirely in accordance with the 'rules of the game' of historical linguistics and that we may have to postulate reconstructed forms which do not meet the very strict requirements of naturalness or realism. The alternative would be to deny relationships which on the basis of recurrent systematic correspondences are established beyond a reasonable doubt.

19.1.1. Example 1: Proto-Indo-European laryngeals

An example would be the case of the Proto-Indo-European 'laryngeals'. As observed in 17.3, there is compelling internal and comparative evidence for postulating such entities. Not to do so would fail to explain not only the morphophonemic alternations in most of the Indo-European languages, but more importantly, it would fail to account for the recurrent similarities between the systems of these languages and that of Hittite (where the 'laryngeals' have distinct reflexes). We would have to claim that these similarities are simply the result of chance. Given the systematicity of the phenomena, such an approach would hardly be acceptable.

At the same time, however, because of an absence of compelling evidence in favor of one interpretation or another, Indo-Europeanists still cannot agree on the phonetic nature of these segments. As a consequence, they generally operate with arbitrary, phonetically unspecified symbols like *A, E, O* which obviously are not in accordance with the requirement that reconstructions be natural or realistic. Still, given the alternatives, this is better than not reconstructing at all.

19.1.2. Example 2: Armenian *erk-*

Similarly, we may at times have to accept the fact that the changes required by a given reconstruction are not in accordance with the 'rules of the game'. We may have to postulate changes which are not natural, or common, or 'explainable'.

Consider for instance the development of PIE **dw-* to Arm. *erk-,* a change which appears to be completely regular, albeit difficult to explain. Cf. the examples in (1).

(1) PIE   Armenian
  *dwō(w)   > erku   'two'
  *dwey-   > erkiwł   'fear'
  *dwāro-   > erkar   'long'

Now, from other evidence such as the data in (2), we know that at a certain stage Armenian regularly added prothetic vowels before initial *r*, whether inherited (as in (2a)) or initial through other developments (cf. (2b)). Moreover, we know that PIE **w* regularly became Arm. *g* before the vowel of the first syllable, as in (3). We know that initial **d* normally becomes Arm. *t* ; cf. (4). Finally, there is precedent for postulating a voicing assimilation of *g* after voiceless obstruent; cf. (5).

(2a) *regʷos   >   erek   'dark, night'
  b) *treyes   > *rekh   >   erekh   'three'

(3) *woyda   >   gitem   'know'

(4) *dek̑m̥   >   tasn   'ten'

(5) *swek̑rū > *sgesur >   skesur 'mother-in-law'

Given all this knowledge, we can get the developments in (6a) and (b). The question which remains, and which is not easily answered, is how we can get from (6a) to (6b), i. e., from the expected outcome **tk-* to the **rk-* presuposed by attested *erk-*. Weakening is perhaps a possibility. Compare the loss of *t* in the cluster **tr-* of example (2b). But the initial, pre-voiceless stop environment in expected **tk-* does not appear to be a natural one for weakening. We may therefore have to accept the change without being able to explain it as an instance of a natural or common process. The alternative, i. e., ignoring the systematic relationship between the words in (1) or attributing it to chance, certainly is far less attractive.

(6a) *dw- > *tg- > *tk-
 b) *rk- > erk-

19.1.3. Example 3: Tocharian dentals

We may even have to accept analyses which violate the principle that sound change is regular. Consider for instance the case of Tocharian. In this group of two closely related languages (commonly referred to as Tocharian A and B), the PIE voiced, aspirated, and voiceless stops regularly merge into voiceless ones. We are therefore not surprised to find voiceless outcomes also for the dental stops. What is surprising, however, is that there are dual outcomes of these stops, namely *t* or *ts,* without there being any apparent conditions for the split. Compare the examples in (7).

(7)	PIE	Tocharian A	Tocharian B	
	*treyes	tre	trai	'three'
	*tu(-)	tu	twe	'you'
	*dek-	täk-		'think (etc.)'
	*dō-		pe-te	'give'
	*dhubro-	tpär	tapre	'high/low'
	*dhē-	tā-	tā-	'put'
vs.	*poti-	pats	pets	'husband'
	*der-	tsär-	tsär-	'separate'
	*dak-	tsāk-	tsāk-	'bite'
	*dheg^{w}h-	tsäk-	tsäk-	'burn'

Although unconditioned split, i. e., sporadic, non-regular sound change, is anathema to historical linguistics, it appears as if we have to accept it here. For again, the alternatives are even worse. We would either have to deny relationship of these forms to the corresponding ones in the other Indo-European languages and thus attribute their recurrent similarities to chance. Or we would have to reconstruct for the proto-language a contrast between *ts and *t, *dz and *d, *$dhzh$ (or the like) and *dh, merely in order to 'account' for a difficulty affecting a single branch of Indo-European — a clear violation of Occam's Razor and of the goal of positing realistic reconstructions. If we followed this procedure for every single difficulty in the development of the various related languages, we would soon arrive at a proto-language with hundreds or even thousands of reconstructed segments, far beyond what one encounters in real, natural languages.

19.1.4. Problem 4: PIE *bh*-cases

Similar situations may arise also in morphology. For instance, the discussion of late Proto-Indo-European dialects (cf. 18.7, as well as 15.3) implied that Baltic, Slavic, and Germanic had a change like (8a), by which the suffix-initial *bh of certain nominal endings was replaced by *m.

    (8a) pl. I   *-bhis   → *-mis
                etc.
      b) sg. D *te-bhey : OCS tebě 'to you'

There are good reasons for believing that this development was not a sound change, for it was restricted to the morphological category of instrumental, dative, and ablative. Elsewhere it did not apply. Moreover, although it applied in the nouns and in most pronouns, one pronominal form did not undergo it, but retained the old form of the ending; cf. (8b). (Note that PIE *bh regularly changes into Slavic *b.)

It is for these reasons that the change in (8a) has been formulated as an analogical replacement — even though there is no known model which would have motivated it. Again we are faced with a violation of one of the basic principles of reconstruction. But again, the alternatives seem to be even less attractive. Either we would have to over-reconstruct, by postulating two sets of coexisting endings for the proto-language, or we would have to attribute to pure chance the recurrent and obvious similarities between the Baltic/Slavic/Germanic endings on one hand and those of the other Indo-European languages (or Proto-Indo-European) on the other. Cf. (9).

(9)   Baltic/Slavic/Germanic   PIE

    pl. I   *-mis/mīs   *-bhi(s)

        D/Ab. *-mos   *-bh(y)os

    du. I/D/Ab. *-ma/mā   *-bh(y)am/bh(y)ām

19.1.5. Conclusion 1

The problem in all of these cases is probably not that our 'rules of the game' are wrong. It is more likely that other linguistic change has obscured the evidence which would make an adequate analysis possible, or that our understanding of the available evidence or of the nature of linguistic change is deficient.

That is, we may not always be able to avoid analyses like the ones above, unless we are willing to sacrifice our goal of accounting for recurrent similarities without over-reconstructing. At the same time, we should retain an uneasy feeling about such analyses. We should subject them to continuing research and reexamination such that eventually they may perhaps be replaced by more adequate analyses. The following sections illustrate the manner in which such an approach might be pursued vis-à-vis the problems discussed in 19.1.1-4.

19.1.6. Proto-Indo-European laryngeals reexamined

In the case of the so-called laryngeals of Proto-Indo-European, there are a number of convergent facts which suggest a possible phonetic identification, however speculative it may be.

One of these facts consists in the *h*-like reflexes found in Hittite and related languages; cf. 17.3 above. To these can be added the evidence of Indo-Iranian, in which the prevocalic combination of voiceless stop + laryngeal resulted in a voiceless aspirated stop; cf. (10). (In Iranian, these stops regularly change into voiceless fricatives.) A possible source for the Hittite and Indo-Iranian reflexes would be an *h* or a voiceless velar fricative; cf. 7.1.1 and 7.3.3.

(10)   PIE *pḷtAu- > Skt. pṛthu-, Av. pərᵊþu- 'broad, wide'

A second consideration is the general consensus noted in 17.3 above that we need to distinguish three laryngeals. And as (11) demonstrates, one of the ways in which these differ from each other is in terms of their effect on a neighboring *e*-vowel: *A* and *O* 'color' a neighboring *e*-vowel into an *a*- or *o*-vowel, respectively, while *E* leaves its 'coloring' unaffected. (This difference in behavior accounts for the common use of the symbols *E, A,* and *O.*)

(11)   PIE   Greek (non-Attic-Ionic)

    *dhi-dhe**E**-mi   ti-thē-mi   'put, place'

    *sti-ste**A**-mi   hi-stā-mi   'stand'

    *di-de**O**-mi   di-dō-mi   'give'

If we look for a place in the PIE obstruent system (cf. (12)) which might accommodate segments of this sort we find one plausible spot, namely the fricative series corresponding to the 'velar' stops *k̑, k,* and *kʷ*. Accordingly, we might rewrite *E, A, O* as the fricatives *x̑, x, xʷ* respectively; cf. (12′).

(12)   p   t   k̑   k   kʷ

    (b) d   g̑   g   gʷ

    bh   dh   g̑h   gh   gʷh

         s

(12′) p   t   k̑   k   kʷ

    (b) d   g̑   g   gʷ

    bh   dh   g̑h   gh   gʷh

         s   x̑   x   xʷ

         (= E   A   O)

Postulating the system in (12′) would have the advantage of not positing any new features for PIE, since [+ fricative] is needed for *s* anyway, and since the features for the three 'velar' series are likewise independently required. Moreover, a frontish quality for *E*, a back-rounded quality for *O*, and a neutral quality for *A* would very well agree with their effects on a neighboring *e*. Although speculative, the reconstruction in (12') therefore would be not only possible but also explanatory. (Some linguists have argued that only two 'velar' series should be reconstructed, since no language has preserved the triple contrast reconstructed for PIE. However, comparative evidence shows that all three 'velars' constrast in the environment before *r;* cf. (13). It is difficult to see how this triple contrast can be derived from an earlier opposition between only two 'velar' series, unless we choose to abandon the principle that sound change is regular. The situation, then, is very similar to the case of the (late) PIE vowels **i, *a,* and **ə,* a distinction which likewise has not been preserved in any of the daughter languages; cf. 19.2.1 below. Curiously, however, few linguists have proposed to reduce this triple contrast to an earlier contrast between only two segments.)

(13) *kred-   'belief, believe'   : Skt. śrad-dhā-, Lat. crēdō,
                                            OIr. cretim
      *krewA-   'raw meat, gore'   : Skt. kraviṣ-, Gk. kreas,
                                            Lat. cruor
      *kʷreyA-   'buy'   : Skt. krī-ṇā-ti, Gk. prias-
                                            thai, OIr. crenid, OW pri-
                                            nit

19.1.7. Armenian *erk-* reconsidered

In the case of Arm. *erku* etc., it turns out that we were perhaps a little too hasty in excluding weakening as an explanation for the change of **tk* to **rk*. We can find a precedent for such a development in the fact that Iranian had weakening of voiceless stops not only before (voiced) non-syllabic sonorants (as in (14a)), but also before (originally) voiceless obstruents (cf. (14b)).

(14) PIE   Avestan
      a) *pro-   > fra-   'forward'
          *trayas   > θrayō   'three'
          *krewA/kruA- > xrūrəm   'raw, bloody'
      b) *pǝtrey > *ptrey > *fθrai > fðrōi   'to the father'
          *psteno-   > fštāna-   'breast'
          *ksep-   > xšap-   'night'

A possible explanation for this development is that it originated in contexts where the words in question were preceded by vowel-final words. Sanskrit evidence shows that under such conditions it is possible to resyllabify word-initial stops into the coda of the preceding syllable; cf. (15). And once in coda position, the stops occur in an environment that is highly conducive for weakening.

(15)   -V ‡ CCV- = [-VC $ CV-]

19.1.8. Tocharian dental stops reconsidered

As for the fate of PIE dental stops in Tocharian, one study has suggested that if we (i) eliminate some of the more dubious etymologies and (ii) allow for a development of PIE *dh to *d by something like Grassmann's Law (cf. (16)), then we can derive the Tocharian outcomes *ts* and *t* by regular sound changes; cf. (17).

(16)   *$dheg^{w}h$- > *$deg^{w}h$- 'burn'

(17a)   *d $> \emptyset / \left\{ \dfrac{\rule{1cm}{0.4pt} C}{V \rule{1cm}{0.4pt} V} \right\}$

            $>$ ts elsewhere

     b)   *t, dh $>$ t

The only apparent flaw in postulating different developments for the voiced vs. the voiceless and aspirated dentals is the fact that in all other stop series, the Proto-Indo-European distinction between voiced, voiceless, and aspirated is completely neutralized (in favor of the voiceless stops). However, this is not a serious flaw. For we find a similar phenomenon in Insular Celtic, where voiced and aspirated stops generally merge and become unaspirated voiced, but where Proto-Indo-European *g^{w} and *$g^{w}h$ retain their separate identities, as *b* and *gw* respectively. Moreover, note that although the Tocharian dentals and the Insular Celtic labiovelars are exceptions to the merger, they do conform to the phonetic 'trend' of the merger: Like all the other reflexes of the Proto-Indo-European stops, Toch. *t* and *ts* are voiceless and unaspirated; and like all the other outcomes of PIE voiced and aspirated stops, Ins. Celt. *b* and *gw* are voiced and unaspirated.

19.1.9. The Proto-Indo-European *bh*-cases reexamined

Even for the PIE *bh*-cases it is perhaps possible to provide a speculative explanation (but see also below):

The Proto-Indo-European instrumental/dative/ablative dual form was given as **bh(y)am/bh(y)ām* in (9). Actually, Sanskrit offers *-bhyām*, Avestan *-bya/byā*, and Old Irish a form [-βʸ] whose effect on following words indicates that it once ended in a nasal (i. e., < **-bhim* or the like). The *-m* which is found in some of these forms recurs in a number of other case forms, such as Skt. sg. D *tubhyam* beside earlier *tubhya* 'to you'. It may at one time have been optionally used to mark the goal or complement of certain verbs. If now we postulate for the prehistory of Baltic, Slavic, and Germanic an 'extended' form **-bhām*, cooccurring with 'unextended' **bhā*, then we might be able to account for the *m*-forms in the following manner: The distant assimilation in (18) would have led to a form **-mām*. (As noted in 5.1.1, distant consonant assimilation usually is not regular. It is therefore not necessary to expect the change in (18) to recur elsewhere.) The initial *m* of this suffix could then be extended to the other *bh*-case endings. The first step perhaps consisted in the optional generalization of *m* to the unextended and therefore unchanged form *-bhā;* cf. (19a). Further extension may then have introduced *m* also in the other endings; cf. (19b).

(18)   *-bhām > *-mām

(19a)   *-mām : *bhā
   → *-mām : *-mā (beside unchanged *-bhā)

   b)   *-bhā : *-mā
       *-bhis : X = *-mis
       etc.

Though there are evidently some 'murky' spots in this explanation, it appears preferable to a formulation like (20). For the latter does not provide any motivation for the change.

(20)   *-bhis → *-mis
       etc.

Other proposed explanations have difficulties of their own. Thus it has been suggested that the *bh*- and *m*-forms are parallel innovations designed to create forms which previously had been lacking in the system. Arguments in favor of this view would include the fact that Hittite, the branch of Indo-European which seems to have broken off earliest, does not have any *bh-* or *m*-case endings. Moreover, there are considerable differences even within the *bh*-languages; cf. e. g. (21).

(21) pl. D.   Skt. -bhyas, Av. -byō   : Lat. -bus, Gaul. -bos
                                            (without *y*)
      du. I/D/Ab. Skt. -bhyām, Av. -byā   : OIr. *-bim

However, there are several problems with this interpretation. First, it can be accused of over-reconstructing. For considering the attested *bh-* and *m*-endings to be parallel innovations requires reconstructing two elements for the proto-language, *-bh-* and *-m-,* from which the attested forms must have developed. Moreover, the analysis does not explain the striking formal agreements between *bh-* and *m*-forms, especially as they are found in Indo-Iranian and Baltic/Slavic. Finally, the analysis does not explain the dialectal distribution of *bh*-forms: The languages exhibiting *bh*-endings (Indo-Iranian, Armenian, Greek, Italic, and Celtic) are not otherwise known for having undergone common innovations. On the other hand Baltic, Slavic and Germanic have done so. Compare the merger of PIE **a, o,* and *ə* (for which see section 18.7 with 15.3 and Map 10). An analysis which accounts for the distribution of *bh*-endings as common archaisms and the *m*-forms as common innovations therefore appears to be preferable.

Perhaps, however, we are here operating on the 'outer fringes' to which the available evidence can carry us, so that all explanations fall short of being completely satisfactory.

19.1.10. Conclusion 2

Analyses which violate the 'rules of the game' or the principles of naturalness and realism thus may not always be replaceable by more acceptable hypotheses. However, as the cases of the PIE laryngeals, of Arm. *erku* etc., and of the Tocharian dentals have shown, looking for alternatives may in many cases eventually lead to more acceptable and more explanatory analyses.

19.2. Phonological reconstruction

The area in which comparative reconstruction generally is most successful is phonology. There are several reasons for this.

First, the number of segments in any given language is much smaller
than the number of words or morphemes. Moreover, morphological
and syntactic patterns tend to be much more complex than phonological
ones.

Secondly, it is much easier to find sufficient relevant evidence for
phonology than for morphology or syntax: Even relatively short texts
offer a virtually complete picture of the segmental inventory of a given
language. On the other hand, the information which such texts provide
for morphology and syntax is quite limited. Gathering sufficient data
therefore requires the study of considerably longer texts. This is not
only more time-consuming; for relatively poorly attested languages, it
is just about impossible.

Moreover, sound change is the area of linguistic change which has
been researched most thoroughly and in which we have the fullest
understanding of what is natural or common. As a consequence, we
are in a much better position for choosing between alternative analyses
than we are for other types of change.

Finally, with the exception of certain well-known subtypes, sound
change is regular. This makes the tracing of historical developments
considerably easier than in other areas of linguistic change.

For these reasons, the primary exemplification of comparative reconstruction will come from the area of phonological reconstruction.

Notice however that what follows is merely an illustration of the
kinds of reasoning which enter into reconstructive work. It should not
be interpreted as a 'how-to' guide to comparative reconstruction. There
simply is no single, sure-fire algorithm for the task of reconstruction.
Rather, as in other areas of linguistics, preliminary hypotheses often
are arrived at by an intuitive 'leap' which defies description. What can
be described are the criteria which make it possible to evaluate and
(one hopes) justify such hypotheses.

Here as elsewhere, reconstruction is based on the oldest attested
stages of the languages, so as to minimize the extent to which independent linguistic changes have brought about the differentiation of related
languages. In addition, the following conventions will be followed in
the presentation of the data:

(i)   Correspondences will be illustrated with a minimum of examples. It is to be understood that unless otherwise stated, the correspondences recur in many other examples. Moreover, unless specifically stated, there are no restrictions on the environments in which the correspondences can be found.

(ii)   Because of lexical obsolescence, etc., words illustrating a given correspondence may not be found in all of the related languages. In cases of this sort, the correspondence will generally be illustrated by more than one word, such that the two vocabulary sets 'overlap'; cf., e. g., (22b) below.

(iii)   For ease of exposition (as well as understanding), data will not be cited from all of the related languages, but just from an illustrative subset of the languages.

(iv)   For similar reasons, the illustrations will be limited to the most common correspondence patterns. Special developments will by and large be ignored.

19.2.1. Occam's Razor in comparative reconstruction — the Proto-Indo-European vowels

We may begin the illustration with a relatively compact example, concerning the reconstruction of the (late, post-'laryngeal') Proto-Indo-European vowel system. Compare the data in (22).

(22)	Sanskrit	Avestan	Greek	Latin	Gothic	
a)	yugam	yugəm	zugon	iugum	juk	'yoke'
b)	idam	idəm		idem	ita	'it, that'
	rikta-	ⁱrixta-	lipto-	re-lictus		'left (behind)'
c)	daśa	dasa	deka	decem	taihun [ɛ]	'ten'
d)	aṣṭau	aštā	oktō	octō	ahtau	'eight'
e)	ajati	azaⁱti	agō	agō	aka (ONorse)	'drive, impel'
f)	pitā	pitā	patēr	pater	fadar	'father'

Here the reconstructions for sets (a), (b), and (e) are easy, since all the languages agree: We must reconstruct *u, *i, and *a, respectively. Also set (c) presents no difficulties, even though there is no complete agreement: Since the majority of languages have e, this is the sound which we will reconstruct for the proto-language.

Examples like these may suggest that reconstruction is governed by the principle that 'the majority wins out'. However, the correspondence sets in (d) and (f) show that this is not correct:

In (d), the majority of languages have *a*; only two have *o*. But note that we have already reconstructed an **a* for set (e); and this **a* does not change into *o* in Greek and Latin. Moreover, the overall evidence of the Indo-European languages does not make it possible to attribute the Greek and Latin contrast between *o* and *a* to a split of earlier **a*. Unless we want to give up the notion of regular sound change, we are therefore compelled to reconstruct a different segment, namely **o*. In addition, we need to stipulate that this **o* changed into *a* in Sanskrit, Avestan, and Germanic. No change is required for Latin and Greek.

Although this reconstruction does 'multiply entities', it does so by 'necessity'. We are thus not in violation of Occam's Razor. (We would, however, be violating that principle if we reconstructed, say, **i*. For such a reconstruction would entail unnecessarily postulating changes not only for Sanskrit, Avestan, and Germanic, but also for Greek and Latin.)

Set (f) poses even greater difficulties: The Indo-Iranian vocalism is the same as in (b), while the vocalism of the other languages is identical to the one in (e). Again there is no evidence which would make it possible to attribute this distribution to a split, either of **i* or of **a*. Unless we abandon the principle of regular sound change — or give up the idea of reconstruction altogether — we are therefore faced with the 'necessity' of setting up another proto-segment, which must be different from either of the two attested segments in (f).

Since this proto-segment must be able to merge with either **i* or **a*, without merging with any other vowels, a central, non-low vowel seems to be the best choice for this reconstruction. And the usual value ascribed to the segment is *ə*. For as (23) shows, this vowel can merge with **i* or **a*, without (incorrectly) merging with some other vowels along the way.

(23)

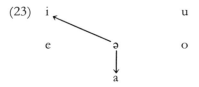

An equally realistic and phonetically acceptable reconstruction would be **i̵*. Note however that the question of how to phonetically identify the proto-segment for set (f) is an issue only if we subscribe to the principle that reconstructions should approximate linguistic reality. For those who do not subscribe to this view, there should in principle be nothing to prevent a reconstruction like '123'. For as can be seen from

(24), such a reconstruction does not require any more changes than one which posits phonetically more realistic ə. (In all fairness it must be admitted that those who argue against the possibility of realism in reconstruction have postulated the same ə as those who argue for it.)

(24 a)   ə   >   i   (Indo-Iranian)
             >   a   (elsewhere)
   b)   123   >   i   (Indo-Iranian)
             >   a   (elsewhere)

Whatever we decide concerning the identity of the reconstructed segment, however, it is clear that also here the principle of 'majority wins' is too simplistic. Occam's Razor, on the other hand, covers not only those cases in which the 'majority wins', but also cases like set (d) and, through its 'necessity provision', even cases like set (f).

19.2.2. The Germanic non-sibilant obstruent system

As an extended example of comparative reconstruction let us take a look at the non-sibilant obstruent systems of the Germanic languages.

In these systems, as exemplified by Old English, Old High German, Gothic, and Old Norse, we find systematically recurring correspondences like the ones in Chart 19.1. Forms are cited in traditional (normalized) orthography. The relevant phonetic correspondences are given on the left. In these formulae, the symbol ~ occurring between two segments indicates that these segments alternate with each other.

Note that the Old English symbol *g* has here been interpreted as having the value [ɣ] in initial environment. For Old English, this interpretation is not completely certain. Other, closely related Germanic dialects, however, have clear evidence for the pronunciation [ɣ]. Interpreting Old English initial *g* as [ɣ] makes it possible to include that evidence, without further proliferation of the data.

There is some uncertainty also about the phonetic interpretation of Gothic *b, d,* and *g* in medial and final environment. The question whether they represent fricatives or stops in this environment seems to be unresolvable.

		Old English	OH German	Gothic	Old Norse	
1	f/f/f/f-		fæder	fatar	fadar	faðir	'father'
2	-f~v/f/f/f~v-	(a)	wulf	wolf	wulf	ulf	'wolf'
		(b)	wulvas	wolfa	wulfōs	ulvar	'wolves'
3	þ/d/þ/þ-		þearf	darf	þarf	þarf	'he needs'
4	-þ~ð/d/þ/þ~ð-	(a)	dēaþ	tōd	dauþ	dauþ	'death'
		(b)	dēaðes	tōdes	dauþaus	dauðar	'of death'
5	h/h/h/h-		hund-	hunt	hund	hund	'hundred'
6	-∅/h/h/∅-	(a)	tēon	zehan	taihun	tjō	'ten'
		(b)	sēon	sehan		sjā	'see'
7	-x/x/x/∅	(a)	seah	sah		sā	'saw'
	(bef. C or #)	(b)	nieht	naht	nahts	nātt-	'night'
8	p/pf/p/p-		pund	pfunt	pund	pund	'pound'
9	p/p/p/p (/s___)		spīwan	spīwan	speiwan	spȳja	'spew'
10	-p/pf/p/p-	(a)	helpan	helpfan	hilpan	hjalpa	'help'
		(b)	sčieppan	skepfan	skapjan	skepja	'create'
11	-p/ff/p/p-	(a)	dēop	tioff	diup-	djūp-	'deep'
		(b)	hlēopan	hlouffan		hlaupa	'leap, run'
12	t/ts/t/t-		twā	zwei	twai	tveir	'two'
13	t/t/t/t (/ [+ fric.]___)		steorra	sterno	stairnō	stjarna	'star'
			(Cf. also set 7b above)				
14	-t/ts/t/t-		settan	setzen	satjan	setja	'to seat'
15	-t/ss/t/t-		sæt	sazz	sat	sat	'he sat'
16	k/kx/k/k-		corn	chorn	kaurn	korn	'grain'
17	č/kx/k/k-		čēapian	chouffōn	kaup-	kaup-	'buy'
18	k/k/k/k (/s___)		scavan	skaban	skaban	skava	'scrape'
19	č/k/k/k (/s___)		(Cf. set 10b above)				
20	-č/kx/k/k-		sæčč	secchia	sakjō		'argument'
21	-k/xx/k/k-	(a)	sacan	sahhan	sakan	saka	'to argue'
		(b)	macian	mahhōn		maka	'do, make'
22	-č/xx/k/k-		līč	līhh	leik-	līk-	'like'
23	b/b/b/b-		bringan	bringan	bringan	bringa	'bring'
24	-b/b/b/b- (/N___)		lamb-	lamb-	lamb-	lamb-	'lamb'
25	-f~v/b/f~b/f~v-	(a)	hlāf	hleib	hlaif	hleif	'bread'
		(b)	hlāvas	hleiba	hlaibōs	hleivar	'breads'
26	d/t/d/d-		dǣlan	teilen	dailjan	deila	'deal, part'
27	-d/t/d/d- (/N___)		(Cf. sets 5 and 8 above)				
28	-d/t/þ~d/þ~ð- ⎫	(a)	gōd	guot	gōþ	gōþ	'good'
29	ɣ/g/g/g- ⎭	(b)	gōdum	guotemu	gōdamma	gōðum	'good' (D)
30	ɣ/g/g/g-		gievan	geban	giban	geva	'give'
31	-g/g/g/g- (/N___)		(Cf. set 23 above)				
32	-x~ɣ~ɣ/g/g/g~ɣ-	(a)	dæg [ɣ]	tag	dag	dag	'day' (A)
		(b)	dagas [ɣ]	taga	dagōs	dagar [ɣ]	'days'
		(c)	burh [x]	burg	baurg	borg	'fort'
		(d)	burga [ɣ]	burgo	baurgē	borga [ɣ]	'forts' (G)

Chart 19.1. Germanic non-sibilant obstruent correspondences

19.2.3. Reconstruction of the basic 'grid'

Of the correspondences in Chart 19.1, the ones in (25) are most easily dealt with. For all languages show the same segment in the same environment. Unless other evidence forces us to reconsider, it would be a gross violation of Occam's Razor to reconstruct anything other than the segments as they are attested.

(25)   1 f/f/f/f-
       5 h/h/h/h-
       9 p/p/p/p- (/ s_____)
      13 t/t/t/t (/[+ fric]_____)
      18 k/k/k/k (/ s_____)
      23 b/b/b/b-
      24 -b/b/b/b- (/ N_____)
      31 -g/g/g/g- (/ N_____)

Also the correspondences in (26) are relatively easy to account for. In these correspondences, only one language differs. In all cases, save one, this is Old High German, which looks as if it has undergone some kind of systematic remaking of the obstruent system. (Exceptions are the environments after *s* and other fricative, where Old High German agrees with the other Germanic languages; cf. sets 9, 13, and 18.) Again, unless other evidence requires reconsideration, it would be a violation of Occam's Razor to reconstruct anything but what is found in the majority of the languages.

(26)   3 þ/d/þ/þ-
       8 p/pf/p/p-
     12 t/ts/t/t-
     16 k/kx/k/k-
     26 d/t/d/d-
     27 -d/t//d/d- (/ N_____)
     28 ɣ/g/g/g-

At this point we can set up a 'grid' of tentatively reconstructed protosegments; cf. (27). Moreover, given that *h* often develops from the voiceless velar fricative *x*, it is possible to (again tentatively) 'smoothe out' the system, by identifying *h* as the reflex of an earlier *x*;

cf. (27′). (Compare section 8.3 above on the tendency for phonological systems to be symmetrical. But see also section 19.5 below.)

(27)

	labial	dental	velar	glottal
'voiceless fricatives'	f	þ		h
'voiceless stops'	p	t	k	
'voiced stops'	b	d	g	

(27′)

	labial	dental	velar
'voiceless fricatives'	f	þ	x
'voiceless stops'	p	t	k
'voiced stops'	b	d	g

We must then proceed to tackle the other, more difficult correspondences.

19.2.4. Further reconstruction

Turning our attention to the 'voiceless fricatives', we may note that in sets 2 and 4 (cf. (28)), Old English and Old Norse agree on having an alternation between voiced and voiceless, and that this alternation is attributable to the environment: Voiced appears in medial voiced environment, voiceless finally. Since the other two languages have non-alternating voiceless fricatives, we can identify these non-initial sets with the initial sets *f* and *þ*, by assuming that Old English and Old Norse had medial voicing. (This being a common process in the world's languages, there is no need to consider it a shared innovation of these two languages.)

(28)   2 -f~v/f/f/f~v-
         4 -þ~ð/d/þ/þ~ð-

We can similarly identify sets 6 and 7 with set 5, which we have tentatively reconstructed as *h* < *x*. Compare (29). The word-final and preconsonantal set 7 in fact offers the velar fricative, a welcome confirmation of our reconstruction *x*. (An exception is Old Norse, where x seems to have been lost finally and before consonant, with compensatory lengthening of the preceding vowel.) The voiced medial set 6, on the other hand, offers *h* in Old High German and Gothic, but $\emptyset$ in Old English and Old Norse. As we have just seen, the latter two languages have independent evidence for medial voicing of voiceless fricatives. This process can be made to account also for the apparent medial loss of *h*; cf. section 3.4 above for discussion. That sets 6 and 7 are related to each other and are differentiated by split is suggested by the alternation in the word 'to see', between $\emptyset$ and *x* in Old English, and between *h* and *x* in Old High German. (Cf. sets 6b and 7a.)

(29)   6 -∅/h/h/∅-
          7 -x/x/x/∅ (/ _____ C or #)
          5 h/h/h/h-

In the 'voiceless stops', the situation in non-initial environment is considerably more complex. We may note that here Old High German offers both affricates (cf. (30a)) and geminate fricatives (cf. (30b)). (For the *č* of Old English see below.) Given that this difficulty is confined to one single language, which also in initial environment has undergone a major change in the obstruent system, one should certainly hesitate reconstructing the opposition between (30a) and (30b) for the proto-language. Rather, one should look for possible alternative explanations.

(30a)   10 -p/pf/p/p-
          14 -t/ts/t/t-
          20 -č/kx/k/k-
     b) 11 -p/ff/p/p-
          15 -t/ss/t/t-
          21 -k/xx/k/k-
          22 -č/xx/k/k-

Closer examination does in fact reveal certain regularities: The affricates occur either after consonant (cf. *helpfan* in 10b) or in contexts where Old English has geminate voiceless stops corresponding to voiceless stop $+ j = $ [y] in Gothic and Old Norse. Since gemination is common before glides (cf. 7.4.1), the Old English geminates can be related to these stop $+ j$ clusters without any difficulty. And if we assume that gemination had occurred also in the prehistory of Old High German, then we can account for the Old High German affricates by means of the same change which is required to produce affricates after consonant. Compare the formulation in (31). That this analysis is on the right track is suggested by the fact that it makes it possible to account for the striking phonetic and semantic similarities between sets 14 and 15, 20 and 21a; cf. (32).

(31)   p   >   pf / C_____
     Hence: helpan   >   helpfan
             skapjan > skeppan >   skeppfan   (> skepfan
                                       by simplification)

(32) 14   settan   setzen   satjan   setja   'to seat'
      15   sæt   sazz   sat   sat   'sat'
      20   sæčč   secchia   sakjō   'argument'
      21a   sacan   sahhan   sakan   saka   'to argue'

Also Old English presents certain difficulties for the reconstruction of our 'voiceless stops'. But these are limited to the velars. Moreover, these difficulties recur in the 'voiced stops'. Corresponding to the velar segments of Gothic and Old Norse, and the various reflexes of velar stop in Old High German, Old English offers both velars and palatals; cf. (33).

(33a) 16   k/kx/k/k-
       18   k/k/k/k (/ s_____)
       21   -k/xx/k/k-
       29   ɣ/g/g/g-
   b) 17   č/kx/k/k-
       19   č/k/k/k (/ s_____)
       20   -č/kx/k/k-
       22   -č/xx/k/k-
       30   y/g/g/g-
   c) 32a/d -x~ɣ~y/g/g/g~ɣ-

Since velars easily change into palatals (but not vice versa) and since there is 'internal' evidence for a morphophonemic alternation between velar and palatal in Old English (cf. especially (33c)), there is no reason for ascribing the Old English contrast to the Proto-Germanic ancestor, even if the conditions for the split of velar into velar and palatal may not be entirely transparent. (A closer look suggests two environments for palatalization: (i) before front-vocalic segments, including *j* = [y] and *ēa* < *au*; cf. sets 17, 19, and 30. (ii) word-finally after front vowels;

cf. sets 22 and 32a. Elsewhere, including before *i* corresponding to OHG *ō* (cf. set 21b), the velar remains unchanged.)

The greatest challenge to reconstruction are the 'voiced stops'. True, the postnasal environment provides solid evidence for voiced stops; cf. (34a); and in initial position the evidence strongly favors stop articulation, with only Old English presenting a fricative — and only in the velar series; cf. (34b).

(34a)	24	-b/b/b/b-	(/ N _____)
	27	-d/t/d/d-	(/ N _____)
	31	-g/g/g/g-	(/ N _____)
b)	23	b/b/b/b-	
	26	d/t/d/d-	
vs.	29	ɣ/g/g/g-	
	30	y/g/g/g-	

In medial and final environment, however, the evidence leans toward fricative articulation. Only Old High German has stops consistently; but then, Old High German has other, independent evidence for a major remaking of the obstruent system. Elsewhere, only Old English has unambiguous evidence for stop pronunciation, and only for the dental; cf. (35a) vs. (35b/c). This is perhaps not surprising, since as noted in section 7.3.4, dental fricatives are relatively unstable and are changed more commonly than other fricatives. (Similarly, in Old High German, only the dental member of the set 'voiceless fricatives' has become a stop.) Given that Old English and Old High German seem to share another innovation, namely gemination before *j* (cf. above), it is quite possible that also the development of *ð to a dental stop was a common innovation of these two languages.

(35a)	28	-d/t/þ ~ d/þ ~ ð-
b)	25	-f ~ v/b/f ~ b/f ~ v-
c)	32	-x ~ ɣ ~ y/g/g/g ~ ɣ-

Also Gothic seems to offer evidence for invariant stop pronunciation, namely in the velar; cf. (35c). However, as noted earlier, the precise phonetic interpretation of the Gothic symbols transliterated as *b, d, g* is not entirely certain. It is at least possible that medially, all of these referred to voiced fricatives. On the other hand, the fact that Old Norse has final g = [g] may be taken as support for an interpretation of Gothic g as a velar stop. (But see also section 19.3 below.)

With these exceptions, the balance of the evidence is in favor of an original fricative pronunciation. For the Old English, Gothic, and Old Norse morphophonemic alternations (cf. (36)) between voiceless and voiced are most easily accounted for in terms of original voiced fricatives which are devoiced word-finally.

(36)   Old English   Gothic   Old Norse
    25 f∼v   f∼b   f∼v
    28   þ∼d   þ∼ð
    32 x∼ɣ   g∼ɣ

The evidence thus points to stop pronunciation in initial and post-nasal environments and to fricative in post-vocalic medial and final positions. It is possible to interpret this as indicating an allophonic distribution in the proto-language. Compare the reconstruction in (37).

(37)   labial   dental   velar
    'voiceless fricatives'   f   þ   x
    'voiceless stops'   p   t   k
    'voiced stops'   b = [b]   d = [d]   g = [g]
                             ∼ [β]   ∼ [ð]   ∼ [ɣ]

However, one may well wonder whether this variability should not be reduced to earlier invariance. Moreover, once we have established evidence for voiced fricatives in medial and final environments, the Old English evidence for initial ɣ- is no longer as easily dismissed as it was earlier, in our first tentative reconstruction. It may rather be taken to indicate an earlier fricative pronunciation for all of the 'voiced stops', in all environments. In that case we would have to assume that already in dialectal Proto-Germanic times, post-nasal voiced fricatives became stops in all the dialects (presumably by assimilation to the stop articulation of the nasal). Similarly, we must assume that initial voiced fricatives became stops in most of the dialects of Proto-Germanic, with only the velar offering some dialectal resistance to the spread of this innovation. On the other hand, in Old Norse and perhaps in Gothic, the velar fricative seems to have been in the vanguard of the change toward stop pronunciation, changing to stop even in final position. (But see section 19.3 below.)

An alternative would be to reconstruct original stops and to derive fricatives, where they occur, by means of appropriate changes.

Neither of these two analyses is entirely free from difficulties. The first analysis suffers from the fact that it needs to explain why voiced fricatives were changed to stops initially and, in the case of *ɣ, also finally in Old Norse and perhaps Gothic. (As the discussion in 19.3 will show, the latter difficulty actually is a pseudo-problem.) In the second analysis, there is the question of why initial *g* should have changed to voiced fricative in Old English, and why only the velar stop, not the others.

As it turns out, certain morphophonemic alternations that must be reconstructed for the proto-language provide evidence which favors the first analysis. Compare for instance the data in (38).

(38)

		Old English	Old High German	Gothic	Old Norse	
a)		weorðan	wertan	wairþan	verða	'become'
		for-weorðan	far-wertan	fra-wairþan		'perish'
	vs.	ā-wierdan	far-werdan	fra-wardjan		'make perish'
b)		hōn	hāhan	hāhan		'hang'
		hengan	hengen		hengja	'make hang'

While the precise conditions which gave rise to this alternation are not recoverable on the basis of the Germanic evidence, one thing is clear: If we reconstruct (recurring) alternations like the ones in (38a) as original alternations between *þ and *ð, then the alternation is simply one of voicing. That is, it could be accounted for by means of a simple voicing or devoicing process. If, however, we reconstruct *þ ~ *d, then the alternation is more complex. We would have to postulate both a voicing/devoicing process and a process which either turns an original fricative into stop or vice versa. Occam's Razor would certainly favor the first analysis.

The alternation in (38b) is especially interesting. For it suggests that voiced fricatives originally were found even after nasal, i.e., in the position where all Germanic languages agree on having a voiced stop.

Though circumstantial, this evidence favors a reconstruction which posits original voiced fricatives; cf. (39)

(39)

	labial	dental	velar
'voiceless fricatives'	f	þ	x
'voiceless stops'	p	t	k
'voiced fricatives'	β	ð	ɣ

This system of reconstructed obstruents, with its contrast between voiced and voiceless fricatives, without a corresponding contrast in the stops, is perhaps not one of the most commonly found obstruent systems. To some linguists' minds, this 'typological markedness' would be reason enough to reject the reconstruction, in which case we would be back to 'ground zero'. However, one might argue that the unusualness of the system is what motivates the general tendency of the voiced fricatives to turn into stops, producing a more natural system. (The issue of typology and reconstruction will be exmined in greater detail in section 19.5 below.)

19.2.5. Justifying the reconstruction

Given the reconstruction in (39), we need to postulate the following changes in order to account for the attested forms and thus to justify the reconstruction. No attempt has been made to account for the manner of articulation of Gothic *b, d, g* in medial position. (Subscript indices, as in $[+\text{cons.}]_1 > [+\text{cons}]_1 [+\text{cons.}]_1$ indicate identical place etc. of articulation.)

(40) $x > h$ $/ \left\{ \begin{matrix} [-\text{ obstr.}] \\ \# \end{matrix} \right\}$ _____ $[-\text{ obstr.}]$

(41) $\begin{bmatrix} +\text{ fric.} \\ +\text{ voice} \end{bmatrix} > [+\text{ stop}] / \text{ N} _____$

(42) $\begin{bmatrix} +\text{ fric.} \\ +\text{ voice} \\ -\text{ vel.} \end{bmatrix} > [+\text{ stop}] / \# _____$

Changes (40)-(42) are shared by all of the dialects and thus probably are of Proto-Germanic provenience.

(43)   ɣ > g   / # _____   (OHG, Goth., ON)

This change is shared by most of the dialects and thus may well date back to dialectal Proto-Germanic.

(44)   ɣ > g   / _____ # (ON, Goth.?; cf. 19.3 below)

(45)   ð > d   (OE, OHG)

(46)   [+ stop]₁ > [+ stop]₁ [+ stop]₁ / _____ j (OE, OHG)

(47)   j > ∅   / (C) C _____ V (OE, OHG)

Also these changes may perhaps go back to dialectal Proto-Germanic. However, they could also reflect later innovations, shared by distinct subgroups of Germanic.

The other changes may be more conveniently listed separately for each language. True, changes (48) and (56) might be common innovations of English and Norse; and (49), (55), and (57) might be shared by English, Gothic, and Norse. However, since the processes in question are quite common, it is not necessary to consider them to be exclusively shared innovations. Moreover, the domains of application seem to be different. For instance, in Old English, *ð did not participate in final devoicing (49), since it had turned into a stop by the earlier change of (45).

Old English:

(48)   [+ fric.]   > [+ voice] / [+ voice] _____ [+ voice]
       (hence h > ∅)

(49)   [+ fric.]   > [− voice] / _____ #

(50)   [+ vel.]   > [+ pal.]   / $\left\{ \begin{matrix} \text{_____} \begin{bmatrix} + \text{voc.} \\ + \text{front} \end{bmatrix} \\ \begin{bmatrix} V \\ + \text{front} \end{bmatrix} \text{_____} \# \end{matrix} \right\}$

Old High German:

(51)   [+ stop]   > [+ affric.] / $\left\{ \begin{matrix} \# \\ \begin{bmatrix} + \text{cons.} \\ - \text{fric.} \end{bmatrix} \end{matrix} \right\}$ _____

       > [+ fric.]₁ [+ fric.]₁ elsewhere

(52) $[+ \text{stop}]_1$ $> \emptyset$ / _____ $[+ \text{affric.}]_1$

(53)   d > t

(54)   þ > d

(55) $\begin{bmatrix} + \text{ fric.} \\ + \text{ voice} \end{bmatrix} > [+ \text{stop}]$

Gothic:

(56) $\begin{bmatrix} + \text{ fric.} \\ (- \text{ vel.?}) \end{bmatrix} > [- \text{voice}]$ / _____ #

Old Norse:

(75) $[+ \text{fric.}]$ $> [+ \text{voice}]$ / $[+ \text{voice}]$ _____ $[+ \text{voice}]$
(hence h $> \emptyset$)

(58) $\begin{bmatrix} + \text{ fric.} \\ (- \text{ vel.?}) \end{bmatrix} > [- \text{voice}]$ / _____ # (cf. 19.3 below)

(59)   x $> \emptyset$ (w. comp. length) / V _____ $\begin{Bmatrix} C \\ \# \end{Bmatrix}$

Among these changes, the following relative chronologies are required:

(40) before (48), (57)
(41), (42), (45) before (53)
(44) before (56), (58) (?)
(45) before (49)
(46) before (47) and (51)
(51) before (52)
(54) must not be ordered before (53). The two changes may be simultaneous, as part of the same overall shift in the obstruent system; or
(53) must precede (54). (Change (55) may perhaps be part of the
same general shift.)

19.3. Refining the reconstruction — 'reconstructing backward'

Once an analysis like the above is completed, it is useful to test its accuracy against data which were not considered in the original reconstruction. Consider now the data in (60).

(60)	Old English	Old High German	Gothic	Old Norse	
	stīgan [ɣ]	stīgan	steigan	stīga [ɣ]	'climb'
	stāh [x]	steig	staig	stē	'he climbed'
	stigon [ɣ]	stigun	stigun	stigu [ɣ]	'they climbed'
	lēogan [ɣ]	liogan	liugan	ljūga [ɣ]	'tell lies'
	lēah [x]	loug	laug	lō	'he lied'
	lugon [ɣ]	lugun	lugun	lugu [ɣ]	'they lied'
	wegan [ɣ]	wegan	wigan	vega [ɣ]	'weigh'
	wah [x]	wag	wag	vā	'he weighed'
	wāgon [ɣ]	wāgun	wēgun	vāgu [ɣ]	'they weighed'

It is quite obvious that in terms of the reconstruction in (39), the root-final consonant in the examples of (60) must be reconstructed as *ɣ. Applying now our sound changes from the preceding section, i. e., reconstructing backward (cf. 18.9 above), we will be able to correctly derive the forms in (60), save the third person singular past-tense forms of Old Norse. Here change (44) would wrongly predict a final *g*. Compare (61). (The numbers on the left side refer to the changes postulated in the preceding section.)

(61 a)		*weɣan	*weɣan	*weɣan	*weɣan
	(55)	– – –	wegan	– – –	– – –
	Other:	wegan [ɣ]	wegan	wegan	vega [ɣ]
b)		*waɣ	*waɣ	*waɣ	*waɣ
	(44)	– – –	– – –	wag	vag
	(49)	wax	– – –	– – –	– – –
	(55)	– – –	wag	– – –	– – –
	Other:	wah [x]	wag	wag	vag*

Cases like these challenge us to find alternative explanations.

In Chapter 3 we have seen the types of alternative explanations which are open to us when confronted with apparent exceptions to the regularity of sound change: We can reformulate our changes, add other sound changes, or invoke analogy or borrowing.

Of these alternatives, borrowing is not a possible solution in the present case, since we have no evidence for an outside source of forms like *vā*. Also analogy must be ruled out, since there is no plausible model for the replacement of expected *vag* by *vā*. Invoking an additional change, by which final *g* is lost with compensatory lengthening, would create more problems than it solves. First of all, it looks like an ad-hoc invention, solely designed to account for these troublesome forms. As such, one suspects, it may constitute a violation of Occam's Razor. Secondly, it would create difficulties for forms like *dag* (cf. set 32a in Chart 19.1). For their *g* should be lost likewise.

At the same time, if forms like **daɣ* appear as *dag,* but forms like **vaɣ* as *vā,* it is clearly impossible to explain both sets of forms as the result of regular sound change.

Now, of the two sets, the type *dag* is synchronically much more transparently related to the forms with which it alternates (cf. *daɣar*) than the type *vā* (cf. *vega, vāgu*). This difference suggests that we should look for an analysis which accounts for *vā* by regular sound change, but *dag* as the product of sound change plus analogy.

Such an analysis can be accomplished by rejecting change (44) for Old Norse and by letting change (57) apply to ɣ in the same way as it applies to the other voiced fricatives. If then we continue reconstructing backward by applying change (58), we will arrive at the outcomes in (62).

(62)   *vaɣ *daɣ
      (57) vax   dax
      (58) vā   dā*

Of these outcomes, *vā* evidently is correct, and *dā** just as evidently is not. However, the predicted paradigmatic alternation between *dā** and the *daɣ-* of forms like *daɣar* suggests a possible explanation for the actually attested *dag,* namely leveling. True, this leveling should produce a form *daɣ**. However, since after change (57) no word-final voiced fricatives are permitted in Old Norse, it is possible to argue that a change like (63) would be well motivated by the structure of Old Norse, in that it eliminates the phonetically aberrant (but morphologically regularized) final γ. Note that as a result, there is a new mor-phophonemic alternation in the paradigm for 'day'. But this alternation is more transparent than the original alternation *dā : da* γ*ar*.

(63) γ > g / _____ #

Our changes therefore need to be adjusted as follows: Change (44) no longer applies to Old Norse. (If it is a genuine change of Gothic, it will have to be listed among the specifically Gothic developments.) Change (57) now applies not only to labials and dentals, but also to velars. And to ensure correct results, it must be ordered such that it feeds (58); cf. (62) above. In addition we have to assume that leveling applied in nominal paradigms such as *da* γ: *da* γ*ar*. Finally, we need to invoke change (63) above to account for the fact that expected (leveled) *da* γ appears as *dag*.

As can be seen from the above illustration, the procedure of recon-structing backward is a very important tool in testing the accuracy of reconstructions and in trying to refine them. Not only did this procedure show that our sound changes for Old Norse were incorrectly formu-lated. Once we reformulated them, the procedure provided the evidence for a paradigmatic morphophonemic alternation which motivated an analogical remaking in the word for 'day'.

Heuristically, this is perhaps the greatest value of reconstructing backward. In many cases the possible motivation for an analogical remaking (or of borrowing) becomes evident only after we have derived the forms which would be expected if only regular changes (or other established changes) had applied. By looking at the relationships of these forms to other contemporary forms, and by comparing them with the actually attested forms, it is frequently possible to determine the causes for the differences between expected and attested forms.

19.4. Non-phonological reconstruction

As noted earlier, there are several factors which make non-phonological reconstruction quite different and more difficult compared to phonol-ogical reconstruction. Beside the question of the sufficiency of available evidence, these factors are (i) the fact that unlike sound change, other

linguistic change normally is not regular, resulting in greater discontinuities in the historical transmission of language; and (ii) our much more
limited understanding of the natural direction of non-phonological
change. As a consequence, the evidence tends to be more diffuse and
complex. Moreover, its interpretation is less certain: In sound change
we can often recognize the probable direction of change. For instance,
an alternation $k : \check{c}$ is unlikely to result from anything but palatalization
of an original velar stop $*k$. On the other hand, there are few specific
criteria which would indicate the directionality of morphological, syntactic, or semantic processes. (Note however that even much of sound
change, including many types of assimilation, lacks built-in 'directionality'. Compare the discussion in section 20.5 below.)

There is however a general criterion which can indicate the probable
direction of change in morphological and syntactic variation. This is
the concept of **archaism**: Since non-phonological change normally is
not regular, it frequently leaves residue which is not affected by the
change. If we can establish which of two competing formations or
structures is archaic and which is innovated, then the task of reconstruction becomes easier. For in that case we can use the evidence of these
archaisms as the basis for reconstruction.

Unfortunately, however, it is not a priori certain what is an archaism
and what an innovation. We cannot appeal to our reconstruction as
evidence that a particular pattern is archaic. For it is circular to argue
that a given structure X is archaic because it agrees with a reconstructed
pattern Y, if that reconstruction was in turn based on the claim that X
is archaic.

However, there are certain criteria which make detection of possible
or probable archaisms simpler, without resort to circular reasoning: As
noted in the discussion of Kuryłowicz's fourth 'law' of analogy (cf.
10.1.4 above), if older forms continue to coexist with the innovated
forms, the latter are used in productive, basic function, while the former
are limited to **marginal functions**.

Moreover, observation of attested language histories shows that
certain types of texts tend to best preserve such marginal forms. These
conservative texts include legal documents, and traditional literary
forms, such as epic poetry, popular ballads, and folk narratives.

Archaisms commonly are deviations from the synchronically more
productive and 'normal' patterns and uses. At the same time, however,
not all deviant patterns are necessarily archaic. Some may be mistakes,
or intentional deviations (especially in non-traditional poetry), or the

harbingers of a coming innovation. Such deviations, however, would not be limited to typically conservative texts. Moreover, if such deviations are synchronically felt to be 'old-fashioned' and if within observable history their use can be seen to be decreasing, it is more likely that we are dealing with archaisms than with, say, incipient innovations.

The case for considering a particular pattern an archaism becomes even stronger if we can find **cumulative** and **convergent** evidence in related languages, such that they show similar deviations, but in very different contexts, at least some of which are typical for archaisms. In that case, common innovation would be highly unlikely, and the only satisfactory historical explanation will be the hypothesis that we are dealing with common inheritance. On the other hand, if we reconstructed only the most productive patterns for the proto-language, then these deviations would remain unexplained.

An example from comparative Romance, concerning the order of the major constituents, subject (S), object (O), and verb (V), may illustrate the relevance of these considerations.

There is virtually universal agreement that in Latin, the (near-)ancestor of the Romance languages, the pragmatically unmarked order of the major constituents was SOV; cf. (64a). And as in other SOV languages, the order of auxiliary (AUX) and non-finite main verb (MV) most commonly was MV + AUX; cf. (64b). Beside SOV, various other orders were possible, many of which can be explained as due to stylistic NP movement processes; cf. (64c). In addition, a marked verb-initial pattern existed, in which the fronted verb signaled focus on the action, stage-setting, etc.; cf. the 'scrambled' word order in (64d). The question arises as to whether reconstruction on the basis of modern Romance evidence can approximate this state of affairs.

(64a)   hi omnes lingua, institutis, legibus inter se differunt
                                                        V
        'all of these differ from each other in speech, political
        institutions, and laws'

   b)   cuius pater ... a senatu populi Romani amicus appellatus
                                                        MV
        erat
        AUX
        'whose father had been called friend by the Roman senate
        and people'

c)   ea res est   Helvetiis per indicium enuntiata
     AUX   MV
    'this matter was made known to the Helvetians through spies'

d)   erant omnino itinera duo
    V
    '(there) were only two roads'

The synchronically most productive and unmarked pattern of the Romance languages clearly is SVO, with the order AUX + MV; cf., e. g., (65). If we were to use this evidence as the basis for reconstruction, then we would fail to arrive at the unmarked SOV and MV + AUX of Latin.

(65) Span. Juan   ha   robado una   manzana
       Fr.   Jean   a   volé   une   pomme
       It.   Giovanni ha   robato una   mela
             S   AUX MV   O
             'John   has   stolen an   apple'

In addition to the productive pattern of (65), the Romance languages also have marginal patterns, i. e., possible archaisms. One of these is pan-Romance, although outside imperatival structures it appears to be on the retreat, especially in French where only a few frozen expressions survive. This is the verb-initial pattern in (66). Disregarding the still-productive imperative structures in (66a), this pattern serves to focus on the verbal action and as a stage-setting device; cf. (66b). Note moreover that the latter pattern contains subjects specified on the surface; and these indicate that the order is in fact ‡VS ...

(66a) Span. vaya con Dios   'go with God'
       Fr.   cherchez la femme   'look for the woman'
       It.   lasciate ogni speranza 'abandon all hope'
    b) Span. fue en esta ciudad   'there was in that city a king'
               un rey ...
       (Fr.   suivent les noms ... '(now) follow the names ...')
       It.   disse il professore ... 'said the professor ...'

Since this pattern is marginal it may possibly be an archaism, of which the predominant SVO would be a secondary replacement. However, the fact that all the Romance languages agree on the specific marked functions of the construction suggests that its marginality, including the markedness of its functions, is inherited from the proto-language, i. e., that in the proto-language verb-initial order coexisted and contrasted with the ancestor of the modern unmarked SVO.

This impression is reinforced by the fact that a similar distinction between verb-initial and other sentence structures is made in the case of verb + clitic pronoun sequences, at least in some of the languages; cf. (67 a/b) vs. (c). And the fact that in French these structures are limited to the only productive verb-initial type, the imperative pattern in (67 a), and that Italian and Spanish have a strong tendency toward a similar limitation suggests that the contrast between verb-initial and other sentence structures is an archaism, not an innovation.

(67 a)		Sp.	mostrad me	'show me'
		Fr.	dis-le	'tell it'
		It.	mostrate mi	'show me'
b)		Sp.	verémos lo	'we will see that'
		It.	disse gli la dama ...	'said the lady to him ...'
c)	vs.	Sp.	(yo) te amo	'I love you'
		Fr.	je t'aime	'I love you'
		It.	(io) ti amo	'I love you'

Beside this marginal ⧣VS pattern, there is cumulative evidence also for marginal (S)OV, verb-final, or MV + AUX patterns. However, unlike the verb-initial type, these patterns are found in very different contexts in the various Romance languages. And these contexts include traditional (popular) poetry.

Evidence for OV is found in the so-called *să*-optative of Rumanian, as in (68). It is also found in frozen, 'idiomatic' expressions like (69 a). Contrast what would be the productive pattern in (69 b). Note that (69 a) is aberrant — and archaic — not only in respect to word order, but also by lacking the indefinite article of the synchronically productive pattern. 'Internal' cumulative evidence of this sort is important and reinforces the cumulativity of the comparative evidence.

(68)   Rum.   dereptate s(ă) aveţi spre tot omu-lŭ
               O   V
       'that you may have justice for every man'

(69a)   Fr.   sans mot dire   'without saying a word'
                 O   V
   b)   Fr.   sans dire un mot   'without saying a word'
                 V   O

Verb-final patterns can be observed in Rumanian and Galician folk poetry of the last century, as in (70).

(70)   Rum.   cu nevesta mě iubesc / după fată mě topesc
                        V   V
               'I am in love with the woman, I pine away for the girl'

A combination of verb-final and MV + AUX is frequently encountered in Sicilian and Sardinian dialects, cf. e. g. (71).

(71)   Sic.   la picilidḍa vattiata è?   'has the girl been baptized?'
               MV AUX

MV + AUX is found in 'frozen' form in the non-Balkan Romance future tense. That forms like (72a) are in fact univerbations of infinitive + 'have' is shown by the evidence of Portuguese and Sicilian, which permit a clitic pronoun to intervene; cf. (72b). Romanian uses a different auxiliary, namely the verb 'want'. And while this auxiliary may agree with the synchronically predominant order and precede its main verb (cf. 73a)), it may also follow; cf. (73b).

(72a)   Span.   amaré = amar + hé   'I will love'
                          inf.   have
                          MV   AUX
    b)   Port.   fazê-lo- hei   'I will do it'
                 MV Clit. AUX

(73a)   Rom.   voǐ cîntà   'I will sing'
                 AUX MV
    b)   Rom.   cîntà voǐ   'I will sing'
                 MV AUX

What is important about these marginal patterns is that the Romance languages diverge greatly, showing no cross-the-board agreement either on the specific patterns or on the contexts in which they are used. At the same time, the patterns converge, all pointing toward the same word order, namely SOV, with verb in final position, and MV + AUX.

If we reconstruct SOV as one of the orders of the proto-language, then we are able to account for these divergent patterns as archaisms, whose survival in a given language and a particular context can be a matter of accident. On the other hand, if we do not reconstruct SOV, then we will have to claim that for some strange and unexplained reason, all of the languages independently underwent innovations which, though taking place in very different contexts, 'happened' to converge in the direction of SOV. Clearly, of these two alternatives, the former provides the better explanation and is to be preferred.

What remains to be settled is whether SOV should be reconstructed as an alternative to the predominant SVO of modern Romance, or in its stead. Evidence for original identity between SOV and SVO may be found in the fact that no special, cross-Romance function seems to be attached to the SOV patterns and that they are just as much in contrast with the specially marked verb-initial pattern as is the synchronically predominant SVO. Also the clitic patterns in (67) argue for an original contrast between two patterns (verb-initial and 'other'), not three (verb-initial, SVO, and SOV). In view of these arguments, it seems preferable to reconstruct SOV as the original unmarked order and to consider SVO an innovation.

A possible counterargument might be that this would entail the dubious assumption that all of the Romance languages independently innovated by changing SVO to SOV, a clear violation of Occam's Razor. However, given that (most of) the neighboring non-Romance languages likewise have SVO and that Romance shares other features with these languages (such as a contrasting pair of definite and indefinite articles, cf. 16.3.7 above), the change of SOV to SVO may be considered a common, areal innovation.

The reconstructions we are left with, then, are verb-initial and SOV. And the fact that these are the two major contrasting patterns of Latin shows that non-phonological reconstruction which is based on the notion 'archaism' can yield results which closely approximate the (near-) ancestral language. True, the evidence examined would not enable us to reconstruct the 'scrambling' exemplified in (64c), or to determine the precise route by which SOV changed to SVO. But as noted in section 19.1, areas of uncertainty exist even in phonological reconstruction, a branch of comparative linguistics which has received much more attention and has had considerably greater success.

According to some linguists, the evidence of the clitic pronouns (cf. (67a/b) vs. (67c)) and the non-Balkan future tense (cf. (72)) would be prima-facie — and sufficient — evidence in favor of reconstructing an original OV order. According to this view, today's morphology is yesterday's syntax. Put differently, morphologically frozen forms like the future tense or nearly-frozen forms like the clitic-plus-verb configurations preserve earlier syntactic patterns which may have been eliminated elsewhere. Now, since in the unmarked structures of (67c), the object clitic precedes the verb, this ordering is considered prima-facie evidence for earlier OV ordering. And similarly, the order MV + AUX in the future tense is argued to directly reflect an earlier OV-type order.

While the argument may well be correct for the future tense, the evidence of the clitic pronouns is less cogent. For the preverbal position of object clitics can be accounted for by a different scenario:

Let us assume that just as in many other languages, the Proto-Romance pronouns were sentence clitics. As such, they would tend to be placed in clause-second position; cf. 13.2.3 above. The resulting patterns are given in (74), where (a) represents the general situation, (b) the specific configuration that results in patterns with initial verb. In either case, the clitic is 'bracketed' with the clause-initial element. (X = clause-initial element other than V, E = clitic pronoun.)

(74a) $[[\sharp \, X \, E] \ldots V \, (\ldots)]$
   b) $[[\sharp \, V \, E] \ldots]$

The subsequent shift from SOV to SVO would change the patterns in (74) to the ones in (74′), where clause-second V directly follows E.

(74′a) $[[\sharp \, X \, E] \, V \ldots]$
   b) $[[\sharp \, V \, E] \ldots]$

Given the fact that clitic pronouns are syntactically and pragmatically linked to verbs as their objects or complements, the patterns in (74′) could be subject to a 'rebracketing' (cf. 13.3.1.4) of the clitic pronoun with the verb. The results of this rebracketing would be precisely the archaic modern Romance patterns in (64), with clitic placed after the verb if it is clause-initial, but before the verb elsewhere. Compare (74″).

(74″a) $[\sharp \, X \, (\ldots) \, [E \, V] \ldots]$
   b) $[\sharp \, [V \, E] \ldots]$

Recent work in historical Romance linguistics suggests that this is in fact the correct scenario and that the hypothesis which views the EV order as a direct archaic retention of the earlier OV ordering is incorrect.

Although the alternative scenario does not necessarily invalidate the claim that today's morphology is yesterday's syntax, it does suggest that we must be cautious about using morphological evidence in syntactic reconstruction. Like most other evidence, it may be amenable to more than one interpretation. Moreover, we must be careful about claims based on very limited evidence, such as the evidence of only the clitic ordering and the non-Balkan Romance future. An approach based on the cumulative and convergent evidence of a variety of different patterns inspires greater confidence.

19.5. Typology and reconstruction

If we accept the view that reconstruction should try to approximate a prehistoric linguistic reality, then it follows that the entities and systems which we reconstruct should be compatible with what is found in real, natural language. The branch of linguistics which is concerned with establishing what types of systems are possible in natural language is commonly referred to as **typology**, a term which is employed also to refer to its findings. (As a consequence, we can talk of 'word-order typologies', 'vowel-system typologies', etc.)

An example of the effect which typological considerations can have on reconstruction was given in section 18.7 above, when it was argued that the three-vowel system in (75) is more usual or common than the one in (76) and thus might be a better reconstruction.

(75) i　　　　　　　u

　　　　　　a

(76) i　　　　　　　u

　　e

The notion that reconstructions should be 'typologically possible' is certainly appealing. However, in practice it has not always led to acceptable results. In part, this is due to the fact that our knowledge of the world's languages is still fairly limited. As a consequence, we can seldom be certain if a pattern which we have not yet observed is impossible or just rare. In part, however, it may also reflect certain unwarranted assumptions about the nature of proto-languages.

19.5.1. Proto-Indo-European word order and typology

The case of Proto-Indo-European word order illustrates both of these problems: Although there is good comparative evidence that the unmarked major constituent order of Proto-Indo-European was SOV, there has been some controversy as to whether the language was a 'genuine' SOV-type language.

This controversy focuses on the fact that, as noted in 13.2.2, there is a crosslinguistic tendency for SOV and SVO/VSO to be correlated with other orderings. For instance, VO languages tend to have the order N + G, prep. + N, AUX + MV. OV languages, on the other hand, prefer G + N, N + po., MV + AUX. In addition, VO languages are said to normally have postnominal relative clauses (RCs) which are introduced by relative pronouns (RPs), while according to an early study, OV languages prefer prenominal RCs that lack relative pronouns; cf. examples (77) and (78).

(77)   [The house [which Mary bought]$_{RC}$]$_{NP}$ is large
              N   RP

(78)   [[sikāgōvule tamur paḍičč-a]$_{RC}$ amerikkaru]$_{NP}$ inge
              'in Ch.'   'Tamil' 'learn'-REL/ADJ. 'Am.'   'here'
          vandāru
          'came'
          'The American who learned Tamil in Chicago came here'

Now, Proto-Indo-European as ordinarily reconstructed had RCs which were introduced by relative pronouns. That is, its RC formation seems to be at variance with the usual pattern of SOV languages. As a consequence, some scholars have argued that Proto-Indo-European, being an SOV language, could not have had these RCs. Others claimed that since Proto-Indo-European had RCs with relative pronouns, it could not have been an SOV language.

However, the typological basis for both claims had been established on an incomplete language sample. More recent investigations have shown that SOV languages may employ several other strategies for relative clause formation. These include the pattern in (79), where the relative clause (marked by a relative pronoun) precedes not its head noun but is placed in front of a correlative main clause (MC) which is marked by a correlative pronoun (CP). (Even Dravidian, a supposedly highly 'consistent' SOV language family has recently been shown to have an inherited RC strategy of this type.)

(79) [yaḥ (puruṣaḥ) kaṭam karōti]RC [saḥ (puruṣaḥ) dēvadattaḥ
      RP 'man'   'mat' 'makes'   CP 'man'   'D.'
      nāma]MC
      'by name'
      'The man who makes the mat is called Devadatta'

As it turns out, the earliest evidence of Indo-Iranian, Hittite, Greek, and Latin indicates that the RC 'strategy' of Proto-Indo-European followed the pattern in (79). (Compare also section 13.3.1.4 above for the very similar structures in early Germanic. These differ from the pattern in (79) by having an uninflected relative marker instead of a relative pronoun and by obligatorily placing the RC after the MC.)

That is, given more recent insights into the typology of RC formation in SOV languages, a Proto-Indo-European with SOV and relative/ correlative structures that employ relative pronouns may be typologically 'natural' after all.

In the present case, the issue clearly extends beyond a premature and therefore erroneous use of typology. For even the early typological study which both the 'anti-RC' and the 'anti-SOV' hypothesis were based on provided clear evidence that the correlations between SOV and other orderings were tendencies, not absolute regularities. (Compare for instance section 13.4 for the quite imperfect correlations that are found in various Indo-European languages.) One may therefore wonder why the two different hypotheses would postulate for Proto-Indo-European a **typological 'consistency'** which is absent in any of the daughter languages or in many other languages around the world.

Perhaps the reason lies in the notion that the cooccurrence of SOV with 'disharmonic' RC strategies constitutes the kind of variation which comparative reconstruction ought to reduce to invariance. However, another element may be the notion that reconstructed languages must somehow be more 'pure' or 'perfect' than actually attested ones. (This certainly was the attitude of pre-neogrammarian linguists; cf. 20.1 below.)

Whatever the motivations, the notion that reconstructed languages must be typologically 'consistent' is questionable. Compare for instance the comparative evidence of Romance: The preceding section has established that SOV must be reconstructed as the unmarked word order of Proto-Romance. At the same time, all the Romance languages have postnominal RCs. If we were to accept the notion that proto-languages must be typologically pure, this would pose difficulties for our reconstruction. For typologically 'consistent' languages have prenominal RCs or relative/correlative structures. We would therefore have to arrive at one of two conclusions: (i) The evidence of the Romance languages notwithstanding, the ancestral language, being SOV, must be reconstructed as having prenominal relative structures or relative/correlative structures. (ii) The evidence for postnominal relative clauses argues against an ancestral SOV.

In fact, however, the relevant chronological layer of Latin had unmarked SOV order AND post-nominal relative clauses. And given the Romance evidence, this is precisely what would be postulated by a reconstruction which does not try to impose on the ancestral language what has been called the 'straight-jacket' of typology.

(In all fairness, the arguments on both sides of the Proto-Indo-European word order controversy included additional elements. For instance, the 'anti-RC' side pointed to the fact that the various Indo-European languages do not agree on the form of the relative pronoun, some languages using a separate morpheme *yo-, others instead employing a form of the interrogative pronoun. Moreover, in many contexts where modern European languages would resort to RCs, most of early Indo-European instead employed participial structures. The 'anti-SOV' side introduced the evidence of adpositions which, as noted in 13.2.2, 13.3.1.2, and 13.4, may either precede or follow their NP in the early Indo-European languages. In addition it pointed to similar variation in the ordering of genitives and nouns, etc. However, these additional arguments are themselves of questionable cogency. For instance, the use of interrogative pronouns as markers of relative clauses is a common tendency (found also in Dravidian) and has led to secondary replacements in languages like English. Their appearance in early Latin and

Hittite therefore can be attributed to independent innovation. And as the discussion in 13.4 above has shown, the adpositions of the attested Indo-European languages result from an early reinterpretation of what originally appear to have been 'adverbials'. Their placement characteristics therefore are irrelevant for Proto-Indo-European.)

19.5.2. Proto-Indo-European obstruents and typology

Questionable uses of typology are not confined to syntax. This section examines a case in which typological arguments have been used in phonological reconstruction.

Nineteenth-century reconstructions of the Proto-Indo-European obstruent system generally postulated four series of stops: voiceless, voiceless aspirated, voiced, and voiced aspirated; cf. (80).

(80) p   t   ǩ   k   kʷ
      ph   th   ǩh   kh   kʷh
      (b)   d   ǵ   g   gʷ
      bh   dh   ǵh   gh   gʷh
      s

However, evidence for a distinct voiceless aspirate series is limited to Indo-Iranian. When it was realized that many of the Indo-Iranian voiceless aspirates can be derived from earlier clusters of voiceless stop plus laryngeal (cf. 19.1.5 above) and that other apparent instances of inherited voiceless aspirates can be accounted for as secondary, it became possible to argue that this series is an Indo-Iranian innovation which should not be reconstructed for Proto-Indo-European.

As a consequence, the obstruent system now is usually reconstructed as in (81).

(81a) p   t   ǩ   k   kʷ
   b) (b)   d   ǵ   g   gʷ
   c) bh   dh   ǵh   gh   gʷh
   d)   s

It has been argued that this system is typologically impossible. For, it is claimed, systems with voiced aspirates but lacking voiceless aspirates do not exist. Voiced aspiration presupposes the presence of voiceless aspiration. Moreover, it has been argued that the (near-)absence of voiced *b* in reconstructed Proto-Indo-European is typologically unusual: If there is a gap in the labial system, it is more commonly found in the voiceless than in the voiced series. Finally, some linguists have claimed that the absence of the glottal fricative *h* in reconstructed Proto-Indo-European is typologically problematic. For aspirated stops presuppose the presence of an independent, segmental *h*.

Based on these arguments, many linguists have postulated a very different obstruent system, distinguishing between a voiceless, a 'glottalized', and a voiced series; cf. (82) (a)−(c), which correspond respectively to (81) (a)−(c). The voiceless and voiced series frequently are considered to have had aspirated and unaspirated allophones.

(82a)	p	t	ǩ	k	kʷ
b)	(p')	t'	ǩ'	k'	k'ʷ
c)	b	d	ǵ	g	gʷ
d)		s			

This system, represented to some extent by some of the Modern Armenian dialects, is considered typologically more acceptable. For it does not have to posit a series of voiced aspirates which lack a corresponding series of voiceless aspirates. Moreover, the labial 'gap' now is comfortably in a voiceless series where it 'belongs', not in the voiced series where it does not. Finally, it has been argued that this reconstructed system provides a better explanation than (81) for certain phonological processes in early Indo-European. On the other hand, however, it has recently been shown that system (82) makes it much more difficult to explain what in the traditional system of (81) would be a simple process of voicing assimilation. The issue of which system better accounts for which phonological processes will therefore be considered moot in the following discussion.

A minority approach has consisted in resurrecting the system in (80), with the addition of a segmental *h* which takes the place of the 'laryngeals'; cf. (83). (This approach therefore has to ignore the evidence for positing at least three distinct laryngeals.)

(83)	p	t	ǩ	k	kʷ	
	ph	th	ǩh	kh	kʷh	
	(b)	d	ǵ	g	gʷ	
	bh	dh	ǵh	gh	gʷh	
	s					h

There are several non-typological problems with these alternative analyses. First, it is by no means certain that the aspirated series in (81) should be identified as voiced. The comparative evidence would equally permit identification of the aspirates as voiceless or as unmarked for voicing (with aspiration being the only distinctive feature):

As the summary in (84) shows, Greek and Italic have (originally) distinctively voiceless reflexes of the aspirates. (For the Italic developments compare 5.2, ex. (58/59).)

The Germanic and Armenian voicing is not probative, since both languages have undergone major sound shifts (if reconstruction (81) is accepted). For Germanic, cf. the discussion of Grimm's Law in section 3.3 above. For Armenian, cf. (85) below. (There is some evidence which suggests that the Proto-Indo-European aspirates at first became distinctively voiced aspirates in Armenian, constrasting with the voiceless aspirates that resulted from the Proto-Indo-European unaspirated voiceless stops.)

The voiced outcomes in Indo-Iranian must be balanced against the fact that this branch of Indo-European has acquired a distinctively voiceless set of aspirates. The voicing of the original aspirates therefore may be attributed to polarization.

In Baltic, Slavic, and a number of other 'central' languages, to be sure, the old aspirates have merged with the old voiced stops, suggesting original voicing. And the same development is found in Celtic. However, it is at least possible that these languages went through a stage similar to Indo-Iranian, in which voiceless stops plus laryngeals resulted in voiceless aspirates (cf. (86a)), the original aspirates therefore became voiced by polarization (86b), and where finally the feature of aspiration was lost (86c). Note that Iranian shows a similar deaspiration of the voiced aspirates and that there is good evidence for early dialect contact between Iranian and the 'central' languages (cf. e. g. 15.2.5 on RUKI and 'palatal assibilation').

Finally, the evidence of Tocharian is ambiguous; cf. the discussion in 19.1.8 above. On one hand, the development of *$dheg^wh$- to *deg^wh- suggests a closer affinity between voiced and aspirated. On the other hand, the fact that *t and *dh merge into t, while *d changes to ts suggests closer affiliation between aspirated and voiceless. (The evidence of Hittite is not certain. There is no complete agreement on whether the language did or did not distinguish between voiced and voiceless obstruents.)

(84)

					Aspirate: voiced or voiceless?
PIE		t	dh	d	?
Greek		t	th	d	voiceless
Italic		t	*θ	d	voiceless
Germanic		*þ	*d	*t	?
Armenian		th	d(h)	t	?
Sanskrit	t ≠ th		dh	d	voiced by polarization
Iranian	t ≠ *th		*dh	d	voiced by polarization
> t ≠ θ			d	d	
Baltic/Slavic		t	d	d	voiced (by polarization?)
Celtic		t	d	d	voiced (by polarization?)
Tocharian		t	t	ts	?

(85a) $\begin{bmatrix} + \text{ stop} \\ - \text{ voice} \end{bmatrix} > [+ \text{ asp.}]$

b) $\begin{bmatrix} + \text{ stop} \\ + \text{ voice} \end{bmatrix} > [- \text{ voice}]$

c) $\begin{bmatrix} + \text{ stop} \\ + \text{ asp.} \end{bmatrix} > \begin{bmatrix} - \text{ asp.} \\ + \text{ voice} \end{bmatrix}$ (or just $>$ [+ voice])

(86a)   tA $>$ th etc.

b) Hence $\begin{bmatrix} + \text{ asp.} \\ \pm \text{ voice} \end{bmatrix} > [+ \text{ voice}]$ (polarization vs. th etc.)

c)   [+ stop] $>$ [− asp.]

(The notation [± voice] in (b) is used as an ad-hoc device to indicate the lack of distinctive voicing in the old aspirate.)

Secondly, reconstruction (82) may well be in violation of Occam's Razor: Under the traditional reconstruction, only two Indo-European languages are characterized by major rearrangements of their obstruent systems, namely Armenian and Germanic. For the other languages, relatively minor adjustments are needed, usually affecting no more than one segment class in any given language. Under reconstruction (82), only Armenian comes close to preserving the old system without a major sound shift. Germanic requires deglottalization of the old glottalized stops and fricativization of the old voiced and voiceless stops. For the other languages it is necessary to posit changes for every segment class; cf. (87). (Special changes which are required under either analysis, such as the development of a distinctively voiceless aspirate series, are ignored.)

(87) Indo-Iranian: Deglottalization and voicing of old glottalized stops;
                        generalization of unaspirated allophones for voiceless stops;
                        generalization of aspirated allophones for voiced stops.

       Greek/Latin: Deglottalization and voicing of old glottalized stops;
                        generalization of unaspirated allophones for voiceless stops;
                        generalization and devoicing of aspirated allophones for voiced stops.

       Baltic/Slavic/   Deglottalization and voicing of old glottalized stops;
       Celtic: generalization of unaspirated allophones for voiceless stops;
                        generalization of unaspirated allophones for voiced stops.

In the reconstruction of (83), the violation of Occam's Razor may lie in the fact that reconstructed elements are multiplied beyond necessity. (However, this reconstruction avoids most of the complications entailed by reconstruction (82).)

What is perhaps most significant is that also the typological arguments in favor of the alternative reconstructions in (82) and (83) are not cogent.

First of all, while it is true that labial gaps are more commonly found in the voiceless stops, a recent publication shows that a fair number of languages have gaps ore near-gaps in the voiced stops. These include languages as diverse as Cherokee, Dargwa, Dehu, Mixe (one variety), or Murle. The traditional reconstruction thus is typologically quite possible.

Secondly, it is possible for a language to have distinctive aspiration without having an independent segmental *h*. Ionic Greek, for instance, lost its *h* at an early time but retained the common Greek voiceless aspirates. The triple distinction between voiced, voiceless, and aspirated in Madurese (cf. below) likewise is accompanied by the absence of *h* in native words. (Madurese, however, has (re-)acquired *h* through borrowings.)

Finally and most importantly, recent publications have drawn attention to the fact that a number of Indonesian languages have aspirates which are voiced or intermediate between voiced and voiceless, but do not contrast with a corresponding voiceless series. Compare the summary in (88). These aspirates are variously described as having a 'murmured, fuzzy quality' (cf. (88a)), as 'voiceless stops with indifferent tension [i. e., neither tense nor lax] followed by heavy aspiration' contrasting with voiceless/tense and voiced/lax stops (88b), or as 'aspirated stops beginning voiced and ending voiceless' (88c). The historical antecedents are not entirely clear. In some languages (those of (88c)), the aspirates seem to have come about from earlier clusters of voiced stop plus *b*. In others, the starting point may have consisted in an allophonic aspiration of originally voiced stops; cf. (88a). In a subset of the latter languages (88b), aspiration seems to have become distinctive (i) by changes like $*w > b$ which introduced new unaspirated stops, and (ii) by borrowings from Malay, etc. The fact that the languages in question are close neighbors suggests that we may be dealing with something like a convergence area.

(88)	Language	Stop system			Location
a)	Javanese:	p	t	etc.	Java
		bh	dh	etc.	
b)	Madurese:	p	t	etc.	Madura and parts of Java
		b	d	etc.	
		bh	dh	etc.	
c)	Kelabit,	p	t	etc.	Sarawak, island of Borneo
	Lun Daye	b	d	etc.	Sabah, island of Borneo
		bh	dh	etc.	

The evidence of these languages demonstrates that even if the aspirates in (81) are interpreted as voiced or as neither distinctively voiced nor voiceless, the traditionally reconstructed system is typologically possible. Given that both alternative analyses may well be in violation of Occam's Razor, there seems to be no strong motivation to abandon the traditional analysis.

19.5.3. Conclusion

The implication of the discussion in the preceding two sections should be obvious: Even the best typologies cannot possibly cover the evidence of all attested languages, not to mention their earlier historical stages or the many languages which have died out unrecorded. Under these circumstances it is premature to reject palpable comparative evidence simply because it does not agree with current typological findings.

20. Linguistic change:
Its nature and causes

The oldest and, outside linguistic circles, probably still the most prevalent view on linguistic change is that it is a matter of decay, caused by slovenly or imprecise speech habits which violate the rules of language. And these rules, in turn, are considered sacrosanct, established for all eternity, at a certain stage of the language which is believed to have been its Golden Age. Or sometimes they are considered to have been established in another language which is considered the most perfect and whose grammar is thought to be the model for the grammars of all other languages.

Consider on one hand the venerability and perfect nature attributed in the Sanskrit tradition to the language described and regulated by the grammarians, or the similar position which the classical language of Caesar and Cicero held in the tradition of Latin. On the other hand, note the influence of Latin grammar on the traditional school grammars of most western languages, lasting well into this century. Similarly, Sanskrit grammar by and large continues to influence the school grammars of most of the modern languages of South Asia.

We find an early reflection of this view of language as decay in the Sanskrit story from the Śatapathabrāhmaṇa that was quoted in the Introduction. But even to the present day, many school teachers, editors, and others concerned with linguistic usage can be found inveighing against the 'slovenly' speech habits, the 'corruption' of 'proper grammar' found in expressions like (1a) below, instead of the 'correct' (1b). Pronouncements of this sort are usually accompanied by dire warnings that if we do not mend our ways, the language will 'go to the dogs' and will cease to be an effective vehicle for communication or rational thought.

(1a)   Me and Joey went to the swimming pool
   b)   Joey and I went to the swimming pool

Unfortunately, however, or perhaps fortunately (?), these pronouncements and dire warnings do not seem to be able to stem the tide of linguistic change: In spite of all the past admonitions that we should speak, or at least write, like Caesar and Cicero, only a few specialists in Classical Latin now are able to write in that fashion, and virtually nobody can speak that way. In the case of Sanskrit, which is still fluently spoken by some Indians and an even smaller number of foreigners, the case may look slightly better. But note that the grammar of this spoken Sanskrit differs from that of the ancient grammarians in several important points. Moreover, the percentage of Indians able to speak Sanskrit fluently is infinitesimal, as well as decreasing at an ever-faster pace.

At the same time, however, our language has not 'gone to the dogs'. We are, it seems, just as able — and sometimes just as unable — to communicate as effectively as the speakers of Classical Latin or Sanskrit.

Moreover, quite frequently the pronouncements of linguistic Cassandras on 'proper' and 'improper' usage turn out to be counterproductive, because they are linguistically and pedagogically naive and address symptoms, not the rule-governed rationale behind much of linguistic change, or even behind the usage which is being propounded as 'correct'. A case in point is the frequent response to statements like (1a), namely (2).

(2)   Don't say *Me and Joey*, say *Joey and I*

Such a statement first of all fails to understand that the use of *me* in (1a) is not just randomly ungrammatical. Rather, it is governed by a rule which is a slightly reinterpreted and extended version of the pronoun marking rule that accounts for the case marking in *That's me*; cf. section 13.3.1.6 above. The only difference is that in this reinterpreted rule, (non-possessive) personal pronouns are marked as nominative only if they directly precede the verb (in unmarked order); elsewhere, the accusative is used. Since the pronoun in (1a) does not directly precede the verb but is separated from it by *and Joey*, it must therefore be marked as accusative.

Moreover, the statement is linguistically and pedagogically unsound. The intended messages, one should suppose, are (i) 'Use the nominative form (*I*) for the subject of the sentence' and (ii) 'It's more polite to refer to someone else first, and then to yourself'. But these two separate issues are not kept distinct. Perhaps even more importantly, the poor listener is given no appropriate rules for 'correct' grammar and usage. Rather, by making the categorical statement 'Don't say *Me and Joey*, say *Joey and I*', the linguistic Cassandra makes it appear as if there were something wrong about the use of the accusative case in conjoined expressions of this sort. A common consequence is the 'ultimate horror', the pattern exemplified in (3), where nominative case is extended into contexts in which both the more innovative grammar and the conservative grammar of the linguistic Cassandra would call for the accusative case. (Like all other linguistic innovations, also this new usage can 'acquire native speakers' in whose grammars it is perfectly grammatical. Note that isolated examples of the type (3) can be found already in Early Modern English. It is not clear whether these came about in a similar fashion or were the results of different 'scenarios'.)

(3) This book is for people like you and I.
Between you and I, this book isn't worth the paper it was written on.
He gave it to Mary and I.

20.1. 'Decay' and 'corruption' versus the uniformitarian principle

In spite of the fact that as we have just seen, the popular view of linguistic change as **decay** and **corruption** is highly dubious as well as frequently counterproductive, it was unhesitatingly accepted by the early practitioners of historical linguistics: The reconstructed Proto-Indo-European parent language and its earliest descendants (Greek, Latin, Sanskrit, etc.), with their complex morphophonemics and clearly marked grammatical endings, were implicitly or explicitly considered pristine and perfect. The increasing loss of morphophonemic complexity and of grammatical endings in later stages of the languages was viewed as the result of decay. And the major vehicle for this decay was thought to consist of changes in speech habits (for the worse) and in what was termed 'false analogy', the reshaping of words on the pattern of other, originally quite different words. Such 'false analogy' was by and large considered unthinkable in the original, pristine parent language or in its earliest descendants.

While their practice did not always reflect their theory, it was one of the major achievements of the neogrammarians to refute this older view. They did so in part by showing that even on the basis of its own premise that, say, loss of endings means linguistic decay, the older view of language change was not tenable. For although the modern languages by and large have lost many or most of the older endings, there have also been developments in the opposite direction. Thus English developed a new adverbial ending -*ly* and nominal affixes like -*hood* and -*dom*; cf. section 9.1.2, ex. (18) above. Similarly, Lat. *(-)ment-* 'mind' developed into an adverbial suffix in Romance, as in Fr. *lente-ment* 'slowly'. Here, then, we would seem to have evidence not for 'decay', but for something like an 'improvement'. Moreover, while endings may have been lost, compensatory grammatical devices such as prepositions were developed which just as effectively signaled grammatical relationships as the older endings.

Most important of all, however, was the neogrammarian insistence that 'decay' (or 'improvement') are notions inapplicable to linguistic change, that reconstructed languages and their early offshoots are no more 'perfect' than their later descendants, and that all of the linguistic phenomena that are observable in the historical development of attested languages must be considered possible also for the proto-language and the earliest stages of its descendants. Consequently, even analogy could now be claimed to have operated in the parent language, or in early Latin, Greek, Sanskrit, etc. It was therefore no longer necessary to label it as somehow deviant by calling it 'false analogy'.

Using a term introduced more recently into linguistics, in a related but different context (cf. 20.10 below), we may refer to this new view as the **uniformitarian principle:** The general processes and principles which can be noticed in observable history are applicable in all stages of language history.

20.2. Neogrammarian views on the nature of linguistic change

With 'decay' or 'corruption' thus eliminated as causes or explanations of linguistic change, it became necessary to look for a new, more plausible, account of the nature and causes of linguistic change.

As noted in Chapter 3 above, the neogrammarians made a fundamental distinction between sound change and all other types of linguistic change. Certain types of phonetic change, such as dissimilation, metathesis, haplology, were likewise considered to differ in their nature from what the neogrammarians called sound change.

The distinction between sound change and other linguistic change was said to lie in the fact that sound change is regular (and thus affects simultaneously all qualifying lexical items), is 'mechanically' conditioned (i. e., only phonetically, not 'grammatically'), is unobservable, and takes place in gradual, imperceptible steps. All other change, on the other hand, can be irregular (and thus can affect different lexical items at different times, sometimes leading to doublets), proceeds according to 'psychological' (and social) principles (such as the mental association between related forms), is observable (through the existence of competing forms), and may take place in terms of highly perceptible, abrupt, quantum leaps. Compare the summary in (4).

(4)	Sound change	Other change
a)	is regular;	is irregular;
b)	affects simultaneously all lexical items that qualify;	can affect different lexical items at different times;
c)	is mechanically (i. e., only phonetically) conditioned;	proceeds according to 'psychological' principles;
d)	is unobservable;	is observable;
e)	takes place in gradual, imperceptible steps.	may take place in highly perceptible, abrupt, quantum leaps.

One may well ask why the neogrammarians chose these different characterizations of the two major classes of linguistic change. Though not much detailed explanation and discussion is offered in their programmatic statements, it is possible to give at least some answers to this question.

The distinction **'regular'** vs. 'irregular' was to a large extent based on the empirical evidence of the various linguistic changes which had been studied up to that time. And it was this empirical evidence which made it necessary to classify phonetic changes like metathesis, dissimilation, and haplology not as sound change, but as a subtype of the changes which frequently or notoriously are irregular.

The distinction **'mechanical'** vs. 'psychological' seemed to be intuitively correct to characterize the difference between sound change and analogy. As far as analogical change is concerned, it was clear that psychological/mental associations between related forms played a major role as the motivation of change. Moreover, since such associations can be made in many different, even contradictory, directions, it was not surprising that this type of change should normally fail to be regular. On the other hand, no such obvious psychological/mental associations seem to be discernible for sound change, which is conditioned only by phonetic factors. Moreover, by taking place without regard to psychological/mental associations it may wreak havoc on the formal manifestations of these associations. (Though usually not specifically mentioned in this context, also semantic and syntactic change would seem to be covered by the label 'psychological'. And borrowing and related processes likewise differ from sound change in that they are motivated by social/psychological factors.)

It is, to be sure, possible to argue that these 'obvious' distinctions between sound change and other linguistic change are meaningless, since ultimately all linguistic activity is psychological or social in nature. Even so, the intuitively appealing neogrammarian distinctions can be justified by observing that while in analogy, borrowing, etc., very specific psychological or social factors are at work, this is not the case for sound change.

Some of the neogrammarians claimed that also the notoriously irregular types of phonetic change (dissimilation, etc.) differ from 'mechanical' regular change by being psychologically motivated. However, this claim is not as intuitively 'obvious' as the ones concerning the distinctions between sound change and analogy or borrowing.

A more appealing distinction was made by Paul, one of the most important theoreticians among the neogrammarians, who pointed out that the varieties of phonetic change which are typically irregular differ from regular change by being of the same nature as speech errors. That is, irregular phonetic change shares with speech errors the fact that it is highly perceptible as a clear, quantum-leap deviation from established norm. (The comparison with speech errors makes it possible to bring a certain 'psychological', or rather perhaps neurological, element into the definition of sound change: Paul compared dissimilation to the difficulty encountered in uttering tongue twisters. The important factor, however, is not neurological control, but a lapse in control.)

On the other hand, the most common types of regular change, namely assimilation and weakening/loss, can be conceived of as starting out as relatively minor and imperceptible deviations from the norm. In fact, phoneticians had pointed out that no two utterances ever are completely alike phonetically, that even in repetitions of the 'same' utterance there are always some small phonetic differences, which are observable only by trained phoneticians. And these differences commonly are of an assimilatory or weakening nature.

It was probably in order to characterize these differences between typically irregular phonetic changes and regular sound change that the neogrammarians had recourse to the criterion of **'imperceptible/ gradual'** vs. 'perceptible/abrupt'.

Finally, the claim that regular sound change differs from other change by being **unobservable** seems to follow as a corollary from the preceding argument, as well as from the regular/irregular distinction. For only irregular change can logically lead to the doublets which indicate that a change is in the process of taking place.

Perhaps this claim was reinforced by the fact that the neogrammarians worked on sound change only ex post facto or 'post mortem' (i. e., long after particular changes had occurred in history). As a consequence they were unable to actually observe a particular change in progress.

Finally, it is also possible that the neogrammarians made this claim in order to maintain the clear, fundamental distinction between sound change and analogy which they wanted to make. For if sound change were observable, then it should be possible for speakers to realize that a given change is destroying morphological (etc.) distinctions. In order to preserve these distinctions, they could therefore be expected to resort to 'preventive analogy' (cf. 3.5 above) before the sound change had actually run its course. Most of the neo-grammarians rejected the concept of preventive analogy, presumably for the following two reasons: (i) In many cases in which the concept had been invoked, close observation showed that analogy had in fact applied as a 'rescue' operation, after the sound change had run its full course. (ii) Admitting the possibility of preventive analogy would have been tantamount to admitting that sound change can be irregular, in so far as analogy can prevent it from taking place under various non-phonetically defined conditions. (See also the discussion in 3.5 above.)

20.3. Neogrammarian views on the causes of linguistic change

As far as the presumable causes of linguistic change are concerned, the neogrammarians concentrated essentially on sound change. Other changes were considered to be caused — and thus explained — by the psychological, social, or speech-error factors which gave rise to them.

Some of the proposed causes for sound change turned out to be hardly more tenable than the older view of sound change as 'decay' or 'corruption'. For instance, attempts to attribute, say, Grimm's Law to changes in climate, other changes in physical environment, or changes in dietary habits run into considerable difficulties. For similar changes have taken place under rather different physical or dietary conditions. (Cf. the Armenian sound shift in 19.5.2, ex. (85).) Non-linguistic explanations of this sort therefore were rather quickly abandoned, although they may occasionally resurface even to the present day.

What remains, then, are two major competing claims concerning the causes of sound change, both of which are clearly linguistic in nature.

According to one view, the basis for phonetic change lies in the fact that (as noted in the preceding section) all speech is characterized by minor phonetic deviations from the established linguistic norm, deviations which are perceptible only to trained phoneticians. While ordinarily these deviations will differ from the norm in a more or less scatter-shot fashion, statistically cancelling each other out, under certain conditions they may turn out to be **cumulative**, leading to a **directional deviation** from the original norm. Compare Chart 20.1. Here the realizations of a given segment *t* range from rather lax, voiced, *d*-like to rather voiceless and aspirated. As a result of cumulative deviation, the voiceless aspirated pronunciation becomes the new norm, and as a consequence, the old norm *t* is heard less frequently. Moreover, a new deviation from the norm, an affricate *ts*, may appear, etc.

At first sight, this conceptualization of sound change is quite appealing. However, a closer look reveals that a crucial element in this scenario is left unmotivated, namely the question why under certain conditions the deviations from the norm should be cumulative, rather than cancelling each other out. True, for the most common changes, such as assimilation and weakening, it may be claimed that there is a 'built-in' directionality, based on the very nature of the changes: A segment will assimilate to another segment, or it will move down on

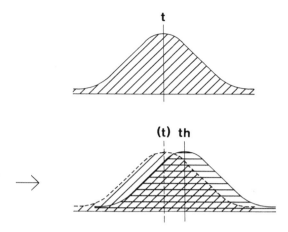

Chart 20.1: Sound change as envisioned by neogrammarians

the weakening hierarchy. However, for other changes, including whole-sale system changes like Grimm's Law, it would be very difficult to find such a natural, 'built-in' directionality. (Even changes like assimilation in the final analysis lack 'built-in' directionality; cf. 20.5 below.)

At least in part because of these difficulties, a different hypothesis was proposed, a hypothesis which to the present day can claim quite a few adherents. According to this view, sound change originates in, and is caused by, errors made in the transmission of language from one generation to another: Children depend on the speech of their parents' generation for learning the language. But as noted, all speech is characterized by certain deviations from the norm. Children therefore may not always correctly perceive the linguistic norms of their predecessors. And as a consequence, they may develop their own norms, which differ from those of their parents' generation.

Unfortunately, this hypothesis suffers from the same difficulty as the preceding one, namely the absence of any explanation for why deviations should be cumulative and directional. The parents' deviations from the norm should be expected to be scatter-shot, canceling each other out. There is therefore no built-in directionality in the older generation's speech. A priori, there is no reason to believe that children's deviations from their parents' norm are any more consistent. However, even if we stipulate that individual children deviate consistently from their parents' norm, we are still faced with the problem as to how and why a large number of new speakers, or all the new speakers of a given language or dialect, should agree on the direction in which they deviate. Especially for whole-sale shifts like Grimm's Law it would be extremely difficult to imagine that out of the vast array of phonetic deviations found in their parents' speech, all of the new speakers would independently select the same variants as their new norm. (In fact, recent studies show that there is only a partial overlap between the deviations found in early child language acquisition and the changes which can be observed in the history of languages. Some common deviations of early child language have no (or hardly any) historical counterparts, and vice versa.)

The only way which (some of) the neogrammarians saw to get out of this dilemma was the assumption that regular sound change originates in the individual dialect or **idiolect** of a particular speaker and that for reasons of prestige it spreads to other members of the speech community. That is, its occurrence in a given dialect or language in the final analysis is the result of borrowing.

It is possible that there have been a few occasions where a sound change did indeed spread in this fashion. The most credible case is that of the wide-spread European change of alveolar [r] to uvular [ʀ], which is said to have originated in the French idiolect of Louis XIV. The fact that in many areas the change is more common in urban centers, combined with the importance of French in early modern European society, lends some plausibility to this hypothesis. However, note that uvular [ʀ] is found also in many rural areas, where French influence is not likely to have played a role. Moreover, it is hardly credible that all regular change should originate in this fashion. In most changes, there is no evidence whatsoever that they were started by some well-known prestigious individual. Even more important is the fact that the postulated spread of the change involves a borrowing process, i. e., a development which is notorious for its general irregularity and sporadicity, even when motivated by prestige. (Compare for instance section 15.2.2 above for the Dutch case of *hūs* vs. *mūs*.) It must therefore remain a mystery how such an irregular mechanism can lead to the appearance of regular sound change in a given dialect or language.

20.4. Functionalism

Some of the difficulties with the neogrammarians' views on the causes of sound change seem to be alleviated relatively easily by supplementing them with a more recent, **'functionalist'** view of language change. As noted in Chapter 8, whole-system changes like Grimm's Law, which lack any obvious, 'built-in' directionality, can be explained as the result of chain shifts or conspiracies which are sensitive to such notions as 'structure' and 'function'. And it is these notions which can be considered to provide the motivation or 'cause' for a given shift in a phonological system.

[margin handwriting: help out Neugram's Cause]

To some degree this is probably true (but see also below). However, upon closer inspection, this approach raises just as many difficulties for the neogrammarian position as it solves. For by emphasizing structural and functional aspects of language, it introduces elements which are not purely phonetic. As may be recalled, the neogrammarians insisted that sound change is conditioned only by purely phonetic factors.

[margin handwriting: But]

Moreover, the cumulativity and directionality of chain shifts requires a certain sensitivity to the nature and effects of a given linguistic change. That is, chain shifts seem to contradict the notion that sound change is unobservable and purely 'mechanical'. True, much of the directionality of chain shifts may be said to result from responses to changes which have already occurred, rather than to changes still in progress. However, the response changes must be properly selected and manipulated in order to bring about the desired goal-oriented effect. More than that, there is reason to believe that response changes do not always have to wait for the completion of the change which initiates the development. For instance, in the Swedish chain shift of 8.4 above, the change of old *å* [ɑ] toward *o* began when the change of old *o* toward *u* had not yet been completed. This suggests that response changes can be sensitive to primary changes which are still in progress and that, therefore, sound change is observable, contrary to neogrammarian doctrine.

Finally, while goal-oriented shifts commonly are regular, the component changes which implement the shift may apply in an irregular fashion. In fact, these component changes may sometimes consist of inherently irregular processes such as borrowing and analogy. (Compare for instance section 8.3 above.)

20.5. The linguistic unpredictability of change

Even to the extent that the functionalist approach seems to provide an explanation of the motivations or causes of wholesale shifts, that explanation to a significant degree is only an apparent one. And similarly, notions such as 'assimilation' and 'weakening' provide only apparent causes for change. In fact, the case is the same for the putative motivations of non-regular change, such as the psychological association of forms which constitutes the basis for analogy. In all of these cases, the apparent explanation does not provide a cause or motivation which is sufficiently explicit and compelling to predict a specific outcome. Rather, we are merely dealing with a label, delineating one of many possible and natural changes, with many possible and natural subvarieties. Which of these a given language may 'choose' at a given time, is a question which these 'explanations' are unable to answer.

To take the case of chain shifts first: While it is true that the starting point for the Swedish chain shift, the fronting of *u*, is a very common phenomenon, the phonetic nature of that fronting may differ from language to language. Some languages show fronted and rounded outcomes (cf. Fr. *ü*), while others have unrounded vowels which moreover may be fronted merely to central position (cf. dialectal American Engl. [ɨw] in words like *boot*). Perhaps even more importantly, the response changes or chains of such changes may differ. In Swedish, the fronting of old *u* occasioned the drag-chain raising of old *o* toward the position vacated by *u*, and the shifting of old *ā* toward *o*. Similar developments are found in early French and ancient Greek. On the other hand, in Central Illinois the fronting of [ʊw] to [ɨw] has brought about a solidarity-chain fronting of all back vowels; cf. section 8.4, ex. (25). Similarly, the raising and diphthongization of [æ] to [æə], [ɛə], etc. has given rise to a drag-chain in Chicago, but a solidarity chain in New York; cf. 8.4, ex. (26/27).

Even in the case of such processes as asimilation, where a 'built-in' directionality seems to be so obvious as not to require further reflection, a closer look reveals that the notion of 'built-in directionality' is a mirage. Given for instance a sequence *tm*, there are at least the following a priori conceivable outcomes by way of assimilation, not counting other possible developments such as the weakening or loss in Span. *atmosfera* = [aθmosfera] or [amosfera].

(5) tm > nm   (Korean pat-mada > pan-mada)
          mm   (Aeol. Gk. kat(a)moros > kammoros)
          nn
          dm
          pm   (Swiss Germ. ātmə(n) > ōpmə)
          bm
          tn   (late Ancient Gk. dial. Patmos > Patnos)
          dn
          tp   (Skt. ātman- > MIAr. dial. atpan-)
          tt   (Skt. ātman- > MIAr. dial. attan-)
          pp   (Skt. ātman- > MIAr. dial. appan-)
          db
          dd
          bb

While some of these developments may perhaps be rarer than others, and a few may lack any attested examples, the fact remains that what at first sight appeared to be a process with 'built-in directionality' can in fact proceed in many different directions. Add to this the fact that in many cases other processes (such as weakening, loss, epenthesis) can likewise apply, and it becomes evident that there is no unidirectional causality in sound change.

Even in other types of linguistic change, the assumption that there is a 'built-in' causality is to a large extent illusory. True, given that a sound change has resulted in morphophonemic alternations, it is quite natural that there should be a leveling process aimed at eliminating the alternations. However, as noted in section 10.2, the direction of leveling is not predictable. Even more significantly, morphophonemic alternations do not always get leveled. In German, for instance, the umlaut alternation in sets like *Gast : Gäste* 'guest : guests' was not eliminated, but extended to other forms which originally did not have umlaut in the plural; cf. section 10.1.

20.6. Further problems

As we have seen in section 20.4, the functionalist approach to linguistic change casts doubt on the neogrammarian claim that sound change is unobservable and motivated purely by phonetic factors. A number of other considerations pose difficulties for the neogrammarian conceptualization of linguistic change.

20.6.1. Numerous objections have been raised against the notion that sound change is gradual and proceeds by imperceptible, gradient steps.

Some of these arguments, to be sure, are pseudo-arguments. Thus the — correct — observation that processes like metathesis by their nature are non-gradual is not a valid counterargument, since the neogrammarians excluded changes like metathesis and dissimilation from their definition of sound change.

Another objection has been that because features such as voice are either present ([+ voice]) or absent ([− voice]), a change such as the voicing of voiceless segments must by definition be abrupt, not gradual. Also this is not a valid counterargument, since the statement that voicing is either present or absent is a phonological, not a phonetic one. The neogrammarians' claims, however, concerned phonetic, not phonological, change. And while phonologically it may be true that voicing is a 'binary' phenomenon which is either present or absent, phonetically there are considerably different degrees of voicing (or voicelessness). Thus, phonologically voiced obstruents seem to be phonetically much more voiced in Hindi or French than in English. (In fact, certain English idiolects offer quite voiceless segments which differ from their 'voiceless' counterparts more in terms of features like 'tense/lax' and aspiration than in terms of voicing.)

Moreover, adherents of the neogrammarian doctrine can defend the view that sound change is gradual by pointing to many instances where phonetically intermediate stages are attested for a given sound change; cf., e. g., the weakening developments in (6).

(6)   Skt. gata- > MIAr. gada- > later MIAr. gaya-
                              > late MIAr. gaa- 'gone'

In all fairness, however, it must be admitted that this particular defence of the neogrammarian view is not necessarily cogent, since it is a priori possible that the attested intermediate stages do not document a completely gradual development, but rather reflect steps in a series of relatively small, but inherently discrete, quantum leaps in phonetic output. (At this point, no evidence seems to exist which might help to decide between the 'gradual' and 'small quantum-leap' hypotheses.)

What is more important is the fact that there is one set of changes
which by their very nature are non-gradient, but which seem to be just
as regular as the other types of sound change that are subsumed under
the neogrammarian regularity doctrine. These are the changes discussed
in section 5.3.5 which involve acoustic confusion or reinterpretation,
such as between velar and labial. Clearly, in articulatory terms there is
no gradual, non-abrupt, way of getting from one pronunciation to the
other. And note that the neogrammarians' notion of graduality was
conceived of in articulatory terms.

20.6.2. Another difficulty for the neogrammarians is that dissimilation
and metathesis, though usually sporadic and irregular, may occasionally
operate in a completely regular fashion. In these cases, they behave
exactly like regular sound changes, their regularity being more or less
instantaneous, unlike the 'regularity' which analogical processes may
sometimes exhibit after the course of many centuries. That is, it appears
that dissimilation and metathesis hold a position intermediate between
'mechanical' regular sound change and 'psychological' (or 'social') non-
regular change. The neogrammarians' binary division of linguistic
change into regular sound change and irregular other change therefore
appears to be an oversimplification.

True, it is now possible to at least speculate under what general
conditions dissimilation and metathesis may be regular, rather than
sporadic. Compare the discussion in section 6.3 above. However, these
conditions are essentially structural and functional, not phonetic as
neogrammarian doctrine would require. Moreover, it is by no means
certain that the presence of these conditions automatically leads to
regular, rather than sporadic, dissimilations.

20.6.3. Yet another type of change argues against the strict separation
of sound change and analogy (and other typically irregular changes):
As noted in sections 8.5 and 9.4, phonetically regular developments
like initial strengthening appear to be motivated by structural, as well
as proportional considerations. And Chapter 11 has shown that processes such as 'rule reordering' take place with complete regularity and
over a relatively short period, even though they are clearly analogical
in character in so far as they involve reinterpretation and secondary
extension. What distinguishes these processes from other, much less
regular, analogical developments is the fact that the non-phonetic
information which motivates or constrains the change is minimal and

very general (e. g., word boundary) and does not contain any references to such specific notions as morphological category or semantic affiliation. In fact, the parameter for some 'rule analogies' may be completely phonetic; cf. the dialectal German extension of final devoicing to syllable-final environment (section 11.1.1 above).

Combined with the evidence of regular dissimilation and methasis, the regularity of rule-governed analogy suggests that the boundary between regular sound change and irregular other change is gradient or 'gradual', not binary or 'abrupt'.

20.7. Problems in the generative approach

As noted in section 11.4, early generative views on historical linguistics went even farther in their denial of a meaningful distinction between sound change and analogy. However, it was also noted that more recently the pendulum has swung back to a view which distinguishes between primary and secondary change and thus is much more compatible with neogrammarian doctrine. Generative claims concerning linguistic change can now by and large be considered extensions of neogrammarian doctrine, not as inherently and diametrically opposed.

One difficulty, however, continues to distinguish generative from older neogrammarian doctrine, namely the fact that generativists usually try to incorporate sound change into synchronic grammar under the notion of rule addition. As observed in section 11.4.1, the difficulty with this view lies in the fact that synchronic rules require synchronic alternations for their justification. Sound change, however, is a diachronic phenomenon and leads to synchronic alternations only in some of its occurrences.

Generativists have tried to resolve this difficulty by claiming that sound change consists in the addition of optional rules at the end of the grammar. And according to some, these optional rules reflect changes in linguistic 'fashion' comparable to changes in clothing (etc.) fashion. The rules, then, are said to become obligatory through restructuring in the grammar formulation of the next generation of speakers.

To the extent that these statements concerning optional rules do not constitute a tacit acceptance of the hypothesis proposed by Labov and his associates (cf. 20.10 below), they give the appearance of being ad-hoc assumptions, designed to resolve a certain theoretical difficulty, but not supported by any concrete evidence.

At the same time, the question raised in generative grammar, namely how diachronic change can be embedded in synchronic grammar, is by no means a trivial one. Providing a satisfactory answer would seem to be as important as addressing the difficulties with the neogrammarians' position which were detailed in earlier sections of this chapter.

20.8. The anti-regularist position 1

The early scepticism of the generativists concerning the neogrammarians' strict distinction between regular sound change and sporadic other change, though now largely superseded, reflects a theoretical tendency whose antecedents go back to the time of the neogrammarians. For the neogrammarians' challenge to earlier historical linguistic theory and practice was met with virtually instantaneous opposition.

To some extent that opposition merely consisted in the reiteration of the old verities: Though sound change displays an amazing degree of regularity, it is silly to expect it to be completely regular. And the neogrammarians' insistence on a strict distinction between sound change and analogy likewise smacks of theoretical excess. It is certainly necessary to accept phenomena like preventive analogy and near-regular, but not completely regular, sound change, whose workings can be blocked by social or formal criteria. In fact, detailed studies of living dialects and their historical developments show almost the exact opposite of the neogrammarians' postulated regularity: 'Each word has its own history.'

To the extent that they were formulated along these lines, the objections to the neogrammarian view of linguistic change were easily dismissed as more or less equivalent to wanting to have one's cake and eat it too: Regularity was admitted where it was convenient, and so was irregularity. No clear criteria were established which in case of doubt might decide whether a regularist or irregularist analysis should be preferred.

Moreover, it was possible to show that many of the anti-neogrammarian arguments are theoretically either unconvincing or irrelevant. Thus, since in observable cases it was always possible — or even preferable

— to assume that a given sound change had run its full course before a response-analogy set in, the notion 'preventive analogy' was a theoretically unnecessary construct. (Cf. also 3.5 above.) Only well-documented case histories showing that in certain languages, at certain times, preventive analogy had in fact set in before the completion of a given sound change would establish the theoretical foundation for that notion. No such case histories, however, seemed to be provided.

Finally, adherents of neogrammarian doctrine would argue that the slogan 'Each word has its own history' is irrelevant, since the neogrammarian regularity principle extends only to sound change, not to the many other types of change which are observable in linguistic history. As a consequence, the neogrammarians were in principle quite ready to admit that millennia of the application of non-regular analogical changes, borrowings, etc. could lead to results which would justify the impression that each word has its own history. (Cf. also section 15.3 above.)

20.9 The anti-regularist position 2 — Schuchardt and beyond

A more formidable, and theoretically more meaningful, attack on the neogrammarian position consisted in the claim that there is no distinction at all between sound change and analogy, that all alleged sound changes can be explained as beginning in one or two isolated words and spreading from these to other lexical items through analogical extension.

This radically different view seems to have first been proposed in 1885 by Schuchardt (who also was one of the pioneers of pidgin and creole studies). Unfortunately however, many of Schuchardt's arguments were indistinguishable from those of the more 'unprincipled' or 'laissez-faire' opponents discussed in the preceding section. Moreover, Schuchardt did not provide any explicit theoretical model which would explain or illustrate his theoretical claims and which would account for how and why analogical change in some cases — the ones labeled sound change by the neogrammarians — should have overwhelmingly regular outcomes, while in others it behaved more like 'classical' analogical change. Finally, Schuchardt's evidence for his view consisted in something like a 'thought experiment', in statements to the effect that it is 'possible' to conceive of sound change as an analogical development. He did not offer any well-documented and convincing case histories which would have unambiguously demonstrated the validity of his claims.

This had unfortunate consequences for later, similar arguments: Because of their 'dubious ancestry', they likewise were easily dismissed, even though they did provide theoretical models or empirical justifications. Such later arguments include the following.

A theoretical model for the Schuchardtian view, which also provided an explicit explanation as to why some types of analogical change come out as 'regular sound change' while others do not, was provided by Sturtevant (1907): What has been called 'sound change' starts in a few isolated words, in the speech of one or two individuals. For reasons such as prestige, this new pronunciation may spread to other speakers. And in this spread, '. . . each person who substitutes the new sound in his own pronunciation tends to carry it into new words . . . Such a spread of a sound change from word to word closely resembles analogical change; the chief difference is that in analogical change the association groups are based upon meaning, while in this case the groups are based upon [phonetic] form.' We may model this development as in (7), where *a, b, c,* etc. refer to segments in given words; *a'* etc. refer to a changed pronunciation of *a* etc. The left and right sides of the proportion represent the old and the new pronunciations, respectively.

(7)   abc : ab'c
       dbc : dXc = db'c
       ebc : eYc = eb'c
       etc.

Empirical evidence for the Schuchardtian view of sound change was provided for instance by Sapir's (1921) description of the very slow change of [ū] to [ŭ] in English dialects, a process still continuing and leading to doublets such as the ones in (8a) vs. other words with invariable, innovated [ŭ] (cf. (8b)) and others which exhibit only the old long vowel (cf. (8c)). The occurrence of doublets, as well as the coexistence of the old state of affairs (in some words) and the new (in others) clearly are features normally associated with analogical and other non-regular change. And the lack of complete regularity, as well as the observability of the change in terms of attested doublets (which

have just begun to undergo the change), <u>contradict important neogrammarian claims about the nature of sound change.</u> *H it's unobservable*

(8a)   room   [rūm]   beside   [rŭm]
       roof   [rūf]   beside   [rŭf]
   b) good   [gŭd]
   c) food   [fūd]

Perhaps the most important empirical study of this sort is the one
initiated by Gauchat (1905) in the French-Swiss mountain village of
Charmey in the early 1900s and continued one generation later by
Hermann (1929). Over the almost thirty years of this study, a sound
change nearly ran its course from early, highly irregular and sporadic,
beginnings to eventual near-regularity. During the period of change,
the sound shift could be observed as being generalized along the three
parameters of time, lexical items affected by the change, and speakers
who displayed the change in their vocabulary. Moreover, there was a
social element associated with the change, a certain correlation between
speakers' age and the degree to which the change was implemented.
(Over time, however, the degree of implementation increased even in
the members of the older generations, as they were advancing in age.)

20.10. Labov and the sociolinguistic motivation of change

Because of their "dubious ancestry" (cf. the preceding section) and also
because of the relatively small number of proponents, these and other
early arguments for the Schuchardtian view of linguistic change could
generally be ignored by the adherents of neogrammarian doctrine.
However, the picture changed radically as a result of the work on
change in progress initiated by Labov (1963) and since then taken up
by many collaborators and followers. For this work is theoretically
quite explicit, well documented by empirical studies, and quite massive
in scope.
Perhaps the most significant of these studies is the one on the
Martha's Vineyard centralization of [a] toward [ə] in the diphthongs
[ay] and [aw]. (Compare also sections 15.1.2 and 15.2.1.)

In many ways the results of this study (and others in the Labovian framework) parallel those of Sapir's discussion of Engl. [ū] > [ŭ] and especially those of the Gauchat-Hermann investigation of sound change in Charmey. Some of the observations, however, especially those concerning the sociolinguistic motivation of linguistic change, go significantly beyond this earlier work and the work of the neogrammarians and other linguistic schools, and lay the foundation for a theory of linguistic change which is sufficiently different to be recognized as a theoretical framework in its own right.

Labov's major observations in the Martha's Vineyard study can be summarized as follows:

(a)   Sound change originates in a relatively small number of lexical items.

(b)   It is generalized to other words in terms of word classes which may be defined phonetically, morphophonemically, morphologically, semantically, syntactically, and/or socially (in terms of age group, sex, etc.).

(c)   During the course of this generalization there is a great degree of irregularity and variability.

(d)   Regularity is found mainly in the eventual outcome of the change, not in its inception.

(e)   The extent to which the change is generalized, both phonetically (in terms of the degree of centralization) and in scope (in terms of phonetic environment or of phonetically, morphophonemically, etc., defined word classes) to a very remarkable degree correlates with social factors (age, sex, class, etc.).

(f)   Perhaps most importantly, the extent to which the change is generalized is correlated with social attitude. It tends to be implemented most thoroughly in the speech of persons who identify themselves as islanders and who have the most polarized, negative attitude toward the mainland. Speakers with a more neutral attitude or those who identify more with the mainland exhibit the change to a much lower degree or not at all.

It is the last observation which probably provided the most significant empirical foundation for a theory which sees social motivation as the most powerful cause of linguistic change. This theory, most clearly stated in Weinreich, Labov, and Herzog 1968 and in Labov 1972, can be summarized as follows.

(i)   The basis for linguistic change lies in the same ever-present low-level variability of ordinary speech that was noticed by the nineteenth-century phoneticians and by the neogrammarians; cf. section 20.3 above.

(ii)   For reasons which linguistically appear to be completely arbitrary, a given phonetic variable, out of the many which are found in ordinary speech, is selected for being socially significant as a marker of group identification. (On Martha's Vineyard, for instance, this was a slightly more centralized variant of [a] which was taken to be a marker of islander identity.)

(iii)   As a consequence of this **sociolinguistic marking** the variable ceases to be a mere 'performance' variant and attains grammatical significance. It becomes a matter of what generativists call 'competence'. This is shown for instance by the fact that over- or under-use of the variable is noticed by speakers much as a speech error or non-native 'accent' is registered.

(iv)   Having thus attained grammatical significance, the variable must be accounted for by the grammar of the (social) dialect, in terms of a **variable rule** which is conditioned both linguistically (in terms of phonology, etc.) and socially.

(v)   This rule in turn, because it is a rule (i. e., 'generalization') and also because of the social reasons that gave rise to it, tends to be generalized or extended to (a) new environments, (b) new word classes, and (c) occasionally to structurally or functionally similar segments. For (a), compare the extension of [a]-centralization from [ay] to [aw] on Martha's Vineyard. The extension to new word classes permits the change to be completely generalized. And the extension to structurally or functionally similar segments allows for the possibility of chain shifts.

(vi)   Social groups hardly ever are completely exclusive of each other, but commonly have overlapping membership; cf. the overlapping group memberships defined by a term like 'White Anglo-Saxon Protestant Professor of Forensic Medicine'. As a consequence, the social parameters for the generalization of the variable rule may be expanded to ever larger groups. (Along the way, the social marking of the variable may well undergo reinterpretation. Compare section 15.1.1 for the reinterpretation of the social function of [æ]-raising and diphthongization outside Chicago.)

(vii)   To the extent that there are no opposing social pressures which might block complete generalization of the variable rule, it may eventually spread through the whole lexicon and throughout the whole

speech community. (It should be noted, however, that such generalization is characteristic only for developments within the speech community. Across different speech communities, the usual developments observed in Chapter 15 will obtain. Because of this notion of 'generalization within the speech community', the Labovian approach avoids the difficulties noted in respect to the neogrammarian attempt to explain the spread of sound change as a borrowing process; cf. section 20.3.)
(viii)   Because generalization usually is not in terms of individual words but of variable **rules**, the ultimate outcome is said to most commonly consist in (virtually) complete regularity.
(ix)   At this point of complete generalization, then, the variable becomes part of the normal, socially unmarked inventory of the speech community and, as a consequence, the variable rule accounting for it ceases to operate. That is, in generative terminology, there is restructuring.
(x)   The fact that this pattern of sound change implementation is observable in all studies of change in progress suggests that also other, completed changes were implemented in this fashion. (It is here that Labov introduced the term **uniformitarian principle**, for which see also section 20.1 above.)

Before examining the ramifications of this theory and the manner in which it manages to resolve the various difficulties discussed in earlier sections of this chapter, let us take a brief look at another recent theory of linguistic change which has been portrayed by its adherents as an alternative or rival theory to Labov's sociolinguistic approach.

20.11. Lexical diffusion

In 1969, Wang proposed the hypothesis that the mechanism of sound change may be **lexical diffusion**, a notion related to, but distinct from, Labov's variable rules. Under this hypothesis sound change application in many cases is specified vis-à-vis individual lexical items:

Phonetic change evidently takes time to be completed. But phonetically (or phonologically), change must be abrupt, in that a given segment either is phoneme X or phoneme Y. Under these circumstances, the only way that change can take time is by being lexically gradual, through the gradual diffusion of the change from one lexical item to another. Thus, at first only a small section of the lexicon is affected by the change X > Y. Along the way, as the change diffuses, there may be some fluctuation between X and Y. Eventually, however, Y will win out — provided the change runs its full course.

In the 1969 version of the hypothesis, the vehicle through which lexical diffusion takes place is tentatively defined as the quasi-analogical generalization process which Sturtevant had proposed (cf. 20.9 above). At this point, then, the difference between lexical diffusion and Labov's sociolinguistic approach is relatively minor. In both views, the variability between old and new phonetic realizations of given forms can give rise to the extension of the new pronunciation to other linguistic forms. The difference lies mainly in the degree or speed of the generalization, which is relatively fast and sweeping for Labov (cf., e. g., the change on Martha's Vineyard), but relatively slow and in terms of individual lexical items for Wang (cf. Sapir's example of Engl. [ū] > [ŭ], section 20.9 above). That is, the difference would roughly correspond to the one between rule-governed analogical change on one hand and the more 'traditional' types of analogy on the other (such as four-part analogy or leveling). In addition, however, there is the difference that Labov invokes a sociolinguistic factor as the starting point for change, but Wang does not.

Later formulations of lexical diffusionist doctrine redefine the differences between the two approaches and in so doing, sharpen them. Lexical diffusion is now claimed to be not the result of change, but its very mechanism. And conversely, variability or variation now is considered the result of change, not its mechanism or cause.

This later theoretical development must be considered unfortunate. For by denying the motivational force of variability, the theory has deprived itself of the ability to explain how lexical diffusion might take place at all: If in fact sound change were to affect each lexical item individually, without at least temporarily being accompanied by variability between the old and new pronunciations, there would be no reason at all for the change to repeat itself in other linguistic forms. That is, if [æ] changes to [æ̧] in *hand*, there would under this theory be no reason that some time later it should undergo the same change in *land*. Rather, given the many different possible ways in which [æ] can change crosslinguistically, there would be nothing to prevent the vowel of *land* from changing to [a], [e], [æ̃], or the like. Only variability between old and new pronunciations can motivate generalization of a given change to other, new forms — either through Sturtevant's analogy or through Labov's variable rules. (Perhaps because of these difficulties, some lexical diffusionist publications operate with the notion that sound change involves the generalization of 'minor rules'. However, there seem to be no alternations which would motivate postulating such rules — unless we accept Labov's view that the variation between old and new pronunciations provides the alternations required for rule formulation.)

Also as regards its empirical foundations, the lexical diffusionist approach suffers in comparison with the Labovian one. Whereas Labov and his associates base their claims on the study of change in progress, much of the early work of lexical diffusionists consisted in the 'postmortem' examination of changes which were believed to confirm the view that sound change is lexical and relatively amorphous in nature and therefore frequently fails to be completely generalized. An example is the case of Middle Chinese 'tone III' words which in some of the modern dialects are reflected either as 'tone 2b' or as 'tone 3b' words, without there being any phonological or semantic/syntactic conditioning for the split. As a consequence, original homonyms became tonally distinct, as in the examples of (9).

(9)   Tone 2b   Tone 3b

    siaŋ 'still'   tsiẽ 'ascend'
    su 'afterwards'   hau 'wait'
    hau 'school'   hau 'imitate'
    tieŋ 'lightening' tõi 'palace'

As it turns out, however, in many of the cases examined, alternative explanations are possible or even preferable. For instance, originally homonymous items like *siaŋ* and *tsiẽ* in (9) differ not only in terms of tone, but also in their segmental representations. These differences find a more satisfactory explanation under an alternative proposal which argues that one set of forms in (9) has been borrowed. Under this analysis, the differences between the two sets result from divergent dialectal developments (affecting tonal as well as segmental features).

Moreover, while some more recent studies do examine changes in progress, most of these developments would not be considered sound changes — or expected to be regular — in the neogrammarian framework: They range from the gradual extension of metathetical developments in Dravidian, to the generalization of a spelling pronunciation in Swedish, to analogical developments, such as the extension of the pattern *pervért* (verb) : *pérvert* (noun) to other English verb/noun pairs.

The best evidence for relatively slow, lexically gradual, generalizations of processes which the neogrammarians would consider sound changes comes from non-lexical diffusionist sources, above all from the work of Labov and his associates. For instance, Labov has noted that the New York change of [æ] to [eə] etc. (cf. 8.4, ex. (27)) is being implemented in a much less sweeping manner than other changes in progress. (Compare also Sapir's change of Engl. [ū] > [ŭ]; section 20.9, ex. (8) above.)

The evidence of such changes clearly shows that in many cases, sound change may be much more 'diffusionist' in its nature than originally envisaged by Labov and his school. However, as noted earlier, the motivation or vehicle for these 'diffusionist' changes must be the same as that for the more rule-governed, sweeping generalizations, namely the variable coexistence of old and new pronunciations in given forms.

20.12. Degrees of regularity and their motivations

As for the conditions which bring about slow, 'diffusionist' change, rather than sweeping, rule-governed generalizations, a recent paper by Labov advances the following, as yet tentative, hypothesis: A distinction must be made between changes which in a generative sense are relatively superficial and which simply change the output of the phonological rule system, and others which are more abstract and which directly affect the lexical or underlying representations of phonological forms. (Changes of the latter type include adjustments in the length or tenseness of vowels, while fronting, raising, and lowering processes belong to the former type.) Labov concludes that relatively superficial changes tend to be generalized in a sweeping, rule-governed fashion, while the more 'abstract' changes which affect the lexical representation of given forms display a tendency toward diffusionist implementation.

Some recent publications suggest that the specifics of Labov's hypothesis may require modification. (What is perhaps more significant than the distinction between 'abstract' and 'superficial' is the fact that sociolinguistic marking is fairly 'weak' in diffusionist changes. For instance, in doublets like [rūm] vs. [rŭm] 'room', the only difference in social connotation appears to be that the long-vowel pronunciation is a little more 'conservative' and 'bookish'. We do not get the strong association between one of the variants and group membership, as we find it for instance in the variation between [æə] and [æ], both in Chicago and outside.)

However, the distinction between relatively minor modifications and more noticeable ones has much to recommend it. For it is along very similar lines that it seems to be possible to explain, within the Labovian framework, why certain types of variability are more easily, more successfully, and more commonly selected for complete generalization than others.

As noted ealier, assimilation and weakening/loss constitute the bulk of phonetic processes which typically result in regular sound change. On the other hand, dissimilation, metathesis, and similar processes occur much more rarely as regular changes. Some of the neogrammarians attributed this difference to the fact that (at least in their initial phases) assimilation and weakening can be conceived of as relatively minor deviations from a given norm, detectable only by trained phoneticians, whereas dissimilation and similar processes are quite perceptible, namely as speech errors.

Similarly, one may argue, analogical replacements (and other types of non-phonetic change) are quite noticeable, even in their initial phases, as violations of established norms. And this noticeability, again, may be considered responsible for the fact that changes of this sort are notoriously irregular.

Unfortunately, however, acoustically-based processes such as the change of *p* to *k* (and vice versa), chain shift generalizations, rule-based analogical generalizations, as well as regular dissimilation and metathesis pose difficulties for the neogrammarian position. Compare sections 20.4 and 20.6 above. At the same time, it should be noted that although the processes just enumerated are regular, they occur much less commonly as regular changes than do assimilation and weakening/loss.

The following hypothesis seems to be able to account to a considerable extent for these differences in behavior.

In the crucial first step of selecting for sociolinguistic marking (and subsequent generalization) one out of the many deviations from the norm which are found in actual speech, selection is favored by **relative imperceptibility** and the **absence of non-phonetic** (or non-phonological) **marking**. The less perceptibly a given variable differs from the norm, the less it is considered already marked as a speech error or a grammatical mistake and thus as not eligible for another, sociolinguistic marking.

This predicts that assimilation, weakening, etc., being the least noticeable, most low-level deviations from the norm (at least in their initial phases), would be most easily and most commonly selected for sociolinguistic marking. Acoustically-motivated changes like $k > p$ involve a much greater phonetic 'leap'; they would therefore tend to be selected mainly in contexts of weakening, where the distinction between [+ velar, + grave] and [- velar, + grave] is less perceptible; cf. 5.3.5 above. Dissimilations, especially those in close contact, where the perceptibility of deviations is greater, would be selected more easily if neutralization makes them less blatant; cf. 6.3.

Elsewhere, processes like metathesis and dissimilation, analogical extensions, and chain-shift generalizations require a **special structural** or **functional motivation** which, moreover, must be relatively purely phonetic or phonological, i.e., **relatively close to the surface** in generative terminology. On the other hand, changes clearly perceptible as non-phonetically or non-phonologically marked, as violations of relatively more underlying grammatical norms, would rarely, if ever, lend themselves to being selected as sociolinguistic markers. And if selected, their generalization would tend to be diffusionist and thus would much more rarely result in complete generalization.

Note that the hypothesis just proposed replaces the neogrammarian binary distinction between regular and sporadic change by a gradient one. In so doing, it provides a resolution for some of the difficulties with the neogrammarian position that have been noted in earlier sections. And it provides a theoretically principled motivation for this resolution, within the framework of the Labovian approach to linguistic change.

20.13. Other ramifications of the Labovian approach

The Labovian approach to historical linguistics makes it possible to provide solutions to a number of other difficulties which beset the neogrammarian framework, as well as the generative one.

As noted in 20.5, one of the greatest difficulties with the neogrammarian approach it that it ultimately fails to provide an explicit, meaningful explanation or cause for given linguistic changes (including chain-shift response changes, and even analogical developments). True, certain types of change are quite common and appear to be well motivated, qua types; but which of these types or what subtype is selected by a given language at a given time seems to be linguistically arbitrary.

In the Labovian framework there is an explanation for this situation: Naturalness and linguistic motivation do play a role in determining the variables which occur, as 'raw material', in actual speech. And relative perceptibility to some extent influences the likelihood of a given variable being selected for sociolinguistic marking. But the ultimately most important step lies in the selection of a given variable as sociolinguistically significant and thus as worthy of generalization. And this process is governed by non-linguistic, social factors. It is the linguistic arbitrariness of this factor which explains why change in the final analysis turns out to be linguistically arbitrary. (Note however that because in most 'post-mortem' analyses of linguistic change it is not possible to recover the social conditions which gave rise to it, we are in most cases dealing with an explanation only in principle: While the actual social determinants of the change may escape us, we can be quite certain that there was some such determinant. Compare section 8.6 for the similar situation concerning chain shifts and whole-system changes like Grimms's Law.)

Linguistic change, then, is governed by two factors: On one hand there are linguistic notions such as naturalness, structure, and function, which provide the 'raw material' for change, plus the notion of perceptibility, which imposes a kind of 'ranking' on the variables of actual speech. On the other hand is a social element which, from the linguistic point of view, arbitrarily selects one of many possible, linguistically motivated, processes for sociolinguistic marking and generalization. (As noted earlier, even in chain shifts, each component part of the chain is linguistically arbitrary in the present sense. It must therefore be assumed that each component change in its own turn is motivated by a non-linguistic, social factor.)

Also the question as to how there can be changes which are sensitive to structural or functional notions (cf. section 20.4) can now be given a satisfactory answer: Since sound change takes place over extended periods and since it is sociolinguistically motivated or 'marked', it is 'observable' and extendable to new, linguistically similar or parallel inputs, in the same sense that other linguistic rules can be said to be 'observable' and extendable. True, this observability and extendability rarely obtains at the fully conscious level. Still, we are not dealing with purely mechanical processes which are completely beyond the speaker's control.

In section 20.7, it was noted that the interesting question of how sound change is embedded in synchronic grammar has not received a satisfactory answer in generative treatments of linguistic change. The Labovian framework provides such an answer, in the concept of socio-linguistically variable rules. Though especially in their initial stages, such rules are motivated by linguistic alternations that are governed by social, rather than purely linguistic factors, the fact that these alternations exist and that they are within the linguistic 'competence' of the speakers provides sufficient justification for postulating corresponding rules within the synchronic grammar. In effect, then, the concept of variable rules eliminates the distinction between diachronic and synchronic linguistics, at least in principle. (In practice, the concerns of historical and synchronic linguistics remain sufficiently different to warrant separate treatment.)

Note however that there may be some questions as to whether heavily 'diffusionist' changes, such as the English change of [ū] to [ŭ], should be accounted for in terms of rules. A quasi-analogical spread along the lines suggested by Sturtevant seems to be empirically more adequate. True, the notion 'minor rule' can be invoked (cf. also section 20.11). However, difficulties arise from the fact that at least in their early phases, also sweeping rule-governed changes are quite limited in their lexical scope and thus should be considered minor rules. A solution may perhaps lie in claiming that both diffusionist and rule-governed changes start out as minor-rule processes and that it is the 'perceptibility' factor discussed in the preceding section or the degree of social marking which determines whether such a minor rule can become more like a major rule in its linguistic behavior.

The Labovian framework, as well as the diffusionist approach (as pointed out in Wang 1969), also makes it possible to provide an explanation in principle for the paradoxical fact that under certain circumstances, sound changes which eventually may turn out regular can lead to irregular outcomes. A probable case in point is the fate of pre-Modern English [ū], which shows the modern outcomes in (10).

(10)	[ū]	[ū] ~ [ŭ]	[ŭ]	[ə]
	aloof	hoof		
		roof		
	bloom	room		
	loom	broom		
	boom			
	gloom			
	groom			
	shoot	(soot)	(soot)	but
	moot	root		
	boot			
	loot			
	food		stood	flood
	brood		wood	blood
	mood		good	
	rood		could	
			hood	
	loon			done
	boon			
	soon			
	spoon			
	loop	hoop		up
	(whoop)	(whoop)		
	stoop			
	spook		book	
			cook	
			look	
			hook	
			shook	
	etc.		etc.	

At first glance the occurrence of different reflexes in identical or near-identical environments (as in *food : good : blood,* all before [d]) would seem to point to quite irregular sound change. True, we can observe certain tendencies, such as unchanged [ū] especially before labial and nasal, short [ŭ] especially before [k]. But these are mere tendencies; cf. *room, broom, hoop* with alternating [ū] and [ŭ] and *up* with [ə], or *spook* with [ū] before [k].

However, once we accept that sound change does not take place suddenly, affecting all lexical items at the same time, it is possible to conceive of sound changes as fully or partly overlapping in time, such that the outcome of one may only partially feed the other. In the present case, there are two changes involved. One consists of the shortening of [ū] to [ŭ] (cf. (11)); the other of the change of [ŭ] to [ə] (cf. (12)). The latter change seems to have run its course over a relatively short time and is no longer active. As far as one can tell, it has been completely regular, in so far as all linguistic items exhibiting [ŭ] at the time of the change did undergo the process. On the other hand, we have seen that change (12) is a very slow, diffusionist development, which even today has not completed its course (although eventually it may well turn out to be regular, in that all items which qualified for the change will have undergone it).

(11)   ū > ŭ

(12)   ŭ > ə

All we need to assume then, in order to account for the 'irregular' outcomes summarized in (10), is that the two changes overlapped in time, such that (11) was implemented early enough in some lexical items that the resulting [ŭ] could undergo change (12), while in other words, change (11) took place too late, preventing the resulting [ŭ] from undergoing (12). Compare the summary in (13).

(13)

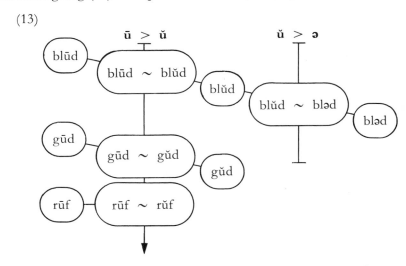

The fact that linguistic change takes time to be implemented and that it proceeds through variability can account also for other developments which are difficult to explain in traditional approaches, as well as in the orthodox lexical diffusionist approach: One of the important factors in the Labovian view of linguistic change is that social factors play a role not only in the inception of the change, but also in its generalization. Now, ordinarily the social motivating factor does not seem to change appreciably during the course of a sound change's implementation. That is the sound change is 'propelled' by social motivations which have the same effect as the original social motivation. However, if there is a complete **reversal in the social evaluation** of a given variable, such that the originally favored variable becomes disfavored, then it is possible that a sound change 'reverses itself'. It is in cases of this sort that there seems to be a genuine **rule inversion.** (On the other hand, 'rule inversions' like the one in section 11.3, ex. (27 a) vs. (30) are indirect reflexes of a restructuring of the grammar, not direct modifications of an 'ongoing' rule.)

A development of this sort seems to have taken place in French: It appears that at a certain time, a sound change $z > r$ (cf. (14a)) was being implemented through some variable process, with the [r] variant being sociolinguistically favored. Somewhere along the way, however, the sociolinguistic marking seems to have been reversed in favor of the [z] alternant. As a consequence, the process was reformulated as in (14b). The result of this rule inversion is that even some [r] segments which had not come about by (14a) changed to [z] by (14b); cf. e. g. the development in (15).

(14a) z > r
   b) r > z

(15) (Gk. kathedra ⇒) Lat. cathedra > OFr. chaire
                                       > NFr. chaise [z] 'chair'

Note however that while developments like the ones in (13) and (14/15) are possible, they do seem to be sufficiently rare not to seriously affect the tenet that for all practical purposes, sound change (as defined by the neogrammarians) is regular.

20.14. Conclusion

The Labovian approach to sound change thus provides important motivations and explanations for phenomena which were difficult to motivate or poorly explained in earlier approaches, especially that of the neogrammarians. Moreover, it makes very different claims about the nature of linguistic change.

The neogrammarians had conceived of sound change as regular, affecting all lexical items simultaneously, unobservable, governed only by phonetic factors, and proceeding by gradual, imperceptible steps. The Labovian approach shows almost all of these tenets to be incorrect or in need of modification — save one: While during much of its implementation, sound change is quite irregular and conditioned by many non-phonetic factors (including of course sociolinguistic ones), in its ultimate outcome it does in the overwhelming number of cases approach the regularity postulated by the neogrammarians. As a consequence, the neogrammarian regularity principle still remains a heuristically useful and important criterion for historical linguistic research.

Moreover, unlike earlier theories, the Labovian approach places a major emphasis on the social motivation of linguistic change. The fact that change is socially motivated casts considerable doubt on occasional attempts, especially by the neogrammarians and the generativists, to locate the motivation of linguistic change in early child language acquisition. (For other difficulties, see section 20.3 above.) While it may well be true that some of the 'raw material' for linguistic change (especially for acoustically based changes) may ultimately derive from errors or reanalyses in child language acquisition, Labovian research shows that the locus for change lies not in the individual dialect or grammar of children, but in the post-early childhood social sphere of peer groups, etc. In fact, as observed earlier, linguistic change-in-progress affects the whole spectrum of society, including the older generations.

Finally, it may be useful to note that though our discussion has focused mainly on sound change, the Labovian approach provides a general, comprehensive theory for all linguistic change. In fact, some of Labov's studies, such as an investigation of variation between 'r-less' and 'r-ful' speech in New York City, have observed a similar variability in dialect borrowing and dialect spread. Studies on analogical and syntactic change have documented that also in these areas, change proceeds through patterned variability. And to the extent that they have focused on change in progress, they have observed a similar correlation between social factors and linguistic change.

Especially in the area of 'traditional' analogy (and of semantic change), the implementation of the change proceeds at a slow, 'diffusionist' pace. What is perhaps surprising is that syntactic change, certainly no less 'abstract' or removed from the surface than analogical change, generally comes out much more sweeping and rule-governed. Moreover, there are difficulties in certain areas of syntactic change, where developments having all the appearances of being rule-governed cannot very easily be accounted for in terms of variable rules. Rather, recent studies suggest that there is variability between entire rule systems or grammatical analyses. These difficulties clearly present challenges for further research, but do not at this point seem to invalidate the essential correctness of the Labovian approach.

Notes

A complete or even representative bibliography of historical linguistics still needs to be compiled. The publications referred to in the notes below constitute only an incomplete selection of the vast published literature. They are listed because (a) they refer to works which were important milestones in the history of historical linguistics, (b) they provide interesting further discussion or references (including opinions differing from the ones advocated in this book), or (c) they serve as sources for data and interpretations that are not in wide circulation. Most of these citations contain references to additional literature. Bibliographical references have been updated and augmented in this second edition and are keyed to the 'References' that follow these Notes.

Many data and interpretations are unattributed, because they are so widely cited in historical linguistics that it would be arbitrary to select one or two publications for reference. This is the case especially in the chapters on sound change. (Further information on such data and their interpretation can be found in handbooks on comparative Indo-European linguistics and on the history of the various Indo-European languages.) A fair number of data come from my own published or unpublished research.

Beside giving bibliographical references, the notes serve as a vehicle for correcting and updating the book. The text of the first edition has otherwise been left essentially unchanged, in order to reduce production costs and to keep the price of the book within affordable limits. For the same reason, corrections are limited to misprints that are not self-correcting and to major factual errors that managed to survive into the first edition in spite of my attempts to keep such errors to the absolute minimum.

In making the revisions reflected in these notes, I have benefited especially from the reviews of the first edition by Ricardo Ambrosini (*Linguistica e letteratura* 11: 213–219 (1986 [1987])), Sheila Embleton (*Diachronica* 3: 203–231 (1986 [1987])), and Brian Joseph (*Language* 65: 162–164 (1989)), as well as from extensive personal comments by W. Keith Perceval and the positive feedback from my colleagues and friends, above all George Cardona, Brian Joseph, Braj B. Kachru, Theo Vennemann, Calvin Watkins, Werner Winter, and Ladislav

Zgusta. The responsibility of all of these persons is, of course, limited to what may be good in this book; the responsibility for the rest remains with me.

Chapter 1
General: *Handbooks*: Introductory: Aitchison 1981; Arlotto 1972; Crowley 1987; Sturtevant 1907, 1947. More advanced: Anttila 1972, 1988; Bloomfield 1933; Boretzky 1977; Bynon 1977; Delbrück 1884; Hoenigswald 1965; Jeffers & Lehiste 1979; Lehmann 1962, 1973; Paul 1920; Polomé (ed.) To Appear; Samuels 1972. (Also useful: Columbus 1974).
Edited readers, paper collections: Ahlqvist 1982; Anderson & Jones 1974a, 1974b; Arbeitman & Bomhard 1981; Baldi 1990; Baldi & Werth 1978; Cherubim 1975; Christie 1976; Dingwall 1971; Fisiak 1978, 1980, 1984, 1985a, 1985b, 1988, 1990; Hamp, Householder & Austerlitz 1966; Hock 1982c; Jazayery et al. 1978; Joos 1957; Keiler 1972; Koopman et al. 1987; Lehmann 1967; Lehmann & Malkiel 1968, 1982; H. Lüdtke 1980; Maher et al. 1982; Pieper & Stickel 1985; Posner & Green 1980; A. G. Ramat et al. 1987; Rauch & Carr 1983; Sebeok 1973; Stump 1983a; Traugott et al. 1980. See also Newmeyer 1989.
Handbooks on Indo-European linguistics: Introductory: Baldi 1983, Krahe 1970. More advanced books and standard handbooks: Brugmann 1897–1916, 1904; Brugmann & Delbrück 1886–1900; Kuryłowicz 1968a; Mayrhofer 1986; Szemerényi 1989; Watkins 1969.
1.2: In the Old English text, correct *scyldum* to *scyldgum*; in the Middle English text (2nd line), read *kyngdom come to* þe. The Old English text is Northumbrian, the Middle English text Wycliffite, the Early New English text from Tyndale.
1.3.1: Cf., e.g., Sturtevant 1940 (for philological interpretation of the phonetics of written texts); Antonsen 1967, Hockett 1959, S. Kuhn 1961, Stockwell & Barritt 1961 (on Old English digraph interpretation); Christie 1982, Fisiak (ed.) 1990 (philology and historical linguistics).
1.4: For the Old English text, see the note on 1.2. The Old High German text is from the 9th century A.D. and comes from Weissenburg. (In line 2 of the text, read: ... *sama sō uuir*). The Gothic text is from Ulfila's bible translation. – In Chart 1.3, the Estonian word for 'ear' should read *kõrv*.

Chapter 2
2.1: H. Andersen 1973, Ohala 1971 (on acoustic basis for sound change); cf. also Thurgood & Javkin 1975 and the references in the Index.
2.1.1: On the sibilant offglide of palatal stops see also 5.1.5 below. A similar phenomenon of 'fricative release' is found in the affricates, for which see 15.2.3 and the note on 7.1.
2.1.6: Because of their stop articulation, nasals are classified as non-continuant in synchronic generative phonology. But this ignores the fact that unlike oral stops, nasals can be audibly extended. The similarity of oral and nasal stops can be accounted for by the feature [+ stop, ± nasal].
2.1.12: The preference for syllable-initial fricative + stop (rather than stop + fricative, with increasing sonority) seems to be motivated by the fact that stops are acoustically more easily identified (as labial, dental, etc.) before vowels than before obstruents. Cf. Hock 1985b and see the note on 6.3.
2.4: Cf., e.g., Bloomfield 1933, Jakobson 1931a, Trubetzkoy 1938 (for 'phoneme', 'contrast', etc.); Darden 1971, Schane 1971 (recent revival of the notion 'contrast').

2.6: See de Saussure 1916 for the distinction 'synchronic' vs. 'diachronic'. (Cf. also Koerner 1987.)
2.7.1: In the list of symbols, add 'or [+ syll.]' to the definition of V.

Chapter 3

General: *Primary sources:* Grimm 1819–1834 and 1893, Rask 1818, Lottner 1862, Verner 1877, Osthoff & Brugmann 1878, Paul 1920 (or earlier editions); cf. also Grassmann 1863. *Discussions:* Christy 1983, Hock 1976a, Jankowsky 1972 and 1976, Schneider 1973, Wilbur 1977. (See also Chapter 20.)
3.4: For relative chronology, cf., e.g., Bremer 1894 and Hoenigswald 1973b; and see Kiparsky 1968b for the terms 'bleeding' and 'feeding'. The terms 'feed' and 'bleed' are used with different connotations in current generative phonology. What is called 'bleed' in this book would be referred to as 'counterfeed'.
3.5: See also chapters 9–11. On morphological conditioning of sound changes and preventive analogy, cf., e.g., Anttila 1972, Cerrón-Palomino 1974 and 1977, Hermann 1931, Kiparsky 1989, Langdon 1975, Malkiel 1968 and 1976, Melchert 1975, Postal 1968, Sihler 1977. Opposing views: Bloomfield 1933, Hock 1976c, Kiparsky 1973b.
3.6: See also Chapter 14. – Engl. *paternal, maternal, fraternal* are indirect borrowings from Latin. The Classical Latin forms are *paternus* etc. – In example (25), read *feoh* and *fæt* (for *fēoh* and *fatu*).
3.7: For onomatopoeia and taboo see also Chapter 12 and the references in the Index.

Chapter 4

General: A. Hill 1936, Hoenigswald 1965, Jakobson 1931a, Juilland 1953, Trubetzkoy 1938, Twaddell 1938.
4.3: The view presented in this section can be contrasted with the view in 4.4 as the 'phonemic' vs. the 'archiphonemic' principle. For the phonemic principle, see, e.g. A. Hill 1936 and Twadell 1938.
4.4: Martinet 1936, Trubetzkoy 1936.

Chapter 5

5.1.1: Halle 1962a (Greek-letter variables); Mayrhofer 1951 (usual, assimilatory interpretation of Pali cluster developments, but cf. Murray 1982). – In example (2), the glosses for *yuŋktha, riŋktha* should read 'ye yoke', 'ye leave'; in (12a), the hyphen (___) should be deleted at the end of the formulation.
5.1.2: An alternative term for 'umlaut', used in some publications, is 'metaphony'.
5.1.3: Cf. H. Kuhn 1970 for Old Norwegian dialectal vowel harmony. (The term ' "locally" predictable' refers to the fact that the contrast is predictable in terms of the 'local' environment , viz. the preceding root vocalism.)
5.1.4: A slightly different view in de Chene 1979.
5.1.5: Neeld 1973 (conditioning hierarchy for palalatization).
5.1.6: Cf., e.g., Hock 1974a, 1975, 1979, 1984 and Steblin-Kamenskij 1965 (vs. Bhat 1973; Emeneau 1954, 1955, 1956, 1962, 1980; Millardet 1933; and others).
5.1.7: Anwar 1974.
5.2: Hock 1976b with 1986a, Cravens 1984 (general); Chen & Wang 1975 ('oral depletion'); Hamp 1974 (further development of nasal fricatives, nasal flaps, etc.). – In ex. (44), note that earlier *veer* has changed to Mod. Span. *ver*; in (49), change Ital. *puoi* to *poi*; and in the note below (58), read $*snig^w h\text{-}es$ > Lat. *nivis*.
5.3.3: Clements 1982, Hayes 1989, Hock 1986a, Hyman 1985, Ingria 1980, Miranda 1984, Wetzels & Sezer (eds.) 1986 (compensatory lengthening); de Chene & Anderson

1979 (weakening + assimilation). See also Garnes 1976, Lehiste 1970, 1972 (phonetic studies on temporary compensation). – Some linguists (e.g., Clements 1982, Hayes 1989) consider developments of the type Lat. *lactem* > It. *latte* to involve compensatory lengthening (of *t* to *tt*, conditioned by the loss of *c* [k]). In many cases, it is possible to propose alternative accounts, such as assimilation ([kt] > [tt]) or weakening + assimilation (e.g., [kt] > [xt] > [ht] > [tt]). However, consider changes of the type PGmc. **rextaz* > ON *rēttr*. Here, the mora of the lost segment, *x*, appears to have split up and attached both to the preceding vowel and to the following consonant. This suggests that, in some cases, compensatory lengthening is indeed manifested as consonant lengthening (or gemination), beside (or instead of) vowel lengthening. (Cf. Hock 1986a.) – An alternative term for 'aphaeresis' is 'aphesis'.
5.3.5: E.g., Hyman 1973c (for [grave]). See also Bonebrake 1979. – In ex. (94), replace PIE (etc.) *ey* by *i* and Lat. *ī* by *i*.
5.4: General: Henderson 1982, Hombert, Ohala & Ewan 1976 and 1979, McCawley 1970.
5.4.2: Dempwolff 1922, Ewan 1976, Hombert 1976, Hyman 1973b (general); Maran 1971 (Jingpho); Bhatia 1975, Ohala 1974b, Purcell, Villegas & Young 1978 (Panjabi).
5.4.5: Becker 1978, Hock 1986a (Slavic); Hamp 1959, Kock 1901, Oftedal 1952 (Scandinavian).
5.4.6: Hock 1986a with references.
5.4.7: Becker 1977a, 1977b; see also Bolinger 1964, Ivić 1976, W. Lüdtke 1959, among others.

Chapter 6

6.1.1: Brugmann 1909, Grammont 1895, Posner 1961, Schwyzer 1933, Togeby 1964.
6.1.2: Cardona 1968, Wurzel 1976.
6.1.3: Labov, Yaeger & Steiner 1972 (but see Hamans 1988), P. Miller 1973, Stampe 1972, Wanner 1975; see also Howell 1988.
6.2: Langdon 1976, Malone 1971, Nakao 1986, Semiloff-Zelasko 1973, Silva 1973, Thompson & Thompson 1969, Ultan 1971 (general); Ekblom 1927, Torbiörnsson 1906, and many others (Slavic vowel-liquid metathesis).
6.3: Grassmann 1863, see also Miller 1977c, Szemerényi 1975b (vs. Kiparsky 1973d); Hopper 1973 (regular glottal dissimilation); Benediktsson 1963, Hock 1987, Schane 1971 (regular dissimilation in position of neutralization); Hock 1985b (regular metathesis). A different view in Hoenigswald 1964. – (Regular) metathesis frequently changes syllable-initial stop + fricative into fricative + stop. For the motivation, cf. the note on 2.1.12 and Hock 1985b. – In the discussion of ex. (22)–(23), read: ... /l/ – the input to the change – and /d/ – the output – do not contrast in the position before /l/.

Chapter 7

7.1.1: Bloomfield 1933, Ohala 1974a and 1974b (epenthesis), see also Howell 1988 (anaptyxis); Allen 1958, Danielsson 1903, Diver 1958, Hock 1985b, Semiloff-Zelasko 1973, Stang 1957 (segmentalization); different treatments of glide epenthesis in Kiparsky 1967, Malone 1971. Cf. also S. Anderson 1976. For aspiration, turbulence, see Abramson 1977, Lisker & Abramson 1964 and 1965. Cf. Árnason 1980, Garnes 1976 for a different view on Icelandic preaspiration, but see also Hock 1986a. – Aspiration, in turn, may be subject to something like wrong timing: In many modern Indo-Aryan dialects, the (highly turbulent) aspiration of voiceless aspirates tends to be 'overlaid' by the place-of-articulation features of the stop element. This is especially the case for the labial; cf. pronunciations like [phal] 'fruit' beside [phΦal], where [hΦ] indicates

labialized, highly turbulent aspiration. Further overlap of aspiration and labiality may lead to 'affricated' stops of the type [pΦ]. Parallels are found elsewhere. E.g., the Modern Danish pronunciation of the famous amusement park *Tivoli* has changed from [thĩvoli], with strong aspiration, to [tsĩvoli]; and similar developments are found in Modern British English dialects. Affricated stops may undergo further developments similar to assibilated stops, resulting in the eventual loss of the stop element (cf. 5.1.5 above). This stage is observable in some modern Indo-Aryan dialects, where we find words like *phal* 'fruit' pronounced as [Φal].
7.2.1: In ex. (28), the gloss of the second word should be 'long'.
7.3.1: Howell 1985 and 1987 (on $r > R$).
7.3.5: Allen 1958, Danielsson 1903, Diver 1958, Hock 1985b, Stang 1957; see also H. Andersen 1973, Ohala 1975 (acoustic explanations).
7.4.1: Hock 1976b, Murray & Vennemann 1983, Vennemann 1988.
7.4.2: 'Checked' syllables are now commonly referred to as 'closed'. In the definition of checked (or closed) syllables, change syllable-final C_o to C.
7.4.3: Cf. also Thurgood & Javkin 1975 (influence of consonants on vowel fronting, rounding, etc.); Beddor 1983, Whalen & Beddor 1989 (nasalization, nasals, and vowel height).
7.4.4: In ex. (70), read: pre-OE *doxtrī*, and change the gloss to 'daughter (Dat. sg.)'.
7.4.5: Labov, Yaeger & Steiner 1972 (but see Hamans 1988, Kiparsky 1989). – For the 'secondary shortening' in ex. (79), see 20.9 and 20.13 below.

Chapter 8
General: Martinet 1958, 1964. See also Hagège & Haudricourt 1978.
8.1: Ex. (2): For 'Loss of conditioning environment' read 'Change in conditioning environment'.
8.2: King 1967, Labov 1982 ('functional load' considered of doubtful importance).
8.3: Moulton 1960 and 1961 (Swiss German); Haudricourt & Juilland 1949 (*u*-fronting).
8.4: King 1969a, Labov, Yaeger & Steiner 1972 (general); Labov 1966a, 1966b, 1972a, 1972b, etc. (New York); Habick 1980 (Central Illinois); Callary 1974 (Chicago).
8.5: Kisseberth 1970 ('conspiracy'); Mayrhofer 1951 (Pali); Martinet 1964 (Slavic); Martinet 1964 (initial strengthening; different interpretation); Kaye 1979 (Ojibwa, with partially different interpretation). – Concerning the Pali two-mora conspiracy there have been repeated attempts to attribute dual developments of the type Skt. *rājñaḥ* > *rañño* beside *rājino* to dialect differences. However, it does not seem possible to isolate dialects in which one or the other development would have been regular. (A good survey of Pali and early Middle Indo-Aryan in general is found in von Hinüber 1986.) – A more accurate formulation of the Ojibwa situation might be that the original contrast was one between 'fortis' (i.e. 'strong') and 'lenis' ('weak') stops, and that in initial position this contrast was neutralized (through merger).
8.6: For English, cf. also Lass 1974. – As for whole-system changes like Grimm's Law, the precise manner in which the change took place is uncertain. One possibility is that the change began with the voiceless stops becoming aspirated, subsequently changing via affricated stops into fricatives (cf. the note on 7.1). In that case, we can assume a drag chain development, with the voiced stops shifting into the voiceless unaspirated position vacated by the original voiceless stops, and the aspirated stops moving into the position thus vacated by the voiced stops. An alternative account would start with the fact that PIE may have had a gap in the voiced labial position and assume that the aspirated labial began shifting into this empty position. Assuming a solidarity shift, by which the other aspirates likewise began to move into the position of the voiced stops, we can postulate a push chain, by which the voiced stops moved into the direction of the voiceless ones, pushing the latter into the direction of aspirates (etc.)

or, alternatively, directly toward fricative pronunciation. (These scenarios are predicated on the traditional reconstruction of the PIE stop system. For recently proposed alternative reconstructions see the discussion in 19.5.2 below.) – For the allophonic differentiation in ex. (47), see the discussion on p. 144 above and note that [a^c] designates a fronted [a] that has not quite reached the position of [æ]. For the 'secondary shortening' in ex. (46), see 20.9 and 20.13 below.

Chapter 9

General: Cf., e.g., Osthoff & Brugmann 1878, Paul 1920, Hermann 1931, Winter 1969; cf. also Anttila 1977, Anttila & Brewer 1977, Fisiak 1980, Zamora 1985.
9.1: Miranda 1974a.
9.1.1: Cf. Hoenigswald 1983 and see 10.1.4 below ('doublets').
9.1.2: de Chene 1975 (on the issue of inter-paradigmatic four-part analogy); Marchand 1969 (English onomatopoeia). – In ex. (18), the Old English type *frēo-dōm* is already attested with the innovated meaning; the original meaning 'realm of the free' is only inferrable.
9.1.4: Cf. Leibiger 1988 for the notion 'inflection'.
9.1.5: Paul 1920, Bloomfield 1933 (English *r/∅*); see also Plank 1965 (rule-oriented approach; cf. Chapter 11). The insertion is limited to contexts where the vowel-final and vowel-initial words occur in the same phonological phrase. (On this prosodic conditioning of *r*-insertion, see, e.g., Vogel 1986.) In some varieties of British English, the *r*-insertion process is now being generalized to word-internal intervocalic contexts, as in *drawing* [drɔ-r-iŋ]. This extension is still highly variable, suggesting an early stage in a Labov-type sound change (for which see 20.10–20.13 below.) A further extension, across syntactic boundary, is noted in Vogel 1986.
9.2: See also Anttila 1975, Hock 1985c, Malkiel 1982, Sturtevant 1907.
9.2.1: Dressler 1977, Menn & MacWhinney 1984, Stemberger 1981; cf. also Cardona 1968, Wurzel 1976 (portmanteau-formation); H. Marchand 1969 (clipping); Benveniste 1968, Fairbanks 1977, Kahr 1975 and 1976 (periphrastic replacements for morphologically simple structures). – In ex. (49b), the form *childen* is inferrable, but apparently not directly attested. The deliberate use of blending can be extended to yield forms which it would be difficult to label 'compromises between competing forms', such as *American Indian* → *Amerindian*, or *television broadcast* → *telecast*.
9.2.2: Dressler 1978, Winter 1969.
9.2.3: A. K. Hale 1973 (Maori, Polynesian recutting).
9.2.4: The form *cranberry* actually is a borrowing from dialectal German *Kranbeere* or *Kronbeere*.
9.2.5: Cf. Mullen 1979.
9.4: Cf., e.g., Trnka et al. 1958 vs. Stankiewicz 1979 (general); Trager 1940 (Eastern Seaboard development); Hock 1974b (Sanskrit *r*-stems).

Chapter 10

General: Kuryłowicz 1947 (also 1964, 1968b), Mańczak 1958 (also 1978 etc.). Evaluations: Anttila 1977, Best 1973, Hock 1976a and 1976c, Vincent 1974. Cf. also Miranda 1974a ('analogy' and 'leveling': two radically different processes).
10.1.2.2: See also Watkins 1962 (on third person singular in general) and Kuryłowicz 1964 (proposed derivation of pre-Gk. sg. 3 *-ei* on the basis of a second-singular pivot). On the clitic origin of the endings of the Polish verb 'to be', cf. especially H. Andersen 1987.
10.1.4: Kiparsky 1974 (recent attack on the validity of the fourth 'law'). – In ex. (9a),

the gloss of the second word should be 'father-in-law'. (The 'correct' inflection of this word is *socer, socer-ī*.) In ex. (10), add the gloss 'dog'.
10.1.5: Cf. Meillet 1909 on German, French, etc. replacement of simple by compound past tense.
10.3: Leopold 1930 (polarity principle); cf. also Kisseberth 1976 and section 11.7 below.

Chapter 11

General: Halle 1962b and especially Kiparsky 1965, 1968a, 1968b, 1971, 1972, 1973b, 1974, 1978, 1989. See also Hogg 1979, King 1969b, Miller 1973, Postal 1968, Stockwell & Macaulay (eds.) 1972, Tsiapera (ed.) 1971. Different views: Anttila 1972 and 1977, Bybee 1980, Fairbanks 1973, Hock 1976a and 1976c, Jeffers 1974, Koefoed 1974, Plank 1965, Schindler 1974, Thomason 1974 and 1976, Vincent 1974, Wagner 1970. See also the more morphologically (or morpho(pho)nologically) oriented approach in publications like Dressler 1985, Klausenburger 1979, and Mayerthaler 1980b, 1981.
11.1.1: Hock 1976c.
11.1.2: W. Friedrich 1901 with references to other studies ('northern' dialects); Kranzmayer 1956 (Bavarian/Southern German); Sadock 1973 (Yiddish, vs. King 1976). What complicates matters is that the standard or northern German distinction 'voiced' vs. 'voiceless' generally corresponds to one of 'tense' or 'fortis' vs. 'lax' or 'lenis' in Bavarian/Southern German.
11.1.3: Vaillant 1958, Hock 1976c (with further references).
11.2: The neogrammarian referred to at the bottom of p. 250 is Paul (1920); the Sanskrit parable comes from Patañjali's *Mahābhāṣya*.
11.3: Vennemann 1972b (rule inversion). – On p. 252 (second full paragraph), the PIE numeral should read **tri-*. In ex. (30), a more accurate formulation for the input to the change would be [+ obstr., -sib., + voice].
11.4.2: Hock 1976a. (The analogy in (32) is not a four-part analogy (in the sense of 9.1.2), but simply a proportional analogy.)
11.4.3: Thomason 1976 (contra simplification); Kiparsky 1971 (paradigm condition).
11.5: Hock 1976c. On the general issue, see also H. Andersen (ed.) 1986. – In ex. (50) and (52), the environment for [- voice] should read 'elsewhere before #'.
11.6: Kiparsky 1968b, 1971, 1973b (general); Campbell 1973, Miranda 1973 (rule loss); Hogg 1976 (rule reordering); Krishnamurti 1978b (rule reapplication).
11.7: Kisseberth 1973 (morphological opacity).
11.8: Sag 1974 and 1976 (synchronic account of Grassmann's Law in Sanskrit); Schindler 1976 (historical development of Grassmann's Law). – In ex. (66) and (67), change OHG *tage* to *taga*.

Chapter 12

General: Bréal 1897; Brown 1979, 1981; Brown & Witkowski 1983; Kronasser 1952; Leumann 1927; Ogden & Richards 1923; Schmitt (ed.) 1977; Stern 1931; Sturtevant 1907; Szemerényi 1962; Thorndike 1947; Ullmann 1957, 1962, 1966; Witkowski & Brown 1983.
12.1: In ex. (4) note that Engl. *evening star* more commonly refers to any planet visible in the western evening sky.
12.2.2: Jespersen 1921 (smallness, feminine gender, and high front vowels); see also Ultan 1978. – In ex. (19), read: *I feel a bit under the weather*; and in ex. (20) (p. 287) read: Finn. *kukko …*
12.2.3: Havers 1946.
12.3.1: Miranda 1975a (Konkani gender).

12.3.3: Gilliéron 1915, 1918 (homonym clash).
12.3.5: Recently, the model of expressions like *Italian-American* has given rise to a new term, *African-American*, which is beginning to replace the older term *black*.
12.4.2: Here and elsewhere replace the terms 'meliorization', 'meliorize', 'pejorization', 'pejorize' with 'melioration', 'meliorate', 'pejoration', 'pejorate'.
12.4.3: See also Pisani 1937, Hilmarsson 1982, Winter 1982 ('tongue').
12.5: Öhman 1951 and Trier 1931, 1973; cf. also Goodenough 1956, Lounsbury 1956 (kinship terms); De Camp 1963 (Jamaican meal time names).

Chapter 13

General: Delbrück 1893–1900; Fisiak (ed.) 1984; Hock (ed.) 1982c; Klima 1965; Lakoff 1968 (but cf. Miller 1974); Li (ed.) 1975 and 1977; P. Ramat et al. (eds.) 1980; Steever et al. (eds.) 1976; Traugott 1965, 1972. See also Faarlund To Appear, Kastovsky To Appear, Lightfoot 1976 and 1979, Stein 1990. (On Lightfoot's claims, cf., e.g., Aitchison 1980, Fischer & van der Leek 1981, Romaine 1981, and the reply in Lightfoot 1981.) See also sections 15.1.2 (with notes), 19.4, and 19.5.1 below. – More formal, mainly synchronic presentations of Relational Grammar in Perlmutter (ed.) 1983, Perlmutter & Rosen (eds.) 1984; cf. also Keenan 1975, Keenan & Comrie 1977; for historical applications see Wallace 1982, 1984 (in part).
13.2.2: Word order typology: Greenberg 1966a (general, see also Hawkins 1979 and 1983 vs. D. L. Payne 1985); Comrie 1979, Derbyshire 1977, Keenan 1978, Pullum 1981 (on O before S languages). Relative clause types in OV languages (general): Andrews 1975 (1985), Downing 1978, Hock 1989a, Keenan 1985, Langdon 1977, Chr. Lehmann 1980 and 1984. Relative clause types in Dravidian: Hock 1988c, Lakshmi Bai 1985, Ramasamy 1981, Steever 1988. Relative clause types in Indo-European: Haudry 1973, Hettrich 1988, Hock 1985c and 1989a, Chr. Lehmann 1979 and 1980, Watkins 1976. On typology in general, see also P. Ramat 1987. For adpositions etc., cf. note on 13.3.1.2 below. Further see the discussion in 19.5.1.
13.2.2: In the discussion of ex. (13), replace 'subject NP' with 'object NP'. In ex. (25), read *tamiṟ*. The example in (26) comes from Sanskrit.
13.2.3: Wackernagel 1892, with Ard 1977a, Steele 1975 and 1977a (sentence clitics in second position). See also Hock 1982d ('initial strings'), 1985a (first position = anything fronted), M. Hale 1987 (partly differing from Hock 1982d). A recent overview and appraisal in Hock 1990.
13.2.4.1: On the promotability hierarchy, see Keenan & Comrie 1977; on different types of passive cf., e.g., Keenan 1975, as well as Perlmutter (ed.) 1983, Perlmutter & Rosen (eds.) 1984, Wallace 1984. – On the development of the ergative, which is often considered derived from an earlier passive, see, e.g., Bubenik 1989, S. Anderson 1977, Hock 1986b, Klaiman 1978, J. R. Payne 1980, Pray 1976, Stump 1983b, Wallace 1982.
13.3: Givón 1977 (Hebrew VSO → SVO).
13.3.1.1: Hock 1982a with Steele 1977b and Garber 1980; cf. also Cowan 1984. Further note Delbrück 1911, Fourquet 1938, Richter 1903, Ries 1907, Rohlfs 1954. Different views: Aitchison 1979; Behaghel 1929; Friedrich 1975, 1976, 1977; Haiman 1974; Hopper 1975; Stockwell 1977, 1984; Vennemann 1974, 1975 (Indo-European languages); Givón 1975, Heine 1976, Hyman 1975, Marchese 1984 and 1986 (African languages; cf. also 16.3.6). (On other historical developments involving AUX, see Harris & Ramat (eds.) 1987.) – In recent transformational approaches, the shift of finite verbs to clause-second position ('V2') is accounted for as movement into a 'base-generated' COMP position, at the left periphery of the clause, which is (optionally) preceded by topicalized (or other fronted) elements; cf., e.g., den Besten 1983, Weerman 1989, Kiparsky In Press. Difficulties with this approach are pointed out in Hock 1990, which reaffirms the origination of 'V2' through AUX-cliticization:

'V2' arises in the 'Phonological Form' component of the grammar (not in the syntax proper), as the phonological attachment of clitic AUXes to clause-initial topicalized elements. Reinterpretations and extensions account for the appearance of other verbal elements in 'V2' and require the reanalysis of 'V2' as a syntactic phenomenon. (As observed in Hock 1990, the 'resistance to change' of dependent clauses referred to on p. 332 may well be limited to the change from SOV toward V2 or SVO.) – What is referred to as 'Behaghel's Law' on p. 332 (and pp. 338, 341, 362) is more accurately called 'Behaghel's Third Law'.

13.3.1.2: Delbrück 1893–1900 with P. K. Anderson 1979, Baldi 1979, P. Friedrich 1987 (early Indo-European 'adverbials'); Watkins 1963, 1964 (Celtic change to VSO). – On p. 341, second paragraph, last sentence, the reference should be to ex. (75'b).

13.3.1.3: Li & Thompson 1974, Li 1976 (Chinese).

13.3.1.4: Hock 1988b; cf. Ard 1976 for the term 'rebracketing'. – In ex. (81a) read: 'then he came ...'

13.3.1.5: Hock 1982b (Skt. passive); Pedersen 1907, Haiman 1983 (reflexive → passive, different view). – The claim that 'it still remains to be seen whether major syntactic processes like the passive are ever comletely lost' (p. 346, sim. p. 348) should perhaps be rephrased as follows: Major syntactic processes like the passive are rarely lost completely. What is more likely to change is their morphosyntactic 'encoding'.

13.3.1.6: Cf. also Klima 1965; Visser 1963–1973 (data).

13.3.1.7: Thurneysen 1961, Ahlqvist 1985.

13.3.1.8: Visser 1963–1973, Wende 1915 (data).

13.3.2: Quirk 1965 (synchronic data for ex. (110/111), cf. also Ard 1977a); Rohlfs 1954 (Sicilian data). For gradual nature of syntactic change: Ashby 1981, Birnbaum 1984, Chung 1977, Chung & Seiter 1980 (Clark 1976 for different analysis of Chung's data), Naro 1981, Timberlake 1977; cf. also Cole, Harbert, Hermon & Sridhar 1978, as well as Ross 1972 (synchronic data). – In ex. (112g) read: *(ne*/?) pas (∅*) de bruit*; in ex. (114), read: *piccilidḍa*.

13.3.3.1: Hock 1986b with Hock 1982b; for a similar development see Timberlake 1976.

13.3.3.2: Visser 1963–1973 (data and some of the interpretation).

13.4: Joseph 1978, 1980, 1983 (Greek/Balkan infinitive). – The Kashmiri change toward SVO (or rather, V2 [cf. the note on 13.3.1.1]) actually has progressed to a stage roughly similar to that of modern German; the table in (ex. 150) should be changed accordingly.

Chapter 14

General: Haugen 1950, Weinreich 1968.

14.1: The French expression referred to on p. 383 should read: *mariage de convenance*.

14.2: Third paragraph, read: OE *fæt* ...

14.3.1: *General:* Byarushengo 1976, Dressler 1973c, Kiparsky 1973c, Lovins 1974 and 1975, Miranda 1977, Ohso 1973, Schmitt 1973, Steinbergs 1984, van Coetsem 1988. *Etymological nativization:* Thurneysen 1961 (early Old Irish borrowings from Welsh), cf. also Winter 1970. *System-based nativization:* P. B. Pandit (personal communication 1973, cf. also apud Kiparsky 1973c). *Phonological structure/phonological rule nativization:* Fowkes 1949, cf. also Dressler 1973c (Japanese) and Thurneysen 1961 (eventual nativization of *p* in Old Irish). (A very different view in Hyman 1970a, 1970b, 1973a; but see Byarushengo 1976, Dressler 1973c, Kiparsky 1973c, Lovins 1974 and 1975, etc.)

14.3.2: Cf., e.g., Thomas 1975, 1978. – In ex. (29), note that the usual Latin form for 'abode of the dead ...' is *inferna*.

14.3.3: Arndt 1970, Whiteley 1967; cf. also Miranda 1977.

14.4: Ferguson 1959a ('diglossia'); different definitions of diglossia in Fishman 1967, Kloss 1966.
14.5.3: Eitel 1970, Forrest 1965 (Chinese); cf. also Thomas 1978 (Czech). – The examples in (43) come from Grimmelshausen's *Simplicius Simplicissimus*.
14.5.4: For German underworld argot and similar secret languages, see Kluge 1901; loans from Wolof in Black Vernacular English have been treated in Dalby 1972.

Chapter 15

General: Chambers & Trudgill 1983, Francis 1983, Mattheier 1983, Niebaum 1983 (recent surveys and discussions). See also Trudgill 1983, 1986, 1988.
15.1.1: Callary 1974 (spread of Chicago shift). – Bailey (1973) claims that in such spreads, the earliest stage of the shift extends over the largest area, with later stages covering increasingly smaller territory. In the case of the Chicago shift, this observation appears to be correct. However, such an interpretation would be difficult in the case of the Old High German sound shift (cf. 15.2.3), where the velars lag behind in the south (suggesting they began to change after the labials), while the labials lag behind in the north (suggesting the opposite scenario). Moreover, Labov's work on sound change in progress (cf. 20.10–20.13 below) shows that in certain cases (such as the Martha's Vineyard shift), a later change may 'overtake' an earlier one.
15.1.2: Labov 1965a, 1965b (Martha's Vineyard shift); Hock & Pandharipande 1976 (1978) (Sanskrit/Middle Indo-Aryan diglossia etc.); Hock 1988b (Sanskrit/Middle Indo-Aryan past tenses, *ta*-participle, ergative. (On the ergative, see also the note on 13.2.4.1 above.)
15.2: On isoglosses and their interpretation, see, e.g., Jaberg 1901 and the general literature cited for Chapter 15. See also Andersen 1988, Trudgill 1989. Although superficially similar, the so-called neolinguistic approach of Italian scholars like Bartoli (e.g., 1925, 1945) and Bonfante (1947) (see also Mańczak 1988) differs on a number of important points; for an evaluation see Hall 1946.
15.2.1: Callary 1974, Labov 1965a and 1965b.
15.2.2: Kloeke 1927, cf. also Bloomfield 1933. – On p. 435, second full paragraph, read: Compare the pockets of solid [ü] territory ... as well as the [ū/ü] enclave in the northeast ...'
15.2.3: Mitzka 1968, Schützeichel 1956. On the way in which the OHG affricates may have originated, cf. the note on 7.1 above. (See also the note on 8.6.)
15.3: J. Schmidt 1872, Meillet 1908, Southworth 1964, cf. also Gilliéron 1915, 1918. On Old High German, see Mitzka 1968. – The issue of Indo-European subgrouping is very complex, not only because of the interaction of the 'wave' and 'tree' models, but also because contact and mutual influence (both in vocabulary and in structure) can continue after dialects have become different languages, namely in situations of bilingualism (cf. Chapter 16). This is most likely the case for Baltic and Slavic, whose similarities may in part reflect common innovations in dialectal Proto-Indo-European and in part bilingual contact after Baltic and Slavic had become different languages. The existence of such alternative explanations for the Baltic and Slavic similarities is no doubt in large measure responsible for the continuing controversy over whether there was a distinct Balto-Slavic subgroup of Indo-European. For a critical evaluation, see Szemerényi 1957. (See Ringe 1988 with references for similar difficulties concerning the question of a special 'Italo-Celtic' subgroup.) – A very different approach to subgrouping, not based on common innovations but on vocabulary retention, is found in Krishnamurti et al. 1983; cf. also Cavalli-Sforza & Wang 1986.
15.4.1: Goepfert 1902, Mendels 1963 (German miners jargon); Billigmeier 1977, Brixhe 1979, Christie 1982, Cowgill 1965, Greppin 1978, Hamp 1982, van Windekens 1979 (Gk. *y- > z-).

15.4.2: Bentur 1978 (effects of orthography on Modern Hebrew phonology).
15.5: On p. 469, end of first paragraph, read: ... on the southeastern periphery of Greek-speaking territory.

Chapter 16

General: Filipović (ed.) 1988, Haugen 1950, Weinreich 1968, Thomason & Kaufman 1988. See also Trudgill 1983, 1986.
16.1.1: Kahane 1986. For Sanskrit as link language, cf. Hock & Pandharipande 1976 (1978); on modern Sanskrit, see Aralikatti 1989, Chatterji 1960, Hock 1983 and 1989b.
16.1.2: Corder 1967 ('interlanguage'); Kachru 1965, 1969, 1982, 1983a (Indian English), cf. also Kachru (ed.) 1983b. The term 'interlanguage' here is used without the negative connotations often found in applied linguistics. The extent to which the effects of interlanguage can become institutionalized can be seen, e.g., in South Asian English: South Asians returning from English-speaking countries with the aspiration of voiceless stops found in native English speech, as in *two* [thū], are told by their relatives and friends to 'stop this [ph ph ṭh ṭh]' and to say [ṭu] instead.
16.1.3: Muysken 1981a (Quechua/Spanish; different interpretation); for another 'unusual' type of 'mixed language', cf. Okell 1965.
16.1.4: *General:* Nielsen 1952, Szemerényi 1964, Tesnière 1939; see also Dressler 1973b, Winter 1973, and section 16.3 below. *Specific:* Schuchardt 1880, Ascoli 1881 (Romance/ Celtic); Martinet 1964 (Basque/Spanish); Millardet 1933 ('substrat X'); Bréal 1907 (Grimm's Law). But see also Haudricourt & Juilland 1949 (*u*-fronting), Martinet 1964 (*u*-fronting, lenition), Rohlfs 1949 (*f > h* in Italian dialects). – In ex. (7), note that Span. *veer* has become *ver*.
16.2: Ferguson 1959b, Hill 1958 ('koiné'); Thumb 1901 (Greek Koiné); Bokamba (personal communication; Lingala/Swahili data); Stucky 1978 (extreme simplification of noun class system in a Bantu koiné; different view in Fehderau 1978). See also Heine 1970, Nida & Fehderau 1970, and section 16.4 below.
16.3: General: Jakobson 1931b and Trubetzkoy 1931, cf. also Petrovici 1957. (A different view in Winter 1973.) For maintenance of different lexica, cf. Pandharipande 1982. See also section 16.1.4.
16.3.3: E.g., Hock 1988a, Schaller 1975, Solta 1980 with references (general); Joseph 1978, 1983 (infinitive).
16.3.4: *General (descriptive, modern period):* Masica 1976 and In Press, Ramanujan & Masica 1969. *(Early) Dravidian influence on Indo-Aryan:* Especially Emeneau 1954, 1955, 1956, 1962, 1980 (general); see also Bhat 1973 (retroflexion), and many others, including Thomason & Kaufman 1988. *Different view:* Cf., e.g., Hock 1975, 1984 (general), 1979 (retroflexion), 1982e (quotative); cf. also Gair 1985.
16.3.5: Gumperz & Wilson 1971. Cf. also Nadkarni 1975 on alleged convergence of Dravidian with Indo-Aryan in relative clause structures; but see Hock 1988c, Lakshmi Bai 1985, Ramasamy 1981, Steever 1988.
16.3.6: *Europe:* Haarmann 1976, Hock 1988a, Lewy 1964 (general); Hock 1982a and the other references in the note on 13.3.1.1 above (SOV → SVO via AUX-cliticization); Meillet 1909 (simple past tense replaced by compound past); see also Adams 1975, Joos 1952 (phonological convergence in sibilant system). *Africa:* Cowan 1984, Garber 1980 (change in 'peripheral' language from SOV to SVO via AUX-cliticization); cf. also Givón 1975, Hyman 1975 (different mechanism for change). A very different view is found in Heine 1976 (SOV etc. areas have innovated); cf. also Marchese 1984 and 1986. – See Campbell et al. 1988 for a Meso-American convergence area. – Regarding the Romance phenomena in ex. (39), note that the relic patterns in (39b) are especially common with the reflexive pronoun *si, se*. In (39), make the following

changes: Substitute *da mmi* 'give to me' for the Italian example in (a); and in (b), substitute Port. *vende-se êste livro* 'this book sells itself' = 'this book is sold' for the first example, and *trovan si molti uomini* 'many people are found' for the second. For Maps 13 and 14, note that the former refers to the situation of (roughly) the 16th century, while the latter depicts the modern situation. This accounts for some differences, such as in the distribution of VSO vs. SVO.

16.4: *General:* R. Andersen (ed.) 1983; Bickerton 1975, 1981; Clyne (ed.) 1981; Corne 1983; De Camp & Hancock (eds.) 1974; Dillard (ed.) 1976; Hall 1966; Heine 1970; Hesseling 1897–1933 (1979); Highfield & Valdman (eds.) 1981; K. C. Hill (ed.) 1979; Hymes (ed.) 1971; Le Page (ed.) 1961; Le Page & De Camp 1960; Mühlhäusler et al. (eds.) 1979; Muysken (ed.) 1981b; Muysken & Smith (eds.) 1986; Nida & Fehderau 1970; Reinecke et al. 1974; Romaine 1988; Schuchardt 1883–1888, 1928, 1978, 1980; Thomason & Kaufman 1988; Turner 1949; Valdman (ed.) 1977; Valdman & Highfield (eds.) 1980; Woolford & Washabaugh (eds.) 1983.

16.4.3: *General:* Schuchardt 1883–1888 (cf. Schuchardt 1928, Gilbert 1976) (general); Ferguson 1971, Ferguson & De Bose 1977 ('foreigner talk'); Baron 1977 (attempt at classifying language contact results in terms of social factors). *Specific:* Naro 1978 (Portuguese teaching of foreigner talk); Clyne 1968 and personal communication (1984), Heidelberger Forschungsprojekt ... 1975, Keim 1978 and 1984, Keim, Nikitopoulos & Repp 1982 (Gastarbeiterdeutsch). For a pidgin not arising in colonial expansion, cf. Neumann 1966 and Nichols 1980.

16.4.4: Silverstein 1972, Thomason 1983 (Chinook Jargon); Broch 1927, Fox 1983 (Russenorsk); cf. also Drechsel 1984 (Mobilian Jargon); Schuchardt 1883–1888, 1928, etc. (Lingua Franca).

16.4.5: Cf. Bickerton 1981 on Hawaiian Creole (but see Schuchardt 1883–1888, Mühlhäusler 1984 on 19th-century existence of a Hawaiian pidgin or creole); Mühlhäusler 1970, 1981, 1983, Woolford 1981, Wurm & Mühlhäusler 1985 (Tok Pisin); Baudet 1981 (West African and Haitian creole data); Le Page & De Camp 1960 ('creole continuum'). – Bickerton's (1981) general claim is that creolization is based on an innate 'bioprogram' which makes it possible to change a pidgin into a creole in one generation and which accounts for the (alleged) fact that all creoles share features absent in many of the relevant substrate and superstrate languages. In Bickerton's view, interlanguage influence from other languages (whether substrate or superstrate) is minimal. This view, especially the rejection of the significance of substrates, has elicited a fair amount of criticism; cf., e.g., Boretzky 1983, Muysken & Smith (eds.) 1986, Singler 1988. Much of the criticism tries to show that we must admit substratal or superstratal influence; but this does not necessarily invalidate the 'bioprogram' hypothesis, since the two phenomena might coexist. Significantly, however, many of the creole features that Bickerton specifically attributes to his 'bioprogram' can be explained as superstratal. A case in point is the fact that many creoles, whether based on English or other languages, have 'pleonastic negation' or 'negation spread'. Bickerton claims that this feature can be attributed only to the 'bioprogram', but the phenomenon is found in all the relevant European superstrate languages, not only in vernacular English (*I don't know nothing*), but with variations also in French (*Je ne sais rien*) and Spanish and Portuguese (cf. Span. *(Yo) no sé nada*). (The fact that present-day educated English rejects negation spread is not relevant, since most of the slave traders must have spoken vernacular English.)

16.4.6: Cf., e.g., Dillard 1976, Turner 1949. For the behavior of the copula in Black Vernacular English see Labov 1969.

16.5: Dressler 1972, 1981; Dressler & Wodak (eds.) 1977; Dorian 1978, 1981, (ed.) 1989; Hock 1983, In Press; A. Schmidt 1985.

Chapter 17
General: Anttila 1973, Austerlitz 1986, Chafe 1959, J. Marchand 1956, Miranda 1975b, Winter 1986.
17.2: For the question of whether rules can be reconstructed directly, see section 19.4 with notes.
17.3: *General:* Cf. especially Miranda 1975b. *PIE* ə, *laryngeals:* de Saussure 1879, Kuryłowicz 1927; cf. also Polomé 1965, Mayrhofer 1986, Bammesberger (ed.) 1988, Vennemann (ed.) 1990 (part 2). (Mayrhofer 1981, 1982 argues that de Saussure's reconstruction was comparative, not internal. A more correct appraisal is that the reconstruction was internal, but based on the results of comparative reconstruction.) – For the 'Indo-Semitic connection', see, e.g., Møller 1907 and 1917, Cuny 1946, and the additional references in the note on 18.5 below. – The Sanskrit data in this section preserve only indirect traces of the full and extended grades: As noted in 5.1.5 (ex. (32)), non-low PIE vowels merged into low vowels in Sanskrit. – An alternative term for 'ablaut' is 'apophony'.

Chapter 18
General: Meillet 1925, as well as Baldi (ed.) 1990, Greenberg 1957, Haas 1960, Hoenigswald 1973a, Joly (ed.) 1988.
Introductory: Jones 1786, Sajnovics 1770; cf. also Gyármathi 1799.
18.1: That the correspondence Mal. *mata* : Mod. Gk. *mati* is entirely fortuitous becomes clear once we examine the history of Mod. Gk. *mati*. The word derives from Class. Gk. *ommátion*, through loss of the initial *o* by aphaeresis and degemination of the resulting initial *mm-* (cf. ex. (93) in section 5.3.4). Now, it is the lost initial *om-* (< **op-* < **okʷ-*) which was the original carrier of the meaning 'eye'; cf. the related form *ṓp-s* 'eye' (PIE *ṓkʷ-s). For similar reasons, the similarities in the Turkish and Basque words for 'one', 'head', and 'mouth' in Chart 1.3 (p. 10), viz. *bir* : *bat*, *baš* : *bürü*, *aɣïz* : *aho*, are most likely due to chance. – Note further that if modern Indo-European languages of South Asia, such as Hindi, are included in Chart 1.3, only the numerals 'two' (*dō*) and 'three' (*tīn*), and possibly the word for 'nose' (*nākh*) look similar to the corresponding words in the related languages of Europe (cf., e.g., Ru. *dva*, *trʲi*, *nos*). On the other hand, the numeral 'one' (*ēk*), and possibly the words for 'ear' (*kān*) and 'nose' (*nākh*) are similar to the corresponding Uralic words, especially those of Finnish and Estonian (cf., e.g, Finn. *üksi*, *korva*, *nenä*, Est. *üks*, *kõrv* [corrected for *wilya-pea*], cf. the note on 1.4], *nina*). In the case of 'one', the similarity (*Vk* : *Vk-*) is clearly accidental: The PIE root for 'one' is **oy-*, and the velar stop of Hindi *ēk* (Skt. *ē-ka-* < PIE **oy-ko-*) is suffixal, just like the *-n-* of the related European languages (< PIE **oy-no-*). The situation is similar for the word for 'ear', but for different reasons: The PIE root was **(a)us-* (cf. Chart 15.2, p. 443); Skt. *karṇa-* > Hindi *kān* constitutes a regional innovation. – The Italian words for 'father' and 'mother' on p. 558 should read *papà* and *mamma*; similarly on p. 560.
18.2: The extent to which borrowing can lead to the appearance of misleading correspondences cannot be underestimated: A fair amount of vocabulary which from a modern, western perspective is not technical, but relatively basic, at one time designated innovations in material culture. And such 'cultural borrowings' may (through borrowing) spread over extensive areas. For instance Engl. *sugar* is ultimately derived from Skt. *śarkara-* 'sand, grit; ground sugar' (as opposed to *khaṇḍa-* 'piece, chunk; piece of unground sugar', which is the ultimate source of Engl. *candy*). The route of borrowing apparently led through Persia (cf. Pers. *shakar*) to Arabic territory (Ar. *sukkar*), from where the word spread into the various European languages, cf. also Fr. *sucre*, Germ. *Zucker*, etc. If such borrowings are made very early, it becomes difficult to distinguish the resulting correspondences (e.g., Skt. *śarkara-* :

Pers. *shakar*, etc.) from genuine cognates. Some of these can be eliminated after the completion of comparative reconstruction; but as shown in section 18.8 below, even then it is not always clear whether given correspondences should be considered inherited or the results of early borrowing. – Syntactic features are considered relevant in Fokos-Fuchs 1962.

18.5: Aalto 1972, Andronov 1972, Austerlitz 1972, Tyler 1968 (Dravidian and Uralic); Collinder 1965, 1966, 1974 (Uralic and Indo-European). Other distant relationships have been proposed, including Indo-European and Semitic/Afro-Asiatic (Cuny 1946, Møller 1907 and 1917), and 'Nostratic', which variously includes Indo-European, Uralic, Afro-Asiatic, Caucasic languages (such as Georgian), Altaic, etc. (Bomhard 1984, Collinder 1974, Illič-Svityč 1971 and 1976, cf. also Birnbaum [no date]). Even larger groupings are being proposed, mainly on the basis of vocabulary comparisons; cf. especially Greenberg 1987 and 1989; but see Campbell 1988, Matisoff 1990, and similar responses. The ease with which chance vocabulary correspondences can be found has been demonstrated, e.g., by Dyen 1970. Cf. additional references in Matisoff 1990, as well as the notes on 18.1 and 18.2 above concerning accidental or misleading vocabulary correspondences. – Greenberg's approach is similar to that of 'lexicostatistics' and the related field of 'glottochronology', which uses lexical correspondences to determine the time depth between presumably related present-day languages and their putative ancestors. (For these approaches, see, e.g., Swadesh 1967, Dyen 1973.) The value of glottochronology has been questioned in many publications; cf., e.g., Bergsland & Vogt 1962, Fodor 1965, Hock 1976c. However, lexicostatistical and similar lexically based statistical approaches continue to find adherents; cf., in addition to Greenberg, Anttila 1988, Cavalli-Sforza & Wang 1986, Embleton 1986, Tischler 1973.

18.6: For Dravidian and Elamite, see the data, discussion, and proposed reconstruction in MacAlpin 1974 and 1975 (the latter including extensive discussion by other scholars, largely negative). A completely different reconstruction is proposed in MacAlpin 1981.

18.7: *General:* J. Schmidt 1872; cf. also Dyen 1969; Hall 1960 (and 1976); Meillet 1908; Pulgram 1953, 1959, 1961. On Indo-European subgrouping, see the note on 15.3 above. See also Schleicher 1868, Lehmann & Zgusta 1979 for attempts to write a story in reconstructed PIE. *PIE vowel system:* For a speculative return to the three-vowel system see Cowgill 1968. The earlier revision from a three-vowel to a five-vowel system reflected the realization (referred to as the 'Law of Palatals') that Indo-Iranian palatalization took place before *a*-vowels corresponding to *e*-vowels in the other Indo-European languages, but not before *a*-vowels corresponding to (non-front) *a*- or *o*-vowels in the other languages. On the question of who discovered the 'Law of Palatals', cf. Collinge 1987. – On p. 568, third paragraph, read: Fr. *il* 'he', *le* 'him', *lui* '(to) him'.

18.8: *General:* Cf., e.g., Thieme 1954, Friedrich 1970, but also Diebold 1988, Hoenigswald 1956, Scherer 1956. A different approach in Shevoroshkin 1987. The discussion goes back to the 19th century, cf., e.g., Schrader 1886, 1906–1907. Further, note Mańczak 1984 on the original homeland of PIE, and Watkins 1989 on the reconstruction of poetic language and even poetic formulas. – A new view of Proto-Indo-European culture, proposed by Renfrew (1987), claims that the present old-world distribution of Indo-European languages generally continues the original situation and that there were no significant migrations or invasions into territories held by speakers of other languages. This view is in conflict with what the early Indo-Europeans tell us about their prehistory, and with the testimony of early attested history. (Note, e.g., the ransacking of Rome and Delphi by the Celts, the imperialist expansions of the Romans, the raids on the Roman Empire by Germanic and other tribes, or the Slavic incursions into the Byzantine empire and much of present-day

Russia.) For evaluations, see also Jasanoff 1988, Szemerényi 1989. *Cautions against merely possible reconstructions:* Bloomfield apud Greenberg 1957, Hock 1985d.
18.9: For subgrouping, cf., e.g., Hoenigswald 1966 and the note on section 15.3 above. For 'reconstructing backward', see the note on section 19.3.

Chapter 19
General: See the notes on Chapter 18; cf. also Birnbaum [no date]. – Boretzky (1981) claims that reconstruction is not possible in many 'exotic' languages, but see Hoenigswald 1990, Schweiger 1984.
19.1.1 & 19.1.6: For parallelism with 'velars', cf., e.g., Hock 1976c. On laryngeals in general see also Bammesberger (ed.) 1988, Mayrhofer 1986. For the 'velar series' controversy, see, e.g., Hamp 1989, Hock 1976c, Kuryłowicz 1971, Magnusson 1967, Melchert 1987, Miller 1976, Szemerényi 1970.
19.1.2 & 19.1.7: Cf. Meillet 1925; for the Iranian developments see also Hock 1976b. Different interpretations of the Armenian situation in Kordtlandt 1989, Szemerényi 1985, etc.
19.1.3 & 19.1.8: Winter 1962.
19.2: Cf. also Hall 1950, Anttila 1972. – In ex. (22), note that Avest. *yug əm* is only indirectly attested and delete Avest. *id əm*. On p. 605, second paragraph after (47), read: True, changes (48) and (57) might be common innovations of English and Norse; and (49), (56), and (58) might be shared by English, Gothic, and Old Norse. P. 606, first ex. under Old Norse: renumber as (57).
19.3: For 'reconstructing backward', cf. Watkins 1963 (who, from a different perspective, uses the term 'reconstructing forward'). – P. 608, fourth paragraph, read: *veɣa, vaɣu.*
19.4: *Examples of syntactic reconstruction:* Behaghel 1929; Delbrück 1893–1900, 1911; Dressler 1969, 1971, 1973a; Fourquet 1938; Hopper 1975; see also below. *Syntactic reconstruction impossible:* Campbell & Mithun 1980; Jeffers 1976; Lightfoot 1979, 1980a, 1980b; Mithun & Campbell 1982; Winter 1984; but see Miranda 1978, Vincent 1980, as well as below. *Reconstruction of rules/synchronically most productive patterns:* Friedrich 1975, 1976, 1977; but see Hock 1985d, Watkins 1976. For phonological reconstruction, cf. also Kiparsky 1973d vs. Miller 1977c, Szemerényi 1975b. *Reconstruction on the basis of archaisms:* Birnbaum [no date], Hetzron 1976, Hock 1985d, Ivanov 1965, Robertson 1975, Watkins 1976; cf. also Eckert 1978, Hoenigswald 1983. For different approaches, see Costello 1983, Gulstad 1974, Hall 1968. Compare also Szemerényi 1975a. *Romance clitics:* Givón 1971; but cf. Pearce 1984 and 1990, Ramsden 1963, Wanner 1985. – In ex. (65), read: *rubato;* in (66b), last line, substitute *tacevano tutti* 'all were silent'; in (67), substitute *da mmi* 'give to me' for the Italian example in (a), and substitute Port. *vende-se êste livro* 'this book sells itself' = 'this book is sold' and *trovan si molti uomini* 'many people are found' for the first and second examples in (b), respectively; in (71), read: *piccili̠dda.*
19.5: General: Jakobson 1958 vs. Kuipers 1968; cf. also Dunkel 1981.
19.5.1: *Typological approach:* Friedrich 1975, 1976, 1977; Houben 1977; W. P. Lehmann 1974, 1982; Miller 1975. Cf. also Hawkins 1979, 1983 (vs. D. L. Payne 1985), Parker 1980. *Counterarguments:* Ard 1977b, Birnbaum 1984, Hock 1985c and 1985d, Smith 1981, Watkins 1976. Cf. also P. K. Anderson 1979, Baldi 1979, Delbrück 1893–1909 (IE adpositions); Comrie 1979, Derbyshire 1977, Pullum 1981 (rare O before S languages). For relative clause strategies in SOV languages, see the note on 13.2.2 above. – In (78), read: *tamir;* and note that ex. (79) is from Sanskrit.
19.5.2:*Typological approach:* Gamkrelidze 1976, 1981, 1988; Gamkrelidze & Ivanov 1973; Hopper 1977; Miller 1977a, 1977b; Vennemann 1984, (ed.) 1989; also Vennemann (ed.) 1990 (part 1); for the Armenian stop system see Vogt 1958. Arguments for

returning to a system with voiceless (beside voiced) aspirates in Szemerényi 1967, 1970 (cf. also Back 1979). Yet a different view in Huld 1986 (traditional aspirates reconstructed as 'ejectives', voiced as 'lenis', voiceless as 'fortis'; moreover, traditional velars are reconstructed as uvulars, and labials as "labiouvulars"). *Counterarguments and evaluations:* Allen 1976, Birnbaum [no date], Collinge 1986, Dunkel 1981, Green 1983. Cf. also Haider 1985. For data and discussion on relevant Polynesian languages, see Dempwolff 1924–1925, Gonda 1950, Horne 1961, Prentice 1974, Stevens 1968. See also Ruhlen 1975.

Chapter 20

20.1–3: Osthoff & Brugmann 1878, Paul 1920; cf. also Christy 1983 and Jankowsky 1972, 1976. (According to a minority view, linguistic change brings about improvement, rather than decay; cf. Jespersen 1941, Whitney 1877. Although different in important details, this view is similar to the early generativists' belief that all linguistic change leads to simplification.)

20.3: *Child language acquisition:* Cf. also H. Andersen 1973, Hsieh 1971, Locke 1983, Stampe 1969; but see Bybee & Slobin 1982, Vihman 1980 on differences between child language acquisition and linguistic change (cf. also Romaine 1989). *[r] > [R]:* Cf., e.g., Howell 1985 and 1987 (including evidence that uvular [R] occurred in German dialects before the time of Louis XIV).

20.4: See Chapter 8 with notes.

20.5: Cf. Hock 1985d.

20.6.1: Cf., e.g., King 1969b. See also Miranda 1974b.

20.6.2: Cf. section 6.3 with notes.

20.6.3–20.7: Cf. Chapter 11 with notes.

20.8: Cf., e.g., Schneider 1973, Wilbur 1977; see also Gilliéron 1915 and 1918.

20.9: Cf. Schuchardt 1885, 1928 with Vennemann & Wilbur 1972; further note Sturtevant 1907, Vennemann 1972a (analogical formulation); Sapir 1921 ($\bar{u}$-shortening; cf. also Dickerson 1975); Gauchat 1905, Hermann 1929 and 1931. See also Anttila 1972; Cerrón-Palomino 1974, 1977; Hermann 1931; Kiparsky 1989; Langdon 1975; Malkiel 1968, 1976, 1979; Melchert 1975; Postal 1968; Sihler 1977.

20.10: Labov 1965a, 1965b, 1966a, 1966b, 1972b, 1981, 1982, as well as Weinreich, Labov & Herzog 1968. See also Habick 1980, Labov, Yaeger & Steiner 1972; Trudgill 1971, as well as Bright & Ramanujan 1964, Householder 1983. Opposing/different recent views: H. Andersen 1973, Bhat 1970 and 1972, Dressler 1976 and 1982, Miranda 1974b, Traugott & Romaine 1985; cf. also the next section and the note on 20.14 below.

20.11: Wang 1969, (ed.) 1977, as well as Chen & Wang 1975, Hsieh 1971, Krishnamurti 1977 and 1978a, Lyovin 1971, Wang & Cheng 1970 and 1971. For critical evaluation see Hashimoto 1981, Hock 1976a.

20.12: Labov 1981, as well as Kiparsky 1980. But see also Janson 1983. For the notion that irregular sound change is more perceptible, cf. Paul 1920.

20.13: See also Wang 1969, Timmers 1977.

20.14: Variable rules or systems in non-phonetic change: Hock 1979, 1980 (analogical change); Labov 1966a (dialect shift); Asbhy 1981, Birnbaum 1984, Chung 1977, Chung & Seiter 1980, Kroch 1989, Naro 1981, Romaine 1984, Timberlake 1977 (syntactic change). For variability between systems, see also Hankamer 1977, Kroch 1989 (syntax); Kiparsky 1989, M. Ohala 1974 (phonology).

It would be inaccurate to claim that the Labovian approach has superseded all earlier approaches. It coexists with a number of other approaches, including the following: (i) A functionalist approach (e.g., Kiparsky 1989); but note Labov's (1982) demonstration that such an approach fails in certain cases. (ii) An account going back to Zipf

(1929) which views change as sensitive to frequency of use (cf. Fidelholtz 1975, Mańczak 1987); but the evidence adduced in favor of this view is limited to phonology and in the majority of cases involves cases of clitic weakening or the irregular reduction in forms of address discussed in 3.7 above. (iii) A 'semiotic' approach (e.g. Anttila 1972 and 1988, Dressler 1982 and 1985, Mayerthaler 1980, Plank 1979); but see the reservations in Hock 1985c vis-à-vis Dressler 1982. Among others, note also Coseriu 1958, 1970 (often cited by adherents of the semiotic approach) and H. Lüdtke (ed.) 1980.

References

Abbreviations

AST = Amsterdam Studies in the Theory and History of Linguistic Science, Series IV: Current Issues in Linguistic Theory. Amsterdam: Benjamins.
BLS = Proceedings of the ...th Annual Meeting of the Berkeley Linguistic Society.
BSL = Bulletin de la Société de Linguistique de Paris.
CLS = (a) Papers from the ...th Regional Meeting of the Chicago Linguistic Society; (b) Chicago Linguistic Society (publisher).
IF = Indogermanische Forschungen.
IJAL = International Journal of American Linguistics.
IJSL = International Journal of the Sociology of Language.
IULC = Indiana University Linguistics Club (publisher).
JIES = Journal of Indo-European Studies.
LIn = Linguistic Inquiry.
LSA = Linguistic Society of America.
KZ = Zeitschrift für vergleichende Sprachforschung.
OSUWP = Ohio State University Working Papers in Linguistics.
POLA = Project on Linguistic Analysis. Berkeley: University of California Phonology Laboratory.
RPLB = Report of the Phonology Laboratory, Berkeley.
SLS = Studies in the Linguistic Sciences. Urbana: Department of Linguistics, University of Illinois.
Stanford
Working Papers = Working Papers on Language Universals, Stanford University.
TCLP = Travaux du Cercle Linguistique de Prague.

Aalto, Pentti
    1972   The alleged affinity of Dravidian and Fenno-Ugrian. In: Asher (ed.) 1972: 262–266.
Abramson, Arthur S.
    1977   Laryngeal timing in consonant distinctions. Phonetica 34: 295–303.
Acson, Veneeta Z., and Richard L. Leed (eds.)
    1985   For Gordon Fairbanks. (Oceanic Linguistics, Special Publication 20.) Honolulu: University of Hawaii Press.
Adams, Douglas Q.
    1975   The distribution of retracted sibilants in medieval Europe. Language 51: 282–292.
Ahlqvist, Anders
    1982   (ed.) Papers from the 5th International Conference on Historical Linguistics. (= AST 21)
    1985   The syntax of relative marking in Old Irish. Folia Linguistica Historica 6: 332–346.

Aitchison, Jean
1979   The order of word order change. Transactions of the Philological Society 1979: 43–65.
1980   Review of Lightfoot 1979. Linguistics 18: 1/2 (= 227/228): 137–146.
1981   Language change: progress or decay? Fontana Paperbacks.
Allen, W. Sidney
1958   Some problems of palatalization in Greek. Lingua 7: 11–33.
1976   The PIE aspirates: Phonetic and typological factors in reconstruction. In: Juilland et al. (eds.) 1976: 237–247.
Andersen, Henning
1973   Abductive and deductive change. Language 49: 765–793. (Repr. in Baldi & Werth (eds.) 1978.)
1986   (ed.) Sandhi phenomena in the languages of Europe. Berlin: Mouton de Gruyter.
1987   From auxiliary to desinence. In: Harris & Ramat (eds.) 1987: 21–51.
1988   Center and periphery: adoption, diffusion, and spread. In: Fisiak (ed.) 1988: 39–84.
Andersen, Roger (ed.)
1983   Pidginization and creolization as language acquisition. Rowley, MA: Newbury House.
Anderson, J. M., and C. Jones (eds.)
1974 (a,b) Historical linguistics. (Proceedings of the First International Conference on Historical Linguistics.) 2 volumes. Amsterdam: North Holland. [Vol. 1 = a; vol. 2 = b.]
Anderson, Paul Kent
1979   Word order typology and prepositions in Old Indic. In: Festschrift für Oswald Szemerényi, ed. by Bela Brogyanyi, 1: 23–34. (= AST 11:1)
Anderson, Stephen R.
1976   Nasal consonants and the internal structure of segments. Language 52: 326–344.
1977   On mechanisms by which languages become ergative. In: Li (ed.) 1977: 317–364.
Andrews, Avery D., III
1975 (1985) Studies in the syntax of relative and comparative clauses. Cambridge: MIT Ph.D. dissertation in Linguistics. (Repr. in 'lightly retouched version', 1985, New York & London: Garland.)
Andronov, M.
1972   Comparative studies on the nature of Dravido-Uralian parallels. In: Asher (ed.) 1972: 267–277.
Antonsen, Elmer H.
1967   On the origin of the Old English digraph spellings. Studies in Linguistics 19: 5–17.
Antonsen, Elmer H., and Hans Henrich Hock (eds.)
1985   Germanic linguistics II: Papers from the Second Symposium on

Germanic Linguistics, University of Illinois at Urbana-Champaign, 3–4 October 1986. Bloomington: IULC.

Anttila, Raimo
1972   An introduction to historical and comparative linguistics. New York: Macmillan.
1973   Internal reconstruction and Finno-Ugric (Finnish). In: Sebeok (ed.) 1973: 317–353. (Repr. as v. 44 of Opuscula Instituti Linguae Fennicae Universitatis Helsingiensis.)
1975   Affective vocabulary in Finnish: An(other) invitation. Ural-Altaische Jahrbücher 47: 10–19.
1977   Analogy. The Hague: Mouton.
1988   Historical and comparative linguistics. [= Revised edition of Anttila 1972.] Amsterdam: Benjamins.

Anttila, Raimo, and W. A. Brewer
1977   Analogy: a basic bibliography. (Amsterdam Studies in the Theory and History of Linguistic Science, Series 5, v. 1.) Amsterdam: Benjamins.

Anwar, Mohamed S.
1974   Consonant devoicing at word boundary as assimilation. Language Sciences 32: 6–12.

Aralikatti, R. N.
1989   Spoken Sanskrit in India: a study of sentence patterns. Tirupati, AP (India): Kendriya Sanskrit Vidyapeetha.

Arbeitman, Yoël L., and Allan R. Bomhard (eds.)
1981   Bono homini donum: Essays in historical linguistics in honor of J. Alexander Kerns. (= AST 16: 1, 2 with consecutive pagination.)

Ard, William J.
1976   Rebracketing in diachronic syntax and Montague Grammar. In: Steever et al. (eds.) 1976: 1–8.
1977 (a) Raising and word order in diachronic syntax. Bloomington: IULC.
1977 (b) Methodological problems in the use of typologies in diachronic syntax. Bloomington: IULC.

Arlotto, Anthony
1972   Introduction to historical linguistics. Boston: Houghton-Mifflin. (Repr. 1981, Washington, D.C.: University Press of America.)

Árnason, Kristján
1980   Quantity in historical phonology. Cambridge: University Press.

Arndt, W. W.
1970   Nonrandom assignment of loan words: German noun gender. Word 26: 244–253.

Ascoli, G. I.
1881   Lettere glottologiche. Rivista di filologia e d'istruzione classica 10: 1–71.

Ashby, William J.
1981   The loss of the negative particle *ne* in French. Language 57: 674–687.

684   *References*

Asher, R. E. (ed.)
1972   Proceedings of the Second International Conference Seminar of
          Tamil Studies, Madras, 1968, v. 1. Madras: International Asso-
          ciation of Tamil Research.
Austerlitz, Robert
1972   Long-range comparisons of Tamil and Dravidian with other
          language families in Eurasia. In: Asher (ed.) 1972: 254–261.
1986   Contrasting fact with fiction: The common denominator in
          internal reconstruction, with a bibliography. In: Kastovsky &
          Szwedek (eds.) 1986: 183–192.

Back, Michael
1979   Die Rekonstruktion des idg. Verschlußlautsystems im Lichte
          der einzelsprachlichen Veränderungen. KZ 93: 179–195.
Bailey, Charles-James N.
1973   Variation and linguistic theory. Washington, DC: Center for
          Applied Linguistics.
Baldi, Philip
1979   Typology and the Indo-European prepositions. IF 84: 49–61.
1983   An introduction to the Indo-European languages. Carbondale
          and Edwardsville: Southern Illinois University Press.
1990   (ed.) Linguistic change and reconstruction methodology. Ber-
          lin: Mouton de Gruyter.
Baldi, Philip, and R. N. Werth (eds.)
1978   Readings in historical phonology. University Park: Pennsylva-
          nia State University Press.
Bammesberger, Alfred (ed.)
1988   Die Laryngaltheorie und die Rekonstruktion des indo-
          germanischen Laut- und Formensystems. Heidelberg: Winter.
Baron, Naomi S.
1977   Trade jargons and pidgins: a functionalist approach. Journal of
          Creole Studies 1977: 5–28.
Bartoli, Matteo
1925   Introduzione alla neolinguistica. (Biblioteca dell' 'archivum
          romanicum', ser. 2, vol. 12.) Genève: Olschki.
1945   Saggi di linguistica spaziale. Torino: Bona.
Baudet, Martha M.
1981   Identifying the African grammatical base of the Caribbean
          creoles. In: Highfield & Valdman (eds.) 1981: 104–117.
Becker, Lee A.
1977 (a) Leftward movement of high tone. Paper at LSA Annual Meet-
          ing.
1977 (b) Perceptually motivated phonetic change. CLS 13: 45–59.
1978   The effects of the fall of the jers on the prosodic system of
          Proto-Serbo-Croatian. Urbana: University of Illinois Ph.D.
          dissertation in Slavic.

Beddor, Patrice S.
1983   Phonological and phonetic effects of nasalization on vowel height. Bloomington: IULC.
Behaghel, Otto
1929   Zur Stellung des Verbs im Germanischen und Indogermanischen. KZ 56: 276–281.
Benediktsson, Hreinn
1963   Some aspects of Nordic umlaut and breaking. Language 39: 409–431.
Bentur, Esther
1978   Some effects of orthography on the linguistic knowledge of Modern Hebrew speakers. Urbana: University of Illinois Ph.D. dissertation in Linguistics.
Benveniste, Émile
1968   Mutations of linguistic categories. In: Lehmann & Malkiel (eds.) 1968: 83–94.
Bergsland, Knut, and Hans Vogt
1962   On the validity of glottochronology. Current Anthropology 3: 115–153.
Best, K.-H.
1973   Probleme der Analogieforschung. München: Hueber.
Besten, Hans den
1983   On the interaction of root transformations and lexical deletive rules. In: On the formal syntax of the Westgermania, ed. by W. Abraham, 47–131. Amsterdam: Benjamins.
Bhat, D. N. S.
1970   Age-grading and sound change. Word 26: 262–270.
1972   Sound change. Poona: Bhasha Prakashan.
1973   Retroflexion: an areal feature. Stanford Working Papers 13: 27–67.
Bhatia, Tej K.
1975   The evolution of tone in Punjabi. SLS 5: 2: 12–24.
Bickerton, Derek
1975   Dynamics of a creole system. Cambridge: University Press.
1981   Roots of language. Ann Arbor, MI: Karoma.
Billigmeier, Jon Christian
1977   The origin of the dual reflex of initial consonantal Indo-European *y in Greek. JIES 4: 221–231.
Birnbaum, Henrik
1984   Notes on syntactic change. In: Fisiak (ed.) 1984: 25–46.
(no date) Linguistic reconstruction: its potentials and limitations in new perspective. (= JIES Monograph 2)
Birnbaum, Henrik, and Jaan Puhvel (eds.)
1966   Ancient Indo-European dialects. Berkeley: University of California Press.
Bloomfield, Leonard
1933   Language. New York: Holt, Rinehart & Winston. (1984 repr., Chicago University Press; chapters on historical linguistics is-

sued separately as 'Language history', New York: Holt, Rinehart & Winston, 1965.)

Bolinger, D.
1964   Intonation as a universal. In: Proceedings of the 9th International Congress of Linguists, 833–845. The Hague: Mouton.

Bomhard, A. R.
1984   Toward Proto-Nostratic: a new beginning in the reconstruction of Proto-Indo-European and Proto-Afro-Asiatic. (= AST 27)

Bonebrake, Veronica
1979   Historical labial-velar changes in Germanic. (= Umeå Studies in the Humanities, 29.)

Bonfante, Giuliano
1947   The neolinguistic position. Language 23: 344–375.

Boretzky, Norbert
1977   Einführung in die historische Linguistik. Reinbek: Rowohlt.
1981   Das indogermanistische Sprachwandelmodell und Wandel in exotischen Sprachen. KZ 95: 49–80.
1983   Kreolsprachen, Substrate und Sprachwandel. Wiesbaden: Harrassowitz.

Bréal, Michel
1897   Essai de sémantique. Paris: Hachette. (Engl. transl. 'Semantics: studies in the science of meaning.' New York: Dover, 1964.)
190   La loi de Grimm. La revue de Paris 14: 6: 52–69.

Breivik, Leiv E., and Ernst H. Jahr (eds.)
1989   Language change: contributions to the study of its causes. Berlin: Mouton de Gruyter.

Bremer, Otto
1894   Relative Sprachchronologie. IF 4: 8–31.

Bright, William, and A. K. Ramanujan
1964   Sociolinguistic variation and language change. In: Proceedings of the 9th International Congress of Linguists, 1107–1112. The Hague: Mouton.

Brixhe, Claude
1979   Sociolinguistique et langues anciennes: à propos de quelques traitements irréguliers en grec. BSL 74: 1: 237–259.

Broch, Olaf
1927   Russenorsk. Archiv für slavische Philologie 41: 209–262.

Brown, Cecil H.
1979   A theory of lexical change (with examples from folk biology, human anatomical partonomy, and other domains). Anthropological Linguistics 21: 257–276.
1981   Growth and development of folk zoological life-forms in Polynesian languages. The Journal of the Polynesian Society 90: 83–111.

Brown, Cecil H., and Stanley R. Witkowski
1983   Polysemy, lexical change, and cultural importance. Man: 18. 72–89.

Brugmann, Karl
1897–1916 Vergleichende Laut-, Stammbildungs- und Flexionslehre der indogermanischen Sprachen. 2 volumes in 5. Straßburg: Trübner. [= Revised edition of Brugmann & Delbrück 1886–1900, vols. 1 and 2.]
1904   Kurze vergleichende Grammatik der indogermanischen Sprachen. Straßburg: Trübner.
1909   Das Wesen der lautlichen Dissimilation. Abhandlungen der Sächsischen Gesellschaft der Wissenschaften, phil.-hist. Klasse 27: 139–178.
Brugmann, Karl, and Bertold Delbrück
1886–1900 Grundriß der vergleichenden Grammatik der indogermanischen Sprachen. 5 vols. Straßburg: Trübner. [Vols. 3–5 = Delbrück 1893–1900.]
Bubenik, Vit
1989   An interpretation of split ergativity in Indo-Iranian languages. Diachronica 6: 181–212.
Byarushengo, Ernest Rugwa
1976   Strategies in loan phonology. BLS 1976: 78–88.
Bybee, Joan L.
1980   Morphophonemic change from inside and outside the paradigm. Lingua 50: 1/2: 45–59.
Bybee, Joan L., and Dan I. Slobin
1982   Why small children cannot change language on their own: Suggestions from the English past tense. In: Ahlqvist (ed.) 1982: 29–37.
Bynon, Theodora
1977   Historical linguistics. Cambridge: University Press.

Callary, Robert E.
1974   Phonological change and the development of an urban dialect in Illinois. In: Language in society, ed. by Dell Hymes, 4: 155–169. Cambridge: University Press.
Campbell, Lyle
1973   Rule loss and rule obliteration. In: Mid-America Linguistics Conference Papers, 1972, ed. by J. H. Battle and J. Schweitzer, 193–206. Stillwater: Oklahoma State University.
1988   Review article on Greenberg 1987. Language 64: 591–615.
Campbell, Lyle, et al.
1986   Meso-America as a linguistic area. Language 62: 530–570.
Campbell, Lyle, and Marianne Mithun
1980   The priorities and pitfalls of syntactic reconstruction. Folia Linguistica Historica 1: 19–40.
Cardona, George
1968   On haplology in Indo-European. Philadelphia: University of Pennsylvania Press.
Cardona, George, and Norman Zide (eds.)
1987   Festschrift for Henry Hoenigswald. Tübingen: Narr.

Cavalli-Sforza, L., and W. S-Y. Wang
1986   Spatial distance and lexical replacement. Language 62: 38–55.
Cerrón-Palomino, Rodolfo
1974   Morphologically conditioned changes in Wanka Quechua. SLS
         4: 2: 40–75.
1977   Cambios gramaticalmente condicionados en quechua: Una
         desconfirmación de la teoría neogramática del cambio fonético.
         Lexis: Revista de Lingüística y Literatura 1: 163–84. (Lima:
         Departamento de Humanidades, Pontífica Universidad Católica
         del Perú.)
Chafe, Wallace L.
1959   Internal reconstruction in Seneca. Language 35: 477–495.
Chambers, J. K., and Peter Trudgill
1983   Dialectology. Cambridge: University Press.
Chatterji, S. K.
1960   The pronunciation of Sanskrit. Indian Linguistics 21: 61–82.
Chen, M. Y., and William S.-Y. Wang
1975   Sound change: actuation and implementation. Language 51:
         255–281.
Cherubim, D. (ed.)
1975   Sprachwandel: Reader zur diachronischen Sprachwissenschaft.
         Berlin: de Gruyter.
Christie, William M., Jr.
1976   (ed.) Current progress in historical linguistics. Amsterdam:
         North Holland.
1982   Philology and historical linguistics. In: Ahlqvist (ed.) 1982:
         414–424.
Christy, Thomas Craig
1983   Uniformitarianism in linguistics. (Amsterdam Studies in the
         Theory and History of Linguistic Science, Series 3, v. 25.)
Chung, Sandra
1977   On the gradual nature of syntactic change. In: Li (ed.) 1977:
         5–56.
Chung, Sandra, and W. J. Seiter
1980   The history of raising and relativization in Polynesian. Language
         56: 622–638.
Clark, Ross
1976   Aspects of Proto-Polynesian syntax. Te Reo Monographs, Lin-
         guistic Society of New Zealand.
Clements, George N.
1982   Compensatory lengthening. Bloomington: IULC.
Clyne, Michael
1968   Zum Pidgin-Deutsch der Gastarbeiter. Zeitschrift für
         Mundartforschung 35: 130–139.
1981   (ed.) Foreigner talk. (= IJSL 28)
Cole, Peter, Wayne Harbert, Gabriella Hermon, and S. N. Sridhar
1978   On the acquisition of subjecthood. SLS 8: 1: 42–71. (Slightly
         expanded version in Language 56: 719–743, 1980.)

Collinder, Björn
1965   Hat das Uralische Verwandte? Eine sprachvergleichende
        Untersuchung. (Acta Universitatis Upsaliensis: Acta Societatis
        Linguisticae Upsaliensis, n.s., 1: 4.) Uppsala: Almqvist & Wiksell.
1966   Distant linguistic affinity. In: Birnbaum & Puhvel (eds.) 1968:
        199–200.
1974   Indo-Uralisch – oder gar Nostratisch? Vierzig Jahre auf rauhen
        Pfaden. In: Antiquitates Indogermanicae ... Gedenkschrift für
        Hermann Güntert ..., ed. by M. Mayrhofer et al., 363–375.
        (Innsbrucker Beiträge zur Sprachwissenschaft, 12.) Innsbruck.
Collinge, Neville E.
1986   The new historicism and its battles. Folia Linguistica Historica
        7: 3–19.
1987   Who did discover the law of the palatals? In: Cardona & Zide
        (eds.) 1987: 73–80.
Columbus, Frederick
1974   Introductory workbook in historical phonology. Cambridge,
        MA: Slavica.
Comrie, Bernard
1979   Book Notice on Jansen (1978): Studies on fronting. Language
        55: 958–959.
Corder, S. P.
1967   The significance of learners' errors. International Review of
        Applied Linguistics 5: 161–170.
Corne, Chris
1983   Review article on Valdman & Highfield (eds.) 1980 and Highfield
        & Valdman (eds.) 1981. Language 59: 176–190.
Coseriu, Eugenio
1958   Sincronía, diacronía e historia: El problema del cambio
        lingüístico. Montevideo: Universidad de la República.
1970   Sprache, Struktur und Funktionen. Tübingen: Narr.
Costello, John R.
1983   Syntactic change and syntactic reconstruction: a tagmemic ap-
        proach. Arlington, TX: Summer Institute of Linguistics and
        University of Texas.
Cowan, J Ronayne
1984   Evidence for the Aux cliticization hypothesis from Nuer. CLS
        20: 34–45.
Cowgill, Warren
1965   Evidence in Greek. In: Evidence for laryngeals, 2nd ed. by
        W. Winter, 142–180. The Hague: Mouton.
1968   A speculative reconstruction of the pre-Indo-European vowel
        system. Paper at LSA Meeting. (Abstract in Meeting Hand-
        book.)
Cravens, Thomas D.
1984   The phonological unity of intervocalic stop weakening in
        Romance. Urbana: University of Illinois Ph.D. dissertation in
        Italian.

Crowley, Terry
1987   An introduction to historical linguistics. Suva, Fiji: University of the South Pacific.
Cuny, Albert
1946   Invitation à l'étude comparative des langues indo-européennes et des langues chamito-sémitiques. Bordeaux.

Dalby, David
1972   The African element in Black American English. In: Rappin' and stylin' out, ed. by T. Kochman, 170–186. Urbana: University of Illinois Press.
Danielsson, O. A.
1903   Zur *i*-Epenthese im Griechischen. IF 14: 375–396.
Darden, Bill
1971   Diachronic evidence for phonemics. CLS 7: 323–331.
De Camp, David
1963   Review of F. G. Cassidy: Jamaica talk. Language 39: 536–544.
De Camp, David, and Ian F. Hancock (eds.)
1974   Pidgins and creoles: current trends and prospects. Washington, DC: Georgetown University Press.
de Chene, Brent
1975   The treatment of analogy in formal grammar. CLS 11: 152–164.
1979   The historical phonology of vowel length. Bloomington: IULC.
de Chene, Brent, and S. R. Anderson
1979   Compensatory lengthening. Language 55: 505–535.
Delbrück, Bertold
1884   Einleitung in das Sprachstudium. Leipzig: Breitkopf & Härtel.
1893–1900 Vergleichende Syntax der indogermanischen Sprachen. Straßburg: Trübner. [= Vols. 3–5 of Brugmann & Delbrück 1886–1900.]
1911   Germanische Syntax II: Zur Stellung des Verbums. (Abhandlungen der Königlich Sächsischen Akademie der Wissenschaften, phil.-hist. Klasse, 28: 8.) Leipzig: Teubner.
Dempwolff, O.
1922   Über Entstehung sekundärer Tonhöhen in einer Südseesprache. Vox 922: 57 ff.
1924–1925 Die *l*-, *r*- und *d*-Laute in austronesischen Sprachen. Zeitschrift für Eingeborenensprachen 15: 19–50, 116–138, 223–238, and 273–319.
Derbyshire, D. C.
1977   Word order universals and the existence of OVS languages. LIn 8: 590–599.
Dickerson, Wayne B.
1975   Variable rules in the language community: a study of lax [u] in English. SLS 5: 2: 41–68.
Diebold, A. Richard, Jr.
1985   The evolution of Indo-European nomenclature for salmonid fish. (= JIES Monograph 5)

Dillard, J. L. (ed.)
1976   Socio-historical factors in the formation of creoles. (= IJSL 7)
Dingwall, William O. (ed.)
1971   A survey of linguistic science. College Park: University of Maryland Linguistics Program.
Diver, William
1958   On the prehistory of Greek consonantism. Word 14: 1–25.
Dorian, Nancy D.
1978   The fate of morphological complexity in language death. Language 54: 590–609.
1981   Language death: the life cycle of a Scottish Gaelic dialect. Philadelphia: University of Pennsylvania Press.
1989   (ed.) Investigating obsolescence: studies in language contraction and death. Cambridge: University Press.
Downing, Bruce T.
1978   Some universals of relative clause structure. In: Greenberg (ed.) 1978: 4: 375–418.
Drechsel, Emanuel J.
1984   Structure and function in Mobilian Jargon: Indications for the pre-European existence of an American Indian pidgin. Journal of Historical Linguistics & Philology 1: 141–185.
Dressler, Wolfgang U.
1969   Eine textsyntaktische Regel der idg. Wortstellung. KZ 83: 1–25.
1971   Über die Rekonstruktion der idg. Syntax. KZ 85: 5–22.
1972   On the phonology of language death. CLS 8: 448–457.
1973 (a) On the reconstruction of Indo-European syntax. In: Indogermanische und allgemeine Sprachwissenschaft, ed. by G. Redard, 11–13. Wiesbaden: Reichert.
1973 (b) Pour une stylistique phonologique du latin: à propos des styles négligents d'une langue morte. BSL 68: 1: 129–145.
1973 (c) Zum Aussagewert der Lehnwortphonologie für die Abstraktheitsdebatte. Die Sprache 19: 125–139.
1976   How much does performance contribute to phonological change? Wiener Linguistische Gazette 12: 3–17.
1977   Phono-morphological dissimilation. In: Phonologica 1976, ed. by W. U. Dressler and O. Pfeiffer, 41–48. Innsbruck: Institut für Sprachwissenschaft.
1978   Tendenzen in kontaminatorischen Fehlleistungen (und ihre Beziehung zur Sprachgeschichte). Die Sprache 22: 1–10.
1981   Language shift and language death: a Protean challenge for the linguist. Forum Linguisticum 1981: 5–28.
1982   A semiotic model of diachronic process phonology. In: Lehmann & Malkiel (eds.) 1982: 93–131.
1985   Morphonology: The dynamics of derivation. Ann Arbor, MI: Karoma.
Dressler, Wolfgang U., et al. (eds.)
1978   Proceedings of the Twelfth International Congress of Linguists. Innsbruck: Innsbrucker Beiträge zur Sprachwissenschaft.

Dressler, Wolfgang U., and Ruth Wodak (eds.)
1977   Language death. (= IJSL 12; published also as vol. 191 of Linguistics, 1977.)
Dunkel, George
1981   Typology vs. reconstruction. In: Arbeitman & Bomhard (eds.) 1981: 559–569.
Dyen, Isodore
1969   Reconstruction, the comparative method, and the protolanguage uniformity hypothesis. Language 45: 499–518.
1970   Background 'noise' or 'evidence' in comparative linguistics: the case of the Austronesian-Indo-European hypothesis. In: Indo-European and Indo-Europeans, ed. by G. Cardona et al., 431-440. Philadelphia: University of Pennsylvania Press.
1973   (ed.) Lexicostatistics in genetic linguistics: Proceedings of the Yale conference, Yale University, April 3–4, 1971. The Hague: Mouton.

Eckert, Rainer
1978   Syntagmatik und Rekonstruktion. In: Dressler et al. (eds.) 1978: 477–480.
Eitel, Ernest John.
1970   Handbook of Chinese Buddhism. Amsterdam: Philo Press.
Ekblom, R.
1927   Zur Entwicklung der Liquidaverbindungen im Slavischen. (Skrifter utgivna av K. Humanistika Vetenskaps-Samfundet i Uppsala, 24: 9.) Uppsala: Almqvist & Wiksell.
Embleton, Sheila M.
1986   Statistics in historical linguistics. Bochum: Brockmeyer.
Emeneau, Murray B.
1954   Linguistic prehistory of India. Proceedings of the American Philosophical Society 98: 282–292.
1955   India and linguistics. Journal of the American Oriental Society 75: 145–153.
1956   India as a linguistic area. Language 32: 3–16.
1962   Bilingualism and structural borrowing. Proceedings of the American Philosophical Society 106: 430–442.
1980   Language and linguistic area: essays selected by A. S. Dil. Stanford, CA: University Press.
Ewan, W. G.
1976   Larynx movement and tonogenesis. RPLB 1: 29–31.

Faarlund, Jan Terje
To Appear Syntactic change: toward a theory of historical syntax. Berlin: Mouton de Gruyter.
Fairbanks, Gordon H.
1973   Sound change, analogy, and generative phonology. In: Kachru et al. (eds.) 1973: 199–209.
1977   Case inflections in Indo-European. JIES 5: 1–31.

Fehderau, Harold W.
1978   The origin and development of Kituba (Lingua Franca Kikongo). In: Jazayery et al. (eds.) 1978: 259–266.
Ferguson, Charles A.
1959 (a) Diglossia. Word 15: 325–340.
1959 (b) The Arabic koiné. Language 35: 616–630.
1971   Absence of copula and the notion of simplicity: a study of normal speech, baby talk, foreigner talk, and pidgins. In: Hymes (ed.) 1971: 141–150.
Ferguson, Charles A., and Charles E. De Bose
1977   Simplified registers, broken language, and pidginization. In: Valdman (ed.) 1977: 99–125.
Fidelholtz, James L.
1975   Word frequency and vowel reduction in English. CLS 11: 200–213.
Filipović, Rudolf (ed.)
1988   Languages in contact. (= Folia Linguistica 22: 1–2)
Fischer, O. C. M., and F. C. van der Leek
1981   Review of Lightfoot 1979. Lingua 55: 301–349.
Fischer, P.
1923   Zur Stellung des Verbums im Griechischen. Glotta 13: 1–11 and 89–205.
Fishman, Joshua A.
1967   Bilingualism with and without diglossia; diglossia with and without bilingualism. Journal of Social Issues 23: 2: 29–38.
Fisiak, Jacek
1978   (ed.) Recent developments in historical phonology. The Hague: Mouton.
1980   (ed.) Historical morphology. The Hague: Mouton.
1984   (ed.) Historical syntax. Berlin: Mouton.
1985 (a) (ed.) Historical semantics, historical word-formation. Berlin: Mouton.
1985 (b) (ed.) Papers from the 6th International Conference on Historical Linguistics. (= AST 34)
1988   (ed.) Historical dialectology: regional and social. Berlin: Mouton de Gruyter.
1990   (ed.) Historical linguistics and philology. Berlin: Mouton de Gruyter.
Fodor, István
1965   The rate of linguistic change: Limits of the application of mathematical methods in linguistics. The Hague: Mouton.
Fokos-Fuchs, D. R.
1962   Rolle der Syntax in der Frage nach Sprachverwandtschaft mit besonderer Rücksicht auf das Problem der ural-altaischen Sprachverwandtschaft. (Ural-altaische Bibliothek, 11.) Wiesbaden: Harrassowitz.
Forrest, R. A. D.
1965   The Chinese language. 2nd ed. London: Faber & Faber.

Fourquet, Jean
1938   L'ordre des éléments de la phrase en germanique ancien. (Publications de la Faculté des Lettres de l'Université de Strasbourg, 86.) Paris: Les Belles Lettres.
Fowkes, Robert E.
1949   Initial mutation of loan words in Welsh. Word 5: 205–213.
Fox, James A.
1983   Simplified input and negotiation in Russenorsk. Andersen 1983: 94–108.
Francis, W. Nelson
1983   Dialectology: an introduction. New York: Longman.
Friedrich, Paul
1970   Indo-European trees. Chicago: University Press.
1975   Proto-Indo-European syntax. (= JIES Monograph 1)
1976   Ad Hock. JIES 4: 207–220.
1977   The devil's case: PIE as type II. In: Juilland et al. (eds.) 1976: 463–480.
1987   The Proto-Indo-European adpreps (spatio-temporal auxiliaries). In: Cardona & Zide (eds.) 1987: 131–142.
Friedrich, W.
1901   Die Flexion des Hauptworts in den heutigen deutschen Mundarten, Schluß. Zeitschrift für deutsche Philologie 33: 45–85.

Gair, James W.
1985   How Dravidianized was Sinhala phonology? Some conclusions and cautions. In: Acson & Leeds (eds.) 1985: 36–55.
Gamkrelidze, T. V.
1976   Linguistic typology and Indo-European reconstruction. In: Juilland et al. (eds.) 1976: 399–406.
1981   Language typology and language universals and their implications for the reconstruction of the Indo-European stop system. In: Arbeitman & Bomhard (eds.) 1981: 571–609.
1988   The Indo-European glottalic theory in the light of recent critique. Folia Linguistica Historica 9: 3–12.
Gamkrelidze, T. V., and V. V. Ivanov
1973   Sprachtypologie und die Rekonstruktion der gemeinindogermanischen Verschlüsse. Phonetica 27: 150–156.
Garber, A.
1980   Word order changes in the Senufo languages. SLS 10: 1: 45–57.
Garnes, Sara
1976   Quantity in Icelandic: production and perception. Hamburg: Buske.
Gauchat, L.
1905   L'unité phonétique dans le patois d'une commune. In: Aus romanischen Sprachen und Literaturen: Festschrift Heinrich Morf, 175–232. Halle: Niemeyer.
Gilbert, G. G.
1976   Hugo Schuchardt's view of simplification in pidgin and creole

languages. In: 1975 Mid-America Linguistics Conference Papers, ed. by F. Ingemann, 136–144. Lawrence: University of Kansas, Department of Linguistics.

Gilliéron, J.
1915   Pathologie et thérapeutique verbales. Paris: Champion.
1918   Généalogie des mots qui designent l'abeille. Paris: Champion.

Givón, Talmy
1971   Historical syntax and synchronic morphology: an archaeologist's field trip. CLS 17: 394–415.
1975   Serial verbs and syntactic change: Niger-Congo. In: Li (ed.) 1975: 47–112.
1977   The drift from VSO to SVO in Biblical Hebrew: the pragmatics of tense-aspect. In: Li (ed.) 1977: 181–254.

Goepfert, E.
1902   Die Bergmannssprache in der Sarepta des Johann Mathesius. (= Zeitschrift für deutsche Wortforschung, supplement to v. 3.)

Gonda, Jan
1950   Indonesian and general linguistics. Lingua 2: 308–339.

Goodenough, W.
1956   Componential analysis and the study of meaning. Language 32: 195–216.

Grammont, Maurice
1895   La dissimilation consonantique dans les langues indoeuropéennes. Dijon: Darantiere.

Grassmann, Hermann
1863   Über die Aspiraten und ihr gleichzeitiges Vorhandensein im An- und Auslaute der Wurzeln. KZ 12: 81–138. (Engl. transl. in Lehmann (ed.) 1967: 109–131.)

Green, G. Michael
1983   An argument against reconstructing glottalized stops in PIE. In: Stump (ed.) 1983a: 50–55.

Greenberg, Joseph H.
1957   Essays in linguistics. (Repr. as Phoenix Book P 119, 1963.)
1966 (a) Some universals of grammar with particular reference to the order of meaningful elements. In: Greenberg (ed.) 1966b: 73–113.
1966 (b) (ed.) Universals of language. Second ed. Cambridge, MA: MIT Press.
1978   (ed.) Universals of human language. 4 volumes. Stanford, CA:
1987   Language in the Americas. Stanford, CA: University Press.
1989   Classification of American Indian languages: a reply to Campbell. Language 65: 107–114.

Greppin, John A. C.
1978   On Greek zeta. JIES 6: 141–142.

Grimm, Jacob
1819–1834 Deutsche Grammatik. 4 vols. Göttingen: Dieterich.
1893   Deutsche Grammatik. Second ed., v. 1. Gütersloh: Bertelsmann. (Engl. transl. of pp. 580–592 in Lehmann (ed.) 1967: 46–60.)

Gulstad, Daniel E.
1974   Reconstruction in syntax. In: Anderson & Jones (eds.) 1974a : 117–158.
Gumperz, John J., and Robert Wilson
1971   Convergence and creolization: a case from the Indo-Aryan/ Dravidian border. In: Hymes (ed.) 1971: 151–168.
Gyármathi, Samuel
1799   Affinitas lingvae hvngaricae cvm lingvis fennicae originis grammatice demonstrata. Göttingen: Dieterich. (Engl. transl. 1983 by V. E. Hanzell, 'Grammatical proof of the affinity of the Hungarian language with languages of Fennic origin', Amsterdam Studies in the Theory and History of Linguistic Science, Series 1, v. 15.).

Haarmann, Harald
1976   Aspekte der Arealtypologie: Die Problematik der europäischen Sprachbünde. (= Tübinger Beiträge zur Linguistik, 72.)
Haas, Mary R.
1960   The prehistory of languages. The Hague: Mouton.
Habick, Timothy
1980   Sound change in Farmer City: a sociolinguistic study based on acoustic data. Urbana: University of Illinois Ph.D. dissertation in Linguistics.
Hagège, Claude, and André Haudricourt
1978   La phonologie panchronique. Paris: Presses Universitaires de France.
Haider, Hubert
1985   The fallacy of typology: remarks on the PIE stop-system. Lingua 65: 1–27.
Haiman, John
1974   Targets and syntactic change. The Hague: Mouton.
1983   Iconic and economic motivation. Language 59: 781–819.
Hale, Kenneth
1973   Deep-surface canonical disparities in relation to analogy and change: an Australian example. In: Sebeok (ed.) 1973: 401–458.
Hale, Mark Robert
1987   Studies in the comparative syntax of the oldest Indo-Iranian languages. Cambridge, MA: Harvard University Ph.D. dissertation in Linguistics.
Hall, Robert A., Jr.
1943   Melanesian Pidgin English. Baltimore: LSA.
1946   Bartoli's 'Neolinguistica'. Language 22: 273–283.
1950   The reconstruction of Proto-Romance. Language 26: 6–27. (Repr. in Joos (ed.) 1957.)
1960   On realism in reconstruction. Language 36: 203–206.
1966   Pidgin and creole languages. Ithaca, NY: Cornell University Press.

1968   Comparative reconstruction in Romance syntax. Acta Linguistica
            Hafniensia 11: 81–88.
1976   Proto-Romance phonology. (Comparative Romance grammar,
            2.) New York: Elsevier.
Halle, Morris
1962 (a)   A descriptive convention for treating assimilation and dissimi-
            lation. MIT Research Laboratory of Electronics, Quarterly
            Progress Report 66: 295–296.
1962 (b)   Phonology in generative grammar. Word 18: 54–72.
Hamans, Camiël
1988   The unnaturalness of naturalness. In: Fisiak (ed.) 1988: 299–234.
Hamp, Eric P.
1959   Final syllables in Germanic and the Scandinavian accent system.
            Studia Linguistica 13: 29–48.
1974   Reassignment of nasality in early Irish. In: Papers from the
            Parasession on Natural Phonology, 127–130. Chicago: CLS.
1982   On Greek z : *y-. JIES 10: 190–191.
1989   The Indo-European obstruent features and phonotactic con-
            straints. In: Vennemann (ed.) 1989: 209–214.
Hamp, Eric P., F. W. Householder, and Robert Austerlitz (eds.)
1966   Readings in linguistics, 2. Chicago: University Press.
Hankamer, Jorge
1977   Multiple analyses. In: Li (ed.) 1977: 583–607.
Harris, Martin, and Paolo Ramat (eds.)
1987   Historical development of auxiliaries. Berlin: Mouton de
            Gruyter.
Hashimoto, M. J.
1981   Review of Wang (ed.) 1977. Language 57: 183–191.
Haudricourt, A. G., and A. G. Juilland
1949   Essai pour une histoire structurale du phonétisme français. Paris:
            Klincksieck.
Haudry, Jean
1973   Parataxe, hypotaxe et corrélation dans la phrase latine. BSL 68:
            1: 147–186.
Haugen, Einar
1950   The analysis of linguistic borrowing. Language 26: 210–231.
Havers, W.
1946   Neuere Literatur zum Sprachtabu. (= Sitzungsberichte der
            Akademie der Wissenschaften Wien, phil.-hist. Klasse, 223: 5.)
Hawkins, John A.
1979   Implicational universals as predictors of word order change.
            Language 55: 618–648.
1983   Word order universals. New York: Academic Press.
Hayes, Bruce
1989   Compensatory lengthening in moraic phonology. LIn 20:
            243–306.

Heidelberger Forschungsprojekt 'Pidgindeutsch'
1975   Sprache und Kommunikation ausländischer Arbeiter. Kronberg: Scriptor.
Heine, Bernd
1970   Status and use of African lingua francas. München: Weltforum.
1976   A typology of African languages. Berlin: Reimer.
Henderson, Eugénie J. A.
1982   Tonogenesis: Some recent speculations on the development of tone. Transactions of the Philological Society 1982: 1–24.
Hermann, Eduard
1929   Lautveränderungen in der Individualsprache einer Mundart. Nachrichten der Gesellschaft der Wissenschaften zu Göttingen, phil.-hist. Klasse, 9: 195–214.
1931   Lautgesetz und Analogie. (= Abhandlungen der Gesellschaft der Wissenschaften zu Göttingen, phil.-hist. Klasse, N.F. 23: 3.)
Hesseling, D. C.
1897–1933 (1979) On the origin and formation of creoles. Engl. transl. by T. L. Markey and P. T. Roberge. Ann Arbor, MI: Karoma.
Hettrich, Heinrich
1988   Untersuchungen zur Hypotaxe im Vedischen. Berlin: de Gruyter.
Hetzron, Robert
1976   Two principles of genetic reconstruction. Lingua 28: 89–108.
Highfield, A. R., and A. Valdman (eds.)
1981   Historicity and variation in creole studies. Ann Arbor, MI: Karoma.
Hill, Archibald A.
1936   Phonetic and phonemic change. Language 12: 15–22. (Repr. in Joos (ed.) 1957.)
Hill, Kenneth C. (ed.)
1979   The genesis of language. Ann Arbor, MI: Karoma.
Hill, T.
1958   Institutional linguistics. Orbis 7: 441–455.
Hilmarsson, Jörundur
1982   Indo-European 'tongue'. JIES 10: 355–367.
Hinüber, Oskar von
1986   Das ältere Mittelindisch im Überblick. (= Sitzungsberichte der Österreichischen Akademie der Wissenschaften, phil.-hist. Klasse, 467.)
Hock, Hans Henrich
1974 (a)   Historical change and synchronic structure: the case of the Sanskrit root nouns. In: Toward tomorrow's linguistics, ed. by C.-J. N. Bailey and R. Shuy, 329–342. Washington, DC: Georgetown University Press. (Repr. in International Journal of Dravidian Linguistics 3: 215–228.)
1974 (b)   On the Indo-Iranian accusative plural of consonant stems. Journal of the American Oriental Society 94: 73–95.

1975 Substratum influence on (Rig-Vedic) Sanskrit? SLS 5: 2: 76–125.
1976 (a) Current trends in historical linguistics. Lektos 2: 1: 25–48.
1976 (b) Final weakening and related phenomena. In: 1975 Mid-America Linguistics Conference Papers, ed. by F. Ingemann, 215–259. Lawrence: University of Kansas, Department of Linguistics.
1976 (c) Review article on Anttila 1972. Language 52: 202–220.
1979 Retroflexion rules in Sanskrit. South Asian Languages Analysis 1: 47–62.
1980 Archaisms, morphophonemic metrics, or variable rules in the Rig-Veda? SLS 10: 1: 59–69.
1982 (a) AUX-cliticization as a motivation for word order change. SLS 12: 1: 91–101.
1982 (b) The Sanskrit passive: synchronic behavior and diachronic development. In: Studies in South Asian languages and linguistics, ed. by P. J. Mistry, 127–137. (= South Asian Review 6: 3.)
1982 (c) (ed.) Papers on diachronic syntax: six case studies. (= SLS 12: 2)
1982 (d) Clitic verbs in PIE or discourse-based verb fronting? Sanskrit *sá hováca gárgyaḥ* and congeners in Avestan and Homeric Greek. In: Hock (ed.) 1982c: 1–38.
1982 (e) The Sanskrit quotative: a historical and comparative study. In: Hock (ed.) 1982c: 39–85.
1983 Language-death phenomena in Sanskrit: Grammatical evidence for attrition in contemporary spoken Sanskrit. SLS 13: 2: 21–35.
1984 (Pre-)Rig-Vedic convergence of Indo-Aryan with Dravidian? Another look at the evidence. SLS 14: 1: 89–107.
1985 (a) Pronoun fronting and the notion 'verb-second' position in Beowulf. In: Germanic linguistics: papers from a symposium at the University of Chicago, April 24, 1985, ed. by J. T. Faarlund, 70–86. Bloomington: IULC.
1985 (b) Regular metathesis. Linguistics 23: 4: 529–546.
1985 (c) Review of Lehmann & Malkiel (eds.) 1982. Language 61: 187–193.
1985 (d) Yes, Virginia, syntactic reconstruction is possible. SLS 15: 1: 49–60.
1986 (a) Compensatory lengthening: In defense of the concept 'mora'. Folia Linguistica 20: 431–460.
1986 (b) *P*-oriented constructions in Sanskrit. In: South Asian languages: structure, convergence, and diglossia, ed. by Bh. Krishnamurti et al., 15–26. Delhi: Motilal Banarsidass.
1987 Regular contact dissimilation. In: Cardona & Zide (eds.) 1987: 143–153.
1988 (a) Historical implications of a dialectological approach to convergence. In: Fisiak (ed.) 1988: 283–328.
1988 (b) Relative clauses and rebracketing in Old English. In: Antonsen & Hock (eds.) 1988: 35–54.
1988 (c) Review article: Finiteness in Dravidian. [On Steever 1988.] SLS 18: 2: 211–231.

1989 (a)   Conjoined we stand: Theoretical implicatons of Sanskrit rela-
            tive clauses. SLS 19: 1: 93–126.
1989 (b)   Spoken Sanskrit in Uttar Pradesh: a sociolinguistic profile.
            Lokaprajñā (Pune, India).
1990   V2 in early Germanic: a „heretical" view. Ninth East Coast
            Indo-European Conference, June 1990, University of Pennsyl-
            vania.
In Press   Spoken Sanskrit in Uttar Pradesh: profile of a dying prestige
            langage. In: Kelley memorial volume, ed. by E. Dimmock, B. B.
            Kachru, and Bh. Krishnamurti. Delhi: Oxford University Press.
Hock, Hans Henrich, and Rajeshwari Pandharipande
1976 (1978) The sociolinguistic position of Sanskrit in pre-Muslim South
            Asia. Studies in Language Learning 1: 2: 106–138. University of
            Illinois. (Condensed repr. 1978: Sanskrit in the pre-Islamic
            context of South Asia. In: Aspects of sociolinguistics in South
            Asia, ed. by B. B. Kachru and S. N. Sridhar, 11–25 (= IJSL 16).)
Hockett, Charles F.
1959   The stressed syllabics of Old English. Language 35: 575–597.
Hoenigswald, Henry M.
1956   Review of Thieme 1954. Language 23: 313–316.
1964   Graduality, sporadicity, and the minor sound change processes.
            Phonetica 11: 202–215. (Repr. in Baldi & Werth (eds.) 1978.)
1965   Language change and linguistic reconstruction. Chicago: Uni-
            versity Press.
1966   Criteria for the subgrouping of languages. In: Birnbaum &
            Puhvel (eds.) 1966: 1–12.
1973 (a)   The comparative method. In: Sebeok (ed.) 1973: 51–62.
1973 (b)   Studies in formal historical linguistics. Dordrecht: Reidel.
1983   Doublets. In: Essays in honor of Charles F. Hockett, ed. by F.
            A. Agard et al., 167–171. Leiden: Brill.
1990   Is the 'comparative' method general or family-specific? In: Baldi
            (ed.) 1990: 375–383.
Hogg, Richard M.
1976   The status of rule reordering. Journal of Linguistics 12:
            103–123.
1979   Analogy and phonology. Journal of Linguistics 15: 55–85.
Hombert, J. M.
1976   Phonetic motivations for the development of tones from
            postvocalic [h] and [ʔ]: evidence from contour tone perception.
            RPLB 1: 30–47.
Hombert, J. M., J. J. Ohala, and W. G. Ewan
1976   Tonogenesis: theories and queries. RPLB 1: 48–77.
1979   Phonetic explanations for the development of tones. Language
            55: 37–58.
Hopper, Paul J.
1973   Glottalized and murmured occlusives in Indo-European. Glossa
            7: 141–166.

1975   The syntax of the simple sentence in Proto-Germanic. The Hague: Mouton.
1977   The typology of the Proto-Indo-European segmental inventory. JIES 5: 41–53.

Horne, Elinor
1961   Beginning Javanese. New Haven, CT: Yale University Press.

Houben, Jeffrey L.
1977   Word order change and subordination in Homeric Greek. JIES 5: 1–8.

Householder, F. W.
1983   Kyriolexia and language change. Language 59: 1–17.

Howell, Robert B.
1985   The origin of uvular *r* in the Germanic languages. In: Germanic linguistics: papers from a symposium at the University of Chicago, April 24, 1985, ed. by J. T. Faarlund. Bloomington: IULC.
1987   Tracing the origin of uvular *r* in the Germanic languages. Folia Linguistica Historica 7: 317–349.
1988   Modern evidence for ancient sound changes: Old English breaking and Old High German vowel epenthesis revisited. In: Antonsen & Hock (eds.) 1988: 65–73.

Hsieh, Hsin-I.
1971   Lexical diffusion: evidence from child language acquisition. POLA 15: 1–12. (Repr. in Wang (ed.) 1977.)

Huld, Martin E.
1986   On the unacceptability of the Indo-European voiced stops as ejectives. IF 91: 67–78.

Hyman, Larry M.
1970 (a) How concrete is phonology? Language 46: 58–76.
1970 (b) The role of borrowings in the justification of phonological grammars. Studies in African Linguistics 1: 1–48.
1973 (a) Nupe three years later. Language 49: 447–452.
1973 (b) Consonant types and tone. (Southern California Occasional Papers in Linguistics, 1.) Los Angeles: University of Southern California.
1973 (c) The feature [grave] in phonological theory. Journal of Phonetics 1: 329–337.
1975   On the change from SOV to SVO: evidence from Niger-Congo. In: Li (ed.) 1975: 113–147.
1985   A theory of phonological weight. Dordrecht: Foris.

Hymes, Dell (ed.)
1971   Pidginization and creolization of language. Cambridge: University Press.

Illič-Svityč, V. M.
1971, 1976 Opyt sravnenija nostratičeskix jazykov, vols. 1 and 2. Moscow: Nauka.

Ingria, R.
1980   Compensatory lengthening as a metrical phenomenon. LIn 11: 465–495.
Ivanov, Vjač. Vs.
1965   Oščeindoevropejskaja praslavjankskaja i anatolijskaja jazykovye sistemy ... Moscow: Nauka.
Ivić, Pavle
1976   Serbocroatian accentuation: facts and interpretation. In: Slavic linguistics and language teaching, ed. by T. F. Magner, 34–43. Columbus, OH: Slavica.

Jaberg, Karl
1908   Sprachgeographie. Aarau: Sauerländer.
Jakobson, Roman
1931 (a) Prinzipien der historischen Phonologie. TCLP 4: 247–267. (Revised version, Fr. transl. 1949, as appendix to Trubetzkoy: Principes de phonologie, Paris: Klincksieck; repr. in Jakobson: Selected writings; Engl. transl. in Keiler (ed.) 1972 and Baldi & Werth (eds.) 1978.)
1931 (b) Über die phonologischen Sprachbünde. TCLP 4: 234–240. (Engl. version in Keiler (ed.) 1972.)
1958   Typological studies and their contribution to historical comparative linguistics. In: Proceedings of the 8th International Congress of Linguists, Oslo, 17–25. (Repr. in Jakobson: Selected writings.)
Jankowsky, K. R.
1972   The Neogrammarians: a reevaluation of their place in the development of linguistic science. The Hague: Mouton.
1976   The psychological component in the work of the early neogrammarians and its foundation. In: Christie (ed.) 1976: 267–284.
Janson, Tore
1983   Sound change in perception and production. Language 59: 18–34.
Jasanoff, Jay H.
1988   Review of Renfrew 1987. Language 64: 800–802.
Jazayery, M. A., et al. (eds.)
1978   Linguistic and literary studies in honor of A. A. Hill, v. 3: Historical and comparative studies. The Hague: Mouton.
Jazayery, M. A., and Werner Winter (eds.)
1988   Languages and cultures: studies in honor of Edgar C. Polomé. Berlin: Mouton de Gruyter.
Jeffers, Robert J.
1974   On the notion 'explanation' in historical linguistics. In: Anderson & Jones (eds.) 1974b: 321–355.
1976   Syntactic change and syntactic reconstruction. In: Christie (ed.) 1976: 1–16.

Jeffers, Robert J., and Ilse Lehiste
1979   Principles and methods for historical linguistics. Cambridge, MA: MIT Press.
Jespersen, Otto
1921   Language: its nature, development, and origin. Repr. 1964, New York: Norton.
1941   Efficiency in linguistic change. (= Det Kgl. Danske Videnskabernes Selskab, 27: 4.)
Joly, André (ed.)
1988   La linguistique génétique: histoire et théories. Lille: Presses Universitaires.
Jones, Sir William
1786   The third anniversary discourse, on the Hindus. Published 1788, Asiatick Researches 1: 422.
Joos, Martin
1952   The medieval sibilants. Language 27: 222–231. (Repr. in Joos (ed.) 1957.)
1957   (ed.) Readings in linguistics, 1. Repr. 1966, Chicago: University Press.
Joseph, Brian D.
1978   Morphology and universals in syntactic change: evidence from Medieval and Modern Greek. Bloomington: IULC.
1980   Linguistic universals and syntactic change. Language 56: 345–370.
1983   The synchrony and diachrony of the Balkan infinitive: a study in areal, general, and historical linguistics. Cambridge: University Press.
Juilland, Alphonse
1953   A bibliography of diachronic phonemics. Word 9: 198–209.
Juilland, Alphonse, et al. (eds.)
1976   Linguistic studies offered to Joseph Greenberg on the occasion of his sixtieth birthday. 3 volumes with consecutive pagination. Saratoga, CA: Anma Libri.

Kachru, Braj B.
1965   The Indianness in Indian English. Word 21: 391–410.
1969   English in South Asia. In: Current trends in linguistics, ed. by T. A. Sebeok, 5: 627–678. The Hague: Mouton.
1982   South Asian English. In: English as a world language, ed. by R. Bailey and M. Görlach, 353–383. Ann Arbor: University of Michigan Press.
1983 (a) The Indianization of English. Delhi: Oxford University Press.
1983 (b) (ed.) The other tongue: English across cultures. Oxford: Pergamon Press.
Kachru, Braj B., et al. (eds.)
1973   Issues in linguistics: Papers in honor of Henry and Renée Kahane. Urbana: University of Illinois Press.

Kahane, Henry
1986   A typology of the prestige language. Language 62: 495–508.
Kahr, Joan C.
1975   Adpositions and locationals: typology and diachronic development. (= Stanford Working Papers 19.)
1976   The renewal of case morphology: sources and constraints. Stanford Working Papers 20: 107–151.
Kastovsky, Dieter
To Appear Historical English syntax. Berlin: Mouton de Gruyter.
Kastovsky, Dieter, and Aleksander Szwedek (eds.)
1986   Linguistics across historical and geographical boundaries, v. 1. Berlin: Mouton de Gruyter.
Kaye, Jonathan Derek
1979   On the alleged correlation of markedness and rule function. In: Current approaches to phonological theory, ed. by D. A. Dinnsen, 272–280. Bloomington: Indiana University Press.
Keenan, Edward L., III
1975   Some universals of passive in Relational Grammar. CLS 11: 340–352.
1978   The syntax of subject-final languages. In: Syntactic typology, ed. by W. P. Lehmann, 267–327. Austin: University of Texas Press.
1985   Relative clauses. In: Language typology and syntactic description, ed. by T. Shopen, 2: 141–170. Cambridge: University Press.
Keenan, Edward L., III, and Bernard Comrie
1977   Noun phrase accessibility and universal grammar. LIn 8: 63–99.
Keiler, A. R. (ed.)
1972   A reader in historical and comparative linguistics. New York: Holt.
Keim, Inken
1978   Gastarbeiterdeutsch. Tübingen: Narr.
1984   Untersuchungen zum Deutsch türkischer Arbeiter. Tübingen: Narr.
Keim, Inken, Pantelis Nikitopoulos, and Michael Repp
1982   Kommunikation ausländischer Arbeiter. Tübingen: Narr.
King, Robert D.
1967   Functional load and sound change. Language 43: 831–352. (Repr. in Baldi & Werth (eds.) 1978.)
1969 (a)   Push-chains and drag-chains. Glossa 3: 3–21.
1969 (b)   Historical linguistics and generative grammar. Englewood Cliffs, NJ: Prentice Hall.
1976   The history of final devoicing in Yiddish. Bloomington: IULC.
Kiparsky, Paul
1965   Phonological change. Cambridge, MA: MIT Ph.D. dissertation in Linguistics.
1967   Sonorant clusters in Greek. Language 43: 619–635.
1968 (a)   How abstract is phonology? Bloomington: IULC.

1968 (b) Linguistic universals and linguistic change. In: Universals in linguistic theory, ed. by E. Bach & R. T. Harms, 171–202. (Repr. in Keiler (ed.) 1972, and in Baldi & Werth (eds.) 1978 [as part of 'Rule reordering'].)
1971 Historical linguistics. In: Dingwall (ed.) 1971: 576–642. (Repr. in Baldi & Werth (eds.) 1978 [as part of 'Rule reordering'].)
1972 Explanation in phonology. In: Goals of linguistic theory, ed. by S. Peters, 189–227. Englewood Cliffs: Prentice Hall.
1973 (a) Three dimensions of linguistic theory, ed. by O. Fujimura. Tokyo: Institute for Advanced Study of Language.
1973 (b) Abstractness, opacity, and global rules. In: Kiparsky 1973a: 57–86. (Also in Koutsoudas (ed.) 1976: 160–186.)
1973 (c) Case studies. In: Kiparsky 1973a: 87–129.
1973 (d) On comparative linguistics: The case of Grassmann's Law. In: Sebeok (ed.) 1973: 115–134.
1974 Remarks on analogical change. In: Anderson & Jones (eds.) 1974b: 257–275.
1978 Analogical change as a problem for linguistic theory. SLS 8: 2: 77–96.
1980 Concluding statement. In: Traugott et al. (eds.) 1980: 410–417.
1989 Phonological change. In: Newmeyer (ed.) 1989: 363–415.
In Press Indo-European origins of Germanic syntax. Indo-European Studies. (Harvard University.)
Kisseberth, Charles W.
1970 On the functional unity of phonological rules. LIn 1: 291–306.
1976 The interaction of phonological rules and the polarity of language. In: Koutsoudas (ed.) 1976: 41–54.
Klaiman, M. H.
1978 Arguments against a passive origin of the IA ergative. CLS 14: 204–216.
Klausenburger, Jürgen
1979 Morphologization: studies in Latin and Romance morphonology. Tübingen: Niemeyer.
Klima, E. S.
1965 Studies in diachronic transformational syntax. Cambridge, MA: Harvard University Ph.D. dissertation in Linguistics.
Kloeke, G. G.
1927 De Hollandsche expansie in de zestiende en zeventiende eeuw. 'sGravenhage: Nijhoff.
Kloss, H.
1966 Types of multilingual communities: a discussion of ten variables. In: Explorations in sociolinguistics, ed. by S. Lieberson, 7–17. The Hague: Mouton.
Kluge, Friedrich
1901 Rotwelsch: Quellen und Wortschatz der Gaunersprache und der verwandten Geheimsprachen. Repr. 1987, Berlin: de Gruyter.
Kock, Axel
1901 Die alt- und neuschwedische Akzentuierung. (= Quellen und

Forschungen zur Sprach- und Kulturgeschichte der germanischen Völker, 87.)

Koefoed, Geert
1974   On formal and functional explanation: Some notes on Kiparsky's 'Explanation in phonology'. In: Anderson & Jones (eds.) 1974b: 277–293.

Koerner, Konrad
1987   The importance of Saussure's 'Mémoire' in the development of historical linguistics. In: Cardona & Zide (eds.) 1987: 201–218.

Koopman, Willem, et al. (eds.)
1987   Explanation and linguistic change. (= AST 45)

Kordtlandt, Frederik
1989   The making of a puzzle. Annual of Armenian Linguistics 10: 43–52.

Koutsoudas, Andreas (ed.)
1976   The application and ordering of grammatical rules. The Hague: Mouton.

Krahe, Hans
1970   Einleitung in das vergleichende Sprachstudium, ed. by W. Meid. (Innsbrucker Beiträge zur Sprachwissenschaft, 1.) Innsbruck.

Kranzmayer, Eberhard
1956   Historische Lautgeographie des gesamtbairischen Dialektraumes. Wien: Österreichische Akademie der Wissenschaften.

Krishnamurti, Bh.
1977   Sound change: Shared innovation vs. diffusion. In: Phonologica, ed. by W. U. Dressler and O. E. Pfeiffer, 205–211. (Supplement to Innsbrucker Beiträge zur Sprachwissenschaft.)
1978 (a) Areal and lexical diffusion of sound change. Language 54: 1–20.
1978 (b) On diachronic and synchronic rules in phonology. In: In memory of P. B. Pandit, 252–276. (= Indian Linguistics 39)

Krishnamurti, Bh., L. Moses, and D. Danforth
1983   Unchanged cognates as a criterion in linguistic subgrouping. Language 59: 541–568.

Kroch, Anthony S.
1989   Function and grammar in the history of English: Periphrastic *do*. In: Language change and variation, ed. by R. W. Fasold and D. Schiffrin, 133–172. (= AST 52)

Kronasser, Heinz
1952   Handbuch der Semasiologie. Heidelberg: Winter.

Kuhn, Hans
1970   Altnordisch. In: Kurzer Grundriß der germanischen Philologie bis 1500, ed. by L. E. Schmitt, 1: 123–143. Berlin: de Gruyter.

Kuhn, Sherman M.
1961   On the syllabic phonemes of Old English. Language 37: 522–538.

Kuipers, Aert
1968   Unique types and phonological universals. In: Pratidānam:

Indian, Iranian, and Indo-European studies presented to F. B. J. Kuiper ..., ed. by J. C. Heesterman et al. The Hague: Mouton.

Kuryłowicz, Jerzy

1927   ∂indo-européen et *h* hittite. In: Symbolae grammaticae in honorem Ioannis Rozwadowski, 1: 95–104. Cracow.

1947   La nature des procès dits analogiques. Acta Linguistica 5: 15–37. (Repr. in Hamp et al. (eds.) 1966.)

1964   The inflectional categories of Indo-European. Heidelberg: Winter.

1968 (a)   Indogermanische Grammatik, 2: Akzent, Ablaut. Heidelberg: Winter.

1968 (b)   The notion of the morpho(pho)neme. In: Lehmann & Malkiel (eds.) 1968: 65–82.

1971   Phonologisches zum indogermanischen Gutturalproblem. In: Donum indogermanicum: Festgabe für Anton Scherer, ed. by R. S. Brandt, 33–38. Heidelberg: Winter.

Labov, William

1965 (a)   The social motivation of a sound change. Word 19: 273–309. (Repr. in Labov 1972a.)

1965 (b)   On the mechanism of linguistic change. Georgetown University Monographs on Languages and Linguistics 18: 91–114. (Repr. in Keiler (ed.) 1972 and Labov 1972a.)

1966 (a)   The social stratification of English in New York. Washington, DC: Center for Applied Linguistics.

1966 (b)   Hypercorrection by the lower middle class as a factor in linguistic change. In: Sociolinguistics, ed. by W. Bright. The Hague: Mouton. (Repr. in Labov 1972a.)

1969   Contraction, deletion, and inherent variability of the English copula. Language 45: 715–762.

1972 (a)   Sociolinguistic patterns. Philadelphia: University of Pennsylvania Press.

1972 (b)   The internal evolution of linguistic rules. In: Stockwell & Macaulay (eds.) 1972: 101–171.

1981   Resolving the neogrammarian controversy. Language 57: 267–308.

1982   Building on empirical foundations. In: Lehmann & Malkiel (eds.) 1982: 17–92.

Labov, William, M. Yaeger, and R. Steiner

1972   A quantitative study of sound change in progress. Philadelphia: US Regional Survey.

Lakoff, Robin

1968   Diachronic change in the complement system. Abstract syntax and Latin complementation. Cambridge, MA: MIT Press. (Repr. in Keiler (ed.) 1972.)

Lakshmi Bai, B.

1985   Some notes on correlative constructions in Dravidian. In: Acson & Leeds (eds.) 1985: 181–190.

Langdon, Margaret
1975   Boundaries and lenition in Yuman languages. IJAL 41: 218–233.
1976   Metathesis in Yuman languages. Language 52: 866–883.
1977   Syntactic change and SOV structure: the Yuman case. In: Li (ed.) 1977: 255–290.
Lass, Roger
1974   Linguistic orthogenesis? Scots vowel quantity and the English length conspiracy. In: Anderson & Jones (eds.) 1974b: 311–343.
Lehiste, Ilse
1970   Temporal organization of spoken language. OSUWP 4: 95–112.
1972   Temporal compensation in a quantitative language. In: Proceedings of the 3rd International Congress of Phonetic Sciences, 929–937. The Hague: Mouton.
Lehmann, Christian
1979   Der Relativsatz vom Indogermanischen bis zum Italienischen. Die Sprache 25: 1–25.
1980   Der indogermanische *kwi/kwo*-Relativsatz im typologischen Vergleich. In: Ramat et al. (eds.) 1980: 155–169.
1984   Der Relativsatz: Typologie seiner Strukturen, Theorie seiner Funktionen, Kompendium seiner Grammatik. Tübingen: Narr.
Lehmann, Winfred P.
1962   Historical linguistics. New York: Holt.
1967   (ed.) A reader in 19th century historical Indo-European linguistics. Bloomington: Indiana University Press.
1973   Historical linguistics. 2nd ed. New York: Holt.
1974   Proto-Indo-European syntax. Austin: University of Texas Press.
1982   Introduction: Diachronic linguistics. In: Lehmann & Malkiel (eds.) 1982: 1–16.
Lehmann, Winfred P., and Yakov Malkiel
1968   (eds.) Directions for historical linguistics. Austin: University of Texas Press.
1982   (eds.) Perspectives on historical linguistics. (= AST 24)
Lehmann, Winfred P., and Ladislav Zgusta
1979   Schleicher's tale after a century. In: Festschrift für Oswald Szemerényi, ed. by Bela Brogyanyi, 1: 455–466. (= AST 11:1)
Leibiger, Carol A.
1988   Inflections and paradigms in German nominal declension. In: Antonsen & Hock (eds.) 1988: 74–80.
Leopold, Werner
1930   Polarity in language. In: Curme volume of linguistic studies, ed. by J. T. Hatfield et al., 102–109. Baltimore: Waverly Press.
Le Page, R. B. (ed.)
1961   Creole language studies. New York: Macmillan.
Le Page, R. B., and D. De Camp
1960   Jamaican creole: an historical introduction. New York: Macmillan.
Leumann, Manu
1927   Zum Mechanismus des Bedeutungswandels. IF 45: 105–108.

Lewy, Ernst
1964   Der Bau der europäischen Sprachen. 2nd ed. Tübingen: Niemeyer.
Li, Charles N.
1975   (ed.) Word order and word order change. Austin: University of Texas Press.
1976   An explanation of word order change: SVO → SOV. Foundations of Language 12: 201–214.
1977   (ed.) Mechanisms of syntactic change. Austin: University of Texas Press.
Li, Charles N., and S. A. Thompson
1974   Historical change of word order: a case study of Chinese and its implications. In: Anderson & Jones (eds.) 1974a: 199–217.
Lightfoot, David W.
1976   The base component as a locus of syntactic change. In: Christie (ed.) 1976: 17–37.
1979   Principles of diachronic syntax. Cambridge: University Press.
1980 (a) Sur la reconstruction d'une proto-syntax. Langages 60: 109-123.
1980 (b) On reconstructing a proto-syntax. In: Ramat et al. (eds.) 1980: 27–45.
1981   A reply to some critics. Lingua 55: 351–368.
Lisker, L., and A. S. Abramson
1964   A cross-language study of voicing in initial stops: acoustical measurements. Word 20: 384–422.
1965   Stop categorization and voice onset time. In: Proceedings of the 5th International Congress of Phonetic Sciences, 389–391. Basel: Karger.
Locke, John
1983   Phonological acquisition and change. New York: Academic Press.
Lottner, C.
1862   Ausnahmen der ersten Lautverschiebung. KZ 11: 161–205.
Lounsbury, F. G.
1956   A semantic analysis of Pawnee kinship usage. Language 32: 158–194.
Lovins, Julie B.
1974   Why loan phonology is natural phonology. In: Papers from the Parasession on Natural Phonology, 240–250. Chicago: CLS.
1975   Loanwords and the phonological structure of Japanese. Bloomington: IULC.
Lüdtke, Helmut (ed.)
1980   Kommunikationstheoretische Grundlagen des Sprachwandels. Berlin: de Gruyter.
Lüdtke, W.
1959   Das prosodische System des Urslavischen und seine Weiterentwicklung im Serbokroatischen. Phonetica 4, Supplement, 125–156.

Lyovin, A.
1971   Sound change, homophony, and lexical diffusion. POLA 15: 13–24.

MacAlpin, David W.
1974   Toward Proto-Elamo-Dravidian. Language 50: 89–101.
1975   Elamite and Dravidian: further evidence of relationship. (With discussion by M. B. Emeneau, W. H. Jacobsen, F. B. J. Kuiper, H. H. Paper, E. Reiner, R. Stopa, F. Vallat, R. W. Wescott, and a reply by D. W. MacAlpin.) Current Anthropology 16: 105–115.
1981   Proto-Elamo-Dravidian: the evidence and its implications. (Transactions of the American Philosophical Society, 71: 3.) Philadelphia.

Magnusson, Walter L.
1967   Complementary distributions among the root patterns of Proto-Indo-European. Linguistics 34: 17–25.

Maher, J. P., et al. (eds.)
1982   Papers from the 3rd International Conference on Historical Linguistics. (= AST 13)

Malkiel, Yakov
1968   The inflectional paradigm as an occasional determinant of sound change. In: Lehmann & Malkiel (eds.) 1968: 20–64.
1976   Multi-conditioned sound change and the impact of morphology on phonology. Language 52: 757–778.
1979   Problems in the diachronic differentiation of near-homophones. Language 55: 1–36.
1982   Semantically-marked root morphemes in diachronic morphology. In: Lehmann & Malkiel (eds.) 1982: 133–243.

Malone, J. L.
1971   Systematic metathesis in Mandaic. Language 47: 394–415.

Mańczak, Witold
1958   Tendences générales des changements analogiques. Lingua 7: 298–325 and 387–420.
1978   Les lois du développement analogique. Linguistics 205: 53–60.
1984   Le problème de l'habitat primitif des Indo-Européens. Folia Linguistica Historica 5: 199–210.
1987   Frequenzbedingter unregelmässiger Lautwandel in den germanischen Sprachen. Wrocław: Polska Akademia Nauk.
1988   Bartoli's second 'norm'. In: Fisiak (ed.) 1988: 349–356.

Maran, La Raw
1971   Tones in Burmese and Jingpho. Urbana: University of Illinois Ph.D. dissertation in Linguistics.

Marchand, Hans
1969   The categories and types of present-day English word formation. München: Beck.

Marchand, James
1956   Internal reconstruction of phonemic split. Language 32: 245–253.

Marchese, Lynell
1984   Exbraciation in the Kru language family. In: Fisiak (ed.) 1984: 249–270.
1986   Tense-aspect and the development of auxiliaries in Kru languages. Dallas: Summer Institute of Linguistics.
Martinet, André
1936   Neutralisation et archiphonème. TCLP 6: 46–56.
1958   Function, structure, and sound change. Word 8: 1–32. (Repr. in Keiler (ed.) 1972 and Baldi & Werth (eds.) 1978.)
1964   Économie des changements phonétiques. 2nd ed. Bern: Francke.
Masica, Colin P.
1976   Defining a linguistic area: South Asia. Chicago: University Press.
In Press The Indo-Aryan languages. Cambridge: University Press.
Matisoff, James A.
1990   On megalocomparison. Language 66: 106–120.
Mattheier, Klaus J.
1983   Aspekte der Dialekttheorie. Tübingen: Niemeyer.
Mayerthaler, Willi
1980 (a) Ikonismus in der Morphologie. Zeitschrift für Semiotik 2: 19–37.
1980 (b) Aspekte der Analogietheorie. In: H. Lüdtke (ed.) 1980: 80–130.
1981   Morphologische Natürlichkeit. Wiesbaden: Athenaion.
Mayrhofer, Manfred
1951   Handbuch des Pali, 1. Heidelberg: Winter.
1981   Über sprachliche Rekonstruktionsmethoden. (= Anzeiger der Österreichischen Akademie der Wissenschaften, 117: 25.)
1982   Über griechische Vokalprothese, Laryngaltheorie und externe Rekonstruktion. In: Serta indogermanica: Festschrift für Günter Neumann, ed. by J. Tischler, 177–192. Innsbruck: Institut für Sprachwissenschaft.
1986   Indogermanische Grammatik, 1. Heidelberg: Winter.
McCawley, James D.
1970   Some tonal systems that come close to being pitch-accent systems but don't quite make it. CLS 6: 526–532. (Repr. in J. D. McCawley (1979): Adverbs, vowels, and other objects of wonder. Chicago: University Press.)
Meillet, Antoine
1908   Les dialectes indo-européens. Engl. transl. 'The Indo-European dialects', 1967, University of Alabama Press.
1909   Sur la disparition des formes simples du prétérit. Germanisch-Romanische Monatsschrift 1: 521–526.
1925   La méthode comparative en linguistique historique. Oslo. (Repr. 1966, Paris: Champion.)
Melchert, H. Craig
1975   'Exceptions' to exceptionless sound laws. Lingua 35: 135–153.
1987   PIE velars in Luvian. In: Studies in memory of Warren Cowgill (1929–1985), ed. by C. Watkins, 182–204. Berlin: de Gruyter.

Mendels, Judy
  1963   Von deutscher Bergwerkssprache. Muttersprache 73: 161–171.
Menn, Lise, and Brian MacWhinney
  1984   The repeated morph constraint: toward an explanation. Language 60: 519–141.
Millardet, G.
  1933   Sur un ancien substrat commun à la Sicile, le Corse, et la Sardaigne. Revue de linguistique romane 9: 346–369.
Miller, D. Gary
  1973   On the motivation of phonological change. In: Kachru et al. (eds.) 1973: 686–718.
  1974   On the history of infinitive complementation in Latin and Greek. JIES 2: 223–246.
  1975   Indo-European: VSO, SOV, SVO, or all three? Lingua 37: 31–52.
  1976   Pure velars and palatals in Indo-European: a rejoinder to Magnusson. Linguistics 178: 47–67.
  1977 (a) Bartholomae's Law and an IE root structure contraint. In: Studies in descriptive and historical linguistics: Festschrift for Winfred P. Lehmann, ed. by P. J. Hopper et al., 365–392. (= AST 4)
  1977 (b) Some theoretical and typological implications of IE root structure constraints. JIES 5: 31–40.
  1977 (c) Was Grassmann's Law reordered in Greek? KZ 91: 131–158.
Miller, Patricia
  1973   Bleaching and coloring. CLS 9: 386–397.
Miranda, Rocky V.
  1973   The nature of rule loss. In: Mid-America Linguistics Conference Papers, 1972, ed. by J. H. Battle and J. Schweitzer, 193–206. Stillwater: Oklahoma State University.
  1974 (a) Analogy and leveling. In: Mid-America Linguistics Conference Papers, 1973. Iowa City: Department of Linguistics, University of Iowa.
  1974 (b) Sound change and other phonological change. Minnesota Working Papers in Linguistics and Philosophy of Language 2: 49–81.
  1975 (a) Indo-European gender: a study in semantic and syntactic change. JIES 3: 199–215.
  1975 (b) Internal reconstruction: scope and limits. Lingua 36: 289–306.
  1977   The assimilation of Dravidian loans to Konkani phonological and morphological patterns. Indo-Iranian Journal 19: 247–265.
  1978   On the reconstructability of syntactic change. In: Dressler et al. (eds.) 1978: 504–507.
  1984   Temporal compensation and phonetic change: the case of compensatory lengthening in Hindi. In: Papers from the Minnesota Regional Conference on Language and Linguistics, 91–104. Minneapolis: Department of Linguistics, University of Minnesota.

Mithun, Marianne, and Lyle Campbell
1982   On comparative syntax. In: Maher et al. (eds.) 1978: 273–291.
Mitzka, Walther
1968   Kleine Schriften zur Sprachgeschichte und Sprachgeographie. Berlin: de Gruyter.
Møller, Hermann
1907   Semitisch und Indogermanisch. Vol. 1. Copenhagen.
1917   Die semitisch-vorindogermanischen laryngalen Konsonanten. (Mémoires de l'Académie Royale des Sciences et Lettres de Danemark, 7me série, 4: 1.) Copenhagen.
Moulton, W. G.
1960   The short vowel system of Northern Switzerland: a study in structural dialectology. Word 16: 155–182.
1961   Lautwandel durch innere Kausalität: Die ostschweizerische Vokalspaltung. Zeitschrift für Mundartforschung 28: 227–251.
Mühlhäusler, Peter
1970   Growth and structure of the lexicon of New Guinea Pidgin. Canberra: Pacific Linguistics, C-52.
1981   The development of the category of number in Tok Pisin. In: Muysken (ed.) 1981b: 35–84.
1983   The development of word formation in Tok Pisin. Folia Linguistica 17: 463–487.
1984   Review of Bickerton 1981. Folia Linguistica 18: 263–277.
Mühlhäusler, Peter, et al. (eds.)
1979   Papers in pidgin and creole linguistics, 2. (= Pacific Linguistics, Series A, 57.)
Mullen, Dana
1979   Back-formation in English: Two approaches to a theory of derivational morphology. Cahiers linguistiques d'Ottawa 7: 1–37.
Murray, Robert W.
1982   Consonant cluster developments in Pāli. Folia Linguistica Historica 3: 163–184.
Murray, Robert W., and Theo Vennemann
1983   Sound change and syllable structure in Germanic phonology. Language 59: 514–528.
Muysken, Pieter
1981 (a) Halfway between Quechua and Spanish: the case for relexification. In: Highfield & Valdman (eds.) 1981: 52–78.
1981 (b) (ed.) Generative studies on creole languages. Dordrecht: Foris.
Muysken, Pieter, and Norval Smith (eds.)
1986   Subtrata versus universals in creole genesis. Amsterdam: Benjamins.

Nadkarni, Mangesh V.
1975   Bilingualism and syntactic change in Konkani. Language 51: 672–683.
Nakao, Toshio
1986   Metathesis. In: Kastovsky & Szwedek (eds.) 1986: 547–556.

714   *References*

Naro, A. J.
1978   A study on the origins of pidginization. Language 54: 314–347.
1981   The social and structural dimensions of a syntactic change. Language 57: 63–98.
Neeld, Ronald L.
1973   Remarks on palatalization. OSUWP 14: 37–48.
Neumann, Günter
1966   Zur chinesisch-russischen Behelfssprache von Kjachta. Die Sprache 12: 237–251.
Newmeyer, Frederick J. (ed.)
1989   Linguistics: the Cambridge survey. Vol. 1. Cambridge: University Press.
Nichols, Johanna
1980   Pidginization and foreigner talk: Chinese Pidgin Russian. In: Traugott et al. (eds.) 1980: 397–407.
Nida, Eugene A., and H. W. Fehderau
1970   Indigenous pidgins and koinés. IJAL 36: 146–155.
Niebaum, Hermann
1983   Dialektologie. (Germanistische Arbeitshefte 26.) Tübingen: Niemeyer.
Nielsen, N. A.
1952   La théorie des substrats et la linguistique structurale. Acta Linguistica 7: 1–7.

Oftedal, M.
1952   On the origin of the Scandinavian tone distinction. Norsk Tidskrift for Sprogvidenskap 16: 201–225.
Ogden, C. K., and I. A. Richards
1923   The meaning of meaning. New York: Harcourt.
Ohala, John J.
1971   The role of physiological and acoustic models in explaining the direction of sound change. POLA 15: 25–40.
1974 (a) Phonetic explanation in phonology. In: Papers from the Parasession on Natural Phonology, 251–274. Chicago: CLS.
1974 (b) Experimental historical phonology. In: Anderson & Jones (eds.) 1974b: 353–389.
1975   Southern Bantu vs. the world: the case of palatalization of labials. BLS 4: 370–386.
Ohala, Manjari
1974   The abstractness controversy: experimental evidence from Hindi. Language 50: 225–235.
Öhman, S.
1951   Wortinhalt und Weltbild: Vergleichende und methodologische Wortfeldtheorie. Stockholm: Norstedt.
Ohso, Mieko
1973   A phonological study of some English loan words in Japanese. OSUWP 14: 1–26.

Okell, John
1965   Nissaya Burmese: a case of systematic adaptation to a foreign grammar and syntax. Lingua 15: 186–227.
Osthoff, Hermann, and Karl Brugmann
1878   (Preface to) Morphologische Untersuchungen auf dem Gebiete der indogermanischen Sprachen, 1. (Engl. transl. in Lehmann (ed.) 1967.)

Pandharipande, Rajeshwari
1982   Counteracting forces in language change: convergence vs. maintenance. In: Hock (ed.) 1982c: 97–116.
Parker, Frank
1980   Typology and word order change. Linguistics 18 (= 229/230): 269-288.
Paul, Hermann
1920   Prinzipien der Sprachgeschichte. 5th ed. Halle: Niemeyer. (Engl. translation of 2nd ed.: Principles of language history, 1889, New York: Macmillan.)
Payne, Doris L.
1985   Review of Hawkins 1983. Language 61: 462–466.
Payne, J. R.
1980   The decay of ergativity in the Pamir languages. Lingua 51: 147–186.
Pearce, Elizabeth
1984   On weak pronoun changes in Romance. University of Melbourne Working Papers in Linguistics 10: 101–117.
1990   Parameters in Old French syntax: infinitival complements. Dordrecht: Kluwer.
Pedersen, Holger
1907   Neues und Nachträgliches: Exegetische und syntaktische Fragen. KZ 40: 129–173.
Perlmutter, David M. (ed.)
1983   Studies in Relational Grammar, 1. Chicago: University Press.
Perlmutter, David M., and Carol G. Rosen (eds.)
1984   Studies in Relational Grammar, 2. Chicago: University Press.
Petrovici, Emil
1957   Kann das Phonemsystem einer Sprache durch fremden Einfluß umgestaltet werden? The Hague: Mouton.
Pieper, Ursula, and Gerhard Stickel (eds.)
1985   Studia linguistica, diachronica et synchronica, Werner Winter sexagenario ... oblata. Berlin: Mouton.
Pisani, V.
1937   Toch. A *käntu* und das idg. Wort für 'Zunge'. KZ 64: 100–103.
Plank, Frans
1965   Rule inversion: Hermann Paul already had an idea-r-of it. York Papers in Linguistics 5: 131–138.
1979   Ikonisierung und De-Ikonisierung als Prinzipien des Sprachwandels. Sprachwissenschaft 4: 121–158.

Polomé, Edgar
1965   The laryngeal theory so far: a critical bibliographical survey. In: Evidence for laryngeals, ed. by W. Winter, 9–78. The Hague: Mouton.
To Appear (ed.) Research guide on language change. Berlin: Mouton de Gruyter.
Posner, Rebecca
1961   Consonantal dissimilation in the Romance languages. Oxford: Blackwell.
Posner, Rebecca, and John N. Green (eds.)
1980   Romance comparative and historical linguistics. (Trends in Romance Linguistics and Philology, 1) The Hague: Mouton.
Postal, Paul M.
1968   Aspects of phonological theory. (Chapters 10 and 11.) New York: Harcourt & Brace. (Repr. in Keiler (ed.) 1972.)
Pray, Bruce R.
1976   From passive to ergative in Indo-Aryan. In: The notion of subject in South Asian languages, ed. by M. K. Verma, 195–211. (South Asian Studies Publication Series, 2.) Madison: University of Wisconsin.
Prentice, D. J.
1974   Yet another PAN phoneme? Oceanic Linguistics 13: 33–75.
Pulgram, Ernst
1953   Family tree, wave theory, and dialectology. Orbis 2: 67–72.
1959   Proto-Indo-European reality and reconstruction. Language 35: 421–426.
1961   The nature and use of proto-languages. Lingua 10: 18–37.
Pullum, Geoffrey K.
1981   Languages with object before subject: a comment and a catalogue. Linguistics 19: 1/2 (= 239/240): 147–156.
Purcell, E. T., G. Villegas, and S. P. Young
1978   A before and after for tonogenesis. Phonetica 35: 284–293.

Quirk, Randolph
1965   Descriptive statement and serial relationship. Language 41: 205–217.

Ramanujan, A. K., and Colin Masica
1969   Toward a phonological typology of the Indian linguistic area. In: Current trends in linguistics, ed. by T. Sebeok, 5: 543–577. The Hague: Mouton.
Ramasamy, K.
1981   Correlative relative clauses in Tamil. In: Dravidian syntax, ed. by S. Agesthialingom and N. Rajasekharan Nair, 363–380. (Annamalai University Publications in Linguistics, 73.) Annamalainagar.

Ramat, Anna Giacalone, et al. (eds.)
1987   Papers from the 7th International Conference on Historical Linguistics. (= AST 48)

Ramat, Paolo
1987   Linguistic typology. Berlin: Mouton de Gruyter.

Ramat, Paolo, et al. (eds.)
1980   Linguistic reconstruction and Indo-European syntax: Proceedings of the Colloquium of the 'Indogermanische Gesellschaft' ... 1979. (= AST 19)

Ramsden, H.
1963   Weak-pronoun position in the early Romance languages. Manchester: University Press.

Rask, Rasmus
1818   Undersögelse om det gamle Norske eller Islandske Sprogs Oprindelse. København: Gyldendal.

Rauch, Irmengard, and Gerald F. Carr (eds.)
1983   Language change. Bloomington: Indiana University Press.

Reinecke, J., et al.
1974   A bibliography of pidgins and creoles. Honolulu: University of Hawaii Press.

Renfrew, Colin
1987   Archaeology and language: the puzzle of Indo-European origins. Cambridge: University Press.

Richter, Elise
1903   Zur Entwicklung der romanischen Wortstellung aus der lateinischen. Halle: Niemeyer.

Ries, John
1907   Die Wortstellung im Beowulf. Halle: Niemeyer.

Ringe, Donald A., Jr.
1988   Laryngeal isoglosses in the western Indo-European languages. In: Bammesberger (ed.) 1988: 415–441.

Robertson, John S.
1975   A syntactic example of Kuryłowicz's fourth law of analogy in Mayan. IJAL 41: 140–147.

Rohlfs, Gerhard
1949   Historische Grammatik der italienischen Sprache und ihrer Mundarten, v. 1. Bern: Francke.
1954   Historische Grammatik der italienischen Sprache und ihrer Mundarten, v. 3. Bern: Francke.

Romaine, Suzanne
1981   The transparency principle: what it is and why it doesn't work. Lingua 55: 277–300.
1984   On the problem of syntactic variation and pragmatic meaning in sociolinguistic theory. Folia Linguistica 18: 409–437.
1988   Pidgin & creole languages. New York: Longman.
1989   The role of children in linguistic change. In: Breivik & Jahr (eds.) 1989: 199–225.

Ross, John Robert
1972   The category squish: Endstation Hauptwort. CLS 8: 316–328.
Ruhlen, Merritt
1975   A guide to the languages of the world. Stanford, CA: Stanford University Language Universals Project.

Sadock, J. M.
1973   Word-final devoicing in the development of Yiddish. In: Kachru et al. (eds.) 1973: 790–797.
Sag, Ivan A.
1974   The Grassmann's Law ordering pseudoparadox. LIn 5: 591–607.
1976   Pseudosolutions to the pseudoparadox: Sanskrit diaspirates revisited. LIn 7: 609–622.
Sajnovics, Joannis
1770   Demonstratio idioma ungarorum et lapponum idem esse. Tyrnania. (Repr. 1968, Indiana University Publications, Uralic and Altaic Series, 91.)
Samuels, M. L.
1972   Linguistic evolution: with special reference to English. Cambridge: University Press.
Sapir, Edward
1921   Language. New York: Harcourt.
de Saussure, Ferdinand
1879   Mémoire sur le système primitif des voyelles dans les langues indo-européennes. Repr. 1968, Hildesheim: Olms. (Excerpts in Engl. transl. in Lehmann (ed.) 1967.)
1916   Cours de linguistique générale. Paris: Payot.
Schaller, H. W.
1975   Die Balkansprachen. Heidelberg: Winter.
Schane, S.
1971   The phoneme revisited. Language 47: 503–521.
Scherer, Anton
1956   Hauptprobleme der idg. Altertumskunde. Kratylos 1: 3–21.
Schindler, Jochem
1974   Fragen zum paradigmatischen Ausgleich. Die Sprache 20: 1–9.
1976   Diachronic and synchronic remarks on Bartholomae's and Grassmann's Laws. LIn 7: 622–637.
Schleicher, August
1868   Eine fabel in indogermanischer ursprache. KZ 2: 206–208.
Schmidt, Annette
1985   Young people's Dyirbal: an example of language death from Australia. Cambridge: University Press.
Schmidt, Johannes
1872   Die Verwandtschaftsverhältnisse der indogermanischen Sprachen. Weimar: Böhlau.
Schmitt, Rüdiger
1973   Probleme der Eingliederung fremden Sprachgutes in das

grammatische System einer Sprache. (= Innsbrucker Beiträge zur Sprachwissenschaft, Vorträge, 11.)
1977   (ed.) Étymologie. Darmstadt: Wissenschaftliche Buchgesellschaft.

Schneider, Gisela
1973   Zum Begriff des Lautgesetzes in der Sprachwissenschaft seit den Junggrammatikern. (= Tübinger Beiträge zur Linguistik, 46.)

Schrader, O.
1886   Linguistisch-historische Forschungen zur Handelsgeschichte und Warenkunde, 1. Jena.
1906–1907 Sprachvergleichung und Urgeschichte: Linguistisch-historische Beiträge zur Erforschung des indogermanischen Altertums. 3rd ed., 2 vols. Jena.

Schuchardt, Hugo
1880   Review of E. Windisch: Kurzgefaßte irische Grammatik. Zeitschrift für Romanische Philologie 4: 124–155.
1883–1888 Kreolische Studien. 8 vols. Wien: Gerold.
1885   Über die Lautgesetze: gegen die Junggrammatiker. Berlin: Oppenheim. (Repr. and Engl. transl. in Vennemann & Wilbur 1972. See also Schuchardt 1928.)
1928   Hugo Schuchardt-Brevier, ed. by Leo Spitzer. Halle: Niemeyer.
1978   The ethnography of variation: selected writings on pidgins and creoles. Translated and selected by T. L. Markey. Ann Arbor, MI: Karoma.
1980   Pidgin and creole languages. Selected and translated by G. G. Gilbert. Cambridge: University Press.

Schützeichel, R.
1956   Zur ahd. Lautverschiebung am Mittelrhein. Zeitschrift für Mundartforschung 24: 112–124.

Schweiger, Fritz
1984   Anmerkungen zu Boretzkys Aufsatz 'Das indogermanistische Sprachwandelmodell und Wandel in exotischen Sprachen'. Folia Linguistica Historica 5: 397–400.

Schwyzer, Eduard
1933   Dissimilatorische Geminatenauflösung als Folge von Übersteigerung. KZ 61: 222–252.

Sebeok, Thomas S. (ed.)
1973   Current trends in linguistics, 11: Diachronic, areal, and typological linguistics. The Hague: Mouton.

Semiloff-Zelasko, Holly
1973   Glide-metathesis. OSUWP 14: 66–76.

Shevoroshkin, Vitaly
1987   Indo-European homeland and migrations. Folia Linguistica Historica 7: 227–250.

Sihler, Andrew L.
1977   Morphologically conditioned sound change and OE past participles in -en. General Linguistics 17: 76–97.

Silva, Clare M.
1973   Metathesis in obstruent clusters. OSUWP 14: 77–84.

Silverstein, Michael
1972   Chinook Jargon: Language contact and the problem of multilevel generative syntaxes. Language 47: 378–406 and 596–625.

Singler, John Victor
1988   The homogeneity of the substrate as a factor in pidgin/creole genesis. Language 64: 27–51.

Smith, Neilson V.
1981   Consistency, markedness, and language change: On the notion 'consistent language'. Journal of Linguistics 17: 39–54.

Solta, Georg Renatus
1980   Einführung in die Balkanlinguistik mit besonderer Berücksichtigung des Substrats und des Balkanlateinischen. Darmstadt: Wissenschaftliche Buchgesellschaft.

Southworth, Franklin C., III
1964   Family-tree diagrams. Language 40: 557–565.

Stampe, David
1969   The acquisition of phonetic representation. CLS 5: 443–454.
1972   On the natural history of diphthongs. CLS 8: 578–590.

Stang, Christian S.
1957   Quelques remarques sur le système consonantique du grec commun. Symbolae Osloenses 33: 27–36.

Stankiewicz, Edward
1979   Studies in Slavic morphophonemics and accentology. Ann Arbor: Michigan Slavic Publications.

Steblin-Kamenskij, M. I.
1965   Om alveolarer og kakuminaler i norsk og svensk. Norsk Tidskrift for Sprogvidenskap 20: 18–27.

Steele, Susan M.
1975   Some factors that affect and effect word order. In: Li (ed.) 1975: 197–268.
1977 (a)   Clisis and diachrony. In: Li (ed.) 1977: 539–582.
1977 (b)   Review of Haiman 1974. Language 53: 209–212.

Steever, Sanford B.
1988   The serial verb formation in the Dravidian languages. Delhi: Motilal Banarsidass.

Steever, Sanford B., et al. (eds.)
1976   Parasession on diachronic syntax. Chicago: CLS.

Stein, Dieter
1990   The semantics of syntactic change: aspects of the evolution of *do* in English. Berlin: Mouton de Gruyter.

Steinbergs, Alexandra
1984   Loanword incorporation processes: examples from Tshiluba. SLS 14: 2: 115–125.

Stemberger, Joseph P.
1981   Morphological haplology. Language 57: 791–817.

Stern, G.
1931   Meaning and change of meaning. Bloomington: Indiana University Press.
Stevens, Alan M.
1968   Madurese phonology and morphology. New Haven, CT: American Oriental Society.
Stockwell, Robert P.
1977   Motivations for exbraciation in Old English. In: Li (ed.) 1977: 291–314.
1984   On the history of the verb-second rule in English. In: Fisiak (ed.) 1984: 575–592.
Stockwell, Robert P., and C. Westbrook Barritt
1961   Scribal practice: some assumptions. Language 37: 75–82.
Stockwell, Robert P., and R. K. S. Macaulay (eds.)
1972   Linguistic change and generative theory. Bloomington: Indiana University Press.
Stucky, Susan U.
1978   How a noun class system may be lost: evidence from Kituba (Lingua Franca Kikongo). SLS 8: 1: 216–233.
Stump, Gregory T.
1983 (a) (ed.) Papers in historical linguistics. (= OSUW 27)
1983 (b) The elimination of ergative patterns of case-marking and verbal agreement in modern Indic languages. In: Stump (ed.) 1983a: 140–164.
Sturtevant, Edgar H.
1907   Linguistic change. Chicago: University Press.
1940   The pronunciation of Greek and Latin. Philadelphia: LSA.
1947   An introduction to linguistic science. New Haven: Yale University Press.
Swadesh, Morris
1967   Lexicostatistic classification. In: Handbook of Middle American Indians, ed. by N. McQuown, 5: 79–115. Austin: University of Texas Press.
Szemerényi, Oswald
1957   The problem of Balto-Slav unity: a critical survey. Kratylos 2: 97–123.
1962   Principles of etymological research in the Indo-European languages. In: II. Fachtagung für indogermanische und allgemeine Sprachwissenschaft, Innsbruck, 10.–15. Oktober 1961. (= Innsbrucker Beiträge zur Kulturwissenschaft, Sonderheft 15.)
1964   Structuralism and substratum. Lingua 13: 1–29.
1967   The new look of Indo-European: reconstruction and typology. Phonetica 17: 65–99.
1970   Einführung in die vergleichende Sprachwissenschaft. Darmstadt: Wissenschaftliche Buchgesellschaft.
1975 (a) Rekonstruktion in der indogermanischen Flexion: Prinzipien

und Probleme. In: Flexion und Wortbildung, 325–345. Wiesbaden: Reichert.
1975 (b) Review of Sebeok (ed.) 1973. Kratylos 20: 1–12.
1985   Armenian between Iran and Greece. In: Pieper & Stickel (eds.) 1985: 783–799.
1989 (a) Einführung in die vergleichende Sprachwissenschaft. 3rd ed. Darmstadt: Wissenschaftliche Buchgesellschaft.
1989 (b) The new sound of Indo-European. Diachronica 6: 237–269.

Tesnière, P.
1939   Phonologie et mélange de langues. TCLP 8: 83–93. (Repr. in Hamp et al. (eds.) 1966.)
Thieme, Paul
1954   Die Heimat der indogermanischen Gemeinsprache. (Akademie der Wissenschaften und der Literatur, Mainz.) Wiesbaden: Steiner.
Thomas, G.
1975   The calque: an international trend in the lexical development of the literary languages in 18th century Europe. Germano-Slavica 1975: 21–41.
1978   The role of calques in the early Czech language revival. Slavonic and East European Review 1978: 481–504.
Thomason, Sarah Grey
1974   On the analysis of inflectional change. Papers in Linguistics 7: 351–379.
1976   Analogic change as grammar complication. In: Christie (ed.) 1976: 401–409.
1983   Chinook Jargon in areal and historical context. Language 59: 820–870.
Thomason, Sarah Grey, and Terrence Kaufman
1988   Language contact, creolization, and genetic linguistics. Berkeley and Los Angeles: University of California Press.
Thompson, Laurence C., and M. Terry Thompson
1969   Metathesis as a grammatical device. IJAL 35: 213–218.
Thorndike, E. L.
1947   Semantic change. American Journal of Psychology 40: 588–597.
Thumb, Albert
1901   Die griechische Sprache im Zeitalter des Hellenismus: Beiträge zur Geschichte und Beurteilung der Koinē. Straßburg: Trübner.
Thurgood, G., and Hector Javkin
1975   An acoustic explanation of a sound change: *-at to -e, *-ap to -o, and *-ak to -æ in Lisu. Journal of Phonetics 3: 161–165.
Thurneysen, Rudolf
1961   A grammar of Old Irish. Dublin: Institute for Advanced Studies.
Timberlake, Alan
1976   Subject properties in the North Russian passive. In: Subject and topic, ed. by C. N. Li, 545–570. New York: Academic Press.

1977   Reanalysis and actualization in syntactic change. In: Li (ed.)
            1977: 141–180.
Timmers, C.
1977   Les vicissitudes de l'*r* en français, ou Comment traiter les ex-
            ceptions à un changement phonétique. Utrecht Working Papers
            in Linguistics 3: 31–71.
Tischler, Johann
1973   Glottochronologie und Lexikostatistik. (= Innsbrucker Beiträge
            zur Sprachwissenschaft, 11.)
Togeby, Knud
1964   Review article: Qu'est ce que la dissimilation? Romance Philol-
            ogy 17: 642–667.
Torbiörnsson, Tore
1906   Antikritische bemerkungen zur slavischen metathesenfrage.
            (Bezzenberger's) Beiträge zur Kultur der indogermanischen
            Sprachen 30: 62–99.
Trager, George L.
1940   One phonemic entity becomes two: the case of 'short a'.
            American Speech 15: 255–258.
Traugott, Elizabeth Closs
1965   Diachronic syntax and generative grammar. Language 41:
            402–415. (Repr. in Keiler (ed.) 1972.)
1972   A history of English syntax. New York: Holt.
Traugott, Elizabeth Closs, et al. (eds.)
1980   Papers from the 4th International Conference on Historical
            Linguistics. (= AST 14)
Traugott, Elizabeth Closs, and Suzanne Romaine (eds.)
1985   Papers on socio-historical linguistics. (= Folia Linguistica
            Historica 6: 1)
Trier, Jost
1931   Der deutsche Wortschatz im Sinnbezirk des Verstandes: Die
            Geschichte eines sprachlichen Feldes, l: Von den Anfängen bis
            zum Beginn des 13. Jahrhunderts. Heidelberg: Winter.
1973   Aufsätze und Vorträge zur Wortfeldtheorie, ed. by A. van der
            Lee and O. Reichmann. The Hague: Mouton.
Trnka, Bohumil, et al.
1958   Prague structural linguistics. Philologica Pragensia 1: 33–40.
Trubetzkoy, N. S.
1931   Phonologie und Sprachgeographie. TCLP 4: 228–234. (French
            version in N. S. Trubetzkoy: Principes de phonologie. Paris:
            Klincksieck, 1957.)
1936   Die Aufhebung der phonologischen Gegensätze. TCLP 6: 29–45.
1938   Grundzüge der Phonologie. (= TCLP 7)
Trudgill, Peter
1971   The social differentiation of English in Norwich. Cambridge:
            University Press.
1983   On dialect: Social and geographical perspectives. New York:
            New York University Press.

1986   Dialects in contact. Oxford: Blackwell.
1988   On the role of dialect contact and interdialect in linguistic change. In: Fisiak (ed.) 1988: 547–564.
1989   Contact and isolation in linguistic change. In: Breivik & Jahr (eds.) 1989: 227–237.
Tsiapera, M. (ed.)
1971   Generative studies in historical linguistics. Edmonton, Alberta: Linguistic Research.
Turner, L. D.
1949   Africanisms in the Gullah dialect. Chicago: University Press.
Twaddell, W. Freeman
1938   A note on Old High German umlaut. Monatshefte für deutschen Unterricht 30: 177–181. (Repr. in Joos (ed.) 1957.)
Tyler, Stephen A.
1968   Dravidian and Uralic: the lexical evidence. Language 44: 798–812.

Ullmann, S.
1957   The principles of semantics. 2nd ed. Glasgow: University Publications.
1962   Semantics: an introduction to the science of meaning. Oxford: Blackwell.
1966   Semantic universals. In: Greenberg (ed.) 1966b: 217–262.
Ultan, Russell
1971   A typological view of metathesis. Stanford Working Papers 7: 1–44.
1978   Size-sound symbolism. In: Greenberg (ed.) 1978: 2: 525–568.

Vaillant, André
1958   Grammaire comparée des langues slaves, v. 1. Lyon: AIC.
Valdman, A. (ed.)
1977   Pidgin and creole linguistics. Bloomington: Indiana University Press.
Valdman, A., and Arnold Highfield (eds.)
1980   Theoretical orientations in creole studies. New York: Academic Press.
van Coetsem, Frans
1988   Loan phonology and the two transfer types in language contact. Dordrecht: Foris.
Vennemann, Theo
1972 (a) Phonetic analogy and conceptual analogy. In: Vennemann & Wilbur 1972: 181–204.
1972 (b) Rule inversion. Lingua 29: 209–242.
1974   Topics, subjects, and word order: From SXV to SVX via TVX. In: Anderson & Jones (eds.) 1974b: 339–376.
1975   An explanation of drift. In: Li (ed.) 1975: 269–306.
1984   Hochgermanisch und Niedergermanisch: Die Verzweigungstheorie der germanisch-deutschen Lautverschiebungen. Beiträge zur Geschichte der deutschen Sprache und Literatur 106: 1–45.

1988   Preference laws for syllable structure and the explanation of sound change. Berlin: Mouton de Gruyter.

1989   (ed.) The new sound of Indo-European. Essays in phonological reconstruction. Berlin: Mouton de Gruyter.

Vennemann, Theo, and Terence H. Wilbur

1972   Schuchardt, the neogrammarians, and the transformational theory of phonological change. Frankfurt: Athenäum.

Verner, Karl

1877   Eine Ausnahme der ersten Lautverschiebung. KZ 23: 97–130. (Engl. transl. in Lehmann (ed.) 1967 and Baldi & Werth (eds.) 1978.)

Vihman, Marilyn May

1980   Sound change and child language. In: Traugott et al. (eds.) 1980: 303–320.

Vincent, Nigel

1974   Analogy reconsidered. In: Anderson & Jones (eds.) 1974: 427–445.

1980   Iconic and symbolic aspects of syntax: prospects for reconstruction. In: Ramat et al. (eds.) 1980: 47–68.

Visser, F. Th.

1963–1973 An historical syntax of the English language. 3 vols. in 4, with continuous pagination. Leiden: Brill.

Vogel, Irene

1986   External sandhi rules operating between sentences. In: Andersen (ed.) 1986: 55–64.

Vogt, Hans

1958   Les occlusives de l'arménien. Norsk Tidskrift for Sprogvidenskap 18: 143–161.

Wackernagel, Jacob

1892   Über ein Gesetz der indogermanischen Wortstellung. IF 1: 333–436.

Wagner, K.

1970   Analogical change reconsidered in the framework of generative phonology. Folia Linguistica 3: 228–241.

Wallace, William D.

1982   The evolution of ergative syntax in Nepali. In: Hock (ed.) 1982c: 147–211.

1985   Subjects and subjecthood in Nepali: an analysis of Nepali clause structure and its challenges to Relational Grammar and Government & Binding. Urbana: University of Illinois Ph.D. dissertation in Linguistics.

Wang, William S.-Y.

1969   Competing changes as cause of residue. Language 45: 9–25. (Repr. in Baldi & Werth (eds.) 1978 and Wang (ed.) 1977.)

1977   (ed.) The lexicon in phonological change. The Hague: Mouton.

Wang, William S.-Y., and C.-C. Cheng
1970   Implementation of phonological change: the Shuāng-fēng Chinese case. CLS 6: 552–559. (Repr. in Wang (ed.) 1977.)
1971   Tone change in Chao-Zhou Chinese: a study in lexical diffusion. POLA 12. (Repr. in Wang (ed.) 1977.)
Wanner, Dieter
1975   A note on diphthongization. SLS 5: 2: 186–202.
1985   Proto-histoire du placement des clitiques en roman. In: Actes du 17ème Congrès International de Linguistique et Philologie Romanes (Aix-en-Provence, 1983), 2: 391–405. Marseilles: Laffitte.
Watkins, Calvert
1962   Indo-European origins of the Celtic verb. Dublin: Institute for Advanced Studies.
1963   Preliminaries to a historical and comparative reconstruction of the Old Irish verb. Celtica 6: 1–49.
1964   Preliminaries to the reconstruction of Indo-European sentence structure. In: Proceedings of the 9th International Congress of Linguists, 1035–1045. The Hague: Mouton.
1969   Indogermanische Grammatik, 3:1: Formenlehre: Geschichte der indogermanischen Verbalflexion. Heidelberg: Winter.
1976   Towards PIE syntax: Problems and pseudo-problems. In: Steever et al. (eds.) 1976: 305–326.
1989   New parameters in historical linguistics, philology, and culture history. Language 65: 783–799.
Weerman, Fred
1989   The V2 conspiracy: a synchronic and a diachronic analysis of verbal positions in Germanic languages. Dordrecht: Foris.
Weinreich, Uriel
1968   Languages in contact: findings and problems. The Hague: Mouton.
Weinreich, Uriel, William Labov, and M. I. Herzog
1968   Empirical foundations for a theory of language change. In: Lehmann & Malkiel (eds.) 1968: 95–195.
Wende, Fritz
1915   Über die nachgestellten Präpositionen im Angelsächsischen. (Palaestra, 70.) Berlin: Meyer & Müller.
Wetzels, Leo, and Engin Sezer (eds.)
1986   Studies in compensatory lengthening. Dordrecht: Foris.
Whalen, D. H., and Patrice S. Beddor
1989   Connections between nasality and vowel duration and height: Elucidation of the Eastern Algonquian intrusive nasal. Language 65: 457–486.
Whiteley, W. H.
1967   Swahili nominal classes and English loan words: a preliminary survey. La classification nominale dans les langues négro-africaines. Paris: Centre National de la Recherche Scientifique.

Whitney, William D.
1877   The principle of economy as a phonetic force. Transactions of the American Philological Association 8: 121–134.
Wilbur, Terence H. (ed.)
1977   The Lautgesetz-controversy: a documentation (1885–86). (Amsterdam Studies in the Theory and History of Linguistic Science, 1: Amsterdam Classics in Linguistics, 9.) Amsterdam: Benjamins.
van Windekens, A. J.
1979   Once again on Greek initial zeta. JIES 7: 129–132
Winter, Werner
1962   Die Vertretung indogermanischer Dentale im Tocharischen. IF 67: 16–35.
1969   Analogischer Sprachwandel und semantische Struktur. Folia Linguistica 3: 29–45.
1970   Some wide-spread Indo-European titles. In: Indo-European and Indo-Europeans, ed. by G. Cardona et al., 49–54. Philadelphia: University of Pennsylvania Press.
1982   IE for 'tongue' and 'fish'. JIES 10: 167-186.
1984   Reconstructional comparative linguistics and the reconstruction of the syntax of undocumented stages in the development of languages and language families. In: Fisiak (ed.) 1984: 613–625.
1986   Bantawa *rv-* < ? An exercise in internal and comparative reconstruction. In: Kastovsky & Szwedek (eds.) 1986: 763–772.
Witkowski, Stanley R., and Cecil H. Brown
1983   Marking-reversals and cultural importance. Language 59: 569–582.
Woolford, Ellen
1981   The developing complementizer system of Tok Pisin. In: Muysken (ed.) 1981: 125–139.
Woolford, Ellen, and William Washabaugh (eds.)
1983   The social context of creolization. Ann Arbor, MI: Karoma.
Wurm, S. A., and Peter Mühlhäusler
1985   Handbook of Tok Pisin. Canberra: Australian National University, Department of Linguistics.
Wurzel, W. U.
1976   Zur Haplologie. Linguistische Berichte 41: 50–57.

Zamora Salamanca, F. J.
1985   La tradición histórica de la analogía lingüística. Revista de la Sociedad Española de Lingüística 14: 367–419.
Zipf, G. K.
1929   Relative frequency as a determinant of phonetic change. Harvard Studies in Classical Philology 40: 1–95.

Index

Page numbers in boldface indicate definition or extensive discussion of a given term. The expression '(and) passim' indicates that in ~~addition~~ to the listed passages, the term is used throughout the boo~~k~~. ~~throughout the chapter). In such cases, enumeration of all occurren~~ would be pointless. For terms beginning with the negative prefix nor~~-~~ the corresponding positive term should generally be consulted.

Philip Baldi (Editor)

Linguistic Change and Reconstruction Methodology

1990. 15.5 x 23 cm. XII, 752 pages. With 5 maps. Cloth.
ISBN 3 11 011908 0
(Trends in Linguistics. Studies and Monographs 45)

This collection of papers on historical linguistics addresses specific questions relating to the ways in which language changes in individual families or groups, and to which methodologies are best suited to describe and explain those changes. In addition, the issue of 'long distance' relationships and the plausibility of recovering distant linguistic affiliations is discussed in detail.

Material by specialists is presented not only from the well-documented Indo-European family, but from Afroasiatic, Altaiac, Amerindian, Australian and Austronesian languages as well.

Despite many claims to the contrary, the method of comparative reconstruction, based on the regularity of sound change, is the most consistently productive means of conducting historical linguistic enquiry.

Equally important is the demonstration that the comparative method has its limitations, and that linguists must be cautious in their postulation of large super-families, whose existence is based too heavily on lexical evidence, and whose scientific foundation is difficult to establish.

mouton de gruyter

Berlin · New York

Edgar C. Polomé (Editor)
Research Guide on Language Change

1990. 15.5 x 23 cm. XII, 564 pages. Cloth
ISBN 3 11 012046 1
(Trends in Linguistics. Studies and Monographs 48)

This collection of 33 invited papers presents a comprehensive survey of the present state of research on the various aspects of language change, focusing on the methodology for the study of the subject and on various theoretical models.

The different types of language change – phonological, morphological, syntactic and lexical – are examined, as well as the topics of language families, contact linguistics, creolization, bi- and multilingualism, and similar contexts of change.

This assessment of the different fields of study provides an introduction to the subject and the presentation is illustrated with numerous examples, mainly from Western languages. Not only are those areas of research which have been explored indicated, but those which need further investigation are also described.

mouton de gruyter

Berlin · New York